The Art of Programming in Java

(Third Edition)

The Art of Programming in Java

(Third Edition)

Yong Qiang Gao

Distributed by

Third Editing and Printing: 2017

ISBN 978-1-387-09726-5

ygao@ohlone.edu

To my lovely wife Kui Zhang,
my son Charles,
my parents Wende Gao and Yuzheng Liang

Contents

Acknowledgements

I would like to thank my editor Lawrence Sanford, my assistant Xiaocheng Qian and Lingqian Chen, without whose help this book would never have been completed.

Foreword

"Dear Professor,

I read your book during my academics and since it is written so simple with lot of examples, made me easy to understand Java fundamentals. Also I referred your book examples while assisting students in the lab. Your book is a great help to students. Thanks."

Teaching Assistant: Yashaswini Bakkesh

"This book is very useful for those who wants to develop their java skills from basic to advance. I like this book very much because the book chapters are well organized in top to bottom fashion so that it's understandable even you have not learnt java before.

The book examples are very effective and more practicable. Last but not least I recommend this book to everyone who really wants to build their java skills in advance. "

Teaching Assistant: Dinesh Madhup

"In every text book I have used previously make me to learn the concept theoretically and the examples used to be complex. When I prefer your book the examples were clear cut and straight away and concepts are clear with sufficient examples, which made me to prefer your book. Thank you! "

Nishanth Reddy Emmadi

"The book written by professor Dr. Y. Gao, actual do embed the concepts into my mind. The light came on about what objects living on the heap were all about and that declaring an object variable is really declaring a reference to an object. Wow! The other books pointed that out, this book MADE the point in the brain.

I could provide lots more examples of how professor have explained the concepts. This has truly different approach to learning. if you understand the underlying concepts, you can design and develop your own java application. To wake up your imagination, the book shows how you can extend Java class format, write your own custom Class Loaders, add arbitrary functionality at run time, etc. There are three reasons why I would love a book: it gives me either conceptual understanding, or details on what's going on "under the hood", or a bunch of practical advice. Thank you"

Vidit Mody

"The textbook was very useful and reliable. It made understanding and learning Java very easy. The good features about the book were the detailed examples in each section. The pictures and tables were also a big help. I also liked that there was usually more than one example that a student can refer to.

Ranjot Singh

"I like this book "Programming Art in Java" because it covers very details about the Java technology. From basic topics like what Java is to more advanced ones like OOP and applets. I also like the way how the examples presented in the book. The examples are all well-commented so it is easy to follow. I especially like the book covers the GUI parts, my experience of reading other Java books is that a lot of them are missing the GUI section. Overall the book is very well organized and presented in a logic manner.

Ryan Chen

"I have enjoyed reading the book Programming Art in Java by Yong Qiang Gao as it explained the core concepts clearly while providing the balanced content for a novice programmer. It made easy for me to work on the exercises and concept questions as the book provided relevant information."

Pujita Munnangi

"Though I read other Java books, this book Programming Art in Java by Yong Qiang Gao provided clear understanding of Java concepts. As I was reading, I used to think of more questions and fortunately they are all explained subsequently in the book. I think it is a well thought out book. Also it helped me prepare for my exams, and projects where this book was so valuable."

Punit Mannangi

"Programming Art in Java" is a nice book written by Yong Qiang Gao for everybody who is interested in Java. This book was very useful; it helped me easily understand a lot of programming concepts, even though I didn't do any java programming before I started reading it. Learning with this book was easy and at the same time it was challenging and interesting. I enjoyed doing lab assignments after each chapter and I was even more excited, when after reading a few chapters I knew exactly how to do them."

Jake Marohl

"While I was learning from Programming art in Java I was also referring to another text book while taking Java, that being "Java Early Objects 5th edition" by Tony Gaddis. Both of them helped guide my perspective on another attempt at learning Java.

Mike Ptak

Preface

Welcome to the Art of Programming in Java, Second Edition. This book is intended for a one- semester or a two-quarter CS1 course. Although it is written for students who don't have any programming background, even experienced students will benefit from its depth of details. This book can also be used as self-learning and training.

The organization of the book can be briefly summarized as follows:

Part I covers fundamental concepts and skills in Java programming for beginners, including Chapter 1 to 5. All basics in Java programming are discussed in details in these five Chapters.

Part II including Chapter 6 to 9, introduces the essential concepts and skills in Object-Oriented Programming (OOP) in Java.

Part III provides more discussion and advanced topics in OOP in Java, including Chapter 10 to 14.

Part IV containing Chapter 15 to 20, shows students how to program in Graphical User Interfaces (GUI) and multimedia in Java.

Part V covers Chapter 21 and discusses the concepts and skills in file input/output programming in Java. In newer edition of this book, it will add Chapter 22 Database Programming and Chapter 23 Network Programming in Java.

Features of the text can be summarized as follows:

3Ws – throughout this book, a learning/teaching method 3Ws (What, Why and hoW) is revealed for better understanding and mastering concepts and skills in OOP in Java.

Example programs – The text provides more than 400 complete and executable example programs, each designed to explain and highlight the topic currently studied. In most cases, these are practical, understandable, and real-world examples. Source code for these examples as can be freely downloadable from author's website: http://www2.ohlone.edu/people/ygao/.

Note, Warning, and More Info – These appear at appropriate places throughout the text. They are short explanations, cautions, and more information about certain Java features, coding techniques, or often misunderstood points relevant to the topic at hand.

Exercises – A thorough and diverse set of review questions and coding exercises is provided at the end of each chapter. These exercises cover the important topics discussed in the chapter and are designed to solidify the student's knowledge of concepts and skills at hand.

Divide and conquer.

-<<Sunzi ‘s Military Strategies>>

Chapter 1 Introduction to Java

Java is originated from the famous coffee beans in Java Island in Indonesia. Throughout this text, of course, we are not talking about coffee, but a popular programming language called Java. However, its name is indeed from the ideas of a group of pioneers in Sun Microsystems, who were seating a coffee shop at Silicon Valley while they enjoyed the coffee and proposed Java as name of programming language they were creating.

1.1 What Is Java?

Java language was developed from C/C++ so that its syntax is similar to C/C++. The first important difference between Java and C/C++ is that Java is 100% object-oriented programming language. That means in Java code, excluding import and package statements for specifying the library classes, there is no any statements outside classes or objects except import and package which are discussed in later chapters. Secondly Java is the first platform-independent programming language in the world. It is declared as “write once, run anywhere”. Table 1.1 lists the important dates in Java version releases. This text introduces Java SE 6, or JDK1.6.

Table 1.1 Important dates for Java version releases

Release Date	Version
January 1996	JDK1.0（Java Development Kit）
February 1997	JDK1.1
December 1998	Java 2（JDK1.2）
August 1999	J2SE（Java 2 Standard Edition）
December 1999	J2EE（Java 2 Enterprise Edition）
May 2000	J2SE1.3
February 2002	J2SE1.4
September 2004	J2SE1.5 (or Java 2 JDK1.5)
November 2005	Java ME (Java Micro Edition)
December 2006	Java SE 6 (or JDK1.6)
June 2011	Java SE 7
March 2014	Java SE 8

More Info: *The commercial name of standard Java version now is called as Java SE plus the major release number, for example, Java 6; its development software package is called as JDK1.6.x. Java is the first 100% Object-Oriented Programming (OOP) language and also the first 100% platform-independence, open-source, and download-free language.*

1.2 What Can Java Do?

The primary purpose of creating Java language was for TV site-top box programming. Although its original goal was not succeed, it has been caught a priceless chance – the age of Internet exploring. 100% OOP and platform-independence have made Java the first choice in software development for the Internet applications. The features of reliability have also made Java suitable in small and middle-scaled software development; it is also capable in large-scaled software development for the Internet applications. Those have been proved by a variety of e-commerce application developments today.

Another feature in Java is its interpreter, or so called JVM (Java Virtual Machine). JVM has become an industrial standard and it is part of all popular Internet browsers today. More and more third-party companies, such as BEA, Apache, Eclipse, including IBM, and Java Community Process (JCP), have released a huge number of supporting and development software packages. These make Java become one of the most popular programming languages today.

Java can be used in software development in desktop applications, Web client programming, server-side programming, cell-phone programming, mobile device and robot programming. Its three major versions provide fundamental software development tools for the areas mentioned above. We discuss some coding examples in later sections of this chapter.

1.3 Java Development Kit

Java development Kit, or JDK, include compiling, executing, debugging, documenting, library classes and other major tools for software developments in desktop applications and Web-client applications, or applets. It is also includes JRE (Java Runtime Environment). JRE includes JVM, Java API (Application Programming Interfaces, or library classes), and other supporting tools.

JVM is software to interpret and execute Java bytecode and it is also called as Java engine. In addition to interpret and execute bytecode, it also optimizes the bytecode if necessary so the translated machine code can be executed more efficiently in a particular rum-time environment. We discuss what bytecode is in section 1.4.2 of this chapter.

1.3.1 What is Java SE?

Java SE is Java standard edition and core of Java language. It is foundation to learn Java programming before you move on to other Java development kits, such Java EE and Java ME. Java SE includes all basic and major functionality in Java language. To program with Java SE 6, you need to download, install, and configure JDK (we will discuss them in Chapter 2). Table 1.2 lists the major file directories in Java SE 6 development kit.

Table1.2 Major file directories in Java SE Development Kit

Directory	Description
Bin	Java program development tools and commands
Jre	Java runtime environment
Lib	Program development libraries
Docs	Java documents (optional)

There are other two important files in JDK: readme.html and src.zip:

readme.html – provides the requirement in Java SE installation; the features of JDK, important links of documents and other information.

src.zip – the source codes for all Java library classes.

More Info: *Java is open-source programming language. Its source codes are all provided in src.zip file.*

1.3.2 What is Java EE?

Java EE is enterprise edition for Java. It not only includes Java SE, but also provides features in network services, component models, management, and communications API. These features make Java EE become new generation software development tools as Service-Oriented architecture (SOA) for businesses. The first edition of Java EE was released in December of 1999. Up to today, the current version of Java EE is SDK 1.6. Java EE is used to develop enterprise applications and large-scaled network services applications. EJB (Enterprise Java Beans) is its major components. Because Java EE includes also the database (mySQL) and operations and management, the reliability and consistence in the performance gain the increasable improvement.

1.3.3 What is Java ME?

Java ME is micro edition of Java in application software development for mobile devices. It was first released in November 2005. Java ME provides flexible user interfaces, reliable and safer in use, self-established graphic protocols, and the dynamic switch and download features in connect/hang up. It is used in embedded programming for application software development in cell-phones, PDAs, GPS, TV site-top boxes, printers, and other wireless communications devices.

1.3.4 What can I learn from the text?

"Rather than giving you a fish, I teach how to fishing". In addition to discuss Java programming concepts and skills step by step systematically, the author, hopefully you will, too, concentrate the great effort in the following areas in learning:

1. Learn how to learn. None book can cover everything. This text emphasizes on essential features and fundamental understanding of concepts and skills in Java programming. It inspires and extends readers interests and ability to learn the ways how to programming in Java in your limited time while exploring the pattern and methodology in mastering new things.

2. Learn from examples. Exam the existing examples are one of the best ways to learn. In addition to examples for every Java programming concept and coding introduced in the text, readers can also download complete codes free from author's Website, for your better understanding and mastering the topics discussed in the examples by scanning over the code, executing, modifying, therefore comprehending the content.

3. Learn from API documents. The key in Java programming is how to learn and use API documentation in your coding. This text will show you step-by-step to discover the knowledge and coding skills in Java by discussion of API docs throughout examples.

4. Learn by practicing. One cannot learn programming just by reading books. The text encourages readers actually to do it. The exercises after each chapter cover all important concepts and programming skills for each topic it is discussed in the chapter. Exercises include concept and coding questions. Some challenge and comprehensive questions as projects are also provided in the exercises. They are listed from easy to comprehensive order and readers are encouraged to practice for better understanding.

5. Emphasize on summarizing and comprehending in learning. For every important concepts and coding skills in Java, the text provides 3W (What, Why and How), summary tables, more info and warning icons to guide students in the learning progress. It attempts to serve as examples and inspires reader's ability to do the same. These emphases are revealed in the exercise questions after the chapters.

1.4 Java Platform

Java platform refers to the working environment for Java programs. More specifically, it includes the operating systems and the configuration of the computer system.

1.4.1 What is Java's platform?

As we mentioned before, Java is the first programming language as platform-independence in the world. It means that, unlike traditional languages, such as C/C++, a Java code can be executed in any operating systems, such as Windows, Unix/Linux, OS, and so on.

Because a Java code can be edited in any text editor, JDK itself doesn't provide text editor or IDE (Integrated Development Environment). A number of third-party companies provide variety of free downloadable Java IDEs, so we can easily edit, modify, save, run, debug, and maintain Java programs.

1.4.2 Why can Java run on any platform?

The reason Java can run on any platforms is because of its unique language structure and the way it compiles and executes the code. Figure 1.1 explains these features.

Different from any existing programming languages, after Java compiler compiles the code, it generates a special machine code called bytecode. Bytecode is a neutral machine code with 0 and 1's, but cannot be executed by any CPU yet. Bytecode must be executed by Java interpreter or JVM, translated line-by-line into particular executable machine code, so that the CPU can run.

Because of all popular Internet browsers today include JVM as industrial standards, or the Java interpreter is provided in all JDKs installed in your computers, so you can "write once, run everywhere."

3W *Bytecode is neutral machine code. It is cannot be executed directly. Installed JVM including Java interpreter translates the bytecode into executable machine language, so it can be run by the CPU. Bytecode separates compiled code and executable code, so it achieves platform-independence.*

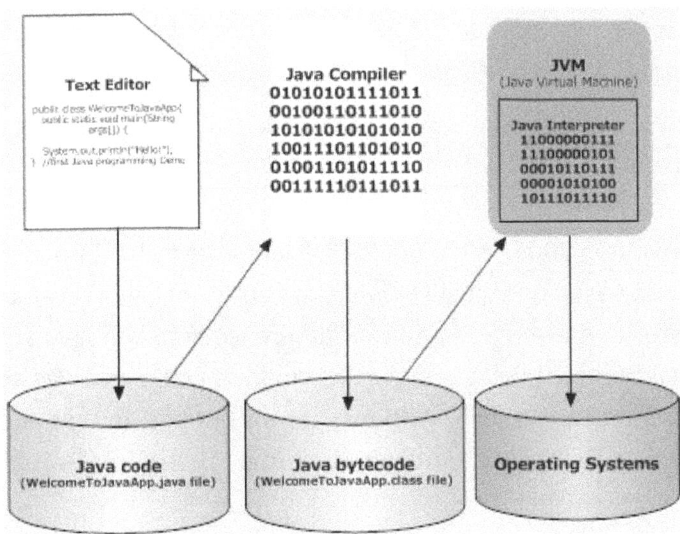

Figure 1.1 How Java achieves platform-independence

1.5 Java vs. Other Languages

In this section we compare Java with other popular programming languages, such as C++ and C#, in terms of syntax, platform, speed, and memory management.

1.5.1 Java vs. C++

Because of originated from C++, the syntax of Java is based on C++ and they are very similar. Due to additional process and interpretation of bytecode, in JVM, the execution speed in Java is slower than C++. However, memory management in Java has been greatly improved and memory leak problems have been reduced comparing with C++.

The significant difference between Java and C++ is that Java is 100% OOP language, while C++ can be both OOP and POP (Procedural-Oriented Programming). This feature makes C++ more flexible in coding but produces some confusion in learning.

Table 1.3 Comparison between Java, C++and C#

Compared field	Java and C++	Java and C#
Syntax	Similar	Similar
Platform	C++ is platform-dependence	C# can only work in Windows
Speed	C++ is faster than Java	C# is faster than Java
Memory management	C++ doesn't provide memory automatic management	Both provide automatic memory management

More Info: *Although the speed of execution in C++ and C# is faster than Java, along with the increasing the speed of CPU and dropping the price of memory, The execution speed in Java is not the major concern in Java.*

1.5.2 Java vs. C#

C# was developed by Microsoft in 2005. It is a 100% OOP language t of .NET and Microsoft Visual Studio. Since development of C# was based on Visual J++ which was the language developed by Microsoft as partner with Sun Microsystems, there is no significant difference between Java and Visual J++ in syntax and structure of the language, except it can only run in Windows platforms. C# also has virtual machine called "Common Language Runtime", or CLR. Although it runs faster than JVM and has some improvement, C# can be only executed on Windows platforms. Therefore, C# is platform-dependence OOP language.

1.5.3 Why study Java

Powerful debugging and exception handling mechanism make Java more reliable, safer and securer. Huge number of API library classes provides software developers in Java application development much faster, convenience in use, and promise in the industrial standardization. The demanding in the Internet applications and e-commerce, and the open-source strategy encourage the third-party companies to develop and release a variety of application development tools in Java. These reasons make Java become one of the most popular programming languages today. Table 1.3 summarizes the comparison between Java, C++ and C#.

The purpose to learn Java is to know how to programming using the world most popular computer language today. Java is a language that can be "write once, run everywhere". It is also an ideal computer language in the Internet programming and Web applications development summarized as follows:

- Java makes Web pages with real-time or dynamic updating
- Java supports multimedia programming with audio, video, color, animation, image, and painting.
- Java makes easier for human-machine interaction
- Java makes coding easier, reliable, supports auto-garbage collection, and multi-threading
- Java SE is foundation of client-server computing, Java EE, and large-scale software development. It is also make wireless/mobile device coding, embedded device coding, or study in Java ME programming much easier.

1.5.4 Common challenges for newbie

Learning how to programming in Java is different from learning other popular computer languages in which you may start with easy concepts and coding skills first. In Java coding, even you start a simple program and try to display "Hello, world!" message, it has already involved many OOP concepts and coding techniques, such as class, object, method, static, output stream, Java API, JVM, and so on. The common problems for newbie in Java learning are listed below:

- Important OOP concepts and coding techniques are overwhelmingly coming to you at day one of learning.

- Tremendous time spent on how to find out the proper API classes to solve your problems.
- How you can determine it is a better or best solution if there are many different ways in coding to solve your problem.

Readers find that these challenges can be overcome and handled by following the discussions, explanations and exercises throughout the text.

1.6 Scales of Java Programming

Java SE is only the core of Java technologies. Java programming also includes many other areas. Java EE and Java ME are examples. Although this text concentrates on Java SE, it is better to have an overview of most important areas and scales of Java applications.

1.6.1 Desktop applications

Desktop applications or applications in short, are used in many off-line applications software development. Because it doesn't involve any Internet uses, in fact, it is a good starting point to learn Java programming with desktop applications. After you know how to code Java applications, you will see how easily you can convert an application to an applet, and vice versa.

The following is a simple example of Java application:

```
 //Simple example of a Java application
public class HelloApp {        //define a class HelloApp
   public staic void main(String[] args) { //define a main method
          System.out.println("Hello, World!");     //display the message
   } //end of main()
}     //end of class HelloApp
```

This code displays the message "Hello, World!" to the computer screen. We discuss it in detail in Chapter 2. Figure 1.2 shows the execute result in Eclipse.

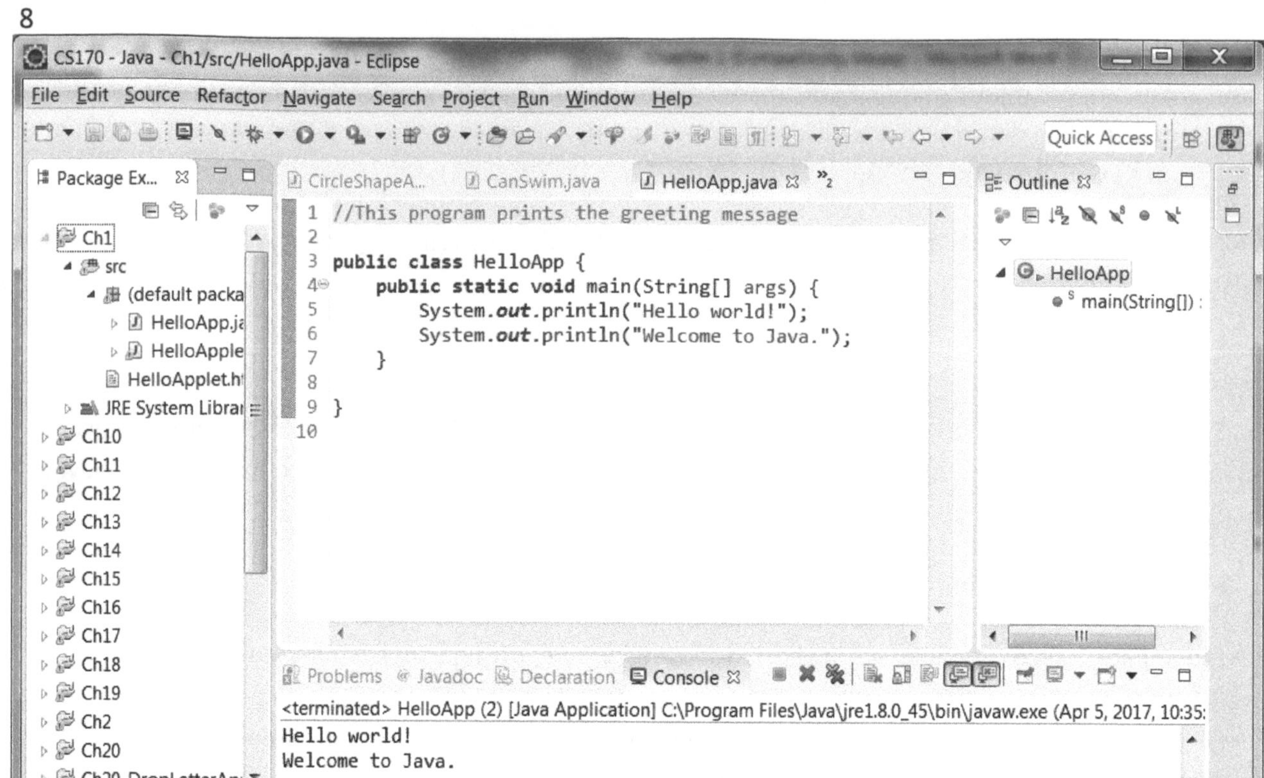

Figure 1.2 Example of output in Eclipse

1.6.2 Applet programming

The power of Java programming is its applet applications, or applets for short. Applets are executed in a HTML file by Internet browsers. There are normally three steps involved in applet programming:

1. Coding an applet
2. Coding a HTML to call the applet
3. After testing, upload the applet to a Web server

The following is a simple applet code that will display “Hello World!” to a webpage:

```
 //Simple Java applet
public class HelloApplet extends JApplet { //define n applet class HelloApplet
   public void paint(Graphics g)      {     //define a method paint()
          super.paint(g);                                //call super class method
          g.drawString("Hello, World!", 25, 30);  //display the message
        } //end of method paint()
} //end of class HelloApplet
```

The following is an example of HTML code to call the applet:

```
<!—HTML code to call HelloApplet.class -->
<html>
   <body>
          <applet code = "HelloApplet.class" width = 250 height = 180> </applet>
   </body>
```

```
</html>
```

An applet must be compiled and the bytecode must be generated before the HTML code can be executed by a Web browser. We discuss applet programming in Chapter 19 after introduction of basic Java programming concepts and techniques. Figure 1.3 shows the execution result of this applet in Mozilla Firefox browser.

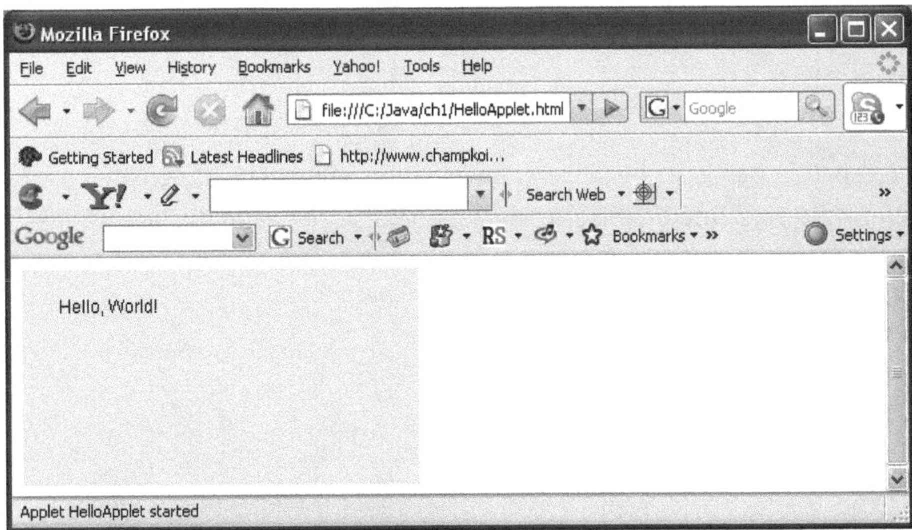

Figure 1.3 Execution result of HelloApplet in Mozilla Firefox

1.6.3 Servlet programming

Applet and Servlet programming construct client-server applications on the Web. Servlet programming is an important part of Java. It is the basis of learning advanced Java programming techniques, such as JSP (Java Server Pages) and Java EE and EJB, after mastering the basic Java programming skills.

The purpose of Servlet programming is to process the requests sending out from the clients, and as a result, sending back the processed information or data to client's Web sites. The power of servlet programming is that it can handle multi-client requests concurrently and provide real-time and dynamic Web page management in client's Web sites.

The following is a simple example of Servlet code. In this example, the server write a new message "Hello, World!" to a client's webpage:

```
//Import API library classes
import javax.servlet.ServletException;
import javax.servlet.http.*;
import java.io.*;

public class HelloServlet extends HttpServlet {   //Define a Servlet class

   protected void doGet(HttpServletRequest request, HttpServlet-
   Response response)
                    throws ServletException, IOException    { //Define method
         response.setContentType("text/html");   //Define sending type
         PrintWriter out = response.getWriter();//Define sending purpose

         out.println("<html>");                             //Begin sending
```

```
        out.println("<body><h1>Hello, World!</h1></body>");
        out.println("</html>");
        out.close();                                        //End of sending
    }                                                       //End of the method
}                                                   //End of HelloServlet class
```

To test out this Servlet code, you must first to download and install the server software package, configure your computer systems, and run the server.

1.6.4 Cell-phone programming

What a cell phone can do today is far beyond our imagination. Actually it has created a new era, shaped up a new generation, and generated significant impact on our society and the way we live, work, and study. Name a few new functions of a modern cell:

- Access the Internet
- Trade stocks
- Play games
- Watch TV
- Listen music
- MP3
- GPS
- Remote controller
- Distance learning

And so on.

Java ME (Micro Edition) is specifically designed for software applications development in cell phones, PDAs, GPS, TV-top boxes, embedded equipment, and robots. The following is part of example code written in Java ME to send a message "Hello World!" to a cell phone:

```
void getViaStreamConnection(String url) throws IOException { //Define a connection


    StreamConnection c = null;
      TextBox t = null;
        c = (StreamConnection)Connector.open(url);     //Establish a connection

        t = new TextBox("Hello World!", 1024, 0);      //Sending a message
      //Display "Hello World!" to cell screen
      display.setCurrent(t);
    }     //End
```

1.6.5 Robot programming

This is a world in which human being and robots will live together. Robots, including bio-robots, will share and control the universe. This is not just in Si-Fi movies or novels. This is going to be fact in the future. We, including many of readers today, will experience this era to come.

More and more robots have been employed in the areas of manufacturing, danger probing and removing, universe discovering, sporting, emulation, entertainment, and house cleaning. The technologies in development of robots have been dramatically improved today.

Java language is the first choice in robot programming, according to the statistics. That is because we can not only use Java SE, but also Java ME, and other Java techniques, to develop the robot software. More and more third-party partners of Sun and JCP (Java Community Process) provide robot developers free-downloadable and open-source API libraries.

The following is part of code that shows how a robot can speech the given words. The code is written in Java using Speech API:

```
//Use Speech API to make robot speech
import javax.speach.*;                //import Speech API
import javax.speach.synthesis.*;      //import speech synthesis API

public void speak(string words) {
        Synthesizer s = Central createSynthesizer(null);//Create a synthesizer
        s.allocate();                                    //Allocate the source
        s.speak(words, null);                            //Make a speech
}       //End
```

1.6.6 Why choose this text

The following may be a summary why readers should choose this text to learn Java programming:

- Guider to get into the door.
- Teacher for self-study.
- Assistant in exercises, practice, and enhancement in learning.
- Demonstrator in clarifying concepts.
- Encourager in summarization.
- Key in mastering Java programming.
- Friend as a companion in learning.

Exercises

1. Why Java is a plate-form independent and 100% Object-Oriented Programming language?
2. What software packages included in Java language?

3. What are included in Java SE package? What is its range in software development?
4. Why we should learn Java SE as a beginner?
5. What is bytecode? Descript its characteristics.
6. What is JVM and what it does?
7. Comparing C++, what are advantages or disadvantages Java has?
8. Comparing C#, what are advantages or disadvantages Java has?
9. What is the purpose of learning Java programming? Why readers should choose this text as first book of Java programming?
10. What are the difficulties the beginners most often are facing in learning Java programming and how you can overcome them?
11. What the meaning of 3W in the text? Discuss also other two indicators introduced in this text.

"Right tool for the right job."

– Confucius

Chapter 2 Java Programming Environment

The Java programming environment includes the Java software packages Java SE and JDK, operating system, system configuration, and programming "workplace," i.e., source code editing facilities, compiling, and executing.

2.1 Installation of Java SE JDK

The latest Java SE – JDK package can be found at the author's website. You can also follow the instructions in the next section and download it from Oracle's website.

2.1.1 Free download of Java SE JDK

All Java software development packages and documentation can be downloaded freely from Oracle's website:

http://www.oracle.com/technetwork/java/index.html

The steps for downloading the Java SE JDK are:

1. Click on Java SE in Top Downloads box
2. Click on Download JDK
3. Click on Download
4. In Platform box, select your Operating systems
5. Fill out the optional information or skip it, and click on Continue
6. Click on the file name you are going to download

The Java SE JDK will be saved to the default directory in your computer.

More Information: *The content and information available at the Oracle—or any website—may be subject to availability and change. You may need to modify the downloading, installation, or other procedures accordingly.*

2.1.2 Steps in Java SE JDK installation

The following are steps to install the Java SE JDK you downloaded to your computer:

1. Find the downloaded JDK file.

2. Run the file

3. Answer the questions in the dialog box (most time you just simply click on the Next button).

When prompted, select the directory to store the JDK. This will usually be the system default directory. For example, if the downloaded file name is jdk-8u131-windows-x64, the system default directory is:

C:\ProgramFiles\Java\jdk1.8.0_131\

4. Click on Finish button to complete your installation.

Congratulations! You have successfully installed Java SE JDK on your computer. Now the system automatically opens README.HTML and introduces the requirements necessary to work with the software, JDK documentation, information about JRE, and other links to related websites.

2.2 Path Configuration

You must configure your computer so it can find the path of the installed Java SE JDK. Establishing the path of execution is a major configuration step that must be completed.

2.2.1 What is an execution path?

An execution path is the location or directory in which the commands to execute a program are stored. For example,

C:\Program Files\Java\jdk1.7.045\bin

is the execution path or directory containing the Java compiler/interpreter in a typical Window's-based installation. It may be more convenient to compile and execute your Java code within any directory your program is saved rather than the directory specified by the execution path. The commonly used Java operational commands are:

1. javac – Java source code compilation command. This command will compile Java source code and generate the bytecode if there are no syntax errors; however, it will stop compilation if a syntax error is found in the code.

2. java – Java execution command. It will execute the bytecode of the Java application generated by the compiler.

Although the execution path is automatically configured when using a Java IDE, such as NetBeans, Eclipse or TextPad, it is good to know the execution path should you wish to compile and execute your code outside the IDE directly under the operating system.

Assume we have installed Java SE JDK in the system default directory as follows:

```
C:\Program Files\java\jdk1.8.0_131\
```

The execution path is:

```
C:\Program File\java\jdk1.8.0_131\bin;
```

However, if the Java SE package is installed in a directory other than the default directory, you may use the Windows search command to locate and identify the directory where the package is stored:

1. Enter keyword "Java" in the search file or folder.
2. Open the Java folder you have found by the search. Find the folder with JDK version number and open it.
3. Find the bin folder and open it.
4. Copy the entire address in the address field located at the top of the window. This address is the execution path.

The following section discusses how to configure the execution path in different operating systems.

2.2.2 How to setup the execution path

The following are the steps to setup the execution path in Windows 2000/NT/XP:

1. Click on Start menu. In Control Panel, double click on System.
2. In System Properties, click on Advanced, then Environment Variables, as shown in Figure 2.1
3. In System Environment dialog box, select Path, then press Edit, as shown in Figure 2.2

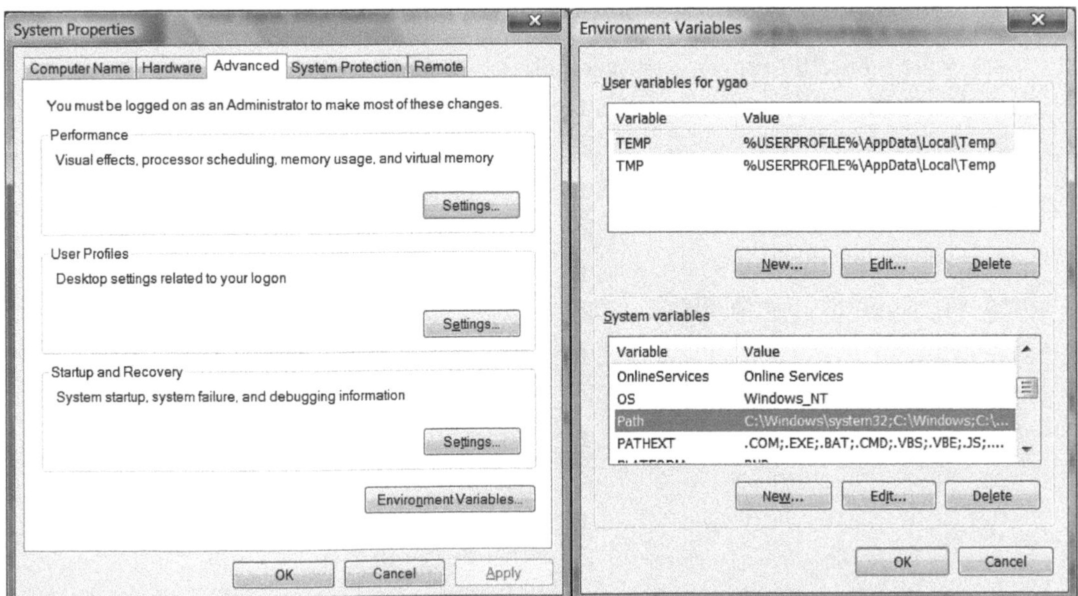

Figure 2.1 Step 2 in the path setup   Figure 2.2 Step 3 in the path setup

4. In the pop-up window of System Environment Variable, click on Variable field, and move the cursor to the end of existing path.

5. Assume the execution path is: C:\Program Files\Java\jdk1.8.0_131\bin. Enter

```
;C:\Program Files\Java\jdk1.8.0_131\bin;
```

at the end of the field. Note: The beginning and ending semi-colons ";" are required.

6. Press the OK button three times to complete your configuration of the execution path.

***Note**: The steps may vary if the version of the operating system is different.*

The following are the steps to setup the execution path in Windows Vista:

1. Click on Start menu, then Select Control Panel.

2. Click on System and Maintenance, then System.

3. Click on Change Settings, Continue, and then Advanced tab. A dialog box will pop up.

4. Use the same procedures described in Steps 4 to 6 above to complete the configuration.

2.3 Test Out Your Installation

You may use the following steps to test if the Java SE JDK software has successfully been installed and configured:

2.3.1 Test steps

1. Click Start menu -> Programs -> Accessories -> Command Prompt and get into the operating system window.

2. Type the following command:

```
javac
```

The installation is successful if the following message shown in Figure 2.3 is displayed. If an error message is displayed, it will be necessary to review the error and re-install the software and/or re-configure the system.

```
C:\Windows\system32\cmd.exe
C:\Users\ygao>javac
Usage: javac <options> <source files>
where possible options include:
  -g                         Generate all debugging info
  -g:none                    Generate no debugging info
  -g:{lines,vars,source}     Generate only some debugging info
  -nowarn                    Generate no warnings
  -verbose                   Output messages about what the compiler is doing
  -deprecation               Output source locations where deprecated APIs are u
sed
  -classpath <path>          Specify where to find user class files and annotati
on processors
  -cp <path>                 Specify where to find user class files and annotati
on processors
  -sourcepath <path>         Specify where to find input source files
  -bootclasspath <path>      Override location of bootstrap class files
  -extdirs <dirs>            Override location of installed extensions
  -endorseddirs <dirs>       Override location of endorsed standards path
  -proc:{none,only}          Control whether annotation processing and/or compil
ation is done.
  -processor <class1>[,<class2>,<class3>...] Names of the annotation processors
to run; bypasses default discovery process
  -processorpath <path>      Specify where to find annotation processors
  -parameters                Generate metadata for reflection on method paramete
rs
  -d <directory>             Specify where to place generated class files
  -s <directory>             Specify where to place generated source files
  -h <directory>             Specify where to place generated native header file
s
  -implicit:{none,class}     Specify whether or not to generate class files for
implicitly referenced files
  -encoding <encoding>       Specify character encoding used by source files
  -source <release>          Provide source compatibility with specified release
```

Figure 2.3 Use javac command to test installation

You may also use the java command

```
java -version
```

to test for a successful installation by displaying the version of the installed JDK.

2.3.2 Class path

JVM may not correctly execute the code even though it contains no compilation errors due to a conflict with other software configurations. It is possible other installed software may have automatically changed the current Java execution path in the class path of your computer system.

The class path is used to tell the operating system where the bytecode generated after compilation is stored. The JRE must also know where all necessary bytecode files, including API files and other execution tools for your application, are stored. Usually, when a Java code is executed, the JRE will automatically run the program from the current execution path where the bytecode is stored and search the directory where the API files and execution tools are located. The JRE will not find these files if the current path is modified by some other software, thereby resulting in an execution error.

The current path denoted as a dot "." in operating systems. We can solve the problem by adding the current path at the beginning of the class path, so your code will be executed correctly.

The following are the steps to add the current path into class path on a Windows platform:

1. Refer to Steps 1 and 2 of Section 2.2.2 to access the Environment Variables.
2. Select Classpath in System Environment box, and press Edit.
3. In the pop-up window, click on variable value, and move the cursor to the beginning.
4. Type **.;** at the beginning.
5. Press all OK buttons in turn to complete the setup.

More Info: *The above steps may vary depending upon the operating system. You may also place the current path at the beginning of the execution path if your code still cannot be executed after setting up the classpath.*

2.4 Java IDE

The JDK does not provide a text editor for source code editing. You may use any text editor, e.g., NotePad, or word processor to type, modify, and save your Java source code. These software tools, however, are not designed for code editing and, therefore, may not be convenient for programming purposes.

2.4.1 What is Java IDE?

Java IDEs (Integrated Development Environment) have been developed by third-party companies or partners of Sun Microsystems. They are designed as Java application software development tools. A typical Java IDE not only provides source code editing capabilities, but also provides functionality for compilation, execution, syntax checking, keyword highlighting, API assistance, project and package creation, and file organization. These functions are displayed in GUI (graphical user interface) windows. There are many popular Java IDEs; most of them are freely downloadable.

We begin our introduction of popular Java IDEs by discussing the downloading, installation, configuration, and use of NetBeans. Other Java IDEs, such as TextPad, Eclipse, and BlueJ, are discussed in later sections.

More Info: *Many Java IDEs support multi-language development.*

2.4.2 Why use NetBeans?

NetBeans IDE, short for NetBeans, is an open-source IDE owned by Oracle. It was originally established in 1996 as the student project Czech. NetBeans is a freely downloadable software development package for Java SE and Java EE.

NetBeans provides multiple environments for use in the software application development process:

1. Text editing.
2. Automatic syntax checking and correction.
3. Java keyword highlighting and color display.
4. Real-time API library assisting.
5. Cross-referencing of API library.
6. Multi-language editing.
7. Debugging.
8. Project creation and organization.
9. Package creation and organization.
10. Plugin manager.
11. Access for many ancillary online services for help.
12. Multi-window view.
13. Quick search and customizable workspace.

It is not too difficult to use these functions since most of them are displayed in the smart-tags as notes.

2.4.3 How to install and use NetBeans

You can download NetBeans from the following website:

http://www.netbeans.org

The default installation mode is usually satisfactory for installing NetBeans. Figure 2.4 shows **HelloApp.java** in the editing window of NetBeans and its result of the code's execution.

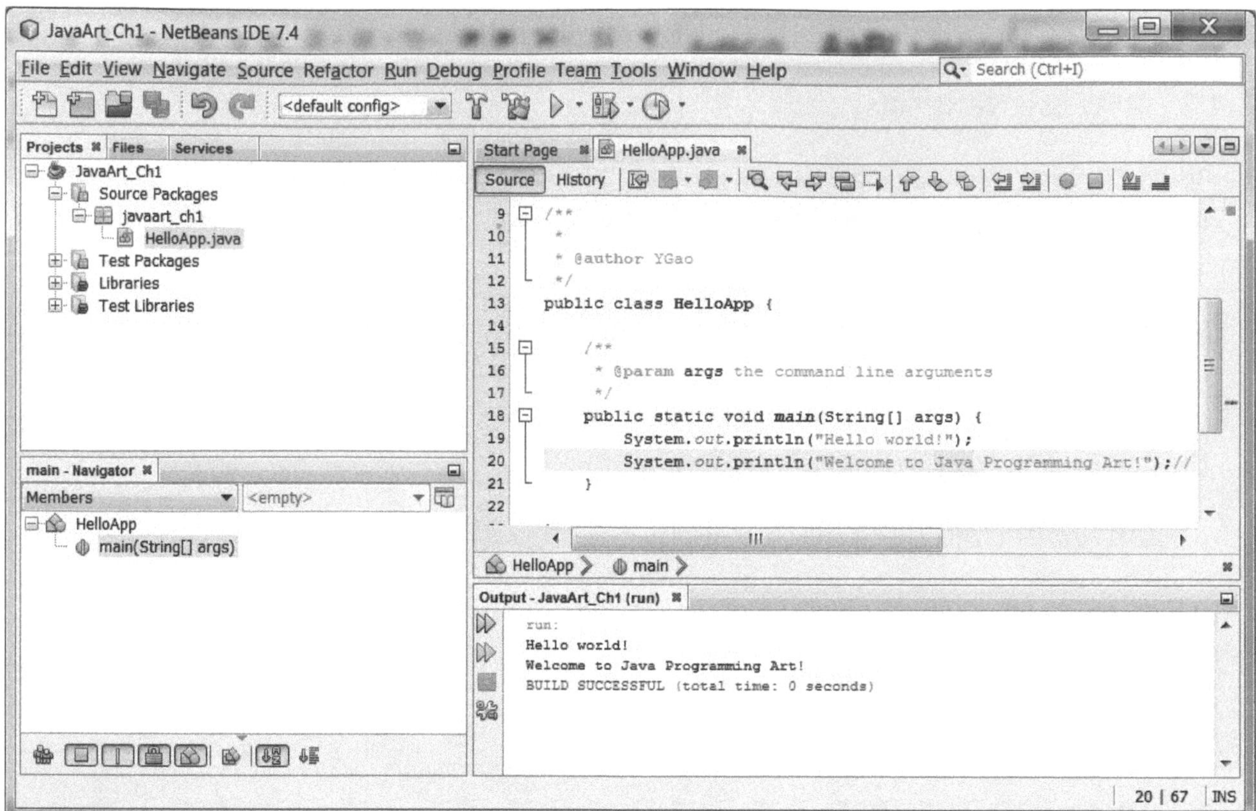

Figure 2.4 HelloApp in editing window of NetBeans and its execution result

The following are the major functions of NetBeans:

- Create Project – click on **File** in menu, select **New Project...**, default selections of **Java** and **Java Application** are displayed in a popup window (you may ignore Filter which is used in Servlets), click on **Next**, type your project name (for example, **Product**), browse to the location you want to store your project; you may deselect **Create Main Class** if you are not creating a driver code for the project, and then click on **Finish**. A code editing window with the default template will be displayed and now you are ready to type the code or copy and paste the existing code into this window. It will automatically display the syntax error if there is any in your code.

- Create file – you may create many files (Java classes) in a project. Click on **File** in menu, select **New File...**, default selections of **Java** and **Java Class** are displayed in a popup window; you may select **Java Main Class** in **File Type** window if you are coding a driver code, click on **Next**, type the class name (for example, **Hello** for a business, or operation class), and then press **Finish**. The editing window will provide code body under class name **Hello**.

- NetBeans automatically checks all syntax errors and compiles your code in the editing window.

- Run Project or File – press Run menu, select Run Project if you want to execute entire project, or select Run File if you want to execute the driver code.

More info: *Since NetBeans automatically checks syntax errors, it will generate the bytecode after all syntax errors have been corrected. As such, it does not provide a separate step to compile the source code. Use of the defined package is discussed in later chapters.*

2.4.4 Compiler errors, run-time errors and debugging

In traditional Java editing packages, a list of any syntax errors is displayed after the code is compiled. NetBeans combines these two steps in one operation by displaying any syntax error made as code is entered in its editing workbench. It even provides possible options to aid in making corrections. This unique functionality guarantees your code contains correct syntax, thereby increasing efficiency in code editing.

Java requires that the source code file name must be the same as the class name and must use **.java** as the file type. This requirement may seem odd and often causes difficulties for beginners learning Java. In NetBeans, the source code file is saved automatically by the editing workbench using the Java file naming extension. If the class name is changed in the source code, NetBeans will automatically change the file name accordingly.

3W *Examples of syntax errors are misspelling, mismatched braces and parentheses, illegal expressions, improper use of Java keywords, et cetera. Source code can be executed only after it has been compiled automatically with no syntax errors.*

More Info: *NetBeans uses its own input/output console to display I/O messages. It will not use the input/output console of the operating system.*

We can also use a variety of debugging modes to execute source code for the purpose of checking logical errors. A logical error is also called a run-time error. Your code will not generate the correct result if it contains a logical error. Debugging tools are used to help detect logical errors at run-time. Figure 2.5 shows the debugging windows wherein the code can be executed step-by-step and any changes of selected variables can be observed throughout the execution.

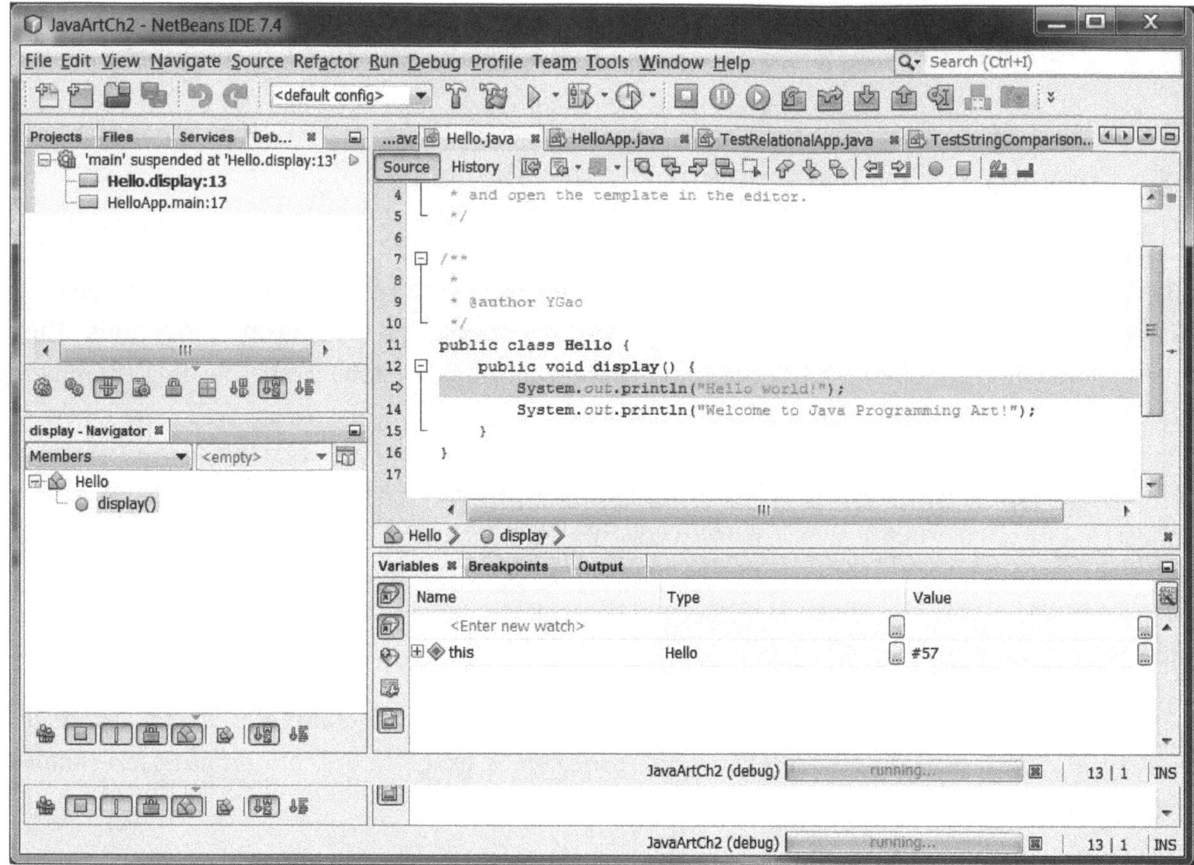

Figure 2.5 Debug windows in NetBeans

We can also set break points in the execution sequence to aid in debugging. Execution will stop at each break point allowing the monitoring of value changes of selected variables. This capability provides valuable clues in making corrections in the code.

3W *Run-time errors are logical mistakes in the code such that the JVM cannot execute correctly. The program may not terminate execution gracefully and possibly not even display the run-time error message(s). Common run-time errors include division by zero, insufficient memory, inability to find a required class, et cetera.*

2.5 Use of Java Commands

All Java commands in NetBans are provided by the JDK installed on your computer. NetBeans provides a more user-friendly interface because these commands are executed through the GUI. As a Java programmer, however, it is much better to know how to directly use Java commands without IDEs. These commands are executed in the Command Prompt window of the operating system.

2.5.1 Javac command

The javac command is short for "Java compiler" and is used to compile source code and generate the bytecode file(s):

```
javac FileName.java
```

Note that all Java commands are case-sensitive, lower-case letters. Assume we have a Java source code file **HelloApp.java**, saved in the following directory:

```
C:\Java\Ch2\HelloApp.java
```

After getting into the Command Prompt window of the operating system, navigate to directory C:\Java\Ch2, type the command **javac** and press the enter key:

```
C:\Java\Ch2\javac HelloApp.java
```

The Java compiler will check the syntax of the code, translate it into bytecode, and save it as file **HelloApp.class** in the current directory. Class files are written in binary format and are non-readable.

If there is any syntax error in the code, the **javac** command will stop the translation and display the error message on the screen noting the line number(s) of the syntax errors in the source code and causes of the errors similar to those as shown in Figure 2.6. No bytecode file will be created.

```
C:\Windows\system32\cmd.exe
Microsoft Windows [Version 6.1.7601]
Copyright (c) 2009 Microsoft Corporation.  All rights reserved.

C:\Users\ygao>cd\

C:\>cd temp

C:\Temp>javac HelloApp.java
HelloApp.java:10: error: ';' expected
        System.out.println("Hello world!")
                                          ^
1 error

C:\Temp>_
```

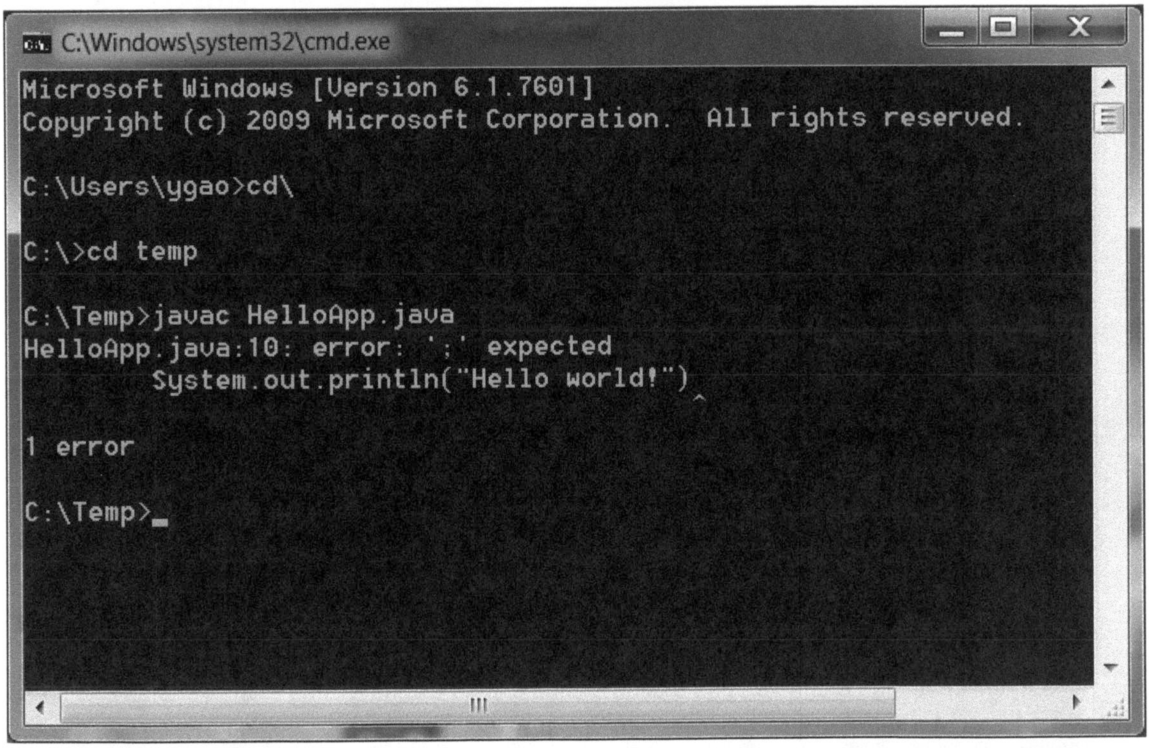

Figure 2.6 javac displays an syntax error message in DOS

This error message indicates a semi-colon is needed in line 6 of **HelloApp.java**. Now you must return to the editing mode, correct the line by adding a semi-colon at the end of the statement, save the file, and recompile the file assuring that no syntax errors remain so the bytecode file will be created.

It may be necessary to use some operating system commands when executing Java commands in various operating systems. Section 2.5.4 discusses commonly used DOS, Linux, and Unix commands.

2.5.2 Java command

The command java is used to execute the byte code:

```
java FileName
```

It will interpret the bytecode line by line and translate the code into executable machine code allowing it to be executed by the CPU. The Java interpreter is an important part of the JVM. The following example shows how to execute the file **HelloApp.class** using this command:

```
C:\Java\Ch2\java HelloApp
```

Note that the file type extension **.class** is omitted in the use of the java command. Figure 2.7 shows the result of the execution.

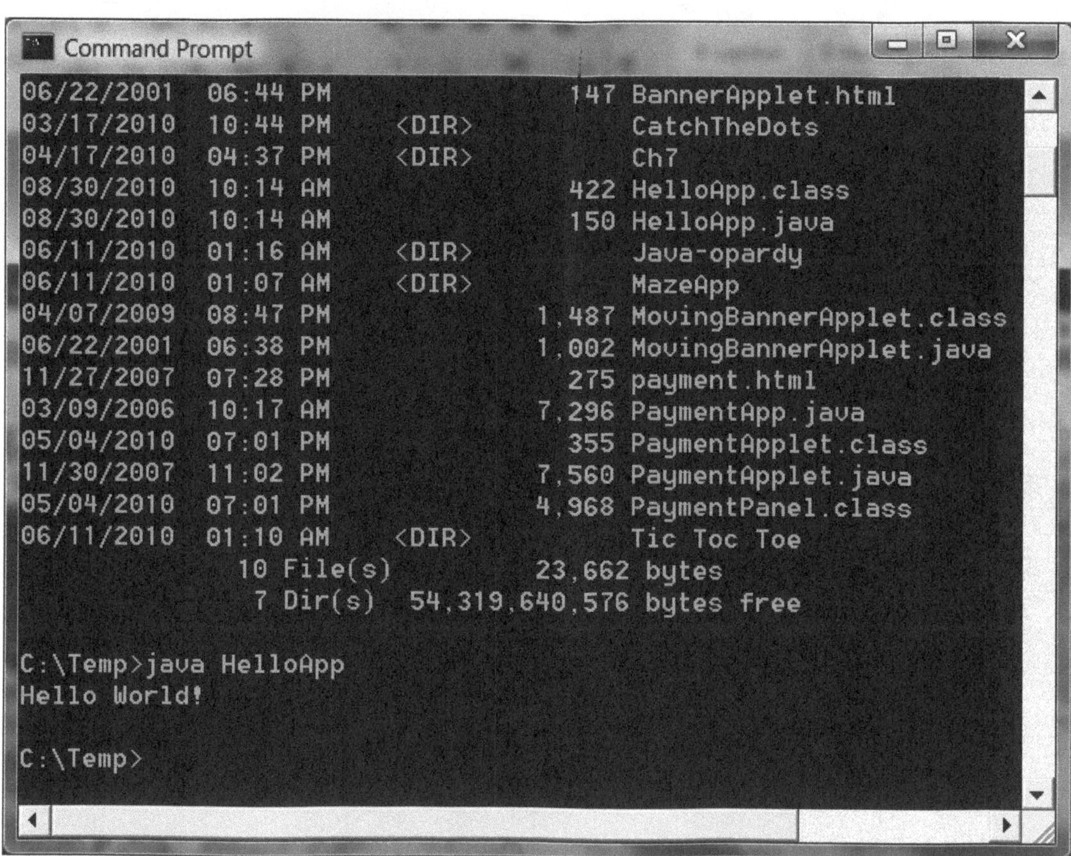

Figure 2.7 Execution result of HelloApp using java command

2.5.3 appletviewer command

The command **appletviewer** is used to execute applets. It will open a simplified internet browser **appletviewer** in JDK for your convenience in applet testing. Assume we modify **HelloApp.java** to become an applet code, **HelloApplet.java**, code a HTML file called **HelloApplet.html**, and save the files in directory **C:\Java\Ch1** as discussed in Chapter 1. After using **javac** to compile the applet, we invoke **appletviewer** to execute the HTML file, thereby calling the **HelloApplet** class file to display the execution result in the simplified browser as shown in Figure 2.8:

```
C:\Java\Ch1\appletviewer HelloApplet.html
```

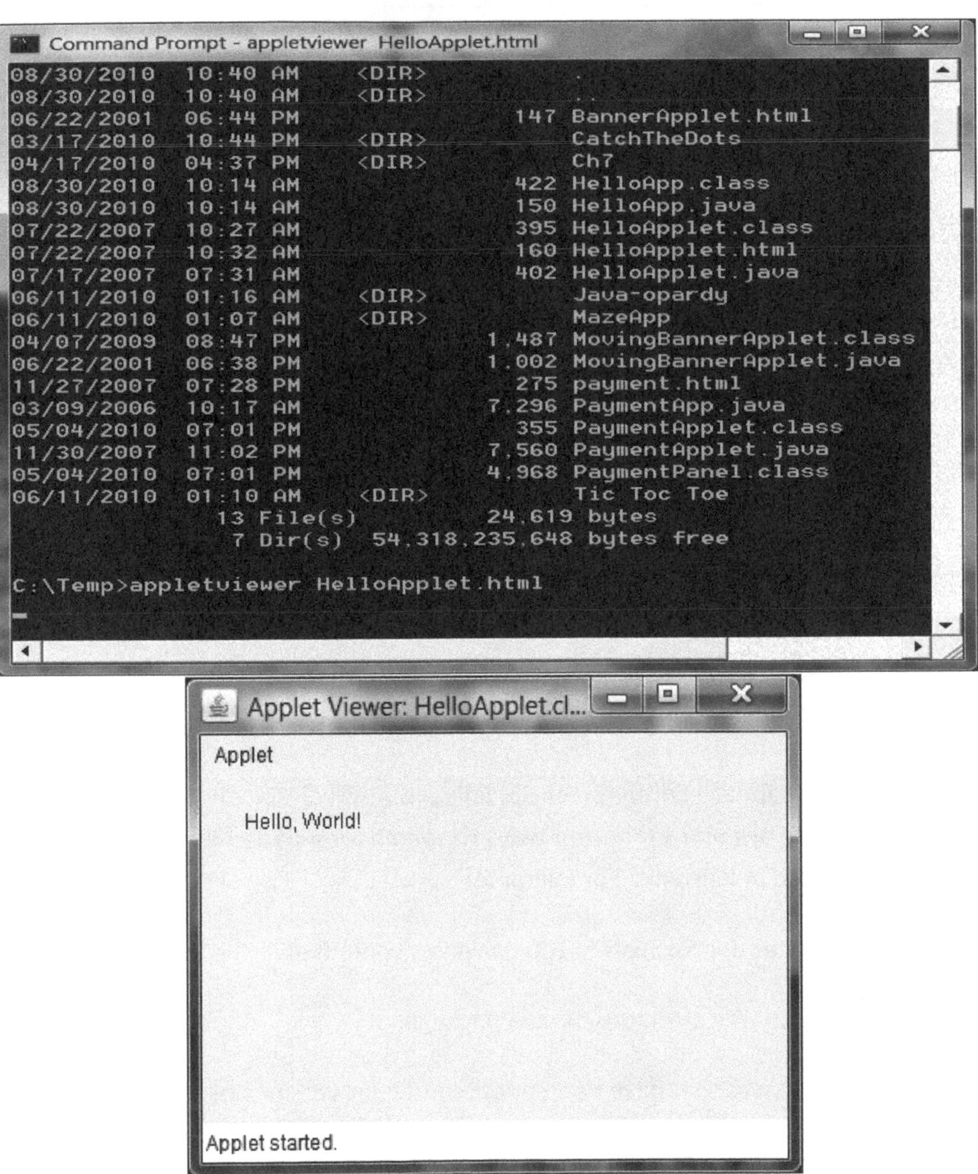

Figure 2.8 Use appletviewer to execute HelloApplet and the result of execution

More Info: ***appletviewer*** *will not provide any error message if there is any syntax error in the HTML file.*

More Info: *In NetBeans, as well as other IDEs, you can directly execute an applet without writing the required HTML file. The IDE will automatically provide this file for you.*

2.5.4 Commonly used DOS/Linux/Unix commands

It may be necessary to use some common DOS, Linux, or Unix commands when compiling and executing Java code directly under operating system control. These commands include the display and changing of file directories, listing of files, et cetera. Table 2.1 lists such commonly used DOS/Linux/Unix commands.

Table 2.1 Commonly used DOS/Linux/Unix commands

DOS	Linux/Unix	Meaning
Dir	ls, or ls –a	Display files and directories
cd\	Cd	Move from current directory to root or home directory
cd..	cd ..	Move from current directory to parent directory
Up and down arrow keys	Up and down arrow keys	Display the stack of executed commands

2.6 First Look at the Java API

The Java API (Application Programming Interface), also called the Java API libraries, are Java classes written by language developers or professionals in third-party companies. All API classes are open-source and are contained in the src.zip file in the JDK directory on your computer.

2.6.1 Understanding the Java API

You can view the Java API documentation and specifications at the following website:

http://www.oracle.com/technetwork/java/api-141528.html

Click on the Java Platform Standard Edition (Java SE) link and it will direct you to the core API documentation page. There are many different ways to search for a particular API class or method which you may be interested in learning. For example:

- Overview – Introduces approximately 200 packages contained in the Java API.
- Tree – Introduces the tree structure of Java packages.
- Deprecated – API classes that have been updated in later versions of the API.
- Index – Search by alphabetical order. This is the most commonly used method of searching.

- Help – Provides a simple explanation of the terminology and keywords used in the API documentation.
- It also lists all API classes in alphabetical order in a scrollable box on the left as shown in Figure 2.9.

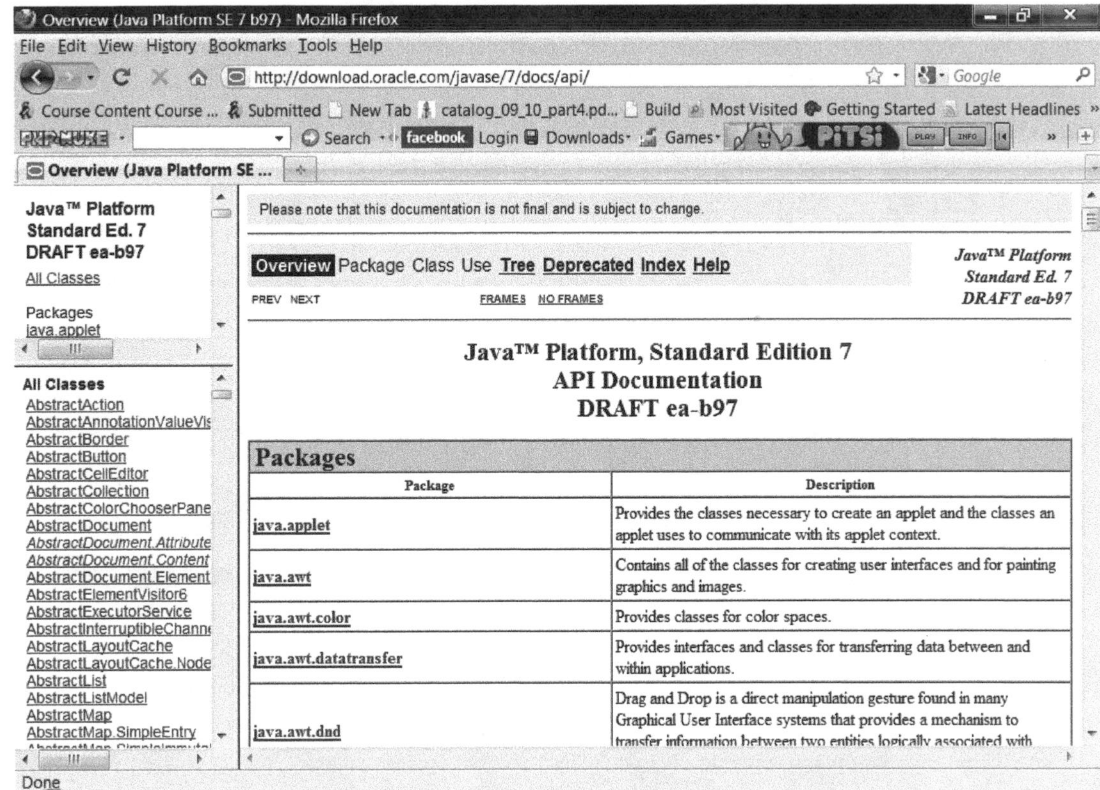

Figure 2.9 Java SE API docs

Assume you are interested in searching for **System.out.println()** method as used in HelloApp. You might begin by selecting the **P** in the Index then locating **println(String x)** in the list. You will then see the technical description of this method. You could also search for **System.out** by clicking on **System** in the class list the further clicking on **out** as shown in Figure 2.10 and Figure 2.11.

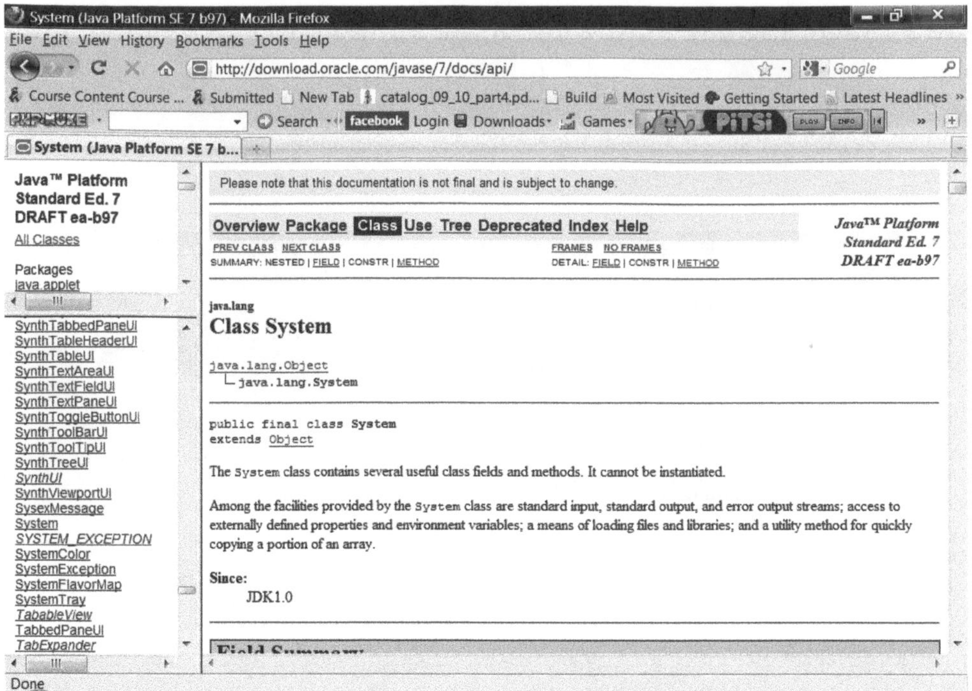

Figure 2.10 Search for explanation of System in API docs

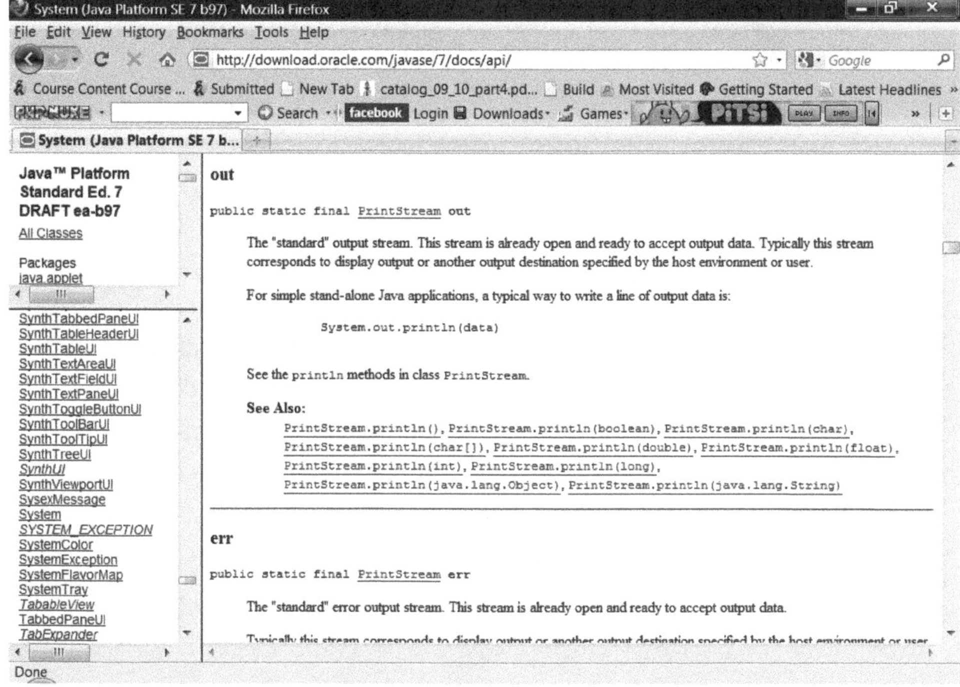

Figure 2.11 Explanation of System.out in API docs

From Figure 2.10 we may see the System class of the Java API belongs to the **java.lang** package and is also defined as a class under **java.lang.Object** representing a subclass or inherited class of Object. For now we may think of a package as a directory containing related API classes. These concepts are discussed further in Chapter 7 and Chapter 12, respectively. We may also see the System class is used to form standard input/output, i.e., accepting input from the keyboard or displaying output on the screen. Initial readings of the Java API descriptions and explanations may seem imposing; this feeling should diminish as you proceed through this text and gain more experience in Java programming.

The Java API docs are the official documentation and specification of the Java language. By using this documentation you will understand the structure of the API package, relationship between the components, and specifications of the packages, classes, data, and methods.

The following list summarizes the API documentation and will hopefully provide a better understanding of its content:

- API is organized by packages.
- Packages may be viewed as directories storing API classes.
- Related classes are included within a package.
- Class names begin with an upper-case letter.
- Many methods and data are included in a class. Each method contains parentheses—even if it uses no parameters—and an associated return type. Each method name begins with a lower-case letter.
- Methods of the same name may appear in different classes and may carry out the same, similar, or different tasks.

For your convenience, the Java API docs can be downloaded to your computer and saved in the JDK directory.

2.7 Other Java IDEs

The following sections introduce several common Java IDEs: TextPad, Eclipse, and BlueJ. These IDEs are freely downloadable.

2.7.1 TextPad

TextPad is developed by Helios Software Co. It is a simplified Java IDE focusing on ease-of-use. TextPad is ideal for beginners learning Java. However, it does not include any debugging capabilities. It can be downloaded from

http://www.textpad.com.

It is easily installed by following the dialog box prompts and pressing the **Next** button; no configuration is required. Figure 2.12 shows the **HelloApp** code in the text edit window of TextPad.

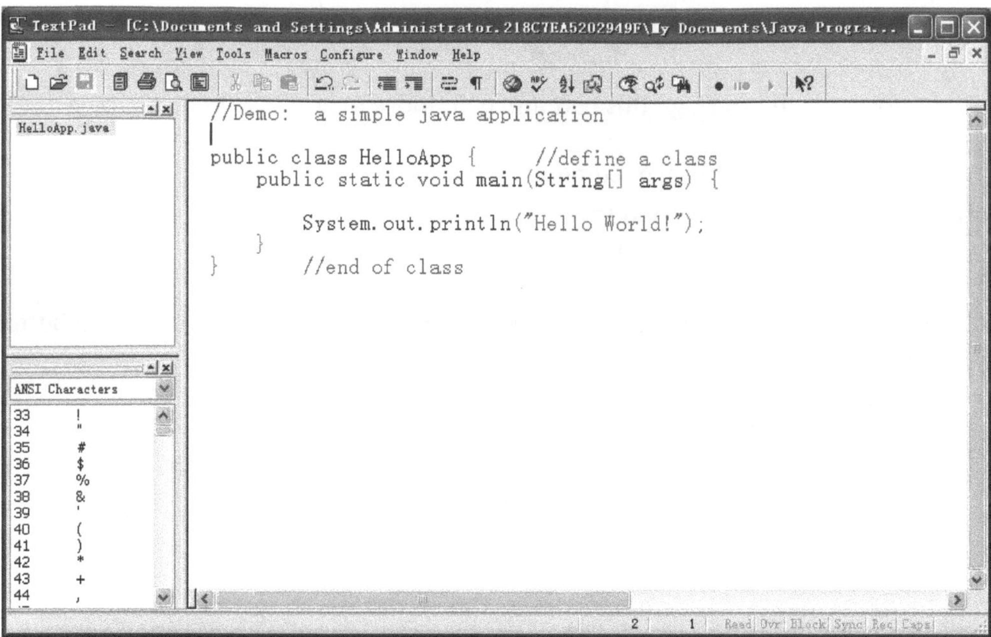

Figure 2.12 HelloApp in text edit window of TextPad

More Info: *TextPad doesn't support for OS, or Linux/Unix.*

The following are commonly used functions in TextPad:

Save file – Press File from Menu, select Save As, in Save as type:, select Java (*.java). Note that file name must be the same as class name. Press Save button.

Compile code – Press Tools from Menu, Select External Tools, Compile Java. If there is any syntax error it will display the error message at the bottom of window. You may also use short-cut Ctrl+1 to compile code. It will automatically save the code after it compiled.

Run application – Press Tools from Menu, select External Tools, and then Run Java Application. It will display the execution result in operating system window. If there is any run-time error, JVM will terminate the execution, and display the run-time error message in operating system window as well. You may also use short-cut Ctrl+2 to run the code.

Run applet – Press Tools from Menu, select External Tools, and then Run Java Applet. TextPad will search if there is HTML file provided by you. It will open the HTML file in appletviewer to run the applet; otherwise, TextPad will automatically write a HTML file to run the applet. You may also use short-cut Ctrl+3 to run the applet.

2.7.2 Eclipse

Eclipse is an open-source community led by IBM. It was originally established in 2001 as the Eclipse Project and later renamed the Eclipse Foundation in 2004. The Eclipse IDE for Java Developers, or

Eclipse, for short, is an open-source, freely downloadable software development package for Java SE and Java EE. Many features in NetBeans are similar in Eclipse.

You can download Eclipse from the following website:

http://www.eclipse.org/downloads/

After downloading the zipped file containing the Eclipse IDE for Java Developers, all you need to do to begin is to unzip the file. Eclipse will automatically create a directory, Eclipse, and save all unzipped files, including eclipse.exe, in this directory.

The following steps must be executed the first time you run Eclipse:

1. Execute Eclipse.exe
2. Click on Workbench, as shown in Figure 2.13.
3. In the Workspace field, enter or select a directory to save your code(s), e.g., C:\JavaBook. You may also use the system default workspace as the directory in which to save your files for the project. Press OK.

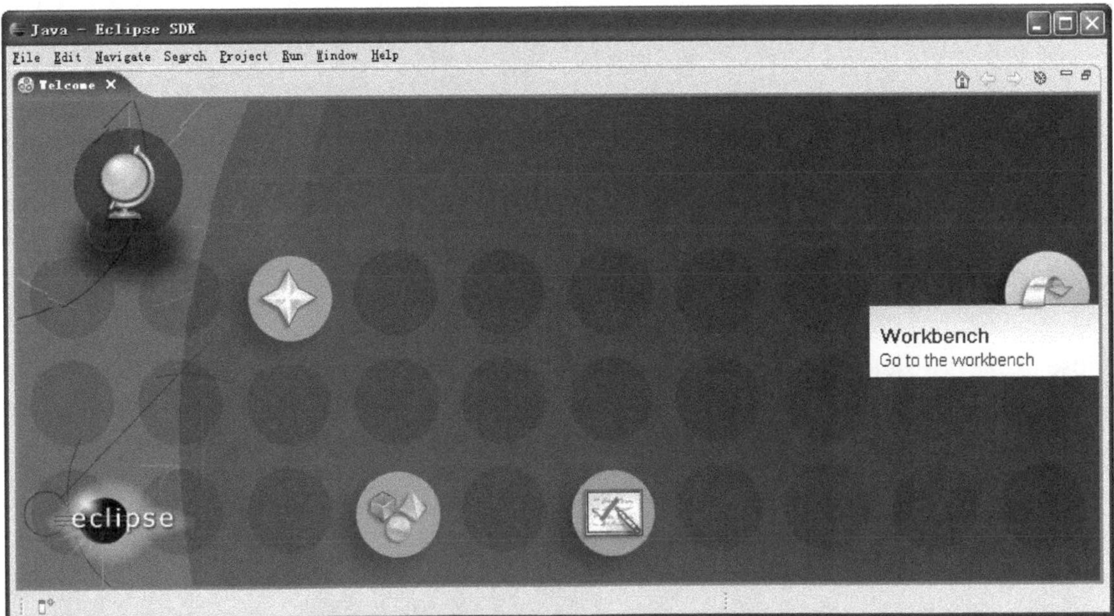

Figure 2.13 Workbench in Eclipse

4. Because all files are organized by project, you must also create a project after establishing a workspace.
5. The next level of file management in Eclipse is to establish a package. Packages are discussed in Chapter 12. After you establish a project, select File → New → Package → in the pop-up window. Enter the package name, e.g., ch2. You may also choose not to use a package and skip this step. A system default package will be used instead.

6. To create a class and begin entering code, select File → New → Class → in the pop-up window. Enter a class name, e.g., **HelloApp**, and press Finish.

Now you can enter your code in an editing window named **HelloApp**, as shown in Figure 2.14.

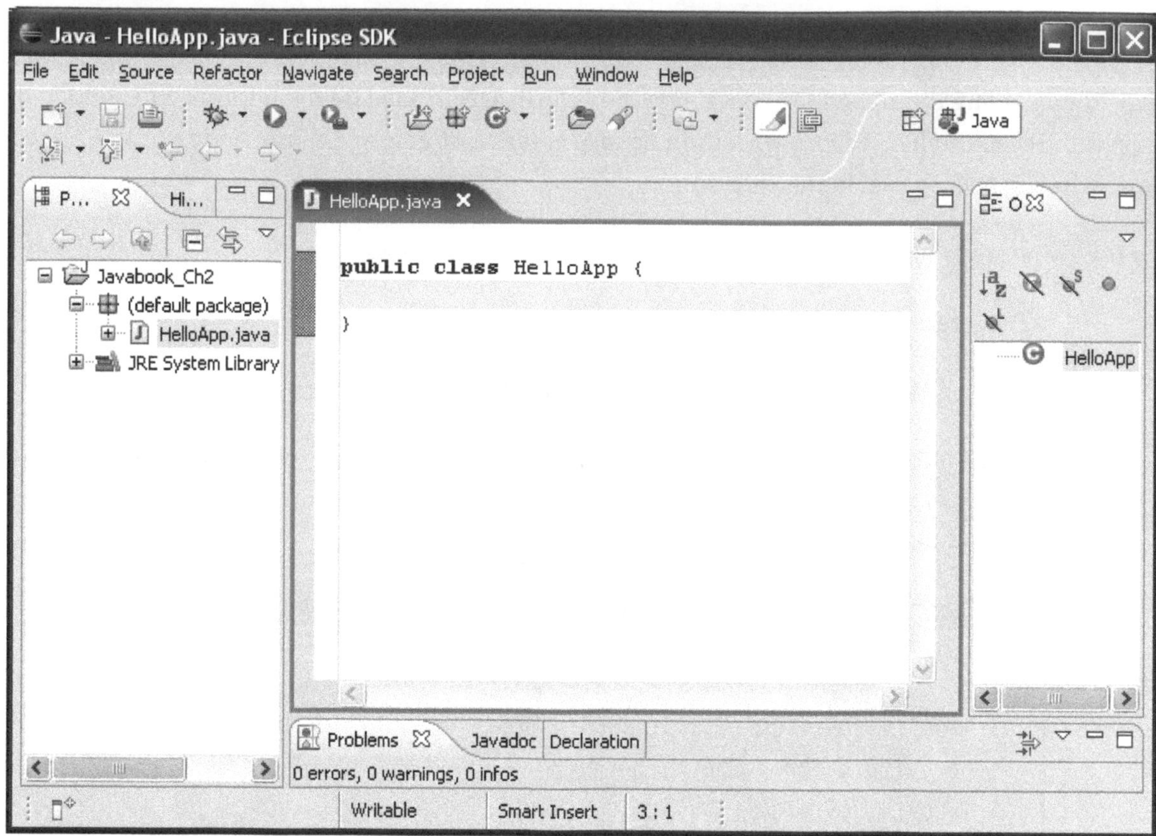

Figure 2.14 An editing window showing code body of HelloApp.java with system default package

Eclipse displays a welcome page the first time it is run. This page shows the major functions, examples, types of assistance, and the workbench. Figure 2.15 shows the source code editing window—the most frequently used workbench of Eclipse. We can see from Figure 2.15 the project name is Ch2. A system default package name is also used. We discuss the concepts and techniques of packages in later chapters.

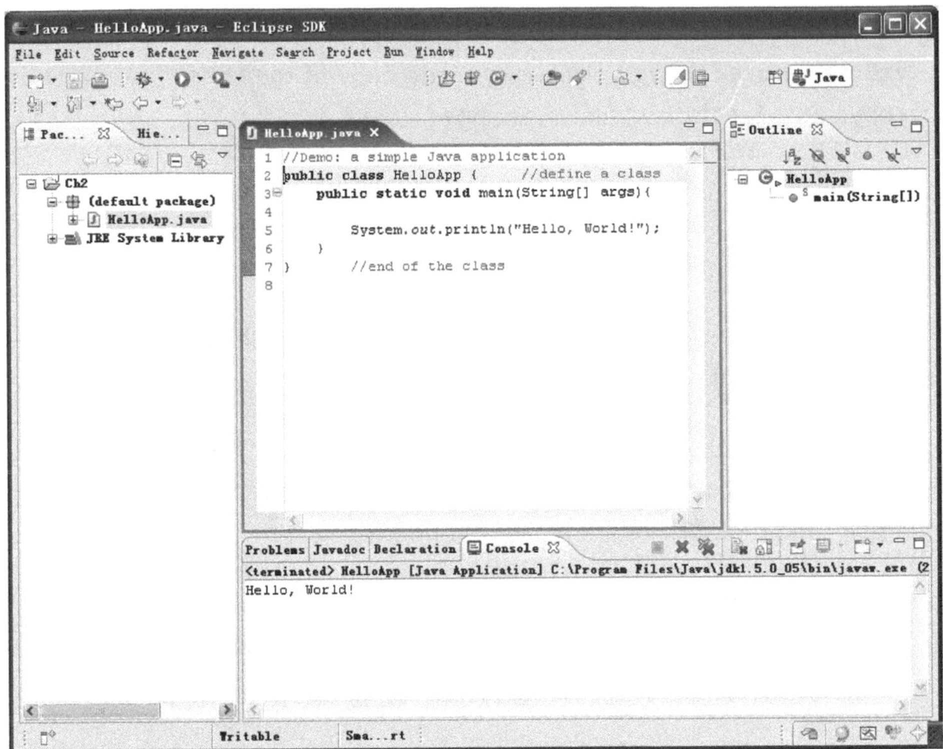

Figure 2.15 Source code workbench in Eclipse

More Info: *Line numbers are displayed for convenience and reference in discussion. They are not part of the actual source code. Eclipse provides a line number display function.*

2.7.3 BlueJ

BlueJ has been developed especially for beginners to learn Java programming and the structure of object-oriented programs in an intuitive way. Its workplace window presents diagrams illustrating the relationship between classes. Although not as popular in use as NetBeans and Eclipse, BlueJ is easy to use and provides the basic functions of editing, compiling, and running the code as well as displaying UML charts. BlueJ also provides simplified debugging functions.

BlueJ is available from: http://www.bluej.org.

The installation of BlueJ is simple and easy. The default installation is usually satisfactory.

The major functions of BlueJ are:

- Create project – click on Project, select new project, select or create a directory you want to save the project from the pop-up window, press create.
- Create class – press new class button, in class name field, type your class name (for example, HelloApp), press OK; if the class is an applet, select applet in class type, and then press OK. It will display an UML chart in the workplace window.

- Edit code – double-click on the class name in the UML chart you want to edit, an editing window will be popped up and display the code body of the class. You can type, modify, delete, and copy and paste the code in this window.
- Compile code – Press Compile in the editing window. It will display syntax error message in color if there is any in your code. For some common syntax errors, it will make automatic corrections.
- Save file – Press the class in the editing window, select save. It will automatically save a compiled code if there is no syntax error.
- Run application – in project workplace window, move your mouse and point to the class in the UML chart. Click the right mouse button, select run method (for example, void main(String[] args)) , and then click on OK in the pop-up window.
- Run applet – in the project work window, move your mouse and point to Applet class in the chart, and click the right mouse button, select run applet in the pop-up window, and then press OK.

Figure 2.16 shows **HelloApp** and **HelloApplet** in BlueJ's editing window.

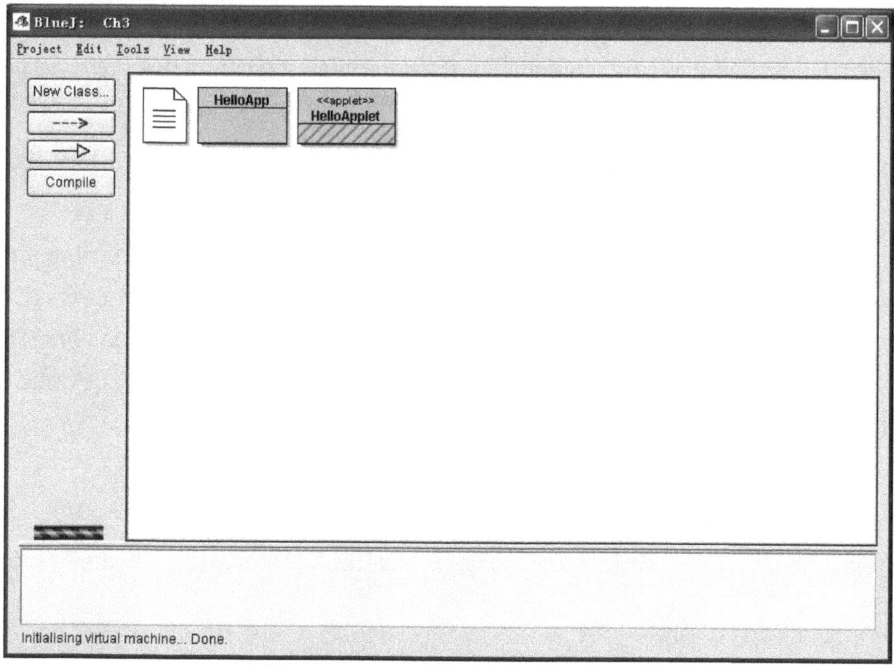

Figure 2.16 HelloApp and HelloApplet in BlueJ's editing window

Exercises

1. Follow the steps in Section 2.1 to download the latest version of Java SE JDK and install it on your computer. Follow the steps in Section 2.2 to establish the configuration path and test if it is correct.

2. Follow the instructions in Section 2.4 and Section 2.7 to select a Java IDE of your choice, download the software, and install it on your computer. Create a project and a Java application. In an editing window of the IDE, open the file HelloApp.java from Chapter 2 as provided from the author's webpage. Copy and paste the code to the window you just created. Change the class name if necessary. Save and execute the code. Modify the code to display "**Java programming world, how are you?**"

3. Create a directory called Temp under root C:\. Copy the source code file you completed in Exercise 2 to this directory. Open the operating system window and change the directory to Temp. Use the **javac** and java commands, respectively, to compile and execute this code. Observe the difference in output between that generated by the java command issued through the IDE and that invoked in the operating system window.

4. Following the discussion in Sections 2.4 and 2.7, select a Java IDE other than TextPad, for example NetBeans, download and install it on your computer. Create a project and new applet file. In another editing window, open the HelloApplet.java file introduced in Chapter 1. This file is available in the Ch1 folder on the author's website. Copy and paste this code to your newly created applet window. Save and run the code. Add a new output statement to display the message: "**Welcome to the Java programming world!**"

5. Create a directory, if it does not already exist, called Temp under root C:\. Copy the source code file you completed in Exercise 4 to this directory. Open the operating system window and change the directory to Temp. Use the **javac** and **java** commands, respectively, to compile and execute this code. Observe the difference in output between that generated by the java command issued through the IDE and that invoked in the operating system window.

6. Following the discussion in Section 2.6, install the latest Java SE API documentation on your computer in a directory called docs. Search for the method: **drawString(String, int, int)**. What class and package does it belong to?

7. Use examples to explain what a syntax error and run-time error are. How can you correct a syntax error? How can you detect and debug a run-time error?

8. Why and how can some advanced Java IDEs run your code directly without having to compile the code first?

9. Search the internet to find tutorials for the Java IDE you have installed on your computer. Select a topic or operation you are interested in and learn how to use it through the tutorial. Save the necessary files in your self-study directory.

"Know the other, know the self, hundred battles without danger."

– Sun Tsu, The Art of War

Chapter 3 Beginning Java Programming

Opportunity is always favorable to the person who prepares well. This is true in programming as well. Starting in this chapter, as your first step in Java programming, the basic concepts and skills in object-oriented programming, particularly in the Java language, will be discussed using examples. You will be able to prepare well if you follow the guidance in this chapter.

3.1 The Basics

Statements are basic elements in a program. Many lines of statements make up a program. For example, if the program were a building, the statements are the building materials. We start with a discussion of the statements in Java.

3.1.1 Statements

The following line is a Java statement:

float average = sum / 5;

This statement tells the Java compiler that the value of the variable **sum** will be divided by 5 and the result will be assigned to another variable **average** as a float to the left of assignment sign =. The statement ends with a semicolon. This statement is called an assignment statement. In Java programming, a statement may begin at any position in an editing screen and continue for any number of lines.

There are many different types of statements in Java. They are used to carry out a variety of calculations and operations in a program. Different types of statements include: incrementing/decrementing statements, branch statements, loop statements, input/output statements, and so on. Although most statements end with a semicolon, a loop statement ends with a closing brace}. Table 3.1 lists the commonly used statements in Java.

Table 3.1 Commonly used statements in Java

Statement	meaning
x = 19.5;	Assignment statement (discussed in 3.2.6)
y++; --i;	Incrementing and decrementing statements (discussed in 3.2.6)

name=JOptionPane.showInputDialog("What is your name? ");	Input statement (discussed in 3.4.7)
System.out.println("Hello! ");	Output statement (discussed in 3.5.1)
if (x > 90) grade = 'A';	Simple branch or if statement (discussed in 3.6.4)

while (count < 10) {
sum +=count;
count++:
}
	Loop or while loop statement (discussed in 3.6.6)

3W: *A statement tells the compiler what to do and normally ends with a semicolon. A program consists of many lines of different types of statements.*

3.1.2 Always use comments

Comments are used to explain what the program does and what specific blocks and lines of statements do. They are part of Java documentation. Their purpose is to increase the program's readability and make maintenance and updating easier. Since the Java compiler ignores comments, the programmer is always encouraged to use them throughout the code. Their use will not affect the operation of the code.

There are two different styles of Java comments: C style and C++ style. A C style comment begins with **/*** and ends with ***/**. It is also called a block comment since it can occupy multiple lines. C style comments are used to document information that applies to the entire program or the block of code. For example:

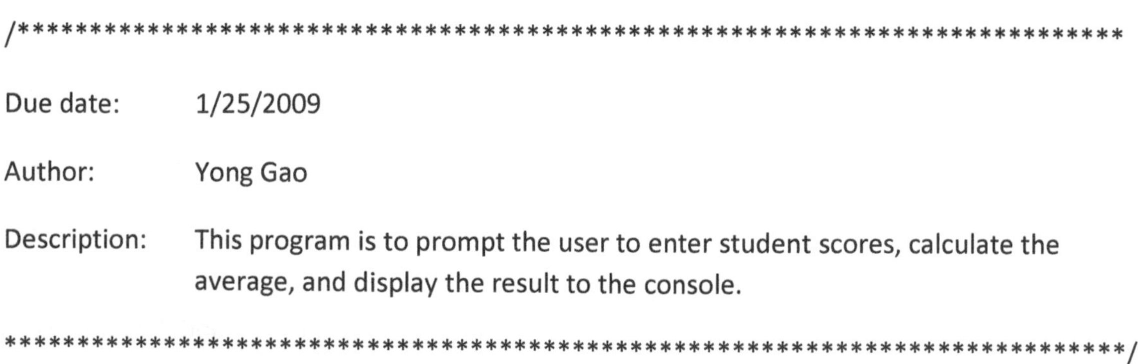

```
/*****************************************************************************

Due date:       1/25/2009

Author:         Yong Gao

Description:    This program is to prompt the user to enter student scores, calculate the
                average, and display the result to the console.

*****************************************************************************/
```

A C++ style comment begins with double slashes **//** and is followed one line of explanation. You must begin each line of a multi-line comment block with **//**. It is used to describe what a specific statement or group of the statements do. For example:

```
float sum, average;        //declare float type of variables
//compute the average and display the result
average = sum / 5;
System.out.println("Average = " + average);
```

Table 3.2 lists commonly used Java comments.

Table 3.2 Commonly used Java comments

Comment	Style and use
/* Author: John Smith Project: customer claim Due date: 6/10/2008 Description: This is just a demo. */	A C style comment. Usually placed at the beginning of a program to provide information about the code. It is also called as a block comment.
//set the count int count = 35;	A C++ style comment. It is used to explain the statement below. It is also called a single line comment.
int count = 35; //set the count	A C++ style comment. It is used to explain the preceding statement. It is also called an end-of-line comment.
/********************************* * This is traditional C style * comment, and it can go over many lines. *********************************/	A C style comment with multiple lines.
/* set the taxRate */ float taxRate = 0.0875;	A C style comment with a single line.

In addition to these two styles of comments, Java also provides a series of commands in document development and management. For example, we can use **javadoc** commands to create the document Web pages of Java classes. We will discuss **javadoc** in Chapter 12. A good programmer must know how to document the code well.

3.1.3 Identifiers

Identifiers are the names created by a programmer within a program. Variable names, class names, and method names are examples of identifiers. Identifiers cannot be any keywords reserved by the Java language. You must use the following rules in creating an identifier:

- An identifier starts with one of any letter, underscore _, or dollar sign $.
- It is followed by the combination of any letters, numbers (0-9), underscores, and dollar signs.
- It cannot be the same as any Java keyword.

The following are 53 Java keywords:

abstract	assert	boolean	break	byte	case	catch
Char	class	const	continue	default	do	double
Else	enum	extends	false	final	finally	float
For	goto	if	implements	import	instanceof	int
interface	long	native	new	null	package	private
protected	public	return	short	static	strictfp	super
switch	synchronized	this	throw	throws	transient	true
Try	void		volatile	while		

Following the introduction in this book, most of the keywords will be discussed using examples.

Although reserved as Java keywords, **const** and **goto** are no longer used and have no function. It is invalid to use Java keywords to name identifiers. The Java compiler will generate an error message if you do so.

According to the rules listed above in naming Java identifiers, the following are valid identifiers:

InvestmentApp	_discountRate	CHRIDSTAMS	Class_name
GameApplet	price	DAY_PER_WEEK	method_name
Employee	Price	x	variable_name
total	customer1	y$	CONST_NAME
total_output	customer_1	i_	_$88_valid_name

Because Java is a case-sensitive language, **price** and **Price** are two different identifiers. It should be noted that identifiers beginning with a dollar sign or an underscore are only used in special circumstances, such as the system calls.

Table 3.3 lists common mistakes in naming identifiers.

Table 3.3 Common mistakes in naming identifiers

Invalid identifier	Description
Investment App	Cannot use space
Float	Cannot use Java keyword
9_loop	Cannot start with a number
*pointer	Cannot start with an asterisk *
total-price	Cannot use dash -

In order to improve code readability, a professional Java programmer must also follow the Java naming conventions in addition to the rules in naming identifiers. Naming conventions are not the syntax, but rather recommendations made by the Java community. For example, a class name starts with a capital letter; a method or variable name begins with a lowercase letter; and a constant should contain all uppercase letters. Meaningful names and other recommendations are also provided. We will discuss more about naming conventions in the book.

3.2 Primative Data Types

Primative data types include numerical data, single characters, and **boolean** data (**true** or **false**). We often create a variable to hold the value for a particular data type so the value can be modified later. Data can be constant in which the value cannot be modified.

In addition to primative data types, Java also provides String and wrapper classes as object data types to perform text and arithmetic calculations. We will discuss wrapper classes in Chapter 5.

3.2.1 8 primative data types

Java provides 8 primative data types to create variables. Table 3.4 lists these data types together with their memory requirements (bytes) and value ranges.

Table 3.4 Eight primative data types in Java

Type	Name	Memory Requirement	Value range
byte	integer in byte	1	-128 – 127

short	short integer	2	-32,768 – 32,767
int	integer	4	-2,147,483,648 – 2,147,483,647
long	integer in long	8	-9,223,372,036,854,775,808 – 9,223,372,036,854,775,807
float	single float	4	-3.4E38 – 3.4E38 (up to 7 significant digits)
double	double float	8	-1.7E308 – 1.7E308 (up to 16 significant digits)
char	single character	2	Unicode character
boolean	boolean	1	true or false

Integer type variables, such as **byte**, **short**, **int**, and **long**, can only store whole numbers, while **float** and **double** variables store data as floating-point numbers. If a single-precision floating-point variable exceeds 7 significant digits, e.g., 123456.75, the eighth digit will be rounded up in the stored value. Java will display bigger or smaller floating-point numbers with scientific notation E. For example, 28600000.0 will be 2.86E7, and .000123 will be 1.23E-4.

Java uses Unicode to represent characters, thus requiring two bytes of storage for each character. As such, there are 65,536 characters in total. This may be compared to the traditional ASCII character set containing only 256 characters. For the purpose of compatibility and ease of use, the first 256 characters are the same as ASCII.

Boolean is a formal data type in Java. It should be noted that the values for Boolean data, **true** or **false**, must be in lower-case letters.

String is not a primative data type. It is provided by the Java language as an API (Application Programming Interface) class, or library class. We can tell String is a class as its name begins with an uppercase letter. Since String is a commonly used data type, Java provides a convenient way, direct referencing (referencing, in short) to define a String object. For example:

String str = "This is a string";   //str referencing to a String object

Although String referencing is the same as defining a primative type variable in its syntax, there are significant differences between them. We will discuss more about String in later chapters. To simplify its use, we consider String referencing as defining a String variable.

3.2.2 Define variables

The following example defines a double-precision variable called **num**:

```
double num;               //define a double type variable called num
```

A variable not only holds the value of the data, but the value can also be modified later. Since Java provides 8 primative data types, we can define 8 different types of variables. The syntax to define any type of variable is as follows:

dataType variableName;

dataType – one of eight data types.

variableName – must be a legal identifier and follow the naming

conventions. The following are more examples in defining variables:

```
byte letter;              //defining a byte type variable called letter
short l;                  //defining a short type variable called l
int count;                //defining a int type variable called count
char ch;                  //defining a char type variable called ch
long population;          //defining a long type variable called population
boolean flag;             //defining a boolean type variable called flag
float interestRate;       //defining a float type variable called interestRate
double total_output;      //defining a double type variable called total_output
```

You can also define many variables of the same type within one statement, e.g.:

```
int x, y, z;              //defining 3 int variables in a statement
double num1, num2;        //defining 2 double variables in a statement
```

Because whitespace (space, tab, return) is ignored during compilation, the following variable definitions are the same as above:

```
int  x,
   y,
   z;
double num1,
        num2;
```

In summary, the general syntax to define a variable is:

dataType varName1 [, varName2, …];

in which the content within square brackets is optional. If more than one variable is to be defined, each must be separated by a comma. The variable definition must end with a semicolon.

More info: *Defining a variable must follow the Java naming convention, so it has clear and meaningful name. The variable name should start with a lower-case letter.*

3.2.3 Variable initialization

Variable initialization is the first time a variable having an assigned value in the code by programmer. It is common to use an assignment statement to do so, for example:

```
int count;
count = 1;              //assign integer value 1 to variable count
double price;
price = 9.89;           //assign double value 9.89 to variable price
```

You can define a variable and assign its value in one statement. The following examples are equivalent to those above:

```
int count = 1;          //define and assign the value 1 to integer variable count
double price = 9.89;    //define and assign the value 9.89 to double variable price
```

You can also define many variables of the same type and initialize them in one statement, for example:

```
byte numberOfMonth = 12, numberOfWeek = 52;
char    firstLetter = 'A',
        lastLetter = 'z',
        letterA = 65;            //the same as letterA = 'A'
```

Since the Unicode representation of the character **A** is 65, variable **letterA** is assigned the value "**A**" and a code conversion is made to the **char** type.

It should be noted each variable assignment is separated by a comma. Table 3.5 lists more examples in defining and initializing variables.

Table3.5 Examples of defining and initializing variables

Example	Description

short numOfDays = 365;	Define and initialize a short type variable with value 365
float tax_rate =0.0875f;	Define and initialize a single float type variable with value 0.00875. Note the use of f to denote a floating-point data type.
float tax_rate = .0875F;	The same as above but use of capital F.
long numberOfBytes = 65536L;	Define and initialize a long type variable with value 65536. Note the use of L to denote a long data type; a lower-case "l" may also be used.
double interestEarned = 9.12E-5, interestRate = 0.0615, price = 0.0;	Define and initialize three double-float type variables with specified values. Note the first variable uses scientific notation.
boolean valid = false;	Define and initialize a Boolean type variable with value **false**
int x = 0, y = 0;	Define and initialize two integer type variables with value 0
char letterA = 'A', letterB = ++letterA;	Define and initialize two character type variables. The first variable is assigned value letter **A**; the second one will increase letterA's value from **A** to **B**, then assign this value to variable letterB

3.2.4 Variables and memories

Variables are related to internal memory in a computer. Defining a variable requests memory space. When the compiler assigns the memory space, it must know how many bytes will be allocated for the requested variable. This information is provided when we define the variable.:-For example, in defining

double price = 25.08;

the compiler knows 8 bytes of memory will be assigned to hold a double-precision floating-point value of 25.08. The variable name represents the memory location of the value—the beginning address of the allocated memory space. This is an advantage of using a high-level computer language, as opposed to using machine language in which the memory address is used to store data.

Figure 3.1 shows the relationship between a variable and its memory location.

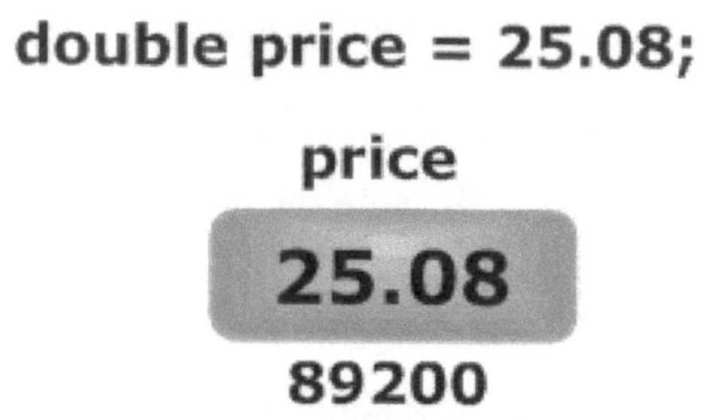

double price = 25.08;

price

25.08

89200

Figure 3.1 The relationship between a variable and its memory location

We can see from the above diagram that variable price represents a double-precision floating-point variable containing the value 25.08, and its beginning address is at memory location 89200.

The memory allocated to a variable during the compilation is called static memory binding; on the other hand, the memory allocated to a variable during the execution time is called dynamic memory binding. We will discuss these topics in Chapter 8.

3.2.5 Initialization of constant data

Constant data means the value an identifier holds cannot be modified. As a variable representing its memory location, the constant data also represents its memory space in which the stored value is fixed. In Java, we use keyword **final** to define constant data. You must assign values or initialize the constant data as you define them. In the Java naming convention, constant data are specified with uppercase letters. The following are examples of defining constant data:

final short DAY_IN_WEEK = 7;

final double SALE_TAX = 0.0875,

INTEREST_RATE = .065;

final Boolean DONE = true;

The syntax to define a constant data is as follows:

final dataType CONST_NAME = value;

or:

final dataType CONST_NAME1 = value1[, CONST_NAME2 = value2, ...];

The square brackets indicate optional items.

3.2.6 Assignment statements

We already used simple assignment statements in variable initialization:

```
int count;                 //define a integer variable count

count = 100;               //assign value 100 to variable count
```

The equal sign = is an assignment operator and assigns the value represented to its right into the variable specified on its left. As such, the following statement will cause a syntax error:

```
100 = count;               //compiler error
```

This is a common mistake for beginners and should be avoided.

The right side of an assignment operator is normally an expression. For example, the following assignment statement:

```
count = 200 + 26;          //do addition first, then result will be assigned to count
```

contains an arithmetic expression on the right side of assignment operator. It will first perform the addition of 200 and 26, then assign the sum 226 to the variable **count**. The original value of **count** will be replaced by the newly assigned result.

3.2.7 Arithmetic expressions

Arithmetic expressions consist of operators and operands. In the previous example:

200 + 26

is a simple arithmetic expression containing the operator **+** and the operands **200** and **26**. This expression performs an addition operation.

Table 3.6 lists the arithmetic operators and their meanings in Java.

Table 3.6 Arithmetic operators in Java

Operator	Meaning	Description
+	Add	Addition of two operands.
-	Subtract	Subtraction of the right operand from the left operand.
*	Multiply	Multiplication of two operands.
/	Divide	Division of the left operand by the right operand.
%	Modulus	Remainder when the left operand is divided by the

		right operand.
++	Increment	Incrementation of the operand by 1, e.g., ++x is equivalent to: x = x + 1;
--	decrement	Decrementation of the operand by 1, e.g., --y is equivalent to: y = y – 1;
+	Positive	The sign indicates a positive number.
-	Negative	The sign indicates a negative number.

The following are some common examples in use of the arithmetic operators and assignment statements:

```
int x = 10, y = 3;

int result1 = x + y;  //result1 = 13

int result2 = x – y; //result2 = 7

int result3 = x * y;  //result3 = 30

int result4 = x / y;  //division of two integers first, then assign the result .  result4 = 3

int result5 = x % y;  //remainder of x divided by y assigned to result5.  result5 = 1

int result6 = x - -y; //the same as x + y, result6 = 13

int result7 = ++x;  //incrementing x by 1，  then assign the result.  result7 = 11, x = 11

int result8 = --y;    //decrementing y by 1，  then assign the result.  result8 = 2, y = 2
```

In the last two examples, we used the incrementing and decrementing operations. They are equivalent to:

```
x = x + 1;                    //x = 11

int result7 = x ;

and:

y = y -1;                     //y = 2

int result8 = y ;
```

Since the operators are placed before the operands, we refer to their operations as prefix incrementing and prefix decrementing.

We can also perform postfix incrementing and postfix decrementing by placing the operators after the operands. In these operations, all other operations in the statement will be performed prior to executing the postfix operations. For example:

```
int x = 10, y = 3;

int result9 = x++;        //result9 = 10, x = 11 (assign first, then increment x by 1)

int result10 = y-- + 5; //result10 = 8, y = 2 (adding  y+5 first, assign the result, then decrement y by 1)
```

In the first example, **x++** denotes postfix incrementation. As such, the assignment operation will be performed first, then **x** will be incremented by 1. In the second example, **y--** denotes postfix decrementation. In this case, the current value of **y** will be added to **5,** and the sum will be assigned to **result10**. Upon the completion of the assignment operation, **y** will be decremented by **1**.

```
int x = 10, y = 3;

int result9 = x;

     ++x;

int result10 = y + 5;

     --y;
```

If a statement contains only an incrementation or decrementation and is not associated with any other operation, the prefix and postfix forms are identical. For example, the result of executing **++x** and **x++** will be the same, as will the result of executing **--y and y--**.

You cannot use square brackets [], angle brackets <>, and braces {} in mathematical expressions within Java. The precedence of all arithmetic operations is the same as in traditional mathematics: expressions within inner parentheses are evaluated first; multiplication and division are performed before addition and subtraction; expressions are evaluated from left to right if all operands are of the same precedence level.

Note that the Java compiler will generate a compiling error in the following expression due to use of illegal brackets and braces:

```
{x – [y + (z – 2)]} X 100;
```

It must be written as follows:

```
(x – (y + (z – 2))) * 100;
```

Warning: *Brackets and braces cannot be used in Java expressions. Multiplication cannot use the "x", and division cannot use the "÷" operators, respectively.*

Table 3.7 Arithmetic expressions

Arithmetic expression	Equivalent to
x + y – 2	(x + y) – 2
x + y / 2	x + (y / 2)
(x + y) / 2	Addition first, then division.
1 - (x + y) / 2	1 – ((x + y) / 2)
(1 – x) * (y – 1)	1-x first, then y-1, finally multiplication.
((x + 1) – (y -1)) /2.5	Inner parentheses first, that is x+1 and y -1; then subtract the results of y-1 from x+1; finally division.

It must be noted that the variables in an expression must be defined; otherwise a compiler error will be generated.

3.2.8 Short-cut assignment operators

The incrementing and decrementing we discussed above actually are examples of short-cut operators. The purpose of using short-cut operators is to simplify coding. Proper use of them will also increase the code's readability. However, the following example:

int result = x++ + ++y - --x + 1;

is a typical example of abusing the use of short-cut operators. Their use in this example, while technically correct, does not increase code readability.

Let's discuss more short-cut operators, or short-cut assignment, operators. Table 3.8 lists these operators and their descriptions.

Table 3.8 Java short-cut assignment operators

Short-cut operator	Description	Example	Equivalent to

+=	Add then assign	count += 5;	count = count + 5;
-=	Subtract then assign	count -= 3;	count = count – 3;
*=	Multiply then assign	price *= .02;	price = price * 0.02;
/=	Divide then assign	total /= 2.5;	total = total / 2.5;
%=	Modulus then assign	num %= 7;	num = num % 7;

Using the short-cut addition operator as an example, we can make the following summary:

varName += value;

is equivalent to:

varName = varName + value;

Here, **varName** is a defined variable name; value is a legal data. A challenge question: Can you summarize other short-cut assignment operators?

It's easily noticed that there are 4 different ways to increase a variable by 1:

```
x = x + 1;      //regular
x += 1;         //short-cut
++x;            // prefix incrementing
x++;            // postfix incrementing
```

The results are exactly the same.

3.3 First Look of Strings

Strings are commonly used in coding. In Java, strings are actually objects. Strings are created by the String class. Java has adopted the same manner of defining strings as C/C++ such that they may be defined as primative types of variables. For example:

String greeting = "Welcome to Java world!";

defines the string object greeting with a value of **"Welcome to Java world!"**. We call this type of string object definition referencing. This means the Java compiler will allocate memory space to hold the characters representing the value of a string object as **"Welcome to Java world!"**. It is referred to by its name called greeting.

We may call the methods of the **String** class since greeting is an object of **String**. For example:

greeting.length();

returns an integer value denoting the length, or number of characters, of the string, i.e., 22.

We will discuss more concepts and techniques about **String** and their use. In the following section, let's discuss the basics of strings.

3.3.1 Strings for beginners

In Java a string consists of one or more characters. These characters can be any from the Unicode set; therefore, each requires two bytes of storage in the memory. A string value is marked by a double quote, but the value of a char variable uses a single quote and must be a single character. The following examples:

char ch = 'a';   //define a char variable called ch with value 'a'

String str = "a"; //define a string called str with value "a"

Although each variable contains the letter "**a**", they represent entirely different entities: **ch** is defined as a **char** (or character) primative variable; **str** is an instance of the **String** class and may be said to define a string variable with the value "**a**".

The following are more examples of defining strings:

```
String    firstName,                //defining 3 strings
          lastName,
          fullName;
firstName = "Xinhua";               //assign value to firstName as "Xinhua"
lastName = "Wang";                  //assign value to lastName as "Wang"
fullName = "Yi Lu";                 //assign value to fullName as Yi Lu"
String firstName = "Xinhua";        //define and assign the value
String lastName = "Wang";           //define and assign the value
String fullName = "Yi Lu";          //define and assign the value
String str1 = " ";                  //define and assign the value as " "
```

String str2 = "";   //define and assign the value as empty

String message = null;   //declare a string reference without memory allocation

String myString;   //define a string with the system default value ""

It can be observed that a space could be assigned to a string str1 as its value. The value of str2 is empty, it has been referenced to a memory location but does not have any value yet. The value of message is null, i.e., it only declared or registered as a referencing without receiving any memory allocation yet.

3.3.2 Understanding string referencing

As we discussed in section 3.2.3, a variable, the value of the variable, and its memory location are closely related internally. This concept can also be applied to the string, the value of the string and the memory location. This relationship can be shown in figure 3.2.

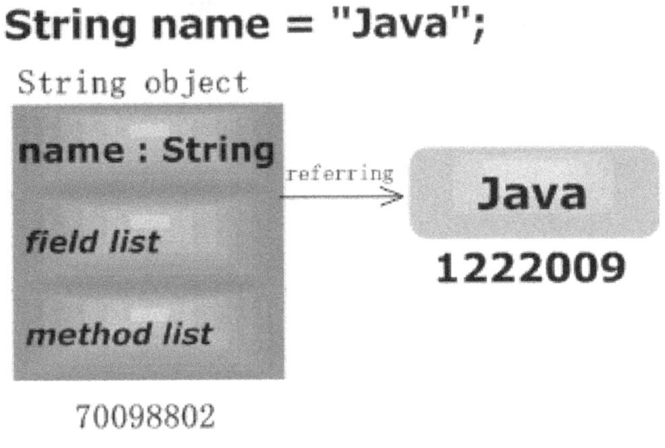

Figure 3.2 String referencing and memory

As we can see from Figure 3.2, as a string is defined with an assigned value, the compiler will create an object of String class and make a reference to the beginning address of memory that stores its value. The size of the memory is determined by the assigned value of the string. In the above example:

String name = "Java";

the value "**Java**" requires 8 bytes to be stored in memory. But in the following example:

String str2 = "";

although the referencing is already defined, no value has been assigned to the variable; it is an empty value, and the memory size is 0. Finally, in the last example:

String message = null;

a potential string referencing called message is registered, but the compiler doesn't create any object of String and allocation of memory space. Therefore, no referencing to the string is created yet.

3.3.3 String join

String join, or string concatenating, means a second string is appended to the end of the first string, thereby generating a new string referencing. In Java, we use the plus sign "+" to perform the string join. We can also append a primative data or variable to the end of a string. The compiler will convert the data or variable into a string, add it to the end of the first string, and generate a new string referencing. The following are examples of string join or concatenation:

```
String   firstName = "Xinhua",
         lastName = "Wang";
String fullName = firstName + " "+ lastName;     //string join
```

After the join operation, the string **fullName** has the value "**Xinhua Wang**".

Another example:

```
double total = 199.89;
String string_total = "total: "+ total;
```

Since variable total is a primative data type of double precision, the compiler will first convert its value to ~~a~~ the string "**199.89**", then perform the join. Thus, string ***string_total*** will contain the value of "**total: 199.89**".

We can also use the short-cut operator to do string join. For example:

```
String   name = "",
         firstName = "Xinhua",
         lastName = "Wang";
 name += lastName;     //the same as: name = name + lastName; name has value "Wang"
 name += " ";          //the same as name = name + " "; name has value "Wang "
 name += firstName;    //the same as name = name + firstName
```

The short-cut join operations are commonly used in the string operations.

The following example will generate a syntax error:

```
String string = 199 + 278.89;     //illegal join
```

It is a syntax error because at least one operand in the join must be a string. This principle can be also applied to other operations in Java code. It will involve data type casting if the operands in an arithmetic operation or string join have different data types. The operator in such an operation will request the compiler to convert a data type with less memory requirement to the data type of the operand with a larger memory requirement, then perform the specified operation. We call this auto data type casting by the compiler, or simply auto data type cast.

Let's go back to the string join example:

199.89 + " is my total price."

The first operand is a double precision value and the second one is a string. Since a string is an object referencing, and it requires more memory space to hold the method loading information, the join operator "+" requests the compiler to convert the double value 199.89 to a string reference of:

" 199.89"

then perform the join operation.

The following example will apply the same principle in auto data type cast:

int bonus = 25;

double payment = 800.77 + bonus;

In the addition operation, the variable bonus is an integer type that requires 4 bytes of memory space; the constant data **800.77** is a double type and requires 8 bytes of memory space. Therefore, the compiler will convert bonus to the double precision value **25.0** then perform the addition.

It seems that the converting or casting is not necessary. Some will say Java is too picky. Yes, it is just because by using of this kind of precision we can get accurate results from the calculations.

Note: *In performing a string join, at least one operand must be a string. Otherwise, a syntax error will be generated.*

3.3.4 Special characters

Table 3.9 lists the commonly used special characters in Java. We must place a backslash "\" before a special character when it is used in a string. This notation is called an escape sequence. The first 3 escape sequences in the table control the cursor's locations. The fourth one is used with a double quote. Since it is already being used to represent string content, you must place a "\" before a quote, "\", if it is part of a string value. The last escape sequence in the table is a backslash "\". Because it is already part of the escape sequence, you must place a "\" before a backslash, "\\", to indicate you want a backslash as a string value.

Table 3.9 Commonly used special characters and examples

Escape sequence	Example	Result
\n	String newline = "\nn";	Move cursor to beginning of next line and display n when string is displayed
\t	String tab = "x\ty";	Separate x and y with a tab character when string is displayed
\r	String begin = "nothing\r";	Position cursor at character "n" when string is displayed
\"	String quotes = "\"Java\" OOP";	Write "Java"OOP when string is Displayed
\\	String double_slash = "C:\\\\dir";	Write C:\\dir when string is displayed

The first example in Table 3.9 indicates that the escape sequence "**\n**" means new line, or return of the cursor to the beginning of the next line; the second "**n**" is a normal character in the string. The last example requires 4 backslashes—one escape sequence for each of the two backslashes representing the directory path. The string **C:\\dir** will be displayed upon output.

It will be a syntax error if the character is not one of these special characters listed in the table. For example:

String something = "\y"; *// illegal value in the string*

The following is an example using an escape sequence:

String content = "Java\tC++\tC";

If we use the following output statement:

System.out.println(content);

The output will be:

Java C++ C

That is, the words **Java**, **C++** and **C** will each be separated by the tabs.

Note: The escape sequences "\t" and "**\r**" will not work if they are used as parameters in the method call **JOptionPane.showMessageDialog()**.

3.4 First Look of Classes and Objects

Classes and objects are the abstract description of the subjects in terms of program design, and a part of Object-Oriented Design (OOD). OOD is a successful technique in which concepts of engineering design and manufacturing are adopted into software development. The separation of data from the operations, such as in Procedural Oriented Programming, e.g., C, to encapsulating data and operations into a unique coding body called a class, such as in Object-Oriented Programming, e.g., Java, is a milestone in the history of software engineering and indicates a maturity of programming concepts and technology.

Classes and objects are the important and major coding parts in OOP. In this chapter we will start to discuss the basic concepts and coding of classes and objects. Throughout this book, there will be more detailed discussion about them.

3.4.1 Understanding classes and objects for beginners

We actually observe classes and objects every day. For example, in the case of human beings such as ourselves, a particular person, e.g., John, David, Lily, is an object. The general description of a human being, such as face, limbs, skin, height, and weight, as well as functioning systems, such as memory, digestion, and reproduction, is the class. The in class of human being, it does not matter if you are talking about John or David or Lily—you can always define them into two parts: attributes and functionalities.

The script of a drama is a class. The play, including actors and actresses, costumes, and the stage, are the objects of the drama class. Your car, her car, my car—any particular car—is an object of the automobile class. The brand, type, color, and number of cylinders are attributes of the class; the ignition, acceleration rate, transmission type, and exhaust system are functionalities of the automobile class.

Your computer, his computer, and my computer are objects of a computer class. The attributes of the computer class are CPU model, memory and storage sizes, monitor specification, and so on. The functionalities of the computer class include operating system, productivity software, virus protection software, and power supply system.

Can you list more examples of classes and objects encountered in your daily life?

How can we create an object from a class? Assume the car class already exists, the following statement will create an object called myCar from Car class:

```
Car myCar = new Car();          //create an object of Car class
```

Here we call **new** as operator of object creation. The object **myCar** is also called as an instance of **Car** class. Therefore, the object creation is also called an object instantiation. The process of an object creation using new operator is called instantiating an object.

The formal syntax in instantiating an object as follows:

ClassName objectName = new ClassName();

wherein:

ClassName—the name of an existing class;

objectName—the name of the object to be created; and

new—the operator of an object creation.

After the instantiation, object **myCar** consists of all properties and functionalities of the **Car** class. We initialize the instance variables of **myCar**, such as **ownerName**, **model**, **engineSize**, **transmissionType**, **sets**, **doorNum**, and so on, to establish **myCar** as a particular vehicle. When we call the methods supplied by the **Car** class, we can actually simulate the operations of **myCar**.

3W: *Class is an abstract definition of an object; class is the blueprint of objects; class contains the building modules of the objects. Attributes are the definition of the data; functionalities are the operations, processes, and calculations. In Java programming, we call attributes as instance variables and functionalities as methods. Instance variables and methods are also called as members of a class.*

3.4.2 First look of access identifiers

Access identifiers specify the rights to access the class and the members of the class. Access identifiers for a class specify how other programs or classes may access it. Access identifiers for the members of the class can be classified as either variable access identifiers and method access identifiers. It is common to assign an access identifier as public within a class so it can be used in other code. A class may define an access identifier as private, or simply call it as a private class, so it can be only used inside the code it is defined. There are other access identifiers, such as protected and package. We will discuss them in detail in later chapters.

The access identifiers for instance variables specify how an object of the class can access its member data; on the other hand, the access identifiers for methods specify how an object of the class can access its methods. We will discuss two commonly used access identifiers, private and public, in this section.

In Java we usually define the instance variables as private to ensure encapsulation, and define the methods as public. Defining methods as public allows an object of the class to directly access or call the class methods using the dot notation. For example, in the following code:

```
public class Car {                          //define the class as public
            private int engineSize;         //define the data as private
            //other instance variables
            ...
```

```
        public void setEngineSize(int size)        //define the method as public
            { engineSize = size; }                 //access the data and assign the value
        //other methods
        ...
    }
```

We define a **Car** class and its access identifier (or simply a public **Car** class). As such, within the class **OtherClass**:

```
public class OtherClass {
    Car myCar = new Car();          //create an object of Car class
    //other statements
    ...
}
```

we can access the **Car** class and instantiate an object of **Car**, **myCar**. It will be a syntax error to create an object of **Car** if its access identifier is private.

In the above example, we defined the instance variables as private. A private variable can only be accessed inside the member method, i.e.,

```
public void setEngineSize(int size)
    { engineSize = size; }     //access private data
```

A syntax error will be generated if you attempt to access a private variable via the dot notation when calling a public method, e.g.,

```
myCar.engineSize = 8;            //illegal access a private data
```

You may notice that we defined the access identifier of the method **setEngineSize()** as public (or simply a public method **setEngineSize()**). Therefore, the object **myCar** can directly call this method by a dot notation:

```
myCar.setEngineSize(8);          //access or call the method to set engine size as 8
```

It would be a syntax error, however, if it had been defined as a private method.

3.4.3 How to code a class

To code a class means to write the instance variables (other variables, such as class variables, will be discussed in later chapters) and its methods. As we discussed earlier, the attributes of the class describe the states of the class. Defining the instance variables is to decide what variables (access identifier, data type, and name) should be included in the class for which all objects of the class can access those data. Coding a method is to design the functionality or the task including the operation, manipulation, calculation, or decision making the method must carry out. A method is normally a subroutine or a block of the code.

The principle to design the instance variables and methods can be twofold: include all necessary attributes and functionality in the specified class; exclude all attributes and functionality that are not in the defined class. It sounds redundant, but this represents an important design idea in OOP – the independence of a class. It means a class should independently exist with all the necessary variables and methods to solve the defined problem.

Let's discuss how to code a method first. The following is a general syntax in coding a method:

```
accessModifier returnType methodName([argumentList]) {
        //the body of the statements
}
```

Here:

accessModifier – can be **public**, **private**, **protected**, or **package**. It is discussed later in Chapter 12.

argumentList—the (optional) parameters required by the method. If a method does not require any parameters, nothing will be specified within the enclosing parentheses.

The syntax of an argument list is as follows:

dataType arg1[, dataType arg2,...]

Every parameter starts with a data type, followed by the parameter name. Each parameter is separated by a comma.

For example, we discussed above:

```
public void setEngineSize(int size)
        { engineSize = size; }      //assign a value to engineSize
```

The access modifier of the **setEngineSize()** method is public. It has a return type of void noting that no data is returned. One parameter, size, is specified as an integer type within the argument list. In the body of the code, it assigned the value of the parameter to the instance variable **engineSize**.

There are important requirements or conventions that everyone in the Java community should follow. These are not Java syntax, but recommendations to follow in coding. These recommendations are based on the experience of the Java language development teams, the Java application software communities, and third party companies in development of Java technologies. As a professional Java programmer or software engineer in Java we should obey these conventions just like we follow the Java syntax. These conventions are:

- Access modifier of an instance variable normally is **private**;
- Access modifier of a method normally is **public**;
- For each instance variable, there **are setXxx()** and **getXxx()** methods;
- **setXxx()** is also called setter. It assigns the value of the parameter to the instance variable it sets.;
- **getXxx()** is also called getter. It returns the value of an instance variable; and
- Other method(s) will carry out a specified task. A method can access the instance variables directly. Normally its return type is void and the argument list is empty.

The following represents the complete coding of the class Payment. It is used to calculate the amount of a bill payment:

```
//Complete code called Payment.java in Ch3 from the author's website
//Demo: Operation class Payment

public class Payment{          //define Payment class
        private double price,      //define an instance variable and a const
                       total;
        private int quantity;
        private final double INTEREST_RATE = 0.0875;    //define a const

   public void setPrice(double cost)                    // setter for price
        { price = cost; }
   public double getPrice()                             //getter for price
        { return price; }

   public double getTotal()                             //getter for total
        { return total; }

   public void setQuantity(int item)          //setter for quantity
        { quantity = item; }
   public int getQuantity()                             //getter for quantity
        { return quantity; }

   public void bill()                                   //define the method
        { total = quantity * price + quantity * price * INTEREST_RATE; }
```

```
} // end of Payment
```

In this example, we followed the Java syntax as well as proper Java convention. We defined 3 instance variables and one const data at the beginning of the class:

private double price,   //define an instance variable and a const

total;

private int quantity;

private final double INTEREST_RATE = 0.0875;   //define a const

It should be noted that you must assign the value to a constant data. Because the instance variable total is used to hold the result of the calculation, it doesn't have setter but getter methods. Its value is assigned by the computing result in the **bill()** method.

public void bill()   //compute the payment

*{ total = quantity * price + quantity * price * INTEREST_RATE; }*

3W: *Defining a class is to define its instance variables and methods. First, we do the analysis to include all necessary attributes and functionality to solve the specified problem, while excluding all others not related to the specified task. This principle is called class independence. Its purpose is to design a class that can be repeatedly used in related applications, thereby increasing the efficiency of the code design.*

3.4.4 How to test a class

A programmer-defined class must be tested to make sure it reaches the objective without any error. To do so, we usually write a driver program to perform the testing. To simplify testing, the driver is normally written in as a Java application class.

The driver has a **main()** method that will be the starting point code for execution by the Java Virtual Machine (JVM). The driver is also called as executable code. The way to code a **main()** method is basically the same for all Java application drivers:

public static void main(String[] args) {

//body of the main()

}   //end of the main()

Here, a driver class and its **main()** method are public. The **main()** method must be declared as a **static** method to be executed by the JVM. The important feature of a static method is that it can be called without creating an object of the class. That means the JVM can execute a **main()** method without instantiating an object of the driver class.

The argument in a **main()** method must be an array of **String** type. Although the **args** parameter may be rarely used in the code, we must follow this required syntax and specify it in the parameter list.

The body of code in a **main()** method creates an object of the testing class then calls its methods for testing.

We will discuss static methods and how the JVM works in later chapters. The following is the driver code for the **Payment** class:

```
//Complete code called PaymentApp.java in Ch3 from the author's website
//The driver code for Payment class
import javax.swing.JOptionPane;
public class PaymentApp {
   public static void main(String[] args) {
      Payment payment = new Payment();      //create an object of Payment
      String str;              //define a local variable
      str = JOptionPane.showInputDialog("Enter a price: ");      //input a price

      //convert to double then call setter
      payment.setPrice(Double.parseDouble(str));
      str = JOptionPane.showInputDialog("Enter a quantity: "); //input quantity

      //convert to int then call  setter
      payment.setQuantity(Integer.parseInt(str));
      payment.bill();  //call method to compute

      //display the result
      JOptionPane.showMessageDialog(null, "Total amount:  " + payment.getTotal());
   }      //end of main()
}         //end of PaymentApp
```

Here, the statement

payment.setPrice(Double.parseDouble(str)); *//convert to double then call setter*

is equivalent to:

double cost = Double.parseDouble(str); *//convert to double*

payment.setPrice(cost); *//call the setter*

It first converts variable **str** denoting the price from a string format to a double value by calling the static method **parseDouble()**of the Java-provided wrapper class Double. It then calls the **setPrice()** method to assign this value to the instance variable price. We will discuss wrapper classes in Chapter 5.

***3W:** Driver is the code that is used to test or execute a programmer-defined class or desktop application. The significant feature of the driver is having a **main()** method that is the starting point of the execution.*

3.4.5 An example

Let's discuss a particular example to describe how to design and define a class. More specifically, we will discuss how to analyze which instance variables and methods should be included in the class. Finally, we will discuss how to write a driver to test out the class.

Assume that we need to define a class used to convert kilometers to miles and verse visa. According to the naming conventions in Java, we call this class **MileageConverter**. Let's discuss what necessary attributes should be included in the class. For example, to be able to convert a defined mileage, the following instance variables or data are necessary:

Kilometers – double

Miles – double

Result – double

To insure encapsulation, we define these variables as **private**.

Let's continue to discuss the methods in the **MileageConverter** class. All variables except the instance variable result should have setter and getter methods. For the conversion, we will use the following formulas:

Kilometers to miles: 1 kilometer = 0.62137 miles

Miles to kilometers: 1 mile = 1.609347 kilometers

In summary, the following methods should be included in the **MileageConverter** class:

setKilometers() -- *set kilometers*

getKilometers() -- *get kilometers*

setMiles() -- *set miles*

getMiles() -- *get miles*

getResult() -- *get result of the conversion*

convertKilometers() -- *convert kilometers to miles*

convertMiles() -- *convert miles to kilometers*

We define these methods as **public** so they can be called directly in the driver. The following is the major part of the code:

```
//Complete code called MileageConverter.java in Ch3 from the author's website


//Define MileageConverter class

public class MileageConverter {

   double kilometers,                        //declare the class variables
          miles,
          result;

   public void setKilometers(double km) //setKilometers() method
          { kilometers = km; }

   public double getKilometers()             //getKilometers() method
          { return kilometers; }

   public void setMiles(double mile)         //setMiles() method
          { miles = mile; }

   public double getMiles()                  //getMiles() method
          { return miles; }

   public double getResult()                 //getResult() method
          { return result; }

   public void convertKilometers()           //convert kilometers to miles
          { result = kilometers * 0.62137; }


   public void convertMiles()                //convert miles to kilometers
          { result = miles * 1.609347; }

 } // end of MileageConverter class
```

The next step is to write a driver code, **MileageConverterApp**, to test the **MileageConverter** class:

```
//The complete code called MileageConverterApp.java in Ch3 from the author's website
//The driver code to test out the MileageConverter

import javax.swing.JOptionPane;
```

```
public class MileageConverterApp {
   public static void main(String[] args) {

         //create an object of MileageConverter
         MileageConverter mc = new MileageConverter();

         String str;          //declare a string
         double distance;     //declare a double

         //receive input data
         str = JOptionPane.showInputDialog("Welcome to Mileage Converter\n"
                                         + "Please enter a distance: ");

         distance = Double.parseDouble(str);     //convert to double

         mc.setKilometers(distance);             //set as kilometers
         mc.setMiles(distance);                  //set as miles

         mc.convertKilometers();                 //convert kilometers to miles

         //display the result as miles
         JOptionPane.showMessageDialog(null, str + " kilometers = " +
mc.getResult() + " miles");

         mc.convertMiles();                      //convert miles to kilometers

         //display the result as kilometer
         JOptionPane.showMessageDialog(null, str + " miles = " + mc.getResult() +
" kilometers");

   } //end of main()
} //end of MileageConverterApp
```

In the driver code we first create an object of **MileageConverter** class called mc, then define two local variables—**str** and distance—that are used to store the input values from the user. **str** is a **String** and distance is a **double**. Because the JVM treats all input and output data as strings, we need to convert accordingly.

We call method **showInputDialog()** in the **JOptionPane** class to prompt the user to enter a distance that needs to be converted. **JOptionPane** is an API class imported from the JDK package. We will discuss it later in this chapter. This method returns the distance variable as string assigned to variable **str**:

str = JOptionPane.showInputDialog("Welcome to Mileage Converter\n"

+ "Please enter a distance: ");

We also call method **parseDouble()** of **Double** class to convert the string to a double value:

distance = Double.parseDouble(str);

We then call setter methods to assign the distance to kilometers and miles, respectively:

mc.setKilometers(distance);

mc.setMiles(distance);

We finally call the **convertKilometers()** method of object mc to convert the distance from kilometers to miles and call the **showMessageDialog()** method of **JOptionPane** class to display the result:

mc.convertKilometers();//convert kilometers to miles

//display the result as miles

JOptionPane.showMessageDialog(null, str + " kilometers = "

+ mc.getResult() + " miles");

In the same way, the distance in miles is converted into kilometers. Figure 3.3 contains screen shots of the execution results.

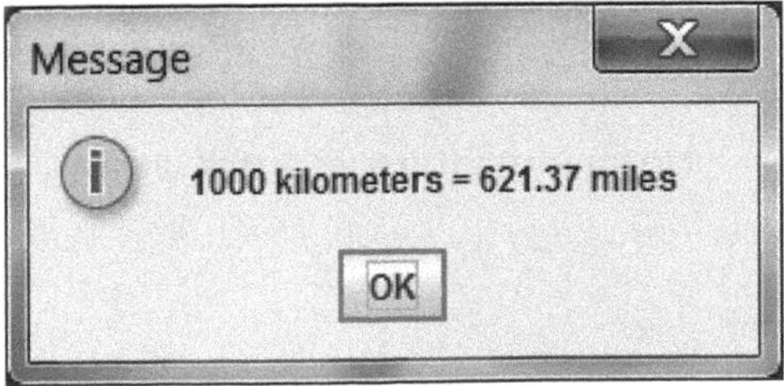

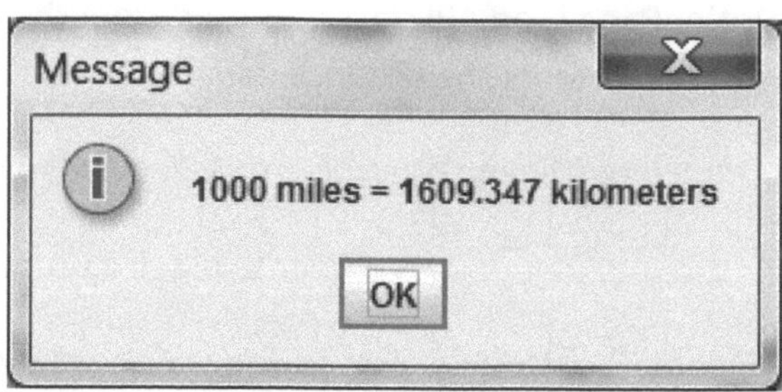

Figure 3.3 The execution result in the kilometers/miles conversion

3.4.6 Use of Java API classes

Java API (Application Programming Interface) is also called Class Libraries. It is part of the JDK and is used in application software development. The API provides the following features for design and coding:

Reliability – developed and tested by professional teams, modified and improved by many version releases, and proven by a rich number of real world applications.

Supportability – includes more than 30 packages and hundreds of classes and methods.

Structure – the best example of the organization and design layout.

Exception-handling – the most unique feature of Java, makes the use of APIs much more reliable by providing better memory management and garbage collection.

Speedy coding – "reinventing the wheel" by using as much of the Java API as possible in code to insure reliability and efficiency in code development.

Extendibility – programmers and developers, including the partner companies, can extend the class libraries and third-party tools in an easy and efficient fashion.

Documentation – all API classes have Webpage documents and can be downloaded with selected language support.

Transparency – All codes of the API classes are open source.

These advantages are making Java one of the most successful programming languages. Java is not only used for regular or small-scaled application coding, but has ability to be used in large-scale and complex software development. It has also changed the traditional way in programming.

In traditional programming we pay more time and effort to creating the code. In programming with Java we can pay more attention to utilizing the existing API classes or extending the specified functionality with the existing APIs.

A rich number of APIs provide us unlimited opportunities in the world of programming; however, this also challenges us in finding the right APIs to fit our particular needs in problem-solving. The professional writing styles and terminologies used in the API documentation also provide challenges for rookies and experienced programmers:

> Which APIs should I use to solve my problems?
>
> How do I correctly use an API?
>
> How do I extend or modify (overload or override) the API to solve my particular problem?
>
> How do I know I have chosen the best API amongst all to solve my problem?

You will become an expert if all these questions can be answered.

Table 3.10 lists commonly used Java API packages and their descriptions.

Table 3.10 Commonly used API packages

Package	Description
java.lang	Default package providing basic and fundamental classes, and primative data types, String, wrapper classes, arithmetic/logical operations, threads, exception handling and system operation management.
java.text	Provides text, date, number, and message processes in a manner of independence of natural languages.
java.util	Provides a variety of utilities for internationalization, collections, and miscellaneous classes.
java.awt	Provides all classes for creating user interfaces, painting graphics, and creating images.
java.awt.event	Provides events and event handling classes and interfaces.
java.io	Provides classes and interfaces dealing with file input and output.
java.sql	Provides classes and interfaces to access and process data stored in databases.
java.applet	Provides the classes necessary to create an applet and the classes an applet uses to

	communicate with its applet context.
javax.swing	Provides a set of all Java-coded components that, to the maximum degree possible, work the same on all platforms.

Because **java.lang** contains all built-in API classes in Java programming, it is the default package and is automatically imported in every Java code.

You must use the import statement to include the particular class name or the package name with the wildcard at the beginning of the code when you specify any Java API. For example:

```
import java.text.NumberFormat;          // include NumberFormat class from java.text package
import java.text.*;                     //include all classes and interfaces from java.text
import javax.swing.JOptionPane;         //include JOptionPane from java.swing
import javax.swing.*;                   //include all classes and interfaces from javax.swing
import java.util.Date;                  //include Date class from java.util
import java.awt.FlowLayout;             //include FlowLayout class from java.awt
import java.awt.event.*;                //include all classes and interfaces from java.awt.event
```

It should be noted that you may use the wildcard "*" to include or import all classes and interfaces from the specified package. However, the wildcard will not import the classes and interfaces in the sub-packages of the specified package. For example:

```
import java.awt.*;
```

specifies all classes and interfaces provided in the **java.awt** package, but will not include any of its sub-packages, e.g., **java.awt.event**, et cetera.

We discuss the packages and interfaces of the java.awt class in detail in later chapters.

Actually, the import statement provides us a convenient way to tell the Java compiler which classes and interfaces will be used in the code. You may use the following way to tell the Java compiler the complete path containing the **JOptionPane** class if you don't use an import statement at the beginning of your code:

```
javax.swing.JOptionPane.showMessageDialog(null, "square is: " + message);
```

The syntax of the complete path for an API class is:

```
packageName.className.methodName();
```

More Info: *In a typical Java program, about 60% or more of the code uses classes and interfaces from Java APIs. The most significant feature in Java coding is how to utilize the correct APIs to solve your particular problems.*

3W: *APIs are class libraries provided by the JDK. We use import statements at the beginning of the code to tell the Java compiler what packages or what particular classes you will use. The purpose of utilizing APIs is to increase the code reliability and efficiency.*

3.4.7 Inside JOptionPane

We have introduced the **JOptionPane** class with some simple examples for data input and output. Let's walk into the **JOptionPane** class and use it as an example showing how to learn and use the classes in a Java API. Figure 3.4 shows the specification in the Java document Webpage for **JOptionPane**.

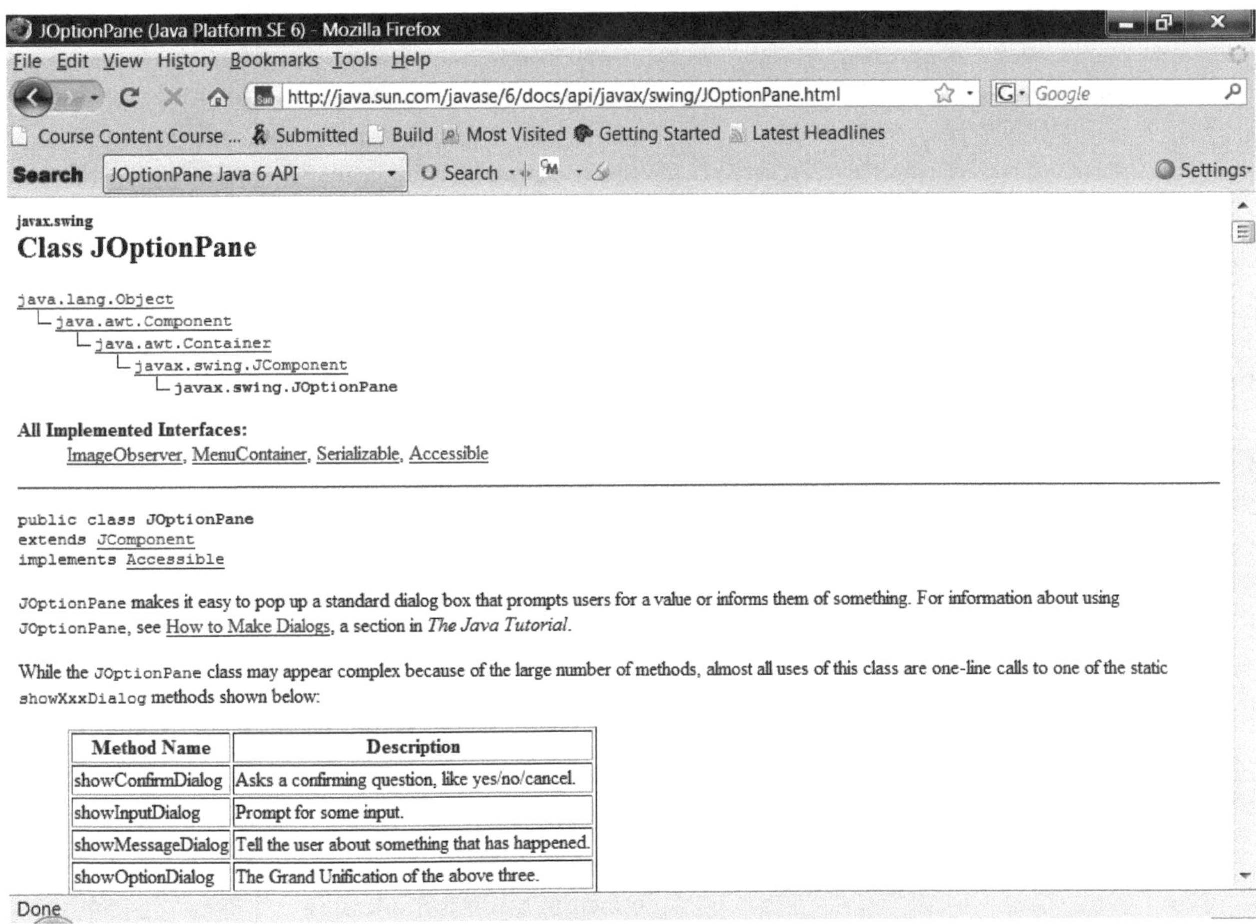

Figure 3.4 Document Webpage of JOptionPane

The top of the Webpage shows the class name and its inheritance hierarchy. We will discuss inheritance in detail in later chapters. The main part of the page explains the general functionality of the **JOptionPane** class and summarizes its methods. Let's start by discussing the two methods we already used in the previous examples first and then move on to another method, **showConfirmDialog()**, that we have not used yet. Hopefully this discussion will serve as a guide to assist you in learning about other API classes. Table 3.11 lists the commonly used methods in **JOptionPane**.

3W : ***JOptionPane*** *class is part of the* javax.swing *package, providing powerful GUI I/O operations in a dialog way. Because all of its methods are static, we can directly call them without creating an object of* ***JOptionPane****.*

Table 3.11 Commonly used methods in JOptionPane

Method	Description
public static String **showInputDialog**(Object message)	Display a dialog window with the message, and return the user's input data as a string. Usually message is a string.
public static String **showInputDialog**(Object message, Object initialSelectionValue)	Display a GUI dialog window with message, and display initialSelectionValue in the input bar as the default value. Return the user's input as a string. Message and initialSelectionValue usually are strings.
public static String **showInputDialog**(Component parentComponent, Object message, Object initialSelectionValue)	In the parent level of GUI component, parentComponent, display a dialog window with message, and display initialSelectionValue in the input bar as the default value. Return the user's input as a string. Usually parentComponent is null-and message and initialSelectionValue are strings.
public static String **showInputDialog**(Component parentComponent, Object message, String title, int messageType)	Display a dialog window in the parent component with message, and also display the title. messageType will be displayed as an icon in the dialog window. Return the user's input as a string. parentComponent is usually null; message and initialSelectionValue are usually strings. See the value and the icon of messageType in Table **3.12**.
public static void **showMessageDialog**(Component parentComponent, Object message)	In the parent component display a dialog window with the message. parentComponent usually is null; message usually is a string or GUI component.

public static void **showMessageDialog**(Component parentComponent, Object message, String title, int messageType)	In the parent component display a dialog window with the message, the title, and the messageType as an icon. parentComponent usually is null; message usually is a string or GUI component. See the value and the icon of messageType in Table **3.12.**
public static int **showConfirmDialog**(Component parentComponent, Object message)	Display a dialog window with *Yes, No, and Cancel* buttons *and* message. Return the user's input as an integer (*Yes=1, No=2, Cancel=3*). The window title is **Select an Option.**

Table 3.12 Message Icon types in JOptionPane

Message Icon Type	Integer value	Icon
ERROR_MESSAGE	0	X
INFORMATION_MESSAGE	1	i
WARNING_MESSAGE	2	!
QUESTION_MESSAGE	3	?
PLAIN_MESSAGE	−1	Non-icon

All methods in **JOptionPane** are static, so we can directly call them without creating an object. We will discuss static methods in detail in later chapters. We can summarize these methods into two categories: The methods providing a dialog window, prompting user input, and returning the input value as a string, such as **showInputDialog()** and **showConfirmDialog()**, and the methods displaying the output message, such as **showMessageDialog()**.

For Java beginners, attempting to learn and understand classes and methods from API document Web pages or the API specification only is impractical. The following outline may serve as some additional guidance:

1. Try to understand the general picture or description of the API class and the summary table.
2. Know the return type and the argument list of a method in the class.

3. Open an IDE, such as Eclipse, and code a driver to test the method. Display the result after the method call.
4. Compare the result using the API with the specification to get a better understanding of the method.
5. Search online and study other examples to master the use of the method.

The following example tests all methods in the **JOptionPane** class. Table 3.13 lists the execution results and comparison with the method calls.

```
//Complete code called TestJOptionPaneApp.java in Ch3 from author's website
//Demo of testing the methods of JOptionPane
import javax.swing.JOptionPane;

public class TestJOptionPaneApp {
public static void main(String[] args) {

        //test the first method listed in 3.11 with one argument
        String str = JOptionPane.showInputDialog("Please enter a number: ");

        //test the second one with 2 arguments. "120" should be the default entry
        str = JOptionPane.showInputDialog("Please enter a number: ", "120");

        //test the fourth one with 4 arguments
        str = JOptionPane.showInputDialog(null, "Please enter a number: ",
                     "Input windows",
                     -1);   //int -1 can be JOptionPane.PLAIN_MESSAGE

        //test the fifth one with 2 arguments
        JOptionPane.showMessageDialog(null, "This is another testing.");

        //test the sixth one with 4 arguments;
        //the JOptionPane.QUESTION_MESSAGE can be 3
        JOptionPane.showMessageDialog(null, "Testing..... " + str,
                                                   "Testing Window",

  JOptionPane.QUESTION_MESSAGE );
        //test the last one: showConfirmDialog()
        JOptionPane.showConfirmDialog(null, "Make a choice: ");
  } //end of main()
} //end of TestJOptionPaneApp
```

Throughout the testing, we may have further understanding that it will display a question mark icon if there is no any message icon type specified in a **showInputDialog()** method; however it will display the **INFORAMTION_MESSAGE** icon if there is no any message type specified in a **showMessageDialog()**; the system default option button is "**Yes**" in a **showConfirmDialog()**.

In later chapters, after the discussion of GUI components and **JFrame**, we will replace null with a parent component object to test the result of execution, and compare the difference between them.

Table 3.13 The common methods and execution results in JOptionPane

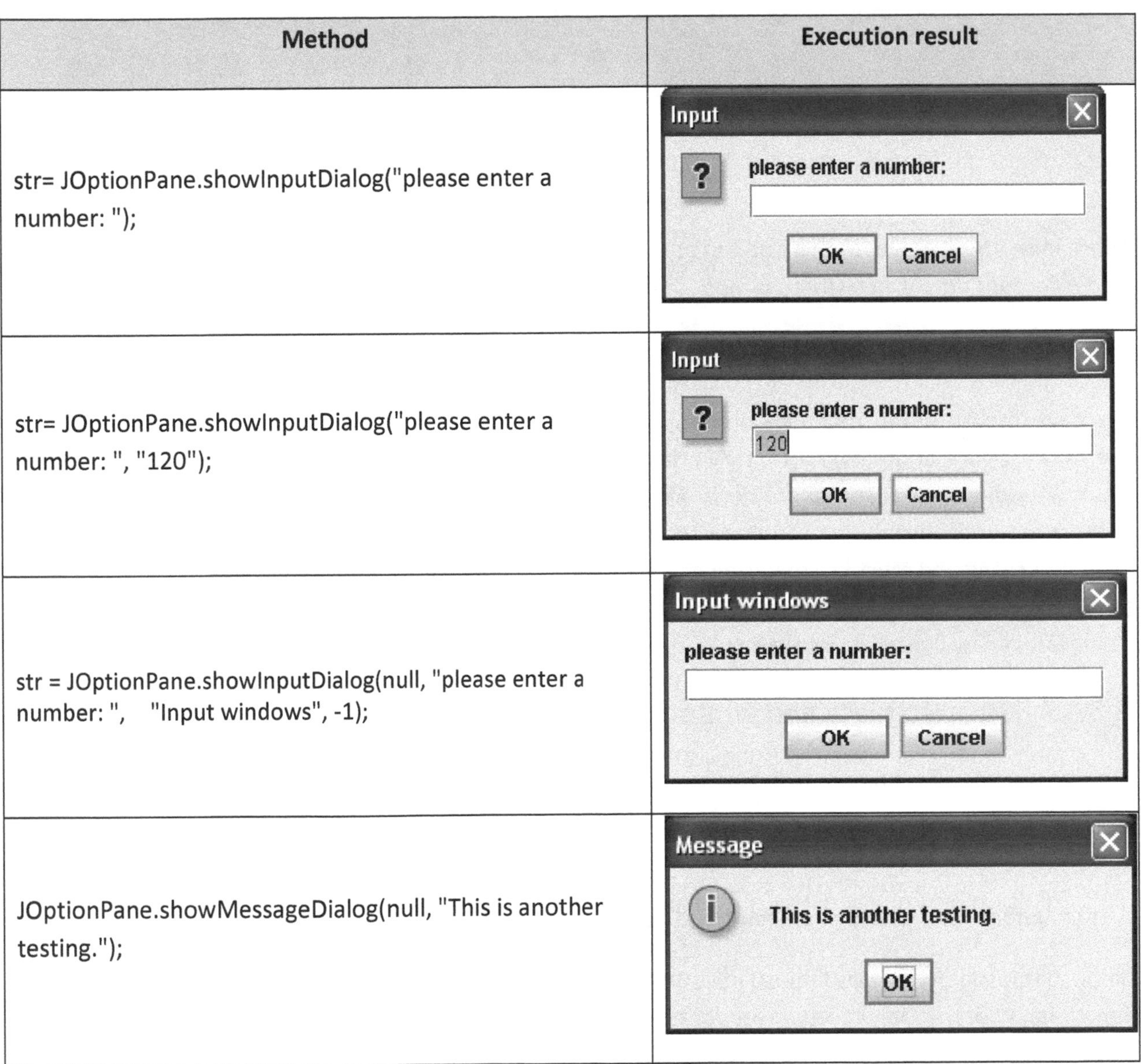

Method	Execution result
str= JOptionPane.showInputDialog("please enter a number: ");	Input please enter a number: OK Cancel
str= JOptionPane.showInputDialog("please enter a number: ", "120");	Input please enter a number: 120 OK Cancel
str = JOptionPane.showInputDialog(null, "please enter a number: ", "Input windows", -1);	Input windows please enter a number: OK Cancel
JOptionPane.showMessageDialog(null, "This is another testing.");	Message This is another testing. OK

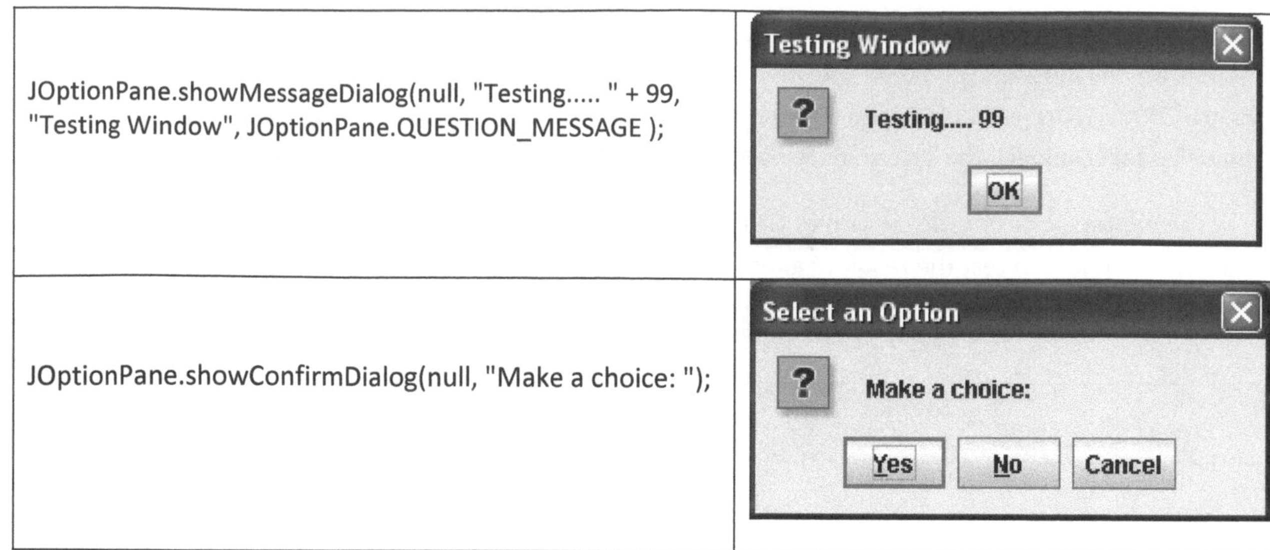

Code	Output
JOptionPane.showMessageDialog(null, "Testing..... " + 99, "Testing Window", JOptionPane.QUESTION_MESSAGE);	
JOptionPane.showConfirmDialog(null, "Make a choice: ");	

More info: *The JVM treats all input and output data as strings, i.e., all input data is converted to a string and all output data is in a string format.*

3.5 More about Input and Output

We have discussed the input and output operations provided by the **JOptionPane** class. In this section we will introduce another important API class provided since JDK1.5 –the Scanner class to handle input data. We will also discuss the traditional API object **System.out** to handle output operations. API object **System.in** treats all input data as character bytes. As such, input data representing numeric values is read as a string and must be converted character-by-character to the numerical value. It is inconvenient to handle input data using **System.in**, and the operation is now largely replaced by the **Scanner** class. Therefore, we will not discuss **System.in**.

3.5.1 Return to black and white

System.out specifies an output stream to the standard output device which usually refers to the computer monitor. **System** is a special API class known as a final class, and its syntax is as follows:

public final class System extends Object;

Here, **extends** denotes inheritance, meaning the **System** will inherit all of the properties and functionality of the **Object** class—the root or ancestor of all other classes. Inheritance is another important feature of the Java language. We will discuss inheritance and final classes in detail in later chapters. You only need to know now that a final class cannot be used to create an object. That is, in the following example, **out** is a static final data of type **PrintStream** used to form a standard output stream,

static final PrintStream out;

forms

System.out

as a standard output object. Table 3.14 lists the commonly used methods and descriptions in **System.out**.

Table3.14 Commonly used methods in System.out

Method	Description
public void print(***var***)	Output of ***var*** to the standard output device. v***ar*** can be any primative data, string or object.
public void println()	Output of a newline "\n" to the standard output device.
public void println(***var***)	Output of ***var*** and a newline "\n" to the standard output device.

System.out is provided by the default **java.lang** package. Therefore, we don't need to import the package. The following are examples using the common methods in **System.out**:

```
//Complete code called TestPrintApp.java in Ch3 from author's website
        System.out.print("price: ");       //print price: to output screen
        System.out.println();              //print a blank line
        System.out.print("\n");            //same as above

        double total = 25.09;
        System.out.println("total: " + total);//print total: and the value
        System.out.print("total: " + total + "\n");  //same as above

        String message = "Welcome to use of System.out.println()";
        System.out.println(message);              //print message string

        char letter = 'A';
        System.out.print("letter = " + letter + 1 + "\n");  //print A1 and return
        System.out.print("letter= " + (letter + 1) + "\n"); //print 66 and return
        System.out.print("letter= " + (char)(letter + 1) + "\n");
```

In the last three output statements, letter is a char variable, and its value is **'A'**. The const data 1 is an integer. **letter + 1** is a string join operation. Therefore, the output is the string "**A1**". However, **(letter + 1)** is an arithmetic expression and will perform an addition operation. It converts the char type data to an integer then adds the value with 1 to obtain a final value of **66**. In the last statement we use the type cast operator (**char**) to convert the integer value of (**letter + 1**), i.e., **66**, to a char data representing the character **B**.

3.5.2 Scanner

API class Scanner has been provided by **java.util** since the release of JDK1.4. It is used for data input from a specified input device, such as a keyboard or file. A method of Scanner class will first read a data from the input device stored in the buffer, convert the data into the specified data type, and finally return the result.

You should use an import statement to include the package at the top of your code:

import java.util.Scanner; *//include the Scanner class*

Because the methods in the Scanner class are not the static, we must create an object of Scanner, before calling them:

Scanner input = new Scanner(System.in); *//create an object of Scanner from the keyboard*

Here, **System.in** is an object, and it specifies input as coming from the keyboard. Table 3.15 lists the commonly used methods in **Scanner**.

Table 3.15 Commonly used methods in Scanner class

Method	Description
public String next()	Return the input as a string from the object of Scanner. The return data will not include any whitespace.
public int nextInt()	Return the input as an integer from the object of Scanner. The return data will not include any whitespace.
public double nextDouble()	Return the input as double from the object of Scanner. The return data will not include any whitespace.
public String nextLine()	Return the input as a string from the object of Scanner. The next scan will start from the beginning of the next newline. The return data will include any whitespace.
public boolean hasNext()	Return true if there is input in the object of Scanner; otherwise return false. It will not affect any input operation.
public boolean hasNextInt()	Return true if there is input representing an integer in the object of Scanner; otherwise return false. It will not affect any

	input operation.
public boolean hasNextDouble()	Return true if there is input representing a double in the object of Scanner; otherwise return false. It will not affect any input operation.
public boolean hasNextLine()	Return true if there is an input line in the object of Scanner; otherwise return false. It will not affect any input operation.

The following are examples of using common methods in the **Scanner** class:

```
    //Complete code called TestScannerApp.java in Ch3 from author's website
Scanner sc = new Scanner(System.in);    //create an object of Scanner
....

System.out.print("Enter a title: ");    //prompt use to enter title  String
title = sc.next();                      //receive a token
System.out.println("title is " + title); //print the title
System.out.print("\nEnter a price: ");   //prompt user to enter a price
price = sc.nextDouble();                 //receive the double

System.out.print("\nenter the quantity: "); //prompt user to enter quantity
quantity = sc.nextInt();                //receive the quantity
total = (price + price * 0.065) * quantity;
System.out.print("\ntotal is " + total);  //print total

sc.nextLine();                      //clear the sc buffer
System.out.println("\n\nenter a line of message: ");//prompt user to enter
message = sc.nextLine();            //receive the line of entry
System.out.println("My message is " + "\"" + message + "\""); //print message
```

It should be noted that when:

String title = sc.next();

is executed, the program will wait for the user's input from the keyboard, i.e., until the return key is pressed. If the user's entry is a string containing spaces and tabs, for example:

This is my (enterkey)

sc.next() only reads characters until encountering a space or tab. In this example, it will stop the scanner after reading "**This**", return it as the input data, and then move the scanner indicator to the beginning of next data, i.e., "**is**". Therefore, the rest of input data from the user is still in the buffer after the statement is executed.

If we have more statements:

```
System.out.print("\nEnter a price: ");        //prompt user to entry

double price = sc.nextDouble();               //scan in a data as double
```

an input data type mismatch exception will occur, and the program will be terminated ungracefully. This is because additional data from the first entry remains in the scanner's input buffer without having been processed. More specifically, the next data, "**is**", in the scanner is not a double.

How can we avoid this error? We must first clear the scanner's buffer before performing the next input process, e.g.,:

```
sc.nextLine();                          //read in a line of data and clear the buffer

System.out.print("\nEnter a price: ");  //prompt user's entry

double price = sc.nextDouble();         //receive the input data
```

sc.nextLine() will consume all data in sc's buffer thereby clearing the buffer after scanning. Therefore, we don't need to worry about the side-effect from the previous operation.

Let's discuss another example:

```
System.out.print("\nenter the quantity: ");            //prompt user 's entry

quantity = sc.nextInt();                               //scan in the input as integer

total = (price + price * 0.065) * quantity;            //compute the total

System.out.print("\ntotal is  " + total);              //display the total

sc.nextLine();                                         //clear the buffer


System.out.println("\n\nenter a line of message: ");   //prompt user's enter message

= sc.nextLine();                                       //scan in a line of string

System.out.println("My message is " + "\"" + message + "\"");  //display the message
```

In this example we use **sc.nextLine()** to clear sc's input buffer, because in *quantity = sc.nextInt();*

the return key "**\n**" the user entered for ending. **sc.nextLine()** would have read the "**\n**" as the input string and assigned it to message if we had continued to the next input

message = sc.nextLine();

without calling

sc.nextLine();

However, there will be no problem if the next statement of the input method call is any one other than **nextLine()**, such as

int someData = sc.nextInt();

because in these methods whitespace, including "**\n**", will be excluded.

Complete code example of using Scanner class called **TestScannerApp.java** is in Ch3 from author's website.

3W: *The Scanner class was released in JDK1.5 and is provided in **java.util** package. It provides a variety of input operations for dealing with different data types in a convenient way as compared to those of **System.in**.*

3.5.3 User-friendly and interactive code

An application must be user-friendly in addition to solving problems so users love to use your program. To create a user-friendly code is one of the goals software developers must achieve. An interactive code is a vehicle to reach this goal.

Interactive means that when the code requests input data from the user or displays the result or information in the code, it will prompt the user in a correct, clear, simple, efficient, and friendly manner, to avoid misleading or frustration for users. If there is any input error, your code will correctly determine the nature of the mistake, display the message of the error, and provide guidance to the user to enter the correct input data.

The same principle applies to output in which correct, clear, efficient, and friendly information is provided to the user.

Usability of an application will increase if it is user-friendly and interactive. The user will clearly know what the requirement is, what is wrong, and what is the result. There is nothing more important than the user's satisfaction.

You might have had this experience and felt somewhat frustrated when you ran a code but it did not display any information at all on the monitor. You may have wondered what you should type in or if you should just wait for some result to be displayed on the screen. You may have asked "Who coded this program?".

To develop a user-friendly and interactive application means that you must think what the user thinks and do what the user needs. Never assume what you understand is what the user wants.

More info: *The user's satisfaction is the only standard to be met in developing a successful application. A successful application must be a user-friendly and interactive code. That is why we are here to learn Java programming.*

3.6 First Look at Control Statements

Control statements in the code are used to control the flow of the execution. Regular statements, such as assignment statements and input or output statements, are executed in a sequential fashion by the JVM. That is, the flow of the execution is the order of the statements. However, we often need to alter this sequential execution so some statements or block of code can be skipped when a certain condition is true or false, to allow specified statements to be executed, or cause some condition to be satisfied so the specified statements or a block of code can be executed repeatedly until the condition is changed. The conditions may include the result of comparison between data in a relational expression, the result of the relationship in a logical expression, or the result of a compound expression consisting of relational expressions or logical expressions.

The above expressions are called conditional expressions. In the rest of this chapter we will discuss the basics of relational expressions and simple control statements, such as if-else and while loop. The logical and compound expressions, multi-branch control statements, and other loop statements will be introduced in later chapters.

3.6.1 Relational expressions

Relational expressions are basic expressions in the conditional expression. A relational expression consists of relational operators and operands as data. We call a relational operator a binary operator because it requires at least two operands to be compared in an expression. Can you recall what other operators are also binary?

Table 3.16 lists the relational operators and examples.

Table 3.16 Relational operators and relational expressions

Operator	meaning	expression	Result
==	Equal to	x == y	If x is equal to y, return true; otherwise return false.
!=	Not equal to	x != y	If x is not equal to y, return true; otherwise return false.

>	Greater than	x > y	If x is greater than y, return true; otherwise return false.
<	Less than	x < y	If x is less than y, return true; otherwise return false.
>=	Greater than or equal to	x >= y	If x is greater than or equal to y, return true; otherwise return false.
<=	Less than or equal to	x <= y	If x is less than or equal to y, return true; otherwise return false.

More info: *Relational expressions are conditional expressions. Conditional expressions also include logical expressions and compound expressions, or any expressions and variables that produce a result of "**true**" or "**false**".*

In the following section we will discuss how to compare the primative data in relational expressions.

3.6.2 How to compare the primative data

We can perform relational comparisons in the eight primative data as follows:

```
boolean result;                 //define a Boolean data
result = 5 >= 4;                //the value of result is true
result = 10 > 11;               //the value of result is false
result = 0.09 != 0.0685;        //the value of result is true
result = 7 <= 7;                //the value of result is true
result = 'a' != 'A';            //the value of result is true
result = 8 == 6;                //the value of result is false
result = 'b' != 98;             //the value of result is false
```

It compared the Unicode of the character **b** which is **98** in the last statement, so the result is **false**.

3W: *Relational operators are used to compare the two operands in a relational expression. The result is either true or false. The purpose of using relational expressions is to control the execution flow.*

It should be noted in the comparison between two floating-point values you must consider the range of significant digits. It will produce a wrong result if the float data exceeds 9 significant digits and double data exceeds 18 significant digits. The Java compiler will not generate any syntax error, and JVM will not produce any run-time exception. In the following output, for example:

System.out.println("123.456789f == 123.4567892f: " + (123.456789f == 123.4567892f));

will display

123.456789f == 123.4567892f: true

actually, in fact, the two values are not equal to each other.

System.out.println("123.45678f == 123.456783f: " + (123.45678f == 123.456783f));

displaying

123.45678f == 123.456783f: true

And in the following statement:

System.out.println("123.45678f == 123.456784f: " + (123.45678f == 123.456784f));

displays

123.45678f == 123.456784f: false

In the comparison of two doubles, it will take "round 4" at the 18th significant digit:

System.out.println("123.45678901234567 == 123.456789012345673: "

+ (123.45678901234567 == 123.456789012345673));

The result is **true**:

123.45678901234567 == 123.456789012345673: true

But:

System.out.println("123.45678901234567 == 123.456789012345674: "

+ (123.45678901234567 == 123.456789012345674));

The result is **false**:

123.45678901234567 == 123.456789012345674: false

The complete code called **TestRelationalApp.java is** in Ch3 from the author's website.

However, compiler errors will be generated for **byte**, **char**, **short**, **int**, and **long** data types used in relational comparisons if the data exceed legal ranges.

More info: *In Java you cannot use **0** to represent a **false** and **1** for **true** as in C/C++.*

3.6.3 How to compare strings

There are two types of relational comparisons involving strings – comparing the contents and comparing the addresses of the strings. Java uses the relational operators we discussed in the last section to compare the addresses of the strings as operands in a relational expression.

To compare the contents of two strings, you must call the methods provided by the **String** class. Table 3.17 lists the commonly used methods in the string comparisons.

Table 3.17 Commonly used methods for string comparisons

Method	Example	Description
public boolean equals(String)	str1.equals(str2)	If the contents of two strings are the same without ignoring the case, return true; otherwise return false.
public boolean equalsIgnoreCase(String)	str1.equalsIgnoreCase(str2)	If the contents of two strings are the same ignoring the case, return true; otherwise return false.

Let's discuss some examples:

```
String  str1 = "My String",      //define a string
        str2 = "My string";      //define another string
 System.out.println(str1.equals(str2));   //print false
```

because the case of '**s**' is different. But:

```
System.out.println(str1.equalsIgnoreCase(str2));        // print true
```

prints **true** since the difference in case is ignored in the comparison.

If we compare the two strings as follows:

```
str1 == str2
```

addresses of each string in memory are compared. For example:

```
System.println(str1 == str2);              //print false
```

System.println(str.equalsIgnoreCase(str2));   //print true

The first output displays false since the two strings are each stored in different memory locations. The second example displays true due to the contents—ignoring case—in the comparison being the same.

You may refer to Figure 3.2 to clarify the relationship between the content and address of a string. As a beginner in Java, it is a common mistake to easily confuse the comparison of the contents and comparison of the addresses of strings. We will discuss topics such as string referencing, string object instantiation, and more about string comparisons of contents and addresses in detail in later chapters.

For learning and testing, the following is a complete example of string content comparisons. It asks the user to enter two strings, makes a comparison, and prints the result. The code terminates after one execution. However, after we have discussed the loop statement, it will be modified to continue execution until the user wants the code to stop.

```
//Complete code called TestStringComparisonApp.java in Ch3 from author's website
//Demo of testing string comparisons

import java.util.Scanner;

public class TestStringComparisonApp {
  public static void main(String[] args) {

         String   str1,              //declare two strings
                  str2;

         Scanner sc = new Scanner(System.in);    //create an object of Scanner

         System.out.println("Welcome to String comparison testing\n");

         System.out.print("Please enter the first string: ");
         str1 = sc.nextLine();              //scan in the first string

         System.out.print("\nPlease enter the second string: ");
         str2 = sc.nextLine();              //scan in the second string

         //display the first and second one
         System.out.println();
         System.out.println("str1 = " + str1);
         System.out.println("str2 = " + str2);

         //display the results of the comparison
```

```
        System.out.println("str1.equals(str2) is " + str1.equals(str2));
        System.out.println("str1.equalsIgnoreCase(str2) is " +
str1.equalsIgnoreCase(str2));

        System.out.println();
        System.out.println("Thank you and please try again...");
    }       //end of the main()
}           //end of TestStringomparisonApp
```

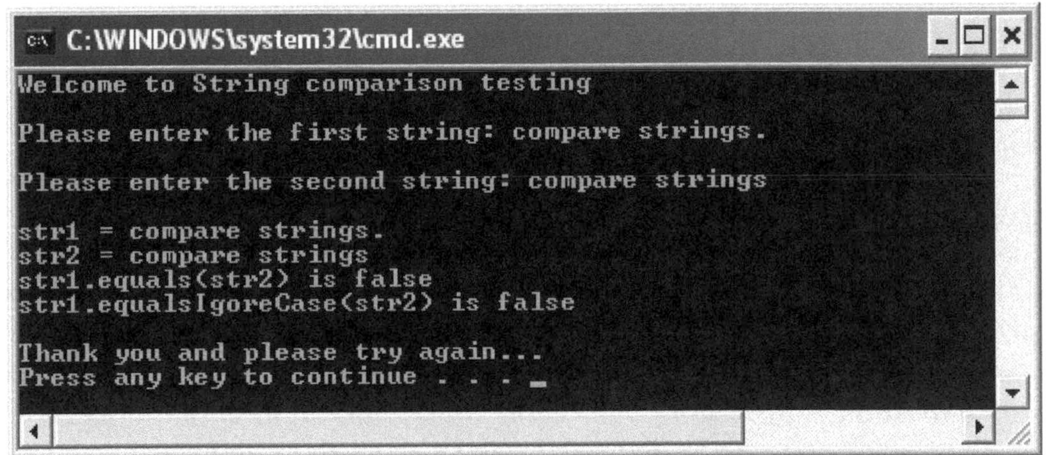

Figure 3.5 A typical output

Figure 3.5 shows a typical execution result.

3.6.4 Simple if statements

" If I save $15,000, then I will buy a Corolla."? This is a typical if statement. You may see that it only states what is going to happen if the condition is true, but does not say what you will do if the condition is not reached. The **if** statement is a single-branch control, and it only takes action if the specified condition is true.

"If it is raining, we will play in the park; else, we will go fishing." This is a typical **if-else** statement. The **if-else** includes two possibilities – what you do if the condition is true and what you do if the condition is not true. Therefore, the **if-else** is a two-branch control statement.

if and **if-else** are the most commonly used control or decision making statements in coding. They are available in most computer languages. We will discuss their simple forms and give examples of their use in this chapter. More complex coding involving branch-control is discussed in later chapters.

Let's look at the **if** statement first. The following notation represents the syntax of the **if** statement:

if (conditional_expression)

statement;

or

if (conditional_expression) {

//a block of statements

statements;

}

Here:

Conditional_expression – any conditional expression. Note that it must be included inside parentheses.

Statements – more than one line of Java statements, or a block of Java statements.

The execution flow is as follows: if the conditional expression is true, it will execute the statement, or statements. If the conditional expression is not true, it will not execute, i.e., skip, the statement or statements. It may be noticed that the braces can be omitted if there is only one line statement under the **if** condition.

Figure 3.6 lists the typical code of the **if** statement and its flow chart and UML chart.

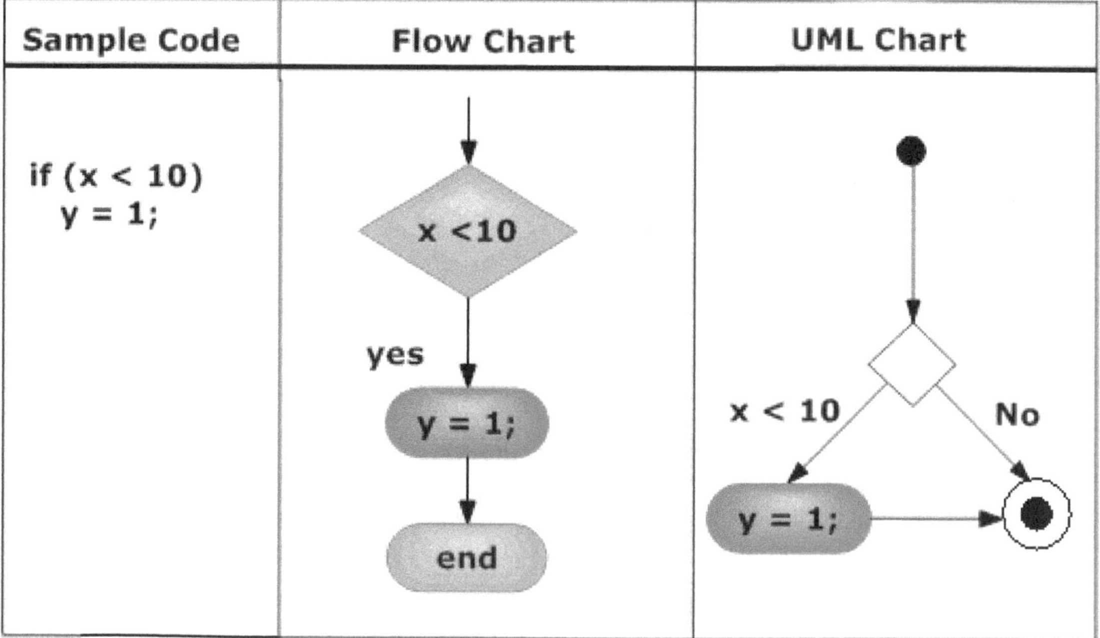

Figure 3.6 if statement flow chart and UML chart

Let's discuss some examples of using **if** statements.

Example 1. There is only one line of code in the **if** statement.

```
discountRate = 0.1;
if (total >= 150)
        discountRate = 0.2;
System.out.println("discount is " + total * discountRate);
```

In this example, if the value of variable **total** is greater than or equal to **150**, **discountRate** is assigned the value of **0.2**, then the output statement is executed; however, if its value is less than **150**, control will skip the assignment statement and **discountRate** will not change. The output statement is then executed.

Example 2. There is a block of code in the **if** statement.

```
discountRate = 0.1;
if (total >= 150) {
        discountRate = 0.2;
        bulkOrder ++;
}
System.out.println("Discount is " + total * discountRate);
System.out.println("Number of bulk order is " + bulkOrder);
//The Complete code called TestIfApp.java is in Ch3 from the author's website.
```

In this example, if the value of **total** is greater than or equal to **150**, the block of the code in the braces will be executed. That is, the **discountRate** will have a new value of **0.2**, **bulkOrder** will be increased by **1**, then the output statement is executed; however, if **discountRate** is less than **150**, this block of the code will be skipped and control will jump to the first statement after the block, that is, in this case, the output statement is executed. So **discountRate** and **bulkOrder** are kept the same.

We should pay more attention in the writing format of the **if** statement. It is encouraged to properly use spaces or tabs to increase the readability, as we did in both examples above. The following writing style:

```
// Discouraged writing format
if (total >= 150)
discountRate = 0.2;
```

```
System.out.println("discount is " + total * discountRate);
```

Or

```
// Avoid writing code like this
if (total >= 150)
{ discountRate = 0.2;
bulkOrder ++;
}
System.out.println("Discount is " + total * discountRate);
System.out.println("Number of bulk order is " + bulkOrder);
```

will certainly decrease code readability. The correct or recommended writing styles are discussed in section 3.7.

3W: *The **if** statement is a single-branch decision making operation. It is used to execute the specified code if the conditional expression is true. You must use parentheses to include the conditional expression. You must use a pair of braces to include the lines of statements if there is a block of code (more than one line of the code) in the **if** statement.*

3.6.5 Simple if-else statements

The **if-else** statement provides a two way decision making functionality. It is also called a two-branch statement. Its syntax is as follows:

```
if (conditional_expression)
        statement;
else
        statement;
```

or

```
if (conditional_expression)
        {
                statements;
        }
```

```
else
    {
        statements;
    }
```

Here, compared to an **if** statement, it has an else branch meaning that if the conditional expression is not **true**, or **false**, the statement or statements in the else branch will be executed. If there is a block of code under the **true** condition or **false** condition, you must use a pair of braces to include those statements.

Figure 3.7 lists the typical code, flow chart and UML chart of the **if-else** statement.

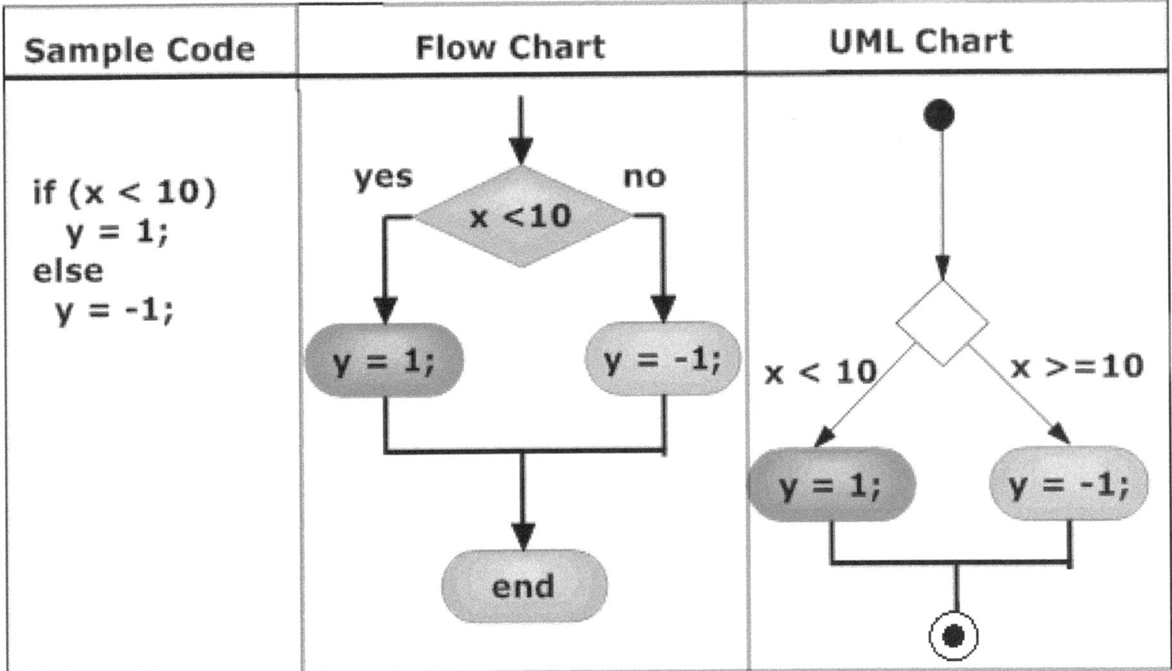

Figure 3.7 if-else statement flow chart and UML chart

Let's look at some examples using **if-else** statements.

Example 1. Simple **if-else**.

```
if (total >= 150)
        discountRate = 0.2;
else
        discountRate = 0.15;
```

```
System.out.println("discount is " + total * discountRate);
```

Compared to the first example using the **if** statement, the above code provides one more choice of decision making. That is, if the **total** is less than **150**, the code in the else will be executed, and **discountRate** will have an assigned value of **0.15**. Otherwise, we need two if statements to do the same tasks:

```
if (discountRate >= 150)

        discountRate = 0.2;

 if (discountRate < 150)

        discountRate = 0.15;
```

Example 2. There are blocks of code in an **if-else**.

```
if (total >= 150) {

        discountRate = 0.2;

        System.out.println("discountRate is: " + discountRate);

  }

 else {

        discountRate = 0.15;

        System.out.println("discountRate is: " + discountRate);

  }

System.out.println("discount is " + total * discountRate);
```

Complete code called **TestIfApp.java** and **TestIfElseApp.java** in Ch3 from author's website.

Because there is more than one line of statements in both the **if** and **else** clauses, a pair of braces must be used.

3W: *The **if-else** is a two-branch statement used to make decisions in either condition is **true** or **false**. You must use parentheses to include the conditional expression. You must use a pair of braces to include the lines of statements if there is a block of code (more than one line of the code) in either the **if** or **else** clause.*

3.6.6 while loop

"Please do not stop the execution, and I need to repeatedly run the code with different data." This is a very common situation in coding. The solution: use a loop statement. In the previous examples, the programs can be only executed once. We often need to run some parts of the code or even the entire code many times with the specified data.

The loop statement is also called an iteration or repetition statement. Java provides 3 loops: **while**, **do-while**, and **for** loop. We will discuss the **while** loop statement first, since it is the basis for other loops.

The following is the syntax of the while loop:

while (conditionalExpression)

{

statements; //the body of the loop

}

The same as in an **if** statement, the conditional expression is evaluated at the beginning of the loop to decide if the body of the loop should be executed. If the expression is **true**, the statements in the braces will be executed; however, if it is **false**, the control will jump out of the loop, and the first statement after the body of the loop will be executed. If there is only one line of the code in the body of the loop, the pair of the braces can be omitted.

Figure 3.8 lists a typical **while** loop, the flow chart and the UML chart. Here, we call **x** as a loop control variable. It must be initialized before the loop is started. The expression **x < 10** is the condition of the looping. It must be in the parentheses of the **while** loop. **x++** is the loop control variable update, and it is usually placed inside the body of the loop. We also call these three parts the three elements of a loop. They specify the behavior of the iteration.

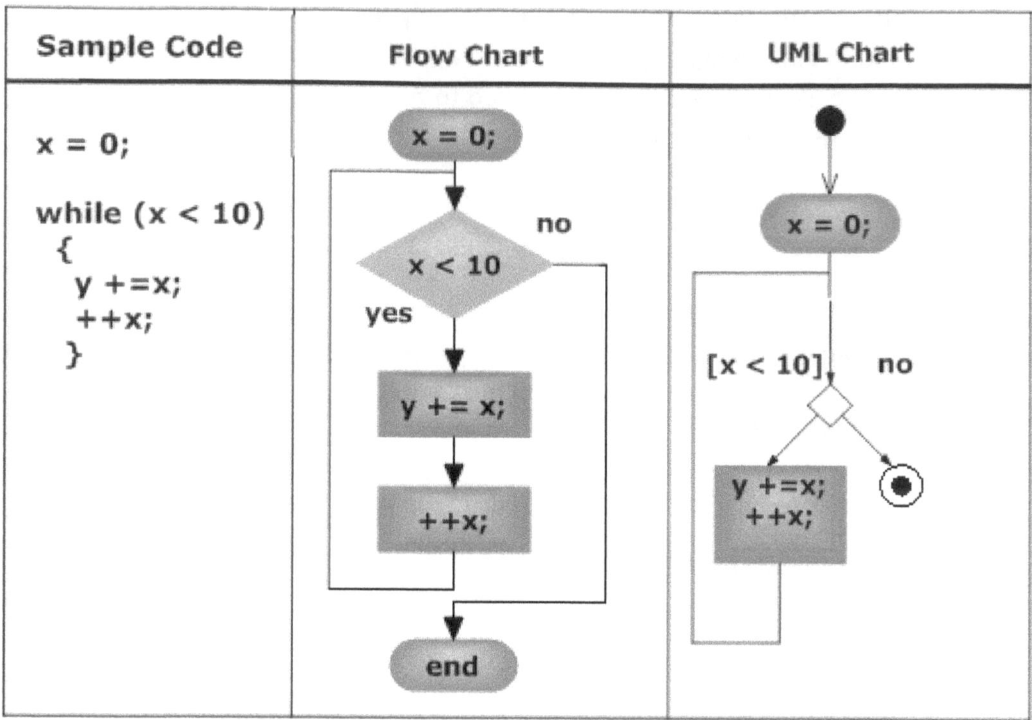

Figure 3.8 while statement flow chart and UML chart

Let's discuss some examples.

Example 1. Use of **while** loop to calculate the sum of 1 to 5.

```
int sum = 0;        //define and initialize the sum
int x = 1;          //define and initialize the loop control variable

while (x <= 5) {          //condition of the looping
    sum += x;             //equivalent to:  sum = sum + x;
    ++x;                  //loop control variable update
}
System.out.println("sum = " + sum);
```

After looping is completed, the **sum** is **15**. Figure 3.18 lists the execution steps.

3W: *The* ***while*** *statement is used to repeatedly execute a block of code. It consists of the loop control variable, the condition of the looping, and the loop control variable update. You must use a pair of braces if there is more than one line of the code in the body of the loop.*

Table 3.18 The steps of the while loop execution in Example 1

x	Condition of looping	Number of repetition	Sum
1	x <= 5 is true	1	1
2	x <= 5 is true	2	3
3	x <= 5 is true	3	6
4	x <= 5 is true	4	10
5	x <= 5 is true	5	15
6	x <= 5 is false; jump out from the loop		

More info: *a loop has 3 elements: the loop control variable, condition of the looping, and the loop control variable update. The loop control variable must be initialized before a loop is started; the condition of the looping can be any conditional expression, and it is used to evaluate if the loop should be continuously iterated. The loop control variable update will change the condition of the looping.*

Example 2. A user controlled **while** loop.

```
//Complete code called TestWhileApp.java in Ch3 from the author's website
//Demo of testing while loop with user control and computing the average score
  …. //statements for variable definitions

  Scanner  sc = new Scanner(System.in);     //create an object of Scanner
  String choice = "y"; //while loop control with default value "y"

  System.out.println("This demo will compute the average score\n");

  while(choice.equalsIgnoreCase("y"))       //loop continue if it's true
  {
     System.out.print("Please enter a student score (1-100): " );
     score = sc.nextInt();                          //receive a score
     total += score;                                //accumulate the total
     count++;                                       //increase number of score by 1

     System.out.println();
     System.out.print("Next student score? (y/n): "); //continue?
```

```
        choice = sc.next();                                  //receive the choice

        System.out.println();
    }
    average = total / count; //calculate the average score

    System.out.println("The number of students is " + count); //display the count
    System.out.println("The average score is " + average); //display the average
    System.out.println("\nThank you for using this example.");
```

The example demonstrates how the user controls the number of iterations. Because the loop control variable is initialized to "**y**", the body of the loop is executed first, the count will be increased by **1**, and the value is displayed. The following statement asks user to enter a choice. If the user types "**y**" or "**Y**", the repetition will continue; however, any other entry will terminate the loop, and the output statement after the body of the loop is executed.

It should be noted that the condition of the looping is not a traditional conditional expression. It is a method of **String** class **equalsIgnoreCase()**. Because the method will return a **boolean** value (**true** or **false**), we often use it to determine if the iteration will continue or not.

3.7 Java Coding Styles

Coding styles refer to the formats and recommendations in programming. Every language has its own preferred coding styles, and this is much more emphasized in Java programming. Let's repeat it again, the coding styles are not the syntax. They are conventions and recommendations and belong to the professional standards and ethics. It doesn't matter if you are a programmer, a software developer, or even a Java coding lover, what you coded cannot be called "good code"—even if there is no syntax error and your program runs well—if you do not follow these recommended coding styles.

3.7.1 Why are Java coding styles important?

According to the development of Java and its application software, the reasons of emphasizing the Java coding styles are as follows:

1. The maintenance cost in software products is about 86% of the total cost.
2. There is no software developed and maintained by a single engineer.
3. It will dramatically increase maintainability if the software follows good coding styles.
4. As in other software products, open-source coding should also follow the principles of simplicity and readability, representing the best standards of the current level of professionalism.

5. Java coding styles make programs readable, consistent in coding and format, so they are certainly easy in modifying and updating.
6. Following Java coding styles helps facilitate maintenance and debugging by making it easier to search for, add, delete, or modify code.
7. Java coding styles improve program extensibility. Extensibility refers to the system ability to new functionality added with minimal or no change to the systems internal structure and data flow.
8. Following Java coding styles improves efficiency. It allows developer and maintenance programmer to focus their attention on problem-solving, logics, and functionality.

We have heard many times of stories how software products are delayed or stopped due to the key engineer leaving the company and not having used good coding style or proper documentation.

Actually, it is not difficult to follow the recommended Java coding styles, the problem is ignorance of them.

3.7.2 Professional Java coding styles

There are particular recommendations provided by Sun in developing software applications with the professional coding styles. These recommendations and conventions can be listed as follows:

- Naming conventions, including files, packages, classes, interfaces, instance variables, final data, methods, local variables, and parameters.
- Use of spaces, tabs, and empty lines.
- The maximum length of the coding line and the style of wrapping back to next line.
- Comment line conventions.
- The recommendations in the use of a variety of statements, such as branches, loops, switches, exception handling, and event handling.
- Documenting.

However, the Java coding styles have their own problems, too. For example, the API classes and user-defined classes follow the same naming conventions. This might confuse code readers since it may be difficult to distinguish the two forms of classes within a code.

The following example shows the three recommended styles of a Java if-else statement:

Style 1:

if (condition) {

```
        statements;
    }
```

Style 2:

```
if (condition)
        { statements;
        }
```

Style 3:

```
if (condition)
        {
          Statements;
        }
```

We can follow these conventions and apply them to the while loop as well.

3.8 Example of an Investment Return

In this section, we apply the concepts and techniques discussed in the chapter so far and write a Java application that will compute return of the investment.

The problem description: calculate the investor's return by giving the monthly investment amount, the period of the investment, and the investment rate. The result of return should be displayed on the monitor. The program should continue until the user wants to quit.

The analysis of the problem: Assume that a user invests a certain amount each month. The period of the investment is yearly, and the return rate is the annual rate. Therefore, the formula to calculate the return is:

futureValue = Σ (futureValue + monthlyInvest) * (1 + monthlyReturnRate)

In Java, the formula can be written:

```
i = 1;
 while (i <= months) {
        futureValue = (futureValue + monthlyInvest) *    (1 + monthlyReturnRate);
   i++;
```

}

This formula also indicates the required input data for the investor to enter:

months – investment period. For the convenience of the user, the investment period will be entered as years and converted to months (months = years * 12).

monthlyInvest—monthly investment amount.

monthlyReturnRate – monthly return rate. For the convenience of the user, the annual rate will be entered as a percent, e.g., 12.5% should be entered as 12.5. The following formula can be used to calculate the monthly return rate: monthlyReturnRate = yearlyRate/100/12.

In addition to these input data, the program will also ask the user to enter the name, so we can facilitate an interactive program. The above data actually represent the instance variables in the class we are going to develop. In this class there are setters and getters in addition to the method to compute the investment return.

Based on the analysis above, we are ready to code the application as follows:

```
//Complete code called FutureValue.java in Ch3 from the author's website
//class FutureValue to compute the future value of the investment

public class FutureValue {
        private String name;                //User name
        private int years;                  //investment in years
        private double  monthlyInvest,      //monthly investment amount
                    yearlyRate,             //annual return rate
                    futureValue = 0;        //return value

        //following are setXx() and getXxx() for class variables
        public void setName(String userName) {
                        name = userName;
                }
        public String getName() {
                        return name;
                }
        public void setMonthlyInvest(double monthlyInvestment) {
                        monthlyInvest = monthlyInvestment;
                }
        public double getMonthlyInvest() {
                        return monthlyInvest;
                }
        public void setYearlyRate(double yearlyReturnRate) {
                        yearlyRate = yearlyReturnRate;
```

```
                    }
        public double getYearlyRate() {
                        return yearlyRate;
                    }
        public void setYears(int investYears){
                        years = investYears;
                    }
        public int getYears() {
                        return years;
                    }
        public double getFutureValue() {
                        return futureValue;
                    }
        public void futureValueCompute() {  //method to compute
                        double monthlyReturnRate = yearlyRate/12/100;
                        int months = years * 12;    //convert to months
                        int i = 1;                  //loop control variable
                        while(i <= months) {
                               futureValue = (futureValue + monthlyInvest) *
                                                      (1 + monthlyReturnRate);
                               i++;                 //month increased by 1
                    }                               //while end
        }           //method futureValueCompute end
}                   //FutureValue class end
```

In the driver, we choose to use the methods provided by API class **JOptionPane** to handle the input and output data. We also use a **while** loop to control the execution.

```
//Complete code called FutureValueApp.java in Ch3 from the author's website
//driver code for future value application using JOptionPane

import javax.swing.JOptionPane;

public class FutureValueApp {
public static void main(String[] args) {

        String choice = "y",              //loop control initial value
                    str,
                    userName;

   while(choice.equalsIgnoreCase("y")) {
        FutureValue futureValue = new FutureValue(); //create an object
        userName = JOptionPane.showInputDialog("Welcome to future value
```

```
application!\n\n" + "please enter your name: ");

         futureValue.setName(userName);          //set user name
         str = JOptionPane.showInputDialog("enter your monthly invest: ");
         futureValue.setMonthlyInvest(Double.parseDouble(str)); //monthly invest

         str = JOptionPane.showInputDialog("enter yearly return rate: ");
         futureValue.setYearlyRate(Double.parseDouble(str));  //set yearly rate

         str = JOptionPane.showInputDialog("enter number of years: ");
         futureValue.setYears(Integer.parseInt(str));         //set invest years

         futureValue.futureValueCompute();

         JOptionPane.showMessageDialog(null, "Your future return is: "
                               + futureValue.getFutureValue());

         choice = JOptionPane.showInputDialog("continue? (y/n): "); //continue?
   } //end of while

   JOptionPane.showMessageDialog(null, "Thank you for using future value
application.");
  } //end of main()
} //end of TestJOptionPaneApp
```

Exercises

1. What is a statement and what are its features? Explain what symbol is used to end an if-else statement.
2. How can the use of comments increase the readability of your code?
3. Use examples to explain two styles of comment lines in Java and differences in their use.
4. What are Java keywords? Why is Java called a “case-sensitive” language?
5. What is the Java naming convention? Why is the naming convention in Java so important?
6. Use examples to explain the naming conventions for classes, objects, methods, driver codes, variables and constant data in Java.
7. What are the primative data types? How many primative data types are integers? How many are floating-point data types?

8. Use examples to explain the differences between character data and strings.

9. Why does Java use Unicode? What are the differences between Unicode and ASCII code?

10. What is the relationship between variables and memory?

11. Use examples to explain the features of constant data.

12. Why it says that "=" doesn't mean equal in an assignment statement? Use examples to explain your answer.

13. What are the differences and similarities between prefixed incrementing and post-fixed incrementing?

14. Answer the following questions:

(1) `int x = 1, y = 2;`

i. `int result = ++x –y-- + 1;`

ii. result = ?   x = ?   y = ?

(2) `int x = 1, y = 2;`

iii. `int result = x++ – --y + 1;`

iv. result = ?   x = ?   y = ?

(3) `int x = 1, y = 2;`

v. `result = (++x + 2)/5 + (y-- - 3)*10;`

vi. result = ?   x = ?   y = ?

15. Convert the following functions to Java expressions:

(1) $(x + y)(x - y)$

(2) $\frac{1}{x + y}$

(3) $\frac{1}{y} + x$

(4) $\frac{x^2}{x + y}(x^2 + y^2)$

16. Why is a string variable actually the reference to the string object? Explain the relationship between string and memory. What is the difference in the relationship between primative data and memory?

17. Answer the following questions:

    (1) Use string to define your name, major, and class.

    (2) Use the join operator to make the strings above a new string named message. Use a space to separate each word.

    (3) Use **System.out.println()** to display the message you defined above.

18. Use special characters and **JOptionPane.showDialog()** to display the following information:

    “path:\\c:\temp\‘myFileName’”

    Note: the double quotes are part of the information to be displayed.

19. When you define a class, why are the member data normally defined as private? Why are its methods normally defined as public?

20. Use examples to explain **setXxx()** and **getXxx()** methods.

21. What is a driver class? Summarize the features of a driver.

22. Use examples to explain the difference between comparing the contents of strings and comparing the addresses of strings.

23. Answer the following questions (assume that variables are already defined):

    (1) Write an **if** statement to satisfy the condition: if the value of variable named **letter** is less than ‘**z**’, variable **x** increases by **1**.

    (2) Write an **if-else** statement to satisfy the conditions: if the value of variable named **letter** is less than ‘**z**’, increases variable **x** by **1**; otherwise, increases variable **y** by **1**.

    (3) Write an **if-else** statement to satisfy the conditions: if the expression **x < y <= z**, use **System.out.println()** to display the value of **y**; otherwise display the values of **y** and **z**.

    (4) Write an **if-else** statement to satisfy the conditions: if the expression **x <= z**, use **System.out.println()** to display the values of **x** and **z**; otherwise if **x > y**, then display the values of **x** and **y**.

24. Answer the following questions:

    (1) Given the following while loop:

        int number = 2;

        boolean done = false;

        while (done != true) {

number += 2;

if (number = 64)

done = true;

}

How many times is the loop executed?

(2) What are 3 criteria of the loop above?

(3) Insert an output statement to display the value of number each time the loop is executed. Also, modify the code so it displays how many times the loop is executed.

25. Write a **while** loop to compute the number of odd and number of even numbers the user entered. The loop should continue until the user enters "**n**" to stop. Display the number of odds and the number of evens after the loop has ended.

26. Using NetBeans or Eclipse open the example **Payment.java** in Ch3 provided by the text and do the following modifications to the exercises:

(1) Insert a double variable named as bonus, and assign the value to bonus according to the following conditions:

if (quantity < 10)

bonus = 10% of total

else if (quantity == 10)

bonus = 15% of total

else if (quantity > 10)

bonus = 20% of total

(2) In the method **bill()**, modify the code so the value of **total** will include the bonus.

(3) Save the code. Compile it, correcting any mistakes until it is error-free.

(4) Open file "**Payment.java**". Compile and execute it. Check if your modifications are correct.

(5) Insert a **while** loop in the driver code **PaymentApp.java** that will make the program continue to run until the user enters "**n**" to stop. Compile and run it. Save the code.

(6) In **PaymentApp.java**, use a method from the Scanner class to replace **JOptionPane.showInuptDialog()** for obtaining the user's input; use **System.out.println()** to

replace **JOptionPane.showMessageDialog()** to display the result. Compile and run your code. Save the modified code.

27. Using NetBeans or Eclipse open the example **MileageConverterApp.java** in Ch3 provided by the text and do the following modifications to the exercises:

    (1) Insert a while loop so the code can be executed continuously until user entered "**n**" or "**N**' to stop. Compile and run the code. Save the modified code.

    (2) Use **Scanner**'s method to replace **JOptionPane.showInuptDialog()** to get the user's input; use **System.out.println()** to replace **JOptionPane.showMessageDialog()** for displaying the result. Compile and run your code. Save the modified code.

28. Using NetBeans or Eclipse open the example **FutureValueApp.java** in Ch3 provided by the text and do the following modifications to the exercises:

    (1) Insert an **if-else** statement to display an error message and terminate the code by calling **System.exit(0)** if the user enters a monthly investment value less than **0**. Compile and run the code. Save the modified code.

    (2) Insert an **if-else** statement to display an error message and terminate the code by calling **System.exit(0)** if the user enters a value for the years of investment that is less than **1**. Compile and run the code. Save the modified code.

    (3) Challenge question 1: Add a loop into the above modified code asking the user to re-enter a corrected value if invalid data is entered. Save the modified code, compile and run the program.

    (4) Challenge question 2: Write a class to accomplish the tasks described in Challenge question 1. There will be at least two methods in this class: one is to make a judgment if the entry of the amount of investment is valid data; the second one is to make a judgment if the entry of the years of investment is valid. A loop should be included in each method to verify the entered data until it is valid. Write a driver code to test the application. Save your code, compile and run the program.

29. Lab project: Write a class that can convert temperatures between Celsius and Fahrenheit. The user will enter a temperature, and the method in the class will display it in both Celsius and Fahrenheit. For example, if user enters 32, your program will display 0.0 C and 89.6 F. Refer to the example **FutureValue.java** in the chapter. Write a driver to test your code. Include documentation and proper naming conventions in your code. Save the project, compile and run your application.

30. Lab Project: Create a class that can perform the conversion between kilograms and pounds. Given a weight, the method in the class can convert it into kilograms and pounds. Refer to the example called **FutureValue.java** in Ch3 from author's website to help you writing this class. Also

write a driver program to test your conversions. Finally, double check if you properly used the naming conventions, comment lines, and documentation in the code.

31. Lab Project (continued from 30 above): Modify the driver program and the weight conversion class- so it prompts the user to enter the weight in kilograms or pounds; depending on the user's entry, you will convert the weight accordingly and display the result. Your program will continue to run until the user enters "n" to terminate the program. Finally, double check if you properly used the naming conventions, comment lines, and documentation in the code.

"Be extremely subtle, even to the point of formlessness. Be extremely mysterious, even to the point of soundlessness. Thereby you can be the director of the opponent's fate."

– Sun Tsu, The Art of War

Chapter 4 Control Statements

Most statements, such as assignments, input and output, and method calls, are executed in sequential order. However, control statements can be used to change the execution flow, thereby altering the order of the execution. In Java, the most commonly used control statements are **if-else**, **switch-case**, loops, **continue**, and **break**. In the previous chapter we discussed the basics of **if-else** and **while** loop statements. In this chapter we will discuss these control statements and their applications in detail.

4.1 Logical Expressions

A logical expression is one form of conditional expression. Logical expressions are used to compare the logical relationship in terms of "AND", "OR", or "NOT" (negation) between two or more relational expressions. Therefore, a logical expression may form more complicated conditional expressions, or compound expressions, in order to control the execution flow.

4.1.1 Logical table

Table 4.1 lists three commonly used logical operations. It is also called a "Truth Table". In Java we use "&&" to denote the logical AND operation, "||" to denote the logical OR operation, and "!" to denote the logical NOT or negation operation.

Table 4.1 Truth table of logical operations

x	*y*	*x && y*	*x || y*	*! x*
true	true	True	true	false
true	false	False	true	false
false	true	False	true	true
false	false	False	false	true

It should be noted that in a logical AND operation, the result is true only if both operands are true. In a logical OR operation, the result is true if one operand is true; otherwise the result is false. A negation operation only involves one operand, and the result is true if the value of the operand is false; otherwise, the result is false if the value of the operand is true.

Short-circuit evaluation is utilized in the evaluation of logical operations in Java. In the logical AND operation **x && y**, the second operand, **y**, will not be evaluated if the first operand, **x**, is false. In the logical OR operation **x || y**, the second operand will not be evaluated if the first operand is true. In some other languages, the full evaluation is performed in such operations.

4.1.2 Precedence

As mentioned before, the use of logical operations can form a complex conditional expression, for example:

a < b + 1 || a >= c – 1 && !(b != d)

Table 4.2 lists precedence of evaluation in Java expressions.

Table 4.2 Precedence of evaluation

Precedence	Operator	Description
1	()	Parentheses always evaluated first
2	!, +, -, ++, --	Single operators
3	*, /, %	Multiply, divide, modulus
4	+, -	Plus and minus
5	<, <=, >, >=	Relational operators
6	==, !=	Equal, not equal
7	&&	Logical AND
8	||	Logical OR
9	=	Assignment

Note: *Evaluation is performed from left to right if operators are of the same precedence.*

Applying Table 4.1, assume in the example mentioned above:

a < b + 1 || a >= c – 1 && !(b != d)

a = 1, **b = 2**, **c = 3**, and **d = 4**. It will be evaluated in the following order:

b != d	*(true)*
Negation of the result of b != d	*(false)*
b + 1 then c – 1	*(3, 2)*
a < the result of b + 1	*(true)*
a >= the result of c – 1	*(false)*
Logical AND "&&"	*(false)*

Finally,

logical OR "||"	*(true)*

4.1.3 Examples

"If the scores of my midterm and final exams are 90 or above, I will qualify for the scholarship; otherwise, I will not be qualified." This is a typical logical question, and we can describe it in a logical expression as follows:

(midtermScore >= 90) && (finalScore >= 90)

Here **midtermScore** and **finalScore** are integer variables.

Excluding the negation operation "!", the precedence of logical AND "&&" and logical OR "||" is lower than that of relational and arithmetic operations. Therefore, the above expression can be simplified without the use of parentheses:

midtermScore >= 90 && finalScore >= 90

We may apply the expression above to an **if-else** statement:

```
if (midtermScore >= 90 && finalScore >= 90)
    applyStatus = true;
else
    applyStatus = false;
```

Assume that **applyStatus** is already declared as a **boolean** variable.

Let's discuss more examples. "You will be awarded $2500 if your midterm or final exam scores are 90 or above." It is a typical logical OR question. We can express it in an **if** statement as follows:

if (midtermScore >= 90 || finalScore >= 90)

grantAmount = 2500;

"You cannot be awarded any amount of the scholarship if your grade in this class is not an "A"; otherwise, you are eligible to apply for the scholarship." Using the negation operation, the description of this problem can be expressed in an if-else statement:

if (!(myGrade.equalsIgnoreCase("A")))

grantAmount = 0;

else

applyStatus = true;

Here **myGrade** is declared as a string and **applyStatus** as a Boolean variable.

The expression can also be stated as:

myGrade.compareIngoreCase("A") != true

You may wish to think if there are any other ways to express the same problem.

Table 4.3 lists more examples using logical expressions. Assume **a**, **b**, and **c** are integer variables.

Table 4.3 More examples of logical expressions

Description	Expression
a is not equal to b and c	a != b && a != c
a is equal to b or c is less than or equal to a	a == b || c <= a
a is less than b +1 or greater than or equal to c-1	a < b + 1 || a >= c – 1
Negation of a > b	!(a > b)

More info: *Java also provides bit-wise logical operations: use of "&" to perform logical AND in which it will produce 1 if input bits from both operands are 1; otherwise resulting 0. Use "|" to perform logical OR in which it will produce 1 if one of input bits from either operands is 1; otherwise resulting 0. Use "~" to perform logical NOT in which it will produce 0 if an input from operand is 1;otherwise resulting 1; Use "^" to perform logical XOR in which it will produce 1 if one of input bit is 0; produce 0 if both of input are*

0 or 1. Noted that the short-circuit rule will not be applied to bit-wise logical AND and OR operations. More detailed discussion of bit-wise logical operations is beyond the scope of the text. Please refer to other texts for details.

The following coding example illustrates the application of logical expressions within a complete code. Its purpose is for you to test and better understand the logical expressions.

```
//test out the basics

System.out.print("Please enter Boolean value of x: ");

x = sc.nextBoolean();

System.out.print("Please enter Boolean value of y: ");

y = sc.nextBoolean();

System.out.print("Please enter Boolean value of z: ");

z = sc.nextBoolean();

System.out.println("x && y: " + (x && y));

System.out.println("x || y: " + (x || y));

System.out.println("!x: " + !x);

System.out.println("x != y && x != z: " + (x != y && x != z));

System.out.println("x == y || x == z: " + (x == y || x == z));
```

The complete example called **LogicTestApp.java** is in Chapter 4 from author's website.

4.2 Nested if-else

In Chapter 3 we discussed the simple uses of **if-else** statements with examples to solve two-branch decision-making problems. Nested **if-else** statements can produce multiple branches; therefore they can be used to solve multiple decision-making problems in coding. Furthermore, the use of nested **if-else** statements incorporating complex conditional expressions allows a variety of logical judgments for solving more complicated problems.

4.2.1 Three typical nested forms

Nested **if-else** statements can be coded into many different forms. For learning purposes, we discuss three typical forms of **if-else** statements that are commonly used in coding. You may create your own forms based on the particular problem you are solving after you have mastered the concept.

Form one:

```
if (booleanExpression)
    { statements; }
else if (booleanExpression)
    { statements; }
else if (booleanExpression)
    { statements; }
...
```

This form will produce multiple selections. It is also called a multiple-switch. The following is an example of its typical code style:

```
if (month ==1)
        monthName = "January";
else if (month == 2)
        monthName = "February";
else if (month == 3)
        monthName = "March";
...
```

Form two:

```
if (booleanExpression)
{
    if (booleanExpression)
            { statements; }
    else
            { statements; }
}
else
{
```

```
        if (booleanExpression)
                { statements; }
        else
                { statements; }
    }
    ...
```

The key feature of this form is the use of additional **if-else** statements inside an **if** and/or **else** statement, thereby allowing multilayer conditional judgments. Note that each **else** must have a matching **if,** or a syntax error will result. The following is an example using this form:

```
    if (today == "Saturday" || today == "Sunday")
        {
      if (rain == true)    //or: if (rain)
          { wakeupTime = "11:00 am";
                goOutStatus = false;
          }
        else
          { wakeupTime = "8:00 am";
            goOutStatus = true;
          }
    }
    else
        { wakeupTime = "6:30 am";
          workStatus = true;
        }
    ...
```

Form three:

if (booleanExpression)

{ statements; }

else if (booleanExpression)

{ if (booleanExpression)

{ statements; }

else

{ statements; }

}

else if (booleanExpression)

...

It can be observed that this form is the combination of **Form one** and **Form two**.

4.2.2 Examples

Assigning a letter grade to a student's score is the classic example using a **nested if-else** in coding. Students will earn a letter grade based on the following criteria:

Score	Letter grade
>= 90	A
80 – 89	B
70 – 79	C
60 – 69	D
< 60	F

The following fragment of code is an example of using a nested **if-else** to solve the problem:

```
//Complete code called Grade.java and GradeApp.java in Ch4 from author's website
//Demo: class Grade will assign a letter grade based on the score

public class Grade {
   int score;
   char grade;

   public void setScore(int s){
```

```
            score = s;
    }
    public int getScore(){
            return score;
    }
    public char getGrade(){
            return grade;
    }
    public void assignGrade(){
            if (score >= 90)
                    grade = 'A';
            else if (score >= 80)
                    grade = 'B';
            else if (score >= 70)
                    grade = 'C';
            else if (score >= 60)
                    grade = 'D';
            else
                    grade = 'F';
    }       //end of method assignGrade()
}           //end of class Grade
```

You can find the complete code in Chapter 4 at the instructor's website. A challenge question for you: Can you use a different form of nested **if-else** to solve this problem?

4.2.3 Conditional operator ? :

Java provides a conditional operator **?:** that can be used as an alternate form of **if-else**. For example:

discountRate = total >= 150 ? 0.2 : 0.15;

is equivalent to:

```
if (total >= 150)
        discountRate = 0.2;
else
        discountRate = 0.15;
```

The syntax of conditional operator **? :** is as follows:

conditionalExpression ? expression1 : expression2

wherein

conditionalExpression – any conditional expression

expression1 and expression2 – constant data, variables or expressions.

Thus, if **conditionalExpression** is true, **expression1** will be executed; otherwise, **expression2** will be executed. Because the conditional expression contains three operands, the operator may be referred to as a ternary operator.

The conditional operator is often used in making a quick judgment and will generate much cleverer code. The following is another example:

System.out.print(grade >= 60 ? "passed" : "failed");

Can you rewrite the above code by using **if-else**?

Warning: *Abuse of the conditional operator may greatly reduce code readability.*

4.3 Multiple Choice Switch

Java provides the **switch** statement to carry out multiple-choice or multiple-selection operations.

4.3.1 Syntax of switch

The syntax of the **switch** statement is:

```
switch (integralExpression) {
        case integralValue_1:     statements;
                                  break;
        case integralValue_2:     statements;
                                  break;
          .
          .
        default:    //optional
                                  statements;
    }
```

Here **integralExpression** and **integralValue_*n*** must be one of the primitive types byte, short, int, or char. The **switch** also works with enumerated types, but will not work with the long primitive type. The use of the keyword **default** is optional. The execution process is as follows:

If **integralExpression** is equal to **integralValue** in any of the listed cases, the statements in that **case** will be executed. The **break** statement in a **case** will cause control to jump out of the **switch**.

If **integralExpression** is not equal to **integralValue** in any of the listed cases, all statements in the default block will be executed, and execution is completed.

If there is no **default** option and **integralExpression** is not equal to **integralValue** in any of the listed cases, no statement in the **switch** will be executed, and control will jump out of the **switch**.

The first statement following the **switch** will be executed after the execution of the **switch** statement is completed.

For example:

```
switch (menuSelector) {

        case 1:    menu.openFile();         //call method of menu object

                   break;

        case 2:    menu.saveFile();

                   break;

        case 3:    menu.exit();

                   break;

        default:   System.out.println("Menu selection error.");

}
```

It should be noted that code execution will continue through successive **case** statements if the executed case does not contain a **break** statement. This attribute may, however, be used to achieve certain desired effects. For example:

```
//Complete code called SwitchTestApp.java in Ch4 from the author's website
      switch(dayOfWeek) {      //switch-case
                case 2:
                case 3:
                case 4:
                case 5:
                case 6:                 day = "Work day";
                                        break;
                case 1:
                case 7:                 day = "Weekend";
         }   //End of switch-case
       System.out.println("day of week: " + day);
```

In this example, we purposely omit **break** statements from **case 2** through **case 6**, representing Monday through Friday, respectively. Variable **day** will be assigned the string "**Work day**" if any of these cases is true. Otherwise, **day** will be assigned the value "**Weekend**" if **case 1** (Sunday) or **case 7** (Saturday) is true. Control will jump out of the **switch** statement if none of the cases is matched, and the first statement after the **switch** will be executed. You may also add a **default** option to provide an error message in this example.

Figure 4.1 shows the flow chart and UML chart of a typical switch statement.

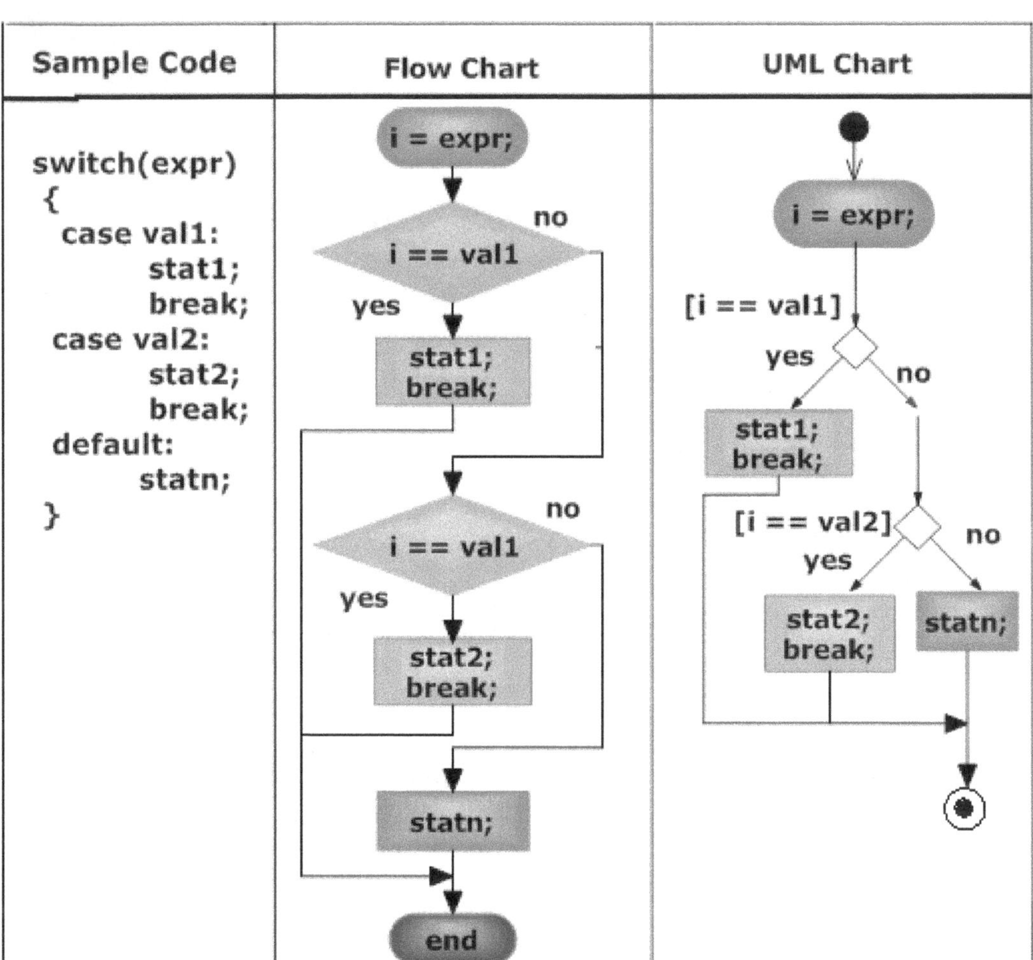

Figure 4.1 Flow chart and UML chart of typical switch statement

4.3.2 Example of the application

The following example uses a **switch** statement to solve the problem of the student grade assignment previously discussed. There are 5 options available for assigning the student grade. Assume each student's score ranges from 0 to 100. After dividing a score by 10, we having the following criteria in the assignment:

Score	Score/10	Grade
90 – 100	9 - 10	A
80 – 89	8	B
70 – 79	7	C
60 – 69	6	D
0 – 59	other	F

We apply the **default** option to deal with the assignment of 0 to 59 as an F grade. This **switch-case** statement can be written as follows:

```
//Complete code called GradeWithSwitch.java and GradeWithSwitchApp.java in Ch4
//from the author's website
  public void assignGrade(){
          int scoreRange = score / 10;
          switch (scoreRange) {
                 case 10:
                 case 9:        grade = 'A';
                                gradeACount++;
                                break;
                 case 8: grade = 'B';
                                gradeBCount++;
                                break;
                 case 7: grade = 'C';
                                gradeCCount++;
                                break;
                 case 6: grade = 'D';
                                gradeDCount++;
                                break;
                 default:grade ='F';
                                gradeFCount++;
          }      //end of switch
   }             //end of method assignGrade()
```

The complete code can be found in Chapter 4 at the instructor's website. In addition to applying the **switch** statement to the assignment of a letter grade, the example code also accumulates the total number of students in each grade category. A **while** loop is used to continue execution until the user enters "**n**" or "**N**" to stop.

4.4 Inside Loops

We have discussed the use of the **while** loop with simple examples. The **while** loop is the foundation of all other types of loops. In this section, we will discuss and summarize four different formats of the

while loop statement and move our discussion to **do-while** and **for** loops. We will also discuss the use of nested loops and examples of their applications.

4.4.1 Inside the while loop

Let's first review the three loop control elements in a **while** loop:

Loop control variable – it must be declared and initialized before the loop

Condition of loop – a Boolean expression to decide if the loop is continued or not

Update of loop control variable – the loop can be eventually stopped

The following are examples of the four typical formats used in a **while** loop:

Format 1: Counter-controlled **while** loop

```
int sum,
    count = 1;              //initialize the loop control variable
while (count <= 10) {       //condition of loop
      sum += count;         // sum = sum + count
      count++;              // update loop control variable
    .
    .
}
```

It is the most common format of the **while** loop, and is used to perform calculations, statistics, selections, and decision making operations. The three elements are very clearly defined and coded in this format.

Format 2: User-controlled **while** loop

```
String choice = "y";                        //Initialize loop control variable
while (choice.equalsIgnoreCase("y") {       //condition of loop
                  //the body inside loop
            .
            .
```

```
            System.out.print("continue(y/n)? ");

            choice = sc.next();            //user updates loop control variable

            .

            .

    }
```

This is a typical interactive example using a **while** loop. The prompt will allow the user to enter a value of the loop control variable, thereby controlling whether the loop will continue execution or end. The feature of this type of loop format is that the number of loops is uncertain.

Format 3: Sentinel-controlled **while** loops

```
double  sum,

        salary = 0.0;              //initialize loop control variable

        while (salary >= 0.0)    {        //condition of loop

            .

            .

            salary = manager.annualSalary(who); //method call to update loop control
                                                //variable

    if (salary >= 0.0)

      sum += salary;

        }
```

In this type of **while** loop, a variable (**salary**) controls the behavior of the loop repetition. For example, if the method call:

```
salary = manager.annualSalary(who);
```

returns any negative number, it indicates the end of salary input has been reached, and this value can be used as a sentinel to terminate the loop. This format is often used in file I/O operations. The number of loop iterations depends on the size of data.

A challenge question for you: Can you use a sentinel-controlled **while** loop to calculate a student's average score?

Format 4: Condition-controlled while loop

```
boolean done = false;
while (!done)        {
        statements;
        .
        .
    if (conditionalExpression)
            done = true;
}
```

This is a typical example of dynamic loop control. During the execution, depending on the result of the logical expression in an **if** statement, the loop control variable will be updated - so the loop can be terminated.

There are various formats of the **while** loop allowing flexibility that may be used to solve problems in the real world. You have to decide which format is best for solving the particular problem.

More Info: *Compared to the* ***for*** *loop, the* ***while*** *loop is more suitable for solving problems in which the number of loop iterations is not fixed.*

4.4.2 Inside the do-while loop

In a **do-while** loop, the condition of looping is examined at the end of the loop. Therefore, the body of the loop will be executed at least once.

The syntax of the **do-while** loop is:

```
do {
        statements;
    } while (conditionalExpression);
```

Braces can be ignored if there is only one statement in the body of the loop. **conditionalExpression** can be any Boolean expression. Figure 4.2 lists the typical code of a **do-while** loop, its flow and **UML** charts.

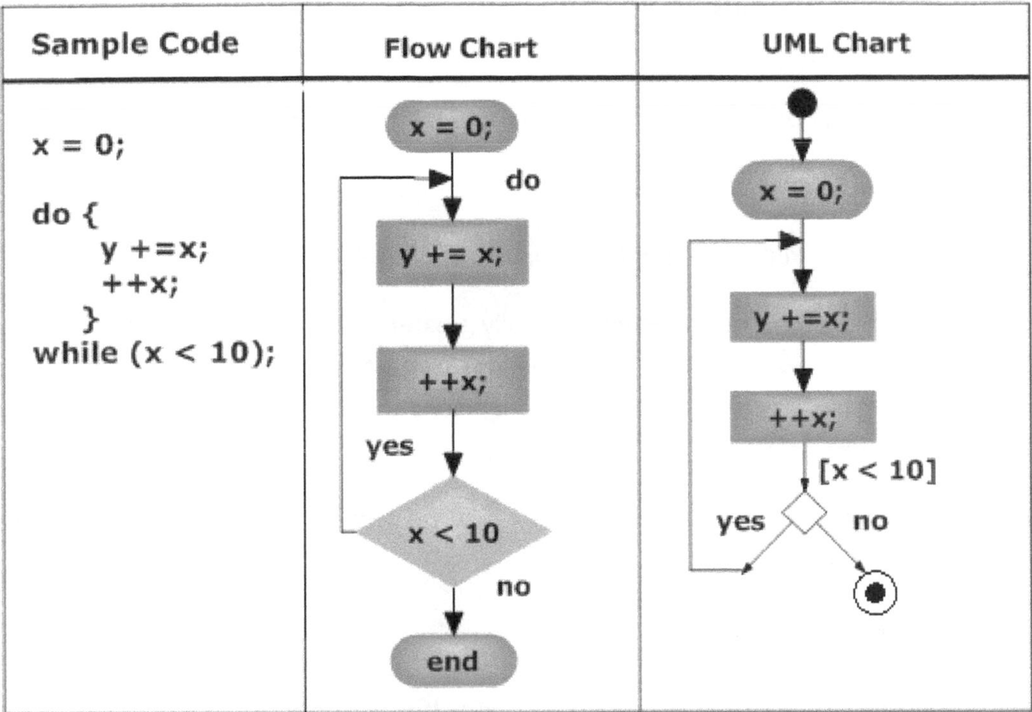

Figure 4.2 Typical code of a do-while loop, flow and UML charts

The following are examples of using a **do-while** loop.

Example 1: Calculate the sum of 1 to 5.

```
int sum = 0;            //store sum
int x = 1;              //initialize loop control variable
do {                    //begin the loop
        sum += x;       //equal to sum = sum + x;
        ++x;            //update loop control variable
    }   while (x <= 5); //condition of loop
    System.out.println("sum = " + sum);
```

After execution, the result of sum is 15. You may wish to make a comparison to see how this example is different from and similar to the example using a **while** loop to solve the same problem.

Example 2: Use of a **do-while** loop to calculate the return of investment.

```
//Assume the variables are already declared and initialized
do {                    //Begin the loop
```

```
        investReturn = (investReturn + monthlyAmount) *  (1 + monthlyInterestRate);

        ++monthCount;                 //Update loop control variable

  }  while (monthCount <= monthInvested)    ;           //Condition for looping

  System.out.println("Return of your investment: " + investReturn);
```

The month of investment, **monthInvested**, is usually greater than or equal to 1 month, and, as such, the use of a **do-while** loop to execute the body of the loop at least once makes sense. An infinite loop condition will be encountered if the loop termination condition is not met. For example, fail to update **monthCount** in this example.

3W: *The* ***do-while*** *loop is similar to the* ***while*** *loop. The body of the loop, however, is executed at least once in a* ***do-while*** *loop.*

4.4.3 Inside the for loop

A **for** loop is similar to a counter-controlled **while** loop. It places three elements of loop control separated by semi-colons inside the parentheses after the keyword **for**. The following is the typical syntax of the **for** loop:

```
for (loopControlVarInitialization; loopCondition; loopControlVarUpdate)
        {
                Statements;
        }
```

loopControlVarInitializaton – initialization of loop control variable

loopCondition – condition of looping

loopControlVarUpdate – update of loop control variable

Actually, the Java compiler will automatically use the syntax of the **while** loop to compile the code of a **for** loop.

Figure 4.3 lists the typical code of a **for** loop, its execution flow and the **UML** chart.

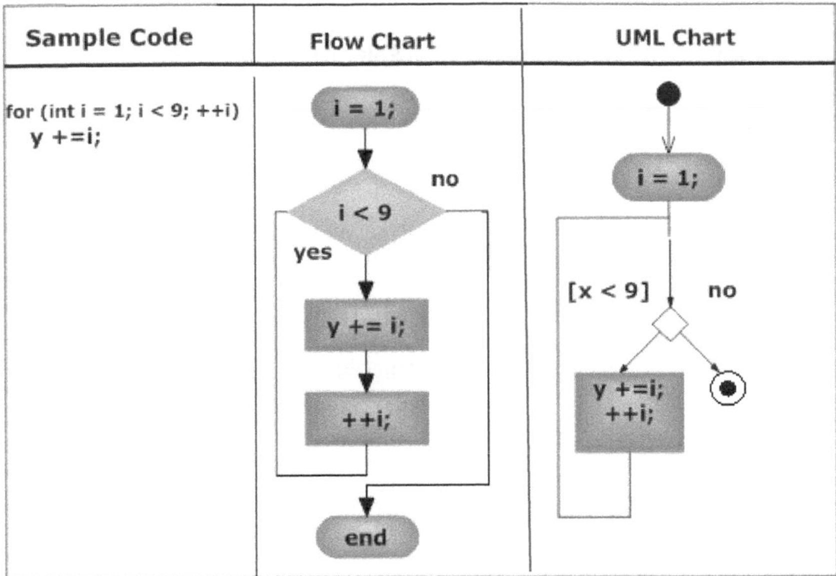

Figure 4.3 Typical code of for loop, flow and UML charts

More Info: *Java also provides the new version of the **for** loop, called the **for-each** loop or **enhanced for loop**. It is used to simplify the access of each element in an array. We will discuss the **enhanced for loop** in Chapter 10.*

3W: *The **for** loop is another form of counter-controlled **while** loop. Three elements of looping are listed in the parentheses and separated by semicolons. Its control flow is the same as a **while** loop. Any **for** loop can be modified to become a **while** loop. The **for** loop is good for solving problems when the number of iterations is given.*

The following are examples of using **for** loops.

Example 1: Compute the sum of 1 to 5.

```
for (int i = 1; i <= 5; i++)
     sum += i;                    //Assume sum already initialized to 0
```

The above code can also be written using a descending order by decrementing the loop counter:

```
for (int i = 5; i >= 1; i--)
     sum += i;                    //Assume sum already initialized to 0
```

Example 2: Use of a **for** loop to compute the return of investment.

```
//Assume all variables are initialized
for (monthCount=1; monthCount<=monthInvested; ++monthCount){    //Beginning of loop
     investReturn = (investReturn + monthlyAmount) * (1 + monthlyInterestRate);
}

System.out.println("Your return is: " + investReturn);
```

The result of execution is the same as in the example using a **do-while** loop.

A **for** loop may have a variety of forms, as well. For example, the following are some commonly used forms of the **for** loop:

1. update loop control variable in ascending or descending order
2. omit some expressions between the semicolons
2. insert some statements between the semicolons
4. separate the elements of loop control

Table 4.4 lists these commonly used forms of the **for** loop.

Table 4.4 Commonly used forms in for loop

Form	Meaning
for (int i = 8; i <= 99; i + = 3)	Loop from 8 to 99 incrementing by 3
for (int i = 100; i >= 1; i -= 2)	Even number looping from 100 to 1 decrementing by 2
for (char ch = 'A'; ch <= 'Z'; ch++)	Loop from 'A' to 'Z'; loop control variable can be **char**
for (double x = 0.0; x <= 9.25; x += 0.07)	Loop from 0 to 9.25 incrementing by 0.07; loop control variable can be **dobule or float**
for (int x = 0, y = 2; x >= 5 || y < 8; --x, ++y)	Insert other statements using commas before the semicolons
for (int i = 1; i <= 5; sum += i++)	Same as example discussed

int i = 0;
.
for (; i <= 5;)
{...
++i;
}
	Separation of three-element of loop control; the semicolons cannot be omitted

The last three forms listed in Table 4.4 are not recommended because of a lack of readability. There is an extreme example of writing a **for** loop:

```
for (; ; ) {
   //other statements
}
```

The Java compiler treats the code as an infinite loop. You must provide the three-elements of loop control within the body of the loop. You may also use **break** statement to terminate the iteration if some desired condition is true. We will discuss the **break** statement in the next section.

More info: ***while*** *and* ***for*** *loops are the most commonly used loop statements in coding according to statistics. You may press* ***ctrl-c*** *or* ***ctrl-b*** *to terminate the looping if there is an infinite loop in the execution.*

4.4.4 Inside nested loops

Following the same concept we discussed in nested **if-else** statement, we can use nested loops to construct more complex coding to solve more complicated problems. In nested loops, there will be an inner loop or inner loops inside an outer loop. Recall in Chapter 3, we have already used a simple nested loop to solve the problem of investment return:

```
while(choice.equalsIgnoreCase("y")) {              //Begin of outer loop
     .
     .
     while(i <= months) {                       //Begin of inner loop
          futureValue = (futureValue + monthlyInvest) *  (1 + monthlyReturnRate);
          i++;                            //Incrementing the month
     }                                    //end of inner loop
                    .
                    .
}  //end of outer loop
```

In this example, an outer loop is used to control the user's choice, and an inner loop is used to calculate the return of investment. It is a typical two-nested loop. You may also use any other loops, such as a **do-while** or **for** loop, to perform the same calculation in the example.

If a single loop is used to solve linear problems, two-nested loops will solve two-dimensional array or table-like problems. Three or more nested loops can be also used to solve more complicated problems, but we are interested in discussing two-nested loops and their applications since they are the foundation of multi-nested loops.

Let's examine the behavior of nested loops by tracing the execution in the following simple example of a nested loop:

```
for(int row = 1; row <= 3; row++)     {      //outer loop controls row
     System.out.println("\nrow = " + row);
  for(int col = 1; col <= 5; col++)          //inner loop controls column
                System.out.print("\tcol = " + col);
}  //end of outer loop
```

The execution result as follows:

```
row = 1
   col = 1        col = 2        col = 3        col = 4        col = 5
row = 2
   col = 1        col = 2        col = 3        col = 4        col = 5
```

```
row = 3
   col = 1        col = 2        col = 3        col = 4        col = 5
```

It is clear in each loop that when the end of the inner loop is reached (**col > 5**) control will jump out of the inner loop, go to the beginning of the outer loop, and make a judgment if **row <= 3** is true within the outer loop. If this condition is true, control will execute the first output statement and restart execution of the inner loop by resetting the inner loop control variable **col** to 1. If this condition is false, i.e., **row > 3**, execution of the outer loop is terminated, and the first statement following the outer loop will be executed.

4.4.5 More examples

Example 1: Print out the multiplication table (9 * 9).

The following is a typical example of using a nested loop. The outer loop controls the line or row number (1 to 9). The inner loop controls the column number, also ranging from 1 to 9. Because the number of iterations is fixed in both loops, we use **for** loops to solve the problem:

```
.
.
System.out.println("\t\t\t\t9 * 9 Multiplication Table\n"); //print out the title
for (int row = 1; row <= 9; row++)  {                       //outer loop from 1 to 9
      for (int col = 1; col <= 9; col++)                    //inner loop from 1 to 9
           System.out.print("\t" + row * col);              //output the result
      System.out.println();                                 //new line
}
.
.
```

The following table is printed upon execution:

```
                              9 * 9 Multiplication Table

1       2       3       4       5       6       7       8       9
2       4       6       8       10      12      14      16      18
3       6       9       12      15      18      21      24      27
4       8       12      16      20      24      28      32      36
5       10      15      20      25      30      35      40      45
6       12      18      24      30      36      42      48      54
7       14      21      28      35      42      49      56      63
8       16      24      32      40      48      56      64      72
9       18      27      36      45      54      63      72      81
```

Example 2: Modify the example of Kilometers – Miles conversion discussed in Chapter 3, Section 3.4.5 to convert Meters – Feet and Kilograms – Pounds. The program will continue to execute until the user chooses to stop.

We design a menu in this application for the user to make a selection. We use a **switch** statement to list the method calls of the various conversions and use a **while** loop to control the execution based on the user's choice. The following code fragment illustrates the conversion modifications:

```
                String menu = "Welcome to Conversion Center\n" + //Menu and prompt
                "1.  Kilometers - Miles\n" +
                "2.  Meters - Feet\n" +
                "3.  Kilograms - Pounds\n\n" +
                "0.  Exit\n\n" +
                "Please make your choice(0 - 3):  ";
String promptEntry = "Enter the data to convert: ";      //Data prompt
String errorSelect = "Wrong selection.  Please redo…";  //error message
boolean notDone = true;       //initialize user's choice

do {
        str = JOptionPane.showInputDialog(menu); //get user's choice
        select = Integer.parseInt(str);                 //convert to integer

        str = JoptionPane.showInputDialog(promptEntry); // get user's selection
        data = Double.ParseDouble(str);                 //convert to double

        switch (select) {
            case 1: cc.setKilometers(data);
                    //Kilometers - Miles
                    cc.setMiles(data);     //Call method to set data
                    cc.convertKilometers();
                    JOptionPane.showMessageDialog(null, str + " kilometers = "
                            + cc.getResult() + " miles");
                    cc.convertMiles();           //Convert Miles to Kilometers
                    JOptionPane.showMessageDialog(null, str + " miles = "
                            + cc.getResult() + " kilomenters");
                    break;
                      .
                      .
             case 0:   notDone = false;                    //Stop
                     break;

             default: str = JOptionPane.showInputDialog(errorSelect);
            }    //End of switch
     }   while(notDone);    //End of while
```

The coding for **case 2** and **case 3** is similar to **case 1**. The only difference in the use of different method calls, i.e., **cc.setMeters(data)** and **cc.convertMeters()** to perform meter-foot conversion and **cc.setKilograms(), cc.convertKilograms()** to perform kilogram-pound conversion.

It should be noted that **case 0** is used to stop the execution in the **switch-case** statement. Furthermore, if the user's selection is not in the menu, the **default** option will be executed, an error message will be displayed, and the menu will be redisplayed.

The code may also be written without the use of **case 0** by using a **while** loop to prompt the user to continue or terminate program execution:

```
String menu = "Welcome Welcome to Conversion Center\n" +    //Menu and prompt
         "1.  Kilometers - Miles\n" +
         "2.  Meters - Feet\n" +
         "3.  Kilograms - Pounds\n\n" +
         "Please make a selection(1 - 3):  ";
   .
   .
String choice = "y";
while (choice.equalsIgnoreCase("y") {                  //continue
         do {
            .
            .
            switch (select) {
                     case 1:  …
                                    .
                     case 2:  …
                                    .
                     case 3:  …
                                    .
                     default: …
                                    .
            }                             //end of switch
     } while (notDone);                   //end of do-while
     //Prompt user to continue or not
     Choice=JOptionPane.showInputDialog("Continue(y/n)? ");

   }                                             //end of while
```

4.5 Break and Continue

In the discussion of the **switch** statement, we have used **break** to end the execution of individual **case** statements and to terminate the **switch** statement. In Java, **break** can also be used to control the behavior of repetition in a loop. The **continue** statement, as opposed to **break**, is used to control the flow of execution. In this section we will discuss the use of **break** and **continue** to control loops. We will also discuss **labeled break** and **labeled continue** statements and their applications. Using these statements in code allows more flexibility, but also provides more opportunities for mistakes. These statements should be applied with caution.

4.5.1 break

Java only allows using the **break** statement in **switch-case** and inside loop statements. The execution of a **break** statement within a loop will cause immediate termination of the iteration.

```
while(i<5){
        i=a.doSomething();
        if (i < 0)
        break;          //jump out of the loop
}
```

If **a.doSomething()** returns a value less than 0, the **break** statement will cause execution to jump out of the loop, thereby terminating the loop iteration.

The following is another example:

```
String choice = "y";    //Initialized value
while (true) {
     if (choice.equalsIgnoreCase("n"))
             break;
      //otherwise continue the loop; else is omitted here
      .
      .
      choice =  JOptionPane.showInputDialog("continue (y/n)?  ");
}
```

If the value of **choice** is either "**n**" or "**N**", **break** will terminate the loop.

The following is an example of using **break** in nested loops to print prime numbers in the given range:

```
int n, x;
for (n = 2;n <= 20; n++ ) {
     for (x = 2; x < n; x++ ) {
       if(n % x == 0)                      //Not a prime number
         break;                            //Out of the inner loop
     }
     if(n == x)                            //Is a prime number
       System.out.print(n + "\t");
 }
```

The execution result is as follows:

```
2    3    5    7    11    13    17    19
```

A non-prime, i.e., composite, number results when **n** can be evenly divided by **x**. Therefore, a **break** statement is used to terminate the inner loop when this situation occurs. Control will resume with the next iteration of the outer loop. If **n** equals **x**, **n** is a prime number, and its value is printed.

It should be noted that although the loop is terminated by the **break** statement, its control variable is not updated. For example:

```
for (int count = 1; count <= 5; count++) {
        if (count == 2)
              break;
            .
            .
}
```

After the loop is terminated by **break**, **count** is still equal to 2. Complete code called BreakTestApp.java can be found in Ch4 from the author's website.

4.5.2 Labeled break

The **labeled break** statement can only be used in a loop, and it can be most effective if it is used in a nested loop. If you want execution to jump out of the outer loop after executing a **break** statement, you may consider using a **labeled break**:

```
outerloop:                                          //label of the break
for(int k = 0; k < 10; k++) {
        while ( i < 5) {
             i = a.doSomething(); //Call a's method
             if (i < 0)
               break outerloop; // Jump out of outer loop
   }                                                     //End of inner loop
   someNum =  i;
}                                                        //End of outer loop
otherNum = k;
```

In this example, the label of the **break** is **outerloop**. We place it outside of the outer loop, so when the **break outerloop** statement is executed control will immediately jump out of the outer loop (it will, of course, first jump out of the inner loop) and execute the first statement after the outer loop:

```
otherNum = k;
```

Java requires that the label of a **break** statement only be placed before the following statements:

- The loop you want to jump out of
- An **if** statement containing a loop
- A **switch** statement containing a loop

We have already discussed the first situation. Let's examine more examples:

```
//Label is placed before an if containing a loop
jmp1:
   if (condition == true) {
          while ( i < 5) {
               i = a.doSomthing();           //Call a's method
               if (i < 0)
               break jmp1;                               //Jump out of the if
          }                                              //End of while
   }                                                     //End of if
   someNum = i;
```

After the **break jmp1** statement is executed, control will jump out of the inner **if** (of course, it will also jump out from the while loop) and execute the first statement after the outer **if**:

```
someNum = i;
```

Another example:

```
//Labeled break must be placed before the switch-case with loop
jmp2:
switch (select) {
```

```
        case 'a':  for(int x = 10; x > 0; x--) {
                      statements;
                      if (condition == true)
                          break jmp2;

                      ...
                   }
        case 'b':  statements;
        ...
    }
obj.doSomethingElse();          //Call obj's method
```

When the **break jmp2** statement is executed, control will jump out of the **for** loop as well as the **switch** statement, and the first statement after the **switch** statement will be executed.

Warning: *Use the **labeled break** statement only when it is necessary. Its use impairs code readability.*

4.5.3 continue

Java's **continue** statement can only be used in the body of a loop. The purpose of using **continue** is to avoid executing the rest of statements in the iteration after a **continue** is encountered. For example:

```
while ( i < 5 )  {
            i = a.doSomething();    //Call a's method
         if (i < 4)
              continue;
      b.doSomethingElse();     //Call b's method
}
```

While **i < 4** is true, the **continue** is executed, control resumes with the next iteration of the **while** statement, and the statement after the **continue**:

```
b.doSomethingElse();
```

is not executed.

It should be noted in the above example than an infinite loop will occur if **i** is never greater than 4.

The following is another example of using **continue** to display the reciprocal of a number in the given range:

```
for(double i = 3; i >= -3; i--) {
      if (i == 0)
        continue;                              //Continue to next loop
      System.out.println(i + "Reciprocal of " + i + " is " + (1 / i));
   }
```

The execution result is as follows:

```
Reciprocal of 3.0 is 0.3333333333333333
Reciprocal of 2.0 is 0.5
Reciprocal of 3.0 is 1.0
Reciprocal of 3.0 is -1.0
Reciprocal of 3.0 is -0.5
Reciprocal of 3.0 is -0.3333333333333333
```

The **continue** statement will cause execution to jump out of the current iteration when **i** is equal to 0, and control will go to the next iteration of the loop. Otherwise, the result will be printed before resuming the next loop iteration.

Note that in a **for** loop the loop control variable will be updated after a **continue** statement is executed; the loop control variable will not be updated following the execution of a **continue** statement within a **while** loop. Ignoring this requirement in coding may cause an infinite loop. For example:

```
int count = 1;
while (count <= 5) {
   if (count % 3 == 0)
          continue;//Infinite loop because the loop control variable is not updated
          System.out.println("in loop: " + count);
          count++;
   }
// insert count++ before the continue will avoid this mistake
```

Because loop control variable **count** is never updated, statement **count % 3 == 0** is always true, thereby causing an infinite loop.

Complete code called ContinueTestApp.java can be found in Ch4 from author's website. A challenge question for you: How can the code be modified to avoid an infinite loop from occurring in this example?

4.5.4 Labeled continue

The **labeled continue** statement is usually used in nested loops. The purpose of **labeled continue** statements is to avoid the specified statements in the body of the loop from being executed. For example:

```
jmp1:                          //Label of continue
```

```
while (someCondition ) {
           for (int i =0; i <4; i++)       {
             if ( a.doSomething()) //Call a's method
               continue jmp1;             //Label of continue is jmp1
               b.doSomethingElse();        //Call b's method
           }
   }
```

When the condition of the **if** statement is true **continue jmp1** will be executed, and control will jump out of the current iteration of the inner loop. The next iteration of the **while** loop will be executed, and method call **b.doSomethingElse()** will be ignored. As discussed above, the loop control variable in the outer **while** loop must be updated to avoid creating an infinite loop.

The following example uses **labeled continue** to find the prime numbers in the given range:

```
int n = 2;
outerLoop:                                  //Label of continue
while ( n <= 20) {
     for (int x = 2; x <= n - 1; x++) {
             if (n % x == 0) {                         //not a prime number
                     n++;                          //Update the loop control variable

                     continue outerLoop;            //Continue to next loop
               }
     }          //End of inner for loop
     System.out.print(n + "\t");                        //Print out the prime number
     n++;                                         //Update the loop control variable
} //End of outer while loop
```

The execution result is as follows:

```
2        3      5      7      11      13      17      19
```

A **while** loop is used in the outer loop to compare its use with a **for** loop. Complete examples using labeled continue can be found in Ch4 from author's website.

More Info: *The use of **continue** and **labeled continue** statements will reduce code readability and increase the opportunity to make mistakes. Some experienced software engineers are opposed to the use of the statements altogether due to their similarity to the **goto** statement. The best suggestion is to avoid using them if you can.*

Exercises

1. Use examples to explain relational expressions, logical expressions, and compound expressions. Also describe the difference between short-circuit evaluation and full evaluation.

2. List the order of evaluation for each of the following expressions and write the result of the expression evaluation:

   （1） (((total/scores) > 60) && ((total/(scores -1) <= 100))， here total = 121， scores = 2

   （2） (x >= y) && !(y >=z)， here x = 10， y = 10， z = 10

   （3） (x || !y) && (!x || z)， here x = false， y = true， z = false

   （4） x > y || x <= y && z， here x = 2， y = 2， z = true

3. We discussed the use of the nested **if-else** statement to assign a letter grade to student scores in Section 4.2.2. Explain why the following coding style should not be used:

```
if (score >= 90)
        grade = 'A';
if (score <=89 && score > 80)
        grade = 'B';
if (score <= 79 && score > 70)
        grade = 'C';
if (score <= 69 && score > 60)
        grade = 'D';
else
        grade = 'F';
```

   Also explain how a nested if-else statement can be used to solve the problem. What is the advantage of using a nested if-else statement?

4. Given the following temperature conditions and associated activities, use a nested **if-else** statement and other possible **if-else** statement variants to write a code segment showing which activity should be performed at a corresponding temperature range:

Temperature	Activities
Greater than 85	Swimming
75 – 85	Picnic
65 – 74	Tennis
50 – 64	Golf
30 – 49	Dance
25 – 29	Ice Hockey
Less than 25	No activity

5. Use a **switch** statement to write a program to display a test score range based upon a student's letter grade (See Section 4.3.2).

6. Given the following scores and results, write code to solve the problem:

Score	Result
Greater than 70	Pass
60 – 70	Repeat
Less than 60	Fail

   (1) Use a nested **if-else** to solve the problem.

   (2) Use a **switch-case** statement to solve the problem.

7. Write a complete driver code that will execute the code in Exercise 6. Use a **while** loop to continue execution until the user wants to stop. During each loop iteration, ask the user to enter a score then display the result. Test your code and save the program.

8. Modify your code for Exercise 7 to use two classes to perform the task. One class, **Result**, will perform the analysis of an entered score and assign the result. The second class, **ResultApp**, is the driver code. Test, document, and save your program results.

9. Open file SwitchTestApp.java in Chapter 4. Use a **do-while** loop to perform the same task. Test your code and save it.

10. Determine which type of loop is best suited to solve each of the following problems:

    (1) Calculate the average score of 30 students.

    (2) Calculate the average score for classes in which the number of students varies.

    (3) The number of iterations of a loop in a given problem is unknown.

    (4) A loop must be executed regardless of circumstances, and the number of iterations is unknown.

11. Modify the following code segments using the specified type of loop to achieve the same purpose. Assume all variables are declared and initialized.

    (1) Modify the following code using a **do-while** loop

```
response = sc.nextInt();
count = 0;
while (response >= 0  && response <= 99) {
        System.out.prinln("response is " + response);
```

```
        response = sc.nextInt();
        count++;
}
```

(2) Challenge problem: Modify the code above using a **for** loop.

(3) Modify the following code using a **while** loop

```
intData = sc.nextInt();
do {
    System.out.println("   " + intData);
    intData = sc.nextInt();
} while (intData >= 10);
```

(4) Modify the following code using a **for** loop

```
sum = 0;
count = 50;
while (count <= 1299) {
    sum += count++;
}
```

12. Modify your code of Exercise 7 using a **do-while** loop to carry out the task. Test your modified code and save it.

13. Use a **for** loop to calculate n!. Ask the user to enter an integer in the range 0 – 25, then display the result of the calculation. (Hint: 5! = 5 x 4 x 3 x 2 x 1).

14. Write a complete driver code to carry out the factorial calculation described in Exercise 13. Save the code as FactorialApp.java. Test the code and save it.

15. Trace the execution in the following code segment and list the result produced in each loop iteration.

```
for (row = 1; col <= 10; row++) {
    for (col = 1; col < = 10; col++)
            System.out.print("*");
    for (col = 1; col <= 2 * row - 1; col++)
            System.out.print("   ");
    for (col = 1; col <= 10 - row; col++)
            System.out.print("*");
    System.out.println();
}
```

16. Assume there is a **switch** statement in the body of a **for** loop. What happens if the **break** statement of the **switch** statement is executed? Will control jump out of the **for** loop? Why or why not?

17. Use nested loops to calculate and print the square and cube of the given numbers as show in the following table:

Number	Square	Cube
1	1	1
2	4	8
3	9	27
4	16	64
5	25	125
6	36	216
7	49	343
8	64	512
9	81	729
10	100	1000

18. Write a complete driver code called **NestedLoopApp.java** to carry out the task described in Exercise 17. Test the code and save it.

19. Modify the code in Exercise 13 using a **while** loop to continuously execute the program until the user wishes to stop it. Test, document and save your code.

20. Open file **BreakTestApp.java** in Chapter 4. Modify it using a **while** loop to carry out the task. Test and save the code.

21. Open file **PrimeNumberApp.java** in Chapter 4. Modify it using a **while** loop to carry out the task. Test and save the code.

22. Open file **FutureValue2App.java** in Chapter 4. Modify its outer loop using a **do-while** loop to carry out the task. Test and save the code.

23. Open file **BreakTestApp.java** in Chapter 4. Modify it using a **do-while** loop to carry out the task. Test and save the code.

24. Open file **PrimeNumber2App.java** in Chapter 4. Modify it using a **for** loop, instead of a while loop, to carry out the task. Test and save the code.

"Garbage in, garbage out (GIGO)."

– An adage of computer men

Chapter 5 Data Control

There is a popular saying in the software engineering community in Silicon Valley: "Garbage in, garbage out." It means if there is a mistake in input data, the output is just like garbage, and you will definitely get the wrong result. To be able to generate the right and accurate result, the first step in coding is to eliminate mistakes from the input data. The Chinese have a saying, "you cannot make dinner without food"; however, an experienced chef will control and select the ingredients for cooking.

We will discuss first in this chapter about the quality control of input data – data testing, then we will move on to formatted output to make it more readable and user-friendly. Finally, we will introduce topics related to the control of data, such as data type casting, **Math** class methods to manipulate data, and the **BigDecimal** class and its applications.

5.1 Eliminate Mistakes at the Beginning

To avoid "garbage in, garbage out," we must examine input data to get rid of possible mistakes from the beginning. Java provides many techniques to accomplish this important step:

- Exception handling. Utilization of Java's powerful exception handling mechanism is not only for input data testing; it is also a good debugging tool in software testing.
- Return status from the methods in API classes. Almost all methods dealing with data input in the API classes will return a status (true or false) denoting if the data are of the correct type. Programmers can use this feature to eliminate or remedy incorrect input data.
- Programmer-defined exception handling. To take advantage of inheritance in OOP, programmers can use the inheritance of functionality from exception handling API classes as well as prepare customized messages to handle particular exceptions in the input data. Software engineers may even provide fault-tolerant code to correct mistakes, thereby making the application more intelligent and user-friendly.

We will discuss these topics in detail throughout in the text.

5.2 First Look of Exception Handling

Let's discuss the basics of exception handling first, then move our discussion to the use of exception handling to control the quality of input data.

What is an exception? An exception refers to a mistake or an unexpected result in code execution. Common examples are:

- Data type errors
- Data overflow
- Division by zero
- Calling a non-existent method, et cetera

Most mistakes involving data type “mismatching” occur with input data. Although some exceptions, such as incorrect user keyboard entry, cannot be controlled by software developers, a good software developer must provide a mechanism in the code to prevent such mistakes from occurring, detect the possible wrong input data, and even provide ways to correct mistakes. Such actions will increase the reliability, usability, and user-friendliness of the code.

5.2.1 Exception handling mechanism – try-catch

We call try-catch Java's traditional exception handling mechanism. Its syntax is as follows:

```
try {
        //Include all statements that possibly generate exceptions
        statements;
    ...
}
catch (ExceptionClass1 objectName)  {
        //Display exception message
        statements;
}
...
catch (ExceptionClassn objectName) {
           //Display exception message
        statements;
}
```

Here:

try – Java keyword. It is called a **try** block, or simply **try**. All statements that could generate exceptions should be included in the **try** block so exception handling will work. If an exception occurs in a **try** block, an object of that exception class will be automatically thrown and possibly caught by the associated **catch** block. It should be noted that the braces must be included even if there is only one statement in a **try** block.

catch – Java keyword. It is called a **catch** block, or simply **catch**. The purpose of a **catch** block is to handle the exception thrown from an associated **try** block. The parameters within the parentheses specify the class name of the exception type and the object name it will create to handle the exception. A **try** block may have many **catch** blocks associated with it to handle a variety of exceptions, but only the code in the first matching **catch** block will be executed.

Let's examine how this exception handling mechanism works using the following example:

```
//Complete example is called TestExceptionApp.java in Ch5 from the author's website
try {
        System.out.print("\nEnter the quantity: ");
        int intData = sc.nextInt();
        System.out.println("intData = " + intData * 10);
  }
catch (InputMismatchException e) {
        sc.nextLine();                                   // Clear sc buffer
        System.out.println("Error!  Invalid integer.  Try again…");
        continue;                                        //Continue to input in the loop
  }
......
```

In the above code, if the user enters any input data other than an integer, the method **nextInt()** of the **Scanner** class will automatically throw an object of **InputMismatchException**. Control will jump out of the **try** block, and the first **catch** after the **try** block will be evaluated. If the thrown exception matches the type listed in the **catch** statement, the statements in this **catch** block will be executed. If the thrown exception type does not match that specified in the first **catch** block, execution will continue through successive **catch** blocks, if present, evaluating if a matching exception type is found. If no **catch** block matches the thrown exception object, the JVM will handle this unmatched exception. In this situation, the program will be terminated ungracefully and the exception message dumped by the JVM will be displayed on the monitor. However, if there is no input error the code will execute normally, and evaluation of the **catch** blocks will be omitted.

The argument name listed after the exception type in the **catch** block can be any Java legal identifier. By convention, ***e*** or ***ex*** is used to denote the exception object.

We could also use the **toString()** method provided by the **Exception** class to display the system default message:

```
catch (InputMismatchException e) {
    System.out.println(e.toString());             //or System.out.println(e);
}
```

The output is:

```
java.util.InputMismatchException
```

Exception objects automatically thrown by API classes are called system thrown exceptions. For example, the **nextInt()** method in the **Scanner** class will automatically throw an instance of the object **InputMismatchException.** In following sections, we will first discuss API exception classes, then introduce the methods in API classes used to examine the input data and types of exceptions they will throw when exceptions occur.

3W *Exception handling is used to process run-time errors or unexpected results occurring in code execution to ensure correctness, reliability, and user-friendliness in programs. Java provides powerful* *exception API classes, exception handling mechanisms, and automatic exception handling systems by the JVM. Programmers can also create customized exception classes inherited from API classes to handle particular exceptions in their applications.*

5.2.2 API exception classes

Java provides a series of API classes to handle exceptions. These API classes are called standard exception classes, or simply API exception classes. Their inheritance chart can be summarized as follows:

```
Exception
    RuntimeException
          NoSuchElementException
                  InputMismatchException
          IllegalArgumentException
                  NumberFormatException
          ArithmeticException
          NullPointerException
```

Exception is the superclass of all other API exception classes. **InputMismatchException**, **IllegalArgumentException**, **NumberFormatException** and **ArithmeticException** are commonly used API exception classes related to input data verification. More discussions about inheritance and exception handling are found in Chapter 7 and Chapter 11.

5.2.3 Throw exceptions

In the Java API documentation, you may notice there are clearly defined descriptions of the types of exceptions which may be thrown for all methods designed using the API exception classes. Table 5.1 lists commonly used methods in the **Scanner**, **Integer**, and **Double** classes for dealing with data verification.

Table 5.1 Commonly used methods in data verification

API Class	Method	Thrown Exception
Scanner	nextChar(), nextByte(), nextShort(), nextInt(), nextLong(), nextFloat(), nextDouble(), nextBoolean()	InputMismatchException
Integer	parseInt()	NumberFormatException
Double	parseDouble()	NumberFormatException

The following code uses the **parseInt()** method of the **Integer** class to examine and test if the user's entry is a whole number, i.e., an integer:

```
try {
     String ageString=JOptionPane.showInputDialog("Please enter your age: ");
     int age = Integer.parseInt(ageString);
     ...
}
```

```
catch (NumberFormatException e) {
      System.out.println("Invalid  entry.    Please  enter  an  integer  as  your
       age." );
       ...
}
```

If the entry is not a valid number, for example, 1abc, the following warning message will be displayed:

```
Invalid entry.  Please enter an integer as your age.
```

5.2.4 Use throw to verify data

The keyword **throw** can be used in Java to explicitly throw a specified exception object in the code. The **Scanner** class provides many methods to check the status of input data in order to verify them. If an exception occurs, these methods will return a boolean value of **false**. We can also utilize these methods to control the data. Table 5.2 lists the commonly used methods in **Scanner** for data verification.

Table 5.2 Methods in Scanner to verify data

Method	Returned Value
hasNext()	Return true if there is an entry; otherwise return false
hasNextInt()	Return true if the entry is an integer; otherwise return false
hasNextDouble()	Return true if the entry is a double; otherwise return false

These methods are designed to verify if the data entered by the user in the buffer are valid. Note that they only check the status by returning a Boolean value and will not do any other operation.

The syntax for the **throw** statement is as follows:

```
throw exceptionObjectName;
```

Here:

throw – Java keyword. It requires the object name of the exception class to be thrown.

exceptionObjectName – specified object name of the exception class.

Or, we can also use the traditional syntax:

```
throw new ExceptionName([message]);
```

Here:

new – Java keyword. Java keyword **new** is used to create the specified exception object.

ExceptionName(message) – the constructor of the exception class. The *message* is an optional string type parameter.

Because the name of the object for handling an exception is not important, the traditional way is commonly used to handle customized exceptions in data verification. It should be noted that the **try-catch** mechanism must be used to handle such exceptions, otherwise a syntax error will be generated.

The following is an example of using **throw** and the methods in **Scanner** to examine data input.

Example 1. Verify if user entered valid data as double.

```
//Complete code in ThrowExceptionTest.java in Ch5 from the author's web site
try {
   System.out.println("Please enter a price: ");
   if (sc.hasNextDouble())                                     //if data is a double
         price = sc.nextDouble();
   else  //otherwise
      throw new InputMismatchException("Invalid price entry. Please enter a
         double." );
}
catch (InputMismatchException e) {
      System.out.println(e);
}
```

The following is an example output resulting from executing the above code:

```
Please enter a price:
$23.56
java.util.InputMismatchException: Invalid price entry. Please enter a double.
```

5.2.5 More in using throw

The examples discussed above verify data in the Java standard data definitions. What happens if the users enters a negative integer as the value of an age? In many applications, we want to verify if data are within a specified range of the defined type, e. g., the range of ages must be between 0 and 199.

Example 1. Use of **throw** to verify if the **age** data are outside the specified range (0 – 199) and display the exception message.

```
//Complete code in ThrowExceptionTest.java in Ch5 from the author's web site
try {
   ageString = JOptionPane.showInputDialog("Please enter your age: ");
   age = Integer.parseInt(ageString);
   if (age < 0 )                                   //Age less than min
         throw new Exception("Age less than 0 error!  Please try again. ");
   else if (age > 199)                             //Age great than max
         throw new Exception("Age greater than 199 error!. Please try again.
                        ");
```

```
    ...
}
catch (NumberFormatException e) {
       System.out.println("Invalid entry.   Please enter an integer as your
       age." );
}
catch (Exception e) {
       System.out.println(e);
}
```

As mentioned above, if input data representing **age** is not an integer, **parseInt()** will throw a **NumberFormatException** object. Furthermore, if an **age** is less than 0, we use **throw** to create an unnamed **Exception** object in which the message indicates the data is less than the minimum value. Similarly, if an **age** is greater than 199, we will do the same with a message indicating the data is greater than the maximum.

We call system thrown exceptions, such as the exception thrown by **parseInt()**, implicitly thrown exceptions. Exceptions thrown by a **throw** statement are called explicitly thrown exceptions.

Example 2. Use of the method **isEmpty()** in the **String** class to verify if the data entered is null, i.e., only the return key is pressed. If the length of a string is 0, **isEmpty()** will return **true** signifying the data entry is null. Use of **isEmpty()** allows the generation of accurate error messages in such exception handling cases. The above example can be modified as follows:

```
try {
      ageString = JOptionPane.showInputDialog("Please enter your age: ");
      if (ageString.isEmpty())              //Only return key is pressed
          throw new Exception("Did not enter any data.   Please enter your
                age. ");
      ...
}
   catch (Exception e) {
          System.out.println(e);
}
```

It is clear in both examples above that API Exception classes can be utilized to handle our specified exception problems. We use them as a “shell” to encapsulate specific exception information passed by an object into the **catch** block. It is very common to use this methodology in coding for data verification. Actually, we may use any of the standard API exception classes, such as **InputMismatchException**, to achieve the same result. For example:

```
   if (ageString.isEmpty())           //Only return key is pressed
       throw new InputMismatchException("Did not enter any data.   Please enter
          your age. ");
   ...
```

```
}
catch (InputMismatchException e) {
        System.out.println(e);
}
```

5.2.6 More examples

Example 1. In Chapter 4 we discussed the assignment of letter grades according to a student's scores as follows:

```
str = JOptionPane.showInputDialog("please enter an integer score: ");
score = Integer.parseInt(str); //convert to int
grade.setScore(score);              //call the method to set the score
grade.assignGrade();                //call the method to assign the grade
```

If the entry is not an integer, the JVM will terminate execution of the code ungracefully and display an exception message. We can improve the code by applying Java's exception handling mechanism to provide an opportunity for the user to re-enter a correct score if input data of the wrong type is incorrectly entered.

To reach this goal, we must first analyze possible statements in the code that will act adversely when provided the wrong type of input data. It is very clear the exception may occur in the method call **parseInt(str)** as follows:

```
score = Integer.parseInt(str); //convert to int
```

Second, we need to understand what type of exceptions the method may throw. In the API documentation, or in our other discussed examples, you may note if **str** is not a string that can be converted into an integer **parseInt()** will throw **NumberFormatException**.

Last, we use a **try-catch** mechanism and a while loop to verify the input data:

```
//Complete code called GradeExceptionApp.java in Ch5 from the author's website
//This is a simple example of using try-catch and a while loop to handle data
//input exceptions

boolean notDone = true;             //Initialize loop control variable
   while (notDone) {
     try {
              //ask for input score
              str=JOptionPane.showInputDialog("please enter an integer score: ");
              score = Integer.parseInt(str);      //convert to int
              notDone = false;                    //Stop loop if data is correct
          }     //End of try
     catch (NumberFormatException e ){
```

```
        JOptionPane.showMessageDialog(null,"Input error.  Enter an integer as
student score");
        continue;                                  //continue loop
      } //End of catch
    } //End of while
    grade.setScore(score);                      //call the method to set the score
    grade.assignGrade();                        //call the method to assign the grade
```

We can also display the exception message provided by the exception object **e** as:

```
System.out.println(e);                  //or: System.out.println(e.toString());
```

or:

```
System.out.println(e.printStackTrace());
```

to display all messages from the exception stack created by the JVM. We discuss this in detail in Chapter 11.

Example 2. The following example uses methods in the **Scanner** class to validate the data input rather than using a **try-catch** mechanism:

```
//Complete code called TestValidationApp.java in Ch5 from the author's website

Scanner sc = new Scanner(System.in);    //Create object of Scanner
//Prompt user to enter a price
...
System.out.print("Please enter the price: ");
if (sc.hasNextDouble() )                       //It's a valid entry
      price = sc.nextDouble();                  //Get the data
else      {
//It's an invalid entry
   sc.nextline();                             //Clear the buffer
      JOptionPane.showMessageDialog(null, "Input error. Enter a price ...");
      continue;                               // Continue the loop
   }
System.out.print("Please enter the quantity: ");   //Prompt user to enter
if (sc.hasNextInt() )                           //It's a valid entry
      quantity = sc.nextInt();                  //Get the data
else      {                                    //It's an invalid data
   sc.nextline();                             //Clear the buffer
      JOptionPane.showMessageDialog(null, "Input error.  Enter an integer...");
      continue;                               //Continue loop
   }
...
```

Note than an integer value entered for price is also a valid entry and will automatically be cast into a double precision value by the JVM. We call this action "data casting". This topic will be discussed in detail in later chapters. In Chapter 10, we will also discuss how to use regular expressions to validate input data.

We can see in the above examples that by using methods provided by API classes, such as the methods in the **Scanner** class, we can avoid having exceptions occur. These methods "take a look" at the entered data before really "reading" it in from the buffer of a **Scanner** object. Although we may use this technique throughout our code for verification of data input without using the **try-catch** mechanism, the use of many if-else statements in the code reduces readability and produces poorly structured and less-reusable code.

5.3 Customized Data Verification Classes

The design and coding of programmer-defined or customized classes to verify data can increase the structure, re-usability, and readability of applications. Utilizing static methods in these classes can also promote flexibility in use. In this section, we will first discuss the concept of static methods and then discuss how to write programmer-defined classes for data validations, Other techniques in data verifications such as **regular expressions** and user-defined exception classes, will be discussed in Chapters 10 and 11, respectively.

5.3.1 A first look at static methods

You may note that many methods in API classes, such as those in **Math**, **Integer**, and **Double**, are **static**. Why are these methods static? What are the advantages of using static methods?

One advantage in using static methods is that you do not need to create an object of the class being called. You can use the class name followed by the dot-notation to call a static method directly. This may be compared to the method of calling a regular dynamic method wherein an object of the class must first be created before making the method call. For example, many methods in **Scanner** are not defined as static. You must first create an object of **Scanner** then call its methods as previously discussed.

The second advantage in using static methods is that static methods are compiled at compile time rather than at run time. This may increase the speed of execution. We will discuss more advantages and disadvantages in using static methods in detail in later chapters.

One may wonder why all methods may not be defined as **static.** Static methods are suitable for situations in which the operations or calculations are directly associated with a class rather than being subject to objects. It does not matter which object calls the static method, as the same task specified in the method will be performed each time. Therefore, static methods do not have a particular object orientation. They are used as utility resources. In the **Math** class, all methods and fields are defined as static. This is done because it does not matter which object will use the methods in the **Math** class—the same formulas and equations are used to perform specified arithmetic calculations.

Why are the methods in the **Scanner** class not defined as static methods? The reason is the object of this class may carry out a variety of operations. For example, the code:

```
Scanner mySc = new Scanner(fileName);        //mySc reads data from a file
Scanner yourSc= new Scanner(textLine);       //yourSc reads data from a string
...
```

carries out different operations for different objects of **Scanner**: **mySc** will get data from a specified file; **yourSc** will retrieve data from a string called **textLine**.

It should be noted that all methods in a driver code must be defined as **static** because the JVM calls them directly without creating an object of the driver.

Considering this feature of static methods, we will code our methods that verify data as **static** methods because they are used as utility resources.

5.3.2 Examples in data verification

Since a data verification class is used as a utility, we should code it in the principle of code re-usability so it can be used as a general data validation toolkit for similar applications. In the following examples, we will apply this principle in coding a data validation class.

Example 1. Use **static** methods in **Scanner** to create class **Validator** to verify the input data. It also demonstrates how to use it in a driver code.

```
//Complete code called Validator.java in Ch5 from the author's website
public class Validator {                                    //Define Validator class
   public static double validateDouble(Scanner sc, String prompt) {
         boolean isValid = false;
         double data = 0.0;

         while(!isValid) {
                    System.out.print(prompt);
                    if (sc.hasNextDouble()) {
                         data = sc.nextDouble();
                         isValid = true;
                    }
                    else    //invalid input
                         System.out.println("\nData input error.  Enter a float…");

                    sc.nextLine();           //Clear the buffer
         } //End of while loop
         return data;
   }       //End of validateDouble()
```

```
   //Define validateInt()
   public static int validateInt(Scanner sc, String prompt) {
      ...
      }      //End of validateInt()
}                 //End of Validator
```

Having this class, we can directly call the static methods of **Validator** in the driver as follows:

```
//Complete code called ValidateDataWithClass.java in Ch5 from the author's website
public class ValidateDataWithClassApp {
   public static void main(String[] args) {
         double price, total;

         int    quantity;

         Scanner sc = new Scanner(System.in);     //Create object of Scanner

          //Call static methods in Validator
         price = Validator.validateDouble(sc, "Please enter a price: ");
         quantity = Validator.validateInt(sc, "Please enter quantity: ");

         total = price * quantity;
         System.out.println("Total: " + total);
      }          //End of main()
}                   //End of ValidateDataApp
```

Example 2. Modify the example above by using a **try-catch** mechanism and a **throw** statement.

```
//Complete code called Validator2.java in Ch5 from the author's website
   try {
   ...
            if ( !sc.hasNextInt() )                          //Illegal integer
                     throw new NumberFormatException();      //Throw          the
exception
            data = sc.nextInt();
            isValid = true;
            ...
         }                                                   //End of try
   catch ( NumberFormatException e) {
          System.out.println("\nInput data error! Please enter correct integer…");
          sc.nextLine();                               //Clear the buffer
         }                                             //End of catch
```

Here, we use API class **NumberFormatException** to verify the input data. In the example above, if data in **sc** is not the expected data type, we use a **throw** statement to throw an unnamed object of

NumberFormatException. In the **catch** block, since the argument is the same type of **NumberFormatException**, it will catch the exception if it occurs in the **try** block and print out the specified message.

You may apply the same principle discussed in these examples to verify the input data as **double**, and create more functionality in your input data validation class.

5.4 Applications in Data Verification – Data Input in Investment Return

In the example **FurtureValueApp.java** previously discussed, we assumed all input data from users were valid. If, however, the user enters wrong data, the JVM will throw an exception, dump and display the message in the stack trace, and terminate the program ungracefully. In the following example, we will apply the exception handling mechanism to improve the code for data verification.

First, we see the input data needing verification are the user name (String), monthly investment and return rate (double), and investment years (integer). We will concentrate on primative data verification first and discuss how to verify strings in a later chapter. In particular, we will add more data validation methods in **Validtor2.java** (above), applying **try-catch**, **throw**, and **static** methods of **Scanner** to enhance our knowledge and skills in data control.

Furthermore, instead of using methods in **JOptionPane** to receive input data, we will use methods in **Scanner** to both receive and verify user-provided data.

The following code is used to verify the **double** input for the monthly investment amount and return rate:

```
//Complete code in Validator3.java in Ch5 from the suhtor's web site
...
try {
      if (!sc.hasNextDouble())      //Not a double
                throw new NumberFormatException();
      else {
                data = sc.nextDouble();     //Receive double
                if (inRange(data))          //In the right range
                   isValid = true;
                else
                   throw new Exception();  //Out of range
      }
 }                                                  //End of try
...
catch (Exception e) {
      System.out.println("\nInput data error!  Please enter right data…");
      sc.nextLine();                               //Clear the buffer
 }                                                 //End of catch
...
return data;
```

After verifying the data type as **double**, we continue by calling the programmer-defined method **inRange()** in **Validator3** to further verify if the value is in the specified range, i. e., a positive double. If the data is valid, it assigns **true** to **isValid**, control jumps to the end of the method, and the data is returned. Otherwise, an Exception object is thrown to be handled by the **catch** block which displays an error message. The code of **inRange()** is as follows:

```
private static boolean inRange(double num) {
        if (num >= 0.0)
             return true;
        else
             return false;
}
```

We define **inRange()** as private because it makes sense to have only the methods inside **Validator3** to call it. It is also fine to define it as a non-static method, if you wish.

To verify the investment year input, we also specify the data range (1 to 150). The code to verify investment years is as follows:

```
//Complete code called Validator3.java in Ch5 from the author's website
public static int validateInt(Scanner sc, String prompt, int min, int max) {
     boolean isValid = false;
     int data = 0;

        while(!isValid) {
        try {
             System.out.print(prompt);
              if (!sc.hasNextInt())
                     throw new NumberFormatException();
              else {
                   data = sc.nextInt();
                   if (data < min)                    //Out of min range
                            throw new Exception();                //Throw it
                     else if (data > max)             //Out of max range
                            throw new Exception();                //Throw it
                     isValid = true;
           }
    }              //End of try
    catch (NumberFormatException e) {
           System.out.println("\n Input data error!  Please enter right data…");
           sc.nextLine();        //Clear buffer
    }                                 //End of catch
    catch (Exception e) {
           System.out.println("\n Input data error!  Please enter right data…");
           sc.nextLine();          //Clear buffer
    }                               //End of catch
```

```
 }                                                      //End of while
    return data;
}        //End of validateInt()
```

Compared to the old version in **Validator2**, method **validateInt()** in **Validator3** has two additional parameters, **min** and **max**, used to specify the range of an integer. If an integer is entered, we will continue to verify if this data is in the valid range. If it is outside the specified range, an exception is thrown, and the matched **catch** block will handle it. Otherwise, the status of **isValid** is set to true and the verified data is returned.

The following code is a sample driver of this application:

```
//Complete code called FutureValue3App.java in Ch5 from the author's website
...
   final int minYear = 1,
             maxYears = 150;
   Scanner sc = new Scanner(System.in);
   FutureValue3 futureValue = new FutureValue3();  //Create object of FutureValue3

   while(choice.equalsIgnoreCase("y")) {
         System.out.print("Please enter user name: ");
         userName = sc.next();
         futureValue.setName(userName);            //Establish user name
         sc.nextLine();                            //Clear buffer

      monthlyInvestment  =  Validator3.validateDouble(sc,  "Please  enter  monthly
investment: ");
         futureValue.setMonthlyInvest(monthlyInvestment);  //Establish the data

         yearlyReturnRate = Validator3.validateDouble(sc,"Please enter return rate
in percent: ");
         futureValue.setYearlyRate(yearlyReturnRate);          //Establish data

         investYears = Validator3.validateInt(sc, "Please enter investment years",
minYear, maxYears);
         futureValue.setYears(investYears);
   //Establish data

         futureValue.futureValueCompute();  //Compute

         System.out.println("Your return is: " + futureValue.getFutureValue());
         System.out.println("Continue? (y/n): ");

          choice = sc.next();     //Receive the status
```

```
        sc.nextLine();                          //Clear buffer
    }                                           //End of while

    System.out.println("Welcome to use the app.  Bye!");
...
```

Variables **minYear** and **maxYears** are defined as **final**.

5.5 Formatted Output

In the above discussion, all output data are displayed using the default format provided by the JVM. Sometimes it is necessary to specify a customized format for data display. For example, we need to display the investment return as a currency format bearing a currency notation, using commas to delineate units of thousands, and display two digits to the right of the decimal:

Your investment return is: $18,290.08

Percent format is another example of formatted output. We need to convert the data into percentage and add the percent sign. Sometimes we also need to control the number of digits to the right of the decimal point. Java provides a variety of API classes for formatting data to satisfy particular needs in real world applications. We will discuss three commonly used data formatting: currency format, percent format, and number format for data output.

5.5.1 Currency format

API class **NumberFormat** provides formatted output for currency and is included in the **java.text** package:

```
import java.text.NumberFormat;
```

Table 5.3 lists the commonly used methods in the **NumberFormat** class for formatted currency output.

Table 5.3 Commonly used methods in **NumberFormat** for formatted currency output

Method	Description
getCurrencyInstance()	Static method, return default currency format ($99,999.99)
getCurrencyInstance(Locale)	Static method, return the currency format specified by Locale object
format(anyNumberType)	Return the output format specified by returned string of this method. The argument can be any numerical data types or object of BigDecimal

Many Java IDEs, e.g., Eclipse, NetBeans, BlueJ, set the default currency type as that specified by the underlying operating system. Other IDEs, e.g., TextPad and the Java compiler in the JDK, set the default currency as the U.S. dollar.

To utilize the formatted currency output, you will first call **getCurrencyInstance()** method in **NumberFormat** to create a reference of **NumberFormat**, then use this reference to call **format()** method, so a string encapsulating the currency format will be returned. For example:

```
//Complete code called TestCurrencyApp.java in Ch5 from the author's website
NumberFormat currency = NumberFormat.getCurrencyInstance();
String price = currency.format(1290.6051);
System.out.println(price);
```

will display the system default output as:

$1,290.61

It will automatically add a dollar sign at the beginning of the currency amount, insert a comma for each "block" of thousands, and appropriately round the cents portion of the currency amount to two places behind the decimal point.

The above example can be coded as a single line statement:

```
String price = NumberFormat.getCurrencyInstance().format(1290.6051);
```

This statement is an example of a cascading call. It will first call the method **getCurrencyFormat()**, then use the returned object of **NumberFormat** to call the **format()** method. A string of the currency type is returned as the final result. Cascading calls are commonly used in Java coding, and we will discuss how to use them in later chapters. However, their incorrect use greatly reduces code readability.

In Table 5.3, we also list a second instance of the **static** method **getCurrencyInstance(Locale)** specifying a parameter of the type **Locale**. This parameter is used to specify currency systems other than the system default. Methods with the same name but having different parameters are called overloaded methods. We will discuss method overloading in detail in later chapters.

In the next section, we will discuss how to use **getCurrencyInstance(Locale)** for displaying formatted currency output of different currency systems.

Note: *The parameter in the* ***format()*** *method must be a numerical data type or an object of* ***BigDecimal****, otherwise a syntax error will result.*

5.5.2 Formatted currency output for different currency systems

We can use the **Locale** class in the **java.util** package to code formatted data in different currency systems, numbers, times, and languages. The **Locale** class provides many static fields to specify its supported country's names, thereby allowing code containing the formatted currency process to be used within those countries and regions. The following is a list of static fields of the **Locale** class used to format currencies, numbers, and times of the noted country or region:

CANADA	CANADA_FRENCH	CHINA	FRANCE	GERMANY	ITALY
JAPAN	KOREA	PRC	TAIWAN	UK	US

Note: *CHINA and PRC [People's Republic of China] both refer to (mainland) China.*

Static fields are similar in nature to static methods in that they are not associated with any particular object. Static fields provide class-wide information. It does not matter which objects are using them as they all provide the same information or values. For example, the static fields in the **Math** class, **PI** and the base of natural logarithms **E**, are good examples of static fields. In later chapters, we will discuss more about static fields in detail.

To use the static fields in **Locale** for a particular country's formatted currency output, we will first establish a reference to the country:

```
Locale locale = Locale.CHINA;                 //或 Locale locale = Locale.PRC;
```

Then we code as discussed above:

```
//Complete code in TestCurrencyApp.java in Ch5 from the author's web site

   //locale defined as CHINA
NumberFormat currency = NumberFormat.getCurrencyInstance(locale);

String price = currency.format(1290.6051);  //Chinese currency format
System.out.println(price);
```

The output is:

￥1,290.61

Of course, we may code the above examples as a cascading call:

```
String price = NumberFormat.getCurrencyInstance(locale).format(1290.6051);
```

or:

```
String price = NumberFormat.getCurrencyInstance(Locale.CHINA).format(1290.6051);
```

The following is another example of formatted output in French currency:

```
System.out.print("In French: " +
NumberFormat.getCurrencyInstance(Locale.FRANCE).format(1234.454));
```

The output is:

```
In French:  1 234,45 F
```

For more complete examples, please refer to **TestCurrencyApp.java** in Ch5 provided by this text.

3W: *Static fields are special fields that can be applied to all objects. A static field provides the same information or value for all objects using it.*

5.5.3 Percent format

We can apply the same process to format percentages. Table 5.4 lists the **static** methods that support percent format in the **NumberFormat** class.

Table 5.4 Methods in the **NumberFormat** for percent format

Method	Description
getPercentInstance()	Static method, return system default percent format (99%)
getPercentInstance(Locale)	Static method, return specified percent format by Locale object
format(anyNumberType)	Return formatted percent specified by the static method of NumberFormat as a string. The argument can be any numeric data types or object of BigDecimal
setMinimumFractionDigits(int)	Set the minimum decimal points for display
setMaximumFractionDigits(int)	Set the maximum decimal points for display

To format a percentage, we first use the **getPercentInstance()** method to establish a reference to **NumberFormat**, then use this reference to call the **format()** method to return a string containing the specified formatted percent. For example:

```
//Complete code in TestPercentApp.java in Ch5 from the author's web site
NumberFormat percent = NumberFormat.getPercentInstance();
String rate = percent.format(0.0651);
System.out.println(rate);
```

will display the result:

```
7%
```

In Java, the default percent format will not keep any digits beyond the decimal point nor round up automatically. To specify the quantity of digits to the right of the decimal point, we can use **setMinimumFractionDigits()** or **setMaximumFractionDigits()** :

```
percent.setMinimumFractionDigits(4);//Keep at least 4 decimal points
```

After we add this line before calling **format()** in above code, its output will be:

```
6.5100%
```

displaying up to 4 digits to the right of the decimal point.

If we change the statement to:

```
percent.setMaximumFractionDigits(1);        //Keep 1 decimal at most
```

it will display:

```
6.5%
```

We can also apply the static fields introduced above to specify the particular percent format notation used within a given country or region. The following code displays a percentage with the format commonly used in Italy:

```
//Complete code called TestPercentApp.java in Ch5 from the author's website
NumberFormat percent = NumberFormat.getPercentInstance(Locale.ITALY); //Italy

   percent.setMinimumFractionDigits(4);          //Keep at least 4 decimals
   System.out.println(percent.format(0.07551));
```

It will display:

```
7,5510%
```

Note: *Because **setMinimumFractionDigits()** and **setMaximumFractionDigits()** do not return any reference of **NumberFormat**, they cannot be used in a cascading call in format processing.*

More Info: ***setMinimumFractionDigits()** and **setMaximumFractionDigits()** can be also used to change system default decimals in currency format.*

5.5.4 Number format

It is often necessary in real-world applications to format numbers. For example, the number of digits beyond the decimal point must be specified, commas must be added to delineate blocks of thousands, a positive sign must be placed before a positive number, et cetera. The **NumberFormat** class also provides support for number formatting. Table 5.5 lists the commonly used methods for number formatting.

Table 5.5 Methods in NumberFormat for number format

Method	Description
getNumberInstance()	Static method, return system default number format (99,999.999)
getNumberInstance(Locale)	Static method, return number format specified by Locale object
format(anyNumberType)	Return the number format specified by static method of NumberFormat as a string
setMinimumFractionDigits(int)	Set the minimum decimal points for display
setMaximumFractionDigits(int)	Set the maximum decimal points for display

The process of number formatting is similar to that of currency and percent formatting. The following is an example code illustrating number formatting:

```
//Complete code in TestNumberApp.java in Ch5 from the author's web site
```

```
NumberFormat number = NumberFormat.getNumberInstance(); //Establish the reference
String num = number.format(1234.5675);            //Use of system default format
System.out.println(num);
```

The execution result is as follows:

1,234.568

It will keep up to three decimal digits and round up from the fourth decimal position. We can also use **setMinimumFractionDigits()**, **setMaximumFractionDigits()**, and **Locale** specifications in number formatting.

Another way to format numbers is to use features from the subclass **DecimalFormat** of **NumberFormat.** The **DecimalFormat** class provides many modes to specify the desired format in a more intuitive way by allowing you to "see" the number format in a template-like notation. We will discuss the following commonly used modes in **DecimalFormat**:

"0" – a digit. Display 0 if there is no such digit in a number.

"#" – any digits in the whole number as a wildcard; will not display if there is no such digit in a number; it only displays a single decimal if it used after decimal point and it will round up.

"." – indicates the decimal point.

"," – Use with "0" mode to include a comma.

Let's discuss the following examples using these modes of NumberFormat:

```
//Complete code called TestNumberApp.java in Ch5 from the author's website
//"0" - a digit.  Display 0 if there is no such digit in a number
NumberFormat formatter = new DecimalFormat("000,000");  //Create an object and
//specify the format


String s = formatter.format(-1234.567);  //Output is -001,235; round up; doesn't
//display decimal; add a comma

//"#" - any digits in the whole number; will not display if there is no such digit
//in a number; it only displays a single decimal if it used after decimal point
//and it will round up

formatter = new DecimalFormat("#");
s = formatter.format(-1234.567);    //Output: -1235 - round up;not display decimal
```

```
s = formatter.format(0);                              //Output: 0
formatter = new DecimalFormat("#00");
s = formatter.format(0);                              //Output: 00

//"." - Indicate decimal point
formatter = new DecimalFormat(".00");
s = formatter.format(-.567);                          //Output: -.57  - round up
formatter = new DecimalFormat("0.00");
s = formatter.format(-.567);                          //Output: -0.57
formatter = new DecimalFormat("#.#");
s = formatter.format(-1234.557);               //Output: -1234.6
```

Note: *Comma mode "," – used to show a comma for each grouping of one thousand—must be used together with "0" mode, otherwise a run-time error will be generated and the JVM will throw an exception.*

5.5.5 More examples in formatted data output

In this section, we will apply the data formatting techniques discussed above to the investment return application **FutureValue3App.java**. We will also modify the application to increase the readability of the code in regard to data output:

```
Your name: Wei Wang
Your monthly investment:  $1,290.00
Your yearly return rate:  8.75%
Your investment years:  19
Your investment return is:  $296,589.20
```

The following is a fragment of the code for data formatting and output:

```
//Complete code called FutureValue4App.java in Ch5 from the author's website
...
//Currency format
NumberFormat currency = NumberFormat.getCurrencyInstance();
investStr = currency.format(futureValue.getMonthlyInvest());
futureValueStr = currency.format(futureValue.getFutureValue());

//Percent format and keep at least 2 decimals
NumberFormat percent = NumberFormat.getPercentInstance();
percent.setMinimumFractionDigits(2);
rateStr = percent.format(futureValue.getYearlyRate()/100);

System.out.println("Your name:  " + futureValue.getName());
System.out.println("Your monthly investment:  " + investStr);
System.out.println("Your yearly return rate:  " + rateStr);
System.out.println("Your investment years:  " + futureValue.getYears());
System.out.println("Your investment return is:  " + futureValueStr);
...
```

The complete code can be found in Ch5 in the instructor's Website.

5.6 Data Type Casting

Data type casting refers to data type conversions associated with the eight primitive data types of Java. Data type casting includes two different operations:

- Automatic data type casting – also called implicit or system default data type casting. It is carried out by the Java compiler.
- Casting – also called explicit data type casting or programmer-defined data type casting.

We will discuss these two casting methods in the following sections, respectively.

5.6.1 Implicit data type casting

Let's begin with the examples we already used before in implied data type casting as follows:

```
String message = "Total price: " + 192.78;
```

and:

```
System.out.println("Your investment return is: " + futureValueStr);
```

Implicit data type casting occurs in operations in which the two operands are of different data types. In the above examples, the Java compiler will first automatically cast or convert the double precision type data into strings then perform the join and output operations.

Another example:

```
System.out.println(11.09);
```

The compiler automatically converts double precision data into a string then performs the output. The compiler applies promotion rules in implicit data type casting. The data type of an operand requiring less memory will be promoted to the data type of the operand requiring more memory space. For example, the memory requirement of a **double** type data is less than a string (since a string is actually an object, and an object requires more memory space to hold all necessary information in addition to string content or value), so **double** will be automatically promoted into a string.

The following is another example:

```
int num = 25 + 'A';              //Auto cast char into integer, then perform addition
float x = 10 - 9.78;             //Auto cast 10 to double as 10.0, then subtraction
double y = y * x;                //Auto cast float x to double
double num = 'A' + 'B';          //Perform ASCII addition b/w A and B, auto cast
                                 //result to double, then assign to num

System.out.println( 'A'+ 192.78 + 20 );     //Auto cast ASCII value of A and 20 to
//double, then perform additions.  Result is auto cast into a string before output
```

You may feel that it is "needless to say", but it is what actually happened and important in the compilation and execution.

Note that the following code produces a syntax error:

```
double someNum = "Total price: " + 192.78;          //Syntax error
```

String is an object that cannot be demoted to a **double** type.

3W: *Implied or automatic data type casting refers to the adjustment of data types among operands into a unique type by applying promotion rules regarding memory requirement size. This is done before any other operation is performed. Specifically, it casts the data type of an operand of a lesser memory size to the data type of the operand having the greater memory requirement. The casting process is automatically performed by the compiler.*

5.6.2 Explicit casting

Explicit data type casting, or simply explicit casting, refers to data type casting defined by programmers. It instructs the compiler to perform the designated cast. It should be noted that the **boolean** type cannot be cast into any other data type. Let's first look at some examples:

```
double average = 10 / (double) 3;    //Or double average = (double) 10 / 3;
```

The value of **average** is:

3.3333333

In the above code, keyword **double** is placed within parentheses, **(double)**, to denote that a casting operation is to be made on the integer value of 3, thereby converting it into a **double** type before the division operation is performed.

If we don't do any casting, the following statement:

```
double average = 10 / 3;
```

assigns the result 3.0 to **average**. A challenge question for you: Why are the quotients different?

The syntax of casting is:

```
(dataType)varName
```

To do explicit data type casting, you need to include a data type in the parenthesis and place it at the front of the data (constant or variable). Here, **dataType** is any primitive data type other than **boolean**.

Explicit casting is not limited to the promotion of a data type. If permitted, a data type can also be "demoted", i.e., a data type casting may be made from a data type with a higher memory requirement to a data type of a lower memory requirement. For example:

(int) 8.95

casts a **double** precision type data into an integer type data having a value of 8. It is necessary to be very attentive when performing a cast for demotion because inaccurate arithmetic values may result from the calculation.

The following are more examples of explicit casting:

```
someInt / (double) 'A';         //Cast char type data to double then divide
(int) (0.499915 * 10); //Multiply first then cast the result to int; result is 4
(char)(130 / (int) 2.5);        //Cast to int, divide, then cast the result to a char
//type.  Result is 'A'
```

It should be noted that all operations within parentheses (for example, as shown in the second line in the above code) are performed *before* the casting is made.

You may want to use explicit casting even in a situation where implied casting is performed to increase readability, e. g.,

```
System.out.println( 'A' + 20 );                          // Original auto casting
```

Adding an explicit cast:

```
System.out.println((int) 'A' + 20 );          //Increase readability
```

may allow a better understanding of the code.

More Info: *The proper use of casting may increase code readability; however, it may also reduce data accuracy when casting in demotion is performed.*

5.7 Math Class

The **Math** class is a commonly used API. It is included in the **java.lang** package. This class is used to perform a variety of arithmetic calculations and operations. Table 5.6 lists the commonly used methods in the **Math** class. All methods in the **Math** class are defined as **static** allowing them to be called directly in code.

Table 5.6 Commonly used methods in the **Math** class

Method	Argument type	Return type	Result
Math.abs(x)	int, long, float, double	Same as arguments	|x|
Math.cos(x)	Double	Double	cos(x)
Math.sin(x)	Double	Double	sin(x)
Math.tan(x)	Double	Double	tang(x)
Math.log(x)	Double	Double	ln(x)
Math.exp(x)	Double	Double	e^x
Math.log10(x)	Double	Double	log(x)

(Continue)

Method	Argument type	Return type	Result
Math.pow(x, y)	Double	Double	x^y
Math.min(x, y)	int, long, float, double	Same as argument	Return minimum value in x and y
Math.max(x, y)	int, long, float, double	Same as argument	Return maximum value in x and y
Math.random()	None	Double	Return a random double that is greater than or equal to 0.0 but less than 1.0, $0.0 \leq x < 1.0$
Math.round(x)	Double	Long	Round up to long
Math.round(x)	Float	Int	Round up to int
Math.sqrt(x)	Double	Double	Square root of x

The following are examples of using methods in the **Math** class.

Example 1. Round up to whole numbers.

```
long lnum = Math.round(3.54012);            //Result: 4
int iNum = Math.round(0.489f);              //Result: 0
```

Example 2. Powers of numbers.

```
double dNum1 = Math.pow(2, 2);              //Result: 4.0
double dNum4 = Math.pow(3.14, 6.18);//Result: 1177.643743030202
```

Example 3. Minimum and maximum.

```
int x = 5, y =10;
double z = 5.01;
int max = Math.max(x, y);                     //Result: 10
int min = Math.min(x, y);                     //Result: 5
double dMax = Math.max(Math.max(z, x), y);   //Result: 10.0
```

Example 4. Random numbers.

```
double x = Math.random();       //Result: any number in range of 0.0 <= x < 1.0
int dice = (int) Math.random() * 6 + 1        //Result: any int in range of 1 to 6
```

5.8 Wrapper Classes

Java has eight classes to provide object methods for the associated eight primitive data types. These classes are called wrapper classes. The purpose of using a wrapper class is to treat a primitive data type as an object of its wrapper class by encapsulating its value inside the object. A wrapper class is also used to pass a reference to a method rather than passing a value of a primitive data type. Wrapper classes provide many methods to easily manipulate data. Wrapper classes are included in the **java.lang** package. Table 5.7 lists the constructors of the eight wrapper classes.

Table 5.7 Constructors in wrapper classes

Constructor	Description
Byte(byte value)	Create an object of Byte with specified value
Short(short value)	Create an object of Short with specified value
Integer(int value)	Create an object of Integer with specified value
Long(long value)	Create an object of Long with specified value
Float(float value)	Create an object of Float with specified value
Double(double value)	Create an object of Double with specified value
Boolean(boolean value)	Create an object of Boolean with specified value
Character(char value)	Create an object of Character with specified value

With the exception of the Character class, all other wrapper classes can also use a **String** type as a parameter for creating an object, e.g., **Byte(String s)**, **Short(String s)**, **Integer(String s)**, **Long(String s)**, **Float(String s)**, **Double(String s)**, and **Boolean(String s)**. The string will be automatically converted into the numeric value it represents.

The following are examples of using wrapper classes to create objects:

```
Integer myInt = new Integer(100); //or: Integer myInt = new Integer("100");
Double rateDouble = new Double(5.69);//or: Double rateDouble = new Double("5.69");
Boolean flagObj = new Boolean(true); //Or: Boolean flagObj = new Boolean("true");
Character chObj = new Character('A');
```

Table 5.8 lists the commonly used methods in wrapper classes.

Table 5.8 Commonly used methods in wrapper classes (excluding Character class)

Method	Description
Byte byteValue()	Return a byte value of the object. Cannot be used for Boolean objects
short shortValue()	Return a short value of the object. Cannot be used for Boolean objects
int intVaule()	Return an int value of the object. Cannot be used for Boolean objects
long longValue()	Return a long value of the object. Cannot be used for Boolean objects
float floatValue()	Return a float value of the object. Cannot be used for Boolean objects
double doubleValue()	Return a double value of the object. Cannot be used for Boolean objects
boolean booleanValue()	Return a Boolean value of the object. Can only be used for Boolean objects
parseByte(Strings), parseShort(Strings), parseInt(String s), parseLong(String s),	Static methods to return the specified numeric data or Boolean value of the object

parseFloat(String s), parseDouble(String s), parseBoolean(String s)	
valueOf(String s)	Static method to return the specified numerical value of the object
toString()	Return the string representing the value of the object

The following are examples of using commonly used methods in the **Integer, Double**, and **Boolean** wrapper classes:

```
Integer myInt = new Integer(100);
byte myByte = myInt.byteValue();  //myByte = 100
int num = myInt.intValue();       //num = 100
long longInt = myInt.longValue(); //longInt = 100
float floatVar = myInt.floatValue(); //floatVar = 100.0
double doubleVar = myInt.doubleValue(); //doubleVar = 100.0
int yourInt = Integer.parseInt("600");  //convert 600 to numerical value
Integer herInt = Integer.valueOf("99");  //return Integer object with value 99
String intString = myInt.toString();  //return a string "100"

Double myRate = new Double(6.79);
byte byteRate = myRate.byteValue();  //byteRate = 6
int intRate = myRate.intValue();     //intRate = 6
float floatRate = myRate.floatValue(); //floatRate = 6.79
double rate = myRate.doubleValue();   //rate = 6.79
double dRate = Double.parseDouble("0.1");  dRate = 0.1
Double rateObj = Double.valueOf("9.15");  //return Double object with value 9.15
String rateString = rateObj.toString();  //rateString = "9.15"

Boolean boolFlag = new Boolean(true);   //create an object of Boolean
boolean flag = boolFlag.booleanValue(); //flag = true
boolean exit = Boolean.parseBoolean("false");  //exit = false
Boolean boolObj = Boolean.valueOf("true");  //boolObj with value true
String boolString = boolObj.toString();   //boolString = "true"
```

To simplify coding, later versions of the JDK have provided mechanisms to facilitate the direct conversion between objects of wrapper classes and primative data types. These mechanisms are called autoboxing and autounboxing. We will discuss them in Chapter 12.

5.9 BigDecimal Class

A Java **double** type data has up to 16 significant digits of accuracy. However, in real-world applications we often need to manipulate data beyond that range. Java provides the **BigDecimal** class included in the **java.math** package to satisfy these calculations. Table 5.9 lists the commonly used constructors and methods in **BigDecimal**.

Table 5.9 Commonly used constructors and methods in the BigDecimal

Constructor/Method	Description

BigDecimal(int)	Create a specified object of BigDecimal with int value
BigDecimal(double)	Create a specified object of BigDecimal with double value
BigDecimal(long)	Create a specified object of BigDecimal with long value
add(BigDecimal)	Add the values in objects of BigDecimal and return the result in an object of BigDecimal
subtract(BigDecimal)	Subtract the values in objects of BigDecimal and return the result in an object of BigDecimal
multiply(BigDecimal)	Multiply the values in objects of BigDecimal and return the result in an object of BigDecimal
divide(BigDecimal)	Divide the values in objects of BigDecimal and return the result in an object of BigDecimal
toString()	Return the value in object of BigDecimal as a string
doubleValue()	Return the value in object of BigDecimal as a double
floatValue()	Return the value in object of BigDecimal as a float
longValue()	Return the value in object of BigDecimal as a long
intValue()	Return the value in object of BigDecimal as an int

Because a floating-point primative data type, such as **double**, cannot accurately represent a number with more than 16 significant digits, the constructor form **BigDecimal(String)** is often used to create an object of **BigDecimal**. It should also noted that traditional arithmetic operators, e. g., +, -, *, and /, cannot be used in **BigDecimal,** since these arithmetic operations are performed inside objects of **BigDecimal**. We must use the corresponding **BigDecimal** methods to perform such operations.

We will discuss in more detail about these constructors and their uses in Chapter 6. The following are the examples of using **BigDecimal** and its methods:

```
//Complete code called BigDecimalTestApp.java in Ch5 from the author's website
//Create objects of BigDecimal

BigDecimal bigNumber = new BigDecimal("89.1234567890123456789");
BigDecimal bigRate = new BigDecimal(1000);
BigDecimal bigResult = new BigDecimal(0);  //bigResult holds 0.0

//multiply the two objects and return the result in bigResult
bigResult = bigNumber.multiply(bigRate);

//Display the result: 89123.4567890123456789000
System.out.println(bigResult.toString());  //or System.out.println(bigResult);

double dData = bigNumber.doubleValue();    //Return the value as double
System.out.println(dData);  //89.12345678901235
```

***Note**: The use of **BigDecimal** methods of the form **xxxValue()** to generate a primitive data type from its **BigDecimal** representation <u>may</u> result in the loss of data accuracy.*

3W ***BigDecimal*** *is used to perform arithmetic operations in numbers in exceeding the range of 16 significant digits. All calculations are performed by calling its methods.*

5.10 Data Format in BigDecimal Class

The method **format()** of the **NumberFormat** class allows us to use **BigDecimal** as a parameter type for the customization of formats of **BigDecimal** objects such as currencies, percentages, and numbers.

Let's use the currency and percent formats as examples to discuss how to customize output in **BigDecimal**. First, we create an object of **BigDecimal**. After performing the desired arithmetic operations, we establish the references from **NumberFormat** by calling **getCurrencyInstance()**, **getPercentInstance()**, or **getNumberInstance()**. We then use the object **BigDecimal** as the parameter in **format()** to return the formatted content as a string:

```
//Complete code called BigDecimalFormatApp.java in Ch5 from the author's website
BigDecimal bigLoanAmount = new BigDecimal(loanAmountString); //Create object

BigDecimal bigInterestRate = new BigDecimal(interestRateString);
BigDecimal bigInterest = bigLoanAmount.multiply(bigInterestRate);  //operation

NumberFormat currency = NumberFormat.getCurrencyInstance();  //referencing

NumberFormat percent = NumberFormat.getPercentInstance();

percent.setMaximumFractionDigits(3);       //Control decimals

//Call format with the BigDecimal object
System.out.println("Loan amount:\t" + currency.format(bigLoanAmount));
System.out.println("Interest rate:\t" + percent.format(bigInterestRate));
System.out.println("Interest:\t" + currency.format(bigInterest));
```

The output is as follows:

```
Loan amount:     $129,876,534,219,876,523.12
Interest rate:     8.765%
Interest:    $11,384,239,549,149,661.69
```

Exercises

1. Use examples to explain the meaning of "Eliminate the error at the first place."
2. What are the differences between an exception and a run-time error?
3. In addition to the examples of exceptions listed in section 5.2, list at least three other exceptions in programming.
4. Use examples to explain what an automatic exception is in Java. Why do programmers need to handle exceptions in coding?
5. What is a system exception throw? What is thrown?

6. Use examples to explain a standard exception.

7. List at least 5 names of exceptions thrown by the methods of **Scanner** which are not discussed in the chapter. What is a common exception thrown by the methods of **BigDecimal**?

8. How can a **throw** statement be used to further examine data? In addition to testing data for being out of range, list some other examples that use a throw statement to validate the input data.

9. Modify the example **GradeExceptionApp.java** in section 5.2.6 so it will accept student scores as a **double** type and handle the exception if scores are invalid. Save the modified code as **GradeExceptionApp2.java**.

10. Modify the code **GradeExceptionApp.java** so that it will use methods in the **Scanner** class to accept and handle exceptions of student scores. Save the modified code as **GradeExceptionApp3.java**.

11. Modify the code **TestValidationApp.java** in section 5.2.6 so that it will use a method of **JOptionPane** to accept student scores and handle the exceptions. Save the modified code as **TestValidation1App.java.**

12. Modify the example **TestValidationApp.java** so that it will use a method of **JOptionPane** to accept student scores and then handle the exceptions. Save the modified code as **TestValidation2.App2.java**.

13. Add a new method called **validateInt()** to **Validator.java** in section 5.3.2 so that it will handle the exception of integer data. Save the modified code as **Validator4.java**. Write a driver to test your code. Save the driver as **Validator4Test.java**.

14. Modify the example **Validator2.java** in section 5.3.2 and create a method called **checkRange(double min, double max)** to examine if the data is in the valid range. Save the modified code as **Validator5.java**.

15. What are three formats provided by the **NumberFormat** class? Use examples to explain the steps in formatting a currency, a percent, and a number.

16. What is a cascading call? What is the requirement for the return type of the calling methods?

17. What is the purpose of Java's **Locale** class? Use examples to explain its use.

18. What are the differences between **setMinimumFractionDigits()** and **setMaximumFractionDigits()**? Use examples to support your explanation.

19. Use examples to explain what is meant by "system default percent format." If you use **setMinimumFractionDigits()** or **setMaximumFractionDigits()** in your code, does the system default format still work?

20. Use **DecimalFormat** class to display the following specified data output formats:

    a. Display 3 decimals in numbers with a comma for each group of one thousand.

    b. Display only 4 decimals after the decimal point.

    c. Always display 2 decimals for any number.

21. Why does a code need automatic data type casting? Why do you need programmer-defined data type casting? Use examples to support your answers.

22. Use the **Math** class to perform the following operations:

    a. Generate random numbers with the range 0 to 100.

    b. Calculate power 10.28 of any number.

    c. Calculate the distance between any given two points.

23. Why should you use a string to create an object of **BigDecimal**? List the steps to perform addition in **BigDecimal**.

24. Code an application using the **BigDecimal** class to calculate the return of an investment. Use the same formula found in **FutureValue4App.java** in section 5.5.5 for the calculation. You must format the currency and percent (keeping 3 positions to the right of the decimal point) and handle any exceptions that may occur from the input data. The valid range of investment amounts is from $1.00 to $1,000,000.00. The valid return rate is from 0.1% to 35%. The valid period of investment years is from 1 to 120. Your program must continue to run until the user enters "n" to terminate the execution. You must validate the user's entry so that only "y" and "n" are accepted. Save your code as file **FutureValueBigDecimalApp.java**.

25. Use methods in **JOptionPane** to write the application described in question above. All described data validations must be performed. Save your code as **FutureValueJOptionPaneApp.java**.

"Isn't it a pleasure to study and practice what you have learned? Isn't it also great when friends visit from distant places? If one remains not annoyed when he is not understood by people around him, isn't he a sage?"

– Confucius

Chapter 6 Inside Classes and Objects

In this chapter we focus our discussion on essential OOP concepts and coding skills—more details concerning classes and objects, and three important features of OOP—encapsulation, inheritance, and polymorphism. We use examples to explain constructors, method overloading, static data, static methods, and static initialization blocks.

6.1 Fundamentals in OOP

Throughout our discussion so far we have observed that OOP is a natural fit within the Java language. All coding, except import and package statements (introduced in Chapter 12), is inside classes. Furthermore, the data and methods are members in the class. Compared with other computer languages, you have no choice but to code your Java programs within the class framework. Let's have a closer look at the typical structure of a class:

```
public class ClassName {                          //Define a class
   dataType dataName1;                            //Define an instance variable
   ...
   public ClassName() {                           //Define a constructor
          dataName1 = 0;
          ...
   }
   public dataType getDataName() {                //Retrieve data
          return dataName1;
   }
   Public void setDataName(dataType dataName) {   //Set data
          this.dataName1 = dataName;
   }
   ...    //Other methods
}
```

The example shows the typical structure of a class and its major components. Since classes are building blocks in OOP, one important challenge is how to design and code classes, create objects, and call methods to solve problems in efficient ways.

6.1.1 Look into classes and objects

Concepts of classes and objects come from the real world. The design processes in transforming classes to objects are the same as going from an abstraction to a particular instance; from generalization and categorization to specialization; from templates to a particular code.

We may also observe the coding of classes and objects is a natural extension of data structures. Recall that early machine languages had only basic primitive variables to represent data. How could arithmetic calculations involving hundreds or thousands of data items be performed? Arrays and loops were developed to meet this need. Since arrays can store only the same data type, data structures such as records and structs were created to group different data types together.

Classes were born in this evolution! Classes are unique data structures combining data and functions (methods) within the same body of code thereby allowing them the same scope of accessibility. Data have defined access modifiers allowing encapsulation inside a class. Classes can be extended to other related classes thereby guaranteeing inheritance. Objects can perform different operations with the same method calls thus ensuring polymorphism. Java even creates a class of classes called collections. Traditional programming concepts and skills have been challenged and changed. The movement from POP to OOP is an evolution from the separation of data and functions to their combination in a class structure. Classes are more reliable, efficient, safer, consistent, and easier in use. In addition, OOP within Java allows the development of large-scaled applications with the internet or network accessibility.

What will be the capabilities and features of the next generation of computer language?

6.1.2 Encapsulation

Encapsulation ensures the protection of instance data by allowing modification of the data only through method calls. The "shell" encapsulating the instance data is the class and its objects. We must define the access modifiers to allow both the data and methods to be encapsulated. Encapsulation guarantees data cannot be modified or accessed directly outside its objects except through method calls.

Let's examine an example in which all instance data are defined as **public** and thereby subject to direct access and modification:

```
public int month, day, year;
public double payment;
public String password;
```

In this case, all instance data can be modified directly by the object through the use of **dot notation**:

```
someObj.month = 13;
someObj.payment = 99999.99;
bankObj.password="8888";
...
```

This format creates two categories of problems. The reliability and safety of the data cannot be ensured, and one must also be aware of details concerning the implementation of the data to avoid mistakes in any desired modification.

Defining instance data as **private** prevents such problems because private data cannot be accessed by means of dot notation:

```
someObj.month = 13;           //Syntax error if month is defined as private
...
bankObj.password="8888";      //Syntax error if password is defined as private
...
```

Sometimes it is necessary to define methods with **private** accessibility to ensure their encapsulation and prevent them from being called directly. The following example includes methods **changePassword()** and **shootMissiles()**, have been previously defined as **public**:

```
someObj.changePassword("0000");
someObj.shootMissiles();
...
```

Obviously you do not want these methods being called directly through the use of dot notation. The above methods must be protected with encapsulation to ensure safety and security. The following method:

```
someObj.login();
```

can be used to verify the user's authority before calling **changePassword()** and **shootMissiles()** inside the **login()** only if such verification is passed.

6.1.3 Inheritance

Inheritance is to obtain something from a preceding generation. Java inheritance allows the access and use of existing code from a superclass so you do not have to rewrite code.

Inheritance in Java is also a "natural born" feature. Every class is automatically inherited from the root class **Object**. Many examples are shown in API documentation in which a package is actually structured in multiple-level inheritance as shown in Figure 6.1.

We call an inherited class a **subclass** or **derived class**. A class from which a subclass receives inherited properties is a **superclass** or **base class**. For example, in Figure 6.1 the **Object** class is the superclass of all other classes. **Exception** is a subclass of **Object** and **Throwable** and a superclass of **RuntimeException**, **NoSuchElementException**, and **InputMismatchException**.

In OOP, a primary consideration in designing a class is to reuse, to the maximum extent possible, existing tested code, thereby increasing code reliability. Inheritance is not the only way to design and code classes since not all classes have a so-called "is-a" relationship. Classes may support each other through a "has-a" relationship. For example, as we discussed before, the **FutureValue** and **Validator** classes have a "has-a" relationship since **Validator** supports the ability of **FutureValue** to verify input data. **Validator** is not an implementation of **FutureValue**. They share nothing in common with the investment calculation. **Validator** is designed as a utility for use by all other classes to verify input data. We will explore these concepts in more detail in Chapter 7.

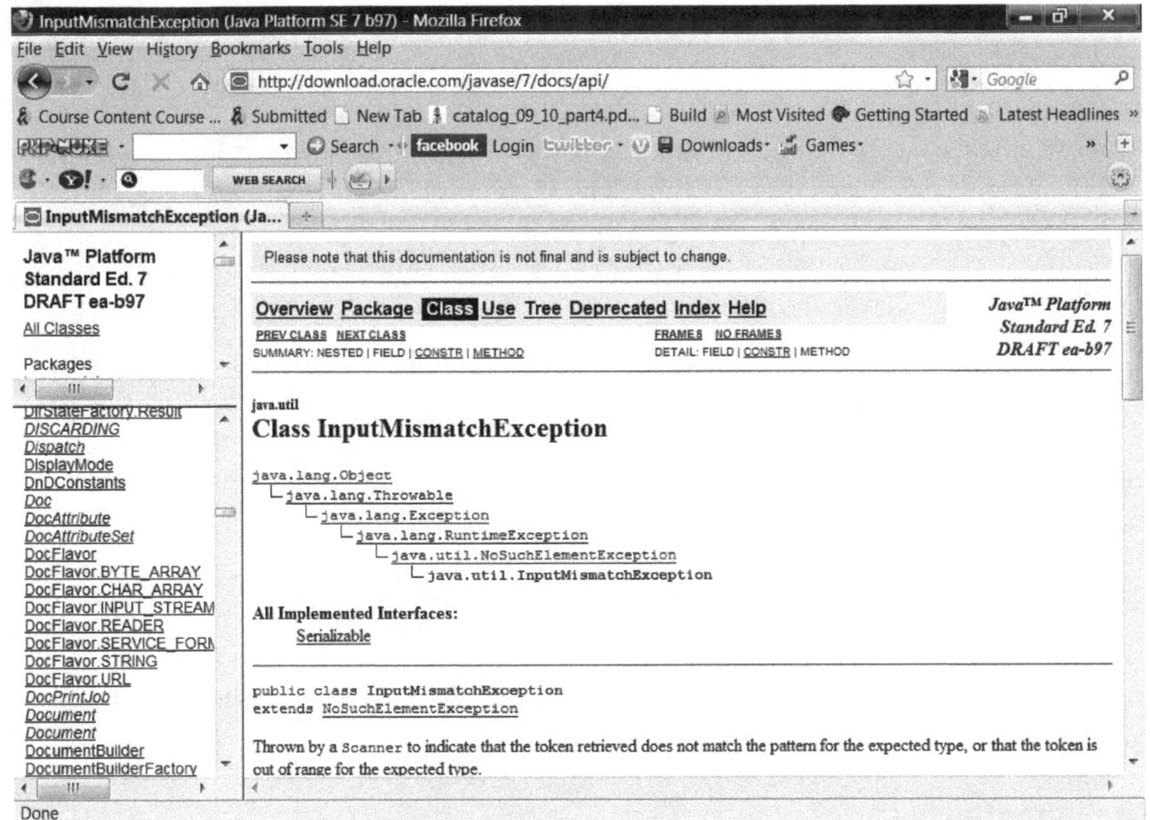

Figure 6.1 Typical inheritance chart in Java API

6.1.4 Polymorphism

Let's first introduce the concept of polymorphism. Detailed coding techniques are discussed in Chapter 8. The term polymorphism is derived from the Greek *poly-* meaning many and Latin *morpheus* meaning form. There are many examples of polymorphism in our world. For instance, "two-in-one", "three-in-one", even "four-in-one" products all exhibit polymorphic features. A facsimile machine can often be used as a telephone, printer, scanner, and copier—in addition to its basic facsimile transmission and receiving capabilities. The device's single "OK" button represents different meanings depending upon the operation being used.

There are examples of polymorphism in software applications. The Microsoft Office suite of applications contains a **Help** menu, but the contents displayed differ in accordance with the application currently in use. We call the **Help** menu a polymorphic feature—use of the same name but with different contents.

The principle of polymorphism in Java is similar to that in the real world. It can be reflected in software development by simulating polymorphic items in software applications.

6.2 Classes Are Blueprints

A class is a blueprint or prototype from which objects are instantiated. The design and code of a class require many important concepts and programming skills: how to categorize the class; how to define its data and methods and their accessibility; and so on. We will discuss these topics by using examples.

6.2.1 Abstraction

Abstraction is the fundamental concept in the design of classes in OOP. Its purpose is to generate the code specification of a designed class using the following principles:

Representability—A class should represent the characteristics of all objects in the defined category. In particular, it represents all the states (data) and behaviors (methods) of its objects in the application.

Specificity—A class represents only its defined objects and nothing else. It will perform specified tasks for all objects and not be a universal tool.

Loose coupling and cohesion—Loose coupling means a class should be self-sufficient in carrying out its defined tasks and its behavior does not rely or depend upon other classes. Cohesion indicates the degree to which a class has a single, well-focused purpose. A class with high cohesion is much easier to maintain and less frequently changed. Incorporation of these concepts increases usability in applications.

Encapsulation—Information hiding. A class should be designed with properly defined access modifiers to prohibit direct access of data and methods.

Hierarchy—The degree of abstraction in class design in a multiple-level inheritance based on the relationship of the member classes. The principles of inheritance ensure abstraction and modularity in class design. Generalization is used in the design of a super class so it can represent all objects contained in its subclasses. Subclasses are designed to inherit all properties from superclasses while performing their own specific tasks. This hierarchy may be envisioned as a pyramid in which the higher the level of class the more abstraction. Use of the hierarchy concept will help you obtain specificity, loose coupling, and high cohesion in class design.

Collaboration—The act of objects working together. A collaboration can be as simple as one object sending a message to another object, or it can be as complex as dozens of objects exchanging hundreds of messages. In fact, an entire application is really a single collaboration involving all the objects within it. An object-oriented application can be broken down into a set of many different behaviors. Each behavior is implemented by a distinct collaboration between the objects of the application. Every collaboration, no matter how small or large, always implements a behavior of the application that contains it.

6.2.2 How to define instance variables

Instance variables must be defined when you design and code a class. The following steps should be considered when making the variable definitions:

1. Careful selection. Instance variables carry out particular operations for all objects of the class. Only those variables involved in these operations should be defined. For example, in the **FutureValue** class discussed previously, instance variables **name**, **monthlyInvestment**, **returnRate**, and **year** are required by all objects in this application to compute the future value of the investment. Instance variables such as **occupation**, **weight**, **height**, and **sex** are irrelevant to the application and should not be defined.

2. Determine access modifier. Ensure encapsulation of instance variables by defining them as **private** to prohibit their access or modification outside the class by the use of dot notation.

3. Static data. If a data item does not depend on objects of the class for its functioning and belongs to the entire class, it should be declared as static data. Examples of static data are a running total of created objects and mathematical constants, such as pi and e. Static data is discussed in the following sections.

4. Type of data. Determine if a datum is one of the 8 primitive data types, a String, or a class type.

5. Constant data. Determine if a datum is a constant or a variable. You must assign values to constant data when they are declared.

6. Naming data. You should follow Java's naming conventions in assigning data names. Using meaningful names can dramatically increase code readability.

The Java compiler automatically assigns values to instance variables when they are declared. It assigns 0 to integer type data; 0.0 to floating-point data; false to boolean data; a space to char type data; and null to strings and objects, as follows:

```
byte byteVar = 0;
short shortVar = 0;
int intVar = 0;
long longVar = 0;
float floatVar = 0.0f;
double doubleVar = 0.0;
char charVar =  ' ';
boolean boolVar = false;
String stringVar = null;
```

```
SomeClass someObj = null;
```

6.2.3 Constructors

Constructors are special methods in a class. The purpose of a constructor is to instantiate or create an object with initialized data. The syntax of a constructor is:

```
public ClassName(dataType argumentName, ...) {
   //body of code
   ...
   }
```

A constructor has the following characteristics:

- The access modifier of a constructor can be **public**, **protected**, **private**, or **package** (no access modifier specified). A constructor is usually defined as public to create objects in any program. Other access modifiers of a constructor are discussed in later chapters.
- A constructor must have the same name as the class.
- A constructor cannot have any return type, including void.

  A constructor is automatically called when an object of the class is created by the **new** operator:

  ```
  SomeClass myObj = new SomeClass(10); //Create an object with initialized data
  ```

  When this statement is executed, object **myObj** will be instantiated and its instance variable initialized to 10.

- The Java compiler automatically provides a default constructor if no constructor is coded in a class. This default constructor contains an empty body of code. No default constructor is provided if a constructor exists. This feature explains why an object can be created in the absence of any constructor in the code.

The following are examples of defining constructors:

Example 1. A constructor with one argument.

```
public class Square {
 double length;
 public Square(double l) {  //Constructor with one parameter
   length = l;
 }  // end of constructor
 ... //other code
}
```

This constructor accepts a double type argument and assigns its value to the instance variable **length**. To increase readability and convenience in coding, the keyword **this** is often used to differentiate the parameter name from the instance variable name:

```
public class Square {
 double length;
 public Square(double length) {    //Constructor with one parameter
   this.length = length;
 }  // end of constructor
 ... //other code
}
```

The keyword **this** refers to the current object in the execution. For example:

```
Square square = new Square(8.95);
```

calls the constructor to instantiate an object of Square called square with an initialized value of 8.95. Keyword **this** in the constructor code represents object square.

We discuss **this** in detail in section 6.2.8. The process of creating an object is also called instantiating an object.

Example 2. A constructor with two parameters.

```
public Rectangle(int width, int height) {   //Constructor with two parameters
   this.width = width;
   this.height = height;
}
```

Using the following code:

```
Rectangle rec = new Rectangle(12, 50);
```

creates a **Rectangle** object with instance variable **width** of 12 and instance variable **height** of 50. Keyword **this** refers to object rec.

Example 3. A constructor with three parameters.

```
public Student(String name, int midterm, int final) {
   this.name = name;
   this.midterm = midterm;
   this.final = final;
}
```

Using the following code:

```
Student student = new Student("Ming Lee", 89, 92);
```

will create an object of **Student** called **student** with the initialized data.

Example 4. A constructor with no parameter.

```
public SomeClass() {   //Constructor without parameter
   //Other statements or empty code
}
```

If a constructor has no code in the body, it is the default constructor provided by the compiler. The following code:

```
SomeClass someObj = new SomeClass();
```

creates object **someObj** with its instance variables set to the system default values.

More Information: *The Java compiler will first attempt to initialize all instance variables with the system default values before assigning any values passed as constructor parameters.*

Example 5. Other constructors.

```
public FutureValue(String name, double invest, double rate) {
   setName(name);
   setMonthlyRate(invest);
   setYearlyRate(rate);
   year = 1;
   }
```

This constructor calls methods of the form **setXxx()** to initialize instance variables **name**, **monthlyInvest**, and **yearlyRate**. It also provides default values to any instance variable for which no value is passed as a parameter of the constructor. For example, **year** is initialized to 1 as default since its value is absent from the parameter list. The reason for calling the **setXxx()** methods to initialize the values of instance data is to increase data reliability when there is a verification operation provided in the **setXxx()** methods.

Example 6. Constructor with class type parameter.

```
public Product(String code, ProductDB dB) {
   this.code = code;
   price = dB.getPrice(code);
}
```

In this example, parameter **dB** must be an object of the user-defined class **ProductDB**. The constructor calls method **getPrice()** from object **dB** to initialize **price**.

6.2.4 Constructor overloading

Constructor overloading is the presence of more than one constructor in a class. Each constructor differs in its signature, that is, by the quantity, type, and order of any parameters. Constructor overloading increases flexibility in object instantiation. The following example uses four overloaded constructors:

```
public Cube() { //No parameter constructor creates a unit cube
   width = height = length = 1.0;
}
public Cube(double size) { //One parameter constructor creates a  cube
   width = height = length = size;
}
public Cube(double width, double height) { //Two-parameter constructor
                                             //uses a unit value as its length
   this.width = width;
   this.height = height;
   length = 1.0;
}
public Cube(double width, double height, double length) {
//three-parameter constructor initializes the size with the passed argument values

   this.width = width;
   this.height = height;
   this.length = length;
}
```

In this example, four different kind of rectangular prism objects can be created based on the argument specifications:

1. No-parameter constructor - it is used to create a unit cubical object. For instance,

   ```
   Cube unitCube = new Cube();
   ```

2. One-parameter constructor – is used to create a cubical object with specified size by this argument. For instance,

   ```
   Cube realCube = new Cube(13.58);
   ```

3. Two-parameter constructor – is used to create a rectangular prism with a unit length and others are specified by two arguments as width and height.

   ```
   Cube rectangle = new Cube(8.09, 12.6);
   ```

4. Complete-parameter constructor – is used to create a rectangular prism object with all specified sizes. For instance,

   ```
   Cube rectangle = new Cube(50.2, 29.8, 18.3);
   ```

In addition to flexibility in instantiating objects, constructor overloading can also reduce the amount of coding work. For example, if there is no one-parameter constructor provided in this code, one must call a complete-parameter constructor to create a cubical object as:

```
Cube cube = new Cube(179.5609, 179.5609, 179.5609);
```

The following are more examples of constructor overloading:

```
//Complete code called MileageConverter.java in Ch6 from the author's website
public MileageConverter() {
   miles = 0.0;
   kilometers = 0.0;
   result = 0.0;
}
public MileageConverter (double distance){
   miles = distance;
   kilometers = distance;
   result = 0.0;
}
```

3W: *Constructor overloading refers to the presence of more than one constructor in a class. Overloaded constructors must have different signatures, that is a differing quantity of parameters, parameter types, and order of parameters, from each other. The purpose of constructor overloading is to allow flexibility in object instantiation.*

More information: *The name of a parameter is not part of the constructor signature and is not sufficient to distinguish it from other constructors.*

6.2.5 A walk through methods

Constructors are considered special methods. However, there are two categories of methods: instance methods and static methods. An instance method represents the behavior of its object and carries out a particular calculation or manipulation of the object; a static method represents the behavior of the entire class, carrying out calculations or manipulations for the entire class rather than individual objects. Static methods are also called class methods.

The syntax of method is defined as follows:

```
[accessType][static][final]returnType methodName([parameterList]){
   //Square brackets indicate optional item
   statements;
   }
```

Here,

[accessType]—optional. An access modifier can be **public**, **protected**, **private**, or **package** (no access modifier specified). A public access modifier is used if an object can directly call the method using the dot notation; otherwise, a private method is defined. A private method can only be called within another method of the object. Section 12.1.6 discusses these four access modifiers and their use in more detail.

[static]—optional. A method can be static. Static methods are discussed in Section 6.4.

[final]—optional. A method can be final. Final methods are discussed in Section 7.6.3.

returnType—A return type can be any primitive data type, class type, or void.

methodName—A method name must be a valid Java identifier. It is highly recommended Java naming conventions be applied to the naming of a method, as discussed in Section 3.1.3.

[parameterList]—optional. A parameter list consists of a valid parameter type and parameter name. A parameter type can be any primitive data type, class type, or interface type. A parameter list is of the form:

```
parameterType1 parameterName1, parameterType2 parameterName2, …
```

You may recall all previous examples of methods were defined as public allowing them to be called using the dot notation syntax. In addition to **setXxx()** and **getXxx()** methods, other methods are coded to perform calculations or manipulations of data, or check the status of data. For example,

```
public void setPrice(double charge) {
   price = charge;
   }
public double getPrice() {
   return price;
   }
public void totalPrice() {
   total = price * amount;
}
```

Note that unless there is type cast, the data type (for example double for **charge**) must match the parameter type and return type must also match the type of assigned data in the calling statement.

Because methods and data are both members of a class, they have the same scope of accessibility, and a method can freely use any data in its operations. This feature dramatically reduces the possibility of mistakes associated with using parameters to pass instance data into and returning it back from a method. It is more convenient for coding. For example, in a calculation method:

```
public void convertKilometers()             //convert kilometers to miles
   { result = kilometers * 0.62137; }
```

the method directly uses instance variables **kilometers** and **result**.

However, sometimes a method may have both a parameter list and return type as well:

```
public int max(int num1, int num2, int num3) {
   return Math.max(num1, Math.max(num2, num3));
   }
```

User-defined method **max()** has three **int** type parameters as well as a return type. It calls API **Math.max()** to return the maximum value of the three integers.

Another example:

```
public Product retrieve(String code){
   return this(code);
}
```

uses instance variable **code** as passed data to instantiate an object of **Product** and return this object as a reference.

6.2.6 Value passing vs. reference passing

In Java, we call a parameter a value parameter if it is a primitive data type and call it a reference if it is an object that actually receives the address of that object.

Value parameters receive copies of the values provided by the method callers. After the parameters receive the values, they do not have any relationship with the original data. The scope of a value parameter is local to the method. It does not affect the original data in the calling program regardless of how the value is changed inside the method. Its life is terminated when the method ends. This concept is explained in Figure 6.2.

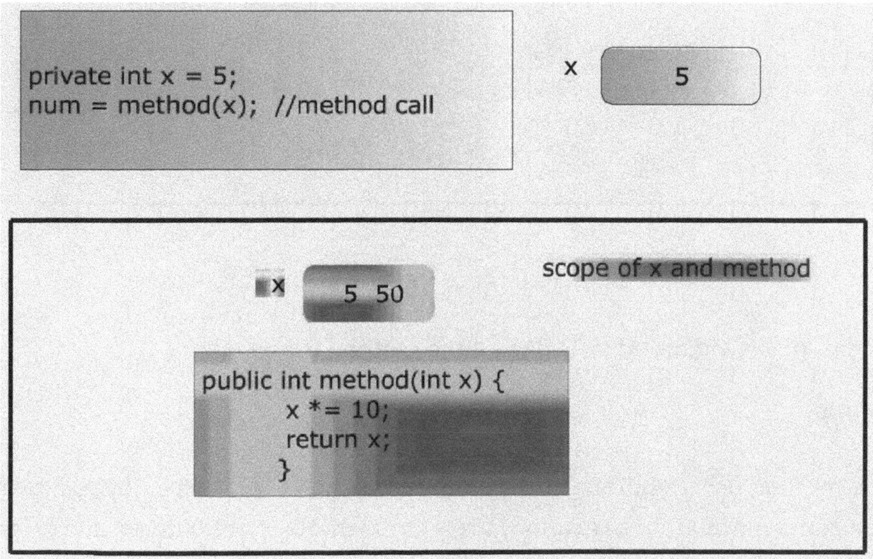

Figure 6.2 Value passing in a method

In Figure 6.2, assume we define instance variable **x** with the value 5. When **method(x)** is called, the calling code passes the value of **x** to **method()**, that is the value 5 is copied and passed to integer parameter **x** of the method. The original **x** is "hidden" (actually, it is pushed onto a stack), and parameter **x** becomes available as a local variable to the method. No matter what value is assigned to **x** within **method()**, the value of **x** in the calling program always remains 5. When execution of the method is complete, the JVM automatically unloads the method and pops the original **x** off the stack without any change. If it is necessary to obtain the result of any change to **x** from within **method()**, as shown in this example, you may return the local value of **x** as a return parameter and assign it to **num**.

Reference passing is the opposite of value passing. Reference passing actually passes the address of the object, not a copy of the object. As such, the scope of the parameter is the same as the original object to which it is referring. When the data of the object changes, it is changing the data of the original object. This modified value is kept following the termination of execution by the method. This explanation is illustrated in Figure 6.3.

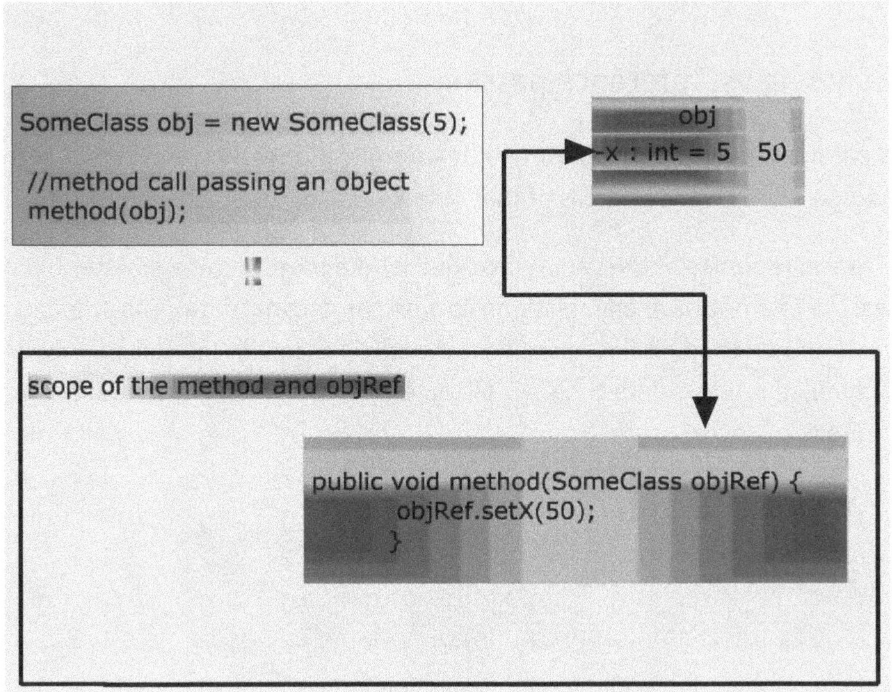

Figure 6.3 Reference passing in a method

Assume instance datum **x** is initialized as 5. When the method is called as

method(obj);

we pass **obj** to the method using **objRef** as the parameter name to reference **obj** as shown in Figure 6.3. When the JVM loads the method for execution, the address of **obj** is not hidden, and referencing is active until execution of the method is terminated. Therefore, when an inside method is called, for example

objRef.setX(50);

it changes the value of instance data **x** within **obj** to 50.

6.2.7 Method overloading

Method overloading, similar to constructor overloading, is a commonly used coding technique. The purpose of method overloading is to have more flexibility in calling methods with the same name but having different parameters. This technique follows the same rules and syntax as constructor overloading, wherein each overloaded method must have the same name but a unique signature so the compiler can differentiate them. As with constructor overloading, the signature includes the name, parameter type, number of parameters, and the order of the parameters. The access modifier, return type, and parameter names are not part of signature definition. The compiler does not consider return type when differentiating between methods so multiple methods with the same signature cannot be declared even if they have different return types. For example:

```
public void method(int num)
```

and

```
public double method(int count)      //Signature is the same as above
```

are not legitimate method overloading constructs because they have the same signature, **method(int)**. The following example:

```
public void method(int num)
```

and

```
public double method(double num)    //Method overloading
```

are legal method overloading constructs because **method(int)** and **method(double)** form different signatures.

Table 6.1 lists more examples of method overloading and side-by-side comparisons.

Table 6.1 Method overloading comparisons

Legal method overloading	Illegal method overloading	Reason
void sum(int count1, int count2)	int sum(int count1, int count2)	Return type is not part of signature
void sum(int count1, short count2)	void sum(int num1, int num2)	Parameter name is not part of signature
void sum(int n1, int n2, int n3)	float sum(int x1, int x2, int x3)	Return type and parameter name are not part of signature

More Info: *Variable parameter is also part of method overloading and it is introduced in Chapter 12.*

The following are more examples of method overloading. Assume the system default currency format is Chinese yuan, as shown in these examples:

```
//Complete code called MethodOverloadTest.java in Ch6 from the author's website
import java.util.*;
import java.text.*;
...
//Use of system default currency format
public void printFormattedCurrency(double amount) {
   String out = NumberFormat.getCurrencyInstance().format(amount);
   System.out.println("System default currency format:  " + out);
}
//Use of user-defined currency format
public void printFormattedCurrency(double amount, Locale locale) {
   String out = NumberFormat.getCurrencyInstance(locale).format(amount);
   System.out.println("User-defined locale" + locale + "format: " + out);
}
//Use of user-defined currency format with control of decimals
public void printFormattedCurrency(double amount, Locale locale, int decimal) {
   NumberFormat currency = NumberFormat.getCurrencyInstance(locale);
   currency.setMinimumFractionDigits(decimal);
   String out = currency.format(amount);
   System.out.println("User-defined locale" + locale + "format with "+ decimal +
"decimal : " + out);
}
```

In the above example, three overloaded methods are defined:

```
printFormattedCurrency(double)
printFormattedCurrency(double, Locale)
printFormattedCurrency(double, Locale, int)
```

Based on different parameters, they produce three types of currency formats as output. The following are the method calls:

```
//Complete code called MethodOverloadTestApp.java in Ch6 from author's website
MethodOverloadTest test = new MethodOverloadTest();      //create object
test.printFormattedCurrency(19.722345);           //Method call with one parameter
test.printFormattedCurrency(19.722345, Locale.US);       //Call with 2 parameters
test.printFormattedCurrency(19.722345, Locale.FRANCE, 4);//Call with 3 parameters
```

The output is as follows:

System default currency format: $19.72

User-defined locale en_US, amount:$19.72

User-defined locale fr_FR, format with 4, amount:19,7223 €

3W: *Method overloading refers to code containing multiple methods of the same name but each method having a different signature to perform different manipulations. It should be noted the access modifier, return type, and parameter name are not part of the signature.*

6.2.8 What is **this**?

The Java language provides a useful keyword, **this**, representing the current object in execution. It can be used in all constructors and methods except static methods. When the current object completes its operation period, the JVM may load another object for the next operation; **this** will refer to the newly loaded object. Therefore, we can say the keyword **this** has polymorphic features. It increases flexibility and convenience in coding. It also increases code readability, as we have used **this** to differentiate the parameter name from the instance data in the previous examples:

```
this.price = price;
```

wherein **price** is a parameter name, and **this.price** is clearly referring to the instance data of the current object.

We must use the keyword **this** in some API classes to reference the current object in event handling. For example, in the statement:

```
okButton.addActionPerformed(this); //Add event handling for okButton
okButton.addActionPerformed(okButton); //Illegal usage
```

this refers to the button object **okButton**. However, literally specifying **okButton** as the method's parameter is illegal in this case. The GUI and **JButton** classes are discussed in Chapter 15.

Common use of **this** in coding can be summarized as follows:

1. Referring to an instance data of the current object.

```
this.varName
```

For example,

```
public method(int n) {
   this.n = n;
}
```

2. Call another constructor in a constructor. For example:

```
//Complete code called TestThisConstructorApp.java in Ch6 from author's website
public class Rectangle {
    private double x, y;
    private double width, height;
```

```
    public Rectangle() {
        this(0, 0, 0, 0);           //Call another constructor with 4 parameters
    }
    public Rectangle(double width, double height) {
        this(0, 0, width, height);  //Call another constructor with 4 parameters
    }
   public Rectangle(double x, double y, double width, double height) {
        this.x = x;
        this.y = y;
        this.width = width;
        this.height = height;
    }
    ...
}
```

It is illegal syntax in Java to directly call a constructor, for example:

```
Rectangle(0, 0, 12.59, 10.08);                    //Illegal constructor call
```

or

```
objName.Rectangle(0, 0, 12.59, 10.08);            //Illegal constructor call
```

It should be noted **this()** must be the first statement executed when calling a constructor:

```
public Rectangle() {
        width = 2.98;
        this(0, 0, width, 0);                     //Syntax error
   }
```

However,

```
public Rectangle() {
        this(2.2, 3.3);
        this(0, 0, width, 0);                     //Syntax error
   }
```

The second statement is illegal.

3. Referring to the returned object. For example:

```
//Complete code called TestClassApp.java in Ch6 from author's website
class TestClass{
    private String message;
    public TestClass( String message) {this.message = message; }
```

```
    public TestClass method () {return this;}       //Return the current object
    public String toString() {return message;}
}

public class TestClassApp {
    public static void main(String[] args) { TestClass
        myObj = new TestClass("Java");
        TestClass yourObj = new TestClass("OOP");
        System.out.println(myObj.method().toString());
        System.out.println(yourObj.method().toString());
    }
}
```

The execution result is:

```
Java
OOP
```

Here, **method()** returns the current object, **myObj** and **yourObj**, respectively.

The above output statements can also be written as:

```
System.out.println(myObj.method());
System.out.println(yourObj.method());
```

The Java compiler will automatically add the **.toString()** method call as a suffix, thereby constructing a cascading statement. Cascading statements are discussed in a later chapter.

4. Return the current object to a caller. For example:

```
//Complete code called TestThisApp.java in Ch6 from the author's website
class Help {
    int n;
    public void setMe (int m) {
        Helper helper = new Helper();
        helper.setValue(this, m);  //this returns the current object  to help
    }
    public void setNum(int num) { n = num; }
    public String toString() { return ("" + n ); }
}

class Helper {
    void setValue (Help help, int num) {help.setNum(num);}
}
//The driver code
```

```
public class TestThisApp {
    public static void main(String[] args) {
        Help help = new Help();
        help.setMe(3);
        System.out.println( help );
    }
}
```

When **help.setMe(3)** is called, method **setMe()** creates an object of **Helper** followed by a call to method **setValue()**, passing the created object and its data as parameters, to initialize the object's data to a value of 3. Though it may seem unnecessary to have intermediate calls or steps to carry out this task, the advantage is verification code in **setValue()** can be added before the data is assigned.

We may also modify this example so method **setValue()** could be defined as a static method:

```
class Helper {
    public static void setValue (Help help, int num) {help.setNum(num);};
}
```

You may also call **setValue()** directly without first creating an object of **Helper** before calling **setValue()** inside method **setMe()**:

```
public void setMe (int m) {
      //Call static method of Helper and pass current object and its data
    Helper.setValue(this, m);
}
```

3W: *The keyword **this** refers to the object currently being executed. It can be used in non-static methods or constructors to refer to the current object. It can be coded in a constructor to call another constructor, but must be coded as the first executable statement. The use of **this** increases readability in assigning a parameter to an instance variable. It is also used as a parameter and return type in methods.*

6.3 A Walk into Static Data

We have discussed the keyword **this** and its uses. The keyword reflects a typical feature of polymorphism—dynamic object reference. However, we also need an operation with opposite functionality—establishing methods and data representing an entire class rather than being associated to particular objects. Java provides static methods and static data to achieve this goal. We will discuss static data in this section and static methods in the next section.

6.3.1 Class data

Static data are shared by all objects of the class and represent all objects in the class. They continue to exist after the completion of a method's execution. Static data are also called class **metadata**. A static datum can be a constant or variable. Static constant data are also called class constant data or static final data. Static variables are also known as class variables. We have often used such data in applications. For example, **Math.PI** and **Math.E** are static constant data provided by the API Math class. The **taxRate** variable in the financial application examples is a user-defined static datum. It does not matter which object performs the financial calculations as they all apply the same defined tax rate. Sometimes, we may want to know how many objects are created and used in an application. A static variable is the best way to maintain such a record. Static data can be private or public.

The following are examples using static data.

Example 1. Define static variables.

```
private static double accountLimit;                  //Define static data as double
private static int userCount = 0;                    //Define a static int data
public static String welcome = "Java is hot!";//Define a static data as String
```

Example 2. More examples in defining static constant data.

```
private static final float TAX_RATE = 0.0875f;            //Define static constants
public static final double EARTH_MASS = 5.972e24;
public static final int MONTH_IN_YEAR = 12;
```

Example 3. Use of static data.

```
public FutureValue() {                          //Constructor
   //Other code
   ...
   userCount++;  //For every created object, increase userCount by 1
}
public FutureValue(String name) {
   this.name = name;
   //Other code
   ...
   userCount++; //Increase userCount by 1 to count objects created
}
```

In the above example, static variable **userCount** maintains the current total of how many objects are created in the code. The following output statement:

```
//Use static method called by the class directly
System.out.println(FutureValue.getUserCount());
```

generates the same result as:

```
System.out.println(myFutureValue.getUserCount()); //Called by an object
```

because method **getUserCount()** is a static method used to retrieve the value of static datum **userCount**. The datum is associated with the entire class rather than being dependent upon a particular object. We discuss static methods in Section 6.4.

6.3.2 Why does static data belong to all objects?

Static data belong to all objects of the class because they are stored in a special memory location—the class access area—that can be accessed by all objects of the class. The access scope is the same as the access scope of the class, not the access scope of the objects. Instance data, on the other hand, are stored in the assigned memory location of the object. If we create 100 objects, there will be 100 assigned memory locations storing the instance data of each object. The scope of accessibility of the instance data is the same as each object's scope of accessibility. Figure 6.4 illustrates the differences between static data and instance data in memory locations.

We discuss this further next.

6.3.3 Principles in the use of static data

The decision of whether or not to use static data in the design of a class is an important one, as static data are part of the class components. You must know the significant differences between static and instance data:

- Instance data apply to particular objects of the class. Each object created in the code has its own instance data. For example, given an instance datum **name**, each object has its own value of **name**. The value of an instance datum is defined by the particular object and is independent of all other objects as well as the entire class.

- Static data are shared among the objects in the class. The data apply to and have the same meaning and value to all objects in the class.

Based on the above analysis, we can summarize the principles of use of static data as follows:

1. Data should be defined as static if it is used as metadata for the entire class.

2. Data used to set upper or lower limits for all objects in the class should be defined as static constant data.

3. Mathematical variables and constants applying to all objects of the class should be defined as static data.

4. Global data used for prompts, greetings, and other messages for all objects in the class should be defined as static constant data.

6.4 A Walk into Static Methods

Many API classes provide static methods. Static methods are convenient to use since you don't need to first create an object then call the methods. Static methods can be called directly by the class without creating objects.

In the previous discussion, we learned how to write and use our own static methods. For example, all methods in a driver code must be static. In another example, the **Validator** class, we defined all methods as static so they can be used as utilities by various applications.

Static methods can also be used to manipulate static data. Although static data can be accessed or modified by any method in the class, it is very common to use static methods to manipulate static data.

6.4.1 Class methods

Static methods, in a manner similar to static data, belong to the entire class, represent all objects of the class, and are not designed to function with particular objects. For example, we have used many class methods in the **Math** class. It does not matter which objects are using them, for they all use the same formulas for all calculations in a particular method call.

A static method can exist without the existence of objects in the class. Although a static method can be called by the objects of the class, it is not necessary to create an object first before calling the static methods. This is because a static method is created and its memory location is assigned before any objects of the class are instantiated. This is the reason the methods in the driver code of a Java application are defined as static. The JVM first loads the driver class, calls **main()**, then directly calls the static methods without creating its object.

Although static data and static methods have many advantages, their improper use will produce negative impacts in coding. Defining all data and methods as static violates the principles of encapsulation and cohesion. It would not be necessary to create objects of the class since each object's operation affects all other objects in the class. An extreme example might be increasing the minimum bank deposit from $1000 to $1500 for an object of a bank customer; the minimum deposit would be raised for all bank customer objects.

The use of the keyword **this** and static represent opposite functionality. Static represents all objects of the class; **this** refers to the current object of execution. Static data and methods are realized by static binding wherein the memory resolution is allocated at compile time; **this** functionality is achieved by dynamic binding and the memory reference is defined dynamically during execution. Keyword **this** is a typical example of polymorphism.

The following are common recommendations in using static data and static methods:

- Avoid use of static data and static methods if you can.
- Consider the use of static method if a method operates independently of all other objects of the class.
- Consider the use of static data if data can be defined as static.

- Use a static method to manipulate static data.

Note It *is illegal to use any instance data, call non-static methods, or use the keyword* ***this*** *in a static method; however, you may access static data or call static methods in non-static methods.*

The following are examples of using static methods.

Example 1. Define a static method that can return the total count of all objects created in the code. Assume static datum **objCount** is already created and increases by 1 each time an object is instantiated.

```
//Complete code in TestStatic.java in Ch6 from the author's website
public class TestStatic {
   //Other statements
   ...
   public static int getObjCount() {
          return objCount;
   }
}
```

Calling **TestStatic.getObjCount()** within the print statement:

```
System.out.println(TestStatic.getObjCount());          //Use class direct call
```

produces the same output as obtaining the object count via the object:

```
System.out.println(obj1.getObjCount());                //Use object to call
```

Example 2. Write a static method called **sqr()** in the class **TestStatic** to calculate the square of a number.

```
//Complete code called TestStatic.java in Ch6 from the author's website
public static double sqr(double num) {
   return num * num;
}
```

Calling

```
System.out.println(TestStatic.sqr(22.98));        //direct call
```

will calculate the square of 22.98.

6.4.2 How are static methods stored?

Static methods are stored in memory locations similar to static data. However, there is a significant difference between them in terms of the way they are stored.

Let's first review how methods of objects are called before discussing the memory allocation of static methods. A "swapping" technique is used when an object's method is called. After a method is loaded for execution, the JVM loads the method's parameters and other information necessary for execution. After the method has completed execution and is now being called by another object, only the parameters from the caller are swapped; the method is resident in memory.

Static methods do not use "swapping" because instance data and instance methods are not permitted in static methods. In a manner similar to static data, static methods are stored in independent memory locations not associated with any objects of the class. Figure 6.4 illustrates the differences between static methods and instance methods.

Assume we have created three objects using a constructor of the **FutureValue** class: **myFutureValue**, **yourFutureValue**, and **herFutureValue**. Each object is stored in its own memory location with its own instance data. However, static datum **taxRate** and static method **getTaxRate()** are stored in different memory locations unrelated to any of the three objects; their access scope is the same as that of the **FutureValue** class. For a given instance method, for example, **getName()**, the JVM will use the "swapping" technique discussed above when any of the three objects calls it. The JVM loads instance data **name** and swaps out the previous instance data **name** associated with the previous object, and performs the specified operation of returning the name. From this figure we may also observe that static data and static methods can also be called by an instance because they are not overwritten in memory.

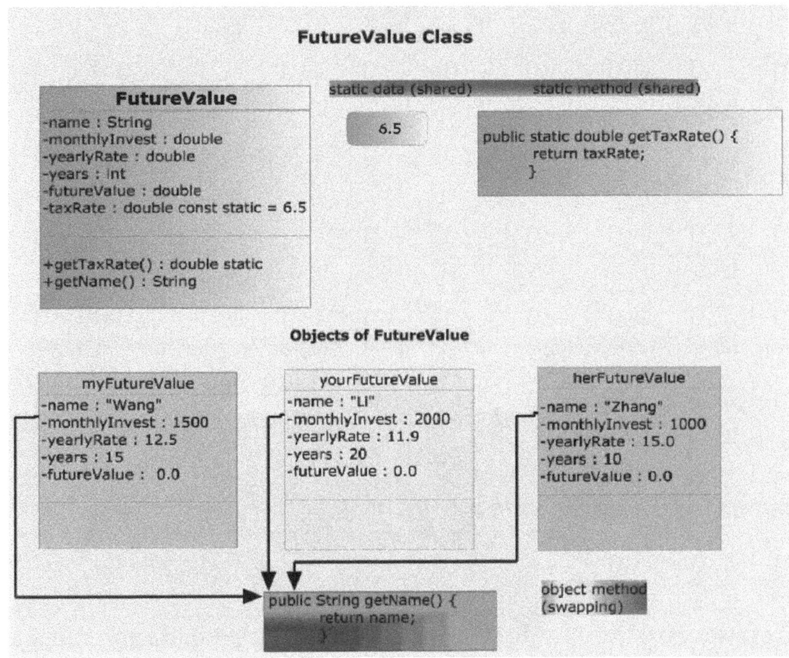

Figure 6.4 Comparison between static data, static methods with instance data and methods

6.4.3 Static initialization blocks

Static data may also be a group of related data, not just an individual datum initialized by a single statement. For example, static data can be an array with many elements (arrays are discussed in Chapter 10).

```
//Declare a static array as double
public static double taxRate[];
```

Assume the value of each of these five elements in array **taxRate** is entered by the user from a keyboard or read from a file. How can you guarantee the array is initialized before being used in the application?

Java provides the static initialization block to solve this type of problem. Its syntax is:

```
static {
   //any statements to initialize static data declared before
   ...
   }
```

Before a constructor or static method is executed, the static initialization block is executed first, thereby guaranteeing the process of static data initialization.

Let's discuss the above example further.

```
//Complete code called StaticBlockTest1.java in Ch6 from the author's website
class StaticBlock1 {
public static double taxRate[] = new double[5];

static { //static initialization block
          Scanner sc = new Scanner(System.in);
          for(int i = 0; i < 5; i++) {
                 System.out.print("Enter the tax rate for county" + i +":");
                 taxRate[i] = sc.nextDouble();
                 System.out.println();
          }
   public static void setup() {
          System.out.println("Begin static data initialization...");
   }
}
```

Assume the first statement in the driver code is:

```
StaticBlock1.setup();
```

Before executing this statement, the JVM first initializes the static initialization block then calls the **setup()** method. In another example, assume an object of **StaticBlock** is initialized in the driver code as:

```
//Complete code called StaticBlockTest2.java in Ch6 from the author's website
StaticBlock staticBlockObj = new StaticBlock();
```

This statement will also activate initialization of the static initialization block first.

6.5 Object Again

In this section, we discuss the use of objects with commonly used techniques such as object instantiating, object referencing, the reuse of object names, and cascading calls.

6.5.1 Object instantiating vs. object referencing

There are two common coding techniques used to instantiate objects: explicit instantiation and implicit instantiation. Both use the **new** operator to create objects; however, implicit object instantiation returns the reference of the object created in a method. Let's first examine an example of explicit object instantiation:

```
SomeClass obj = new SomeClass(x);    //explicitly create an object
```

When this statement is executed, the constructor of **SomeClass()** is called, instance data is initialized, and a memory location is specified for the object. Created object **obj** points to the beginning address of this memory location. This process is called, as we know, instantiating. Therefore, object creation is associated memory allocation and reference to the execution address.

We may increase encapsulation by instantiating objects as many API classes do through the use of implicit object instantiation. For example, we have used implicit object instantiation and referencing in **NumberFormat** for formatted currency:

```
NumberFormat currency = NumberFormat.getCurrencyInstance();
```

In fact, the **getCurrencyInstance()** method contains a statement to create an object of **NumberFormat**:

```
public static NumberFormat getCurrencyInstance() {
   NumberFormat object = new NumberFormat();
   return object;
}
```

Therefore, **currency** is actually a reference to the returned object, **object,** of **NumberFormat** from **getCurrencyInstance()**. Writing in this way achieves information hiding for better code abstraction and encapsulation for a static method.

We may employ this principle in our user-defined methods in object creation. For example:

```
//Complete code called ObjectCreateReferenceTest.java in Ch6 from author's website
public static SomeClass getSomeClassInstance() {
   SomeClass object = new SomeClass();
   return object;
}
```

So we can use implicit object instantiation and object reference as:

```
SomeClass myObj = SomeClass.getSomeClassInstance();
```

We can use method and constructor overloading to write different signatures for method **getSomeClassInstance()** to provide additional coding convenience.

Object referencing refers to the state in which one or more names are associated with an existing object. This is the opposite of explicit object instantiation and implicit object instantiation in that no new memory is allocated. For example:

```
SomeClass obj1 = new SomeClass(10); //Instantiate an object
SomeClass obj2 = obj1;              //Use obj2 to refer obj1
SomeClass obj3 = obj2;              //Use obj3 to refer obj2, therefore obj1
```

In this example, **obj1** has two other names: **obj2** and **obj3**. **obj2** and **obj3** both refer to the memory location of **obj1**. Any operations performed in either **obj2** or **obj3** will affect their referred object, **obj1,** and vice versa. They are just different names for the same memory location storing data and operations. For instance,

```
obj2.setX(100);
System.out.println(obj3.getX());    //Or
System.out.println(obj1.getX());
```

will display:

100

However, as compared to object instantiation:

```
SomeClass myObj = new SomeClass(10);//Create an object
SomeClass yourObj = new SomeClass(10);     //Create another one
```

although **myObj** and **yourObj** have the same data value, they are actually two different objects of **SomeClass**. The objects are stored in two different memory locations with no relationship between them despite the fact they belong to the same class. Figure 6.5 illustrates the concept of object instantiation versus object referencing.

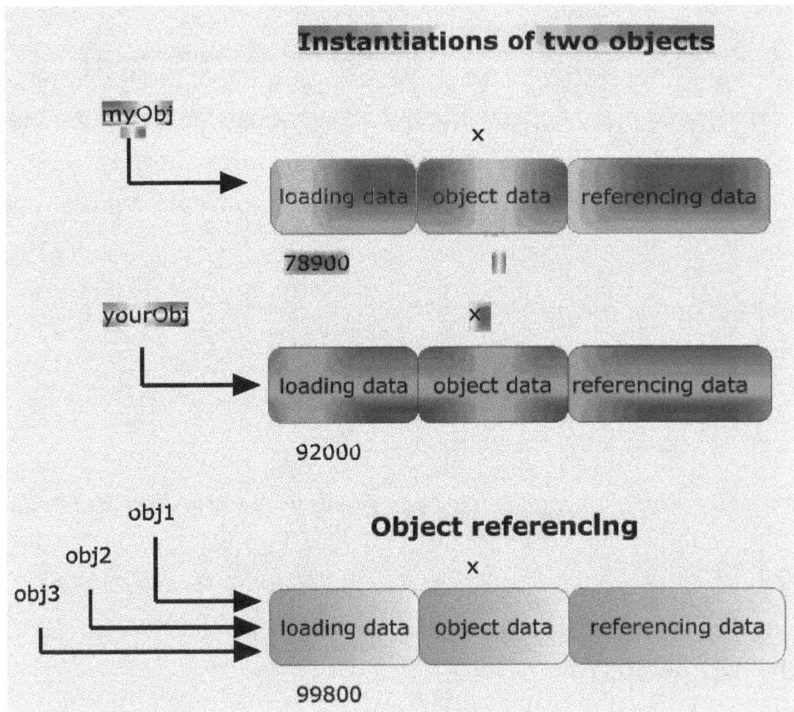

Figure 6.5 Object instantiation vs. object referencing

It is clear to see in Figure 6.5 the name of an object represents the beginning address of the memory location in which the object's data and loading information (method loading and reference data) are stored. In summary, object instantiation involves memory allocation and object referencing associates an existing memory location of the object with the object to which is being referred.

More info: *The declaration of an object, for example **SomeClass obj;**, does not perform object instantiation.*

6.5.2 Reuse of an object name

In Java, an object name can be reused for instantiating other objects of the same class. For example:

```
//Complete code called ObjectNameReuseTest.java in Ch6 from the author's website
...
int count = 1;
SomeClass obj;                                  //Declare an object of SomeClass
  while(count <=3)
   {
    obj = new SomeClass(5*count);               //obj is reused 3 times
   ...    //other method calls
    System.out.println("otherObj's x = " + obj.getX());
    count++;
   }
   obj = new SomeClass(20);                     //reuse again
```

```
...
```

In the loop, object name **obj** is reused three times. In each iteration of the loop, the life cycle of any existing **obj** is terminated, its memory located is gathered in garbage collection by the JVM, and a new object with the same name and same data is instantiated. This process is repeated three times. Following completion of the looping process, **obj** is reused again to create another object with different data.

NOTE: *In reusing an object name, the newly created object must be of the same class as the old object, otherwise a syntax error will occur.*

6.5.3 Cascading calls

We have already discussed some examples of cascading calls in previous chapters. The statement

```
String futureValueStr = NumberFormat.getCurrencyInstance().format(2987655.
32276);
```

is a combination of the two method calls:

```
NumberFormat currency = NumberFormat.getCurrencyInstance();
String futureValueStr = currency.format(2987655.32276);
```

Although cascading calls can simplify code writing, not all methods can be cascaded. The syntax requirement for a cascading call is:

```
Identifier.method1().method2().[methodn_1()].methodn()
```

wherein **Identifier** can be an object or class.

With the exception of the last method, **methodn()**, all other methods in the cascading call must return the object, class type, or reference to the object as specified by the identifier, otherwise a syntax error will occur.

The principle of cascading calls is obvious. A method in the cascade can be continually called because the previous call returns the address used to call the next method. The last call does not necessarily have to satisfy this requirement because no more methods are present in the cascade. However, if a cascading call is used in an output statement, the last method must return the value to be displayed or written.

Note: *Abuse of cascading calls can reduce code readability.*

6.6 Improved Example: Investment Return

In this section we utilize the concepts and techniques introduced in this chapter to improve the example of investment return discussed in Chapter 5 as follows:

1. Add constructor and constructor overloading to increase flexibility in object instantiation. In the improved code, several objects of **FutureValue** created with different signatures show how these overloaded constructors are used:

```
//Complete code called FutureValueApp.java in Ch6 from the author's website
//Use constructor overloading to create different objects and call their methods
FutureValue noNameFutureValue = new FutureValue();
   noNameFutureValue.futureValueCompute();
FutureValue noInvestFutureValue = new FutureValue("John");
   noInvestFutureValue.futureValueCompute();
FutureValue noRateFutureValue = new FutureValue("Wang", 1000);
   noRateFutureValue.futureValueCompute();
FutureValue noYearsFutureValue = new FutureValue("Liu", 2000, 9.85);
   noYearsFutureValue.futureValueCompute();
FutureValue myFutureValue = new FutureValue("Gao", 1590, 10.28, 25);
   myFutureValue.futureValueCompute();
```

2. Add static data and static methods. They are used to count the number of objects created in the code and represent the tax rate for all objects in this class:

```
private static int count = 0;
public static final double TAX_RATE = 0.085;
public static int getCount() {
   return count;
}

public static String getFormattedMessage(FutureValue futureValue) {
  //Cascading call
String        investStr        =        NumberFormat.getCurrencyInstance().format(future
Value.getMonthlyInvest());
String futureValueStr=NumberFormat.getCurrencyInstance().format(futureValue.getFutu
reValue());

  //Percent format to keep up two decimals
  NumberFormat percent = NumberFormat.getPercentInstance();
  percent.setMinimumFractionDigits(2);
  String rateStr = percent.format(futureValue.getYearlyRate()/100);

  String message =  futureValue.getName() + "\n"
                              + investStr + "\n"
                              + rateStr + "\n"
                              + futureValue.getYears() + "\n"
                              + futureValueStr + "\n\n";
  return message;
}
```

3. Use of keyword **this** to differentiate the parameter names from the instance data:

```
public FutureValue(String name, double monthlyInvest, double yearlyRate, int
years) {
   this.name = name;
   this.monthlyInvest = monthlyInvest;
   this.yearlyRate = yearlyRate;
   this.years = years;
   futureValue = 0.0;
   count++;
}
```

4. Use of cascading calls:

```
//Cascading call to setup currency format
String investStr = NumberFormat.getCurrencyInstance().format(futureValue.
getMonthlyInvest());
futureValueStr = NumberFormat.getCurrencyInstance().format(future
Value.getFutureValue());
```

5. Reuse of object names in the loop.

6. Improvement of output information. For example, use static methods for all objects to generate a formatted output and display the statistics of object created in the application:

```
//Call static methods for formatted output
System.out.println(FutureValue.getFormattedMessage(noNameFutureValue));
System.out.println(FutureValue.getFormattedMessage(noInvestFutureValue));
System.out.println(FutureValue.getFormattedMessage(noRateFutureValue));
...
//Call static method to display the statistics of objects created
System.out.println("Total users created " + FutureValue.getCount() + "\n\n" );
```

Exercises

1. Use examples to explain the relationship between class and object.

2. Use examples to explain three important characteristics in OOP.

3. Why is the class a module of programming in OOP? What are the principles of abstract design in writing classes? Use examples to explain how to use these principles in your design and coding of classes.

4. Define an instance variable.

5. What is a constructor? What are the characteristics of a constructor?

6. What is constructor overloading? Why do you use constructor overloading?

7. Write overloaded constructors of a **Circle** class in which there are the following parameter options for the instantiation of objects of **Circle**:

a. No parameters—It will initialize the radius to 0.0.

b. One parameter – It will initialize the radius.

c. Two parameters – It will use (0, 0) as the center of the circle and these two parameters as another point on circle to determine the radius of the circle.

d. Three parameters – It will use the first parameter as the arc length, the second parameter as the arc sine, and the third parameter as the central angle.

e. Four parameters—It will use the first two parameters as the coordinates of the center of the circle and the last two parameters as the coordinates of a point on the circle to determine the radius of the circle.

8. What are differences between constructors and methods?

9. Use examples to explain passing-by-value and passing-by-reference. Explain when you should use passing-by-value and passing-by-reference.

10. Why are method parameters not used as frequently in Java as in other programming languages?

11. Write a method to calculate the area of a circle. The method should accept the radius (double precision) as a parameter and return the computed area (double precision). Assume the class and a constructor with one parameter representing the radius have been written. Write a driver code to create a circle object with a radius of 15.34 and call the method you wrote to compute and display the area of the circle.

12. What is the signature of a method? What are the components of a method signature?

13. What is method overloading? Why do we need method overloading? What are the differences between constructor overloading and method overloading?

14. Use method overloading to write three overloaded methods to compute the average of data as double precision. These methods have two to four parameters and return the average, respectively.

15. Write three overloaded methods to print greeting messages. The first form will display the string parameter as a greeting message. The second form will display the two parameters as name and greeting, respectively. The third form will display the first and second parameters as strings representing name and greeting, respectively, and the third parameter (integer) will indicate the number of times the named greeting will be repeated.

16. Use examples to define the Java keyword **this**. List four reasons for using the keyword **this**.

17. What are static data? What are differences between instance data and static data?

18. List three examples likely to use static data and write the statements defining these three static data.

19. What is a static method? What are differences between instance methods and static methods?

20. Write three static methods to display the three static data as defined in Question 18.

21. Assume a class exists that will convert seconds, minutes, and hours to days or number of weeks, as appropriate. Which data in the class should be defined as static data? Which methods in the class should be defined as static methods? Explain your answers.

22. What is a static initialization block? List its coding and executing features.

23. Write a static initialization block to initialize the static data defined in **Question 21**.

24. Use constructor and method overloading, static data, and static methods to code a complete class that can covert seconds, minutes, and hours (or a combination thereof) to days. If the number of days exceeds 6, the result will be converted to the number of integral weeks and any remaining portion expressed as days. Write a driver code to test your class using a variety of data to create corresponding objects based upon the entries and display the results of the conversions. Save all of your files.

25. Improve your answer to Question 24. Instead of using hard-coded data, ask the user to enter a variety of data, then create the corresponding objects converting these data to days (or weeks), and display the result. Your driver code will continue to run until the user enters 'n' to stop.

26. Modify your answer to Question 25 to use implicit object instantiation, as discussed in this chapter, to create objects for all constructors.

27. What is a cascading call? What is its syntax requirement?

28. Assume that there are three existing methods:

    a. **Object computeAverage(double midterm, double final);** - It will compute the average of two exams, assign the average to an instance data **average**, and return this object.

    b. **Object assignGrade();** - It will use average to assign a letter grade.

    c. **String toString();** - It will return the average and grade as strings.

    Write code performing the above three requirements as a single cascading call.

"Don't reinvent the wheel."

– Silicon Valley Engineer community

Chapter 7 Inheritance

Inheritance is one of the natural-born features in Java. All classes, whether API- or programmer-defined, are automatically inherited from a root class—**Object**. In fact, **Object** represents all common features found in all other classes. In this chapter, we discuss in detail the concept of inheritance and explain why inheritance is so important in Java programming. We also use examples to illustrate step-by-step how to use inheritance and inheritance-related techniques in coding.

7.1 Nature Of Inheritance

Characteristics of inheritance are similar to those in real world; inheritance means reuse the existing code, or code-reusable. For example, programmers can inherit an API class, plus adding some new features to solve the particular problem, so you don't need to rewrite everything from beginning.

From a programming point of view, it is not difficult to apply inheritance to your code. However, it requires care to properly use inheritance. Inheritance involves understating basic concepts, conducting categorical analysis, and correct application in coding. For example, assume we wish to write code simulating operations in different types of cars. First, we immediately realize most operations performed by vehicles are similar regardless of vehicle model or type. Second, we do not want to repeatedly write an entire simulation program for each type of vehicle, but would rather analyze categories of vehicles – such as sedan, semi-tractor trailer, SUV, sports car, jeep, and so on. We may draw the following summary based on the categorization:

- All cars have common parts, such as wheels, engine, steering wheel, seat, transmission, exhaust system, et cetera. We already know in OOP these can be defined as "state" and "behavior", or data and methods in a defined class.
- Similar parts in different vehicles may be of different designs. For example, engines in sports cars need faster acceleration and higher speed; truck engines require greater horsepower.

Based on the above analysis, we can design common parts and operations in super classes from which these data and methods may be inherited by subclasses to represent different features for different vehicles. Figure 7.2 shows our analysis in terms of an inheritance chart.

We see inheritance involves a relationship between at least two classes—a super class and subclass.

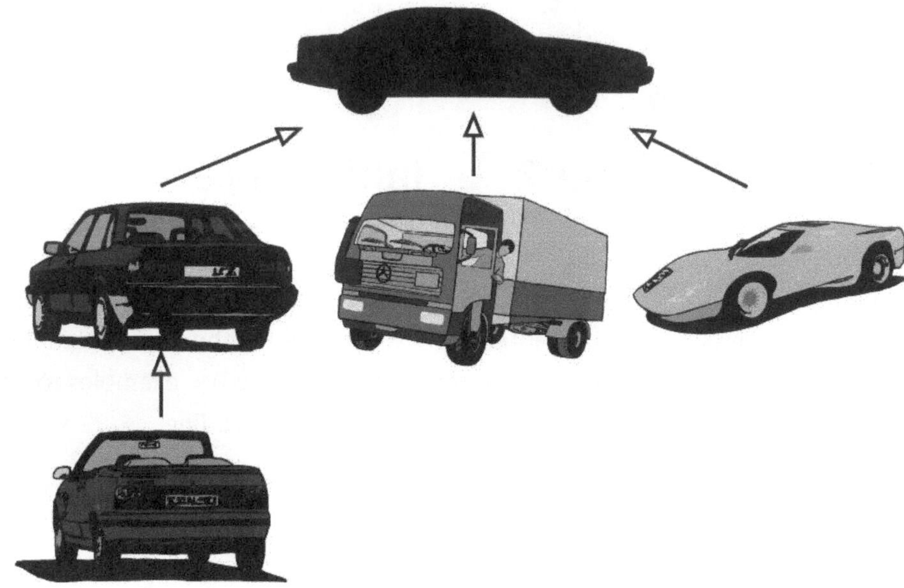

Figure 7.1 Inheritance chart of different vehicles

Based on the above discussion, we see inheritance in Java is about defining relationships between classes in terms of states and behaviors, or data and methods. We call the base class covering all its subclasses a super class. A subclass may also be referred to as a derived class. In reality, an inheritance hierarchy contains many levels. A subclass can be a super class to the next level of inheritance. We discuss different types of inheritance in a later section of this chapter. The relationship between a super class and a subclass is known as an "is a" relationship. This means a subclass is part of a super class and belongs to the same category or similar type of object. It is also implicitly stating code of the super class can be reused by its subclasses, thereby avoiding the need to "reinvent wheels." We can therefore concentrate on the new states and behaviors not available or described in the super class.

Not all classes have an "is a" relationship. Some classes may form involving a "has a" relationship because the relationship between these classes is supportive or compositional. Most utility classes are supporting classes. Business logic classes form a "has a" relationship with utility classes to verify input data. We will discuss relationships between classes in more detail in later chapters.

The use of inheritance involves categorization and analysis. It requires the correct definition of an "is a" or "has a" relationship between the classes of the inheritance hierarchy. We discuss these techniques in the following secton.

7.1.1 Analysis of categorization

Analysis of categorization is based on the particular problem you are going to solve. It involves the following steps:

- Generalization
- Specialization
- Module design

For example, given a problem that involves printing college student transcripts, we must first analyze the characteristics comprising a college level course. The generalization of a student course allows us to summarize common features of college students related to printing transcripts, e. g., ID, name, address, major, GPA, et cetera. The generalization may include some operations applying to all college students in the printing of their transcripts, such as statistics, grade calculation, formatting. Generalization is a foundation for designing a super class(es).

We move further in our analysis to specialization based on generalization. College students can be of different types in terms of academic goals: undergraduate and graduates. Graduates may include both master degree students and PhD students. Specialization is used to define particular subclasses and determine the "is a" relationship in the inheritance hierarchy. It also involves defining states (data) and signatures of functionalities (methods) in each class.

Module design involves the use of classes as modules to write code. Code reusability is purposely emphasized in module implementation. We will discuss a particular example in later section of this chapter.

Categorization of a super class also involves abstraction and interface design. It may also lead to the use of polymorphism in coding. We discuss interfaces in Chapter 8 and polymorphism in Chapter 9.

7.1.2 "is a" and "has a" relationships

Assume the existence of two classes: **Employee** and **Manager**. It is clear the relationship between these classes is a "is a" relationship because a **Manager** is an **Employee** and an **Employee** includes a **Manager**. They are in the same category. Features defined in the **Employee** class, such as ID, name, address, department, job title, work load calculation, and salary calculation, can be reused with or without modification of the **Manager** class.

Assume the existence of another class: **Computer**. Obviously, a computer is not an employee, and, as such, no "is a" relationship can exist between the **Computer** and **Employee** classes. However, an employee may have a computer and the **Computer** class could support the **Employee** class. The relationship between these two classes is a "has a" relationship. It would make no sense to reuse any code in the **Computer** class within the **Employee** class; however, we can instantiate an object of type **Computer** in **Employee** and call methods of the **Computer** class to help or support **Employee** objects in performing some defined tasks.

Analysis of the relationship between classes and clarification if the two classes form an "is a" or "has a" relationship will help us verify the possibility of establishing inheritance for allowing code reusability.

7.1.3 Code reusability

Code reusability refers to the ability of a subclass to reuse existing code, including data and methods, from its super class by virtue of inheritance. Furthermore, a subclass can also extend or add new data and methods not available in its super class to perform customized or particular tasks.

In an inheritance hierarchy, a subclass may have many levels of super classes forming a chain of inheritance as shown in Figure 7.2.

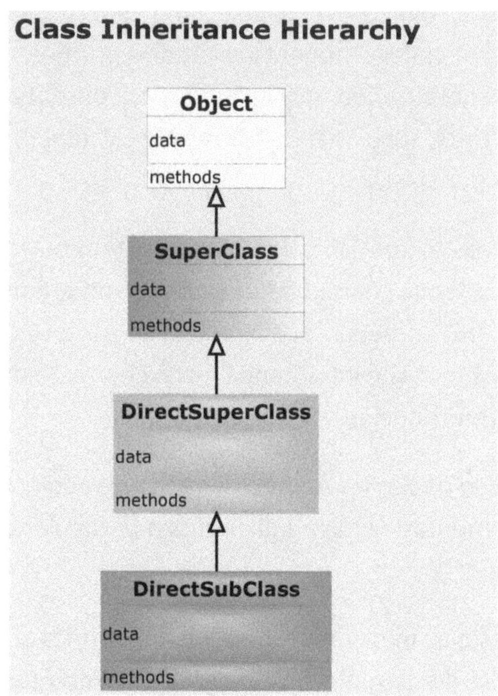

Figure 7.2 Inheritance Hierarchy

We call the class immediately above a subclass a direct super class. Similarly, that specific subclass is a direct subclass of the super class. A subclass may have many levels of indirect super classes. Regardless of the number of levels of inheritance, a subclass inherits all properties (data and methods) from its direct and indirect super classes. All Java classes inherit from the "ancestor" class **Object**.

From a design point-of-view, a top-down walk through an inheritance hierarchy represents a progression from abstraction to specialization, from the general to the specific. Following this principle of inheritance design guarantees code efficiency and reusability.

7.1.4 Code reliability

The vast number of API classes provides ample opportunities to apply inheritance in Java coding. These API classes have been written, tested, and improved by Java language developers from the language's earliest days to the present. The use of API classes as super classes increases code reliability. Modular structure in inheritance hierarchy is also a key factor in obtaining code reliability.

7.1.5 Other advantages

Inheritance in coding can simplify code design, increase coding efficiency, and increase program maintenance. It is also a foundation of polymorphism.

Simplify code design – It is much easier to inherit API classes than write your own. One might imagine how difficult writing the code for such classes as **JFrame** or **JPanel** for frame and panel management would be in designing a GUI application without the use of inheritance.

Increase coding efficiency – Simplification of code design results in greater coding efficiency. In the above example, one need not be concerned how the **JFrame** and **JPanel** classes are designed and coded; one only need be concerned with the classes' methods and calling sequences for use in the application code.

Increase program maintenance – Inheritance reflects the essential features in OOP: modular design and encapsulation. Program development can focus on the design and modification of the appropriate user-defined subclasses rather than the entire application or super classes from API libraries. Encapsulation ensures us in program maintenance without knowing details in coding.

Foundation of polymorphism – Inheritance is the foundation upon which polymorphism in achieved in coding. Polymorphism cannot be performed without use of inheritance. We discuss polymorphism in Chapter 8.

7.1.6 Disadvantages

There are several disadvantages and shortcomings regarding the use of inheritance in Java:

- Java only supports single direct super class inheritance, rather than inheritance from multiple direct super classes, as in C++. We discuss this topic in section 7.1.8.

- After an object has been instantiated from a subclass, the object cannot change its role or function. For example, an **Undergraduate** object cannot be changed to a **Graduate** object.

- Java inheritance may compromise data safety. For example, it is necessary to grant data accessibility to all objects of a subclass even though only a specific object needs to access these data from its super class.

- Multithreading objects of a subclass may cause synchronization problems. We discuss multithreading and synchronization in Chapter 14.

7.1.7 How inheritance is used in API classes

We discussed some basic concepts of inheritance relating to exception handling API classes in Chapter 6. Converting Figure 6.1 to an inheritance hierarchy chart (Figure 7.3) allows us to further discuss and explain the use of inheritance in API classes. We will apply these techniques to our inheritance design.

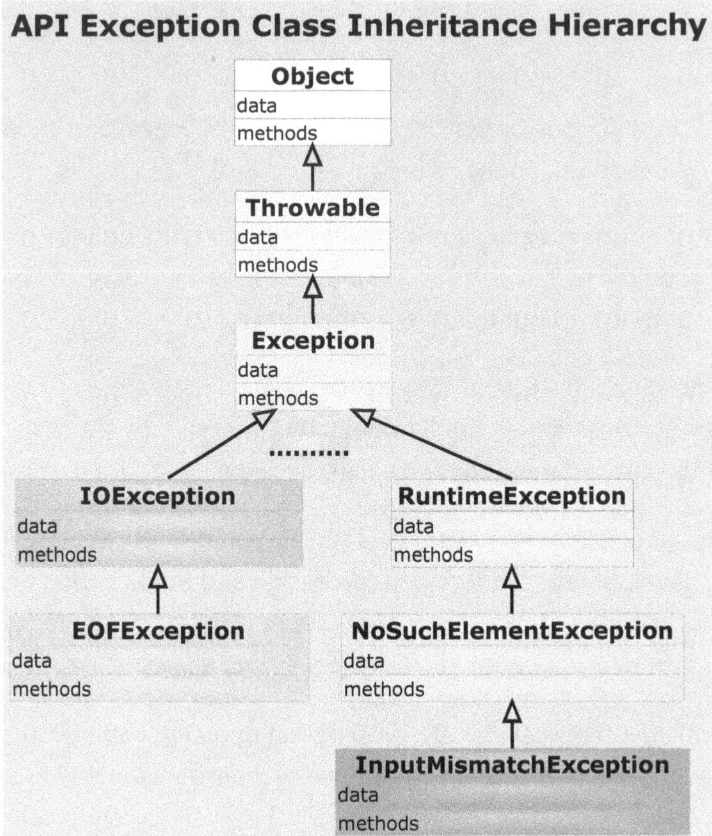

Figure 7.3 Inheritance hierarchy in exception handling API classes

We may see the following points from Figure 7.3:

- There are many levels of inheritance. It is a common feature within all API classes. Super classes and subclasses are relative terms; a subclass may be a super class for the next level of inheritance. However, once the "is a" relationship is defined the position of a super class and a subclass is fixed. This methodology can be also applied to our own inheritance design.

- Proceeding from top to bottom, each level of inheritance represents a progression from abstraction to specification, from general to specific. A subclass can directly or indirectly access all data and methods of its super classes in the inheritance hierarchy. This principle is also true in programmer-defined inheritance coding.

- A super class can be inherited by more than one subclass, i.e., a parent class may have many child classes. For example from Figure 7.3, **Object** is inherited by all other classes. You may also see this from API documentation of the **Exception** class: it has almost 80 direct subclasses. This feature of inheritance is very commonly applied in the design of large scale application software development.

- Although multiple inheritance is not allowed in Java, i.e., a subclass cannot have more than one direct super class, we can apply indirect multiple inheritance by allowing a subclass to have a direct super class and more than one interface in inheritance. We discuss interfaces in Chapter 9.

7.1.8 Three basic types of inheritance

There are three basic types of inheritance in Java: simple inheritance, multiple-level inheritance, and indirect multiple inheritance.

Simple inheritance – a super class derives one or more direct subclasses. This type of inheritance is the foundation of all other forms of inheritance. Figure 7.4 shows simple inheritance.

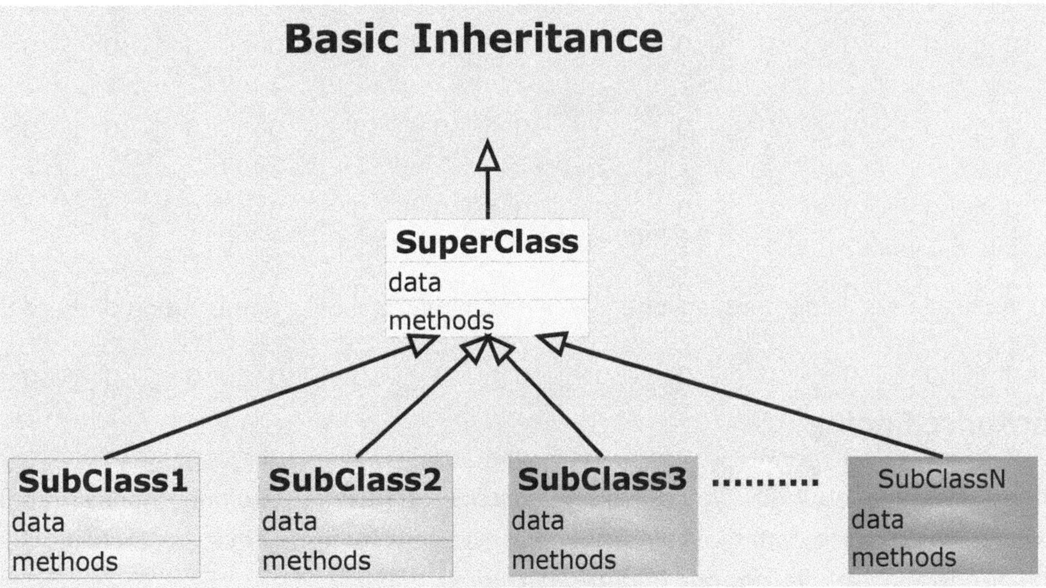

Figure 7.4 Simple inheritance

Multiple-level inheritance – There is more than one level of indirect super class or indirect subclass in the inheritance schema, as shown in Figure 7.2, Figure 7.3, and Figure 7.6.

Indirect multiple inheritances – a subclass has a direct super class and one or more interfaces in the inheritance schema, as shown in Figure 7.5. We discuss interfaces in Chapter 9.

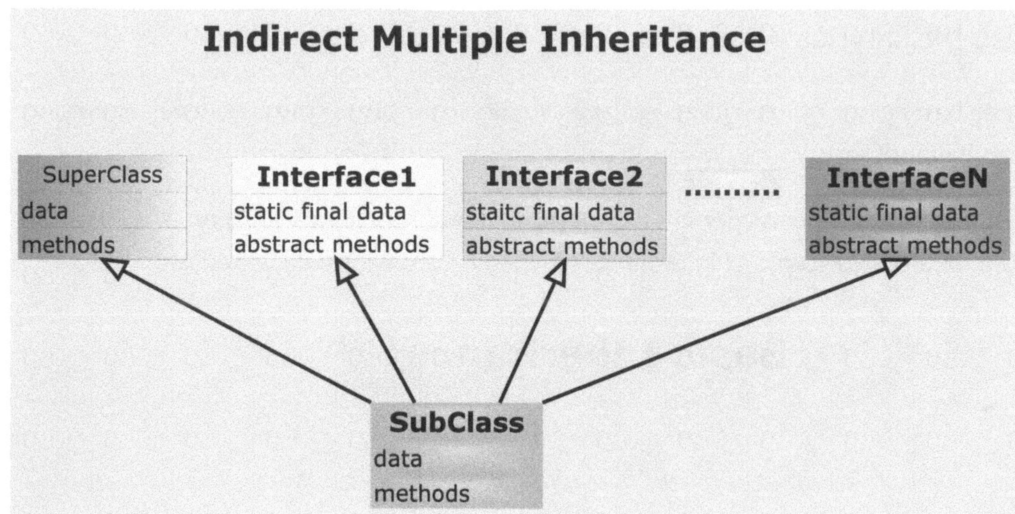

Figure 7.5 Indirect multiple inheritances

In real world application development, an inheritance design may involve a combination of these three inheritance types.

7.2 Inheritance Coding

We use examples to demonstrate how you can apply concepts and techniques of inheritance in coding. Assume we wish to design a program that calculates areas and/or volumes of circles or circular objects. First, we would like to analyze the common features of a circle. A circle can be defined by specifying:

- The coordinates of two points.
- The coordinate of one point and the radius.
- A diameter.

The circular objects can be:

- Circles, rings, and sectors in two-dimensions.
- Spheres, cylinders, cones, tori, and fans in three-dimensions.
- Consider ovals and ellipsoids as special cases of circles and circular objects.

We continue the analysis by specifying the formulas required to calculate the areas and volumes of circles or circular objects:

Area of circle: $= \pi r^2$

Surface area of sphere $= 4\pi r^2$

Volume of sphere = $4/3\pi \cdot r^3$

We also observe there are common factors in the formulas to compute circles or circular objects. For example, assuming a circle and a sphere of the same radius, the surface area of a sphere is 4 times the area of a circle; the volume of a sphere is one and one-third of the circle's area multiplied by its radius.

The above analysis clearly indicates the design forms an "is a" relationship for the calculations, as shown in Figure 7.6.

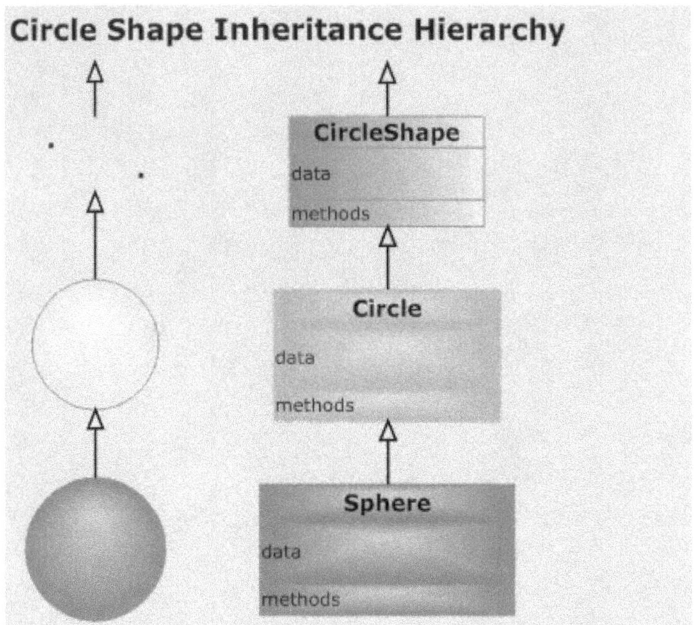

Figure 7.6 Multiple-level inheritances in circular objects

You may extend the chart to include more objects, such as sectors, rings, cylinders, tori, or cones, showing they also have "is a" relationships. You may list the formulas for computing the area, surface area, or volume of these objects to see common factors in the calculations. In summary, the common factors in a formula from a super class can be inherited by its subclasses to avoid recalculating these components. We discuss how this code can be reused in the following sections of this chapter.

7.2.1 How to code super class

Coding a super class involves highly abstractive processing. The major principle of coding a super class is to include all common features (data and methods) that apply to all of subclasses in the specified applications and eliminate all special features applying only to subclasses. For example, in the calculation of circular areas and volumes, super class **CircleShape** should include the following data and methods:

Math.PI

radius

Coordinates for two points (x1, y1), (x2, y2)

```
CircleShape();                      //Constructor
CircleShape(double radius);         //Overloaded constructor
CircleShape(double x1, double y1, double x2, double y2); //Overloaded constructor
setRadius(double radius)
setXY(double x1, double y1, double x2, double y2);
computeRadius(); //use coordinates of 2 points to compute radius
getRadius();                        //retrieve radius
```

The use of getters and setters for **x1**, **x2**, **y1**, and **y2** are irrelevant to area and volume calculations and are omitted.

The following is example code of the **CircleShape** super class:

```
//Complete code called CircleShape.java in Ch7 from the author's website
//Superclass
public class CircleShape {
   protected double radius,     //subclass may direct access the data
                    x1, y1, x2, y2;
   public CircleShape() {            //Constructor and overloaded constructors
         radius = 0.0;
         x1 = y1 = x2 = y2 = 0.0;
   }
   public CircleShape(double radius) {
         this.radius = radius;
   }
   public CircleShape(double x1, double y1, double x2, double y2) {
         this.x1 = x1;
         this.y1 = y1;
         this.x2 = x2;
         this.y2 = y2;
   }
   public void setRadius(double radius) {    //setter and getters for radius
         this.radius = radius;
   }
   public double getRadius() {
         return radius;
   }
   public void computeRadius() {     //use 2 coordinates to compute radius
```

```
        radius = Math.sqrt((x1 - x2)*(x1 - x2) + (y1 - y2) * (y1 - y2));
    }
}
```

We define all data in **CircleShape** as **protected**, allowing them to be directly accessed by subclasses. A subclass could not directly access these data if we had defined them as **private**. Access modifiers are discussed in section 7.3.

7.2.2 How to code subclass

In addition to inheriting the properties from its super class, a subclass will add its special data and methods to solve particular problems. Continuing our circular area and volume calculations from the previous section, assume we have a subclass **Circle** to compute areas of circle objects. It should have the following properties:

- New data added in **Circle – area**, double type
- Overloaded constructors – **Circle()**, **Circle(double radius)**, and **Circle(double x1, double y1, double x2, double y2)**.
- **computeArea()** – calculate the area.
- **getArea()** – return the area.

The following is the code of **Circle**:

```
//Complete code called Circle.java in Ch7 from the author's website
//Subclass Circle inherited from CircleShape
public class Circle extends CircleShape{   //Inherits CircleShape
    private double area;

    public Circle() {
        super();                                    //Call super class constructors
    }
    public Circle(double radius) {
        super(radius);
    }
    public Circle(double x1, double y1, double x2, double y2) {
        super(x1, y1, x2, y2);
        super.computeRadius();                          //Call super class method
    }
    public void computeArea() {                         //Compute area
        area = Math.PI * radius * radius;
    }

    public double getArea() {
```

```
        return area;
    }
}
```

We use keyword **super** with specified arguments to call the inherited constructors from the super class. Keyword **super** is also used to call inherited methods from super class **CircleShape**, so we don't need to rewrite the existing methods.

Note: *The calling statements of super class constructors super() must only be used in the constructors of the subclass, and they must be the first statements in the constructors.*

We may also code **Circle** as a super class with a little modification for the next level of inheritance to calculate surface areas and volumes of three-dimensional circular objects.

We modify the access modifier of **area** of **Circle** from **private** to **protected** so subclass **Sphere** can directly access its inherited data from **Circle**.

```
protected double area;
```

The complete code of **Sphere** is:

```
//Complete code called Sphere.java in Ch7 from the author's website
//Sphere inherits Circle

public class Sphere extends Circle{
    private double volume;                              //Define a new data
    public Sphere() {
        super();                                        //Call super class constructors
    }
    public Sphere(double radius) {
        super(radius);
    public Sphere(double x1, double y1, double x2, double y2) {
        super(x1, y1, x2, y2);
    }

    public void computeArea()          {                //Compute surface area
        super.computeArea();                            //Call super method
        area = 4* area;                                 //The final result
    }
    public void computeVolume() {                       //Compute volume
        super.computeArea();       //Code reuse: area of circle
        volume = 4.0/3 * radius * area;                 //The final result
    }
    public double getArea() {
        return area;
```

```
    }
    public double getVolume() {
            return volume;
    }
```

In **Sphere**, we add new data **volume** to hold the result of the volume of a **Sphere** object. In calling constructors for code reusability in **Sphere**, we first call the corresponding super class constructors. Control then goes to that constructor in **Circle.** It, in turn, will call the specified constructor in **CircleShape**. For example, in **Sphere**, we call:

```
public Sphere() {
        super();                                  //Call constructor in its super
    }
```

Then in super class **Circle**:

```
public Circle() {
        super();                                  //Call constructor in its super
    }
```

Eventually the constructor of root super class **CircleShape** will be called:

```
public CircleShape() {          //Constructor to initialize data
        radius = 0.0;
        x1 = y1 = x2 = y2 = 0.0;
    }
```

This forms a chained call, and data of a **Sphere** object is actually initialized by its super class. This works in a similar manner for other super class constructor calls.

In calculating the surface area of a **Sphere** object, we note the surface area is 4 times the area of a circle of the same radius. So, we first call **super.area()** to compute the area, then multiply the returned result by 4 to get the surface area of the sphere. A similar methodology is used in calculating the volume of a sphere. The formula to compute the volume of a sphere:

Volume of sphere = $4/3\pi \cdot r^3$

may be rewritten as:

Volume of sphere = the circle area · 4/3 · r

Therefore, we first call **super.computeArea()** to compute the area of the circle, then multiply **area** by 4/3 * r.

Although the complete formulas to compute the surface area and volume of a **Sphere** object may be directly applied in their calculation, the above examples are presented as an application of code reusability.

7.3 Access Modifiers

Data in super classes are commonly defined as **protected**, rather than **public**, so subclasses can access these data directly, without loss of encapsulation. You may also define data in super classes as **private**. In this case a subclass must call the proper methods inherited from the super class to access the data indirectly, if such methods are available in its super class. So far, we have discussed the following three types of access modifiers:

- **public**
- **protected**
- **private**

Java also provides another access modifier called **package access**, or **package**, for short. Package access will be discussed in detail in Chapter 12.

Here we discuss these three access modifiers in terms of inheritance and summarize the following rules in defining access modifiers of data in inheritance:

In super classes, most data, including static data, should be defined **protected**. Data may also be defined **private** for safety or special protection purposes. Subclasses can only access **private** data of the super class via method calls, such as getters, provided by the super class.

Sometimes the access modifiers may be defined as **private** in a super class. In this case, a subclass must call indirectly to invoke the **private** methods in its super class. For example:

```
public class SuperClass {
   ...
   private void someMethod() {
   ...
   }
   public void otherMethod() {
          someMethod();              //Call private method
   }
}
class SubClass extends SuperClass {
   ...
          otherMethod();                    //Call public method
```

```
    }
}
```

After an object of Subclass is created:

```
SubClass subClass = new SubClass();
```

We call the inherited method:

```
subClass.otherMethod();
```

to indirectly access the **private** method in a manner similar to the indirect accessing of **private** data defined in a super class.

More Info: *Although the access modifier for a method can be defined as* ***protected,*** *it can only be accessed in the same package. Detailed discussion is in section 12.1.6.*

7.4 More Discussion About Inheritance

In addition to using constructor and method overloading, method overriding is also commonly used in inheritance. We will use examples to discuss this coding technique. In this section, we also discuss object casting, object comparison, and how to use an API class to obtain information about objects.

7.4.1 Overloading

Overloading in inheritance is not limited to operations within a class but applies to the entire inheritance hierarchy. Because private constructors or methods of a super class are hidden from its subclasses, we shall pay more attention to public and protected constructors and methods. For example, a subclass can overload any public or protected methods defined in its super class. In addition, a super class or subclass can overload any of its own constructors or methods without consideration of access modifiers. We will use example of calculating areas of circular objects to explain in detail overloading in inheritance.

- Subclass overloads a method in super class. For example, **Circle** overloads **computeRadius()** method of **CircleShape**:

```
  //Complete code called CircleOverload.java in Ch7 from the author's website
public void computeRadius(double x1, double y1, double x2, double y2) {
                radius = Math.sqrt((x1 - x2)*(x1 - x2) + (y1 - y2) * (y1 - y2));
   }
```

We may call this method in a driver code to compute the area of circular objects as follows:

```
//Complete code in CircleShapeOverloadApp.java in Ch7 from the author's website
CircleOverload myCircle = new CircleOverload();
myCircle.computeRadius(0, 0, 1, 1);             //Call overloaded method
myCircle.computeArea();
System.out.println("My circle area: " + myCircle.getArea());
```

- Overload its own methods in a super class or subclass. For example, the following code overloads **computeArea()** in **Sphere**:

```
//Complete code in CircleOverloadApp.java in Ch7 from the author's website
public void computeArea(double radius) {          //method overloading
        setRadius(radius);
        super.computeArea();
        area = 4 * area;
}
```

We may call it in a driver code as:

```
//Complete code in SphereOverload.java in Ch7 from the author's website
mySphere = new SphereOverload();
mySphere.computeArea(5.5);    //Call overloaded method with radius
...
```

7.4.2 Overriding

Method overriding, or overriding for short, means methods defined in a subclass have the same signature as the methods defined in its super class or super classes. F For example, method **computerArea()** has been discussed in association with **Circle** and **Sphere**. Overriding only applies to inheritance dealing with methods in subclasses and super classes in the hierarchy. Assume a super class contains a method:

```
public class SuperClass {
   ...
   public int method(double n) {
   ...
   }
}
```

In its subclass, we define a method with the same name:

```
public class SubClass extends SuperClass {
   ...
   public int method(double n) {
   ...
   }
}
```

These two methods have the same signature, i.e., return type, name, parameter type, number of parameters, and parameter order, but perform different operations. The JVM will not confuse which method is to be executed because addresses of method calls are unique and mutually exclusive. For example, in the code:

```
SubClass subObj = new SubClass();
int num = subObj.method(10);    //call method of subclass object
```

caller **subObj.method(10)** will generate a reference to the method in the subclass. In a similar manner, the following code:

```
SuperClass superObj = new SuperClass();
int num = superObj.method(99);
```

explicitly calls the method of its super class.

An overridden method in a super class can also be called by its subclasses. It is necessary, however, to use the keyword **super** at the beginning of the calling statement. For example, the code

```
public void computeArea() {   //Compute surface area of sphere
   super.computeArea();       //Call super class overridden method first
   area = 4* area;            //Compute the surface area
}
```

shows that within method **computeArea()** of class **Sphere** the overridden method **computeArea()** in super class **Circle** is being called, thereby promoting code reusability.

Overloading and overriding are both commonly used in coding. However, their use may cause confusion for beginners. Table 7.1 shows the differences between overloading and overriding.

Table 7.1 Differences between overloading and overriding

Overloading	Overriding
Methods with different signatures – type, number, or order of parameters is different. Return type is not part of judgment for legal overloading. Can be in the same class or in different classes in the hierarchy. Normally overloaded methods carry out the same operation.	Methods with the same signature – type, number, order, and return type of parameters are the same. Must be in different classes in the hierarchy. Normally carry out different operations.
someMethod(int, double, long)	someMethod(int, double long)
someMethod(double, int)	someMethod(int, double, long)

Note: *Access modifier of an overriding method in a subclass must be the same or higher than the method in its super class; otherwise a syntax error will occur.*

7.4.3 Hidden data

In inheritance, by applying the same principle of method overriding, we may define data with exactly the same data types and names in super classes and subclasses. When a subclass accesses its own data, the inherited data with the same names as in its super class will be automatically hidden. However, if a subclass wants to access the inheritable data from its super class, the keyword **super** must be used to differentiate them. For example,

```
public class SuperClass {
   protected int n;
```

```
   void method() {...
     }
}

class SubClass extends SuperClass {
    protected int n;
    public void method() {
         n = 100;              //Access its own data, data in super class is hidden
         super.n = 10;         //Access super class data
    }
}
```

instance variable **n** is defined in both the super class and subclass. When **n** is directly accessed as instance variable within its method in the subclass , **n** in the super class will be hidden. However, in using the form **super.n**, the reference goes to **n** in the super class and instance variable **n** in the subclass will be automatically hidden.

It should be noted the name of a parameter may be the same as the name of an instance variable. The concept of hidden data is not applicable to parameters. For example,

```
public class SomeClass {
   int n = 5;                  //instance data
   void method(int n) {        //Parameter as a local variable
         n = n + 10;           //Only change locally; no relation to instance data
   }
}
```

in **method(int n)**, **n** represents a parameter serving as a local variable to method **method**. After **method** is called and receives the value of **n** from the calling routine, no relationship or association exists outside of **method** with the class. The scope of parameter **n** is only inside the method, and after execution of the method is completed it will be cleared by the JVM garbage collector. However, it is recommended that the use of the same name for parameters and instance data be avoided to increase code readability and understanding.

3W Overloading *refers to the concept of methods of the same name using different signature;* ***overriding*** *refers to many methods different classes of the hierarchy sharing the same signature. Data-hidden means data having the same name defined in super classes and subclasses will be mutually-exclusive. The JVM will automatically hide data in the super class when the data is accessed in its subclass. The keyword* ***super*** *is used to indicate to the JVM the data in the super class is being accessed.*

7.4.4 Object information

In coding we often need to know information about an object, for example, the name of the object, the class name to which an object belongs, the super class or inheritance hierarchy information of an object, knowledge if two objects belong to the same class, et cetera. The use of methods in API classes **Object** and **Class** allows us to conveniently retrieve this information. Table 7.2 lists commonly used methods in **Object** and **Class**.

Table 7.2 Commonly used methods to retrieve object info in **Object** and **Class**

Method	Class	Function
boolean equals(Object)	Object	Returns true if the address of calling object is the same as address as the object in the argument; otherwise return false.
Class getClass()	Object	Returns string representing class name of Class to which object belongs.
String toString()	Object	Returns class information including class name and hexadecimal address represented by @hash code.
static Class forName(String)	Class	Returns the object of Class specified by the string argument as the class name. Must provide exception handling.
String getName()	Class	Returns name of the class or interface as string.
Class getSuperclass()	Class	Returns the super class of calling object.

Let's first discuss how to use some of the methods listed in Table 7.2.

Example 1. Use methods **equals()** and **toString()** of Object to display object information.

```
//Complete code in ObjectClassTest.java in Ch7 from the author's Website
Circle circle1 = new Circle();
Sphere sphere = new Sphere();
Circle circle2 = circle1;            //referencing
Circle circle3 = new Circle();       //creating another object of Circle

if (circle1.equals(circle2)) //Call Object's equals() method
   System.out.println("Two objects are equal\n" + circle1 + "equals"
    + circle2);
else
   System.out.println("Two objects are not equal\n" + circle1 + " not equal"
    + circle2);

if (circle1.equals(circle3))
   System.out.println("Two objects are equal\n" + circle1 + " equals"
    + circle3);
else
   System.out.println("Two objects are not equal\n" + circle1 + " not equal"
    + circle3);
```

Obviously, **circle.equals(circle)** is **true** because **circle2** is an alias of **circle**. However, **circle1.equals(circle3)** is **false** because these entities represent two different objects, despite having exactly the same initialized data. The execution result of the code is:

```
Two objects are equal
Circle@61de33 equals Circle@61de33
Two objects are not equal
Circle@61de33 not equal Circle@14318bb
```

Note that in the code:

```
System.out.println("Two objects are the equal\n" + circle1 + "equals"
```

```
    + circle2);
```

circle2 is short for **circle2.toString()**. Overriding the virtual **toString()** method provided by **System.Object** allows us to display the name of the class to which **circle2** belongs and its hexadecimal address after the "at sign", @, rather than only the name of the class.

Example 2. Use of **getClass()** in Object and **getName()** in Class to obtain object information.

```
//Complete code in ObjectClassTest.java in Ch7 from the author's Website
Circle circle = new Circle();
Class theClass = null;              //Define a reference of Class
theClass=circle.getClass();         //Return the class of circle
System.out.println("Class name of circle: " + theClass.getName());

   if (circle.getClass().getName().equals("Sphere"))
          System.out.println("it's a Sphere object");
   else
          System.out.println("it's not a Sphere object");
```

The execution output as:

```
Class name of circle: Circle
it's not a Sphere object
```

Example 3. Write a utility class using static methods to retrieve information about the object.

```
//Complete code in MyClass.java in Ch7 from the author's Website
public class MyClass {         //Utility class
    public static void printClassName(Object object) {  //print class of object
                System.out.println("The class of " + object + " is " + object.
          getClass().getName());
     }
    public static String getInheritanceTree(Class aClass){//print hierarchy chain
                //Use of API StringBuilder class to append strings
          StringBuilder superclasses = new StringBuilder();

                superclasses.append( "\n");              //append method
          Class theClass = aClass;

while ( theClass != null ) { //obtain all super classes of the object
          superclasses.append( theClass );
          superclasses.append( "\n" );
          theClass = theClass.getSuperclass();    //Return the super class
          }
          superclasses.append( "\n" );
          return superclasses.toString();//Return all super class names as string
   }
```

```
}
```

The following test code calls the methods in the above utility class to print information about the object:

```
//Complete code in ObjectClassTest.java in Ch7 from the author's Website
Circle circle = new Circle();
MyClass.printClassName(circle);                          //Call static method

Class theClass = null;
   theClass = circle.getClass();                    //Return the class of object
try {
       theClass = Class.forName("Sphere"); //obtain the reference of Sphere
       System.out.println(MyClass.getInheritanceTree(theClass));
      //Call method to print the inheritance hierarchy list
}
catch(ClassNotFoundException e){
       System.out.println(e);
}
```

Because method **forName()** in **Class** requires exception handling, we provide a try- catch mechanism to satisfy it. The following is the result of execution:

```
The class of Circle@61de33 is Circle
class Sphere
class Circle
class CircleShape
class java.lang.Object
```

We see the output represents an inverted hierarchy of the inheritance for class **Sphere**.

Example 4. Use of methods provided in **Object** and **Class** demonstrating how to overload and override methods **equals()** and **toString()** of **Object**. This will allow **equals()** to determine if two objects belong to the same class. It can also be used to judge if two objects have exactly the same data. After overriding **toString()** in this example code**,** it will return the information about the object's data.

```
//Complete code in Circle.java in Ch7 from the author's Website
//Overload Object's equals() to compare if two objects belong to the same class
public boolean equals(String className) {
         if (this.getClass().getName().equals(className))
            return true;
         else
                return false;
}
//Override Object's equals() to compare if data in two objects are same
public boolean equals(Object object) {     //equals() overriding
```

```
  if (object instanceof Circle)           //See if two objects in the same class
    {
        Circle circle = (Circle) object;
        if (radius == circle.getRadius())        //Data are the same
          return true;                           //Return true
        }
        return false;                            //Return false
  }
//Override Object's toString(), so it returns data of Circle object
public String toString() {                  //override the toString() method
  if (x1 == 0.0 && y1 == 0.0 && x2 == 0.0 && y2 == 0.0 && radius != 0.0)
                                            //return radius
        return ("radius: " + radius + "\n");
  else {
    String message = "(" + x1 + "," + y1 + "), ("
                                  + x2 + "," + y2 + ")\t"
                                  + "radius: " + radius + "\n";
    return message;
  }
}
```

In this example, the first occurrence of method **equals()** overloads method **equals()** in **Object** to compare if two objects belong to the same class. It utilizes **getClass()** in **Object** and **getName()** in **Class** to make the judgment. The second **equals()** overrides the **equals()** method in **Object** to compare if two objects have exactly same data in **radius**. It also uses special operator **instanceof** to see if two objects belong to the same class. Its syntax as follows:

objectName instanceof ClassName

wherein:

objectName – object name as first operand.

ClassName – class name as the second operand.

It carries out the following operation: if **objectName** is an object of **ClassName**, return **true**; otherwise return **false**.

It is very common to override **toString()** in **Object** to return data of a particular object. In an output statement, we often use the object name to call **toString()** as:

```
System.out.println(myCircle);
```

It is equivalent to:

```
System.out.println(myCircle.toString());
```

The JVM automatically connects **toString()** to the object and makes the method call. If the object does not override **toString()**, **Object**'s method **toString()** will be used to return the address of the object.

The following code demonstrates how to call the methods in **Example 4**:

```
//Complete code in OverridingEqualsTest.java in Ch7 from the author's Website
Circle circle = new Circle();
if (circle1.equals("Circle"))
      System.out.println("It's a Circle object");
else
   System.out.println("It's not a Circle object");

Circle circle2 = new Circle(10.09);
Circle circle3 = new Circle(10.09);
Circle circle4 = new Circle(0, 0, 1, 1);

if (circle2.equals(circle3))
   System.out.println("Two objects are the same.");
else
   System.out.println("Two objects are not the same.");
System.out.println("circle4 data: " + circle4);
```

The following results will be displayed after execution:

```
It's a Circle object.
Two objects are the same.
circle4 data: (0.0,0.0), (1.0,1.0)  radius: 1.4142135623730951
```

Note: *Only the overridden form of* ***toString()*** *can be directly called by the object name.*

7.5 Abstract Class

Abstraction is a very important design and coding concept in OOP. In Java, we use the keyword **abstract** to denote an abstract class. This is to be compared with C++, which requires no keyword and the concept is virtually recognized. In this section, we discuss features of abstraction in super classes, and then move on to the design and coding of abstract classes using particular examples.

7.5.1 High generalization - abstraction

By examining the super classes in hierarchy charts in API classes or user-defined super classes, for example, **Object,** or **CircleShape**, the following conclusion may be drawn: The higher the level of super class, the higher abstraction it represents. We may say abstraction is the highest generalization of design and coding in application development.

Design and code abstract classes are based on this concept. For example, in area or surface area calculations for circular shapes, super class **CircleShape** has abstractly covered the one common feature of circle-related objects – radius. It does not include other data associated with special circular shapes, such as height for cylinders, outside diameter for rings, et cetera. These special features do not apply to all circle-related objects, therefore they should not be included in super class **CircleShape**.

If we raise the abstraction to a higher level to define all geometric objects or shapes, we may add another super class, **Shape**, on top of **CircleShape**. Class **Shape** not only includes circle-related shapes, but also covers lines, rectangles, cubes, triangles, and higher-order polygonal objects. The data applying to all objects in the **Shape** class should be the coordinates of two points. These data will be inherited to it subclasses.

Because of the extremely high level of abstraction in abstract classes, it is meaningless to instantiate any objects from these classes: abstract classes cannot create objects in Java. We discuss this concept further in Chapter 8.

Now let's introduce how to code an abstract class.

7.5.2 Abstract classes and abstract methods

We use keyword **abstract** to define an abstract class as follows:

```
public abstract class ClassName {
   //Define data
   ...
   //Define methods
   ...
   //Define also abstract methods
   public abstract returnType methodName(argumentList);
}
```

Although an abstract class may contain all regular methods, it normally includes some abstract methods. The abstract methods serve as prototypes and must be implemented by the subclasses inheriting the abstract class. The constructors in an abstract class can only be called internally by its methods and cannot be used to instantiate an object.

As discussed in the above section, an abstract class is a high level class in the hierarchy and is normally placed at the top of the hierarchy. It represents all features of its subclasses. There may be more than one abstract class in a large-scale or complicated application.

Let's discuss some particular examples in coding abstract classes.

Example 1. Modify **CircleShape** and make it as an abstract class.

```
//Complete code in Shape.java in Ch7 from the author's Web site
public abstract class CircleShape {
   protected double radius;
   protected double x1, y1, x2, y2;
   //Other statements
   ...
```

```
    public abstract void computeArea();           //Define an abstract method
    public abstract void computeVolume();
}
```

Example 2. Define an abstract class representing all human beings as a person.

```
//Complete code in Person.java in Ch7 from the author's Website
//abstract class
public abstract class Person {
    protected String lastName, firstName;
    protected char sex;
    protected byte age;
    protected String address;
    public  Person(String  lastName,  String  firstName,  char  sex,  byte  age,
    String address) {
            this.lastName = lastName;
            this.firstName = firstName;
            this.sex = sex;
            this.age = age;
            this.address = address;
    }
    public String toString() {
            String  message  =  "Last  name:  "  +  lastName  +  ",  "  +  "first  name:  "
            + firstName + "\n"
                                        + "Sex: " + sex + "\n"
                                        + "Age: " + age + "\n"
                                        + "Address: " + address + "\n";
             return message;
            }
}
```

This abstract class can be used for all programs dealing with people, because it represents all basic features of a person. Overridden method **toString()** returns the data defined in **Person**. You may note there is no abstract method in **Person**.

In an application that calculates the salary of employees, we may code a subclass **Employee2** that inherits **Person** as follows:

```
//Complete code called Employee2.java in Ch7 from the author's Website
public abstract class Employee2 extends Person {
    protected String employeeID;
    protected String jobTitle;
    protected byte seniority;
    protected double salary;

    public Employee2(String lastName, String firstName, char sex, byte age,
```

```
                                String address, String employeeID, String jobTitle,
byte seniority) {
          super(lastName, firstName, sex, age, address);
          this.employeeID = emloyeeID;
          this.jobTitle = jobTitle;
          this.seniority = seniority;
   }
   public abstract void computeSalary();    //Define an abstract method
   public String toString() {               //Override Person's toString()
          String message = super.toString() + "EmployeeID: " + employeeID + "\n"
                                + "jobTitle: " + jobTitle + "\n"
                                + "Seniority: " + seniority + "\n";
          return message;
   }
}
```

***3W** An abstract class is a high-level generalization of its subclasses and is placed at the top of hierarchy. An abstract class is defined by keyword **abstract**. We may define all types of data and methods in an abstract class; however, normally an abstract class only includes abstract methods. An abstract method is also defined by keyword **abstract**. An abstract method is the prototype of a method only and does not provide any body of code. An inherited subclass must implement the abstract method to avoid a syntax error.*

7.5.3 Apply abstract class in geometric computing

In this section we use the knowledge and coding skills discussed in abstract classes to calculate the areas and volumes of geometric objects. We modify **CircleShape** so it will:

1. Add abstract class **Shape** at the top of **CircleShape**. This class represents all geometric objects.
2. Inherit **Shape** class and modify **CircleShape** as an abstract class called **CircleShape2**.
3. Modify **Circle** class so it will inherit **CircleShape2** and override **toString()** in **CircleShape2**.
4. Write a driver code to test the program.

The following is abstract class **Shape**:

```
//Complete code called Shape.java in Ch7 from the author's Website
public abstract Shape {
   protected double x1, y1, x2, y2;
   public Shape() {
          x1 = y1 = x2 = y2 = 0.0;
   }
   public Shape(double x1, double y1, double x2, double y2) {
```

```
                this.x1 = x1;
                this.y1 = y1;
                this.x2 = x2;
                this.y2 = y2;
        }
    public abstract void computeArea();             //Define abstract methods
    public abstract void computeVolume();
}
```

The following is the modified **CircleShape2**:

```
//Complete code called CircleShape2.java in Ch7 from the author's Website
public abstract class CircleShape2 extends Shape { //Abstract class defines
        //another abstract class

    public CircleShape2(double x1, double y1, double x2, double y2) {
            super(x1, y1, x2, y2);              //Call constructor
    }
...
public String toString() {              //Overrides Shape's toString()
            return super.toString() + "Radius: " + radius + "\n";
    }
}
```

The following is a code segment from **Circle2**:

```
//Complete code called Circle2.java in Ch7 from the author's Website
public class Circle2 extends CircleShape2 {
    ...
    public void computeVolume() {}              //Implement abstract method

    public String toString() {                  //override the toString() method
            return super.toString() + "Area: " + area + "\n";
      }
}
```

Although there is no volume calculation in a circle object, we have to implement the method **computeVolume()** with an empty body of code to satisfy the requirement of implementation; otherwise it will be a syntax error. In overriding **toString()**, we call **toString()** in CircleShape2 first to obtain the **radius**, and then call **toString()** in **Shape** to return the coordinates of two points on a circle. Note that if the radius, rather than two points on a circle is used when the circle object is instantiated, **toString()** from **Shape** will display the coordinates as (0.0, 0.0), (0.0, 0.0).

We can also write code to calculate other geometric objects, such as rectangles. The following code shows class **Rectangle** inherits from **Shape**:

```
//Complete code called Rectangle.java in Ch7 from the author's Website
public class Rectangle extends Shape {              //inherit from Shape
   protected double height, length;
   protected double area;
   public Rectangle(double x1, double y1, double x2, double y2) {
         super(x1, y1, x2, y2);                               //Call constructor
         computeHeight();
         computeLength();
   }
   public Rectangle(double height, double length) {      //Constructor overloading
         this.height = height;
         this.length = length;
   }
   ...
   public void computeHeight() {                              //Calculate height
         double height = Math.abs(x1 - x2);
         setHeight(height);
   }
   public void computeLength() {                              //Calculate length
         double length = Math.abs(y1 - y2);
         setLength(length);
   }
   public void computeArea() {                                //Compute area
         area = height * length;
   }
   public void computeVolume() { }                   //Must implement it
   ...
}
```

In this example, there are two ways to create an object of **Rectangle**: if two point coordinates are given to create a square, the constructor in **Shape** is called by **super()**; if the height and length are given, the constructor in **Rectangle** is called. This code also uses the **abs()** method in class **Math** to correctly calculate the **height** and **length**. It should be noted again that although there is no volume associated with a rectangle, we must implement the method **computeVolume()** with an empty body of code.

The drive code is shown as follows:

```
//Complete code called ShapeApp.java in Ch7 from the author's Website
Circle2 circle = new Circle2(12.98);
circle.computeArea();
System.out.println("Circle area: " + circle);
```

```
Rectangle rec1 = new Rectangle(0, 0, 1, 1);
rec1.computeArea();
System.out.println("Rec1: " + rec1);
```

The output is shown as follows:

```
Circle area: (0.0,0.0), (0.0,0.0)
Radius: 12.98
Area: 529.2967869138698

Rec1: (0.0,0.0), (1.0,1.0)
Height: 1.0
Length: 1.0
Area: 1.0
```

7.6 What Is A Final Class?

There are many final classes in Java API libraries, e. g., **String**, **Math**, et cetera. Although There are many final classes in Java API libraries, e. g., **String**, **Math**, et cetera. Although programmers may not often code their own final classes, final classes and final methods have unique features for use in code: a final class cannot be inherited and cannot be overridden; a final method is executed faster than a regular method. Let's discuss final classes in detail.

7.6.1 Why final class cannot be inherited

For purposes of code safety and robustness, we sometimes need to prohibit the inheritance of a class by a subclass. For example, in class **Math** inheritance is prohibited to guarantee correctness and accuracy of the class's inherent calculations. A final class is placed at the bottom of the hierarchy. In addition to automatically inheriting the **Object** class, a final class may exist independently and perform designated operations and calculations, such as the management of passwords, obtaining database information, et cetera.

Final classes also execute faster than regular classes. Because final methods cannot be overridden their address bindings are completed at compile-time rather than run-time. The use of final classes is recommended when no inheritance is expected or required by the application. It is important to note the differences between a final data and a final class. A final data is constant and its value cannot be modified after initialization; a final class cannot be inherited.

7.6.2 Define a final class

A class is defined as a final class through the use of the keyword **final** in the class definition:

```
public final class SomeClass {
   ...
}
```

or

```
public final class SomeClass extends SuperClass {
   ...
}
```

The methods of a final class are also defined as final. This classification does not apply to the data definitions in either the class or its methods.

7.6.3 Cannot override final methods

A method may be defined as final within any regular class. Although a class with a final method can be inherited, the final method in the class cannot be overridden by its subclasses. Many API classes have final methods. For example, **print()** and **println()** in **System.out** and all methods in **Math** are defined as final methods. In application software development, methods performing special calculations or operations are often defined as final methods. The syntax to define a method as final is to place the keyword **final** at the beginning of the method after the access modifier:

```
public final String printVersion() {          //Define a final method
   return version;
}
```

7.6.4 Final parameters

A final parameter cannot have its content or value modified after it receives the data from its argument:

```
public void setVerison(final String version) {    //Define a final parameter
   this.version = version;
}
```

A final parameter cannot have its content or value modified after it receives the data from its argument:

```
version = "other version…";                                     //invalid operation
```

7.6.5 Improve speed of execution

A final class can improve speed of execution because:

- It does not involve inheritance and overriding.

- It uses static binding. That means the address referencing and class loading are completed during the compiler-time, rather than run-time.

- It doesn't require extra time and space for JVM to produce dynamic address referencing due to overriding. And

- The above mentioned structure and constraints of a final class require less time associated with simplified JVM garbage collection requirements.

But in some cases, use of final methods alone may not achieve increasing speed of execution. That is because the method referencing and loading may not occurr during compiler-time for all final methods.

Assume class **C** inherited from class **B** and class **B** inherited from class **A**, which contains a final method. For **C**, calling the final method of **A** is indeed an inline compilation or static binding. However, for **A** and **B** there may be no such method call at all. Another situation may exist at run-time wherein the JVM may not load the final method that object **C** wanted to call. In these cases, the speed of execution may not be improved.

Assume class **C** inherited from class **B** and class **B** inherited from class **A**, which contains a final method. For **C**, calling the final method of **A** is indeed an inline compilation or static binding. However, for **A** and **B** there may be no such method call at all. Another situation may exist at run-time wherein the JVM may not load the final method that object **C** wanted to call. In these cases, the speed of execution may not be improved.

Exercises

1. Use examples to explain the meaning of the expression: "Don't reinvent wheels."

2. Why and how can inheritance increase code-reliability?

3. List a minimum of three pairs of classes that have an "is a" relationship in each pair. List a minimum of three pairs of classes having a "has a" relationship in each pair. Explain your answers.

4. Use examples to explain the characteristics and design features between a super class and its subclass(es).

5. Why can a super class represent its subclasses?

6. Use examples to support the statement "a super class and a subclass are relative term."

7. Given the following classes, list them in order of inheritance hierarchy from super class to subclasses:

a. Worker

b. Manager

c. GeneralManager

d. Person

e. Employee

8. Given the following list of classes, indicate which classes have "is a" relationships and which have "has a" relationships.

    a. Product

    b. Computer

    c. Book

    d. Dog

    e. Person

    f. Cat

    g. Pets

9. Continued from Question 8: Draw an inheritance hierarchy chart showing all classes having "is a" relationships.

10. What are the three basic inheritance models in Java? Explain the characteristics of each model.

11. Assume that each side has the same length in the triangle and triangular pyramid. Apply inheritance to write a super class and subclass to compute the area of triangle and the surface area of tri-vertebral. Pay attention in code-reusable in your coding. You need also to override **toString()** methods in both of super class and subclass so they will return the data of an triangle object and the data of tri-vertebral object respectively. Write a driver code to test your classes, document and print your source code, and save the files.

12. Use principles of inheritance to write code calculating the area, surface area, and volume of rectangular objects. First, write a super class, then write a subclass that inherits from the super class to compute areas of rectangles, including squares. Finally, write another subclass that inherits from the super class above to compute surface areas and volumes of cuboids. Pay attention to code reusability in coding. Override **toString()** methods in all developed classes to return the proper data from each object. Write a driver code to test your program. Create different rectangular objects with a variety of data for use in computing their areas, surface areas, and/or volumes, as applicable to the instantiated objects. Document and print the source code. Save all files.

13. Summarize the information that should be included in retrieving object data. How would you analyze and include these data? How would you return these data for a particular object in the code? Show examples.

14. Using example code **MyClass**, discussed in 7.4.4, modify the classes created in Exercise 12 to print out information about the object data. Write a driver code to test your program. Document and print the source code. Save the files.

15. What is an abstract class? Why would you use a n abstract class? List at least two examples of abstract classes.

16. List the features of a final class. In what situation(s) would you use final classes and final methods?

17. Explain the differences between a final class, a final method, and a final argument.

18. **Project**: Geometry computing program. Based on **Question 11** and **Question 12**, design an abstract class respectively in triangular program and rectangular program. This abstract class will cover all features (data and methods) of triangles and tri-vertebral related objects or features of rectangles and cuboids. You should define these added methods as abstract. Modify the existing methods if necessary. Write a driver code to test your program. Create a variety of object with different data. Display the calculation results. Document and print the source code. Save the files.

19. **Project**: Bank account program. Design an abstract class called **BankAccount** first. This abstract class should include the following data and abstract methods:

    a. Balance

    b. Number of deposits

    c. Number of withdrawals

    d. Interest rate = 0.055 (static data)

    e. Service charge = $2.00 (static data)

    f. **deposit()** – method to process the deposits. Use amount of deposit as argument. It should update the balance and number of deposits.

    g. **withdraw()** –method to process the withdrawals. Use amount of withdrawals as an argument. It should update the balance and number of withdrawals.

    h. **calculateInterest()** – Use the following formula to calculate the monthly interests earned:

        i. monthly interest rate = interest rate/12

        ii. monthly interest = balance * monthly interest rate

        iii. balance = balance + monthly interest

i. **chargeProcess()** – an abstract method to calculate the service charge.

Write an inherited class called **SavingsAccount**. In addition to inheriting all features from super class **BankAccount**, it should have the following data and methods:

a. **inactive** – boolean type data; default: true.

b. **SavingAccount()** – constructor. Process the initial account balance.

c. **chargeProcess()** – abstract method implemented from its super class. The formula for calculating the service charge is:

   Service charge = $2.00 * (number of deposits + number of withdrawals)

d. **deposit()** - override the super class method. First, it will check the status of **inactive**. If **inactive** is false, display the status and stop further processing. Otherwise, call method **deposit()** from its super class to update the balance. Incorporate code reusability.

e. **withdraw()** – override the super class method. First, it will check the status of **inactive**. If **inactive** is false, display the status and stop further processing. Otherwise, verify the current balance to make certain the amount of the withdrawal is less than or equal to the balance. If the amount of the withdrawal is not valid, display the information and cancel the transaction.

Write the driver code to test your program. Create different accounts and call a variety of methods to verify they are working properly. Display the outputs. Document and print the project. Save all files.

"Kill two birds with one stone."

– Chinese idiom

Chapter 8 Polymorphism

We all experience and use many kinds of polymorphism in our daily lives, from the description of a person's behavior, e.g., "multiple personalities", to "three-in-one" household products and "multi-function" devices. Computers may be the best known example of polymorphism. Polymorphism makes our lives more convenient.

Polymorphism is one of the three most important coding features in OOP. In Java polymorphism is realized by using inheritance, overriding, and superclass type-casting. In this chapter, we will first discuss the characteristics of these techniques and then introduce how to use polymorphism in coding to solve specified problems.

8.1 General Introduction Of Polymorphism

A computer language is not considered a powerful dynamic-binding language if it does not support polymorphism. Java provides improved polymorphic coding techniques over C/C++ and makes them much more simple, standardized, and applicable to solving problems in software development. For example, Java eliminated operator overloading, which sometimes proves confusing to programmers. It also eliminated some special requirements, such as virtual member functions, in using polymorphism.

Applying polymorphism in coding is not an easy job, and it involves many coding techniques. For example, to achieve polymorphism in Java you must meet special requirements for the methods performing the polymorphic calls in a superclass. It also requires that the subclass override or implement these methods to perform the particular tasks in polymorphic ways. And, it involves the writing of specialized driver code to perform dynamic binding in the execution of the polymorphic tasks.

8.1.1 Polymorphic problems

Let's discuss some typical examples of using polymorphism in software development.

Problem 1. A credit card company needs to send account information to thousands of customers. Each customer is represented as an object within the Java accounting software. How would you write code to solve this problem in an efficient way?

Problem 2. Define special keys/functions on a standard keyboard. For example, based upon different applications, a function key, for example, F1, may have different meanings or actions to take. How would you write code to perform such a task?

Problem 3. How can you write code to efficiently compute areas of related geometric objects discussed in Chapter 3?

Our answers to solve these problems are to use polymorphism.

8.1.2 The benefits of using polymorphism

There are five advantages or benefits to be gained by using polymorphism in programs:

1. Substitutability. You can easily add more functionality by simply replacing existing code with new code designed to carry out the new task. For example, if polymorphism works for circle objects, it will also work for circle-related related objects such as spheres, cones, rings, and cylinders. Figure 8.1 shows this concept.

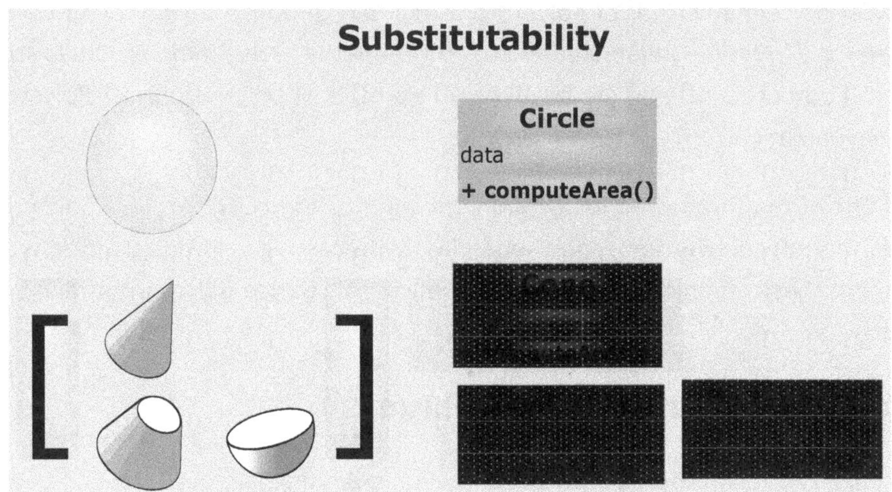

Figure 8.1 Substitutability in polymorphism

2. Extensibility. Polymorphism can easily extend an existing functionality to a new one without affecting the existing features of polymorphism, inheritance, and execution of the original environment. It is easily obtained by incorporating new subclasses. For example, based on a working polymorphism for cones, half-cones, and half-spheres, it will be much easier to add new sphere-related objects, as shown in Figure 8.2.

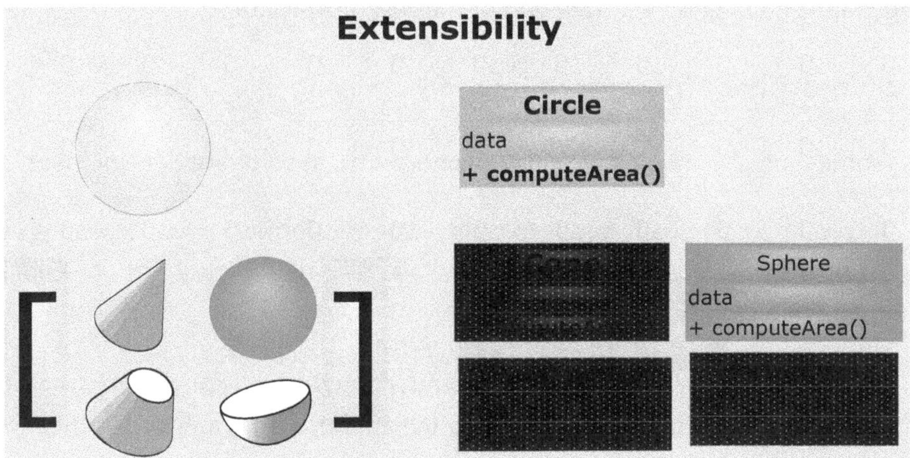

Figure 8.2 Extensibility in polymorphism

3. Interfaceability. Polymorphism is achieved in Java by first providing a method signature in a superclass for its subclasses. We may consider this mechanism to be an interface declared in the superclass and implemented by its subclasses to carry out particular calculations, as shown in Figure 8.3.

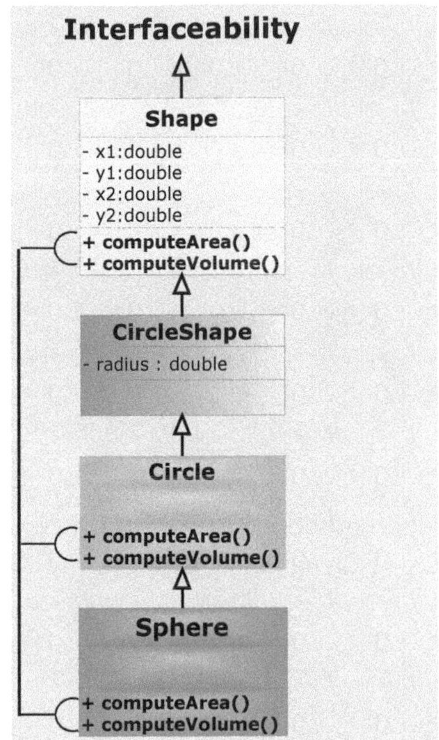

Figure 8.3 Interface-ability in polymorphism

For example, superclass **Shape** declares two methods, **computeArea()** and **computeVolume()**, for its subclasses **Circle** and **Sphere**. **Circle** and **Sphere** must, in turn, implement or override these two methods to execute in a polymorphic manner.

4. Flexibility. It is obvious polymorphism in coding can be achieved in a different ways.
5. Simplicity. Polymorphism simplifies code modification and code maintenance, especially in large-scale software development.

It should be noted the use of polymorphism will not increase execution speed; it may even reduce execution speed. Polymorphism is based on dynamic binding in which memory allocations are resolved by the JVM at execution time. Dynamic binding and static binding are discussed in Section 8.4.

8.1.3 A walk in polymorphism

Let's first observe the result of execution from the following code:

```
//The complete code called SuperClass.java in Ch8 from the author's website
//demo polymorphic method
public class SuperClass {
```

```
 public String method() {
   return "from SuperClass...";
  }
 public void otherMethod()
   {System.out.println("from SuperClass otherMethod()...");}
 }

class SubClass extends SuperClass {
 public String method() {                    //Override super class method
   return "from subClass...";
   }
 }
```

In this example, **Subclass** overrides **method()** in its superclass. Note the superclass contains another method, **othermethod()**, that is not overridden by **Subclass**. The following is the driver code:

```
//Complete code in Ch8 called PolymorphismTest.java from the author's website

public class PolymorphismTest {
   public static void main( String args[] )
   {
      SubClass b = new SubClass();

      SuperClass supper = b;        //or SuperClass supper = (SuperClass) b;
                                    //it makes object cast to its superclass

      System.out.println(supper.method());        //call subclass method
      supper.otherMethod();                       //call superclass method
   }
}
```

We created a **Subclass** object, **b**, and then cast it to its superclass type, **SuperClass**. The result of execution is:

```
from subClass...
from SuperClass otherMethod()...
```

It may seem surprising **supper.method()** invokes **method()** from its subclass rather than its own **method()**. As **otherMethod()** is not overridden by the subclass, there should be no doubt it is invoked in the execution of **super.otherMethod()**.

Let's keep this as a mystery for a while and make some changes in the code by re-establishing the superclass an abstract class and its **method()** as an abstract method:

```
//Complete code called SuperClass2.java in Ch8 from the author's website
```

```
public abstract class SuperClass2 {
   public abstract String method();  //abstract method

   public void otherMethod()
          {System.out.println("from SuperClass otherMethod()...");}
}
```

Due to the fact **SubClass** has already implemented **method()** it inherited, we do not need to make any change in **SubClass**. After execution, it shows exactly the same result as the original coding scenario.

Based on these facts from our observation, we may draw the following conclusion: When a subclass overrides a method from its superclass—even though the object of the subclass has been cast as a reference to its superclass—it still calls the method from the subclass, not the method in its superclass. This is a rule of polymorphism.

From the conclusion above, we may extend our example by adding more subclasses to examine the rule:

```
//Complete code called SuperClass3.java in Ch8 from the author's website
public class SuperClass3 {
 public String method() {
    return "from SuperClass3...";
 }

 public void otherMethod() {
   System.out.println("from SuperClass3 otherMethod()...");
   }
 }

class SubClass3 extends SuperClass3 {
 public String method() {
   System.out.println("SubClass3 calls SuperClass3 method: " +
   super.method());                                 //Call super class method
   return "from SubClass3...";
   }
 }

class SubClass4 extends SuperClass3 {
   public String method() {
          return "from SubClass4...";
   }
}
class SubSubClass extends SubClass4 {
   public String method() {
          return "from SubSubClass...";
```

```
    }
}
```

We added another subclass, **SubClass4**, and extended the inheritance hierarchy to **SubSubClass**. In addition to these changes, **method()** of **SubClass3** has been augmented to call **super.method()** to examine the overridden method of the superclass. The overridden method in the superclass can still be called from its subclass in this manner. The following is the modified driver code:

```
//Complete code called PolymorphismTest3.java in Ch8 from the author's website
public class PolymorphismTest3 {
    public static void main( String args[] )
    {
        SubClass3 b3 = new SubClass3();
        SubClass4 b4 = new SubClass4();
        SubSubClass bb = new SubSubClass();

        SuperClass3 supper = b3;                          //Cast to super class
        System.out.println(supper.method());

        supper = b4;
        System.out.println(supper.method());

        supper = bb;
        System.out.println(supper.method());

        supper.otherMethod();                         //Call non-overridden method
    }
}
```

The result of execution is:

```
SubClass3 calls SuperClass3 method: from SuperClass3...
from SubClass3...
from SubClass4...
from SubSubClass...
from SuperClass3 otherMethod()...
```

From the output, we can see that as long as a subclass overrides or implements the methods from its superclass and the calling class has been cast as a reference of its superclass, the newly cast class will always call the methods from the subclass(es), not from its superclass. This methodology can be applied to a situation wherein multiple casting of objects of subclasses to invoke all overridden or implemented methods from different objects can be made dynamically during execution.

8.2 Coding Polymorphism

In summarizing the above discussion, we can draw the following conclusions regarding the coding of polymorphism:

1. Both a superclass and associated subclass must exist to establish polymorphism.

2. The superclass provides the polymorphic method(s)--either regular method or abstract method—signatures. The methods must be implemented by the subclass.

3. A subclass using polymorphism must override or implement each method performing the specific polymorphic operations.

4. Code the driver program or application code to cast the object of the subclass to its superclass reference, thereby allowing the polymorphic operations to be performed.

In the following section we use examples to discuss how to code polymorphism.

8.2.1 Super class provides polymorphic methods

Let's use the example of area calculations for circular objects to begin our discussion of polymorphism. We will first review the requirements for the superclass.

```
//Complete code called Shape.java in Ch8 from the author's website
public abstract class Shape {
   ...
   // The following are polymorphic methods
   public abstract void computeArea();
   public abstract void computeVolume();
   public abstract double getArea();
   public abstract double getVolume();

}
```

In addition to the original existing methods, **computeArea()** and **computeVolume()**, we now add methods **getArea()** and **getVolume()** to begin establishing the polymorphism paradigm.

A superclass with polymorphism need not be defined as an abstract class and the polymorphic methods in the superclass need not be defined as abstract methods. However, in most such situations, superclasses are not able to provide specific, detailed polymorphic operations for their subclasses. Therefore, it is very common that these methods in the superclasses are defined as abstract.

The following example of performing employee salary calculation:

```
// Use an abstract method to provide a polymorphic method
public abstract class Employee {
   ...
   public abstract double earnings();    //Define polymorphic method
}
```

can also be defined as a regular method:

```
//A regular method that will be overridden by the subclass to perform polymorphism
 public class Employee {
     ...
     public double earnings () {return 0.0};
```

8.2.2 Subclass overrides/implements polymorphic methods

In the example of calculating circular-object areas or volumes, **CircleShape2** inherited **Shape**, **Circle** inherited **CircleShape2**. **Circle** implemented the abstract methods to perform polymorphism as follows:

```
//Complete code called Circle.java in Ch8 from the author's website
public class Circle extends CircleShape2 {
   ...
   double volume = 0.0;                              //Circle doesn't have volume
   public void computeArea() {                       //Implements computeArea()
          area = Math.PI * radius * radius;
   }
   public double getArea() {                         //Implements getArea()
          return area;
   }
   public void computeVolume() {}             //Implements computeVolume()
   public double getVolume() {                //Implements getVolume()
          return volume;
   }

}
```

The code implements all four methods as abstract methods to perform polymorphism. Because volumes are not applicable to circle objects, **computeVolume()** is coded as an empty body and **getVolume()** will return 0.0.

Based on the above analysis and coding, we continue our application development by coding **Sphere** to perform polymorphism for **Sphere** objects:

```
//Complete code called Sphere.java in Ch8 from the author's website
public class Sphere extends Circle{
   ...
   public void computeArea() {                //Override Circle's method
          super.computeArea();                //Call inherited method from Circle
          area = 4* area;
   }
   public void computeVolume() {              //Override Circle's method
          super.computeArea();                //Call inherited method from Circle
          volume = 4.0/3 * radius * area;
```

```
    }
}
```

Because **Sphere** inherits **Circle**, we only override **computeArea()** and **computeVolume()** to calculate the surface areas and volumes of **Sphere** objects. All other code remains the same.

Applying the sample principle, we can code the subclass with polymorphism in calculating employee salary as follows:

```
//Demo code
public class Manager extends Employee {
   ...
   public double earnings () {
          return baseSalary + meritPay + bonus;
   }
```

In summary, subclasses must override the regular methods or implement the polymorphic methods coded in their superclass to perform polymorphism.

8.2.3 How to perform polymorphism

We now cast the objects of a subclass as references to the superclass to perform polymorphism. The casted object will polymorphically and dynamically call its specified methods from the subclass during execution. For example:

```
Circle myCircle = new Circle(20.98);
Shape shape = myCircle;                      //Cast to the superclass
shape.computeArea();.                        //polymorphic call
...
```

By applying linked lists and loops within our code, we can perform polymorphism on a large number of objects or perform a large number of polymorphic method calls for a variety of objects from different polymorphic-ready subclasses.

The following code is an example of performing polymorphism in calculating area and volumes of circular objects:

```
//Complete code called CircleShapeApp.java in Ch8 from the author's website
public class CircleShapeApp{
   public static void main(String[] args) {
          Circle circle = new Circle(12.98);
          Sphere sphere = new Sphere(25.55);

          Shape shape = circle;              //Cast to its super class
          //Polymorphic calls
          shape.computeArea();
          shape.computeVolume();
```

```
            System.out.println("circle area: " + shape.getArea());
            System.out.println("circle volume: " + shape.getVolume());
            //polymorphic calls
            shape = sphere;
            shape.computeArea();
            shape.computeVolume();
            System.out.println("Sphere area: " + shape.getArea());
            System.out.println("Sphere volume: " + shape.getVolume());
    }
}
```

The result of execution is:

```
circle area: 529.2967869138698
circle volume: 0.0
Sphere area: 2050.8395382450512
Sphere volume: 69865.26693621474
```

We may use arrays and loops in cases involving many objects associated with polymorphic calls:

```
...
for(int i = 0; i < objNum; i++) {                        //looping for objNum times
   shape[i].computeArea();                               //i from 0 to objNum-1
   shape[i].computeVolume();
   System.out.println("The area: " + shape[i].getArea());
   System.out.println("The volume: " + shape[i].getVolume());
}
```

Arrays are discussed in Chapter 10. The use of linked lists to perform polymorphism is introduced in later chapters.

8.3 Another Example Of Polymorphism

Figure 8.4 shows a hierarchy chart of employee salary calculations. We will use it as an example to discuss coding in polymorphism.

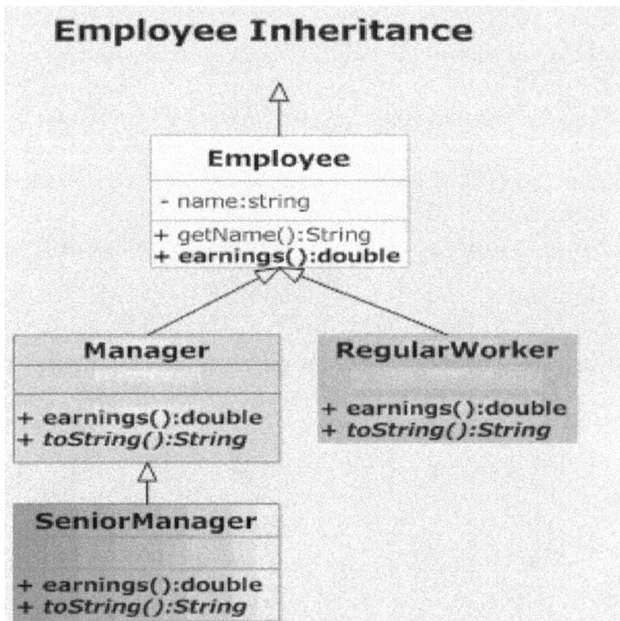

Figure 8.4 Inheritance hierarchy of Employee

We will only apply basic data and polymorphic methods in this example. Ancillary methods may be added by the interested reader.

The following is code for the superclass **Employee**:

```
//Complete code called Employee.java in Ch8 from the author's website
public class Employee {
   private String name;

   public Employee(String name ) {
      this.name = name;
   }
 public String getName() { return name; }
 public String toString() { return "name " + getName(); }  //polymorphic method
 public double earnings(){return 0.0;}                    //polymorphic method
}
```

In the superclass **Employee** we defined two polymorphic methods, **toString()** and **earnings()**. A subclass must override each method to perform polymorphic operations. Method **toString()** overrides **toString()** in the **Object** class to return the employee's name. It should noted that although we did not provide a **toString()** method in **Employee**—one will be included in the subclass **Manager** (see below)--calling **toString()** by superclass referencing, e.g., **employee.toString()**, will invoke the **toString()** method contained in **Manager**, not **Object**. Method **earning()** returns an initialized **salary** value of 0.0.

The following code shows **Manager** inherits **Employee** and overrides the polymorphic methods defined in its superclass:

```
//Complete code called Manager.java in Ch8 from the author's website
//Manager class derived from Employee
public class Manager extends Employee {
```

```
  protected double salary;
  public Manager( String name, double salary) {
     super( name );                              //Call super class constructor
     this.salary = salary;
  }
  public double earnings() { return salary; }    //Override polymorphic method
  public String toString() {
     return "Manager " + getName();        //Call inherited method getName()
  }
}
```

Continue our example, **SeniorManager** inherits **Manager**, and also overrides these two polymorphic methods:

```
//Complete code called SeniorManager.java in Ch8 from the author's website
//SeniorManager class derived from Manager
public final class SeniorManager extends Manager {
  private double meritPay;
  public SeniorManager( String name, double salary, double meritPay) {
  super( name , salary);                         //Call super class constructor
       this.meritPay = meritPay;
  }
  public double earnings() { return salary + meritPay; }
                                                 //Overrides polymorphic methods
  public String toString() {
  return "Senior Manager " + getName();
  }
}
```

Concluding our example, class **RegularWorker** inherits **Employee** and overrides the two polymorphic methods:

```
//Complete code called RegularWorker.java in Ch8 from the author's website
//RegularWorker class derived from Employee
public class RegularWorker extends Employee {
  protected double salary, overtimePay;
  public RegularWorker( String name, double salary, double overtimePay)
  {
       super( name );                            //Call super class constructor
       this.salary = salary;
       this.overtimePay = overtimePay;
  }
  public double earnings() { return salary + overtimePay; }
                                                 //Overrides polymorphic methods
  public String toString() {
     return "Regular worker: " + getName();
  }
```

```
}
```

The following is the driver code to test the polymorphism:

```
//Complete code called PolymorphismApp.java in Ch8 from the author's website
import javax.swing.JOptionPane;
import java.text.DecimalFormat;

public class PolymorphismApp {
   public static void main( String args[] ) {
      Employee[] ref = new Employee[3];  //Superclass referencing an array
      String output = "";

      Manager manager = new Manager( "Wang", 5800.00 );
      SeniorManager senior = new SeniorManager( "Smith", 6250.0, 1500.0);
      RegularWorker regular = new RegularWorker( "Lee", 2980.00, 270.0);

      DecimalFormat precision2 = new DecimalFormat( "0.00" );

      ref[0] = manager;        //Superclass referencing manager
      ref[1] = senior;         //Superclass referencing senior manager
      ref[2] = regular;        //Superclass referencing regular worker

      for(int i = 0; i < 3; i++)     //Loops to create polymorphic output
        output += ref[i].toString() + " earned $" +
                precision2.format( ref[i].earnings() ) + "\n";

      JOptionPane.showMessageDialog( null, output, //Display the output info
         "Demonstrating Polymorphism",
         JOptionPane.INFORMATION_MESSAGE );
   }
}
```

In the driver code, we create three types of objects, **manager**, **senior**, and **regular**, and use an array, cast from the respective subclasses, for superclass referencing each object's polymorphic methods. We use a **for** loop to perform the polymorphic calculations for the salaries and build up the display information in the output. This technique allow us to use **showMessageDialog()** and **JOptionPane()** to display the result shown in Figure 8.5.

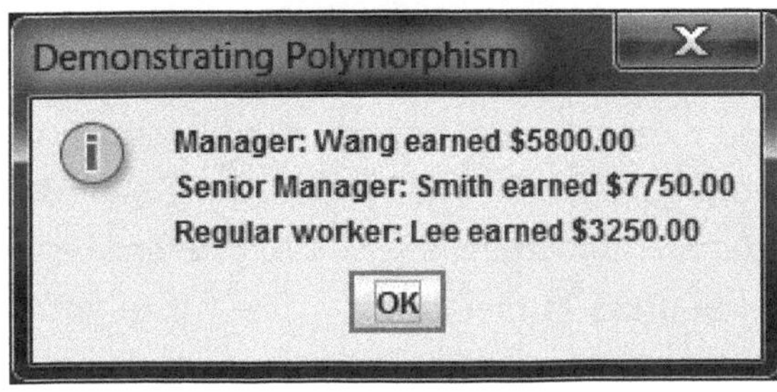

Figure 8.5 The execution result

8.4 Inside Method Binding

Method binding is the procedure for handling memory allocation associated with processing a method call, the stack operations, and processing of parameters and local variables. During execution, the JVM uses this information provided by the method binding to execute the method call. As constructors are special methods, method binding also applies to their processing. We have discussed in previous chapters two types of method binding in Java: static method binding and dynamic method binding. Static method binding occurs during compilation and is completed by the compiler; dynamic method binding, on the other hand, occurs during execution and is carried out by the JVM.

8.4.1 Static binding

Because static method binding is resolved at compile time, it can improve execution speed. Methods that may have static method binding are:

- Static methods.
- Constructors.
- Private methods.
- Method calls that use keyword **super**, including the use of **super(),** to call a constructor in the super class and the use of **super.superMethod()** to call the method in the super class.

8.4.2 Dynamic method binding

If the compiler is not able to resolve a method call at compilation time, the binding is done at run-time. This is known as dynamic binding. In dynamic method binding, the JVM allocates memory during execution and produces the necessary references and links as it interprets the byte code. Because of the additional processing required, code execution speed in Java is often slower than comparable code written in C or C++.

8.4.3 Inside method binding and method calling

Static method binding and dynamic method binding both involve the process of converting symbolic references to direct memory references within the code, verifying their validity, loading objects and parameters, and maintaining the stack.

- Symbolic reference to direct memory reference – A symbolic reference provides recognition and description to a method by associating the class name to which the method belongs, the method name, parameter information, and the return type of the method. During the process of binding, based upon this associated information, a symbolic reference is replaced by a direct reference to the method's physical address in memory for direct reference by the JVM during execution. Direct memory referencing may involve a pointer to the memory address or the offset of the memory address.

- Verification of validity – During the binding process, the method and method call must be verified according to Java language specifications. This includes verifying if a method call is legal and safe to execute, for example, verifying that a private method is called inside another method of its object. The compiler or JVM will produce a syntax error or run-time exception, respectively, if verification fails.

- Loading the object and parameters – If the method involved in binding is an object method, the object reference and parameters of the method must be loaded onto the stack. However, if the method is static, only the parameters are loaded onto the stack.

- Use of the stack – During the method call, the JVM produces a stack frame associated with the method's execution. The stack frame includes the memory locations for all local variables, operations of the stack, and other data required during execution. The memory requirements for the local variables and stack operations are already provided by the bytecode, so the JVM will know how much memory is needed for execution. Stack operations include pushing and popping of the code and data.

8.4.4 Invokespecial and invokevirtual

The **invokespecial** is instruction issued by JVM automatically when the code invokes instance initialization methods involving static bindings, private methods, and methods of a superclass of the current class. **ClassName.methodName()** and **super()** are examples of method instances using **invokespecial**. **Invokevirtual** invokes a method based upon the class of an object and is associated with dynamic binding, e.g., **obj.methodName()**. Note that in a method call of the form **superReference.methodName()**, if **methodName()** is a polymorphic method and the subclass has overridden or implemented, and the object of the subclass has been cast to its superclass, **superReference.methodName()** then becomes of the form **invokevirtual**. Let's discuss this using examples.**superReference.methodName()** is actually an **invokevirtual**.

```
//Complete code called InvokeTest.java in Ch8 from the author's website
//demo: invokespecial vs. invokevirtual
class SuperClass5 {
   public String method() {
           return "from SuperClass5...";
   }
   public void otherMethod() {
          System.out.println("In SuperClass5 otherMethod()...");
          //invokespecial
          System.out.println("SuperClass5 otherMethod() calls method(): " +
          method());
   }
 }
```

```
class SubClass5 extends SuperClass5{
   public String method() {
          return "from SubClass5...";
   }
   public void subMethod() {
          //call SuperClass5 method()
          System.out.println("SubClass5 calls super.method(): " +
          super.method());
   }
}
```

The driver code is:

```
//invokespecial vs. invokevirtual test

public class InvokeTest {
   public static void main( String args[] ) {

      SubClass5 b = new SubClass5();
      SuperClass5 supper = b;                    //Cast to superclass type
      System.out.println(supper.method());    //invokevirtual referring to b

      b.subMethod();
      b.otherMethod();
   }
}
```

And the execution result is:

```
from SubClass5...
SubClass5 calls super.method(): from SuperClass5...
In SuperClass5 otherMethod()...
SuperClass5 otherMethod() calls method(): from SubClass5...
```

It is clear **supper.method()** is an **invokevirtual** and the **super.method()** call from **subMethod()** of **SubClass** is an **invokespecial**.

Exercises

1. List at least three examples of polymorphic products used in your daily life and describe their polymorphic features.
2. Polymorphism is used in much application software. List and explain at least three such features in applications you have used.
3. What are five benefits of polymorphism described in the text? List them.
4. Summarize the steps to perform polymorphism in coding.

5. Use examples to explain the polymorphic method and how you would code such methods in a subclass to perform polymorphism.

6. Use examples to describe how to override polymorphic methods.

7. Using one of your programs involving inheritance, explain how you would modify it to use polymorphism within the code.

8. Obtain example code files **Shape.java**, **Circle.java**, **Sphere.java**, and **CircleShapeApp.java** from **Ch8** of the author's website. Compile and execute the example and understand the polymorphism it performs. Modify the application as follows:

   a. Code a class called **Cone** inherited from class **Circle**. **Cone** will override the **computeArea()** and **computeVolume()** methods from its superclass to calculate the area and volume of a **Cone** object.

   b. Modify the driver code, **CircleShapeApp.java**, so it will also create an object of **Cone** with a height of 12.5 and diameter of 10.48. Modify the polymorphic calls to calculate and display the result of the calculations.

   c. Document your source code and save your work.

9. Obtain example code files **Employee.java**, **SeniorManager.java**, **Regularworker.java**, and **PolymorphismApp.java** from **Ch8** of the author's website. Compile and execute the example and understand the polymorphism it performs. Modify the application as follows:

   a. Code a class called **SeniorWorker** which inherited from **Employee,** in addition to **name**, **salary** and **overtimePay**, it adds a double type data called **meritPay** which is calculated as 10% of the salary. It overrides **earnings()** and **toString()** methods to compute the total salary of **SeniorWorker** and return the proper data of **SeniorWorker**, respectively.

   b. Code a class called **SeniorWorker** inherited from class **Employee** which, in addition to **name**, **salary**, and **overtimePay**, includes a double type data, **meritPay**, calculated as 10% of the salary. The class will override the **earning()** and **toString()** methods to compute the total salary of **SeniorWorker** and return the proper data of **SeniorWorker**, respectively.

   c. Document your source code and save your work.

10. What is static method binding? What is dynamic method binding? Use of examples to explain your answers.

11. Obtain example code files **InvokeTest.java** from **Ch8** of the author's website. Compile and execute the code. Understand the meaning and differences between **invokespecial** and **invokevirtual**.

"The accomplished scholar is not a utensil."

– Confucius

Chapter 9 Interfaces

In this chapter we discuss another important coding technique of Java—interfaces. First, we introduce and define interfaces, note the differences between an abstract class and an interface, and discuss the purpose of using interfaces. We also discuss the use of interfaces in multiple inheritance, the inheritance for an interface itself, and applications using interfaces through the use of examples.

9.1 What Is An Interface?

An interface is a special class in which only the headers or prototypes of methods and static final data are allowed. These unfinished methods in an interface must be implemented by a class to perform their functions. Compared with abstract classes, interfaces have more coding restrictions. For example, instance data in an interface can only be declared **static final** and methods cannot have an associated body of code within an interface. The purpose of using an interface is to serve as a protocol or form of guidance for the class that implements it. However, an interface makes no requirement or specification upon the class regarding the manner of implementing the methods; it only requires that the class use the defined prototypes or signatures of the methods. The following is an example of an interface:

```
public interface Pluggable {
   static final String componentID = "CPU";            //Optional
   void plugin(argumentList);                          //Optional
}
```

It should be noted that both **static final** data and method prototypes are optional in an interface. In the most extreme case, an interface may have neither data nor a method prototype at all—only the name of the interface. For example, the interface **Cloneable** from the Java API is an empty interface. The purpose of such an interface is to establish the signature or naming for classes to follow. We discuss **Cloneable** and its use in a later section of this chapter.

9.1.1 Inheritability

A class that implements an interface inherits the **static final** data and prototypes of the methods, if any, from the interface. Since a class may extend a superclass and implement more than one interface, Java supports "indirect multiple inheritance" (see Figure 7.5). The following is an example of indirect multiple inheritance:

```
public class SubClass extends SuperClass implements Interface1, Interface2,
InterfaceN {
   ...
}
```

Since **SubClass** only inherits the method prototypes from all interfaces using the comma operator, in addition to any possible **static final** data from each interface, it must provide the implementation code for each method.

9.1.2 "like a" relationship

When a class implements an interface it forms a "like a" relationship. It is explicitly indicated that a class implementing an interface must use the defined signatures of the stated methods. No specification or requirement is made concerning how a method must be coded to implement the desired functionality. In other words, a "like a" relationship between a class and an interface acts upon the principle that as long as a class uses the method prototypes specified in the interface it may be coded in any manner.

9.1.3 Abstraction

Interfaces reflect abstraction and form a "pure abstract class" as compared with ordinary abstract classes. Recall that in an abstract class regular data and methods are allowed. However, only static final data and method prototypes are allowed in an interface.

An abstract class may contain an abstract method serving as a protocol allowing a subclass that inherits the abstract class a means of implementing it. In an interface, all methods must be abstract and any class implementing the interface must provide code for each of the stated methods. This arrangement allows a separation between regulation and implementation. It also reflects an important principle of object-oriented design (OOD): "loose coupling" and "tight cohesion". For example, an abstract class:

```
public abstract class SomeAbstractClass {
   ...
   public abstract void someMethod();
}
```

can be rewritten as an interface:

```
public interface SomeInterface {
   public abstract void someMethod();
}
```

And the resulting class implementing the interface will be of the form:

```
public class SomeClass implements someInterface {
   ...
   public void someMethod() {...}
}
```

The benefits of using an interface are:

- Promoting the concept of a "contract" between the interface and the class concerning the establishment of method prototypes/regulations within the interface and their independent implementation within the class methods.

- Reduction of class complexity.
- Stating the functionality of an API, thereby freeing users from the concerns of the API implementation.

9.1.4 An introductory walk into Interfaces

The following syntax defines an interface:

```
public interface InterfaceName {
   public static final varType CONSTANT_NAME = value;          //Optional
   public abstract returnType methodName(argumentList);        //Optional
}
```

wherein:

interface – Java keyword to define an interface.

varType – any primative data type declared **public** and **static final**. Access modifier **public** and keywords **static final** can be omitted.

returnType – return type. It can be any primative data type, object, or **void**.

argumentList – list of parameter types and names, as required.

Note that the access modifier **public** and keyword **abstract** in the method prototype can also be omitted. The simplest syntax format to define an interface is:

```
public interface InterfaceName {
   varType CONSTANT_NAME = value;            //Optional
   returnType methodName (argumentList);     //Optional
}
```

It should also be noted the presence of data definitions and method prototypes are optional.

The following are examples of defining interfaces:

Example 1: An interface, **Printable**, with a method prototype, **print()**, containing neither an argument list nor return type.

```
public interface Printable {
   void print();
}
```

This interface requires that the class implementing it must provide code for method **print()**, and the method must be written with no arguments and no return type, i.e., **void**.

Example 2: An interface, **DepartmentCode**, containing only **static final** data representing a department code.

```
public interface DepartmentCode {
   int ADMINISTRATION = 1;
   int FINANCE = 2;
   int MARKETING = 3;
   int SERVICES = 4;
}
```

This interface only defines a collection of **static final** data. The class that implements the interface can use the list of specified department codes from the interface.

Example 3: An interface, **Positionable**, containing initialized data representing the beginning coordinates of geometric objects and the prototypes of all required methods.

```
public interface Positionable {
   short X0 = 0;
   short Y0 = 0;
   short getX();
   short getY();
   void setX(short x);
   void setY(short y);
}
```

Example 4 – Java API **Cloneable** interface

```
public interface Cloneable {
}
```

The Java API **Cloneable** interface is an example of an empty interface. However, the class implementing the interface must override the **Object.Clone()** method, as noted in the interface documentation. The **Cloneable** interface is discussed in detail later in this chapter.

9.1.5 Interfaces vs. abstract classes

Although interfaces have many similarities with abstract classes, for example, neither can instantiate any object, there are significant differences in syntax, coding, and use between the two entities. Table 9.1 lists these differences.

Table 9.1 Differences between Interfaces and Abstract Classes

Interface	Abstract class
Static constant data only	Regular data Constant data Static data Static constant data

Abstract methods only	Regular methods Static methods Abstract methods
Use keyword **interface**	Use keyword **abstract**

It can easily be seen that an interface has more restrictions than an abstract class. Abstract classes are a special case of regular classes using the keyword **abstract**; interfaces are "pure abstract" classes.

- Specification of event handling: Event handling interfaces, e.g., **EventListener**, **ActionListener**, **WindowListener**, **MouseListener**, must be implemented to handle specified events. Event handling is discussed in Chapter 15.
- Specification of object recognition: Java API interfaces **Comparable** and **Cloneable** are examples of object recognition interfaces. Their name and purpose enforce Java naming convention practices.
- Specification of I/O: Java API interfaces **Printable**, **appendable**, and **Readable** are examples of I/O interfaces.
- Specification of connectivity: Java API interface **Connection** is used in establishing database connections.
- Specification of special constant static data: Java API interface **Enumeration** facilitates the establishment of this special data type.
- Specification in inheritance and structure control in high-level API classes: Java API interfaces **Collection** and **List** are examples of these interface functionalities.
- Specification of utility classes: Interfaces providing for functionality associated with **Recyclable**, **Colorable**, **Positionable**, and other "**-able**" capabilities are examples of such utilities.

Table 9.2 shows the comparison between interfaces and abstract classes in application code.

Table 9.2 Comparison between Interfaces and Abstract Classes in Application Code

Application Range	Interface	Abstract class
Multiple interfaces	A class can implements multiple interfaces, thereby allowing it to perform indirect multiple inheritance.	A class can only inherit one abstract class as a direct super class.
"like a" and "is a" Relationships	Usually specify the utility or peripheral functionality; it is not for core code.	Usually define the code or high-level functionality.
Similarity	Used in different applications sharing common signatures and specifications.	Used as references for polymorphism.
Freedom	"like me"	"is me" or "like me"

Code Maintainability	Same	Same
Speed	Relatively slow	Relatively fast
Simplicity	High	Low
Extensibility	Must modify all classes if a new method specification is added to an existing interface.	It is not necessary to modify subclasses if a new *regular* method is added to an existing abstract class.

9.1.6 Commonly used Java API interfaces

Every Java API package specifying an interface provides the necessary information to code and correctly implement the interface. The types of exceptions that may require handling by the programmer are also noted. Table 9.3 lists commonly used Java API interfaces.

Table 9.3 Commonly used Java API interfaces

Interface	Data/Method	Package	Function	Chapter Discussion
Cloneable	Object.clone()	java.lang	Copy objects	9
Comparable	int compareTo(Object o)	java.lang	Sort objects	10
Runnable	void run()	java.lang	Threading	14
AudioClip	void loop() void play() void stop()	java.applet	Audio functions	20
ActionListener	void actionPerformed(ActionEvent)	java.awt.event	Handle events	17, 18
WindowConstants	int DISPOSE_ON_CLOSE int DO_NOTHING_ON_CLOSE int EXIT_ON_CLOSE int HIDE_ON_CLOSE	javax.swing	Control windows	18

These and other interfaces are discussed in later chapters.

9.2 Implementing Interfaces

The manner in which an interface is implemented depends on the particular application using the interface. From this point of view, implementing interfaces is actually a form of application-oriented programming. Indirect-multiple inheritance can be coded using interfaces; interfaces can perform multiple inheritances; and interfaces can be used as parameter types. In this section, we discuss these concepts and coding techniques of interfaces.

9.2.1 Implementation of Interfaces

The implementation of an interface actually refers to the embodiment of the method prototypes declared in the interface. Java uses the keyword **implements** to perform such implementation. The class that implements an interface must follow the prototypes of the methods in the interface. If the interface contains only **static final** data definitions, it is not necessary to do anything in the implementation, and the class implementing the interface will automatically inherit these data.

Example 1. Use of example **CircleShape2.java** to implement interface **Printable**, as discussed **in 9.1.4**:

```
//Complete code called CircleShape2.java in Ch9 from the author's website
public abstract class CircleShape2 extends Shape implements Printable {
   protected double radius;
   ...
   public void print() {
         System.out.println("radius: " + radius);
   }
   ...
}
```

Any subclass of **CircleShape2**, such as **Circle** or **Sphere**, can also override the implemented method, **print()**, to allow the addition of more printing operations.

Example 2. Use of example **Employee.java**, discussed in Chapter 8, modified to use an interface to perform polymorphism.

```
//Complete code called AccountPrintable.java in Ch9 from the author's website
//Accounting Printable interface
import java.text.*;
import java.util.*;
public interface AccountPrintable{
   void print();
   NumberFormat currencyFormat(Locale locale);
}
```

We will begin by defining the interface **AccountPrintable**. This interface specifies that the class implementing it must provide code for methods **print()** and **currencyFormat()**. Method **currencyFormat()** must also contain a parameter of type **Locale**.

```
//Complete code called Employee2.java in Ch9 from the author's website
public abstract class Employee2 implements AccountPrintable {
   ...
   public abstract double earnings();    //It will be used to perform polymorphism
   public void print() {                 //Implement print()
         System.out.print("Name: " + name + "\t");
   }
   public     NumberFormat     currencyFormat(Locale     locale)     {     //Implement
```

```
currencyFormat()
        NumberFormat currency = NumberFormat.getCurrencyInstance(locale);
        return currency;
   }
}
```

Subclass **Manager2** can override method **print()** implemented by its superclass, **Employee2**:

```
//Complete code called Manager2.java in Ch9 from the author's website
public class Manager2 extends Employee2 {
   protected double salary;
   ...
   public double earnings() { return salary; //overridethe method toretrieve
    //salary
   public void print() {                          //override print()
          super.print();                          //call super class print()
          System.out.print("Salary: " + currencyFormat(Locale.US).
          format(earnings()) + "\n");             //cascading calls
   }
}
```

Overriding method **print()** allows the coding of additional printing operations, e.g., the ability to call the superclass implementation of **print()** to print **name** and the superclass implementation of **currencyFormat()** to specify the printing format of manager objects.

No code modifications are required for **SeniorManager**, and a minor modification for **RegularWorker** is made as follows:

```
//Complete code called RegularWorker2.java in Ch9 from the author's website
public class RegularWorker2 extends Employee2 {
   ...
   public void print() {                          //Override print()
          super.print();                          //Call super class print()to print name
          System.out.println("Salary: " + currencyFormat(Locale.CHINA).
          format(earnings()) + "\n");
   }
}
```

We purposely used the currency format of Chinese renminbi to demonstrate the flexibility of the interface. With a little modification of the driver code in Chapter 8, the following can be a result of execution:

```
Name: Wang      Salary: $5,800.00
Name: Smith     Salary: $7,750.00
Name: Lee       Salary: ¥3,250.00
```

9.2.2 Multiple inheritances in interfaces

Java allows a subclass to implement multiple interfaces:

```
public class SubClass extends SuperClass implements Interface1 [, Interface2,
…, InterfaceN] {
   ...
}
```

The above syntax shows **Subclass** inheriting **SuperClass** as well as providing capabilities to implement more than one interface . The use of brackets indicates the presence of optional items. This type of inheritance is called indirect-multiple inheritance. A subclass inherits all properties of its superclass, and all **static final** data and method signatures from any interface. The subclass must provide code to implement each method specified in the interface(s).

Example 1. A simple example of indirect multiple inheritance.

```
//Complete code called CanSwim.java in Ch9 from the author's website
public interface CanSwim {                     //interface 1
  void swim();
}
interface CanFly {                             //interface 2
  void fly();
}
interface CanWalk {                            //interface 3
  void walk();
}
```

Each interface describes a behavior, mobility, shared by such entities as animals, humans, robots, vehicles, et cetera. Each behavior can be implemented by any type of such classes. For example:

```
//Complete code called SomeOne.java in Ch9 from the author's website
abstract class Action {             //Superclass
  public void doingList() {
  System.out.println("Here is what I can do: ");
  }
}
//Subclass performs indirect-multiple inheritance
public class SomeOne extends Action implements CanSwim, CanFly, CanWalk {
  public void swim() {
         System.out.println("I can catch fish.");
  }
  public void fly() {
         System.out.println("The sky is my limit.");
  }
  public void walk() {
         System.out.println("I can even run.");
  }
}
```

The following is the driver code to test this example:

```
//Complete code called MultipleInheritanceTest.java in Ch9 from author's website
public class MultipleInheritanceTest {
   public static void main(String args[]) {
      SomeOne guessWho = new SomeOne();
      guessWho.doingList();
      guessWho.swim();
      guessWho.fly();
      guessWho.walk();
       System.out.println("\nWho am I?");
   }
}
```

The following result will be displayed after the example is executed:

```
Here is what I can do:
I can catch fish.
The sky is my limit.
I can even run.

Who am I?
```

In the exercises of this chapter you will create a class designed to ask a user to enter a guess in response to the question and display the correct answer.

Example 2. Define an interface **AccountPayable** with an abstract method **payment()**:

```
public interface AccountPayable {
   double payment();
}
```

The interface can be used in applications dealing with payments, including the example of computing an employee's salary discussed earlier. The following code modifies **Employee2.java** and implements two interfaces for the salary computations:

```
//Complete code called Employee3.java in Ch9 from the author's website
public class Employee3 implements AccountPayable, Printable {
   ...
   public double payment(){return 0.0;}          //Implements the method
         ...
}
```

Any subclasses used in the example, such as **Manager** and **RegularWorker**, can override **payment()**, thereby allowing the computation of their respective salaries. For example:

```
//Complete code called Manager3.java in Ch9 from the author's website
public class Manager3 extends Employee3 {
   ...
   public double payment() { return salary; } //override method to return salary

   ...
```

```
  public void print() {                              //override print()
     super.print();
     System.out.print("Salary: " + currencyFormat(Locale.US).
     format(payment()) + "\n");
  }
}
```

9.2.3 Inheritances in interfaces

All inheritance techniques can be applied to interfaces. The following examples show various forms of inheritance used in association with interfaces:

1. Simple inheritance of interfaces.

```
public interface SubInterface extends SuperInterface {
...
}
```

   For instance:

```
public interface Shooting {
   double DISTANCE = 2000.0;
   void target();
}
interface Fight extends Shooting {
   void weapon();
}
```

   Interface **Fight** inherits all properties, i.e., **static final** data and the prototype of method **target()**, from interface **Shooting**.

2. Multiple-level inheritance of interfaces. Continuing the above example:

```
public interface CasualtyReport extends Fight {
    int casualty();
}
```

   The interface **CasualtyReport** inherits all properties from **Fight** and **Shooting** and adds a new method prototype, **casualty()**.

3. Multiple inheritance of interfaces. For example:

```
public interface CanDo extends CanSwim, CanFly, CanWalk {
   ...
}
```

The interface **CanDo** inherits all properties from **CanSwim**, **CanFly**, and **CanWalk**. It is important to note this type of inheritance cannot be applied to classes. Using the multiple inheritance capabilities of interfaces, **SomeOne.java** (discussed in **9.2.2)** can be simplified as follows:

```
public class SomeOne extends Action implements CanDo {
    ...
}
```

9.2.4 Interface parameters

Interfaces can be used as parameter types in methods. All objects that implement the interface can be legal arguments of the methods. The syntax for interface parameter types is:

```
public void someMethod(InterfaceName objectName, otherArgumentList);
```

wherein,

objectName – object implementing interface **InterfaceName**.

otherArgumentList – any remaining user-defined parameters

The following example uses an interface as a parameter of a method:

```
//Complete code called SomeOne2.java in Ch9 from author's website
public void canDoList(CanDo object) {
   object.swim();
   object.fly();
   object.walk();
}
```

The statement to call this method is:

```
//Complete code called InterfaceAsArgumentTest.java in Ch9 from author's website
...
SomeOne2 goose = new SomeOne2();
canDoList(goose);
```

The following output is displayed upon execution of the code:

```
I can catch fish.
The sky is my limit.
I can even walk.
```

More Info: *Methods using interfaces as parameters can be static methods with any type of access modifiers.*

Interfaces can also be used as a return type of a method. The method returns the object that implemented the interface. For example:

```
public interfaceName someMethod(argumentList);
```

The following code uses an interface as a return type:

```
//Complete code called SomeOne3.java in Ch9 from the author's website
public CanDo canDo(int swimSpeed, int flySpeed, int walkSpeed) {
   this.setSwimSpeed(swimSpeed);
   this.setFlySpeed(flySpeed);
   this.setWalkSpeed(walkSpeed);

   return this;
}
```

The following driver code snippet calls the method:

```
//Complete code called InterfaceAsReturnTypeTest.java in Ch9 from author's website
SomeOne3 goose = new SomeOne3();
System.out.println("Goose info: ");

//Return the object that implemented CanDo, and then call its toString()
System.out.println(goose.canDo(25, 129, 16));

//Returned object can be used by brownAfricanGoose as reference
CanDo brownAfricanGoose = goose.canDo(10, 200, 9);

System.out.println("Brown African Goose info: ")
SomeOne3.canDoList(brownAfricanGoose);            //Call static method canDoList()

System.out.println(brownAfricanGoose); //Call brownAfricanGoose's toString()
```

Executing the code produces the following result:

```
Goose info:
My swim speed is 25
My flying speed is 129
My walk speed is 16

Brown African Goose info:
I can catch fish.
The sky is my limit.
I can even walk.
My swim speed is 10
My flying speed is 200
My walk speed is 9
```

9.3 The Java API Interface Cloneable

The interface **Cloneable** in **java.lang** is used to copy or clone objects. Not all objects are cloneable. In particular, only instances of classes that implement the **Cloneable** interface can be cloned. Attempting to clone an object that does not implement the **Cloneable** interface throws the exception **CloneNotSupportedException**. Most classes in the Java API do not implement **Cloneable,** so instances of their objects are not cloneable.

9.3.1 Implementing the Cloneable Interface

The interface **Cloneable** is an empty interface:

```
public interface Cloneable {}
```

However, it is required that any class implementing **Cloneable** must override the **Object** class method **clone()** to allow the copy operation of the objects to be made.

```
protected Object clone() throws CloneNotSupportedException {
   return super.clone();
}
```

The **clone()** method requires handling of the **CloneNotSupportedException** exception in the event an attempt is made to clone an object that does not support the cloning operation. The above example uses the **throws** operator to propagate this exception to the caller of the method. Such "must be handled" exceptions in Java are called checked exceptions. Programmers must provide code to handle these exceptions. Checked exceptions and their handling are discussed in Chapter 11.

A class needing a copying functionality may add the above code to allow object cloning:

```
class SomeClass implements Cloneable {
   protected Object clone() throws CloneNotSupportedException {
   return super.clone();
 }
}
...
SomeClass object1 = new SomeClass();        //Create object1
...
SomeClass object2 = (SomeClass)object1.clone();   //Call clone()method

                                                  //object1 is copied to object2
```

It is important to note **clone()** returns an **Object** type that must be recast to the class type being copied. Failure to recast the **Object** type will cause a compiler error.

The resulting entity derived from invoking the **clone()** method is referred to as a "shallow copy." Shallow copies and the related concept of "deep copies" are discussed in the following sections.

9.3.2 Reference vs. copy

The reference to an object and a copy of an object are significantly different concepts. Referencing associates an object by another name; referencing actually points to the address of an object and does not involve any memory allocation. For example:

```
SomeClass object = new SomeClass();
...
SomeClass object2 = object;          //object2 references to object
```

Any operation performed on **object** will similarly affect **object2**, and vice versa. For example, executing

```
object.setValue(10);                 //set a new value
System.out.println(object2.getValue());
```

sets the value of **object** to 10 *and* sets the value of **object2** to 10.

A copy or clone of an object involves memory allocation and binding, as a new entity is created. However, it may also involve object referencing if the result of a copy operation is a shallow copy.

9.3.3 "Shallow copy" vs. "deep copy"

"Shallow copy" means if there is any member data as an object type in the source object you want to copy from (except the String objects and wrapper class' objects), **clone()** method just only generates a reference to such objects, and does not actually copy the member data of them. However, **clone()** method does copy all of the primitive member data, strings, and objects of all wrapper classes. That is, it will allocate memory space and copy the values to the cloned objects.

In a shallow copy, any change made to object data in either the source objects or in copied objects affects the other. However, the primitive data in either object will not be affected. Let us study an example case dealing with the class **SomeClass**:

```
//Complete code called CloneableTest.java in Ch9 from the author's website
class SomeClass implements Cloneable{
   OtherClass other;          //member object:  will be "shallow copy"
   Integer myInt;             //Wrapper class object data: will be "deep copy"
   int n;                     //primitive data:  will be "deep copy"
   SomeClass(String title, int n) {
          other = new OtherClass(title);
          myInt = new Integer(100);
          this.n = n;
   }
   void setTitle(String title) {
          other.setName(title);
   }
   void setN(int n) {
          this.n = n;
   }
   void setInteger(int n) {
```

```
        myInt = n;
    }
    public String toString() {
        return "other: " + other + ", n: " + n + ", myInt: " + myInt;
    }
    protected Object clone() throws CloneNotSupportedException {
        return super.clone();
    }
}
```

SomeClass contains two object member data types: **OtherClass**, a user-defined class, and **Integer**, a wrapper class. We have also defined a primitive member data type, **n**, as **int**. **SomeClass** implements the **Cloneable** interface, thereby allowing a copy operation to be performed. In order to satisfy the requirement of checked exception handling required by **clone()**, the code will throw any **CloneNotSupportedException** exception to the JVM.

The code of **OtherClass** is:

```
class OtherClass {
    String name;
    OtherClass(String name) {
        this.name = name;
    }
    void setName(String name) {
        this.name = name;
    }
    public String toString() {
        return name;
    }
}
```

For purposes of this example, we have only defined a **String** type member data, **name**, and a few member methods. In fact, we call clone() method of instantiated object and then cast resulting object to **SomeClass** before assigning this copy to **targetObj**:

```
public class CloneableTest {
    public static void main(String[] args) throws CloneNotSupportedException {
        SomeClass sourceObj = new SomeClass("Java", 10);
        SomeClass targetObj = (SomeClass) sourceObj.clone();
        System.out.println("content of sourceObj: " + sourceObj);
        System.out.println("content of targetObj: " + targetObj);

        targetObj.setTitle("JSP");
        sourceObj.setN(20);
        sourceObj.setInteger(0);
        System.out.println("After modify: ");
```

```
        System.out.println("content of sourceObj: " + sourceObj);
        System.out.println("content of targetObj: " + targetObj);
   }
}
```

Executing the above code produces the following result:

```
content of sourceObj: other: Java, n: 10, myInt: 100
content of targetObj: other: Java, n: 10, myInt: 100
After modify:
content of sourceObj: other: JSP, n: 20, myInt: 0
content of targetObj: other: JSP, n: 10, myInt: 100
```

This clearly shows **clone()** performs a shallow copy of member data **other** from **sourceObj**. Any modification performed on **other** in either **targetObj** or **sourceObj** will manifest itself in the other object. However, wrapper class member data **myInt** and primitive member data **n** represent deep copies, wherein each object is a unique entity and any modification made to one object will not affect the other.

In order to achieve a deep copy operation, the overridden **clone()** method above may be modified in the following manner:

```
protected Object clone() throws CloneNotSupportedException {
   SomeClass2 someClass = new SomeClass2(this);
   return someClass;
}
```

Providing a copy constructor within **SomeClass** allows the performance of "deep copy" functionality. The following is the modified code of **SomeClass**:

```
//Complete code called DeepCloneableTest.java in Ch9 from the author's website
class SomeClass2 implements Cloneable{
   OtherClass other;                              //object member data
   Integer myInt;                                 //object member data
   int n;                                         //primitive data
   SomeClass2(SomeClass2 someClass) {             //copy constructor
        other = new OtherClass(someClass.other.toString());
                                                  //return string as name
        myInt = someClass.getInteger();           //return myInt
        n = someClass.getN();                     //return n
   }
   SomeClass2(String title, int n) {
        other = new OtherClass(title);
        myInt = new Integer(100);
        this.n = n;
   }
   void setTitle(String title) {
```

```
            other.setName(title);
    }
    void setN(int n) {
            this.n = n;
    }
    void setInteger(int n) {
            myInt = n;
    }
    int getN() {
            return n;
    }
    Integer getInteger() {
            return myInt;
    }
    public String toString() {
            return "other: " + other + ", n: " + n + ", myInt: " + myInt;
    }
    protected Object clone() throws CloneNotSupportedException {
            SomeClass2 someClass = new SomeClass2(this);
            return someClass;
    }
}
```

The following is the result of executing the same driver code from the previous example:

```
content of sourceObj: other: Java, n: 10, myInt: 100
content of targetObj: other: Java, n: 10, myInt: 100
After modify:
content of sourceObj: other: Java, n: 20, myInt: 0
content of targetObj: other: JSP, n: 10, myInt: 100
```

We can see copied object **targetObj** has "deep copies" of all member data elements, as well as the **OtherClass** object, **other**. Both **targetObj** and **sourceObj** are now two independent objects; any changes made to or by one object will not affect the other object.

9.3.4 Application example – Use of a superclass to implement Cloneable

We may also consider the implementation of the **Cloneable** interface by a superclass within an application containing multiple-level inheritance to perform cloning operations. We have discussed such an application, **CircleShapeApp**, in Chapter 8. To allow all subclasses, e.g., **Circle** and **Sphere**, to perform copy operations, we will use **CircleShape** to implement **Cloneable**. Although **CircleShape** is an abstract class, it will not affect its subclasses in their inheritance of such a feature. The following is the modified code of **CircleShape**:

```
//Complete code called CircleShape.java in Ch9 from the author's website
```

```
public abstract class CircleShape implements Cloneable {
   ...
   public Object clone() throws CloneNotSupportedException {
          return super.clone();
   }
}
```

Assume two objects of **Circle** and **Sphere** are instantiated and perform the following operations in the driver code:

```
...
Circle circle = new Circle(1);
circle.computeArea();
System.out.println("Circle area: " + circle.getArea());
                                        //Print the circle area: 3.141592653589793
Sphere sphere = new Sphere(1);
sphere.computeArea();
System.out.println("Sphere area: " + sphere.getArea());
                                        //Print the sphere area: 12.566370614359172
```

The following code performs the copying operations of the **Circle** and **Sphere** objects, respectively:

```
//Complete code called CircleShapeApp.java in Ch9 from the author's website
...
try {
      //clone()requires handling of the CloneNotSupportedException exception
      Circle otherCircle = (Circle) circle.clone(); //Copy circle to otherCircle
      Sphere otherSphere = (Sphere) sphere.clone(); //Copy sphere to otherSphere
      otherCircle.setRadius(100);
      otherCircle.computeArea();
      System.out.println("Other circle area: " + otherCircle.getArea());

      otherSphere.setRadius(10);
      otherSphere.computeArea();
      System.out.println("Other sphere area: " + otherSphere.getArea());
   }
catch (CloneNotSupportedException e) {
      System.out.println(e);
 }
```

In this example, **try** and **catch** blocks are used to perform the required exception handling of **clone()**. The result of executing the above code is:

```
Circle area: 3.141592653589793
Sphere area: 12.566370614359172
Other circle area: 31415.926535897932
Other sphere area: 1256.6370614359173
```

Exercises

1. Use examples to explain the similarity between interfaces in hardware and interfaces in software. What are the features of Java interfaces?

2. What are differences between interfaces and abstract classes? What are the advantages of using interfaces?

3. Code the following interfaces:

    a. An interface called **Accountable** with **void withdraw(double)** and **double getPayment()** methods.

    b. An interface called **AccountReceivable** with a **void deposit(double)** method.

    c. Save these two interfaces in separate files.

4. Code a class, **BusinessAccount**, that implements the two interfaces defined in Exercise 3. Define and code the necessary instance variables and constructors. Override **toString()** so it will return the amount of a business account. Apply the particular operations required in implementing the interfaces. Create at least two objects of **BusinessAccount** with instance data of your choice in the driver code to test the class. Save all code.

5. Download files **CanSwim.java**, **SomeOne.java**, and **MultipleInheritanceTest.java** from Ch9 of the author's website. Study and understand each program. Use the three interfaces defined in **CanSwim.java** to code a class for the implementation. Write a driver code to test your class. In a loop within the driver code, prompt the user to (repeatably) enter guesses until the correct guess is made. Terminate the loop and display the correct guess and greeting message. Save all code.

6. What is inheritance as it relates to interfaces? What is the key feature?

7. What is an interface parameter? How do you use it?

8. Code the following interfaces, implement them, and use the interface as a parameter, respectively:

    a. An interface called **Printable** with a **void print()** method.

    b. An interface called **EmployeeType** with **FACULTY** and **CLASSIFIED** integer data. The value of **FACULTY** is 1 and **CLASSIFIED** is 2.

    a. A class called **Employee** to implement the two interfaces. Its constructor will initialize three instance data as **name**, **employeeType**, and **salary**. Implementation of method **print()** will display **name**, **employeeType**, and **salary**; **salary** is to be displayed as a currency format. You may use an **if-else** construct to identify the nature of the

employeeType—**FACULTY** or **CLASSIFIED**—so the particular information of each category can be shown.

b. Write a static method called **printInfo()** with a **void** return type in a class called **Output**. The first parameter is a **Printable** type, and it will accept the object of **Employee** as an argument. The second parameter is an integer type representing the quantity of printings. The method will display all employee information with the specified number of printings.

c. Write a driver code to test the above code. Create at least three objects with instance data of your choice. Call **printInfo()** to display the information of each object, respectively. You may decide how many times to print the information.

9. Extend the **Employee** class to implement the **Cloneable** interface, thereby allowing it to copy objects. In the driver code above, add two statements that will clone objects of **Employee** and then call **printInfo()** to display the information of these two objects.

"Reviewing what you have learned and learning anew, you are fit to be a teacher."

– Confucius

Chapter 10 Arrays And Strings

In this chapter, we discuss concepts and coding skills associated with arrays and strings, explore arrays as objects, arrays of strings, strings as objects, and API classes that support array and string processing.

10.1 General Discussion

Attempting to process a large amount of data without arrays is very difficult, if not virtually impossible. Java arrays are actually represented as objects and a number of API classes are provided to work with arrays. However, since arrays are commonly used data structures, Java retains traditional array operations, such as array declaration and initialization. Unlike C/C++, array boundaries in Java are automatically checked by the JVM, thereby eliminating the need to use terminators or null pointers in maintaining character arrays. Such features improve code readability and reliability by eliminating the need for testing for a terminator or attempting to process memory beyond the bounds of the array.

10.1.1 Understanding arrays

An array is a collection of related data having the same data type. These data, or items, are called array elements and are accessible by specified subscripts of the array. As Java arrays perform "zero-based" addressing, each subscript, or index, is a unique integer ranging from 0 to *array_size* – 1. The type classification of the array indicates the data type stored in the array. It may be any primitive data type or object.

If an array is an **Object** type the elements may theoretically be of any type of objects of the class and its subclasses. For example, an array of type **Object** may have any objects of the **Object** class and its subclasses as elements. However, to prevent any form of unsafe operations occurring on elements of different data types, Java provides type safe operations. We discuss this topic in Chapter 13.

The size or length of an array must be an integral value represented by an integer type. Once the array is declared, its size cannot be modified except in instances of re-declaring another array with the same name and same data type or specialized circumstances of array copying. This concept is called array name reuse and is discussed in a later section of this chapter.

An array can be one-dimensional or multidimensional. Multidimensional arrays are often used to represent complex data structures. The access and performance of operations on individual elements of an array is usually controlled by loops governing the array index or indices. A primary purpose in using arrays is to speed up the processing of a large amount of data. One might imagine hundreds or thousands of data items in an application needing to be calculated, sorted, or searched without using the efficiency of arrays and loop operations.

10.1.2 Array and object

In Java, an array is actually an object inherited from class **Object**. An array name represents the object using a subscript(s) to reference a given element of the array. This concept is illustrated in Figure 10.1.

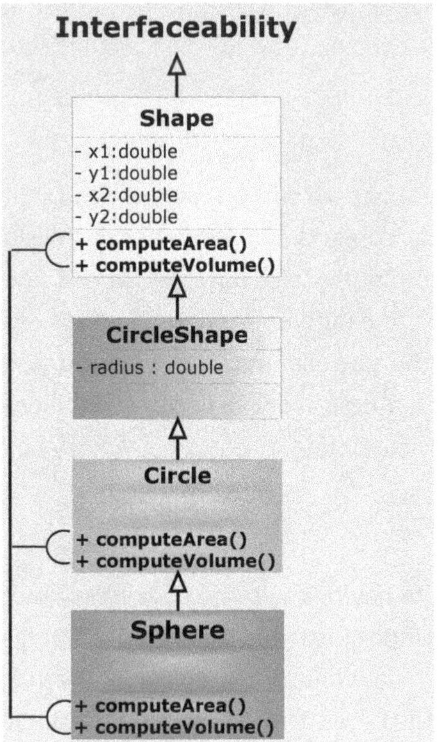

Figure 10.1 Array and address referencing

The upper portion of Figure 10.1 demonstrates the use of subscripts to reference the address of the elements in an integer type array. The element is referencing a particular data. The lower portion of the figure illustrates the referencing of the elements of an object array of class **Circle**. In the object array, each element is actually a reference to the beginning address of the particular object.

Once an array is declared, the number of elements in the array—the length of the array—is determined by a constant member data called **length**. The length of an array can be accessed using the syntax

arrayName.length

The use of **length** prevents many array out-of-bounds problems, thereby making the use of arrays a robust feature in Java.

As with other objects in Java, the array is an object of class **Object** and may be used with any members of the **Object** class. Since all Java-defined array types (primitive data types, **String** type, and wrapper class types) have implemented the **Cloneable** interface, the **clone()** method can be used to make copies of arrays. In addition, the **Arrays** and **System** classes in the Java API also provide many methods to perform a variety of operations on arrays, such as comparing, filling, copying, sorting and searching, et cetera.

Arrays may be considered as the basis of many modern data structures. Other data structures, such as **ArrayList** (array lists), **LinkedList** (linked lists), and **Vector** (vectors), are expansions of arrays. Arrays represent the default data structure within Java and do not require the importation of any Java API library. **Array** is also a final class and cannot be used to perform inheritance, overloading, and overriding.

10.1.3 An Introduction to arrays

Java uses dynamic memory allocation to assign a region of memory for array storage. It should be noted *declaring* an array does not create an array object or allocate space in memory—the declaration merely creates a variable with a reference to an array. The JVM automatically initializes all elements of an array when *created* according to the following scheme in Table 10.1:

Table 10.1 Default assignments in arrays

Array	Default Assignment of Array Elements at Initialization
Oolean	FALSE
Byte	0
Character	empty (space): '\u0000'
Short	0
Int	0
Long	0L
floating point	0.0f
Double	0.0d
Object	Null
String	Null
Array	Based on array type

Java provides several different methods to create, declare, and initialize arrays.

Method 1. Use of the **new** operator to create arrays according to the following syntax:

```
dataType[] arrayName = new dataType[n];
```

wherein,

dataType – any data type. The trailing square brackets must be empty.

n – quantity or size of elements. **n** must be any integer type (**byte**, **char**, **short**, or **int**) except **long**.

The JVM will allocate memory space according to the specified data type and size **n** and initialize the elements in the array. For example,

```
int[] gradeArray = new int[30];
```

creates an integer array called **gradeArray** with 30 elements. Its subscript range is from 0 to 29. All elements are initialized to 0 automatically by the JVM.

Method 2. Declaration is separated from initialization:

```
int[] gradeArray;               //Declare an integer array
...
gradeArray = new int[30];       //initialize the array
```

The declaration of an array does not involve memory allocation. Memory is only allocated and initialized using the **new** operator. Note that the square brackets must be empty when an array is declared, otherwise a syntax error will be generated.

When an array is declared, the position of the empty brackets denotes a specific meaning. For example, the statement

```
int []array, number;
```

or

```
int array[], number;
```

declares an integer type array, **array**, and an integer type variable, **number**. Such a notation allows the intermixed declaration of arrays and scalar variables in the same statement.

However, the statement

```
int[] array, number;
```

declares two integer type arrays, **array** and **number**, respectively.

Memory for each array may, in turn, be allocated and initialed

```
array = new int[10];
number = new int[50];
```

It is important to note that although an array of size 0 may be created:

```
int[] array = new int[0];
```

such a statement results in the creation of an array containing zero(0) elements, i.e., its length is 0. As the meanings of size and length are not the same as index, attempting to access an element within the array will cause an **ArrayOutBoundException** exception. This concept, however, is used in instances of array name reuse and is discussed in later sections.

Method 3. Use of C/C++ "traditional" ways to create arrays. The syntax as follows:

```
dataType[] arrayName = {value1, value2, ..., valueN};
```

wherein,

dataType – any data type. The trailing square brackets must be empty.

value*x* – initial values to be assigned to consecutive elements in the array. The values must match the declared data type or a syntax error will be generated.

For example, the statement

```
int[] scores = {90, 82, 75, 99, 62, 95, 88};
```

declares and initializes an integer array, **scores**, containing 7 elements with each element (0 through 6) being assigned the value 90, 82, 75, 99, 62, 95, and 88, respectively.

This method of creating arrays is efficient for small sized arrays. It is important to note that separating the initialization from the declaration will result in the generation of a syntax error.

The square brackets can be in different positions with different meaning, as discussed above. For example,

```
double[] rateArray = {0.098, 0.0875, 0.0681, 0.1052},
         loanArray = {12908, 50980.55, 766.49};
```

creates two double type arrays, **rateArray** and **loanArray**, while the statement

```
double rateArray[] = {0.098, 0.0875, 0.0681, 0.1052}, num = 2.3;
```

creates a single array double type, **rateArray**, and a double type scalar variable, **num**.

This method can be applied to any type of array. For example,

```
char[] name = {'W', 'a', 'n', 'g'};
```

or

```
char []name = {'W', 'a', 'n', 'g'}, ch1 = 'm', ch2 = 's';
```

or

```
char name[] = {'W', 'a', 'n', 'g'}, ch1 = 'm', ch2 = 's';        //same as above
```

Note that Java does not require the use of a terminating '\0' element at the end of **char** type arrays. The JVM will automatically check the boundaries of the array.

The following are more examples in creating arrays:

```
// create a String array with 5 elements
String bookTitles = {"Java", "C++", "C#", "JSP", "Java EE"};
```

```
//Create a wrapper class Integer array with 2 elements
Integer[] IntObjs = {new Integer(100), new integer(200)};

//Create a user-defined class type Book array with 3 elements
Book[] books= {new Book("001","Java",28.98), new Book(), new Book("C++",89.00)};
```

Figure 10.2 describes the elements, subscripts, and memory allocation of a **char** type array called **name**:

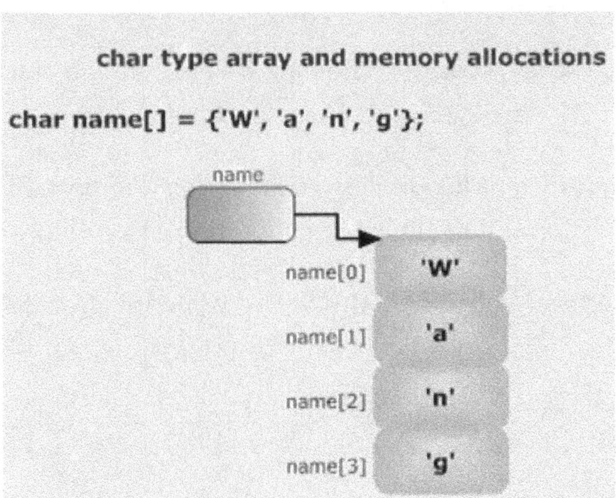

Figure 10.2 **char** type array and use of subscripts

Object type arrays are also commonly used in coding. The statement

```
Object[] objArray = new Object[100];
```

creates an **Object** type array called **objArray** containing 100 elements with each element initialized to null. The array can be used to store any **Object** elements since **Object** is a superclass for all classes. This form of array construct is generally avoided as intermixing object types in such an array may cause exceptions to be generated when operations are applied to the elements.

By way of another example, the statement

```
Circle[] circles = {new Circle(2.98), new Circle(0.92), new Circle(91.03)};
```

creates and initializes a **Circle** type array with 3 elements of **Circle** objects called **circles**. Direct use of the **new** operator in instantiating an object without an object name is called anonymous object creation. In this technique, especially when used in conjunction with arrays, the names of objects are not important as the subscripts represent each element of the objects. This technique illustrates the lower portion of Figure 10.1, by describing the memory allocation, element referencing, and member data for each element.

There are three important considerations that must be addressed in the use of arrays:

- In the traditional way of creating an array, a comma can be added after the last element value:

```
int[] array = {1, 3, 5, 0, };
```

This is a legal Java statement and is the form often used in code prepared by automatic code generators.

- An array name can be reused. For example,

```
byte[] grades = new byte[30];
...
grades = new byte[50];                    //Reuse of array name "grades"
```

However, the data type must remain the same in the "reused" array as in the original array.

- When using an expression to compute the size of an array, it is important to remember the assignment is made *before* the exception occurs. For example, in the statement

```
int array = new int[var1 = var2 * var3];
```

if the value of **var1** exceeds 2,147,483,648, an **ArrayIndexOutOfBoundsException** will be thrown *after* **var1** has been assigned the wrong value.

More Info: *In Java a multidimensional array can contain a different number of elements in each row. We discuss these topics in Section 10.3.*

10.2 Array Operations

Array operations include element access, assigning values to array elements, arithmetic calculations, array copying, array referencing, and the reuse of array names. We also discuss the use of loops in performing array operations and introduce enhanced for-loops in accessing array elements in the following sections.

10.2.1 Access array elements

A subscript, or index, is used to access an element after the array is created:

```
arrayName[index]
```

wherein,

index – subscript of the array element, ranging in value from 0 to **length** – 1. **length** is a constant member data representing the size, or number of elements, of the array.

The following are common examples of accessing array elements:

Example 1. Assign values to array elements.

```
int NUM = 3;                          //or final int NUM = 3;
…
double[] score = new double[NUM];     //Create a double type array with 3 elements
score[0] = 99.89;
score[1] = 87.29;
score[2] = 88.95;
score[3] = 77.45;             //This will throw an ArrayIndexOutOfBoundsException
```

Attempting to access an element outside the bounds of the array's range of elements causes the JVM to throw an **ArrayIndexOutOfBoundsException** exception.

We can also reassign a value of an array element:

```
score[1] = 80.0;
```

Example 2. Assign values to elements of a **String** type array.

The statement

```
String[] name = new String[1];        //Create a String type array with one element
name[0] = "Ling Li" ;
```

creates a **String** array containing one element, a **String** variable containing the value "Ling Li". The one element array, **name**, is similar—but not the same—in meaning to the statement

```
String name = "Ling Li";
```

The second statement denotes a scalar variable **String** referencing.

As a point of information, the statement

```
char[] name2 = {'Ling', ' ', 'Li'};
```

is an example of a **char** type array containing three elements. Array **name2** is <u>not</u> a **String** array and cannot have methods of the **String** class applied to it.

The following statements create a **String** type array with 4 elements:

```
String[] languages = {"Java", "C++", "C#", "JBoss"};
```

or:

```
String[] languages = new String[4];
languages[0] = "Java";
languages[1] = "C++";
languages[2] = "C#";
languages[3] = "JBoss";
```

These two examples are equivalent. The first uses the traditional way of declaring and assigning initial values to the array; the second way separates the declaration of the array and the assignment of values to the respective elements.

Figure 10.3 illustrates the memory allocation scheme, assignment of element values, and their relationship with the array subscripts in a **String** array. It is important to note the subscript in a **String** array refers to the beginning address of the character string serving as the value of the element.

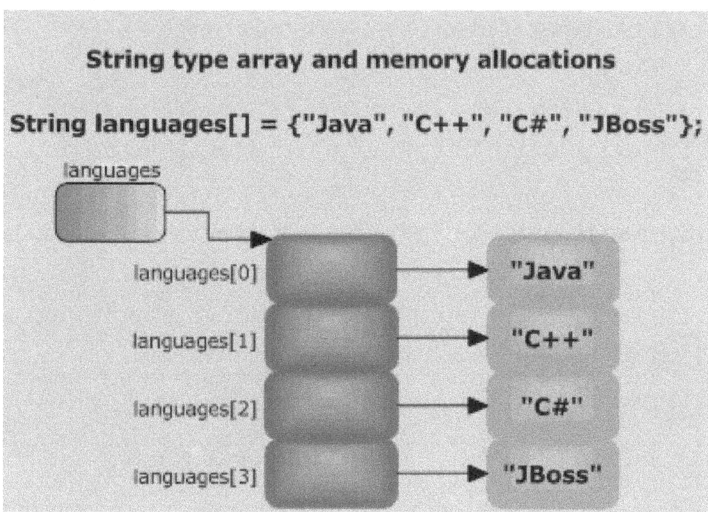

Figure 10.3 Address referencing in a **String** type array

We can reassign the value of any particular array element:

```
languages[3] = "Python";              //"JBoss" is replaced by "Python"
```

Example 3. Assign objects of a user-defined class, **Manager**, to the elements of an array.

```
Manager[] manager = new Manager[2]; //Create an Manager type array with 2 elements
Manager ourManager = new Manager("Zhang Shuang", 2900); //Create object of Manager
manager[0] = ourManager;              //assign the object to the element
Manager yourManager = new Manager("Huang Zhan", 2800);
Manager[1] = yourManager;             //assign the object to the element
```

The five preceding statements are equivalent to:

```
Manager[] manager = {new Manager("Zhang Shuang", 2900), new Manager("Huang Zhan",
2800)};
```

It is important to note the following statement

```
manager[0] = {new Manager("Zhang Shuang", 2900)};        //Syntax error
```

will cause a syntax error because it can only be used in code combining array declaration and initialization within one statement.

The following statements

```
manager[0].setName("Qiu Bai");                  //Call setName() of the first element
System.out.println(manager[1].earnings());  //Call   earnings()   of   the   second
element
```

call the methods of the object element, **setName()** and **earnings()**, respectively, of the array.

You may assign a new object of **Manager** to an element of the array:

```
// Create an object of Manager
Manager otherManager = new Manager("Smith Li", 3290);
manager[1] = otherManager;           //Assign the object to the second element
```

The previous object, **yourManager**, contained in the second element of the array is replaced by the new object, **otherManager**.

Example 4. Use of **clone()** to copy an array.

```
int[] values = {78, 90, 100, 88, 76, 80};
int[] scores = values.clone();              //copy all elements of values to scores
```

Since **values** is an integer array and has implemented the **Cloneable** interface (see Chapter 9), we can call the **clone()** method to make a copy of **values** to **scores**. The reader is strongly urged to be mindful of the cautions and pitfalls associated in using the **clone()** method.

10.2.2 Arrays and loops

The access and processing of elements in large arrays is almost always achieved through the use of loops.

Example 1. Assign double precision random numbers to an array containing 50 elements.

In the following Java code

```
double[] randomArray = new double[50];
for (int i = 0, i < randomArray.length; i++) {
   randomArray[i] = Math.random() * 100.0;
}
```

a series of fifty double precision random numbers, ranging from 0.0 to less than 100.0, is generated and assigned to the fifty elements of array **randomArray**. The constant member data **length** associated with the array limits the upper bound of the array.

Example 2. Print the value of each element in an array:

```
int[] numbers = {5, 20, 3, 9, 6};
for (int i = 0; i < numbers.length; i++)
```

```
   System.out.println(numbers[i]);
```

Example 3. Calculate the average of the elements in an array.

```
int sum = 0;
double average;
for (int i = 0; i < numbers.length; i++) {
   sum += numbers[i];                        //Calculate the sum
}
average = (double) sum / numbers.length;     //calculate the average
```

The above code can also be written

```
int sum = 0;
double average;
for (int i = 0; i < numbers.length; sum += numbers[i++]);
average = (double)sum / numbers.length;     //Calculate the average
```

wherein the incrementation of the array index is "incorporated" within the statement incrementing the sum. This form of coding, however, reduces code readability.

Example 4. Search array **languages** for the presence of the key **C#.**

```
boolean find = false;
for (int i = 0; i < languages.length; i++) {
   if (languages[i].equals("C#") {
          find = true;
          break;
   }
} //End of loop
if (find)
   System.out.println("languages[" + i + "] = " + languages[i]);
else
   System.out.println("The array languages doesn't contain C#");
```

The code examines each element of the array testing for the presence of the value "C#" matching the key. If the key is present in the array, the looping process is terminated by the **break** statement; if the key is not present, looping terminates upon completion of the "for-loop" processing. The result of the search is displayed.

10.2.3 Enhanced for loop

Java provides an "enhanced" for loop known as a "for each" loop. This loop is designed specifically for iterating over arrays and collections by eliminating much of the programming overhead involved in managing array indices and collection iterators. This feature became available in JDK 1.5.

The syntax of the enhanced for loop is:

```
for (dataType varName : arrayName) {
   ...
   //Satements in the loop
}
```

wherein:

dataType – specifies the primitive data type or object type of the array.

varName – variable name used to refer to an element.

arrayName – an existing array name.

This enhanced for loop iterates **arrayName.length** - 1 times, from 0 to *array_size* – 1, thereby accessing each element of the array.

Let's discuss examples using the enhanced for loop.

Example 1. Modify **Example 1** in the previous section to use an enhanced for loop.

```
double[] randomArray = new double[50];
for (double randomNum : randomArray)
   randomNum = Math.random() * 100.0;
```

Example 2. Modify **Example 2** in the previous section to use an enhanced for loop.

```
int[] numbers = {5, 20, 3, 9, 6};
for (int number : numbers)
   System.out.println(number);
```

The following numerical sequence corresponding to the elements of the array is displayed upon execution:

```
5
20
3
9
6
```

Example 3. Modify **Example 3** in the previous section to use an enhanced for loop.

```
int sum = 0;
double average;
for (int number : numbers)
   sum += number;                             //Sum
average = (double)sum / numbers.length;     //Average
```

It is important to note the square brackets form of array subscript notation cannot be used in conjunction with an enhanced for loop. The following statement is illegal:

```
for (int number : numbers; sum += numbers[i++];)  //Illegal use of square brackets
```

Warning: *You cannot modify or delete any element in an array using an enhanced for loop. The use of an array index is only inferred.*

10.2.4 Examples in applications

Sorting, searching, copying, inserting, and referencing are common operations associated with arrays. The **Arrays** and **System** classes in the Java API provide a rich number of methods to assist in these operations. These methods are discussed in Section 10.4. The following example illustrates a statistical array application. A second example computes the average and total of areas in a user-defined class **Circle** type array.

Example 1. Randomly generate whole numbers to simulate the roll of a die and run the code 10,000 times to show the statistics relating to the appearances of each number.

```
//Complete code called DieStatisticsTest.java in Ch10 from author's website
//demo: simulating the frequency of each side in a die
import java.util.Random;            //Use Random in API to generate random numbers

public class DieStatisticsTest {
   public static void main( String[] args ) {

      int side = 1;
      int[] frequencies = new int[6];       //Use arrays to hold the statistics

      Random randomNumber = new Random();  //Create Random object

      for(int roll = 1; roll <= 10000; roll++)
         // NOTE:  Method "nextInt(6)" generates random numbers in the range:
         //         0 - 5, inclusive, to simulate the six(6) sides of a die
         ++frequencies[randomNumber.nextInt(6)]; //accumulate appearances

       System.out.println("Side\t" + "Frequency");
       for (int frequency : frequencies)
          System.out.println(side++ + "\t" + frequency);
   }
}
```

This example uses the **Random** class of the Java API **java.util** package to generate random numbers. Method **nextInt(n)** generates a random number from 0 to n - 1 (in this example, from 0 to 5). Class **Random** also provides many other methods for operations involving random numbers.

The first loop in the code is used to store the appearances of each number appearing on the top side of a die rolled 10,000 times. Each array subscript represents a side of the die in a one-to-one correspondence with the randomly generated numbers. When a random number is generated, the value of the array element denoted by the subscripted random number is incremented by 1. The second loop uses an enhanced for loop to display the statistics. The following is a typical result of code execution:

```
Side      Frequency
1         1607
2         1720
3         1668
4         1666
5         1676
6         1663
```

Example 2. Modify **CircleShapeApp**, discussed in Chapter 8, to use an array of objects in calculating the total area and average of the areas in the **Circle** objects in the array.

```
// Complete code called CircleShapeApp.java in Ch10 from the author's website
public class CircleShapeApp{
   public static void main(String[] args) {
      //Create a Shape array with 3 Circle objects and 2 Sphere objects
      Shape[] shapes = {new Circle(10.02), new Circle(6.54), new Circle(0.69),
                        new Sphere(67.23), new Sphere(1.28)};
      double totalArea = 0.0;
      double average = 0.0;

      // Use enhanced for loops
      for(Shape shape : shapes)
         shape.computeArea();                       //Compute the area

      for(Shape shape : shapes)
         totalArea += shape.getArea();              //Compute total area
      average = totalArea/shapes.length;            //Compute average

      System.out.println("The total of the areas " + totalArea);
      System.out.println("The average of the areas " + average);
   }
}
```

This example creates a **Shape** array containing five elements: three **Circle** objects and two **Sphere** objects. The code also demonstrates the use of polymorphism and enhanced for loops in computing the areas of objects and the total areas in the array.

10.3 More Techniques With Arrays

While one-dimensional arrays, such as those discussed in previous sections, are used to handle data in lists, two-dimensional arrays are used to handle data in tables with rows and columns. In the following sections, more concepts and coding techniques using two- and higher-dimensional arrays, array parameters, and array returns types are discussed.

10.3.1 Two-dimensional arrays

A two-dimensional array can be considered as array of arrays, i.e., an element of the array points to a single-dimensioned array. A **String** array is a typical example of such an array. An element of the **String** array is a string. Examining the content of each string, each character can be considered as an element of a **char** type array.

As in the declaration, creation, and initialization of one-dimensional arrays, Java provides a variety of methods to manipulate two-dimensional arrays.

Method 1. Use of **new** operator to create a two-dimension array.

In this example,

```
int[][] values = new int[2][3];
```

an **int** array, **values**, is declared, created, and initialized to contain two rows and three columns. Each array element is initialized to 0.

```
values[0][0] = 0        values[0][1] = 0     values[0][2] = 0
values[1][0] = 0values[1][1] = 0     values[1][2] = 0
```

Method 2. Array declaration is separated from the instantiation.

```
int[][] values;         //may also be written:  int [][]value; or int values[][];
...
values = new[2][3];
```

It is important to remember, however, that a statement such as

```
double[][] rates, prices;
```

only <u>declares</u> two **double** type two-dimensional arrays, **rates** and **prices**, respectively, while the statement

```
double [][]rates, price;      //or double rates[][], price;
```

declares a two-dimensional **double** type array, **rates**, and a **double** type variable, **price**.

Although the following array creation and initialization

```
Object[][] objects = new Object[3][2];      //Create an Object type 2-D array
```

are legal, assigning different types of objects to the array elements:

```
objects[0][0] = new Integer(10);
objects[0][1] = new Float(2.78);
objects[1][0] = new Double(92.873);
objects[1][1] = new Character('a');
objects[2][0] = new String("Java");
objects[2][1] = new Circle(20.05);
```

causes a type-unsafe problem. Although all arithmetic operations can be performed on the numerical elements of the array, attempting such operations on the **String** and **Circle** elements will generate run-time errors. Type-unsafe issues are discussed in Chapter 13.

Method 3. Use of braces to declare, create, and initialize a two-dimensional array.

In the statement

```
int[][] scores = { {89, 92, 87}, {99, 90, 82} };
```

two inner sets of braces separated by a comma form the two rows of an **int** type two-dimensional array. Inside each pair of inner braces are three **int** data separated by commas forming the three columns—one column associated with each row—of the array. This is the traditional way of combining the declaration, creation, and initialization of a two-dimensional array into one statement.

As previously discussed, the position of the square brackets denotes different meanings to the statement. For example, the statements

```
int[][] scores = { {89, 92, 87}, {99, 90, 82} };
```

and

```
int scores[][] = { {89, 92, 87}, {99, 90, 82} }, count = 2;
```

each declare, create, and initialize a 2 x 3 two-dimensional array, **scores**, and an **int** variable, **count**, respectively.

However, the statement

```
int[][] scores = { {89, 92, 87}, {99, 90, 82} }, counts = {{1, 3}, {2, 4}};
```

declares, creates, and initializes two-dimensional **int** arrays, **scores** and **counts**, respectively.

As with one-dimensional arrays, a comma may be placed at the end of last column:

```
String[][] names = {{"Zhao Linlin", "Qian Linyi", "Sun Linsan", "Li Linsi"},
{"Zhang Yilin", "Guan Yiyi", "Li Yier", "Dai Yisan"}, };
```

All above discussions have dealt with regular, or rectangular, two-dimensional arrays. A rectangular two-dimensional array has two associated measurements—rows and columns: **arrayName.length** measures the number of rows and **arrayName[*i*].length** measures the number of columns in row ***i***.

The most common method of accessing each element in a two-dimensional array is to use nested loops: an outer loop using **arrayName.length** to control the access of elements in each row and an inner loop using **arrayName[i].length** to control the access of columnar elements in each row. Let's discuss an example:

```
//Complete code for TwoDArrayTest.java is available in Ch10 from author's website

// Outer loop controls rows
for( int row = 0; row < scores.length; row++) {
   // Inner loop controls columns
   for( int col = 0; col < scores[row].length; col++) {
      System.out.print(scores[row][col] + "\t");         //Print element
      sum += scores[row][col];                           //Sum
   }
   System.out.println("\n");
}
average = (double)sum / (scores.length * scores[0].length);     //2 * 3:  6 elements
System.out.println("Average score: " + average);
```

The following is the result of execution:

```
89      92      87

99      90      82

Average score: 89.83333333333333
```

We may also apply the enhanced for-loop to this example:

```
// Outer loop specifies rows
for (int[] row : scores) {
   // Inner loop specifies columns in each row
   for(int col : row) {
         System.out.print(col + "\t");              //Print element
         sum += col;                                //Sum
   }
   System.out.println("\n");
```

```
}
average = (double) sum / (scores.length * scores[0].length);    //2 * 3:  6 elements
System.out.println("Average score: " + average);
```

The result of the code execution is the same.

10.3.2 Jagged arrays

A two- or higher-dimensional array containing rows or columns of varying length is called a jagged array. There are three different methods typically used in creating a jagged array.

Method 1. Use of **new** operator to create a two-dimensional array with an empty column length.

The establishment of a jagged two-dimensional array with varying column lengths, for example,

```
float[][] pyramid = new float[4][];
```

first requires the specification of the length of the rows. The length of each column must then be specified before using the array:

```
for(int i = 0; i < pyramid.length; i++)
   pyramid[i] = new float[i + 1];
```

The above code snippet generates a triangle-, or pyramid-shaped array:

```
pyramid[0][0] = 0.0
pyramid[1][0] = 0.0            pyramid[1][1] = 0.0
pyramid[2][0] = 0.0            pyramid[2][1] = 0.0         pyramid[2][2] = 0.0
pyramid[3][0] = 0.0            pyramid[3][1] = 0.0         pyramid[3][2] = 0.0
pyramid[3][3] = 0.0
```

We may, of course, also create an analogous jagged array containing rows of varying lengths.

Method 2. Array declaration is separated from the instantiation.

The following sequence of Java statements constructs a jagged **String** array in a step-by-step manner with each array column containing a **String** of a differing length:

```
String[][] addresses;                         //Declaration
...
addresses = new String[3][];                  //Create rows
addresses[0] = new String[5];         //Create column for the first row
addresses[1] = new String[10];                //Create column for the second row
addresses[2] = new String[1];         //Create column for the third row
...
```

Method 3. Use of braces to declare, create, and initialize a two-dimensional jagged array.

The Java statement

```
CircleShape[][] CircleObjects = { {new Circle(9.65), new Circle(21.03), new
Circle(7.01)}, {new Sphere(3.98)}, new Sphere(66.29)} };
```

creates a two-dimensional jagged array of **CircleObjects**. The first row contains three columns of **Circle** objects; the second row contains two columns of **Sphere** objects.

The following example creates a "pyramid" array, similar to that shown above, and assigns a random number ranging from 0 through 99 to each element:

```
for( int[] row : pyramid)
   for(int col : row)
          col = (int) Math.random() * 100;
```

The above coding techniques can be extended to higher-dimensional jagged arrays. The use and meaning of the three different positions of the square brackets notation discussed in relation to defining one-dimensional arrays is also applicable to multidimensional jagged arrays.

10.3.3 Array parameters

We have used an array as a parameter in our first programming example:

```
public static void main(String[] args) { //Or String args[]
...
}
```

The use of a **String** array as a parameter in **main()** is required in a "driver" code by the JVM for proper code execution. Let's examine the following example to better understand how this parameter is used:

```
//The complete code called ArrayArgsTest.java in Ch10 from thd author's Website
public class ArrayArgsTest {
   public static void main(String[] args) {
      for(int i = 0; i < args.length; i++)
         System.out.println("args[" + i + "] = " + args[i] + "\t");
      System.out.println();
}
```

After compilation, the driver code may be executed with a list of arguments specified in the command line, as shown in the following example:

```
java ArrayArgsTest This is Array arguments test
```

The five words comprising the list of arguments are assigned to the first five elements of the **String** array **args**:

```
args[0] = "This"
args[1] = "is"
args[2] = "Array"
args[3] = "arguments"
args[4] = "test"
```

Let's develop another example using the array arguments provided on the command line to perform an arithmetic calculation:

```
//Complete code called CommandLineTest.java in Ch10 from the author's Website
public class CommandLineTest{
   public static void main(String[] args) {

      int x = Integer.valueOf(args[0]);      // Or Integer.parseInt(args[0]);
      int y = Integer.valueOf(args[1]);      // Or Integer.parseInt(args[1]);

      System.out.println("x * y = " + x*y);
   }
}
```

After compilation, the driver code may be executed with the parameters specified in the command, for example:

```
java CommandLineTest 10 20
```

Command line input strings "10" and "20" are assigned to **args[0]** and **args[1]**, respectively. It is important to remember that all parameters provided on the command line are treated as character strings, despite their numerical "appearance." As such, each element of **args** must be converted to a numeric value. In the above example, this conversion is performed by calling method **Integer.valueOf()** and assigning the method's integer return values to integer variables **x** and **y**, respectively.

The following examples illustrate techniques using arrays as arguments.

Example 1. Using a one-dimensional array as an argument.

The method signature of **method()**

```
public void method(int[] array) {            //Or method(int array[])
   //The statements using array in the task
   for(int element: array)
      System.out.println(element);
   ...
}
```

requires an integer array, **array**, to be provided as a parameter to the method.

An array may be passed to a method by specifying the array's name as the method's parameter, for example:

```
objectName.method(array);  //array is the name of a defined array
```

Recalling that a row of a two-dimensional array is, in fact, a one-dimensional array in itself, a given row of the array may be passed to a method. Using the pyramid-shaped jagged array discussed previously, we may pass the array representing the elements of row "0" of **pyramid**:

```
objectName.method(pyramid[0]);       // pyramid is a two-dimensional array;
                                     // pyramid[0] is a one-dimensional array
```

to **objectName.method()**.

Note that the **int** type array is a referenced argument and any changes in the argument array will affect to the original array.

It is important to note and recall pyramid is an **int** type array being used as a referenced argument. As such, any changes made to the argument within **objectName.method()** will affect the original array in the calling program.

Example 2. Using a two-dimensional array as an argument.

The method signature of **method2()**

```
public void method2(double[][] doubleArray)
```

requires the presence of a two-dimensional array to be provided by the calling code.

```
public void method2(double[][] doubleArray) {
  //Statements to use doubleArray for specified task
  for(double[] row: doubleArray)      // outer loop controls row
     for(double col:row)              // inner loop controls column
        System.out.println(col);      // display each element in passed 2-D array
}
```

The calling routine need pass only the array name as the argument for the method:

```
objectName.method2(array);  //array is the name of a defined array
```

10.3.4 An array as the return type of a method

An array can be the return type of a method. In actuality, the method returns the reference of the array. For example:

```
//Complete code called ArrayUse.java in Ch10 from the author's website
public static double[] append(double[] array1, double[] array2) {
   double[] join = new double[array1.length + array2.length];
   for(int i = 0; i < array1.length; i++)
      join[i] = array1[i];
   for (int i = 0; i < array2.length; i++)
      join[array1.length + i] = array2[i];
   return join;
}
```

This static method combines the contents of two **double** type arrays into a single array and returns the resultant array to the calling program. In the method, a new array, **join**, is created with a length equaling the sum of the lengths of the two target arrays. The first loop copies each element of **array1** into the beginning element sequence of **join**. The second loop copies each element of **array2** into the remaining elements of **join**. At the completion of code execution, **join** is returned as a reference to the calling code.

The following is the driver code used to test this method **append()**:

```
//Complete code is called ArrayReturnTest.java in Ch10 from the author's Website
public class ArrayReturnTest {
   public static void main( String args[] ) {
      //Create and initialize two double arrays
      double[] firstArray = { 89.2, 192.09, 87.77, 299.102, 920.02, 82.2 };
      double[] secondArray = { 0.934, 0.087, 0.056, 0.0625};

      //Create another double array to receive the reference from append()
      double[] combinedArray;

      //Call append()
      combinedArray = ArrayUse.append(firstArray, secondArray);

      //Display the result
      for(double element : combinedArray)
         System.out.print(element + "  ");
      System.out.println("\n");
   }
}
```

The elements of the concatenated array are displayed

```
89.2  192.09  87.77  299.102  920.02  82.2  0.934  0.087  0.056  0.0625
```

upon executing the code.

Multidimensional arrays can also be the return type of a method. As in the case of one-dimensional arrays, the method returns the reference to the multidimensional array. Code snippet **method()**

```
public double[][] method() {
   //Create a 2-D array and other statements
   ...
   return doubleArray;
}
```

returns a reference to a two-dimensional array. The calling statement may be of the form:

```
double[][] doubleArray = objectName.method();
```

or

```
double doubleArray[][] = objectName.method();
```

10.4 Arrays Class

The **Arrays** class provided in the **java.util** package of JDK1.6 is used to perform filling, comparison, copying, sorting, and searching operations associated with arrays. Prior to JDK1.6, method **arrayCopy()** in the **System** class was used to copy arrays.

If an array is a user-defined class type array, the **Comparable** interface must be implemented to perform sorting of the array elements. This interface is discussed in the following section.

10.4.1 Commonly used methods in class Arrays

Table 10.2 lists the commonly used methods in the **Arrays** class.

Table 10.2 Commonly used methods in Array class

Method	Description
boolean equals(arrayName1, arrayName2)	Returns **true** if both arrays , on an element-by-element basis, are the same; otherwise returns **false**. User-defined array types must implement the **Comparable** interface to use this method.
fill(arrayName, value)	Fills each element of **arrayName** with specified **value**.
fill(arrayName, index, n, value)	Fills **n** elements of **arrayName** beginning at **arrayName[index]** with specified **value**.
dataType[] copyOf(arrayName, length)	Returns copied array of the specified **length,** truncating or padding with zero or null, according to **dataType**, as required. The **dataType** of copied array must be same **dataType** as **arrayName**.
dataType[] copyOfRange(arrayName, index1, index2)	Returns copied array from **arrayName[index1]** to **arrayName[index2]**. Length of target array is **index2** - **index1** + 1. The **dataType** of copied array must be same **datatType** as **arrayName**.
sort(arrayName)	Sorts array into ascending order, according to natural ordering of elements . User-defined array types must implement **Comparable** interface.
sort(arrayName, index1, index2)	Sorts array elements within specified range into ascending order,

	according to natural ordering of elements. User-defined array types must implement **Comparable** interface .
int binarySearch(arrayName, value)	Searches **arrayName** for specified **value** key Returns index of element if **value** key is found; otherwise , returns a negative value.
String toString(arrayName)	Returns a String representation of the contents of **ArrayName**.

The above table serves as an overview of important **Arrays** class sorting methods. The JDK documentation should be consulted for full implementation details, particularly in cases involving sorting of floating-point numbers, **Object** arrays, and arrays of user-defined types.

Let's discuss examples using the above methods.

Example 1. Call **fill()** method to assign a value to all elements of an array.

```
int[] educationYears = new int[8];

// "fill" all elements of array with integer value: 10
Arrays.fill(educationYears, 10);
```

Example 2. Call **fill()** method to assign a value to specified range of elements in the array.

```
int[] educationYears = new int[8];

// "fill" first four elements of array, i.e., elements 0 - 3, with integer
// value:  15

Arrays.fill(educationYears, 0, 4, 15);
Arrays.fill(educationYears, 4, 4, 10);
```

Example 3. Call **equals()** method to compare contents of two arrays.

```
//Complete code called ArraysMethodsTest.java in Ch10 from the author's Website
String[] names1 = {"C", "C++", "Java"};
String[] names2 = {"c", "C++", "Java"};

if(Arrays.equals(names1, names2))
   System.out.println("They are equal");
else
   System.out.println("They are not equal");
```

The result of execution is:

```
They are not equal
```

Note: *The* ***equals()*** *method in the* ***Object*** *class compares the addresses of two arrays.* ***Arrays*** *class does not provide* ***equalsIgnoreCase()*** *method.*

Example 4. Another example of using **equals()** method to compare two arrays as **Object** types.

```
Object[] objects1 = {new Double(10.20), new Integer(20)};
Object[] objects2 = {new Double(10.20), new Integer(20)};

if (Arrays.equals(objects1, objects2))
   System.out.println("They are equal");
else
   System.out.println("They are not equal");
```

Because the objects in the two arrays are exactly the same, the message

```
They are equal
```

is displayed.

Example 5. Use **toString()** to print elements in the array from **Example 2**.

```
System.out.println(Arrays.toString(educationYears));
```

The following result is displayed:

```
[15, 15, 15, 15, 10, 10, 10, 10]
```

10.4.2 Sorting and searching

The **sort()** and **binarySearch()** methods in the **Arrays** class are used to perform sorting and searching of arrays with primitive data, **String**, and wrapper class types. For user-defined class type arrays it is necessary to implement method **compareTo()** in the **Comparable** interface before performing any array sorting and searching operations. The **compareTo()** method is discussed in section 10.4.4. The following examples illustrate common sorting and searching operations used with arrays.

Example 1. Use of the **sort()** method to sort an **int** array.

```
//The complete code called ArraysMethodsTest.java in Ch10 from author's Website
int[] scores = {2, 4, 0, 1, 10, 9, 5, 3, 8};
Arrays.sort(scores);
for(int score : scores)
  System.out.print(score + "    ");
```

The following is the execution result:

```
0  1  2  3  4  5  8  9  10
```

Example 2. Use of the **binarySearch()** method to find a key in a sorted array. The array must be sorted prior to using the **binarySearch()** method. If the array is not sorted, the result is undefined.

```
String[] javas = {"Java SE", "JSP", "Java EE", "Java ME", "Servlets", "Applets",
                  "Java"};
Arrays.sort(javas);                                        //sort first
int index = Arrays.binarySearch(javas, "Java");            //search
```

After sorting, the elements of the array are in ascending order:

```
Applets   JSP   Java   Java EE   Java ME   Java SE   Servlets
```

and the **binarySearch()** method may be successfully applied. The index of the successful search key in the array is 2.

Example 3. Sort and perform a binary search in a **Double** type two-dimensional array.

```
Double[][] doubles = { {new Double(2.98), new Double(19.23), new Double(0.09)},
                       {new Double(1.02), new Double(20.34), new Double( 2.09),
                        new Double(8.201), new Double(0.01)} };

Arrays.sort(doubles[0]);                      //Sort in the first row

Arrays.sort(doubles[1]);                      //Sort in the second row
for (Double[] row : doubles) {                //Display the result
   for(Double col : row)
          System.out.print(col + "    ");
   System.out.println();
}

// Perform binary search for selected key in second row of array and display
// result.

System.out.println("index of 2.09 = " + Arrays.binarySearch(doubles[1], 2.09));

// Perform binary search for selected key of non-existent value in first row of
// array and display result.

System.out.println("index of 2.98001 = " + Arrays.binarySearch(doubles[0],
2.98001));
```

The following is the result of the execution:

```
0.09   2.98   19.23
0.01   1.02   2.09   8.201   20.34
index of 2.09 = 2
```

```
index of 2.98001 = -3
```

Because search key 2.98001 represents a non-existent value in the array, a negative result is returned. The return value of -3 represents: (-(*insertion point*) – 1). The *insertion point* is defined as the point at which the key would be inserted into the array, i. e., the index of the first element greater than the key, or **array.length** if all the elements in the array are less than the specified key. This mechanism guarantees the return value will be greater than or equal to 0 if and only if the key is found.

NOTE: *An array must be sorted prior to calling the* ***binarySearch()*** *method. If sorting and binary searching operations are to be performed on a two-dimensional array, each row of the array must be dealt with as a one-dimensional array.*

10.4.3 Copying arrays

Let's first discuss the difference between an array reference and a copy of array. The following is an example of an array reference:

```
int[] values = {10, 5, 20, 100};
int[] valuesRef = values;          //valuesRef is a reference to values
```

valuesRef is actually a reference to **values**. **valuesRef** does not have its own copy of the elements contained in array **values; valuesRef** is merely another name of **values.**

When we create an array:

```
int[] others = {2, 3, 4, 5};
```

and use this variable name to reference another array:

```
others = values;
```

all memory, i.e., the elements, associated with array **others** will be reclaimed by the garbage collection facilities of the JVM because the "original" array no longer has any references to it. Upon completion of execution of the statement, any modification in the **others** array will actually be performed in **values,** and vice versa.

Let's discuss an example of copying array using the **clone()** method:

```
int[] values = {10, 5, 20, 100};
int[] others = values.clone();          //Copying array
```

Method **clone()** performs a copying operation. It first creates an array named **others** with the same length as **values**, and then copies each element from **values** to **others** in the proper order.

Methods **copyOf()** and **copyOfRange()** in the **Arrays** class and **arraycopy()** in **System** provide more flexibility in copying arrays. Let's discuss some examples using these methods.

Example 1. Use of **copyOf()** to copy an array.

```
//Complete code called ArraysMethodsTest.java in Ch10 from author's Website
//Copy grades to copyGrades
double[] grades = {98, 78, 89, 82, 100, 67};
double[] copyGrades = Arrays.copyOf(grades, grades.length);
```

Example 2. Use of **copyOfRange()** to clone the specified range in a target array to a destination array.

In this example, the elements in the second half of **grades (**82, 100, and 67) are copied to destination array **copySome**.

```
double[] grades = {98, 78, 89, 82, 100, 67};
double[] copySome = Arrays.copyOfRange(grades, 3, grades.lentgth - 1);
```

Example 3. Use of **arraycopy()** in **System** class to copy an array.

```
double[] grades = {98, 78, 89, 82, 100, 67};

//Create an array with the same length of grade double[]
 copyGrades = new double[grades.length];
 System.arraycopy(grades, 0, copyGrades, 0, grades.length);
```

Five parameters are required in the use of method **arraycopy()**: target array; beginning subscript of the target array; destination array; beginning subscript of the destination array; and length of element range in target array to be copied.

It is important to note that if the target array is a user-defined class type array, all of these methods associated in copying arrays, e.g., **arraycopy()**, **copyOf()**, **copyOfRange()**, and **clone()**, perform "shallow" copying of the array elements as discussed in Chapter 9. As such, the full "depth" of data in the target array may not be copied, and any modification in the target array will affect the destination array, and vice versa.

Example 4. Use of **arraycopy()** to copy a user-defined object array ("shallow copy" or copy reference).

```
Object[] sourceObjects = {new Circle(5.26), new Circle(19.20)};

// Create a target array
Object[] targetObjects = new Object[sourceObjects.length];

//Create a destination array and copy the reference
System.arraycopy(sourceObjects, 0, targetObjects,0,sourceObjects.length);
```

This operation is equivalent to the following coding using methods **copyOf()**:

```
// Copy reference
targetObjects = Arrays.copyOf(sourceObjects, sourceObjects.length);
```

or **copyOfRange()**:

```
// Copy reference
targetObjects=Arrays.copyOfRange(sourceObjects, 0,  sourceObjects.length);
```

in the **Arrays** class to perform the same copying functionality.

In addition, the **clone()** method can also be used to make an actual duplication of the contents of the array, not just a copy of the references to the arrays and objects:

```
   targetObjects = sourceObjects.clone();                    //Copy reference
```

It is important to remember that when method **clone()** is used in copying user-defined object arrays, you must first implement the **Cloneable** interface.

10.4.4 Understanding the Comparable Interface

The **Comparable** interface defines a method, **compareTo()**, that provides information for performing **quickSort()**. The **quickSort()** method, based upon Hoare's algorithm of the same name, performs the underlying sorting mechanism for sorting user-defined class type arrays when method **sort()** in the **Arrays** class is called.

The syntax of **compareTo()** is:

```
public interface Comparable {
   int compareTo(Object object);
}
```

The argument type **Object** can be any type of object. In the implementation, the **this** object is compared for order with the specified object. The return value is a negative integer, zero, or positive integer if the comparison of the two objects is such that the **this** object is less than, equal to, or greater than the specified object, respectively.

Let's discuss a particular example in which a user-defined object containing numerical data is sorted. We will first implement the **Comparable** interface:

```
//Complete code called Item.java in Ch10 from the author's Website
public class Item implements Comparable {          //Implement Comparable
   private int number;
   private String name;

   public int getNumber() {
      return number;
   }
```

```
  public String getName() {
     return name;
  }

 // Implement compareTo() method
 public int compareTo(Object object) {
    Item item = (Item) object;      //Convert object to Item

    // compare "this" object with specified object:  numbers
    if (this.number < item.getNumber())
      return -1;      // first object is less than second object, return -1

    if (this.number > item.getNumber())
      return 1;       // first object is greater than second object, return 1

    // objects are equal, return 0
    return 0;
 }
}
```

The following is the driver code used to sort the user-defined array:

```
//Complete code called ItemSortTest.java in Ch10 from the author's Website
Item[] items = new Item[4];          //Create a user-defined array with 4 elements
items[0] = new Item(25, "Java");     //Use of the object reference
items[1] = new Item(100, "JSP");
items[2] = new Item(12, "Servlets");
items[3] = new Item(88, "JDBC");

Arrays.sort(items);                  //Call sort()to sort number in the array

for (Item item : items)              //Display result
   System.out.println(item.getNumber() + "\t" + item.getName() );
```

The following is the result of execution:

```
12      Servlets
25      Java
88      JDBC
100     JSP
```

The reader is strongly encouraged to note the Java documentation strongly recommending, but not strictly requiring, that **(x.compareTo(y)==0) == (x.equals(y))**. Generally speaking, any class implementing the **Comparable** interface that violates this condition should clearly indicate this fact. The recommended language is: "Note: this class has a natural ordering that is inconsistent with equals." See the Java documentation relating to the Comparable interface for further information.

If the data to be sorted in a user-defined array are **String** type, you may use the following code to implement the **Comparable** interface:

```
public int compareTo(Object object) {
    Item item = (Item) object;

    return this.name.compareTo(item.getName());
}
```

Note: *Method* ***compareTo()*** *in the* ***Comparable*** *interface can only implement one type of data in the sorting array; you cannot perform more than one data sorting in a specified array unless a multi-level inheritance is involved in forming the objects in the array.*

If the objects to be sorted in the array are formed through multilevel inheritance, we should select the higher level superclass to implement the **Comparable** interface. This will allow objects from the subclasses to call the **sort()** method to sort the data. A subclass can also override the implemented **compareTo()** method, thereby allowing another selected data in the object to be sorted. An example of this technique is discussed in the next section.

10.4.5 I need sorted data

The following example illustrates the sorting of radii, i.e., variable **radius**, in the **Circle3** and **Sphere** classes. The **Comparable** interface is implemented in class **CircleShape3**.

```
//Complete code called CircleShape3.java in Ch10 from the author's Website
public abstract class CircleShape3 extends Shape implements Comparable {
   ...
        public int compareTo(Object object) {
        CircleShape3 circleShape = (CircleShape3)object;

        //Converted to object of CircleShape3
        if (this.radius < circleShape.getRadius())      //Sort radius
              return -1;
        if (this.radius > circleShape.getRadius())
              return 1;
        return 0;
   }
}
```

In the following driver code, an array, **shapes**, containing five **Circle3** class type objects is created. Three elements are references to objects of **Circle3** and two elements are references to objects of **Sphere**. In addition to sorting the radius of each object, the method also calculates the area of each object.

```
// Complete code called CircleShape3App.java in Ch10 from the author's Website
Circle3[] shapes = {new Circle3(10.02), new Circle3(6.54), new Circle3(0.69),
                    new Sphere(67.23), new Sphere(1.28)};
   for(Circle3 shape : shapes)
         shape.computeArea();              //compute area for each element

   Arrays.sort(shapes);

   for(Circle3 shape : shapes)
         System.out.println(shape);
```

The following is the execution result:

```
(0.0,0.0), (0.0,0.0)
Radius: 0.69
Area: 1.4957122623741002

(0.0,0.0), (0.0,0.0)
Radius: 1.28
Area: 20.58874161456607

(0.0,0.0), (0.0,0.0)
Radius: 6.54
Area: 134.3709443422812

(0.0,0.0), (0.0,0.0)
Radius: 10.02
Area: 315.4171590574766

(0.0,0.0), (0.0,0.0)
Radius: 67.23
Area: 56798.397991198384
```

Note that the **radius** of each object is sorted.

The **compareTo()** method may be overridden to perform another sorting. For example, the **Sphere** class might override the **compareTo()** method implemented by **Circle** to sort the volumes of the **Sphere** objects, as shown in the following code that may be added to the driver code above:

```
//Complete code called CircleShapeApp3.java in Ch10 from the author's Website
Sphere[] spheres = {new Sphere(98.23), new Sphere(6.56), new Sphere(10.88)};

for(Sphere sphere : spheres)
sphere.computeVolume();

Arrays.sort(spheres);
System.out.println("Sorted by volumes in spheres array: ");
for(Sphere sphere : spheres)
System.out.println(sphere.getVolume());
```

The following execution result is from the added code above:

```
Sorted by volumes in spheres array:
1182.497217347923
5394.799336126033
3970279.135344333
```

10.5 Walking Into String

The **String** class is another important subclass of the **Object** class. It is a **final** class and cannot be inherited. Once a **String** object has been created, its contents cannot be modified; it is "immutable." However, the reference to a **String** object can be changed. A string can reference another string, and the previous reference is automatically discarded by the JVM. We will discuss this topic in detail in later sections. Package **java.lang** also provides two API classes, **StringBuilder** and **StringBuffer**, designed to modify and manipulate strings. **String** objects created by these two classes are "mutable" and their contents may be altered. In addition, **java.util** provides the **StringTokenizer** class containing methods to perform tokenization and related operations to strings.

The **String** class has a close relationship with arrays of **byte**, **char**, **short**, and **int** types. For example, **char** type arrays may be used as arguments to create a **String** object and **String** objects can be referenced by **char** type array elements. However, arrays of **char** and **String** are two different classes.

The **String** class provides a rich number of constructors and methods for performing a wide variety of string-related operations. We first discuss string referencing and string instantiation and commonly used constructors and methods in the **String** class. We will then discuss the **StringBuilder**, **StringBuffer**, and **StringTokenizer** classes.

10.5.1 String referencing vs. String instantiation

In Java, establishing a reference does not normally involve memory allocation; the action merely "refers" to an existing object. It is an alias of an object:

```
String name = new String("Java");    //Instantiate an object of String
String language = name;              //Establish a reference to variable "name"
```

wherein, **language** is a reference or alias to **name**. Continuing our example, in the code snippet:

```
//Reuse language to instantiate a new object
String language = new String("C++");

//Discard any existing content of name; establish name as a reference to language
name = language;
```

we "reuse" **language** in the instantiation of a new object containing the **String** object "C++". In the assignment of **language** to **name**, the memory associated with **name**, i.e., the string "Java", is no longer referenced, the memory will become subject to garbage collection by the JVM, and **name** now becomes a reference of **language**.

It should be noted that statements

```
String string1 = new String("Java");
```

and

```
String string2 = "Java";
```

are different in their purpose and intent. The first statement is the instantiation of a **String** object called **string1**; the second statement establishes the **String** object **string2** only as a reference to a string whose content is "Java". **String** objects **string1** and **string 2** are distinct objects and have different memory addresses.

However, in the following code sequence:

```
String s1 = "Java";
String s2 = s1;
String s3 = "Java";
```

each **String** object instantiation refers to content "Java" and each will share the same memory address. If the reference of **s1** is modified:

```
s1 = "JSP";
```

s1 will no longer refer to "Java". Instead, it now becomes a reference to "JSP" and its address will be different from the memory address of **s2** and **s3**. In summary, the content of a string cannot be modified because it is immutable. However, its reference can be changed.

Continuing the above example, in the statements

```
String s4 = new String("JSP");
String s5 = new String("JSP");
```

s4 and **s5** represent two distinct objects of **String**. Although the objects have exactly the same content, their memory addresses are different.

If we assign a new reference to **s1**, for example,

```
s1 = s5;
```

the JVM garbage collector will first discard the previous reference of **s1** and then let it serve as a reference to **s5**. The complete code for this exercise in string referencing can be found in **StringReferencingTest.java** in **Ch10** from the author's website.

10.5.2 String constructors

Table 10.3 lists some commonly used constructors of the **String** class.

Table 10.3 Commonly used constructors in **String**

Constructor	Description
String()	Constructs a new **String** object as an empty character sequence: ""
String(dataType[] arrayName)	Constructs a new **String** object based upon the contents of arrayName. **dataType[]** may be **byte** or **char** type arrays. **byte** arrays will be decoded using the platform's default **charset**. The contents of **char** arrays represents a sequence of characters in the array.
String(dataType[] arrayName, int startIndex, int count)	Constructs a new **String** object of length **count** beginning at the **startIndex** of **arrayName**. **dataType[]** may be **byte** or **char** type arrays.
String(String str)	Constructs a new **String** object containing the sequence of characters in the specified string.
String(StringBuilder strBuilder)	Constructs a new **String** object containing the sequence of characters in the specified **StringBuilder** object.

The following are examples using the above constructors:

Example1. Define a **byte** array and use it to instantiate a **String** object.

```
// platform-dependent charset representation of: "China"
byte[] countryArray = {67, 104, 105, 110, 97};

String country = new String(countryArray);            // Use content of
countryArray
String countryCode = new String(countryArray, 0, 2); // "Ch"
```

String **countryCode** is formed from the two-character subset of **countryArray** beginning at element 0: "Ch".

Example 2. Define a **char** type array and use it to instantiate a **String** object.

```
char[] cityName ={'B', 'e', 'i', 'j', 'i', 'n', 'g'};
String city = new String(cityName);
String cityCode = new String(cityName, 3, 4);
```

The content of **cityCode** is "jing", the last four character bytes in the array **cityName**.

Example 3. Define an **int** array and use it to instantiate a **String** object.

```
int[] unicodeArray = {74, 97, 118, 97};                    //"Java"
```

```
String unicode = new String(unicodeArray);
```

The content of **unicode** is "Java".

10.5.3 More methods in the **String** class

Methods provided by the **String** class can be divided into the following categories:

- Those returning the position of a specified substring in a string;
- Those returning a modified or updated string; and
- Those comparing the strings.

Because the content of a string is immutable, all operations on a string relating to any form of modification return a new resultant string. To maintain consistency with collections and array operations, strings are formed with zero-based indices, i.e., the first element of a string is associated with an index of "0".

Table 10.4 lists commonly used methods that return a substring or the position of a substring in the string operation.

Table 10.4 Commonly used methods returning a substring or the position of a substring

Method	Description
int length()	Returns length of the string.
int indexOf(char ch)	Returns position as index of the first occurrence of the specified character **ch** in the string, or -1 if character is not present.
int indexOf(String str)	Returns position as index of the first occurrence of the specified substring **str** in the string, or -1 if substring is not present.
int indexOf(String str, int index)	Returns position as index of the first occurrence of the specified substring **str** beginning at the specified **index** in the string, or return -1 if substring is not present.
int lastIndexOf(char ch)	Returns position as index of the last occurrence of the specified character **ch** in the string, or -1 if character is not present.
int lastIndexOf(String str)	Returns position as index of the last occurrence of the specified substring **str** in the string, or -1 if substring is not present.
int lastIndexOf(char ch, int index)	Returns position as index of the last occurrence of the specified substring **str** beginning at the specified **index** in the string, or return -1 if substring is not present.
int lastIndexOf(String str, int index)	Returns position as index of the last occurrence of the specified substring **str** beginning at the specified **index** in the string, or return -1 if substring is not present.

The following example illustrates the use of the **length()**, **indexOf()**, and **lastIndexOf()** methods.

Example 1. Using the **length()**, **indexOf()**, and **lastIndexOf()** methods.

```
// The complete code of StringMethodsTest.java in Ch10 form the
// author's website

String title = "Java Programming in Practice";
int titleLength = title.length();                 //titleLength = 28
int index  = title.indexOf('a');                  //index = 1
int index1 = title.indexOf("in");                  //index1 = 13
int index2 = title.indexOf("in", 14);              //index2 = 17
int index3 = title.lastIndexOf('a');         //index3 = 22
int index4 = title.lastIndexOf('a', 5);           //index4 = 3
int index5 = title.lastIndexOf("Pr", 19);         //index5 = 5
int index6 = title.indexOf('R');                  //index6 = -1
```

Table 10.5 lists commonly used methods that return a new created **char** or **String** object as the result of applying the method.

Table 10.5 Commonly used methods that return a new **char** or **String** object

Method	Description
String substring(int startIndex)	Returns a substring starting at the specified location.
String substring(int startIndex, int endIndex)	Returns a substring starting at the specified **startIndex** and extends to the character at **endIndex** – 1. The length of the returned substring is **endIndex – startIndex**.
String replace(char oldChar, char newChar)	Returns a new string in which all occurrences of **oldChar** are replaced by **newChar**.
char charAt(int index)	Returns the specified character located at **index**.
char[] toCharArray()	Returns the string as a **char** type array.
String[] split(String delimiter)	Returns a **String** array consisting of substrings separated by the specified regular expression deliminter.
String trim()	Returns a string with leading and trailing whitespace removed, if any.
String toLowerCase()	Returns a string with all characters converted to lower case.
String toUpperCase()	Returns a string with all characters converted to upper case.

The reader should review the Java documentation for all details, return codes, and other information regarding the above methods.

The following examples illustrate the use of **String** class methods in which a new **char** or **String** object is returned.

Example 2. Using methods **substring()**, **replace()** and **split()**.

```
String greeting = String new ("Welcome to the Java Programming Community!");
String substring = greeting.substring(0);          //Copy greeting to substring
String substring1 = greeting.substring(15, 19);  //substring1 = Java
```

Note in the last statement only those characters beginning at index 15 and ending at index 18, i.e., 19 – 1, are included in **substring1**.

```
String replaceString = greeting.replace("Java", "JSP");   //Replace Java with JSP
String[] splits = greeting.split(" ");
```

The above statement generates an array of **String** objects containing the following six elements:

```
splits[0] = "Welcome";
splits[1] = "to";
splits[2] = "the";
splits[3] = "JSP";
splits[4] = "Programming";
splits[5] = "Community!";
```

The following examples illustrate the use of **String** class methods to modify case, extract individual characters from a string, and perform string "housekeeping."

Example 3. Using methods **toLowerCase()** and **toUpperCase()**.

```
String greeting = new String("Welcome to the Java Programming Community!");
String lowerCaseString = greeting.toLowerCase();
String upperCaseString = greeting.toUpperCase();
```

The string **lowerCaseString** contains a lowercase representation of **greeting**. The string **upperCaseString** contains an uppercase representation of **greeting**.

Example 4. Using methods **charAt()** and **toCharArray()**.

```
String greeting2 = new String("Java");
char ch = greeting2.charAt(3);                        // ch = 'a'
char[] charArray = greeting2.toCharArray();
```

String **greeting2** contains the character '**a**' representing the last character in the string "Java". The **char** type array, **charArray**, contains the individual character components comprising the string "Java", as contained in **greeting**:

```
charArray[0] = 'J'
charArray[1] = 'a'
charArray[2] = 'v'
charArray[3] = 'a'
```

Example 5. Using method **trim()**.

```
String countryName = "          People's Republic of China   ";
String country = countryName.trim();
```

After execution, string **country** contains "People's Republic of China", an analogue of **countryName** with leading and trailing whitespace removed.

Table 10.6 lists commonly used methods in analyzing string characteristics.

Table 10.6 Commonly used methods in analyzing string characteristics

Method	Description
boolean equals(String str)	Returns **true** if two strings are equal and not null; otherwise returns **false**.
boolean equalsIgnoreCase(String str)	Same as above, but ignoring case considerations.
boolean startsWith(String str)	Returns **true** if string starts with specified string; otherwise returns **false**.
boolean startsWith(String str, int startIndex)	Returns **true** if string starts with specified string at the specified location; otherwise returns **false**.
boolean endsWith(String str)	Returns **true** if string ends with specified string; otherwise returns **false**.
boolean isEmpty()	Returns **true** if string has no content: **length()** = 0; otherwise return **false**.
int compareTo(String str)	Compares two strings lexicographically. Returns 0 if the two strings are equal; otherwise returns a positive integer if **this** string is lexicographically greater than **str**; returns a negative integer if **this** string is lexicographically less than **str**.
int compareToIgnoreCase(String str)	Same as above, but ignoring case considerations.

The following examples illustrate selected methods to analyze string characteristics or obtain data relating to the content of a string.

Example 6. Using methods **equals()**, **equalsIgnoreCase()**, **startWith()**, **endWith()**, and **isEmpty()**.

```
String fullName = "Wang Chang Ling";
String name = "Wang chang ling";
boolean result0 = fullName.equals(name);                    //result0 = false
boolean result1 = fullName.equalsIgnoreCase(name);          //result1 = true
boolean result2 = fullName.startsWith("W");                 //result2 = true
boolean result3 = fullName.startsWith("W", 1);              //result3 = false
boolean result4 = fullName.endsWith("G");                   //result4 = false
boolean result5 = fullName.isEmpty();                       //result5 = false
```

The following example illustrates methods of string comparison.

Example 7. Using methods **compareTo()** and **compareToIgnoreCase()**.

```
String fullName = "Wang Chang Ling";
String name = "Wang chang ling";

int flag0 = fullName.compareTo(name);                     //flag0 = -32
int flag1 = fullName.compareToIgnoreCase(name);       //flag1 = 0
```

10.5.4 Application example - Calculator

We will write a calculator application that performs addition, subtraction, multiplication, and division of an infix expression. The example we will use is the expression:

```
5 + -10.02 - 2 * 8.5 / 3.4 - -6 + 100.89
```

A space must exist between an operator and an operand. Operands may be both positive (including 0) and negative integers and floating-point values. The calculator will evaluate an expression from left to right.

Analysis of the problem

We must design a class that can read the user's expression and perform the calculation. The class has the following specifications:

Class name: **Calculator**

Data: **String expression** – store expression to be evaluated

char operator – store operator

double currentTotal – store first operand and result.

double operandValue – store second operand.

Method:

void requestInput() – request expression to be evaluated

void parseExpression() – perform parsing of expression and conversion to individual operator and operand "tokens".

void compute() – perform calculation.

String toString() - return calculation result as a string.

Driver code:

A driver code, **CalculatorApp.java**, is to be written to test the code.

We begin by developing the **Calculator** class:

```
// Complete code called Calculator.java in Ch10 from the author's Website
import javax.swing.JOptionPane;

public class Calculator {
   private String expression;
```

```
    private char operator;
    private double operandValue, currentTotal;

    public Calculator() {               //Constructor
       expression = null;
       operator = ' ';
       operandValue = 0.0;
       currentTotal = 0.0;
    }
    public void requestInput() {  //handle the user's entry
       expression = JOptionPane.showInputDialog("Please enter your expression:  ");
    }
    public void parseExpression() {  //Translate to operators and operands
       // form operator and operand tokens using "split"
       String[] expressions = expression.split(" ");
       currentTotal = Double.parseDouble(expressions[0]); // obtain first operand

       for (int i = 1; i < expressions.length; i += 2) {
           // obtain remaining operators and operands
          operator = expressions[i].charAt(0);
          operandValue = Double.parseDouble(expressions[i+1]); // obtain operand
          compute();    // compute result
       }
    }
    public void compute() {
       switch (operator) {
          case '+':  currentTotal += operandValue;
                      break;
          case '-':  currentTotal -= operandValue;
                      break;
          case '*':  currentTotal *= operandValue;
                      break;
          case '/':  currentTotal /= operandValue;
                      break;
          default:   System.out.println("invalid operator...");
                      break;
       }
    }
    public String toString() {          //Return the expression and result
       return expression + "\nThe total after the calculation: " +
       currentTotal;
    }
}
```

Code Review:

The **String** class method **split()** performs the key task of **parseExpression()**: parsing the expression into individual operators and operands. Because of the project requirement that the user must both begin the expression with a space and enter a space between an operator and an operand, parsing is facilitated by allowing us to use a space as a delimiter in "splitting" the expression string into tokens. The first operand is initially stored in **currentTotal**. Subsequent operators and operands are obtained from the expression array, and method **compute()** performs the calculation process.

The following is the major part of the driver code to test the **Calculator** class:

```
// Complete code called CalculatorApp.java in Ch10 from the auhtor's Website
Calculator calculator = new Calculator();  //Create an object
String choice = "y";

while (choice.equalsIgnoreCase("y")) {
   try {                                   //Handle exceptions
        calculator.requestInput();         //request for entry
        calculator.parseExpression();      //translate expression
        JOptionPane.showMessageDialog(null, calculator);//display result
   }
   catch (NumberFormatException e) {
      System.out.println("The expression is wrong…\nPlease try again.");
   }
   choice = JOptionPane.showInputDialog("Do you want to continue(y/n)? ");
}
```

10.6 StringBuilder class

The **StringBuilder** class of the Java API is used when the internal content of a string itself needs to be modified, rather than return a new, modified string derived from the **String** class.

The **StringBuilder** class was first introduced in JDK1.5. It is included in the default package **java.lang**. In the following sections, we use examples to discuss commonly used constructors and methods in **StringBuilder**.

10.6.1 Mutable vs. Unmutable

The execution speed associated with using methods of the **StringBuilder** class is much slower than methods of the **String** class. This is primarily due to the fact that strings derived from methods in the **StringBuilder** class are mutable whereas strings associated with the **String** class are immutable. As such, the reader should consider avoiding the use of the **StringBuilder** class if the content of a string is not to be modified during code execution.

10.6.2 Constructors

Table 10.7 lists three commonly used constructors in the **StringBuilder** class. The length of any string established by the **StringBuilder** class is automatically set to 16 bytes by default. This length can be overridden in instantiating an object of class **StringBuilder**.

Table 10.7 Commonly used constructors in **StringBuilder**

Constructor	Description
StringBuilder()	Instantiates an empty string with the capacity of 16 bytes.
StringBuilder(int length)	Instantiat s an empty string with the specified capacity.
StringBuilder(String str)	Instantiates the specified string with a length of the original string plus an additional 16 bytes of capacity.

The following example uses these three constructors to create objects of **StringBuilder.**

```
// Create a string with a capacity of 16 bytes
StringBuilder futureString =new StringBuilder();

// Create a string with a capacity of 2 bytes
StringBuilder countryID = new StringBuilder(2);

// Create a string containing the content "Wuhan" with an additional capacity of
// 16 bytes
StringBuilder cityName = new StringBuilder("Wuhan");
```

As discussed in previous sections regarding referencing, the statement:

```
//nickName is an alias to cityName
StringBuilder nickName = cityName;
```

makes **nickName** a reference to the existing object of **StringBuilder** called **cityName**. A change to either entity affects the other.

10.6.3 Commonly used methods in the **StringBuilder** Class

Table 10.8 lists commonly used methods that can be used in both the **StringBuilder** and **String** classes.

Table 10.8 Commonly used methods in both the **String** and **StringBuilder** Classes

Method	Description
int length()	Returns length of the string.
int indexOf(String str)	Returns position as index of the first occurrence of the specified substring **str** in the string, or -1 if substring is not present.
int indexOf(String str, int index)	Returns position as index of the first occurrence of the specified substring **str** beginning at the specified **index** in the string, or return -1 if substring is not present.
int lastIndexOf(String str)	Returns position as index of the last occurrence of the specified substring

	str in the string, or -1 if substring is not present.
int lastIndexOf(String str, int index)	Returns position as index of the last occurrence of the specified substring **str** beginning at the specified **index** in the string, or return -1 if substring is not present.
String substring(int startIndex)	Returns a substring starting at the specified location.
String substring(int startIndex, int endIndex)	Returns a substring starting at the specified **startIndex** and extends to the character at **endIndex** – 1. The length of the returned substring is **endIndex – startIndex**.
int lastIndexOf(char ch, int index)	Return the index of specified character appeared in the string after the specified index; otherwise return a negative integer.

Table 10.9 lists the commonly used methods available only in **StringBuilder**.

Table 10.9 Commonly used methods in **StringBuilder**

Method	Description
int capacity()	Returns the current capacity.
int setLength(int length)	Sets the length of the character sequence.
append(dataType item)	Appends the specified item to the end of the string. **item** can be any primitive data types, **char** array, **Object**, **String**, or **StringBuffer**.
insert(int index, dataType item)	Inserts the specified item into the specified location. Item can be any primitive data types, char array, or **String**.
replace(int startIndex, int endIndex, String str)	Use str to replace the content from the specified starting index to the endIndex -1.
delete(int startIndex, int endIndex)	Deletes the characters from the specified starting index to the endIndex - 1.
deleteCharAt(int index)	Deletes the character at the specified location.
setCharAt(int index, char ch)	Use **ch** to replace the character at the specified location.
String toString()	Returns the content of **StringBuilder** object as a **String**.

It is important to note two important details the **StringBuilder** class:

1. The capacity of a **StringBuilder** object will automatically be extended to accommodate an increased size of the character string array, and
2. The **StringBuilder** class is not thread-safe.

The following examples illustrate the use of various **StringBuilder** methods.

Example 1. Using the **capacity()**, **length()**, and **setLength()** methods.

```
// Complete code called StringBuilderMethodsTest.java in Ch10
// from the author's Website
```

```
StringBuilder phone = new StringBuilder("510-651-5168");
int length = phone.length();
System.out.println("length = " + length);                //length = 12
int capacity = phone.capacity();
System.out.println("capacity = " + capacity);            //capacity = 28

phone.setLength(3);
System.out.println("phone = " + phone);                  //phone = 510
System.out.println("capacity = " + phone.capacity());    //capacity = 28

phone.setLength(12);
System.out.println("phone = " + phone);                  //phone = 510
System.out.println("capacity = " + capacity);            //capacity = 28
```

It can be seen that method **setLength()** reduces the actual length of the string, but does not change the capacity. Calling method **setLength()** again to reset to the original length of the buffer may be done, but the previous content of the object cannot be recovered.

Example 2. Using the **append()**, **insert()**, **replace()**, **delete()**, **deleteAt()**, and **setCharAt()** methods.

```
StringBuilder phone2 = new StringBuilder("510-651-5168");
phone2.append(" ext. 299");        //phone2 = "510-651-5168 ext. 299"
phone2.delete(4, 7);               //phone2 = "510--5168 ext. 299"
phone2.insert(4, "659");           //phone2 = "510-659-5168 ext. 299",  or
phone2.replace(0, 3, "408");       //phone2 = "408-659-5168 ext. 299"
phone2.deleteCharAt(7);            //phone2 = "408-6595168 ext. 299"
phone2.setCharAt(2, '9');          //phone2 = "409-6595168 ext. 299"
```

Example 3. The arguments of **StringBuilder** methods **append()** and **insert()** can be any primitive data type. The following example demonstrates the use of **int** and **boolean** data as parameters in calling **append()** and **insert()**.

```
StringBuilder builder = new StringBuilder();
builder.append(129.87);         //"129.87"
builder.append(true);           //"129.87true"
builder.insert(6, 25);          //"129.8725true"
```

Note: *In the* ***substring(), delete()*** *and* ***replace()*** *methods, the ending index actually is endIndex-1.*

10.6.4 Application example: Standardized format of telephone numbers

Write an application that can standardize the format of telephone directory information to be of the form: last name, first name (xxx)xxx-xxxx. If, for example, the input data is

```
Chris West9195551618
```

or

```
Chang Lin Wang9195551666
```

the standardized formats would be

```
West, Chris (919)555-1618
```

and

```
Wang, Chang Lin (919)555-1666
```

respectively. Similarly, input of the form:

```
Jon N. Smith9992221223
```

would be standardized as

```
Smith, Jon N. (999)222-1223
```

The application includes a user-defined class called **StringBuilderFormatter** that uses methods from the **StringBuilder** class to evaluate the input and perform any required formatting tasks.

```
// Complete code called StringBuilderFormatter.java in Ch10 from author's Website
public class StringBuilderFormatter {
   StringBuilder formatter(String message) {
      int phoneIndex = 0,
      lastNameIndex = 0;
      StringBuilder str = new StringBuilder(message);

      // find ending index of person's name
      for (int i = 0; i < str.length(); i++) {
         //Find the location of the telephone number within input string
         if (str.charAt(i) != ' ' && str.charAt(i) != '.' && str.charAt(i) < 'A'){
            phoneIndex = i; //Phone index
            break;
         }
      }
      for (int i = phoneIndex; i >= 0; i--) {        //Last name index
         if (str.charAt(i) == ' ') {       //A space exists before last name
            lastNameIndex = i + 1;         //Last name index
            break;
         }
      }

      String lastName = str.substring(lastNameIndex, phoneIndex); //Last name
```

```
        lastName += ", ";                          //Add a comma
        str.insert(phoneIndex, " (");              //Format the phone number
        str.insert(phoneIndex + 5, ")");
        str.insert(phoneIndex + 9, "-");
        str.delete(lastNameIndex, phoneIndex);        //Delete last name
        str.insert(0, lastName);                      //Insert last name at beginning

        return str;
    }
}
```

From the Unicode or ASCII code table, we may see that a number must be in the following range:

```
str.charAt(i) != ' ' && str.charAt(i) != '.' && str.charAt(i) < 'A'
```

The driver code for this application is as follows:

```
//Complete code called StringBuilderFormatterApp.java in Ch10 from the author's
//Website
import javax.swing.*;
public class StringBuilderFormatterApp {
   public static void main( String args[] ) {
   String choice = "y";
   while (choice.equalsIgnoreCase("y")) {
      String message = JOptionPane.showInputDialog("Please enter string to be
      formatted:  ");
      StringBuilderFormatter format = new StringBuilderFormatter();
      StringBuilder str = format.formatter(message);

      JOptionPane.showMessageDialog(null, str);
      choice = JOptionPane.showInputDialog("Do you want to continue(y/n)?");
   }
  }
}
```

Examples of driver code execution results are presented at the beginning of this section.

10.6.5 StringBuffer class

There is no significant difference between the capabilities of the **StringBuilder** and **StringBuffer** classes. Both classes have similar constructors and methods. The definitions and operations of the methods are basically the same. The main differences between these two classes are in their applications dealing with strings:

- The **StringBuffer** class uses synchronized methods for use in multithreaded applications using threads. A thread refers to a block of code performing a specified task. In a multithreaded application an object with synchronized methods can be accessed by multiple threads concurrently. Multithreading can significantly increase the speed of program execution; however, multithreading also requires more operational processes. As such, **StringBuffer** methods are usually slower than similar methods in the **StringBuilder** class in dealing with strings. Multithreading techniques are discussed in Chapter 14.

- The **StringBuffer** class incorporates features of synchronization for thread-safe applications.

- In applications that do not involve multithreading, **StringBuilder** methods should be used instead of **StringBuffer** methods in string modification applications.

Because the commonly used constructors and methods of the **StringBuffer** class are similar to those in the **StringBuilder** class, the list will not be repeated. The reader may refer to Table 10.6 through Table 10.8 and the accompanying examples discussed in the previous sections for more information and details.

10.7 StringTokenizer Class

The **StringTokenizer** class in the Java API is specially designed to tokenize a string. Tokenization is the process of breaking a string into its component parts, which are called tokens. The **StringTokenizer** class is provided in the **java.util** package.

```
import java.util.StringTokenizer;
```

Although the **split()** method in the **String** class can be used to perform string tokenization, the method always produces a new array of strings consisting of tokens. In many applications this may not be necessary. The **StringTokenizer** class avoids this functionality, thereby making string tokenization more flexible and faster.

10.7.1 What is a token?

A token is a single atomic unit of a language. Examples of tokens in the Java language are keywords, identifiers, and symbol names. Tokens can be identified or isolated through the use of separating delimiters. For example, in the string:

"Java Programming World"

each word, or token:

"Java" "Programming" "World"

is delimited by whitespace. In the string:

"8990|Washington Avenue|Fremont|CA|94539"

the tokens

“8990” “Washington Avenue” “Fremont” “CA” “94539”

are delimited by the “|” symbol.

10.7.2 Constructors and methods

Table 10.10 lists constructors in the **StringTokenizer** class.

Table 10.10 Constructors in the **StringTokenizer** class

Constructor	Description
StringTokenizer(String str)	Constructs a string tokenizer for the specified string using whitespace as the default delimiter.
StringTokenizer(String str, String delimiter)	Constructs a string tokenizer for the specified string using the specified delimiters.
StringTokenizer(String str, String delimiter, boolean delimiterIncluded)	Constructs a string tokenizer for the specified string using the specified delimiters. If **delimiterIncluded** is **true** the delimiting characters are also returned as tokens. If **delimiterIncluded** is **false** the delimiting tokens are not returned as tokens.

The following Java statements are examples using **StringTokenizer** to create objects of string tokens:

```
// Construct StringTokenizer object consisting of tokens:
// "Java", "JSP", "Servlets", and "JavaBeans"
// using whitespace as delimiting characters.

StringTokenizer token = new StringTokenizer("Java JSP Servlets JavaBeans");

// Construct StringTokenizer object consisting of tokens:
// "10", "15", and "2007"
// using "-" as a delimiting character.

StringTokenizer dateToken = new StringTokenizer("10-15-2007", "-");

// Construct StringTokenizer object consisting of tokens:
// "10", "-", "15", "-", and "2007"
// using "-" as a delimiting character.  The delimiting character is also returned
// in the token list.

StringTokenizer dateToken2 = new StringTokenizer("10-15-2007", "-", true);
```

Table 10.11 lists of commonly used methods in the **StringTokenizer** class.

Table 10.11 Commonly used methods in the **StringTokenizer** class

Methods	Description
int countTokens()	Returns the number of tokens remaining in the **StringTokenizer** object.
boolean hasMoreTokens()	Returns true if **StringTokenizer** object contains more tokens.
String nextToken()	Returns the next token from the **StringTokenizer** object.

The following example calls these three methods to tokenize a string.

```
// Complete code called StringTokenizerTest.java in Ch10 from the author's Website
StringTokenizer dateToken = new StringTokenizer("10-15-2007", "-", true);
   while(dateToken.hasMoreTokens() ) {
      System.out.println(dateToken.nextToken());
      System.out.println("Number of tokens left: " + dateToken.
      countTokens());
   }
```

The result of execution is:

```
10
Number of tokens left: 4
-
Number of tokens left: 3
15
Number of tokens left: 2
-
Number of tokens left: 1
2007
Number of tokens left: 0
```

10.7.3 Example of a StringTokenizer application

The following code segment is a modification of the Calculator application (see Section 10.5.4) method **parseExpression()** using **StringTokenizer** to form a token sequence of the expression string operators and operands.

```
// Complete code called Calculator2.java in Ch10 from the author's Website
public void parseExpression() {
   String operatorStr;                       // Store tokenized string
   char[] operatorArray = new char[1];       // Store operators

   StringTokenizer tokens = new StringTokenizer(expression);
   currentTotal = Double.parseDouble(tokens.nextToken());

   // Tokenize input stream, converting operands to numerical values, as required
   // Store current calculation
```

```
    while (tokens.hasMoreTokens()) {
        operatorStr = tokens.nextToken();           //Read in operators
        operatorArray = operatorStr.toCharArray();  //Convert to char array
        operator = operatorArray[0];                //Convert to char
        operandValue = Double.parseDouble(tokens.nextToken()); //Next operand

        compute();
    }
}
```

10.8 Regular Expressions

Regular expression processing capabilities in Java were formally introduced in JDK1.4. These capabilities provide a variety of dynamic operations involving strings and text, such as searching, matching, selecting, verifying, and other forms of editing.

Regular expressions are used in many computer languages and are considered a form of dynamic verification modeling languages. The range of regular expression capabilities and uses is broad. This text only covers the basic capabilities of regular expressions used in Java for pattern recognitions and data verifications.

10.8.1 A first look at regular expressions

Consider an application code to verify if a U.S.-based email address is legal. Without the use of regular expression processing, one would have to consider the use of the **String**, **StringBuilder**, or **StringTokenizer** classes to perform the verification. It would be a complicated task. However, the use of regular expression processing provides a wonderful solution in a much easier and more efficient manner. In regard to the email verification task stated above, the regular expression notation

```
(\\w+)(.\\w+)*@(\\w+\\.)(com|edu|net|org|gov)
```

forms the underlying evaluation structure to evaluate an email address.

The regular expression used to verify an email address would specify that an email address may start with any letter, number, an underscore, or optional period in any quantity of repetitions, followed by an **@**, and continue with any letter, number, underscore, or period sequence before ending with a character string of: **.com** , **.net**, **.org**, or **.gov**.

As noted above, we can consider using one of the following steps to validate a string:

- Use of a regular expression to create a verification model. This topic is discussed in the following section; or
- Call **matches()** method in the **String** class to perform verification:

```
if ( myEmail.matches("(\\w+)(.\\w+)*@(\\w+\\.)(com|edu|net|org|gov)") )
        isValid = true;
else
        isValid = false;
        ...
```

However, if more operations beyond string verification, such as validating and editing a text file, the **Pattern** class in the Java API provided in the **java.util.regex** package to process such operations:

```
// Define a regular expression
String emailExp = "(\\w+)(.\\w+)*@(\\w+\\.)(com|edu|net|org|gov)";
// Compile the regular expression
Pattern p = Pattern.compile(emailExp);
```

The Java API class **Matcher** in the **java.util.regex** package is then used to perform the verification:

```
String email = JOptionPane.showInputDialog("Please enter your email address:");
Matcher m = p.matcher(email); //Perform verification
boolean matchFound = m.matches();    //Call matches()to verify the result
if (matchFound)
   isValid = true;
else
...
```

In the example snippet, the **matches()** method in the **Matcher** class returns **true** if **email** matches the pattern specified in the regular expression built in **Pattern** object **p**.

In the following sections, we first introduce regular expression constructs and instantiation. Examples are shown to explain the use of regular expressions in a variety of pattern verifications and recognitions.

10.8.2 Regular expression constructs

Constructs in regular expressions can be classified into the following categories:

- Constructs of character classes
- Constructs of boundaries
- Constructs for logic determination
- Constructs for the definition of quantifiers

Table 10.12 lists the constructs of character sequences in regular expressions.

Table 10.12 Constructs of character sequences

Character structure	Description
.	Any single character
X	A single character including escape sequence s: \t, \n, \r, \\, \f
Xxx	A string
[abc]	a or b or c
[^abc]	Not a or b or c
[a-zA-Z]	a through z or A through Z (inclusive)
\s	Whitespace
\S	Not whitespace
\d	Digits (0-9)
\D	Non-digits
\w	Text character, any one of [a-zA-Z_0-9]
\W	Non-text character

Note: *In order for the Java compiler to recognize a character sequence construct beginning with "\", an additional, leading "\" must preface the sequence. A regular expression must be defined as a string within double quotes.*

Table 10.13 lists the constructs of some regular expression boundary conditions.

Table 10.13 Constructs of boundary conditions

Definition	Description
^	Beginning of a line
$	End of a line

The following are examples using regular expression boundary constructs. The definition of the **(.)*** notational syntax is explained in Table 10.14.

"^cat(.)*" any string beginning with "cat"; examples: "cat", "catalog", but not "indicate".

"(.)*cat$" any string ending with "cat"; examples: "cat", but not "indicate".

Table 10.13 lists constructs of regular expression logic operations.

Table 10.13 Constructs of regular expression logic operations

Definition	Description
XY	X followed by Y. X or Y can be any single character or a string
X|*Y*	X or Y

Examples using logical operations:

"(\\d)|(\\s)" any digits from 0-9, or any whitespace.

"[y/n]|[Y/N]" capital or lowercase letter y or n only.

Table 10.14 lists the quantifier constructs of regular expressions.

Table 10.14 Definition of regular expression quantifier constructs

Definition	D
X?	X: Match once or not at all
*X**	X: Match zero or more times
X+	X: Match one or more times
X{n}	X: Match exactly **n** times
X{n,}	X: Match at least **n** times
X{n, m}	X: Match at least **n** times, but not more than **m** times

The following are examples of using regular expression quantifier constructs:

"a?" match an empty string or at most one occurrence of string **a**.

"(Java)*" match "Java" zero or more times.

"(Java)+" match "Java" one or more times.

"(Java){2}" match "JavaJava".

"(Java){2,} match at least two occurrences of "JavaJava".

"(Java){1, 3}" match "Java", "JavaJava", or "JavaJavaJava".

"(\\d){3}-(\\d){2}-(\\d){4}" match any legal Social Security Number (nnn-nn-nnnn).

"^(\\d)+(\\s)*([a-zA-Z]+(\\s)*[a-zA-Z]+)+,(\\s)*[a-zA-Z]+,\\s+[A-Z]{2}(\\s)*(\\d){5}$"

match any valid mailing address. The street address must start with digits and may contain whitespace space. The street address must then continue with any letter sequence and may have embedded whitespace or commas, or it may contain no comma. This sequence is followed by a city name, a comma, and may have embedded whitespace. A city name is followed by a comma followed by optional whitespace. The state abbreviation consists of two capitalized letters. The mailing address may have optional whitespace separating the state name and before ending with a five digit zip code. As an example

```
1234 First Street, Oakland,  CA 93455
```

is considered as a legal mailing address.

10.8.3 Regular Expression matching using the String class matches() method

An easier way to verify a string pattern is to use the **matches()** method provided by the **String** class. Its syntax is:

```
boolean matches(String regex)
```

The method returns **true** if character string matches the regular expression pattern specified by the method parameter, **regex**. If the pattern fails to match, the method returns **false**.

Let's use method **matches()** to establish the validity of a mailing address:

```
//Complete code called PatternTest.java in Ch10 from author's Website

boolean isValid = false;
Scanner sc = new Scanner(System.in);
String address = "^(\\d)+(\\s)*([a-zA-Z]+(\\s)*[a-zA-Z]+)+,(\\s)*[a-zA-Z]+,\\s+[A-
Z]{2}(\\s)*(\\d){5}$";
...

while(!isValid) {
   System.out.println("Please enter your mailing address: ");
   if (sc.nextLine().matches(address))
      isValid = true;
   else
      System.out.println("Invalid address!  Please try again…");
}
...
```

10.8.4 Pattern and Matcher classes

Pattern and **Matcher** classes were specially designed to work with regular expression object instantiations, pattern recognition, and matching-related operations. Additional methods were added in JDK1.5 making pattern verification much easier and convenient. Table 10.15 lists the commonly used methods in the **Pattern** class.

Table 10.15 Commonly used methods in the **Pattern** class

Method	Description
Pattern compile(String regex)	Compiles regular expression **regex** into a pattern.
Matcher matcher(CharSequence input)	Creates a matcher that will match specified **input** against the pattern.
static boolean matches(String regex, CharSequence input)	Static method that compiles regular expression **regex** and attempts to match input pattern against it. Returns **true** if **regex** matches input; otherwise returns **false**.
String pattern()	Returns regular expression from which this pattern was compiled.
String toString()	Returns string representation of this pattern.

More Info: ***CharSequence*** *can be a* ***String*** *type.*

The following code snippet example uses methods from the **Pattern** and **Matcher** classes:

```
// Complete code called PatternTest.java in Ch10 from the author's Website

// The following regular expression is similar to: "\\d+{3}-\\d+{2}-\\d+{4}"
Pattern ssnPattern = Pattern.compile("[0-9]{3}-[0-9]{2}-[0-9]{4}");

// Note:  Additional erroneous spacing included in Social Security Number
Matcher ssnMatcher = ssnPattern.matcher("111 -   11   -  1111");

if (ssnMatcher.matches())
   System.out.println("SSN Matches!");
else
   System.out.println("SSN does not Match!");
System.out.println("pattern: " + ssnPattern.pattern());
System.out.println("toString(): " + ssnPattern);
```

The specified pattern does not match the template of a properly formed Social Security Number due to the extra spacing within the pattern:

```
SSN does not Match!
pattern: [0-9]{3}-[0-9]{2}-[0-9]{4}
toString(): [0-9]{3}-[0-9]{2}-[0-9]{4}
```

The above example can be modified to call the **Pattern** class **matches()** method to achieve the same functionality:

```
//NOTE:  Social Security Number "candidate" has correct formatting

if (Pattern.matches("[0-9]{3}-[0-9]{2}-[0-9]{4}", "111-11-1111"))
   System.out.println("SSN Matches!");
else
   System.out.println("SSN does not Match!");
```

The execution result is:

```
SSN Matches!
```

Table 10.16 list commonly used methods in the **Matcher** class.

Table 10.16 Commonly used methods in the **Matcher** class

Methods	Description
boolean matches()	Attempts to match the entire region against the pattern. Returns **true** if

	there is a match; otherwise returns **false**.
String group()	Returns input subsequence matched by the previous match operation.
String group(int group)	Returns input subsequence captured by the given group during the previous match operation.
String groupCount()	Return the number of capturing groups in this matcher's pattern.

The following example uses several of these methods:

```
//Complete code called PatternTest.java in Ch10 from the author's Website

// Match any strings containing pattern:  "cat"
Pattern catPattern = Pattern.compile("(.*)cat(.*)");
Matcher catMatcher = catPattern.matcher("OOP in Java catalogue");

if (catMatcher.matches())
    System.out.println("Pattern contains sequence:  cat");
else
    System.out.println("Pattern does NOT contain sequence:  cat");

System.out.println("group(): " + catMatcher.group());
for(int i = 0; i <= catMatcher.groupCount(); i++)
    System.out.println("group[ " + i + "] = " + catMatcher.group(i));
```

The following is the execution result:

```
Pattern contains sequence:  cat
group(): OOP in Java catalogue
group[ 0] = OOP in Java catalogue
group[ 1] = OOP in Java
group[ 2] = alogue
```

10.8.5 Application code examples using Pattern and Matcher

Example 1. Verify if a string both begins and ends with the character sequence "Java".

The regular expression can be written as:

```
"^(Java)(.)*|(.)*(Java)$"
```

The following code snippet calls method **matches()** in the **String** class to verify the string:

```
String javaString = "Java Programming is fun";
String javaPattern = "^(Java)(.)*|(.)*(Java)$";
if (javaString.matches(javaPattern))
```

```
    System.out.println("String matches required Java pattern!");
else
    System.out.println("String does NOT match required Java pattern!");
```

The execution result

```
String does NOT match required Java pattern!
```

shows the failure of the "matches" test because the string does not end with the character sequence "Java".

Example 2. Verify if user entered "y" or "n" in either lower- or uppercase format to terminate the execution.

The regular expression can be written as:

```
"[yn]|[YN]"
```

The following code calls **matches()** in the **String** class to verify the user's input:

```
while (!done) {
   choice = JOptionPane.showInputDialog("Continue? (y/n): ");

   if (choice.matches("[yn]|[YN]"))
      done = true;
  else
     JOptionPane.showMessageDialog(null, "Wrong entry. You can only enter y
    or n" + "\nCheck your entry and try again...");
}
...
```

Example 3. Use regular expressions to code a **Validator** class to validate telephone numbers.

```
// Complete code called RegexValidator.java in Ch10 from the author's Website
public class RegexValidator {
   public static String validateTelephoneNumber(Scanner sc, String prompt) {
      boolean isValid = false;
      String telephoneNumber = null;
      String phonePattern =
         "[1-9][0-9]+{2}-[1-9][0-9]+{2}-(\\d)+{4}|(\\([1-9][0-9]+{2}\\))
          [1-9][0-9]+{2}-(\\d)+{4}";

      while(!isValid) {
         try { System.out.print(prompt);
              telephoneNumber = sc.nextLine();
```

```
            if (telephoneNumber.equals(""))
                  throw new NullPointerException();
            else {
                  System.out.println("\nYou entered: " + telephoneNumber);
                  if (email.matches(phonePattern))
                        isValid = true;
                  else
                        throw new Exception();
            }
        } // End of try
        catch (NullPointerException e) {
              System.out.println("\nYou are in telephone number verification.");
        }
        catch (Exception e) {
              System.out.println("\nInvalid telephone number.");
              System.out.println("\nCheck your entry and try again.);
        }
    } // End of while
  return email;
}  // End of validateTelephoneNumber()
...
```

The regular expression to verify telephone numbers

```
String phonePattern =
"[1-9][0-9]+{2}-[1-9][0-9]+{2}-(\\d)+{4}|(\\([1-9][0-9]+{2}\\))[1-9]
[0-9]+{2}-(\\d)+{4}";
```

Allows the user to enter telephone numbers of the form:

```
111-111-1111
```

as well as

```
(111)111-1111
```

In addition, the regular expression construct also regulates that:

- the first digit of area code and the prefix cannot be 0;
- there must be a hyphen, "- ", between the area code and the prefix if parentheses are not used with the area code; and
- a hyphen, "-", must be present between the prefix and suffix segments.

Exercises

1. What is an array? What are an array's key features? We do we need and use arrays?

2. Explain why arrays are a default class, **Arrays**, in Java.

3. Use examples to show three ways to define an array. Explain the situations and circumstances in which each way is used to define an array.

4. Explain the purpose of square brackets when declaring an array. Explain the purpose of the three different locations of the square brackets in relation to the name of the array.

5. Why can an array of **Object** include elements of all types of objects? Discuss any problems that can arise for intermixing objects of different types within an array.

6. Define the following arrays:

    a. A **char** type array called **grade**.

    b. A **float** type array called **average**.

    c. A **boolean** type array called **flags**.

7. Create arrays defined in Step 6 above:

    a. **grades** array with 50 elements.

    b. **averages** array with 160 elements.

    c. **flags** array with 29 elements.

8. Create the following arrays:

    a. A **double** array called **rates** with 4 elements.

    b. A **float** array called **prices** with 3 elements.

    c. A **String** array called **names** with 5 elements.

    d. A **Book** array called **books** with 4 elements.

9. Modify Questions 6 – 8 above so the creation and initialization of the arrays are performed in the same statement. Use your own data to do the initialization. Assume the constructor of the **Book** class has three arguments: a **String** type for the name of the book; a **double** type for the price; and an **int** type for the quantity of books.

10. Use loops to do the following exercises:

a. Use a traditional "for" loop to print the elements of each array created in Questions 8 and 9, respectively.

b. Use an enhanced or "for-each" loop to print the elements of each array created in Questions 8 and 9, respectively.

11. Write Java code to calculate the average price and average quantity of books created in an array called **books** in Question 9. You will first code a **Book** class with the necessary constructor(s) and methods. Write a driver code in which data contained in four(4) elements of the **books** array are used to perform the calculations. Use an enhanced "for" loop to perform the computing. Document and save all source code.

12. List two ways to define a two-dimensional array. Explain how to use each form of array.

13. What is rectangular arrays? What is a jagged array? How do you create a jagged array?

14. Create the following two-dimensional arrays:

    a. 3 X 2 **String** type array called **grades**.

    b. 4 X 5 **int** type array called **matrix**.

    c. 2 X 3 **Book** type array called **textbooks**.

15. Use your own data to initialize each array in Question 14 above.

16. Use your own data to create and initialize the following two-dimensional arrays:

    a. 2 X 2 **String** type array called **students**.

    b. 3 X 1 **char** type array called **letters**.

    c. 1 X 3 **String** type array called **myBooks**.

17. Use the **Book** class written in Question 11 and write a driver code in which a 2 X 2 two-dimensional array of **Book** objects is created and initialized using your own data. Use an enhanced "for" loop to calculate the average **price** and **quantity** of books.

18. Why are the contents of copied arrays "shallow" copies? How would you perform "deep" copying of the contents of an array.

19. Use command-line execution to input three double data and compute the sum and average. Write a driver code to test your program. Document and save your code.

20. Code a **ArrayCompute** class containing the following static methods:

a. **doubleAverage()**: accept a **double** type one-dimensional array as an argument and return a **double** scalar type. The method computes and returns the average of the passed array.

b. **total()**: accept a **double** type one-dimensional array as an argument and return a **double** scalar type. The method computes and returns the total value of the passed array.

c. **max()**: accept a **double** type one-dimensional array as an argument and return an **int** scalar type. The method returns the index of the element of the maximum value in the passed array.

d. **min()**: accept a **double** type one-dimensional array as an argument and return an **int** scalar type. The method returns the index of the element of the minimum value in the passed array.

21. Continuing Question 20, write a driver code to test all methods written in the **ArrayCompute** class. Use the **random()** method in the **Math** class to generate fifty **double** type data ranging from 0.0 to 100.0. Assign the data to an array. Call each method to perform the calculations and display the results. Document your code and save all files.

22. Write a driver code to sort and select the maximum and minimum values in the array created in Question 21 and print the results. Document your code and save all files.

23. Write a driver code using methods **clone()**, **arrayCopy()**, **copyOf()**, and **copyOfRange()** to perform the copying operations of the array created in Question 21. Use these four methods to copy the array to newly created arrays: **array1** through **array5**. When using method **copyOfRange()**, assume only the first half of the array is copied to a new array. Print all elements in each copied array. Document your code and save all files.

24. Implement the **Comparable** interface in the **Books** class defined in Question 11 to compare the instance data **price**. Write a driver code and use your own data to create a **double** type array with four elements containing instances of **price**. Sort the array. Display the sorted array. Prompt the user to search the array for a desired **price** and display the result (success or failure) of the search. Document your code and save all files.

25. Use examples to explain differences between string referencing and string creation. Why are **String** objects immutable?

26. Use methods provided by the **String** class to write an application that will reverse the order of a string. First, write a class with a static method to perform the reversion process and a static method to display the result. Code a test driver that asks the user to enter a string, invoke the static methods, and display the result. The program will continue to run until the user chooses to stop execution. Document your code and save all files.

27. Use methods provided by either the **StringBuilder** or **StringBuffer** class to write an application that will reverse the order of a string. First, write a class with a static method to perform the reversing process and a static method to display the result. Code a test driver that asks the user to enter a string, invoke the static methods, and display the result. The program will continue to run until the user chooses to stop execution. Document your code and save all files.

28. Augment the capabilities of the **Validator** class by writing static methods incorporating regular expression handling to:

    a. Verify if the user enters **y/n** in either lower- or uppercase letter format to stop program execution. The method will return the correct entry.

    b. Verify if the user enters an integer within a specified range. The range is passed to the methods as a minimum and maximum. The method will return the success/failure status denoting if the value is within range.

    c. Verify if the user enters an double precision number within a specified range. The range is passed to the methods as a minimum and maximum. The method will return the success/failure status denoting if the value is within range.

    Document the **Validator** class and save the file.

29. Write a driver code testing all the methods defined in Question 28. Prompt the user to enter the correct data. In the event the user enters incorrect data display an error message from the static method in the **Validator** class and allow the user to continue entering data until it is correct. Display the correct data entry. Document your code and save all files.

"There were four things from which the Master was entirely free. He had no foregone conclusions, no arbitrary predeterminations, no obstinacy, and no egoism."

– Confucius

Chapter 11 Exception Handling

This chapter discusses exception handling. An exception is a run-time error that occurs during code execution. Java provides a rich number of exception handling classes in its API and powerful exception handling mechanisms to deal with a variety of exceptions. Java also allows programmers to define custom designed classes to handle specific exceptions that may occur in particular applications.

11.1 Exception Classes in the Java API

Figure 11.1 lists commonly used exception classes in the Java API and their relational hierarchy.

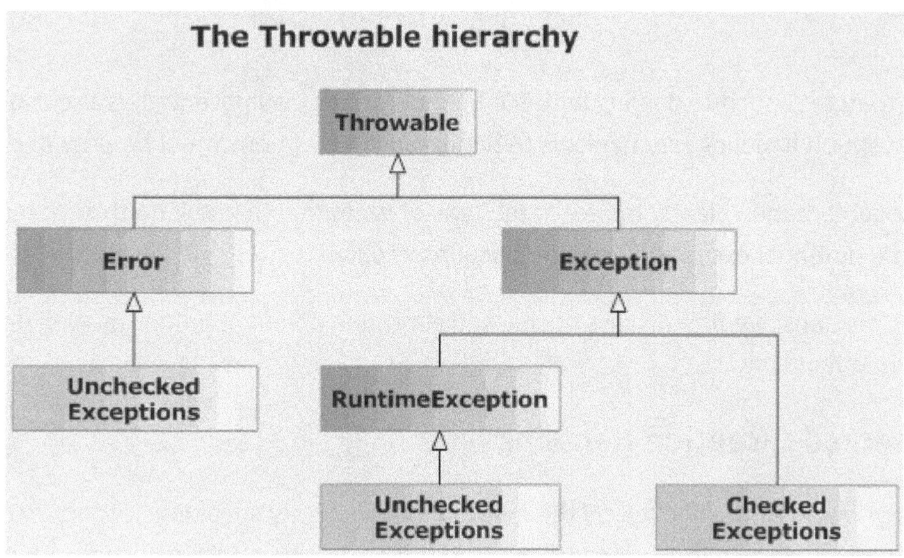

Figure 11.1 Commonly used exception classes in the Java API and the hierarchy chart

We may see from the chart that all exception classes in the Java API are inherited from the **Throwable** class. These exception classes can be categorized into two types: checked exceptions and unchecked exceptions. All exception classes inherited from the **Error** and **RuntimeException** classes are unchecked exceptions. An unchecked exception typically represents a condition that, as a rule, results from errors in program logic and cannot be reasonably recovered from at run time. The unchecked exception is handled by the JVM whenever it occurs during program execution. Common defined unchecked exception classes inherited from are:

```
ArithmeticException
IllegalArgumentException
```

```
   NumberFormatException
IndexOutOfBoundsException
   ArrayIndexOutOfBoundsException
   StringIndexOutOfBoundsException
NullPointException
```

Other unchecked exception classes are inherited from the **Error** class. They deal with system and hardware errors, such as JVM errors, threading errors, I/O device errors, and system configuration errors. Normally these types of unchecked exceptions rarely occur. Until this point, all exceptions covered in our discussions have been unchecked exceptions.

All subclasses directly inherited from the **Exception** class are checked exceptions. The programmer must provide an exception handling mechanism to handle all checked exceptions; failing to provide such mechanisms will result in the generation of syntax errors during compilation. Common checked exception classes in the Java API are:

```
ClassNotFoundException
IOException EOFException
   FileNotFoundException
NoSuchMethodException
```

It is important to note that code dealing with file I/O operations may potentially raise checked exceptions. Exception handling mechanisms to handle such exceptions must be provided.

The Java API documentation clearly indicates the type of exception that will be thrown by a method should a potential exception issue be encountered.

In the following sections, we first discuss unchecked exception handling before moving on to checked exception handling.

11.2 Unchecked Exception Handling

Unchecked exceptions are not checked by the Java compiler. Strictly speaking, it is not necessary for the programmer to write code to handle unchecked exceptions. However, in the absence of programmer-provided code to handle these exceptions, the JVM will produce the following actions upon encountering an unchecked exception:

1. Terminate program execution ungracefully, and
2. Display technical information regarding the source and type of exception occurring the execution.

The following are common causes of unchecked exceptions:

- Division by 0
- Array out of bounds
- Data type mismatch

- Use of Illegal argument
- Use of Illegal object

Most unchecked exceptions are the result of typographical or logical errors in coding made by the programmer. Careful programming may avoid the occurrence of unchecked exceptions.

Exceptions may occur due to unforeseeable errors in the code user's entry of data. In an effort to prevent "garbage in, garbage out" scenarios, we should provide exception handling code to verify these data before using them. This action will produce more reliable code.

11.2.1 Discover unchecked exceptions

A key principle of exception handling is to discover the first place in the code where a given exception may occur and provide code to handle the exception. Common first places an exception may occur are:

- Constructors that instantiate an object.
- Input statements or method calls to acquire user data. Examples include method calls in the **Scanner** class and methods of the form **parseXxx()** that convert the data to other types.
- Statements performing calculations that may produce data out of bound exceptions.
- Statements accessing elements of arrays.
- Method calls associated with objects that do not exist, thereby causing a **NullPointerException**.

We should perform exception analysis using these criteria to make exception handling more efficient.

11.2.2 Why handle unchecked exceptions?

Why should programmers even consider handling unchecked exceptions, given their automatic handling by the JVM? Some literature states unchecked exceptions should not be handled by programmers but only by the JVM.

The primary reason in providing capabilities permitting programmer handling of unchecked exceptions is to allow necessary corrections in data acquisition and computing and let the code continue to execute, thereby avoiding an ungraceful termination of execution. Code reliability and fault-tolerance are our goals in exception handling. A good application should not stop executing due to logic errors or invalid data entry. Rather, it should provide exception handling mechanisms and the opportunity for the user to make corrections for the submission of valid input data.

11.3 Checked Exception Handling

Checked exceptions are exceptions that must be handled by the programmer. Failure to implement the required exception handling will result in compiler syntax errors. Methods or constructors in the API class documentation explicitly specifying checked exceptions that may be produced must have programmer-provided exception handling mechanisms to deal with such exceptions in the code.

11.3.1 Discover checked exceptions

Checked exceptions may occur in:

- Method calls for file I/O operations, e.g., **FileNotFoundException**, **EOFException**.
- Method calls for threading operations, e.g., **InterruptedException**.
- Method calls for database operations, e.g., **SQLException**.
- Method calls for network connections and operations, e.g., **URLException**, **IOException**.

  Method implementations for interfaces in API, e.g., **CloneNotSupportedException** in the **Cloneable** interface implementation.

Proper exception handling mechanisms for checked exceptions must be implemented by the programmer. The Java compiler requires their proper handling in order to run the code.

11.3.2 Checked exceptions

The Java API documentation clearly states all information concerning the checked exceptions a method may throw. The names of the checked exceptions are referenced in association with the Java keyword **throws**. For example, in a constructor dealing with the file input process **FileReader()**, the API documentation specifies the following signature:

```
public FileReader(File file) throws FileNotFoundException
```

indicating that in using an instantiation of this constructor for file input the programmer must provide an exception handling mechanism to deal with the **FileNotFoundException** exception. Another example may be found in the **close()** method used in file I/O. The API documentation for the **close()** method specifies:

```
public void close() throws IOException
```

requiring the programmer to provide exception handling code to deal with **IOException**.

More Info: *In file I/O, especially in sequential file I/O,* ***EOFException*** *is commonly used to indicate when the end of the file has been reached; it is a special case. A detailed discussion of this topic is provided in Chapter 21.*

11.4 Exception Handling Mechanisms

Exception handling mechanisms in Java for both checked and unchecked exceptions can be summarized in four basic models:

- Traditional **try-catch-finally** mechanism.
- Use of **throws** to throw a list of exceptions to the calling procedure.
- Combination of the above two models.
- Use of the **throw** statement to throw or re-throw exceptions.

11.4.1 Traditional exception handling mechanism

The "try-catch-finally" model is also known as the traditional exception mechanism. The use of a **finally** block is optional. It can be described as follows:

```
try {   //try block
    //Including all statements that possibly throw exceptions
   ...
}
//catch clause
catch (ExceptionName1 e) {
   //Exception handling message
   ...
}
catch (ExceptionName2 e) {
   //Exception handling message
   ...
}
...
catch (ExceptionNameN e) {
   //Exception handling message
   ...
   }
finally {  //Optional
   //Message that must be processed
   ...
}
```

Important concepts of the traditional exception handling mechanism are:

- A **try** block normally has at least one **catch** block. It may also have an optional **finally** block. If a **try** block does not have a **catch** block, however, it must have a **finally** block, otherwise a syntax error will occur.
- A **catch** block must be associated with an accompanying **try** block.
- A **finally** block is always executed whether or not an exception occurs.
- A **try** block may have multiple **catch** blocks but only one optional **finally** block. The **finally** block must be placed after all **catch** blocks or after the **try** block if no **catch** block is provided.

- A pair of braces must be used in each block of the try-catch-finally mechanism, even if only one statement is present in the block. Missing braces within block will result in the generation of a syntax error.

Let's discuss what happens when an exception occurs in the following code snippet:

```
try {
   int value = Ingeter.parseInt("12ab");
   //Other statements
   ...
}
```

We hard-coded an illegal data element as the parameter for the for **parseInt()** method. Executing the statement will automatically throw a **NumberFormatException** object. This action is also known as an "implicit throw," since it is thrown automatically by the JVM. The flow of code execution will then jump out of the **try** block, ignoring any remaining statements in the **try** block, and resume at the first **catch** block provided in the code. An evaluation is performed at this point to determine if there is a match with the object that has been thrown. If the match is successful, code execution continues within the **catch** block. In the absence of a **catch** block, code execution continues in the mandatory **finally** block. Now, let us assume the code contains two **catch** blocks:

```
catch (InputMismatchException e) {
   //Process the exception and display the message
   ...
}
catch (NumberFormatException e) {
   //Process the exception and display the message
   ...
}
```

In the evaluation process following the throwing of the exception, code execution once again transfers to the first **catch** statement. The evaluation test determines the exception object does not match the specification of this **catch** statement and execution transfers to the second **catch** block. The second **catch** block is executed because a match exists between the thrown object and the specified argument type. The statements in the second **catch** block are executed and the exception is handled. In situations wherein more than one thrown object matches the argument specified in the **catch** blocks, only the first matched **catch** block will be executed.

Note: *The order of specifying **catch** blocks is important since only the first **catch** block will be executed if more than one **catch** block matches the thrown object. As such, **catch** blocks should be listed in order from most specific to general.*

If a thrown exception fails to match any exception specified in the list of **catch** blocks, the JVM will automatically trigger its own exception handling mechanism. The program will be terminated ungracefully, and the message of the exception handling will be recorded in a **stackTrace** displayed on the output console. The **stackTrace** is discussed in the following section..

If no exception occurs during the execution of statements contained in a **try** block, all listed **catch** blocks will be ignored. The **finally** block is always executed—whether an exception occurs or not.

A **finally** block should be used in the following situations:

- When statements must be executed after completing the successful processing of statements in the **try** block, e.g., to stop thread execution.

- When statements must be executed after an exception has been handled, e.g., issuing a **return** statement of a method class to close a file.
- When statements must be executed in the absence or failure to match the exception specified in the provided list of **catch** blocks before the JVM assumes processing of the exception. Examples include releasing memory space and closing audio, video, or picture display mode.

The following is an example using a **finally** block:

```
...
finally {              //Execute the return statement due to exception
  System.out.println("A default null has been returned due to the exception
  ... ");
   return null;
}
...
```

Another example:

```
...
finally {        //Execute the close() due to the exception
   fileOutput.close();
}
```

And another one:

```
...
finally {
   System.out.println("Your verification of the data has failed after 4 attempts. "
                        + "Your session will be logged off. ");
   verifying.off();     //close the operation
}
```

If a **return** statement is used in a try-catch-finally mechanism, good coding practice dictates that a viable **return** statement be processed in the event of an exception to avoid the syntax error: "lack of return statement." Consider the following code snippet producing a exception in which no **return** statement exists within the **catch** block::

```
public int validateInt() {
    try {
            ...
            return Integer.parseInt(intString);  //produce the syntax error
        }
        catch (NumberFormatException e) {
            ...
        }
}
```

The code may be modified to avoid the syntax error in the event of handling an exception as follows:

```
public int validateInt() {
   ...
  while (!valid) {
   try {
         intString = requestInput();        //Call requestInput()to receive data
         value = Integer.parseInt(intString); //May throw NumberFormatException

         valid = true;                      //If no exception, stop the loop
     }
   catch (NumberFormatException e) {
         System.out.println(ExceptionMessage);    //Display message
         continue;                                //Continue the loop
    }
}
return value;                                     //Return the verified data
}
```

11.4.2 Propagation of exceptions

Exception propagation refers to the practice of using the Java keyword **throws** after a method name to propagate or pass one or more exceptions to the method caller(s). In nested method calls, exception propagation may propagate the thrown object(s) to its associated hierarchy of methods calls on the stack of nested calls maintained by the JVM.

A common example of exception propagation is to use **throws** to pass exception objects to the JVM:

```
public static void main(String[] args) throws IOException,
InputMismatchException {
   ...
}
```

The above code structure throws both a checked **IOException** object and an unchecked **InputFormatException** object to the JVM. The reasons to do such propagation may be threefold:

- Trigger the JVM to handle the specified exceptions if no exception handling code is provided in the application.;
- Increase code readability. Although it may not be necessary in the event of unchecked exception handling, code readability and understanding is increased by examining the method header to learn what exceptions may potentially exist.; and
- You may still provide a **throws** list of exceptions even though an exception handling mechanism is provided in the code. However, the exception object will not be propagated to its method caller if a successful match of an included **catch** block exists to handle such an exception.

It must be pointed out that if a propagated exception is not passed to JVM, but another method, you must provide code either to handle passed exception or to propagate it to next level of method call.

It must be noted passing a propagated exception to another method rather than the JVM requires the presence of code to either handle the passed exception or to propagate the exception to the next level of method call.

Exception propagation in nested method calls is discussed in Section 11.6.2. In the case of implementation of a **Cloneable** interface, particularly in overriding the **clone()** method, we use **throws** to pass **CloneNotSupportedException** to the superclass of the **clone()** method to handle the exception:

```
public Object clone() throws CloneNotSupportedException {
   return super.clone();
}
```

The above code will generate a "missing return statement" error if a traditional try-catch-finally mechanism is used in the code without the use of exception propagation.

11.4.3 More discussion of exception messages

In API exception classes, all subclasses propagate exception messages to the superclass **Throwable** using the statement **super(message).** This mechanism allows us to easily use the methods provided in **Throwable** to retrieve these messages. Table 11.1 lists the methods commonly used to retrieve these messages.

Table 11.1 Commonly used methods in **Throwable** to retrieve exception handling messages

Method	Description
String getMessage()	Return the current exception handling message.
printStackTrace()	Display the exception handling message associated with this throwable recorded in the stack and its backtrace to the standard error stream.
String toString()	Return the exception handling message including the exception class name associated with this throwable.

For example, after executing the code snippet

```
try {
   int number = Integer.parseInt("123abc");        //Throws NumberFormatException
}
catch (NumberFormatException e) {                  //Handle the exception
   System.out.println(e.getMessage());             //Display the exception message
   e.printStackTrace();                  //Display the message recorded in the stack
   System.out.println(e);                //Or e.toString()
}
```

statement **System.out.println(e.getMessage())** produces the following information:

```
For input string: "123abc"
e.printStackTrace()displays the following message:
java.lang.NumberFormatException: For input string: "123abc"
        at java.lang.NumberFormatException.forInputString
        (NumberFormatException.java:48)
        at java.lang.Integer.parseInt(Integer.java:456)
        at java.lang.Integer.parseInt(Integer.java:497)
        at ExceptionHandlingTest1.main(ExceptionHandlingTest1.java:7)
```

and **System.out.println(e.toString())** or **System.out.println(e)** generates the following output:

```
java.lang.NumberFormatException: For input string: "123abc"
```

11.4.4 Examples

In this section more examples are presented using the concepts and coding techniques of exception handling previously discussed.

Example 1. Exception handling in **main()** method. Assume the code demonstrates sorting an array and the size of the array is determined by the user's data entry:

```
//Complete code is called ArrayValidationTest1.java in Ch11 from the author's
//Website
public class ArrayValidationTest1 {
   public static void main(String[] args) {
   ...
     while (choice.equals("y")) {
     try {
          System.out.print("Please enter an integer for the size of the array: " );
          size = sc.nextInt();        //May throw InputMismatchException
          int[] intArray = new int[size];
                                      //May throw NegativeArraySizeException
           System.out.println();

           ArrayDemo.fillArray(intArray);     //Call the static method
           Arrays.sort(intArray);             //Array sorting
```

```
            ArrayDemo.display(intArray);       //Display the sorting result
        }
        catch (InputMismatchException e) {  //Handle InputMismatchException
            System.out.println("You must enter an integer for array size...");
            count++;                                    //Increase the count
            sc.nextLine();                              //Clear the buffer
            continue;                                   //Continue to loop
        }
        catch (NegativeArraySizeException e) {
    //Handle NegativeArraySizeException
            System.out.println("You must enter a positive integer for array
            size...");
            count++;                                    //Increase the count
            sc.nextLine();                              //Clear the buffer
            continue;                                   //Continue to loop
        }
        finally {
            if (count >= 3) {
                    System.out.println("The application is terminated due to 3
                    wrong entries...");
                    System.out.println("Review your entries and try run the program
                    again. Bye!");
            break;                  //Or: System.exit(0); Terminate the loop
            }
    }
...
```

The code handles two types of exceptions: **InputMismatchException** and **NegativeArraySizeException**. It provides three opportunities for the user to correct erroneous data entry. A counter is increased by 1 in each **catch** block to keep track of the quantity of user data entries. The **continue** statement resumes the next loop iteration for data verification. Since the **finally** block is always executed whether or not an exception has occurred, it will print the message prompting the user to review the input data only if three or more attempts have been made. A **break** (or **System.exit(0)**) statement terminates the code execution.

Example 2. M Modify the code in **Example 1** to use a default array size if the user enters invalid data more than three times:

```
//Complete code called ArrayValidationTest2.java in Ch11 from the author's Website
...
    finally {
    if (count >= 3) {
                System.out.println("You've entered 3 wrong entries...");
                System.out.println("A default array size 100 has been assigned
                ...");
```

```
                int[] intArray = new int[100];
                ArrayDemo.fillArray(intArray);          //Call static method
                Arrays.sort(intArray);                  //Array sorting
                ArrayDemo.display(intArray);            //Display result
                break;
            }
    } ...
```

Example 3. There is another coding technique to handling exceptions – design a verification class, for example, **Validator**, as a utility class with a number of static methods to verify data and handle a variety of exceptions. In following code:

```
//Complete code called ArrayValidationTest3.java in Ch11 from the author's Website
while (choice.equals("y")) {
   size = Validator4.arraySize(sc, "Please enter an integer for the
   array size: ");
   int[] intArray = new int[size];          //size is already verified

      ArrayDemo.fillArray(intArray);
      Arrays.sort(intArray);
      ArrayDemo.display(intArray);

      System.out.print("Continue? (y/n): ");
      choice = sc.next();
}
...
```

static method **Validator4.arraySize()** is called to verify the size of the array using an application-specific user prompt as the method parameter. We code method **arraySize()** in the **Validator4** class as follows::

```
//Complete code called Validator4.java in Ch11 from author's Website
public static int arraySize(Scanner sc, String prompt) {
         boolean done = false;
         int count = 0;
         int size = 0;
         while (!done) {
         try {
             System.out.print(prompt );
             size = sc.nextInt();    //May throw InputMismatchException
             if (size < 0)
               throw new NegativeArraySizeException();

                 System.out.println();
                 done = true;
             }
          catch (InputMismatchException e){//Handle InputMismatchException
```

```
                System.out.println("You must enter an integer for array
                size...");
                count++;                                //Increase count
                sc.nextLine();                          //Clear buffer
                continue;                               //Continue to loop
            }
            catch (NegativeArraySizeException e) {
                                                //Handle NegativeArraySizeException
                System.out.println("You must enter a positive integer for array
                size...");
                count++;                                //Increase count
                sc.nextLine();                          //Clear buffer
                continue;                               //Continue to loop
            }
            finally {
                if (count >= 3) {
                    System.out.println("You've entered 3 wrong
                    entries...");
                    System.out.println("A default array size 100 has been
                    assigned…");
                    size = 100;
                    break;
                }
            }
        }
    return size;
}
```

In handling the situation in which an array size is less than 0, a **throw** statement is used to throw an anonymous object of **NegativeArraySizeException**. We discuss the **throw** statement in the next section. In the **finally** block, if **count >= 3**, a default size of 100 is used to establish the array length.

Example 4. It is recommended that an **Exception** class object be used in the last **catch** block of an exception handling "sequence" to handle any exception that may not be explicitly handled (or missed) in the code:

```
…
catch (Exception e)      {                    //The last catch block
   System.out.println("A exception occurred that cannot be handled in the code.\n
                    The following is the stack trace information: \n");
   System.out.println(e.print Stack Trace());           //Or: e.getMessage();
}
```

Since **Exception** or **Throwable** is a superclass of all exception classes, it will catch any type of exception. As such, it will not miss "capturing" any exception that has occurred and handled in the code.

11.5 Use of the throw Statement

It is important to note the difference between the **throw** statement and the **throws** statement. A **throws** statement is declarative for the method. It tells the compiler the particular exception will be handled by the calling method. The **throw** statement, however, is used to force the code to explicitly throw an anonymous object of the exception if some condition is satisfied. It can also be used in a **catch** block or a **finally** block in which an object of the exception could be (re-)thrown to propagate the exception.

11.5.1 Automatically throw by the JVM

As previously discussed, if an unchecked exception occurs during code execution the JVM, or system, will automatically and implicitly throw an object of the exception. The JVM will also automatically handle the processing of the exception. This form of exception is known as an implicitly thrown exception. An implicitly thrown exception is handled by the JVM if the user does not provide code to handle the exception. For example, the JVM will automatically, i.e., implicitly, throw an object of **InputMismatchException** if an invalid data, such as a floating-point number, is entered in the statement:

```
int value = sc.nextInt();               //sc is an object of Scanner
```

In effect, the JVM uses a **throw** statement to throw this exception as:

```
throw new InputMistachException();
```

Although the object of **InputMismatchException** does not have a name (it is not important here), the JVM will retrieve the message recorded in the stack and display it if no exception handling code is provided in the program.

11.5.2 I can throw, too

Programmers may use a **throw** statement to explicitly throw an exception. For example:

```
try {
   if (!sc.hasNextInt())              //May produce InputMismatchException
          throw new InputMismatchException(); //Throw this exception
}
catch (InputMismatchException e) {   //Handle this exception
   System.out.println("Incorrect integer entry.  Please check and try again...");
}
...
```

There is another constructor with a **String** type argument provided in any API exception classes

```
public InputMismatchException(String message)
```

that may be used to throw an exception with a specified message, for example:

```
throw new InputMismatchException("Incorrect integer entry.  Please check and try
again...");
```

In the **catch** block associated with the exception,

```
catch (InputMismatchException e) {
   System.out.println(e);
}
```

the following message will be displayed:

```
Incorrect integer entry.  Please check and try again...
```

A **throw** statement can also be used in a **catch** block to explicitly throw another exception:

```
...
catch (IOExcetion e) {
   System.out.println(e);
   throw new FileNotFoundException();
}
```

In the above code snippet, the **catch** block throws a new **FileNotFoundException** to the method caller or the upper level of exception handling stack after it processes the caught exception. Note that the original exception handling message will be lost if it immediately throws a new exception. We discuss this topic in section 11.8.1. The following list describes situations in which a **throw** statement might be used in a **catch** block:

- Although the **catch** block handles the caught exception, more exception processing is required to produce a more accurate or specific exception handling message.
- The matched **catch** block may not suitable to handle the matched exception and will need to throw it or throw a new exception to the next level of exception handling code.

***Note**: When using a **throw** statement to throw an exception, it must be the last statement in the **try, catch**, or **finally** block; otherwise a syntax error will result. If an exception is **RuntimeException**, it is common practice to use a **throws** statement to throw it to the JVM rather than use a **try-catch-finally** structure to handle it. An example can be found in **RuntimeExceptionTest.java** in Ch11 from the author's Website.*

11.5.3 Re-throw an exception

Re-throwing an exception refers to the situation in which a **catch** block, after catching an object of an exception from a **try** block, uses a **throw** statement to re-throw the object yet again to the calling method or upper level of exception handling stack maintained by the JVM to be handled. It should be noted when a **catch** block re-throws such an exception a **throws** statement must be included in the method header listing the exception:

```
...
public void someMethod() throws Exception {//List the re-thrown exception
   try {
         ...
         throw new Exception ();    //Throw an exception
```

```
    }
    catch (Exception e) {
        ...
        throw e;                    //Re-throw the exception
    }
}
```

In the **catch** block, statement **throw e** re-throws **Exception**, thereby throwing the object of **Exception** to its caller or the next upper level of exception handling in the stack. If the re-thrown event occurs in the **main()** method, the JVM will handle this exception.

The purpose of re-throwing is similar to the use of the **throw** statement in a **catch** block—both throw an object of an existing exception.

11.6 Nested Exception Handling

An exception handling mechanism can be of a nested structure format within the coding. An example of this was discussed in the last section. The purposes of using nested exception handling are:

- Inner exception handling code is used to handle a more specified exception than the outer exception handling code.; and
- If the inner exception handling mechanism cannot fully handle the exception it can automatically propagate to its outer exception handling code.

Nested exception handling can also happen in nested method calls. It has its own features that are different from the regular exception propagation discussed at the beginning of this chapter. In this section, we discuss these important concepts and coding techniques.

11.6.1 Nested models

The following possibilities may occur during code execution:

- If no exception occurs, the program will execute normally and the **finally** blocks (if present) in both the inner and outer exception handlers are always executed.
- If the inner exception mechanism does not match any thrown exception, its **finally** block (if present) is always executed. Program control will propagate the exception to the first **catch** block in the outer exception handling, with each **catch** block will be evaluated and the **finally** block being executed (if present). The JVM, however, will step in to complete the exception handling if no matched **catch** block in outer exception handling mechanism is executed.
- If the exception occurs in the outer exception handling mechanism, each **catch** block will be evaluated and its **finally** block executed (if presented). If there is no matched **catch** block, the JVM will step in after the **finally** block is executed and all inner exception handling code, including its **finally** block, will be omitted.
- A **throw** statement may be used to perform an explicit exception throw in an outer or inner exception handling mechanism. For example, a **throw** statement used in the inner exception handling code will throw the exception to its outer exception handling code.

- The code may also re-throw an existing exception in nested exception handling. For example, a **catch** block in the inner exception handling mechanism may re-throw an exception to its outer exception handling code, and a **catch** block in the outer exception handling code may re-throw an exception to its caller or the next level of the exception handling in the stack.

It is important to note that the abuse of a nested exception handling mechanism will reduce execution speed and code readability. It should be used properly.

Model 2:

```
...
try  {
   method1();                 //Call method1()
   ...
   method2();                 //Call method2()
}
catch (...) {
   ...
}
finally {                     //Optional
```

```
    ...
}
...
public void method1() {
    try {
            ...
    }
    catch (...) {
            ...
    }
    ...
}
public void method2() {
    try {
            ...
    }
    catch (...) {
            ...
    }
    ...
}
```

In this model, each method has its own exception handling mechanism. This form is commonly used in more sophisticated coding applications. Similarly, it may explicitly throw an exception or re-throw an existing exception in any **catch** block to the next level of exception handling.

11.6.2 Propagation in nested exception handling

We first discuss a typical example of exception handling propagation in a nested exception handling mechanism using Model 2 (see above) wherein each method throws the same exception to its caller. Figure 11.2 illustrates this concept.

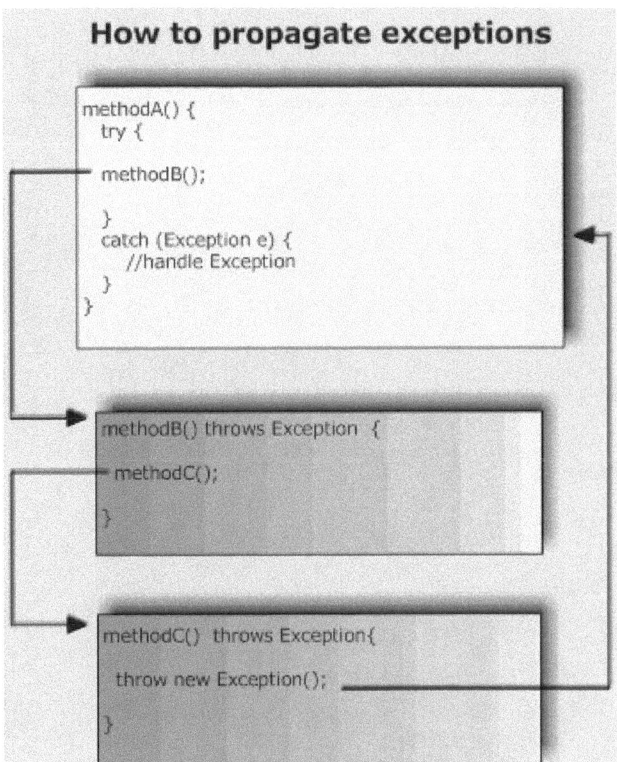

Figure 11.2 Propagation in a nested exception handling

In Figure 11.2, **methodA()** provides the uppermost level of exception handling below the JVM. Should **methodA()** throw this exception, the JVM will step in to handle the propagated exception. The propagation changes the normal execution flow: instead of executing the unfinished code in each nested method, the execution directly jumps up to the exception handling mechanism, **methodA()**, to handle the exception.

Propagation in a nested exception handling is commonly used in complicated networking programming, remote method calling, and Web services applications.

11.6.3 Nested exception re-throw

Nested exception re-throw refers to a coding scenario involving nested method calls in which each method provides an exception handling mechanism. In each **catch** block, a **throw** statement is used to re-throw the existing exception to the method's caller. Figure 11.3 illustrates this concept.

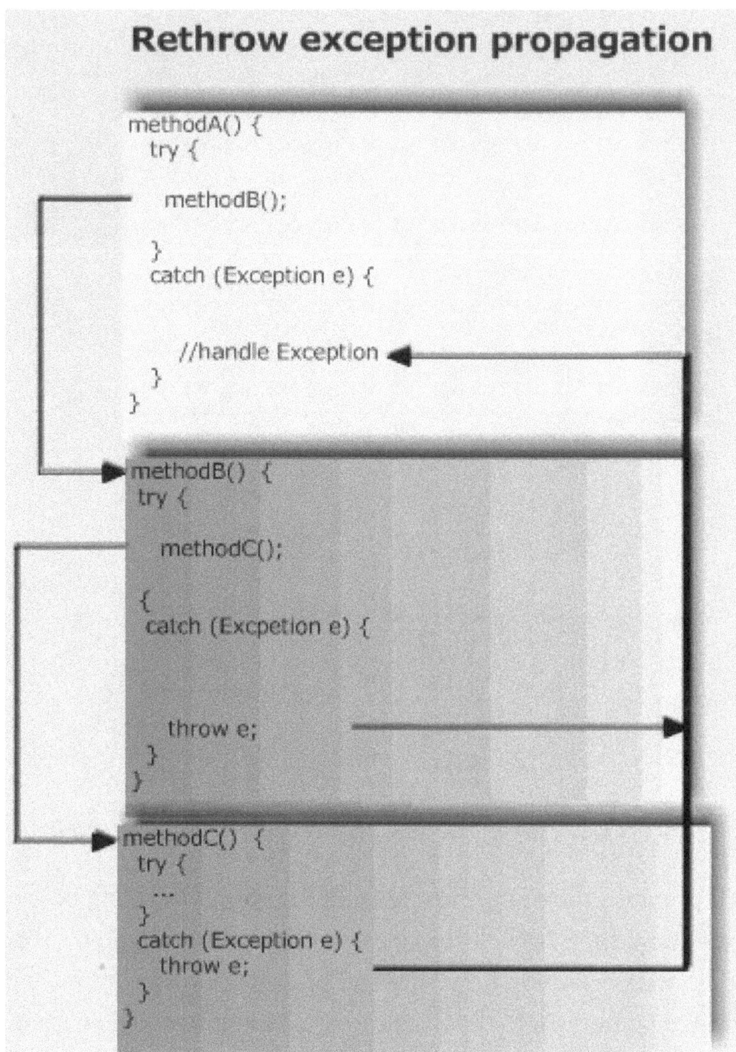

Figure 11.3 Re-throw the exception in nested method calls

In Figure 11.3, the **catch** block of **methodC()** re-throws a caught exception to its caller, **methodB()**. In **methodB()**, the exception is, in turn, propagated to **methodA()**. The exception may be handled in **methodA()** or re-thrown to the JVM.

Propagation in a nested re-throw is similar to propagation in a nested exception handling. The key difference, however, is that propagation in a nested re-throw will cause the flow of execution to travel through each nested method until it reaches the exception handling code. In the propagation of nested exception handling, execution will jump directly to the origin of the occurring exception. This technique is commonly used in large scale applications in networking, remote method calls, and Web services.

11.7 Programmer-Defined Exception Classes

Although we may use the standard **Exception** class to handle a specified exception:

```
try {
    // If there is an exception handle with custom handler
    //  NOTE:  We may use any API exception class
    if (someCustomException)
```

```
        throw Exception ("Custom message about the exception...");
}
catch (Exception e) {
   System.out.println(e);              //Display the specified message
}
```

in this example we "borrow **Exception** to make a gift to our application" by using the **Exception** constructor form with a **String** argument to pass the particular custom message as result of the exception handling. Programmers often define their own exception classes using inheritance from the API **Exception** class to handle more specified or custom exceptions for particular applications. Of course, we may use any of standard exception class to do the same thing above.

11.7.1 Define your own exception classes

The commonly used template to code a user-defined exception class is:

```
public class CustomException extends Exception {  //Inherit an API exception class
   public CustomException()  {}                    //No argument constructor
   public CustomException(String message) {        //An argument constructor
         super(message);                           //Call the super constructor
   }
}
```

You may inherit **Throwable** as the superclass to define your own exception class. Although the constructor without an argument may not be used very often, it does provide a measure of convenience in the instantiation of the exception object. The second constructor will pass the particular message of the exception handling to the superclass where the message will be recorded. The message can be retrieved by calling **toString()**, **getMessage()**, or **printStackTrace()**.

Let's discuss an example. Assume we need to verify if a user-provided data for age is a positive value. We may code this exception using the template:

```
public class NegativeAgeException extends Exception { //Or: extends Throwable
   public NegativeAgeException()  {}
   public NegativeAgeException(String message) {
         super(message);
   }
}
```

The following code snippet uses an exception handling code that applies this user-defined exception class, **NegativeAgeException**:

```
//Complete code called NegativeAgeExceptionTest.java in Ch11 from the author's
//Website
...
```

```
try{
   String ageString = JOptionPane.showInputDialog("Enter your age: ");

   if (Integer.parseInt(ageString) < 0)
        throw new NegativeAgeException("Please enter a positive age");
   else
        JOptionPane.showMessageDialog(null, ageString, "Age", 1);
}
catch(NegativeAgeException e){
    System.out.println(e);
}
...
```

You may also use the constructor without an argument to create an object of **NegativeAgeException** and then print the specified message in the **catch** block:

```
   throw new NegativeAgeException();
   ...
 catch(NegativeAgeException e){
    System.out.println("Please enter a positive age.");
}
...
```

This will produce the same result as previous example.

11.7.2 Programmer-defined exception handling

The mechanism of programmer-defined exception handling refers to a code structure wherein a **try** block containing an **if** statement is used to test and throw a programmer-defined exception and an associated **catch** block "matching" the thrown exception object handles the exception in a more specific manner. This can be defined as follows:

```
try {
   ...
   if (someExceptionConditon == true) {
          throw new CustomException("A custom exception xxx occurred. Please
          check your entry...")
   ...
   }
catch (CustomException e) {
   ...
}
```

The exception handling message can be included in the constructor as its argument or provided in the **catch** block with code to print out the message.

It is very important to note that a standard exception may occur before the custom exception. For example, in a code needing to verify that an age is a positive integer, user-defined data for the age may not be a legal integer type. As such, a **NumberFormatException** exception will occur before a (possible) **NegativeAgeException** exception. You must provide code to handle both exceptions. Placing the **catch** block associated with handling the **NumberFormatException** exception first may provide better coding efficiency and readability:

```
try {
   ...
   if (Integer.parseInt(ageString) < 0)
          throw NegativeAgeException("Please enter a positive age");
   else
          ...
   }
   catch (NumberFormatException e) {
          System.out.println(e);
   }
   catch (NegativeAgeException e) {
          System.out.println(e);
   }
   ...
```

Using the above code snippet as an example, if **ageString** receives an illegal integer data, e.g., "25abc", method **parseInt()** will throw **NumberFormatException** automatically and the first **catch** block will handle this exception. The **throw** statement relating to **NegativeAgeException** will not be executed.

11.7.3 Modified Validator class

Based on our discussion of exception handling so far, we may modify the **Validator4** class to include more exception handling functions:

```
//Complete code called Validator5.java in Ch11 from the author's Website
public class Validator5 {
   ...
public static int intWithRange(Scanner sc, String prompt, int min, int max)
{
   boolean done = false;
   int count = 0;
   int data = 0;
   while (!done) {
     try {
      System.out.print(prompt );
      data = sc.nextInt();     //May produce InputMismatchException
      if (data < min)          //Exceeded the min
        throw new IntegerOutOfRangeException("Data out of minimum "+ min +
        " range exception.");
      if (data > max)          //Exceeded the max
           throw new IntegerOutOfRangeException("Data out of maximum "+ max
           + " range exception.");
      System.out.println();
      done = true;
     }
```

```
    catch (InputMismatchException e) {//Handle InputMismatchException
         System.out.println("You must enter an integer...");
         count++;                        //Increase count
         sc.nextLine();                  //Clear buffer
         continue;                       //Continue loop
    }
    catch (IntegerOutOfRangeException e) {
                                        //Handle IntegerOutOfRangeException
         System.out.println(e);
         count++;                       //Increase count
         sc.nextLine();                 //Clear buffer
         continue;                      //Continue loop
    }
  }
  return data;
  }
  ...
}
//User-defined exception class
class IntegerOutOfRangeException extends Throwable {
                                                     //Or: extends Exception
  public IntegerOutOfRangeException() {}
  public IntegerOutOfRangeException(String message) {
         super(message);
  }
}
```

11.8 Exception Chaining

The purpose of exception chaining is to prevent the loss of a previously occurring exception when a successive exception is thrown. It is a common situation in which a user-defined exception is thrown in response to another exception occurring. For example, in the **catch** block responding to **NumberFormatException** you may subsequently throw **NotIntegerException**. Exception chaining uses the constructor and methods provided in class **Throwable** to chain these two related exceptions together so information in **NumberFormatException** will not be lost.

11.8.1 "Losing" an exception

The following code

```
catch (IOException e) {                        //Handle IOException
   throw new CustomIOException();              //Throw another exception
}
```

illustrates a typical example of losing an exception. After a new exception, **CustomIOException**, has been thrown the message stored in the previous exception, **IOException**, is erased by the JVM.

11.8.2 Realizing exception chaining

The **Throwable** class was introduced in JDK1.4. It can be used to realize exception chaining, thereby providing a successful means of avoiding the loss of previously occurring exceptions. Commonly used constructors and methods used in exception chaining are listed in Table 11.2.

Table 11.2 Constructors and methods used for exception chaining in **Throwable**

Constructor/Method	Description
Throwable(Throwable cause)	Create an object of Throwable with the specified cause and a detail message of (cause==null ? Null : cause.toString()) which typically contains the class and a detail message of cause.
Throwable(String message, Throwable cause)	Create an object of Throwable including the message and the exception object
Throwable getCause()	Retrieve the object of exception from the upper level or null if the cause is nonexistent or unknown.
initCause(Throwable cause)	Set the object as a upper level exception source. Initializes the cause of this throwable to the specified value. It cannot be used if a constructor already created an object of the exception from the upper level.

Exception chaining may be performed in two different ways:

Way 1:

- In user-defined exception handling, use the **Throwable(Throwable)** constructor to chain or record the previous exception together with the custom exception handling. For example:

```
public class CustomIOException exdends Exception {
   public CustomIOException() {}
   public CustomIOException(Throwable cause) {//cause is previous exception
          super(cause);                        //Record or save this exception
   //other exception handling statements
   ...
   }
}
```

- In the **catch** block, **throw** the user-defined exception with the information of the previous exception:

```
catch (IOException e) {
 throw CustomIOException(e); //Message in IOException recorded to CustomException
}
```

- When the method caller or the exception handling in the next level of exception handling stack handles this thrown exception it will call method **getCause()** method to display all messages associated with the chained exceptions:

```
catch (CustomIOException e) {
   System.out.println("Custom IO Exception info: " + e);
                                    //Display the custom exception message
    System.out.println("Previous IO Exception info: " + e.getCause());
```

```
                                        //Display the previous exception message
}
```

Way 2:

Assume there is no **Throwable** constructor used in a user-defined exception class. We may directly use the **initCause()** method in class **Throwable** to perform exception chaining as follows:

```
try {
  ...
  if (!inputFile.canRead())   {     //If the file cannot be read in
     cannotRead = new CustomIOException();  //Create an object of custom exception
     cannotRead.initCause(new IOException()); //Chained with IOException
     throw cannotRead;                         //Throw both exceptions
  }
  ...
```

Since method **initCause()** accepts **Throwable** as its argument it can be used when a previous exception is passed into the current exception object, thereby chaining together the exceptions. This form of exception chaining is commonly used in exception handling requiring the processing of both exceptions.

11.9 Assertion

The **assert** statement was introduced in JDK1.4. It is specifically designed for code debugging and testing. It may be placed at any place within the code as a statement, and is often referred to as a "run break." A condition for a run break is provided after the keyword **assert** to declare a termination of the execution if the condition is not satisfied. For example, the run break code statement:

```
assert age > 18
```

will cause code execution to stop if the assertion "**age** is greater than 18" fails.

Assertion evaluation must be enabled before code execution. The following sections discuss the use of assertion.

11.9.1 Coding an assert statement

The syntax of the **assert** statement is:

```
assert booleanExpression [: message];
```

wherein

assert – Java keyword.

booleanExpression – Java boolean expression to declare a condition that must be satisfied.

[:**message**] – optional display message.

As with other Java statements, the **assert** statement must end with a semicolon.

For purposes of code readability, we use parentheses to identify the boolean expression in an **assert** statement.

Let's discuss several examples using assertions:

Example 1.

```
//Complete code called AssertTest.java in Ch11 from author's Website
int age = 17;
assert (age > 18) : "Age must be greater than 18.";
```

The code will terminate because **age** is less than 18. The JVM will display the following message with the specified information:

```
Exception in thread "main" java.lang.AssertionError: Age must be greater than 18.
at AssertTest.main(AssertTest.java:11)
```

In actuality, the JVM treats the assertion failure as a thrown **AssertionError** exception. The **assert** statement will be omitted and the code will continue to execute if age is greater than 18.

Example 2.

```
//Complete code called AssertTest.java in Ch11 from author's Website
double total = 219.98;
assert (total > 0 .0 && total < 200.0) : "total: " + total + " - out of range.";
```

Code execution will halt because the value of **total** (219.98) fails to meet the requirements of the **assert** statement. The JVM will display the following message:

```
total: 219.98 - out of range.
at AssertTest.main(AssertTest.java:10)
```

11.9.2 Enabling and disabling assertion processing

The methods of enabling and disabling assertions depend on the manner in which the code is to be executed. If the program is executed in command line console mode under the operating system, the following command will enable the processing of assertions and execute the code:

java –ea ClassName

Option **ea** is short for enable. This option will enable assertion processing in the Java execution command. The following command sequence

java ClassName

without the **ea** option disables assertion processing.

More info: *You may also use **java –da ClassName** to execute the code disabling the assertion. Option **da** is short for disable.*

Executing code in an IDE, e.g., Eclipse or TextPad, requires that assertions be enabled in the following configurations:

Eclipse:

In the **Run** menu,

```
Run...
Arguments
```

select parameter **arguments.** In the **VM Arguments** window, enter:

-ea (or **enableassertion**)

and then select **apply** and **run**.

If you would like to disable the assertion, go to VM window and delete the **–ea** option.

TextPad:

To enable assertions, access the **Configure** menu, select **Preference**, **Tools**, and **Run Java Application**. In the **Parameter** window, enter:

-ea followed by a space

Then click **OK** to confirm.

If you would like to disable the assertion, go to the **Parameter** window and delete the **–ea** option.

Exercises

1. What is a checked exception? What is an unchecked exception? Use examples to explain.
2. What are commonly used exception handling mechanisms? Use examples to explain.
3. What is a clause of **catch** blocks? Use examples to explain. Explain the best way in which to order a clause of **catch** blocks in a Java program.
4. Use examples to explain the features of a **finally** block. What code should be included in a **finally** block?
5. What is exception propagation? Use examples to explain how you would propagate an exception.

6. Open the file **ArrayValidationTest.java** in Ch11 from author's Website, add the code that will verify the max size of an array cannot exceed to 1000 using the following two ways:

    a. Verify using the **Throwable** and **Exception** classes; and

    b. Verify by using a programmer-defined class called **ArrayOutOfMaxException**.

7. Open file **Validator4.java** in Ch11 from the author's Website. Using the example shown in Section 11.4.4 as a guide, add the following static methods into the class to validate positive integer and double values:

    a. **validatePositiveInt(Scanner sc, String prompt, int num)** – num is the data you want to verify.

    b. **validatePositiveDouble(scanner sc, String prompt, double num)** – num is the data you want to verify.

8. Write a driver code to test **Validator4** you have modified in **Question 8**. Doc your source code and save the files.

9. Use examples to explain the differences between the **throws** and **throw** statements.

10. What is meant by the concept of re-throwing an exception? Why is re-throwing needed?

11. Use examples to explain the different ways in which exceptions can be nested.

12. What is the propagation of a nested exception? Explain the differences between a nested exception and the propagation of a nested exception.

13. What is meant by the concept of re-throwing in a nested exception? Explain the differences between a re-throw in a nested exception and nested exception propagation.

14. Write the following programmer-defined exception classes to handle the specified exception. Each class must include a non-argument form of a constructor::

    a. **IllegalSelectionException** – handle a selection exception that is out of the range

       in the given selection items.

    b. **IntOutOfRangeException** – an integer out of range exception.; and

    c. **PriceOutOfRangeException** – a price outside a specified range.

    Write a driver code to test the three user-defined exception classes. Hint: You may wish to provide a series of prompts to the user regarding a list of items from which to select, a range of integers, and a range of prices. Code should be written to handle any pattern of occurring exceptions.

15. What is meant by the term "exception losing?" Explain this concept using examples.

16. What is exception chaining? How do you realize or implement exception chaining?

17. What is an assert statement? What is the purpose of assertion?

18. Open file **ArrayValidatorTest.java** in Ch11 from the author's Website. Add an **assert** statement to verify the specified array size has not exceeded 1000 elements. If the assertion fails, display a message indicating the array size has exceeded 1000 elements. Document your code and save the files.

"The Master said, 'There may be those who act without knowing why. I do not do so. Hearing much and selecting what is good and following it; seeing much and keeping it in memory - this is the second style of knowledge.'"

– Confucius

Chapter 12 More OOP Technology

Java technology includes not only numerous API libraries, but also consists of many object-oriented programming tools. Package technology permits better class management and access. The **javadoc** command is used to create documentation web pages for source code. The **Enum** class is used to increase source code readability. In addition to these topics, auto-boxing, auto-unboxing, and variable-length arguments are also discussed in this chapter.

12.1 Package

The Java package mechanism provides an effective means to manage and access classes. A package consists of related classes established in accordance with the Java namespace specification, using Java archive or zip technology. The classes are stored in a specified file directory. In real world applications, all classes are categorized into packages.

The **package** statement exists outside the "bounds" of a class. The keyword **package** is used at the beginning of a class to establish the class as a packaged class:

```
package com.classes.java;
```

com.classes.java represents the package name and specifies the directory in which the class package is located. Using the **javadoc** command with the option **-d** also creates a package:

```
C:\javac -d com\classes\java javabook\src\ch12\PackageTest.java
```

wherein, for example, **com\classes\java** specifies the file directory. Using the **javadoc** command to create your own packages and packaged files and access them will be discussed in later sections of this chapter.

The mechanism of package technology is also related to class accessibility, i.e., the package access. In Java, if no access keyword is specified the class is considered as having package access. For example,

```
class PackageClass {          //Class has package accessibility
   int value;                 //Instance variable has package accessibility
   ...
   void method() {            //Method has package accessibility
          ...
   }
   ...
}
```

We will discuss package accessibility in section 12.1.6 and other accessibilities are also summarized in that section.

12.1.1 Package specification

Java provides the following naming conventions for packages in order to guarantee name uniqueness:

- The package name must be specified in lowercase letters.
- The package name must follow the syntax of Java identifiers.
- It is recommended that a package name use the reverse order of a company's website. A country or regional code may be incorporated to provide further uniqueness.
- Avoid using Java API package names, e.g., **java.lang**, **javax.swing**.

Example 1. Names of user-defined packages.

```
 Website URL                                          Package Name
FreeSkyTech.com                                       com.freeskytech
Ohlone.edu/faculty/CS                          cs.faculty.edu.ohlone.usa
```

Example 2. For the purpose of training and learning, the author recommends using meaningful names as package names, e.g.:

```
C:\javabook\classes\ch12\
```

12.1.2 Creating packaged files

There are two common ways to create and use packaged classes or files:

- Specification of a CLASSPATH.
- Use of the Java JAR command.

Let's first discuss how to use CLASSPATH to create and use packaged files. Assume, for purposes of illustration, we are using the Windows OS. The following steps will create a packaged file:

- Create a directory to store the packaged file. Java specifies that a packaged file must be stored at least three subdirectory levels below the root directory. For example, the following directory:

```
C:\javabook\classes\ch12\
```

satisfies the subdirectory requirement and specifies **ch12** as the package name.

- At the beginning of the class being packaged, specify the package name **ch12** using the Java keyword **package**:

```
package ch12;
public class PackageTest {
public void print() {
        System.out.println("Here is message from Package Test ...");
    }
}
```

3. Create a CLASSPATH. The CLASSPATH tells the Java compiler the location at which the package files may be found and loaded. According to the Java specification, a CLASSPATH must be one level higher than the package directory. In this example, the CLASSPATH should be:

```
C:\javabook\classes;
```

In the **Control Panel**, select Systems -> Advanced -> Environment Variables (N) -> New Setup. In the window **Name of Environment Variables**, type:

```
CLASSPATH
```

And then in the window **Value of the Variable**, type:

```
.;c:\javabook\classes;
```

Click on OK -> OK -> OK.

However, if there is an existing CLASSPATH, then select "Edit ->". At the beginning of the existing CLASSPATH, type:

```
.;c:\javabook\classes;
```

And then press OK all way through.

4. Create the directory to store the source code files for the package. For example:

```
C:\javabook\src\ch12
```

5. Copy and paste the source code file(s) to the above directory.
6. Compile the packaging file with the **-d** option:

```
C:\javac -d javabook\classes javabook\src\ch12\PackageTest.java
```

7. In this compilation command, option **–d** instructs the compiler to store the generated bytecode files in the first specified directory. The second argument indicates the location where the source code file to be packaged is located. If the directory contains more than one file needing to be packaged, you may use the wildcard "*" to compile all the files:

```
C:\javac -d javabook\classes javabook\src\ch12\*.java
```

After executing the above command, the Java compiler will store the bytecode files in **C:\javabook\classes\ch12**. Subdirectory **ch12** is automatically created as the package name.

You may also consider using two subdirectories to store the packaged file as:

```
package ch12.share;
public class PackageTest2 {
        ...
}
```

Note the CLASSPATH is still the same:

```
C:\javabook\classes\
```

The compilation command will remain the same, but the compiler will automatically create the two subdirectories as **ch12\share** after the specified CLASSPATH **C:\javabook\classes**.

Note: *In Windows OS, you may use either forward slash or backward slash to indicate a subdirectory.*

12.1.3 Import packaged files

We use the **import** statement to retrieve and include a packaged file for access within the code as is done with an API class or classes in Java libraries.

```
import ch12.PackageTest1;
import ch12.PackageTest2;

public class PackageTestApp {
   public static void main(String[] args) {
          PackageTest1 myPackage = new PackageTest1();
          myPackage.print();
          PackageTest2 yourPackage = new PackageTest2();
          yourPackage.print();
   }
}
```

We may also use the wildcard "*" in the **import** statement:

```
import ch12.*;
```

Note that **PackageTestApp.java** can be stored in any directory and perform the compilation and execution.

12.1.4 JAR files

Another way to create packaged classes is through the use of the Java **JAR** (Java Archive) zip command. The JDK directory **jre\lib\ext** allows users to store packaged files with JAR zipped format. A **JAR** file may include one or more packaged classes for efficiency of loading; it will be automatically unzipped by the compiler. The use of JAR files will avoid the establishment of CLASSPATH.

The JAR command is included in the JDK. The following illustrations use the JAR command for packaging the example used in CLASSPATH above.

```
package ch12;
public class PackageTest1 {
public void print() {
   System.out.println("Here is Package Test 1 message...");
   }
}
```

and:

```
package ch12;
public class PackageTest2 {
public void print() {
   System.out.println("Here is Package Test 2 message...");
   }
}
```

The following steps are used to create and use the packaged classes:

- Create a directory to store the packaged file(s). This requirement is the same as that using CLASSPATH. You must have at least three subdirectory levels below the root:

```
C:\javabook\classes\ch12\
```

2. Copy and paste the source code file(s) that will be packaged in the directory created above. It is the same as that using CLASSPATH.
3. Use the compilation command to compile the packaging files:

```
C:\javac -d javabook\classes javabook\src\ch12\*.java
```

4. Create the JAR file. Relocating to the directory one level above the package directory, type the following JAR command:

```
C:\javabook\classes\jar cvf ch12.jar ch12\*
```

This command will automatically create the subdirectory within the current directory **C:\javabook\classes**, generate a zipped bytecode archive file, and store it into **C:\javabook\classes\ch12**.

The definition of three options **cvf** specified in the JAR command are:

c – create an archive file

v – use of verbose display listing each file name as it is incorporated into the JAR file archive

f – direct the output to the file specified immediately following the **f** option rather than *stdout*

The use of the wildcard specifier "*" in the JAR command causes all appropriate files, including source code files, to be archived. For example, invoking the following JAR command places only the bytecode files in the archive file:

```
C:\javabook\classes\jar cvf ch12.jar ch12\*.class
```

Note the use of the Java naming convention requiring lower case letters for the archive file name. [NOTE: I do not understand the application of "can be any legal identifiers." LAS]

5. Copy and paste the generated archive file to the subdirectory of the JDK installed on your computer:

   \jer\lib\ext

6. Use the **import** statement to retrieve the packaged classes. For example:

```
import ch12.*;       //import all package classes
public class PackageJarTestApp {
   public static void main(String[] args) {
       PackageTest1 myPackage = new PackageTest1();   //Use of packaged class
       myPackage.print();  // Call the method

       PackageTest2 yourPackage = new PackageTest2(); //Use of packaged class
       yourPackage.print();
   }
}
```

The use of the **import** statement is the same as with the Java API classes. If you only need to import a specific packaged class, you may specify the class name explicitly:

```
import ch12.OtherClass;
```

12.1.5 Packages in IDEs

All popular Java IDEs use the package mechanism to manage classes and files. Beginning in this chapter, all example programs will use the package mechanism provided by the Eclipse IDE.

IDE package mechanisms provide a convenient way of managing and loading packaged classes by relieving the programmer of the need to manually create packages and packaged classes as we discussed in the previous sections. The automatic creation of package archives eliminates errors that might otherwise arise in the creation and importing of the packaged files.

The following section uses the Eclipse IDE as the example basis in discussing how to setup packages within an IDE. We will use the examples of the previous sections, **PackageTest1.java** and **PackageTest2.java**. First, we must delete the **package** statement from the source code:

```
//package ch12;  //no longer needed because it is automatically handled in Eclipse
public class PackageTest1 {
   public void print() {
      System.out.println("Here is Package Test 1 message...");
   }
}
```

We will do the same in **PackageTest2.java**.

Eclipse provides many different ways to set up packages. The following is a typical method:

1. Create the Project first. Select **File -> New -> Project -> Next**. Type in your project name, e.g., **PackageTest**, and press **Finish**.
2. Under the project name, in this case **PackageTest**, select **File -> New -> Package. I**n the window **Name:**, type the package name, e.g., **ch12**, and press **Finish**.
3. Under the project name, create a subdirectory, e.g., **classes**, to store the packaged files.
4. Copy and paste the classes that will be packaged in the subdirectory **classes**, thereby completing the package setup phase. Note that Eclipse automatically adds the following statement as the new beginning of each source code file:

package classes;

```
package ch12;

import classes.*; //include all packaged classes
   public class PackageTestApp2 {
         public static void main(String[] args) {
         PackageTest1 myPackage = new PackageTest1();
         myPackage.print();

         PackageTest2 yourPackage = new PackageTest2();
         yourPackage.print();
      }
}
```

If the packaged classes are stored in the same directory as the driver code, it is not necessary to use the **import** statement.

12.1.6 A walk through access identifiers

Understanding the package mechanism will help you know more about the Java default access identifier—packaged access. As you know, there are four types of access identifiers in Java: **public**, **protected**, **packaged** (without any keyword), and **private**.

Table 12.1 lists the four access identifiers and their accessibilities.

Table 12.1 Access identifiers and their accessibilities

	In same class	In class of the same package	In subclass of the same package	In subclass of different package	In class of different package
Public	Yes	Yes	Yes	Yes	Yes
protected	Yes	Yes	Yes	Yes	No
Package	Yes	Yes	Yes	No	No
Private	Yes	No	No	No	No

Let's use an instance variable called **data** and a method called **myMethod()** to explain the meaning of the access identifiers and their accessibilities, as listed in Table 12.1. For the purpose of discussion, we will assume all classes are defined as **public**.

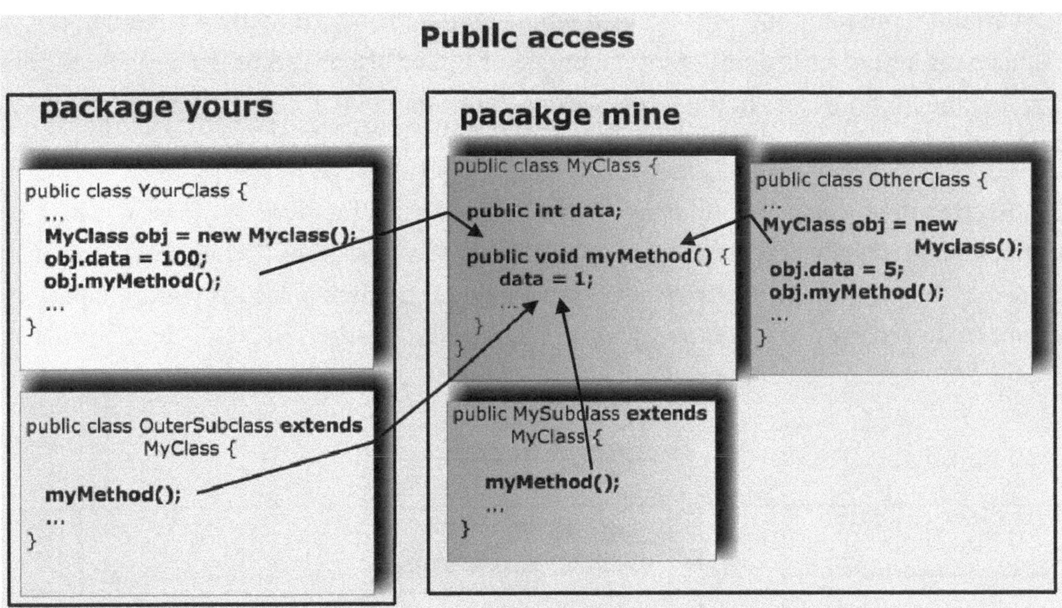

Figure 12.1 **public** access identifier and its accessibilities

From Figure 12.1 we may see if an instance variable (**data**) is defined as **public**, it can be accessed directly in the same class. It can be accessed by using the dot notation after creating an object of the class in all packages. By defining a method as **public**, it can also be called directly in the same class and can be called using the dot notation after creating an object of the class in all packages. As such, the **public** access identifier has the widest range of accessibility and allows access in all scopes.

Figure 12.2 illustrates an instance variable and a method with **protected** accessibilities. You may see

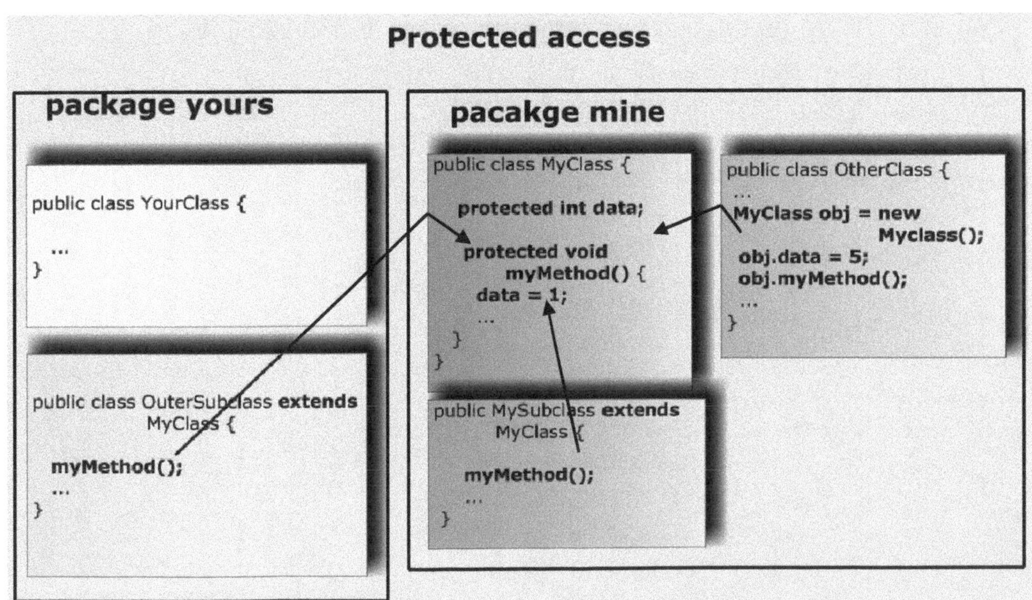

Figure 12.2 **protected** access identifier and its accessibilities

that instance variables and methods with the **protected** identifier can be directly accessed in the same class or its subclasses in the same or different packages. They can also be accessed by the dot notation after creating an object of the class in the same package, but cannot be accessed in a class that is not in the same package.

Figure 12.3 illustrates the **package** identifier and its accessibilities. A member of a class having a **package** access identifier can be directly accessed in the same class or the subclasses in the same package. It can also be accessed by the dot notation after creating an object of the class in a class within the same package. It cannot be accessed in any other classes in different packages.

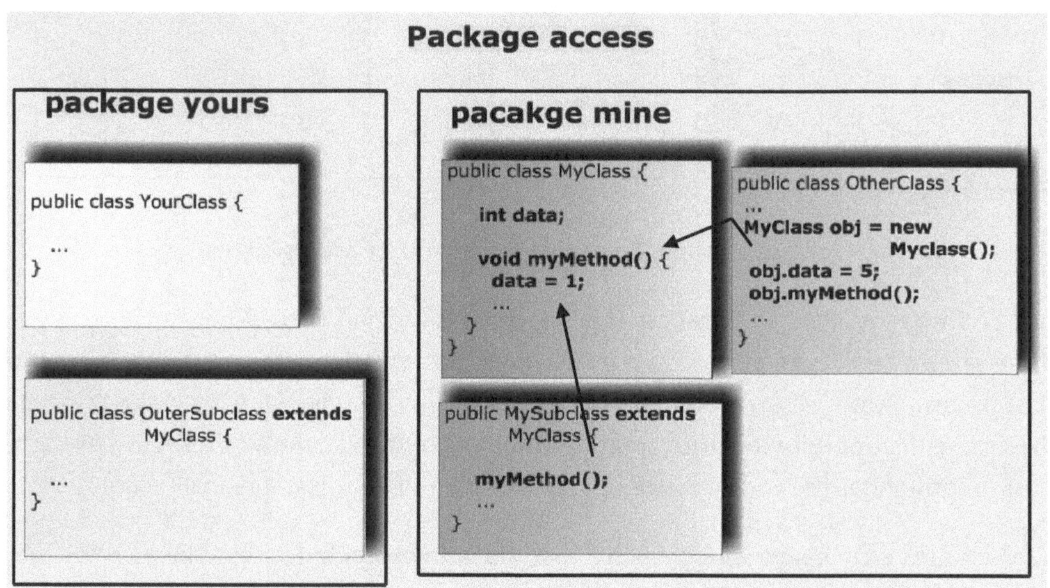

Figure 12.3 **package** access identifier and its accessibilities

Figure 12.4 illustrates the **private** access identifier and its accessibilities. A member of a class having a **private** identifier can by directly accessed only in the same class. The **private** identifier is the most restricted access identifier.

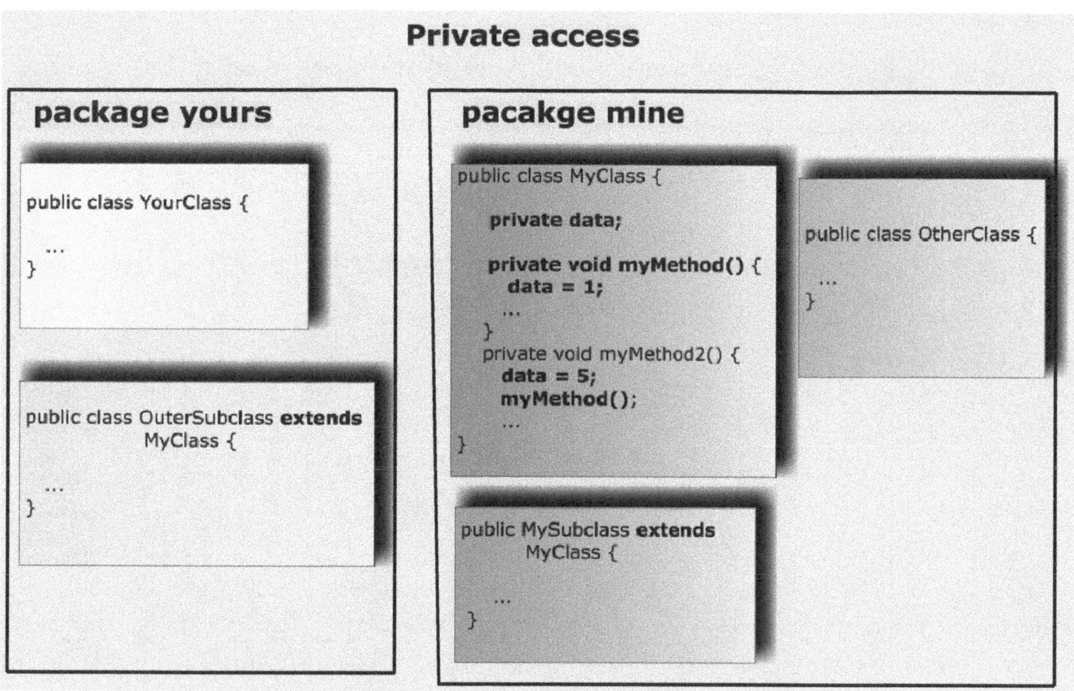

Figure 12.4 **private** access identifier and its accessibilities

12.2 Javadoc and Documentation

The JDK **javadoc** command provides the capability to create web page documentation of user-defined classes, such as API libraries. Although some IDEs provide proprietary features to generate such web page files, it is still beneficial for programmers and developers to understand the use of the **javadoc** command.

12.2.1 Documenting source code

Before you use the **javadoc** command to create web pages files, you must follow the specification of the command to document your source code:

The **javadoc** command specifies the following requirements for documenting Java source code:

- A documented line must use C-style comments starting with **/**** (note the double asterisk "**" requirement) and ending with ***/**. Extra asterisks can be applied within the comment and will be ignored by **javadoc**.
- Documented lines must be placed directly above of the class, constructor, method, or variable being documented. Intervening space is not allowed.
- The documented lines are used to describe the content of the code. The content will be displayed in the generated web page files.
- **javadoc** supports the use of other languages in documented lines.

It is also important to note **javadoc** does *not* provide syntax checking of the source code.

Note: *You may use **C++** style comment lines in your source code; they will be omitted by **javadoc**.*

The following example uses the specification of **javadoc** to document a source code file:

```
//Complete code called Manager.java in Ch12 from author's Website
package ch12;
import java.text.*;

/**
Class Manager inherits Employee class.  It is used to instantiate an object of
Manager and return salary and the name of the object.
*/

public class Manager extends Employee {
/**
* Instance variable.  The value must be greater than or equal to 0.
   **/

   protected double salary;
/*************************************************
*Constructor to instantiate object of Manager
************************************************/

   public Manager(String name, double salary) {
      super(name);  // call superclass constructor
      this.salary = salary;
   }
...
```

In above example, we arbitrarily use entire lines of asterisks.

In general, the content of documented lines follows the format:

```
/**
*Summarized statement for documented line
*Provide more information about the documented item
*Use of tags in javadoc provides more information for the arguments and return
*type (optional)
*/
```

The following section discusses how to use tags provided in **javadoc** and HTML to document the comment lines.

12.2.2 How to use tags in **javadoc** documentation

able 12.2 lists important tags provided by **javadoc** for use in documentation.

Table 12.2 Tags in **javadoc** command for documentation

Javadoc Tag	Description
@author	Author's name. Default: omitted in generated web files.
@version	Version of the code. Default: omitted in generated web files.
@param	Arguments for constructors and methods

@return	Return type
@exception	Exception being thrown

You may override the default status in tags of **@author** and **@version** to display the specified content (see example in section 12.2.3).

HTML tags can be used in the documented source code. Table 12.3 lists common HTML tags used in the documentation.

Table 12.3 Common HTML tags used in javadoc documentation

HTML Tag	Description
<b>...</b>	Emphasizing, or use <code>...</code>
 	Line break
<p>	Same above, but having a space line.
<pre>...</pre>	Predefined paragraph format

The following is an example of using these tags:

```
//Complete code called Manager.java in Ch12 from author's Website
/**
* Class <b>Manager</b>inherits <b>Employee</b>.
* <b>Manager</b> is used to instantiate objects, return salary and the name of
* object.
*
* @author Yong Gao
* @version 1.1.0
***/
public class Manager extends Employee {
/**
* Instance variable and its value must be greater or equals to 0.
***/
        protected double salary;
```

```
/**
*Constructor to instantiate objects
*
*@param name A <b>String</b> - object name.
*@param salary A <b>double</b> - salary
***/
...
```

12.2.3 The **javadoc** command

After documenting the source code according to **javadoc** requirements, you may invoke the **javadoc** command to generate the web pages files. The format of the **javadoc** command is:

```
javadoc -option directory ClassName.java
```

wherein:

-option – optional arguments (see Table 12.4).

directory – the directory to store the generated web page files.

ClassName.java – name of the documented source code file.

For example, issuing the following **javadoc** command:

```
C:\javabook\src\Ch12\javadoc -d docs Manager.java
```

will store the generated web page files of **Manager** class in the **docs** subdirectory of the current folder. Figure 12.5 shows the web pages content revealed by opening **Manager.html** in the **docs** directory.

Table 12.4 Commonly used javadoc options

Javadoc option	Description
-d directory	Store the generated files to the directory. Create this directory from the current directory first if it doesn't exist.
-author	Include information written in @author to the generated file.
-version	Include information written in @version to the generated file.
-source version	Provide JDK version in the generated file.

Another example:

```
javadoc -d docs -author -version Manager.java
```

overrides the **@author** and **@version** tags to include information concerning the author and version of the **Manager** class in the web page files.

More Info: *If the specified directory doesn't exist,* ***javadoc*** *will create the directory from the current directory first.*

12.2.4 More examples

Using the **javadoc** specification, the source code file **Employee.java** is prepared as follows:

```
//Complete code called Employee.java in Ch12 from author's Website
/**
* Super class <b>Employee</b>
* Method <b>getName()</b> and <b>earnings()</b> are used to perform polymorphism,
* <br> return the referenced name and salary of the object.
*

* @author Yong Gao
* @version 1.1.0
***/
public class Employee {
/**
* Private instance variable to store name.
***/
   private String name;

/**
*Constructor to instantiate object of Employee.
*
*@param name A <b>String</b> Name of the object
***/
   public Employee(String name ) {
      this.name = name;
   }
/**
*Return the name
*
*@return <b>String</b> for the name.
***/
   public String getName()
      { return name; }
/**
*Return the salary
*
*@return <b>double</b> for the salary.
***/
   public   double earnings(){return 0.0;}
}
```

Assume this documented class and the **Manager.java** file previously discussed are saved in the directory:

```
C:\javabook\src\ch12\
```

Going to this directory and issuing the **javadoc** command:

```
C:\javabook\src\Ch12\javadoc -d docs -author - version *.java
```

will generate all the web page files and store them in the specified subdirectory **docs**. Figure 12.5 shows the content of a web page file in the web browser.

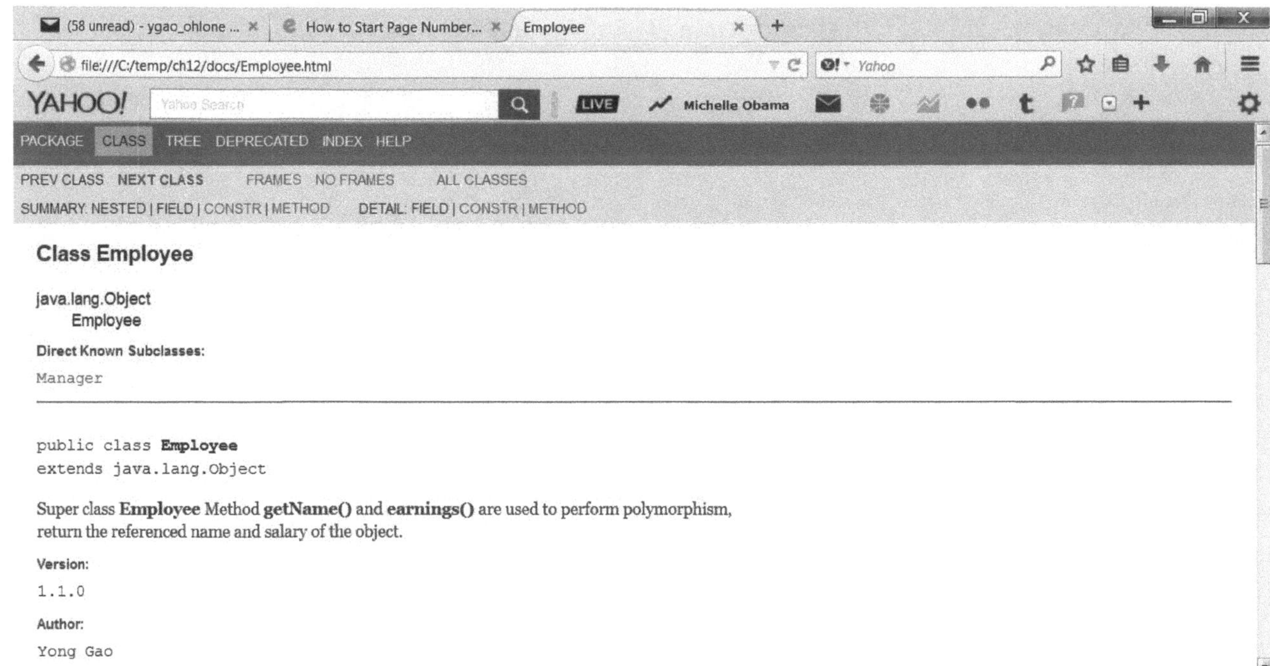

Figure 12.5 Screenshot of documented Employee class

12.3 More Uses of Classes

An application may consist of many classes. In addition to classes with "is a" and "has a" relationships, classes may be coded as file classes, inner classes, inner static classes, nested inner classes, or local classes according to the purpose(s) of the application. We will discuss more uses of classes in this section.

12.3.1 Inheritance or composition

Two classes having an "is a" relationship form the basis of inheritance. However, it is not always true that all classes in an application should have an "is a" relationship. Furthermore, many programmer-defined classes, such as classes used as utilities, e.g., verifications, exception handling, file I/O processing, formatted output, et cetera, may have "has a" relationships with the major operation classes in the application. These are compositional or supporting classes. We have discussed inheritance and the "is a" relationship between classes in Chapter 7. Now let's discuss more characteristics of utility classes in compositions:

- Java naming convention reflects the nature of the class: composition or supporting, e.g., **Validator**, **NegativeAgeException**, **FileReader**, **Formatter**, et cetera.
- Class member data or methods are defined as **static.** As a utility class, it will provide the services for all objects, not just individual ones. There is no need to instantiate an object before calling its method.
- The classes are normally defined as **final** classes.

- The internal structure of a utility class may consist of inheritance and/or compositional components to provide more functionality and services.

The classes are usually included in a package to allow importing and provide documentation generated by **javadoc**.

12.3.2 File classes

File classes are contained along with the public class in the source code. The file is stored under the file name of the public class. For example,

```
public class SomeClass {                    //Begin SomeClass
   ...
}                                           //End SomeClass
class FileClass1 {                          //Begin file class:  FileClass1
   ...
}                                           //End FileClass1
   ...                                      //More file classes
class FileClassN {                          //Begin file class:  FileClassN
   ...
}                                           //End FileClassN
```

Because only one public class is allowed in a given source code file, a file class cannot be defined with the **public** attribute. It may only have the **package** access identifier. The use of other access identifiers will generate a syntax error.

A file class normally provides support of or belongs to its public class. As such, the relationship between a public class and a file class is a "has a" relationship.

12.3.3 Inner classes

An inner class simply means that a class is contained or nested within another class. For example,

```
public class OuterClass {
   ...
```

```
    class InnerClass1 {                  //Inner class
          //Can access all members of OuterClass
          ...
    }                                    //End of InnerClass
    ...
    class InnerClassN {                  //More inner class
          //Can access all members of OuterClass
          ...
    }                                    //End of InnerClassN
} //End of OuterClass
```

An outer class may have more than one inner class. An inner class may have its own members and has access to all members of the outer class. It is an implicit form of inheritance.

The purpose of using an inner class is to increase code readability, maintainability, and manageability. An inner class normally processes the extended "mechanics" of the calculation, operation, or manipulation of its outer class. An inner class should consist of tightly knit code written to perform one particular task not included in its outer class. For example, inner classes provide such functions as sorting, searching, threading, event handling, et cetera.

The following is an example of using an inner class:

```
//Complete code is called InnerClassTest.java in Ch12 from the author's website
public class InnerClassTest {
   public static void main( String args[] ) {
        OuterClass outer = new OuterClass();     //Create an object of outer class
        OuterClass.InnerClass    inner1    =    outer.new    InnerClass();
                                                  //Create an object of inner

        OuterClass.InnerClass inner2 = new OuterClass().new InnerClass();
                                      //Create an object of another inner class
        outer.outerMethod();
        inner1.innerMethod();
        inner2.innerMethod();
   }
}
class OuterClass {                                          //Outer class
        private int n = 10;                                 //Private member data
        void outerMethod() {
        System.out.println("from OuterClass...");
   }
        class InnerClass {                                  //Inner class
        private int m = 5;
              void innerMethod() {
              int sum = n + m;          //Can access all members of outer class
              System.out.println("from InnerClass sum = " + sum);
```

```
                outerMethod();
                }
        }               //End of inner class
}               //End of outer class
```

In the example above, we see there are two different ways to instantiate an object of an inner class:

1. Create an object of the outer class. Use this object as a reference to create an object of the inner class:

```
OuterClass outer = new OuterClass();
//Create an object of inner class
OuterClass.InnerClass inner = outer.new InnerClass();
```

2. Directly create an object of the inner class:

```
//Directly create an object of the inner class
OuterClass.InnerClass inner2 = new OuterClass().new InnerClass();
```

The following is the result of the code execution:

```
from OuterClass...
from InnerClass sum = 15
from OuterClass...
from InnerClass sum = 15
from OuterClass...
```

You may also nest an inner class within another inner class:

```
class Outer {
   private void foo()   {
   }
   class AInner {
          private void goo() {
          }
          class BInner {
                 void hoo () {
                        foo(); //Directly access all members of Outer class
                        goo(); //Directly access all members of AInner class
                 }
          }      //End of BInner
   }             //End of AInner
}                //End of Outer
```

The following example shows how to create different objects based upon the above code:

```
Outer outer = new Outer();            /Create an object of the Outer class
Outer.AInner aInner = outer.new AInner();
Outer.AInner.BInner bInner = aInner.new BInner();
bInner.hoo();
```

You may also use the following method to create an object of the innermost class:

```
Outer.AInner.BInner bInner2 = new Outer.AInner.BInner();
```

12.3.4 Static inner classes

In a manner similar to a standard inner class, a static inner class is coded within an outer class. For example,

```
public class OuterClass {
   ...
   static class StaticInnerClass1 {                //Inner static class
          //Can only access static members of the OuterClass
          ...
   }//End of StaticInnerClass1
   ...
   static class StaticInnerClassN {                //More inner static class
      //Can only access static members of the OuterClass
      ...
   }      //End of StaticInnerClassN
}  //End of OuterClass
```

You cannot use ***this*** operator inside an inner static class and can only access static data and static methods from the outer class. The purpose of using static inner class is similar to code an inner class: if an inner class doesn't belong or have no relationship to any object of its outer class, you may code it as a static inner class.

The following code demos how to code a static inner class:

```
//Complete code saved as StaticInnerClassTest.java in Ch12 from the author's website
    public class StaticInnerClassTest {
       public static void main( String args[] ) {
              OuterClass2 outer = new OuterClass2();
              OuterClass2.StaticInnerClass.innerMethod();
                                             //Call static method in an inner static class
              OuterClass2.outerMethod();
              //Create an object of an inner static class
```

```
        OuterClass2.StaticInnerClass staticInner = new OuterClass2.Static
    InnerClass();
        int num = staticInner.innerMethod2(); //Call method of inner static class
    }
}
class OuterClass2 {                     //Outer class
    private double x = 0.0; //Cannot access no-static member of outer class
        static private int n = 10;          //Can access static data of outer class
        static void outerMethod() {         //Static method of outer class
        System.out.println("from OuterClass...");
    }
    void outerMethod2() {
        System.out.println("from OuterClass' instance innerMethod2()...");
    }
        static class StaticInnerClass {  //Static inner class
        static private int m = 5;        //Static data
        static void innerMethod() {      //Static method
            int sum;
            n = 20;                      //Can access static data of outer class
            sum = n + m;
            System.out.println("from InnerClass sum = " + sum);
            outerMethod();      //Can access static method of outer class
            }
        int innerMethod2() {
            n = 100;
            outerMethod();
            System.out.println("from InnerMethod2() n = " + n);
            return n;
        }
        }            //End of static inner class
}           //End of outer class
```

12.3.5 Local classes

A local class is a class inside a method of another class. It is also called local inner class. For example:

```
public SomeClass {
    void method() {
        class LocalClass {
            localMethod() {
                ...
            }
        }            //End of the local class
        ...
    }                //End of the method
}                    //End of the outer class
```

As with a local variable, a local class can only be used inside the defining method. A local class can access any member of its outer class, including the local variables of the method. Therefore, it is a special case of inheritance. You can use a local class only if its scope is within the method. Proper use of local classes can increase encapsulation, readability, and maintainability.

The following is an example of code using a local class:

```
//Complete code is called LocalClassTest.java in Ch12 from the author's Website
public class LocalClassTest {
   public static void main( String args[] ) {
       SomeClass obj = new SomeClass();
       obj.someMethod();
   }
}
class SomeClass {
   private int m = 5;
   void someMethod() {
          class Local {                                   //Local class
                 private in n = 10;
                 int localMethod() {
                        return m + n;
                 }
          }                                               //End of local class
          //n = 100; is illegal
          Local local = new Local();              //Create object of local class
          int x = local.localMethod();            //Call method of the local class
          System.out.println("from SomeClass someMethod()  m + n = " + x);
   }                                              //End of someMethod()
}                                                 //End of SomeClass
```

As indicated in the example code, a local class must be defined before the instantiation of the object of a local class. A local class may have its members, but cannot have any static members. You cannot access any members of the local class outside of the local class. For example, the member data ***n*** of the local class cannot be accessed outside of **Local** in **someMethod()**.

The following is the execution result:

```
from SomeClass someMethod() x = 15
```

12.3.6 Anonymous classes

Anonymous classes are also called anonymous inner classes. An anonymous class is actually a local class without a name. The steps of defining the class and instantiating a class object are coded in one statement. For example:

```
//Complete code called AnonymousClassTest.java in Ch12 from the author's website
public class AnonymousClassTest {
   public static void main( String args[] ) {
      System.out.println(new Object() {           //Anonymous class
         public String toString() {
            return "toString() in Object class will return the address of " +
                     super.toString();
         }
      });
   }
}
```

In this example, anonymous class inside **System.out.println()** is used to override **toString()** to print the information and address of the anonymous class. The result of execution is:

```
toString() in Object class will return the address of AnonymousClassTest$1@c17164
```

"$1" is referring to the anonymous class.

Anonymous classes are usually used to override the methods of Java API classes. They may have object data and constructors but cannot have static members. An anonymous class can also be used to implement interfaces, thereby avoiding the coding structure of the **implements** form. Anonymous classes are often used in event handling routines of GUI programming:

```
...
AddButton = new Jbutton("Add");

//Establish anonymous class to handle AddButton event
AddButton.addActionListener(new ActionListener() {

   public void actionPerformed(ActionEvent e) {
      Add();     //Call method to add
   }
});
...
```

This coding technique within GUI event handling is also called "callback." Because almost every GUI component has an event to be handled, the use of anonymous classes to handle the events can greatly simplify the coding.

12.3.7 Summary of using classes

We have discussed many kinds of classes and their coding techniques. File classes are actually classes coded and following a public class. The relationships between the public class and the file classes are compositional. Member classes consist of inner classes, static inner classes, local classes, and anonymous classes. From the coding point of view, inner classes and static inner classes are actually members of an outer class. Local classes and anonymous classes are coded within a method of another class. From the application point of view, inner classes, inner static classes, and anonymous classes perform specific and relatively short tasks. They can access all members of the outer class, thereby allowing better encapsulation. This compositional relationship allows better readability. They do not exist as independent code units, so the quantity of files of an application is reduced, thereby increasing maintainability. However, because inner member classes are only used in the special cases of specif applications, they are not in popular use. Table 12.5 summarizes the characteristics of member classes.

Table 12.5 Summary of member classes

	Inner class	Static inner class	Local class	Anonymous class
Feature	Access all members of its outer classes; simplify in interface coding.	Same as inner classes, but it depends on the objects of outer classes.	Same as inner classes.	Event handling in GUI.
Accessibility	All members of outer classes.	All static members of outer class.	Same as inner classes.	Same as member classes.
Access identifiers	All access identifiers.	Same as inner classes.	Same as inner classes.	Same as inner classes.
Nested	Yes	No	Yes	Yes

12.4 Enumeration

Java uses the keyword **enum** to define a class of enumeration. **enum** is inherited from the **Object** and **Enum** classes, and as such we can use **enum** to define and create objects of **Enum**. The enumeration type typically defines a group of related constant data, or values of enumeration. Examples might include the definition of directions, such as **NORTH**, **SOUTH**, **EAST**, and **WEST** or the definition of colors **RED**, **GREEN**, and **BLUE**. The enumerated terms are capitalized because they are constant values. Because you are defining the object of **Enum**, you may also define methods, or override methods from its superclasses. The purposes of coding or overriding these methods is to expand the operations of defined enumerations in superclasses. It may also increase the readability of the code.

12.4.1 Enumeration types

The syntax to define an enumeration is:

```
accessModifier enum EnumName {
   FIELD_LIST;
   accessModifier EnumName(argumentList) {              //Constructor; optional
          statements;
   }
   accessModifier returnType methodName(argumentList) {  //Optional
          statements;
```

wherein:

accessModifier – Java access modifier: **public**, **protected**, **private**, or **package**.

enum – keyword to define enumeration type.

enumName – name of enumeration. It is automatically defined as **final**.

FIELD_LIST – defined value list of enumeration. Each field is named with capital letters and is separated by a comma. The fields are automatically defined as **static final**. In special cases, there may be sub-value inside a field. You may also define methods, if necessary. More examples are discussed in Section 12.4.3 and 12.4.4.

returnType – return type of method; can be **void**.

methodName – name of method.

argumentList – list of arguments; can be empty.

Constructors and methods in an enumeration can be optional and overloaded.

The following is example of defining an enumeration data:

```
//Complete code is named as EnumTest.java in Ch12 from the author's Website
enum DiscountType {                    //Define an enumeration
    BASIC_DISCOUNT,                    //Constant fields
    EXTRA_DISCOUNT,
    SUPER_DISCOUNT;
}
```

In using an enumeration, we first create an object:

```
DiscountType discount;
```

Of course, you may define more objects:

```
DiscountType myDiscout = DiscountType.BASIC_DISCOUNT,
                 yourDiscount = DiscountType.SUPER_DISCOUNT;
```

The following is an example of using an enumeration in an **if** statement:

```
if (myDiscount == DiscoutType.BASIC_DISCOUNT)
   System.out.println("Basic discount for new customers: 10%");
```

The Java compiler automatically defines each field value starting with 0. In the above example, **BASIC_DISCOUNT** is assigned 0; **EXTRA_DISCOUNT** is assigned 1; and **SUPER_DISCOUNT** is assigned 2. It is important to note these values represent internal assignments and can only be used by the method call. Thus, the following code is illegal:

```
if (myDiscount == 0)  //illegal statement
  ...
```

Because **enum** is inherited from the **Object** and **Enum** classes, you may call these methods form its superclasses to perform a variety of operations. Table 12.6 lists commonly used methods of **enum**:

Table 12.6 Commonly used methods in enum

Method	Description
int compareTo(Enum object)	Compare the enum with the specified object for order. Returns a negative if it is smaller than compared value; return 0 if they are equal; and return a positive value if it is greater.
Boolean equals(Object)	Compare the enum with the specified object for equality. Returns true if they are equal; otherwise, returns false.
String name()	Returns the name of the enum constant, exactly as it is defined in the enum declaration. Most programmers should use toString() in preference to this methods, as it returns a more user-friendly name.
int ordinal()	Returns the ordinal of this enumeration constant (its position in its enum declaration, where the initial constant is assigned an ordinal valueof zero). This method is designed primarily for use by sophisticated enum-based data structures, such as `EnumSet` and `EnumMap`.
String toString()	Return the value as a string of the field as defined in the declaration.
Enum[] values()	Return the specified values of the fields as an array of **Enum**.

Continuing from our discussion above, the following example demonstrates the use of the methods in Table 12.6:

```
//Complete code is called EnumTest.java in Ch12 from the author's website
myDiscount = DiscountType.BASIC_DISCOUNT;
System.out.println(myDiscount.name());                //Call name()
System.out.println(myDiscount.toString());
                              //Call toString(), or System.out.println(myDiscount);
System.out.println(myDiscount.ordinal());             //Call ordinal()

DiscountType yourDiscount = myDiscount;               //Assign another value

if (myDiscount.equals(yourDiscount))        //Call equals()to compare
   System.out.println("We received the same basic discount for new customers: 10%");
if (myDiscount == yourDiscount)                       //Call == to compare the addresses
   System.out.println("We are referring to the same memory location.");

int compareResult1 = myDiscount.compareTo(yourDiscount);//Call compareTo()
System.out.println("compareResult1 = " + compareResult1);

int compareResult2 = myDiscount.compareTo(DiscountType.SUPER_DISCOUNT);
                                                           //Call compareTo()
System.out.println("compareResult2 = " + compareResult2);
```

The following is the result of execution:

```
BASIC_DISCOUNT
BASIC_DISCOUNT
0
```

```
We received the same basic discount for new customers:  10%.
We are referring to the same memory location.
compareResult1 = 0
compareResult2 = -2
```

It should be noted methods **name()** and **toString()** return the value of **myDiscount**. Method **ordinal()** returns the internal serial number of **myDiscount,** i.e., 0.

You may also assign another value to a field:

```
DiscountType yourDiscount = myDiscount;          //Assign another value
```

DiscountType yourDiscount now will refer to the value of **myDiscount**; their addresses are equal.

The method **values()** is discussed in Section 12.4.3.

Note: *In consideration of data type safety, objects of enumeration cannot be copied. Attempting to use* ***clone()*** *to copy the objects of an enumeration is illegal.*

12.4.2 Static import

The purpose of static import is to simplify the coding of enumeration data. With the use of static import, the statement

```
DiscountType myDiscount = BASIC_DISCOUNT;
```

becomes illegal. The statement must now be coded as:

```
DiscountType myDiscount = DiscountType.BASIC_DISCOUNT;
```

The syntax of static import is:

```
    static import packageName.className.*;
```

wherein,

static import – keyword phrase used to establish static import.

PackageName – package name.

ClassName.* – Package name of the enumeration data to be statically imported. The wildcard "*" indicates all enumeration data is to be statically imported. You may also specify the particular member of the enumeration.

Assume we want to statically import all members of **DiscountType** from package **ch12**. You may write the statement:

```
static import ch12.DiscountType.*;
```

allowing direct use of the data in the code, e.g.,:

```
DiscountType yours = EXTRA_DISCOUNT;
```

You may also simplify the **compareTo()** statement discussed above as:

```
int compareResult2 = myDiscount.compareTo(SUPER_DISCOUNT);     //Call compareTo()
System.out.println("compareResult2 = " + compareResult2);
```

Static import is not limited to use with enumerations; it can also applied to classes with static data or static methods to simplify coding. For example, in the **Validator** class, we have coded many static methods to verify the data. Now the statements can be simplified using static import:

```
import static ch12.Validator;
...
// Directly call method intWithRange();
intWithRange(sc, "Please enter your score: ", 0, 100);
```

However, abuse of static import may reduce code readability.

12.4.3 Walk into enumeration

Enumeration data are objects, so they have members. In addition, an enumeration field may further define subfields. Subfields are parenthesized and separated by commas. For example:

```
//Complete code called DiscountType2.java in Ch12 from the author's website
enum DiscountType2 {                                    //Define enumeration type
    BASIC_DISCOUNT("for new customers", "10%"),        //Each has two subfields
    EXTRA_DISCOUNT("for returning customers", "20%"),
    SUPER_DISCOUNT("for royal customers with 3 years", "30%");
    final private String explain;                                  //Private data
    final private String rate;
    private DiscountType2(String explain, String rate) { //Constructor
           this.explain = explain;
           this.rate = rate;
    }
    public String getExplain() {                                   //Getter methods
           return explain;
    }
    public String getRate() {
           return rate;
    }
}
```

In this example, each field of **DiscountType2** has two subfields. The constructor initializes the value of each subfield. Arguments **explain** and **rate** represent the values of each subfield, respectively. Two "getter" methods are coded to access the values of each subfield.

NOTE: *The argument type and order must be the same as listed in the subfields to avoid a syntax error.*

The following driver code demonstrates how to use the enumeration data and their subfields:

```
//Complete code called EnumTest2.java in Ch12 from author's website
import static ch12.DiscountType2.*;         //Static import
import java.util.EnumSet;                    //Call range() from EnumSet
public class EnumTest2 {
   public static void main( String args[] ) {
      for (DiscountType2 type : DiscountType2.values())          //Call values()
         System.out.println("type: " + type.getExplain() + " rate: " +
                              type.getRate());

      for (DiscountType2 type : EnumSet.range(EXTRA_DISCOUNT, SUPER_DISCOUNT))
          System.out.println("type: " + type.getExplain() + ", rate: " +
                              type.getRate());
   }
}
```

The code uses static import, thereby allowing enumeration data to be directly referenced. Using an enhanced for-loop and calling method **values()** from the **Enum** class, each field and subfield of **DiscountType2** is printed. The second for-loop uses the **range()** method from the **EnumSet** class to specify the range of the output. The following is the result of execution:

```
type: for new customers, rate: 10%
type: for returning customers, rate: 20%
type: for royal customers with 3 years, rate: 30%
type: for returning customers, rate: 20%
type: for royal customers with 3 years, rate: 30%
```

Because objects of enumeration are created without using the **new** operator (use of referencing), the constructor is defined as **private**. The constructors may be overloaded to carry out different initializations of the subfields.

The subfield of an enumeration can be defined as a method, but it must define as an **abstract** type. For example:

```
//Complete code called EnumTest3.java in Ch12 from the author's website
enum Coins {
   PENNY { int value() { return 1; }},
   NICKEL { int value() { return 5; }},
   DIME { int value() { return 10; }},
   QUARTER { int value() { return 25; }};
   abstract int value();                              //Must be defined as abstract
}
```

The above code can also be coded as:

```
public enum Coins {
   PENNY (1),
   NICKEL (5), DIME
   (10), QUARTER
   (25);
   private int value = 0;
   private Coins(int value) {                              //Constructor
      this.value = value;
   }
   private int getValue() {
     return value;
   }
}
```

12.4.4 More examples

The following example demonstrates how to use enumeration data in an application displaying information about sports cars.

The enumeration data are defined:

```
//Complete code called SportsCarType.java in Ch12 from author's website
enum SportsCarType {                          //Define enumeration type
    PORSCHE("Made in Germany", 120000),       //Each field has two subfields
    FERRARI("Made in Italy", 150000),
    JAGUAR("Made in England", 110000);

    final private String make;
    final private int price;
    private SportCarType(String make, int price) {         // Constructor
       this.make = make;
       this.price = price;
    }
    public String getMake() {                 //Define methods to access subfields
       return make;
    }
    public int getPrice() {
       return price;
    }
}
```

The following class uses enumeration data to display information about the sports car based on the user's selections:

```
import static ch12.SportsCarType.*;         //Static import
import java.text.DecimalFormat;             //Formatted output
class SportsCar {
   SportsCarType type;                      //Create enumeration data
   public SportsCar (String choice) {       //Constructor
      if (choice.equals("P"))
          type = PORSCHE;
      else if (choice.equals("F"))
          type = FERRARI;
      else if(choice.equals("J"))
          type = JAGUAR;
   }
   public String toString() {               //Override toString()
      DecimalFormat dollar = new DecimalFormat("#,##0.00");    //Formatted output
      String info = type.getMake() + "\nPrice: $" +
                    dollar.format(type.getPrice());
      return info;
   }
}
```

The following is the driver code:

```
import javax.swing.*;                  //Use methods in JOptionPane
public class SportsCarApp {
   public static void main( String args[] ) {
      //Get the selection from user
      String car = JOptionPane.showInputDialog(null, "Select your sports car (P -
Porsche, F - Ferrari, J - Jaguar): ");
      //Create object
     SportsCar yourCar = new SportsCar(car);
     //Output information
     JOptionPane.showMessageDialog(null, "Info of your car: \n" + yourCar);
   }
}
```

Figure 12.6 shows a typical execution result:

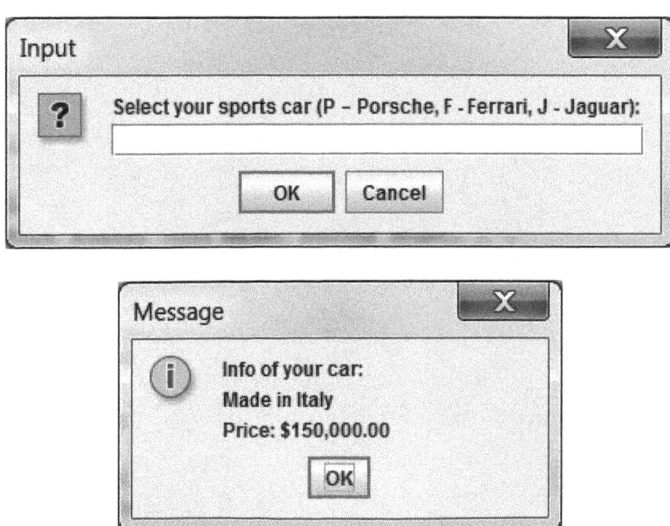

Figure 12.6 A typical execution result using enumerations

12.5 Auto-Boxing

Auto-boxing was first released in JDK 1.5. Auto-boxing is the conversion of a primative type data to its corresponding wrapper class object. For example:

```
int x = 5;
Integer myInt = x;              //auto-boxed to the object of Integer
```

Auto-boxing is not a magical box – it actually creates an object of the wrapper class and encapsulates the primative data into it:

```
Integer myInt = new Integer(x);
```

Its purpose is to promote a primative type data to its wrapper class object.

Note: *Abuse of auto-boxing may reduce code readability.*

12.5.1 Auto-boxing is very easy

The syntax for auto-boxing is:

```
WrapperClassName objectName = expression;
```

wherein:

WrapperClassName – a wrapper class; it can be one of 8 primative data type wrapper classes.

objectName – the object created.

expression – data or expression to be auto-boxed into the object; it must match the corresponding wrapper class.

The following code snippet shows several examples of auto-boxing:

```
Integer intObj = 10;    //10 is auto-boxed into intObj.
                        //similar to Integer intObj = new Integer(10);

double x = 19.88, y = 0.56;
Double myDouble = x + y * 5;           //Arithmetic result is auto-boxed into myDouble

Boolean choice = true;                 /true is auto-boxed into choice
```

12.5.2 Referring or creating?

Because the object of auto-boxing is immutable, in a manner equivalent to an object of the **String** class (see Section 10.6), it involves the concepts of object referring and object creating. For example, in examining the code

```
Integer n1 = 127;        //Auto-boxing
Integer n2 = 127;
Integer n3 = 128;
Integer n4 = 128;
```

one might come to the conclusion that if object referring is present, the result of comparing the addresses of the several variables using "==", **n1 == n2** or **n3 == n4**, will be **true**, because they are referring to the same objects. Similarly, if object creation is represented, the result of comparing objects **n1** and **n2** or objects **n3** and **n4** will be **false** because they are different objects and have different addresses:

```
//Complete code called AutoBoxingTest.java in Ch12 from author's webxite
System.out.println(n1 == n2);        //Print out the result
System.out.println(n3 == n4);
```

Executing the above code yields the following result:

```
false
true
```

Why does the seeming discrepancy occur? For objects of an **int** type, auto-boxing will create an object to encapsulate the data if it is smaller than 127 and use referencing if it is greater than 127. For **short**, **int**, and **char** type data in the range [-128, 127], the JVM creates a single object referenced from different locations in performing auto-boxing operations. Multiple objects are created and referenced for **int** values outside this range. For **Boolean**, **byte**, **float**, **long**, and **double** type data, object creation is used in performing auto-boxing.

12.6 Auto-unboxing

In a manner analogous to auto-boxing, auto-unboxing converts an object of the wrapper class to its primative data value, e.g.,

```
int n = myInt; //Assume myInt is an object of Integer
```

In actuality, the Java compiler will automatically call the **intValue()** method of class **Integer** to do the conversion, as might be performed by the following code:

```
int n = myInt.intValue();
```

Method **inValue()** returns the data encapsulated in **myInt** and assigns it to **n**.

Auto-unboxing is provided as a counterpart to auto-boxing by providing a convenience in coding for the programmer. It does not reduce any processing for the compiler and JVM.

12.6.1 Auto-unboxing is much easier

The syntax of auto-unboxing is:

```
variableType variableName = WrapperExpression;
```

wherein,

variableType – any primative data type.

variableName – a name of the primative data type.

wrapperExpression – an object of the wrapper class or an expression with objects of the wrapper class. It must match the primative data type or satisfy the rules of autocasting.

For example,

```
Double myDouble = 9.12;                                         //Auto-
boxing              Integer              myInt          =             15;
//Auto-boxing double result =  myDouble + myInt + 100;    //Auto-unboxing
and computing
```

It is equivalent to the following code:

```
double result = myDouble.doubleValue() + myInt.intValue() + 100;
```

Let's discuss another example:

```
//Complete code called AutoBoxingTest.java in Ch12 from the author's website
boolean flag = true;                   //Define a primative data type variable
Boolean myBoolean = true,                     //Auto-boxing
       yourBoolean = false;                   //Auto-boxing
if (flag && myBoolean && yourBoolean)         //Auto-unboxing
   System.out.println("result is true.");
else
  System.out.println("result is false.");
```

The execution result is:

```
result is false.
```

Note: *Abuse of auto-boxing and auto-unboxing will reduce code readability and the efficiency of code execution.*

12.6.2 Testing auto-boxing execution speed

The following code tests the execution speed of code performing mathematical operations with and without auto-boxing for the same data. It also tests execution speed using arrays with and without auto-boxing.

```
//Complete code called AutoBoxingPerformanceTest.java in Ch2 from author's website
long time1 = 0;
long time2 = 0;
Integer[] integerValues = new Integer[2147483];   //Create an array of Integer
time1 = System.currentTimeMillis();               //Begin the timer

// Use auto-boxing to assign the elements to the array
for(int i =0;i<2147483;i++){
   integerValues[i]=i;                            //Auto-boxing
}
// Multiplication
```

```
for(int i=0;i<2147483;i++){
   integerValues[i] *= 10;           //Auto-boxing; any number for multiplicand
}

time2 = System.currentTimeMillis();                //End of timer
System.out.println("Auto-boxing with Integer array: "+(time2-time1)+"ms");

int[] intValues = new int[2147483];                //Create an array of int
time1 = System.currentTimeMillis();                //Begin the timer
for(int i=0;i<2147483;i++) {
   intValues[i] = i;                               //Without auto-boxing
}
// Multiplication
for(int i=0;i<2147483;i++){
   intValues[i] *= 10;                             //Without auto-boxing
}

time2 = System.currentTimeMillis();                //End of the timer
System.out.println("Using an int array without auto-boxing: "+(time2-time1)+ "ms");

time1 = System.currentTimeMillis();                       //Begin the timer
for(int i = 0;i < 2147483; i++) {
   intValues[i] = intValues[i] * 10;               //Directly computing in the array
}
time2 = System.currentTimeMillis();                //End of the timer
System.out.println("Directly using an int array: "+(time2-time1)+"ms");
...
```

The following is the execution results:

```
AutoBoxing with Integer array: 1332ms
Without autoboxing with an int array:
30ms Directly using an int array : 20ms
```

It clearly showed the auto-boxing reduces the speed of execution.

Note: *The result of execution may be vary.*

12.7 Variable-Length Arguments

The concept of variable-length argument lists was introduced in JDK 1.5. This feature provides an extremely helpful convenience in the coding of overloaded methods. As with many Java capabilities, it does have some conditions and limitations in its use.

12.7.1 The best example of method overloading

You may have encountered the following experience while coding: The arguments of a method are changeable and cannot be determined at compile-time. Assume you want to write an application to print a list of the participants at a party. A method called **printInvitation()** will perform the printing according to the arguments associated with the participant's names. However, the name list is unknown at compile-time. One technique is to write several overloaded methods to perform the task:

```
void printInvitation(String name);
void printInvitation(String name1, String name2);
void printInvitation(String name1, String name2, String name3);
...
```

The key problem with this technique lies in the fact that the number of overloaded methods is unknown and may rapidly become an unmanageable quantity. An array might be considered, but the same problem remains.

The use of a variable-length argument list will easily solve the problem:

```
//Complete code called VarargsTest.java in Ch12 from the author's website
void printInvitation(String...names) {      //use of variable arguments
   for (String name : names) {
      makeCard(name);                          //Call the method
      System.out.println("Recording info: invitation card has been printed for " +
                         name);
   }
}
```

In the above code, a variable-length argument, **(String...names)**, is provided as a parameter to the method. Any number (including zero) of names, declared as **String** type data, may be provided as parameter(s) to the method. In practice, the parameter specification is converted to an array type argument during compilation:

```
void printInvitation(String[] names)
```

The following example calls method **printInvitation()** with a varying number of names in the argument list:

```
printInvitation("Li Gong", "David Smith");
printInvitation("Greg Wu", "Paul Nguyen", "Liu Wei", "Zhang Xin");
printInvitation();                      //No argument
```

When the method is called with no argument, as in the last method invocation above, no code will be executed in the method.

The following list of party invitees is printed as a result of executing the above code:

```
Recording info: invitation card has been printed for Li Gong
Recording info: invitation card has been printed for David Smith
Recording info: invitation card has been printed for Greg Wu
Recording info: invitation card has been printed for Paul Nguyen
Recording info: invitation card has been printed for Liu Wei
Recording info: invitation card has been printed for Zhang Xin
```

12.7.2 How variable-length arguments work

The JVM processes variable-length arguments by treating the argument list as an array whose elements are all of the same type. This allows the method body to manipulate the parameter values in the above example as an array of **String**.

The simplified syntax of variable-length arguments is:

```
methodName([argumentList,] dataType...argumentName);
```

wherein,

argumentList – optional list of "traditional", i.e., non-variable-length arguments, regular argument list.

dataType – primative or object type. It will be automatically converted to the array type.

... - ellipsis denoting the method is to receive a variable number of arguments of the specified data type dataType.

argumentName – argument name.

Note: *It is important to note the use of the ellipsis can occur only <u>once</u> in a parameter list. The ellipsis, together with its type, must be placed at the end of the parameter list following any "regular", i.e., non-variable-length, parameters.*

The following are more examples of using variable-length arguments:

```
//Complete code called VarargsTest.java in Ch12 from the suthor's website
public static int sumInts(int...numbers) { //the variable argument is it type
   int sum = 0;
   for (int num : numbers)
          sum +=num;
   return sum;
}
```

and:

```
public void totalTax(String name,double rate, double...amounts) {
                         //The regular arguments must be before varargs.
   double total = 0.0,
          tax = 0.0;
   for (double amount : amounts)
          total += amount;
   tax = total * rate;
   System.out.println("Name: " + name + "\nTotal: " + total + "\ntax: " +    tax);
}
```

The variable-length arguments can also be used in a constructor:

```
public class Supper {
   public Supper(char...characters) {
   ...
   }
```

and in its subclass to override the constructor:

```
class SubClass extends Supper {
   public SubClass(char...characters) {
          ...
   }
}
```

12.7.3 Variable-length arguments overloading

Variable-length arguments can be overloaded. For example:

```
void someMethod(int count, double...prices) {
   //Statements
   ...
   }
void someMethod(double...prices) {                        //Overloading
   //The body of the code
   ...
   }
double someMethod(String...names) {                 //Overloading
   //The body of the code
   ...
}
...
```

It should follow all the syntax requirements in variable arguments overloading.

12.7.4 Application examples using enumerations and variable-length argument lists

The following example uses enumerations and variable-length arguments to modify the example we discussed in Section 12.4.4. It adds the following two methods using enumerations to process the color and payment methods associated with the sports car:

```
//Complete code called VarargsApp.java in Ch12 from author's website
enum ColorType {
   WHITE {String getDescription(){
          return "Selection: White, Gray White, and Bright White";
        }
   },
   SILVER {String getDescription() {
           return "Selection: Silver, Grey Silver, and Pure Silver";
          }
   },
   BLACK {String getDescription() {
          return "Selection: Black and Off Black";
         }
   };
   abstract String getDescription();
```

```
}
enum PaymentType {
   CASH("10% discount"),
   CREDIT("Accept credit cards"),
   LOAN("Interest rate is 0.56%");
   final private String payment;

   private PaymentType(String payment) {
      this. payment = payment;
   }
   public String getPayment() {
      return payment;
   }
}
```

Methods using variable-length arguments to process the type, color, and payment after the user selects a sports car:

```
class SportCar {
   SportCarType type;                               //
   ColorType color;
   PaymentType payment;
   public SportCar (String...choices) {    //Variable arguments
         type = null;                               //Initialize
         color = null;
         payment = null;
         processInfo(choices);                      //Call the method
   }
   private void processInfo(String[] choices) {
      if (choices.length == 1) {             //Process type of the car
         processType(choices[0]);
      }
      else if (choices.length == 2) {        //Process type and color
        processType(choices[0]);
        processColor(choices[1]);
                }
      else if (choices.length == 3) {        //Process type, color and payment
           processType(choices[0]);
           processColor(choices[1]);
        processPayment(choices[2]);
      }
 }
```

```
private void processType(String type) {    //Process type of the car
         if (type.equals("P"))
                this.type = SportCarType.PORSCHE;
         else if (type.equals("F"))
            this.type = SportCarType.FERRARI;
         else if(type.equals("J"))
                this.type = SportCarType.JAGUAR;
}
...
```

The driver code for the class is:

```
public class VarargsApp {
 public static void main( String args[] ) {

    SportCars yourCar = new SportCars("P");
    System.out.println("Car Info: \n" + yourCar + "\n");

    SportCars myCar = new SportCars("J", "S");
    System.out.println("Car Info: \n" + myCar + "\n");

    SportCars herCar = new SportCars("F", "B", "C");
    System.out.println("Car info:\n" + herCar + "\n");


   }
}
```

The execution results are:

```
Car Info:
Made in Germany
Price: $120,000.00

Car Info:
Made in England
Price: $110,000.00
Selection: Silver, Grey Silver, and Pure Silver

Car info:
Made in Italy
Price: $150,000.00
Selection: Black and Off Black
10% discount
```

Exercises

1. What is a package? What are the features of a package? Why are packages used?

2. What is the naming convention of packages? How can you ensure the uniqueness of package names?

3. Use CLASSPATH to create a package as follows:

    a. Select a class you have written, e.g., **Validator.java**, and call its methods to verify it executes properly. Add the statement **package utilpackage;** at the beginning of the class.

    b. In your computer, create the following file directory:

        C:\javaArt\classes\utilpackage

    c. Follow the steps discussed in section 12.1.2 to create this package file.

    d. Write a driver code using the package you created. Call its methods to verify it executes properly.

    e. Save the driver code and execution results.

4. Modify the code in Exercise 3 using a JAR file to create and use a package. Save the testing file and execution results.

5. Follow the steps discussed in section 1.1.5 to create a package in Eclipse IDE, and use it to manage all of your written codes.

6. What is a package access identifier? What are its features?

7. What is a documented source code? How is it created?

8. Why should source code be documented?

9. Following the discussion and examples in Section 12.2 as a guide, select a class you have written, document the source code, and use **javadoc** to create the associated web files. The files should be saved in a subdirectory called **docs** in the directory in which the source code is saved. Open file **index.html** to check if the web files have successfully been established.

10. Use examples to explain the differences between inheritance and composition.

11. What is a file class? Why and under what circumstances should a file class be used?

12. Modify an application code you have written so it will be saved as a file class. Compile and execute the modified code. Save the code and results of execution.

13. Use examples to explain the differences and similarities between an inner class and a static inner class.

14. Modify the code in Exercise 12 to use inner class(es). Compile and execute the code. Note the file names created by the compiler and explain the meaning of the "$" in the compiled file names.

"It is a very simple code if a program has objects with only fix and known lifecycle"

– Bruce Eckel

"However, it may be a dangerous program if the lifecycles of all of the objects are unknown. We need something in between."

– Java Generics and Collections, JavaOne International Conference

Chapter 13 Collections

API interface **Collection** is not included in the core API libraries; it is in the extension. **Collection** can encapsulate any type of object, so it provides great flexibility in coding. However, it also raises issues concerning type safety. **Generics** were first introduced in JDK 1.5 and have changed Java syntax and code notation. A generic type, as a new coding concept and technology, is applied to collections and may help solve type-safety problems. Similar to its C/C++ origins, **Generics** can be applied to any type of data definition and operation.

13.1 Collections of Objects

An object of **Collection** can store one or more objects or elements of any type. For example, **ArrayList** is a commonly used subclass of **Collection**. You may create an object of **ArrayList** to store strings:

```
Collection<String> code = new ArrayList<String>();
//or: ArrayList<String> code = new ArrayList<String>();
code.add("Java SE");          //Add elements into code
code.add("JSPS");
code.add("Java EE");
```

Variable **code** is an object of **Collection** and we can add one or more strings to it by calling the **add()** method. Thus, **code** is a collection of three objects of **String**, and **<String>** is denoted as the type argument or concrete type in **Generics**. We discuss **Generics** and type arguments in Section 13.13. The following output statement:

```
System.out.println("Number of elements in code: " + code.size());
System.out.println(code);          //Or: System.out.println (code.toString());
```

calls the **size()** method of **ArrayList** to display the number of elements in **code**. The second statement displays all elements in **code**. The result is:

```
Number of elements in code : 3
[Java SE, JSPS, Java EE]
```

You may also use the enhanced **for** loop to display each element in **code**:

```
for(Object element : code)
   System.out.println(element);
```

13.1.1 Collection vs. Array

The **Collection** class and arrays have a close relationship, sharing similarities and differences. The basic similarity between a Collection and an array is each has the capability to store objects. ArrayList, in fact, uses arrays to store objects. The key differences between each are:

- **Collection** is the extension of API classes; an array is a core Java data structure.
- **Collection** stores objects dynamically; an array is fixed in size.
- **Collection** can only store objects; arrays may store data with the primative types or objects.
- Elements are accessed, added, deleted, or modified by calling methods in **Collection**; these operations are performed by specifying the index of an element in the array.
- There are a rich number of methods that can be called in **Collection**; only a few methods can be used with arrays.

Note that although you cannot use an index to access the elements in a **Collection**, the concept of indexing is applied by indicating the location of the element within the **Collection**.

13.1.2 General discussion of Collection

Figure 13.1 lists the hierarchy in **Collection**. The figure is also called the **Java Collection Framework**. You may see there are two interfaces in **Collection**: **Collection** and **Map**. **Set** and **List**, as secondary interfaces, inherit **Collection** and derive three commonly used subclasses: **HashSet**, **ArrayList**, and **LinkedList**. Two classes are derived from **Map**: **HashMap** and **TreeMap**.

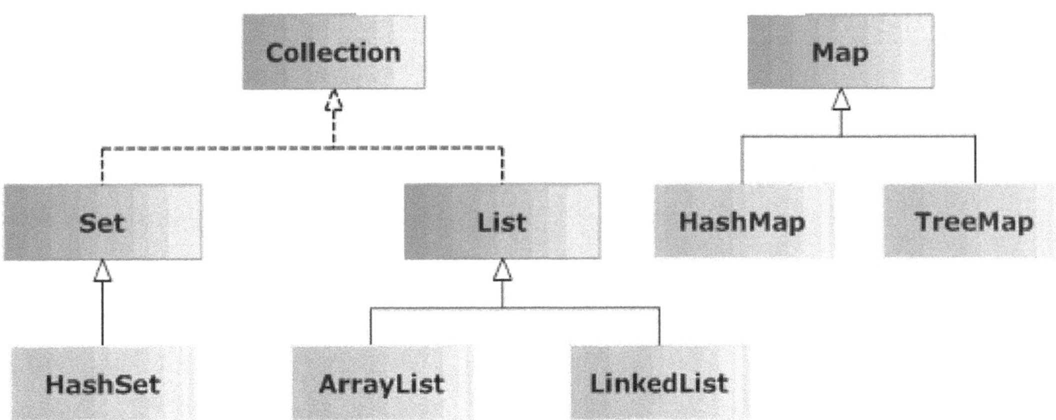

Figure 13.1 Java Collections Framework

The essential methods are defined in **Collection** and are implemented by **HashSet**, **ArrayList**, and **LinkedList**. Interfaces **Set** and **List** divide the collections into two categories: **HashSet**, in which no duplicate elements are allowed, and **ArrayList** and **LinkedList**, which allow the duplication of elements. **Collection** and **Map** are provided in the **java.util** package.

Although there are two distinct interfaces in **Collection**, they share similar operations. The key difference is in the way they store the elements. For example, in **Map** an elements is stored as a key-value pair. *Key* is used to identify the associated value of the element. Table 13.1 presents a summary of the four interfaces in **Collection**.

Table 13.1 Summary of interfaces in Collection

Interface	Description
Collection	Defines essential methods of interface, e.g., size(), isEmpty(), contains(), add(), remove(), iterator(); inherited from Iterable interface.
Set	Defines essential methods in collections in which duplicated elements are not allowed; inherits all methods defined in Collection. .
List	Defines essential methods in collections in which duplicated elements are allowed; inherits all methods from Collection.
Map	Defines essential methods of interface, for example, containsKey(), containsValue(), keySet(), put(), values().

It is important to remember that no duplicated elements are allowed in **HashSet**; otherwise, an exception will be thrown. **ArrayList** and **LinkedList** allow duplication of elements and the order of adding elements is retained.

Table 13.2 provides a brief explanation of the classes in **Collection**.

Table 13.2 Classes in Collection interface

Class	Description
ArrayList	Array structured collection class with dynamic sizing. Position of an added element is fixed. Efficient in random and sequential access of elements. Not efficient if element is not added at the end of the structure.

LinkedList	Similar to ArrayList, but uses linked node structure. Efficient if elements are not added at the end of the structure.
HashSet	Uses a hash code in a Hash table to store non-duplicated elements. Elements must implement hashCode() method. Position of added element is not fixed and not retained.

Example. Assume **arrayList** is an object of **ArrayList** containing 5 elements. Calling its **add()** method:

```
arrayList.add(3, objName);
```

will insert **objName** as the 4th element in **arrayList**. This operation is slow because of the array structure. However, using **LinkedList** to insert the element:

```
LinkedList<Product> linkedList = new LinkedList<Product>();//Create a linkedList
...
linkedList.add(n, objName);                          //Insert objName in any position
...
```

is much faster than using **ArrayList.** Commonly used methods in **HashSet**, **ArrayList**, and **LinkedList** are discussed in Sections 13.2.1 and 13.2.2.

HashSet and **Map** use a hash code to store unique elements. The elements must implement the **hashCode()** method to generate the hash code defining the position to store the elements in the structure. However, each element in **HashMap** and **TreeMap** is stored as a key:value pair. Furthermore, the order of the elements in **Treemap** is automatically defined using the key values.

Table 13.3 Commonly used collection classes in Map interface

Class	Description
HashMap	Similar to HashSet; but each class is in a different interface. Uses key-value pair to store an element. No duplicated keys are allowed and a key can only refer to a value. Automatically ordered by keys.
TreeMap	Similar to HashMap, but uses tree structure to store elements. Uses key-value pair to store an element. No duplicated keys are allowed and a key can only refer to a value. Automatically ordered by keys.

In the following example, method **size()** of **HashMap** returns the number of elements stored in the object **employeeMap**. The second output statement displays the entire set of elements in the object. The result of execution is:

```
Size of employeeMap:3
{1110=Ming Zhu, 1112=Lee Wong, 1115=John Smith}
```

Adding the following statement to the end of the code:

```
employeeMap.put("1115", "Geo King");
```

replaces the original element ("1115" , "John Smith"), resulting in the new collection of elements:

```
Size of employeeMap:3
{1110=Ming Zhu, 1112=Lee Wong, 1115=Geo King}
```

As we discuss more concepts and coding techniques in Collection, more examples and applications will be provided.

13.1.3 Generic types

Generics are used in C/C++ and serve as a template to define abstract data types, including primative data types. In Java, however, generics can only define types of **Object** and its subclasses. Generics cannot be used with static variables and static initialization blocks. The following is a simple example using generics in Java code:

```
class SomeClass<T> {
   T value;
   SomeClass(T value) {
      this.value = value;
   }
   ...
}
```

The codes defines a generic type, **SomeClass<T>**. The angle brackets denote a generic indicator in which you may code any legal identifier as a generic type. We usually use an uppercase letter to define a generic type argument; here, it is **T**, or **<T>**. When you use a generic type to create a particular object, you must us an instantiable class type, or argument type, to replace the generic argument type, e.g.,:

```
SomeClass<Integer> obj = new SomeClass<Integer>(100);
```

Here an object of **SomeClass** with **<Integer>** argument type, **obj**, is created with an initialized value of 100. Note that you must still use angle brackets to indicate the particular argument type. Of course, you may also create other objects of **SomeClass** with any instantiable class type:

```
SomeClass<Double> obj2 = new SomeClass<Double>(100.99);
SomeClass<Product> myProduct = new SomeClass<Product>("1100", "Java", 89.28);
```

Another example of using generics is in establishing the definition of a **Collection** interface:

```
public interface Collection<E> {
   //Define the methods to be implemented
}
```

As such, **E** is replaced by **String** and it creates an **ArrayList** object, code, with **String** type elements. Because **Collection** is the superclass of **ArrayList**, it can refer to any **ArrayList** object:

```
Collection<String> code = new ArrayList<String>();
```

We have discussed it before. Here, **E** is replaced by **String** and it created an **ArrayList** object called **code** with **String** type elements. Because **Collection** is the super class of **ArrayList**, it can be used to refer to any **ArrayList** object.

Generics can also be used to define the data type in classes, the only requirement being that the data must be an object type, not a primative data type. The following example defines three generic type arguments, each being separated by a comma:

```
//Complete code is called GeneItems.java in Ch13 from the author's website
 class GeneItems<T1, T2, T3> {
   private T1 firstObj;
   private T2 secondObj;
   private T3 thirdObj;

   public GeneItems(T1 obj1, T2 obj2, T3 obj3) {
          firstObj = obj1;
          secondObj = obj2;
          thirdObj = obj3;
   }
   public void setFirstObj(T1 obj1) {
          firstObj = obj1;
   }
   public T1 getFirstObj() {
          return firstObj;
   }
   ...
}
```

Note that in defining a generic with multiple arguments, if one argument type, e.g., **T1**, already defines a particular type argument, e.g., **firstObj**, the other type arguments, **T2** and **T3**, cannot be used to redefine **firstObj**, unless the redefinition is achieved through casting. The following code:

```
public void setFirstObj(T2 obj1) {
   firstObj = obj1;
}
```

is illegal since **T1** already defines **firstObj**.

The following code:

```
//Complete code called Geneltems.java in Ch13 from the author's website
Geneitems<String, Integer, Double> items = new GeneItems<String, Integer,
Double>("Java", 15, 79.89);
```

creates an object of **Geneltems** called **items** with three particular type arguments: **String**, **Integer**, and **Double**.

The type arguments discussed above are called concrete type parameters and the argument types are called concrete parameterized types.

We will now explore four important concepts in generics:

Unbounded wildcard <?>

The unbounded wildcard uses **<?>** to define a concrete type argument of any element type. For example:

```
//Complete code called WildcardTest.java in Ch13 from the author's website
List<?> bList;          //Declare a collection of any type element
```

In the above code snippet, **<?>** represents an unbounded wildcard defining **bList** of **List**. It can be of any concrete element type, e.g., **<Integer>**, **<Double>**, **<String>**, **<Product>**, et cetera. In the following code:

```
 List<Integer> iList = new ArrayList<Integer>();  //Create a collection of Integer
iList.add(8);                                     //Add an element (autoboxing)
iList.add(88);
bList = new ArrayList<Integer>(iList); //bList can have a collection of Integer
```

bList may have any type of elements; we have assigned it the **Integer** elements in **iList**. Continuing the above example:

```
List<Double> dList = new ArrayList<Double>();     //Create a collection of Double
dList.add(0.8);                                  //Add elements
dList.add(0.08);
bList = new ArrayList<Double>(dList);       //bList may have collection of Double
```

Note that you cannot directly add an element to a collection that is defined using an unbounded wildcard. For example,

```
bList.add(19.22);                //Illegal
```

will cause data type safety issue since any type of element can be added into **bList**.

Unbounded wildcards can also used as method arguments:

```
//Complete code called Test.java in Ch13 from the author's website
class Test <T>{
   static void printList(Collection<?> c) {
      for (Object obj : c)
         System.out.println(obj);
   }
}
```

In this example, an unbounded wildcard is used as an argument in method **printList()**, indicating it can represent any concrete object type. The code can is successfully print the elements in the collection using **Object** as a reference. Continuing the example above:

```
Test.printList(dList);          //Or: Test.printList(bList);
```

dList or **bList** are collections of **Double** and can be used as argument in **printList()**. The execution result is:

```
0.8
0.08
```

The following code demonstrates the use of an unbounded wildcard in **printList(Collection<?>c)**:

```
//Complete code called WildcardTest.java in Ch13 from the author's website
ArrayList<String> arrayList = new ArrayList<String>();
                              //String is concrete type in printList()
arrayList.add("abc");
arrayList.add("xyz");

Test.printList(arrayList);           //Can be collection of String
```

Variable **arrayList** is a collection of **String**, so it is a member of **Collection**. The execution result is:

```
abc
xyz
```

Note: ***Collection** is not an **Object**. You cannot use **Object** in the place of an unbounded wildcard. For example, it is illegal to code: **printList(Object c)**.*

Upper bounded wildcard <? extends T>

An upper bounded wildcard **<? extends T>** declares elements or concrete type arguments that are subclasses of **T** including **T**. For example,

```
List<? extends Number> aList;
```

elements in **aList** must be objects of **Integer**, **Long**, **Float**, **Double**, **BigDecimal**, and **Number**, e.g.,

```
aList = new LinkedList<Integer>();
bList = new ArrayList<Double>();
```

Statements

```
aList = new ArrayList<String>();
```

and

```
aList = new LinkedList<Object>();
```

are illegal since **String** is not a subclass of **Number** and **Object** is the superclass of **Number**.

Let discuss one more example. Assume that **Item** and **Book2** are programmer-defined classes:

```
//Complete code called UpperBoundTest.java in Ch13 from the author's website
class Item {                                                  //Superclass Item
   protected String name;
   Item(String name){
      this.name = name;
   }
   public String toString(){
      return "Name: " + name;
   }
}
class Book2 extends Item {                                    //Subclass Book2
   private int quantity;
   public Book2(String name, int quantity)  {
      super(name);
      this.quantity = quantity;
   }
   public String toString(){
      return super.toString() + "\nQuantity: " + quantity;
   }
}
  }
```

Assume the following upper bounded wildcard is used to define a static method:

```
//Complete code called UpperBoundTest.java in Ch13 from the author's website
static void printList(List<? extends Item> c){
   for(Item item : c)
      System.out.println(item);
   }
}
```

Method **printList(List <? Extends Item> c)** declares that the argument used to call this method must be an object of **Book2** or **Item**.

In the following code:

```
List<Book2> bList = new ArrayList<Book2>();
bList.add(new Book2("Java", 5));                              //Add Book2elements
bList.add(new Book2("JSPS", 10));
```

```
List<? extends Item> list = new ArrayList<Book2>(bList); //Book2 extends Item
Test.printList(list);                  //Call the method
```

list is a copy of **bList**, so its elements are objects of **Book2**.

The execution result is:

```
Name: Java
Quantity: 5
Name: JSPS
Quantity: 10
```

The following code is also legal in above example:

```
List<Item> iList = new LinkedList<Item>();
iList.add(new Item("software"));
iList.add(new Item("hardware"));
Test.printList(iList);                 //Call the method using iList
```

The execution result is:

```
Name: software
Name: hardware
```

But the following code:

```
List<String> sList = new LinkedList<String>();
sList.add("xyz");
Test.printList(sList);                                    //Compiling error
```

will cause the syntax error because **String** is not subclass of **Item**.

Let's change the argument **Item** in **printList()** method to a generic type:

```
//Complete code called Test.java in Ch13 from the author's website
class Test <T> {
   static <T> void printList(List<? extends T> c){
      for (T item : c)
         System.out.println(item);
   }
}
```

In this application, generic type **T** is replaced by any concrete type, e.g., **Item**, **Book2**, or **String**. This method will also accept **sList as a** parameter. Furthermore, **<? Extends Object>** is equivalent to an unbounded wildcard, since it can accept all types of elements.

Lower bounded wildcard <? Super T>

Lower bounded wildcard **<? Super T>** declares that the element type or concrete argument type must be superclass of **T** including **T**. For example:

```
List<? super Integer> aList;
```

declare that the elements in collection **aList** must be of type **Number**, **Object**, or **Integer**. Another example:

```
Collection<? super String> sList;
```

specifies elements in **sList** must be type of **Object** or **String**.

Let's use the example of **Item** and **Book2** we have discussed before. We modify method **printList()** as follows:

```
//Complete code called LowerBoundTest.java in Ch13 from author's website
class Test3 {
   static void printList(List<? super Book2> c){ //Or Collection <?  super Books> c
      for (Object item : c)
         System.out.println(item);
   }
}
```

Note that the superclass of **Book2** may be **Object**, so you may have to use **Object** as a reference to the collection of **c**.

Let's first create and add elements to **iList**, and then call **printList()** in **Test3**:

```
 List<Item> iList = new ArrayList<Item>();
iList.add(new Item("software"));
iList.add(new Item("hardware"));
List<? super Book2> list = new ArrayList<Item>(iList);

//list has elements of Item in iList
Test3.printList(list);                                  //Legal call
```

The elements in List are objects of **Item**, which is the superclass of **Book2**. It satisfies the requirement of the lower bounded wildcard **<? Super Book2>** and is legal.

In real world applications, lower bounded and upper bounded wildcards are often used together to restrict the elements in defined collections. For example, the search method defined in **java.util.Collections**:

```
int binarySearch(List<? extends Comparable<? super T>> list, T key)
```

specifies two arguments. The first argument uses a lower bounded wildcard to specify that the elements in **list** must be the subclass that implements **Comparable**. The second argument specifies the search key. All the classes provided in the JDK satisfy this requirement. However, programmer-defined classes must first implement the **Comparable** interface before calling this method.

Let's discuss an example that uses upper bounded and lower bounded wildcards in a programmer-defined method, **copy()**.

```
//Complete code called Test.java in Ch13 from the author's website
public static <T> void copy(List<? super T> dest, List<? extends T> src) {
   for (int i = 0; i < src.size(); i++) {
      dest.set(i, src.get(i));
   }
}
```

The method specifies two arguments: The first specifies the elements in dest must be the superclasses of T included T; the second specifies the elements in src must be the subclasses of T including T. To satisfy both conditions, the collections must have the following conditions:

- The elements are objects of both of **dest** and **src**; or

There is an inheritance relationship in **dest** and **src**, i.e., the elements in **src** must be objects of subclasses of **dest**.

The following code demonstrates the copy operation that satisfies these conditions:

```
//Complete code called WildcardCopyTest.java in Ch13 from the author's website
List<String> str1 = Arrays.asList("abc", "xyz"); //Call asList() in Arrays

List<String> str2 = Arrays.asList("11");
Test.copy(str1, str2);                          //Copy

System.out.println(str1);

//Return the collections
List<Object> objs = Arrays.<Object>asList(1, 2.89, "three");
List<Integer>  ints = Arrays.asList(100); //Return the collection of Integer
Test.copy(objs, ints);        //Legal copy since Integer is subclass of Object
```

```
System.out.println(objs);      //Return the collection of Item
List<Item> items = Arrays.<Item>asList(new Item("Java"), new Item("JSPS"));

//Return the collection of Book2
List<Book2> books = Arrays.<Book2>asList(new Book2("J2EE", 10));
Test.copy(items, books);       //Legal since Book2is subclass of Item
System.out.println(items);
```

The execution result is:

```
[11, xyz]
[100, 2.89, three]
[Name: J2EE
Quantity: 10, Name: JSPS]
```

For convenience in adding elements, the example uses the **asList()** method in **java.util.Arrays** to accept one or more arguments and return the collections of the specified type. Because **ArrayList** implements the **List** interface, we use **List** as a reference. You may see that since **dest** and **src** are the same collections, the code will first perform the copy operations. For example, **String**, **Integer**, or **src** is an object of the subclass of **dest**. Of course, if **src** is the collection of **Integer**, legal collections for **dest** also include **Number** and **Integer**.

Table 13.4 summarizes commonly used terminology and descriptions in Generics. The table uses **Collection** and **ArrayList** as examples, but these may be applied to any facet of **Collection**.

Table 13.4 Commonly used terminology and description in generics

Example	Description
Interface Collection<E>{}	Define a generic type interface called Collection. E or <E> are type arguments.
ArrayList<Integer> list = new ArrayList<Integer>();	Create a collection of ArrayList called list. ArrayList<Integer> is an argument type and Integer is a concrete type.
Collection<String> list = new ArrayList<String>();	Create a collection of ArrayList called list. Use Collection as its reference.
void method(Collection<?> list) {}	Define a method with an argument type of any Collection. <?> is an unbounded wildcard.
List<? extends Super> list	Define a collection called list using upper bounded wildcard. It is legal if concrete types are subclasses of Super including Super.
List<? super Subclass>list	Define a collection called list using lower bounded wildcard. It is legal if concrete types are super classes of Subclass including Subclass.
List<? extends T>list	Define a collection called list using generic upper bounded wildcard. Generic type T must be specified as a concrete type. Elements in list must be objects of subclasses of T including T.
List<? super T> args1, List <? extends T> args2	args1 must be collection of superclasses of T including T; args2 must be collection of subclasses of T including T. T must be specified as a concrete type.
class Foo<T extends Number & Comparable> {}	Defined a class called Foo with generic type T that must be subclasses of Number and implemented as a Comparable interface. T must be specified as a concrete type.

13.1.4 Type safety

Prior to establishing generic types, Java allowed the addition of any type of element in a **Collection** without performing any check of type safety:

```
ArrayList myList = new ArrayList ();//Collection without using generic
myList.add("Java");                      //Add String element
myList.add(89.89);                       //Add Double element
myList.add(new Product());               //Add programmer-defined
element
...
```

Although adding elements in collections without using generics as the basis of type checking may provide a seeming convenience in coding, this technique cannot guarantee the validity and consistency of the member elements in a specified collection. Such a practice is extremely likely to cause errors in operations, such as arithmetic procedures, in the collections. The above definition of the collection is thus formed by what is called the definition of raw type parameters.

In example above, the collection is actually created using **Object** as the default type:

```
ArrayList<Object> myList = new ArrayList<Object>();
```

13.2 A Walk Into Collection Classes

Let's first discuss **ArrayList** and **LinkedList** that implement **Collection** and **List**. We will then discuss the **Set** and **HashSet** classes in Java collections.

13.2.1 ArrayList

ArrayList uses an array as its underlying structure. However, unlike arrays, the size of an **ArrayList** object is dynamic and can expand or contract during run-time. This dynamic quality requires the JVM to perform extra work, and, therefore, operations will be slower when elements are added or deleted from other than the end of the object. **ArrayList** can accept any type of **Object** as its elements, with the exception of primative type data. All operations are performed by call the object's methods in **ArrayList**. Table 13.5 lists commonly used constructors and methods in **ArrayList**.

Table 13.5 Commonly used constructors and methods in ArrayList

Constructor/Method	Description
ArrayList()	Creates an empty list collection of ArrayList with an initial capacity of 10 elements. Element safety is not checked.
ArrayList<E>()	Creates an empty list collection of ArrayList with an initial capacity of 10 elements of type <E>. Element safety is not checked.
ArrayList<E>(int capacity)	Creates an empty list collection of ArrayList with an initial capacity of *capacity* elements of type <E>. Element safety is not checked.
ArrayList<E>(Collection (? extends E) c)	Creates an empty list collection of ArrayList having elements of another specified collection of c in which elements must be objects of subclasses of E including E. Element safety is not checked.
boolean add(E element)	Appends specified element of type E at end of list. Returns true if successful; otherwise returns false.
void add(int index, E element)	Inserts specified element of type E at specified index in list.
void clear()	Removes all elements from collection.
boolean contains(Object element)	Returns true if collection contains specified element; otherwise returns false.

E get(int index)	Returns element at specified index in list. Throws IndexOutOfRange if index exceeds bounds of collection.
int indexOf(Object element)	Returns index of first occurrence of element in collection; returns -1 if element is not in collection.
boolean isEmpty()	Returns true if collection is empty; otherwise returns false.
Iterator<E> iterator()	Returns an iterator over elements in this list in proper sequence.
E remove(int index)	Removes element at specified position in this list (optional operation). Shifts any subsequent elements left, i.e., subtracts one from their indices. Returns element removed from list.
boolean remove(Object element)	Removes first occurrence of specified element from this list, if present (optional operation). If list does not contain element, it is unchanged. Returns true if removal operation is successful.
E set(int index, E element)	Replaces element at specified position in list with specified element (optional operation). Returns replaced element.
int size()	Returns number of elements in collection.
Object[] toArray()	Returns array containing all elements in this list in proper sequence, i.e., from first element to last element). Returned array will be "safe," such that no references to it are maintained by this list. Method must allocate new array even if list is backed by an array. Caller may modify returned array.
String toString()	Returns names of all elements in collection as String. If not over toString() in a programmer-defined collection, it also returns address of element reference.

NOTE: *The default size of an **ArrayList** object is 10 elements. You may provide an initial specification of the size of **ArrayList**, and its size will dynamically change during program execution.*

The following are examples using constructors and methods in **ArrayList**.
Example 1. Create collections of **ArrayList** with varying sizes using different constructors.

```
//Complete code called ListTest.java in Ch13 from the author's website

//Create non-type-safe ArrayList
ArrayList noSafeList = new ArrayList();

//Create String type nameList
ArrayList<String> nameList = new ArrayList<String>();

//Create Double type priceList with size of 80 elements
ArrayList<Double> priceList = new ArrayList<Double>(80);

//Create Product type productList with default size of 10 elements
ArrayList<Product2> productList = new ArrayList<Product2>();

//list has all elements contained in nameList
ArrayList<String> list = new ArrayList<String>(nameList);
```

In the last statement of the above example, a copy constructor of **ArrayList** is used to duplicate all elements in **nameList** into **list.** A deep copy operation is performed, thereby allowing **list** and **nameList** to be two independent collections.

Example 2. Call **add()** method of **ArrayList**.

```
nameList.add("Lee");          //Add element at the beginning
nameList.add("Smith");        //Add element "Smith" before "Lee"
```

```
priceList.add(129.65);          //Perform autoboxing; place element at beginning
priceList.add(0, 89.76);        //Perform autoboxing; place element at index 0

//Add an unnamed element of Product2 at beginning
productList.add(new Product2("1011", "software", 59.85");
```

The last statement in the above example creates an unnamed object of **Product2** and adds it at the beginning of the collection.

Example 3. Call other methods in **ArrayList**.

```
//Continuing from above examples ...
System.out.println(priceList.contains(129.65));    //Result: true
System.out.println(nameList.get(1));          //Result: Smith
System.out.println(nameList.indexOf("Lee"));       //Result: 0

ArrayList<String> list2 = new ArrayList<String>(nameList);
System.out.println(list2.isEmpty());          //Result: false
list2.remove(1);                 //Or: list2.remove("Smith"); Delete element "Smith"
list2.set(0, "Fan Yi");                            //"Lee" is replaced by "Fan Yi"
System.out.println("Size of List2 = " + list2.size()); //Result: Size of list2 = 1
System.out.println("Size of nameList = " + nameList.size());//Size of nameList = 2
Object[] doubleArray = priceList.toArray();        //Return priceList as array
System.out.println(doubleArray[0]);                //Result: 89.76
System.out.println(priceList); //or: System.out.println(priceList.toString());
```

The last line of the code will be compiled as:

```
System.out.println(pricelist.toString());
```

resulting in the display of the following output:

```
[89.76, 129.65]
```

However, the following code:

```
System.out.println("productList = " + productList.toString());
//Or: System.out.println(productList);
```

because programmer-defined class **Product2** does not override the **toString()** method of **Object,** prints the address of the collection **productList**.

```
[Product2@c17164]
```

The iterator listed in the table is discussed in section 13.2.4.

13.2.2 LinkedList

A **LinkedList** collection uses a node linking structure to order and associate the elements in the linked list, thereby increasing the efficiency of adding or deleting an element that is not at the end of the list. In all other aspects, it is similar in function to **ArrayList**.

Table 13.6 lists commonly used constructors and methods in **LinkedList**. It has additional methods that operate on elements at the beginning and end of the linked list; in other all other aspects, it is similar to methods in **ArrayList**.

Table 13.6 Commonly used constructors and methods in LinkedList

Constructor/Method	Description	Constructor/Method
LinkedList()	Creates an empty list collection of LinkedList. Element safety is not checked.	
LinkedList<E>()	Creates an empty list collection of LinkedList of type <E>. Element safety is not checked.	
LinkedList<E>(Collection (? extends E) c)	Creates an empty list collection of LinkedList having elements of another specified collection of c in which elements must be objects of subclasses of E including E. Element safety is not	
boolean add(E element)	Appends specified element of type E at end of list. Returns true if successful; otherwise	
void add(int index, E element)	Inserts specified element of type E at specified index in list.	
addFirst(E element)	Adds specified element at beginning of LinkedList object.	
addLast(E element)	Adds specified element at end of	addLast(E element)
void clear()	Removes all elements from collection.	void clear()
boolean contains(Object element)	Returns true if collection contains specified element; otherwise returns false.	
E element()	Returns, but does not remove, first element (head) in collection without moving location	
E get(int index)	Returns element at specified index in	E get(int index)
E getFirst()	Returns first element in collection.	E getFirst()
E getLast()	Returns last element in collection.	E getLast()
int indexOf(Object element)	Returns index of first occurrence of element in collection; returns -1 if element is not found.	
boolean isEmpty()	Returns true if collection is empty; otherwise returns false.	
Iterator<E> iterator()	Returns an iterator over elements in this list in proper sequence.	
int lastIndexOf(Object element)	Returns index of last occurrence of element in collection; returns -1 if element is not found.	
E remove(int index)	Removes element at specified position in this list (optional operation). Shifts any subsequent	
boolean remove(Object element)	Removes first occurrence of specified element from this list, if present (optional operation). If list does not contain element, it is unchanged. Returns true if removal operation is	
E set(int index, E element)	Replaces element at specified position	E set(int index, E element)
int size()	Returns number of elements in	int size()
Object[] toArray()	Returns array containing all elements in this list in proper sequence, i.e., from first element	
String toString()	Returns names of all elements in	String toString()
Constructor/Method	Description	
LinkedList()	Creates an empty list collection of LinkedList. Element safety is not checked.	

Comparing Table 13.6 with Table 13.5, you can see most methods of the **ArrayList** and **LinkedList** classes are similar. The following examples show some differences in functionality between the two classes:

Example 1. Assume a collection, **nameList**, of **ArrayList** is already created. Create a collection of **LinkedList** that includes the data contained in **nameList**.

```
//Complete code called ListTest.java in Ch13 from author's website
LinkedList<String> linkedList = new LinkedList<String>(nameList);
```

This statement will deep copy all elements from **nameList** to **linkedList**.

Example 2. Call methods **addFirst()** and **addLast()** in **LinkedList**.

```
linkedList.addFirst("Jiang");
linkedList.addLast("Duke");
System.out.println("linkedList = " + linkedList); //or: linkedList.toSring()
```

The execution result is:

```
linkedList = [Jiang, Lee, Smith, Duke]
```

Example 3. Call other methods in **LinkedList**:

```
Object obj = linkedList.getFirst(); //obj = "Jiang"
System.out.println("Last index of \"Lee\" = " + linkedList.lastIndexOf ("Lee"));
```

The result of execution is:

```
Last index of "Lee" = 1
```

The use of **Iterator** in Table 13.6 is discussed in Section 13.2.4.

13.2.3 HashSet

HashSet differs from **ArrayList** and **LinkedList** in the following ways:

- It is formed using **HashTable**.
- Duplicate elements are not allowed.
- Elements are not stored in their order of addition due to the **HashTable** structure.
- Programmer-defined elements must override **hashCode()** to be able to generate **Hash** code.

HashSet provides means achieving simple and fast search related operations in the collections.

Table 13.7 lists commonly used constructors and methods in **HashSet**.

Table 13.7 Commonly used constructors and methods in HashSet

Constructor/Method	Description
HashSet()	Creates an empty set with an initial capacity of 16 elements and a load factor of 0.75.
HashSet<E>(int capacity)	Creates an empty set with an initial capacity of *capacity* elements of type <E>.
HashSet<E>(Collection (? extends E) c)	Creates an empty set having elements of another specified collection of c in which elements must be objects of subclasses of E including E. HashSet is created with initial load factor of 0.75 and sufficient capacity to contain elements in specified collection.
boolean add(E element)	Appends specified element of type E at end of list. Returns true if successful;

	otherwise returns false.
void clear()	Removes all elements from collection.
boolean contains(Object element)	Returns true if collection contains specified element; otherwise returns false.
boolean isEmpty()	Returns true if collection is empty; otherwise returns false.
Iterator<E> iterator()	Returns an iterator over elements in this list in proper sequence.
boolean remove(Object element)	Removes specified element from this list, if present. If list does not contain element, it is unchanged. Returns true if removal operation is successful.
int size()	Returns number of elements in collection.
Object[] toArray()	Returns array containing all elements in this list in proper sequence, i.e., from first element to last element). Returned array will be "safe," such that no references to it are maintained by this list. Method must allocate new array even if list is backed by an array. Caller may modify returned array.
String toString()	Returns names of all elements in collection as String. If not over toString() in a programmer-defined collection, it also returns address of element reference.

The following are examples using the constructors and methods listed in Table 13.7.

Example 1. Create collections of **HashSet** and add elements.

```
//Complete code called HashSetTest.java in Ch13 from the author's website

//Create a collection with 16 elements
//NOTE:  type-safety is not checked—compiler warning will be issued
HashSet mySet = new HashSet();

//Create a collection of Character type with size of 16
HashSet<Character> set = new HashSet<Character>();

//Create a collection of String type with size of 9
HashSet<String> hisSet = new HashSet<String>(9);

//Create a collection of Double type with size of 16
Collection<Double> yourSet = new HashSet<Double>();

//Create a collection that has all elements from mySet
Collection<?> herSet = new HashSet(mySet);

hisSet.add("Wang");  //Adding elements to the collections
hisSet.add("45");

herSet = new HashSet<String>(hisSet);  //herSet has all elements from hisSet
System.out.println("herSet = " + herSet);  //Call toString()
```

The first statement in the example will cause the compiler to issue a warning message reporting there is no type safety checking performed for the collection. The example also demonstrates the use of the wildcard **Collection<?>** to create **herSet** having all elements from **mySet**. This constructor is also called as a copy constructor, as previously discussed. Elements in **herSet** can be any specified type, since it is created using the **Collection** type. Collection **herSet** is reusable, and, as such, can become a collection with all elements from **hisSet**; the original content of **herSet** is replaced. The last statement generates the following message in **herSet**:

```
herSet = [45, Wang]
```

Example 2. Continued from **Example 1**, Call other methods in **HashSet**.

```
if(!mySet.add("Java"))
   System.out.println("the element is aready in the set.");
else
   System.out.println("the element has been successfully added into the set.");
```

HashSet method **add()** returns true if the element has been successfully added to the collection. The execution result is:

```
the element has been successfully added into the set.
```

13.2.4 Iterator

Iterators have been mentioned in the **ArrayList**, **LinkedList**, and **HashSet** classes. They are used to return the reference of the specified Iterator, so the iterator's methods can be called to go through all the elements in the collection. Although the elements can be scanned using a standard loop, as discussed at the beginning of the chapter, **Iterator** provides more methods associated with the iteration of the elements. Table 13.8 lists three commonly used methods in **Iterator**.

Table 13.8 Three important methods in Iterator

Method	Description
boolean hasNext()	Return true if there is element in the collection; otherwise return false.
E next()	Return the next element.
void remove()	Delete the element pointed by the iterator.

Continuing from Section 13.2.2, we will use **Iterator** to iterate the elements in the linked list:

```
//Complete code called ListTest.java in Ch13 from the author's website
Iterator<String> iterator = linkedList.iterator(); //Create the iterator

int i = 1;
while (iterator.hasNext()){
   System.out.println(i + "th element: " + iterator.next());  //Get the element
   i++;
}
```

or:

```
for(Iterator iterator = linkedList.iterator(); iterator.hasNext();)
   System.out.println(iterator.next());
```

The execution result is:

```
1th element: Jon
2th element: Lee
3th element: Smith
4th element: Duke
```

However, the following result is displayed if a **for** loop is used to display all the elements in the collection:

```
Jon
Lee
Smith
Duke
```

13.2.5 Application example

The following application example uses **ArrayList** to create a collection to record product purchasing data and print out the total amount of a purchase. It includes three classes: **Product**, **Order**, and **OrderInvoiceApp**.

Product class includes product name, order amount, and product price as instance data. It also contains the constructor and getters as follows:

```
//Complete code called Product.java in Ch13 from the author's website
class Product {
  private String name;
  private int  quantity;
  private double price;

public Product(String name, int quantity, double price) {//Constructor
   this.name = name;
   this.quantity = quantity;
   this.price = price;
 }
public getName() {  //getters
   return name;
 }
public getQuantity() {
   return quantity;
 }
public getPrice() {
   return price;
 }
```

```
}
```

The **Order** class uses **ArrayList** to create a collection, **orderList**, of **Product** type. It has methods to add and search a product order, as well as a statistical method to compute the order total and quantity of order.

```
//Complete code called Order.java in Ch13 from author's the website
class Order {
  private ArrayList<Product> orderList;    //Declare a collection of Product type
  NumberFormat currency = NumberFormat.getCurrencyInstance();  //Currency format

  public Order() {                                          //Constructor
      orderList = new ArrayList<Product>();
  }
  public void addOrder(Product product) {  //Add an order
      orderList.add(product);
  }
  public String getOrderInfo(String name) {       //Search an order
      Iterator<Product> iterator = orderList.iterator(); //Create the iterator
      int totalQuantity = 0;
      double totalAmount = 0.0;
      String message;
      Product order;
      while (iterator.hasNext()) {                //iterating
            order = iterator.next();
            if (name.equals( order.getName()))   //Comapring
                  totalQuantity += order.getQuantity(); //acculalate
            totalAmount = order.getPrice();              //Get the price
            }
      totalAmount *= totalQuantity;                             //Compute total
      message = "Product name: " + name + "\nTotal quantity: " + totalQuantity
                  + "\nTotalAmount: " + currency.format(totalAmount) + "\n";
      return message;                                   //Return the info
      }
   public String getInvoiceTotal() {              //Compute total amount
      double total = 0.0;
      for(Product order : orderList)                   //Use of for-each loop
            total += order.getPrice()*order.getQuantity();

      return "Grand Total: " + currency.format(total) + "\n";
   }
}
```

For demonstration purposes, the code uses Iterator and a for-each loop to go through the elements in the collection.

The following is the driver code of this application:

```
//Complete code called OrderInvoiceApp.java in Ch13 from the author's website
public class OrderInvoiceApp {
  public static void main(String[] args) {

  Product myOrder = new Product("Java", 15, 89.69);       //Demo for 3 orders
  Product herOrder = new Product("JSPS", 12, 78.99);
  Product hisOrder = new Product("Java", 20, 89.69);

  Order invoice = new Order();                            //Create the collection
  invoice.addOrder(myOrder);                              //Add the orders
  invoice.addOrder(herOrder);
  invoice.addOrder(hisOrder);

  System.out.println("Invoice info\n" + invoice.getInvoiceTotal());   //Print

  System.out.println("Get order info\n" + invoice.getOrderInfo("Java")); //Search
  }
}
```

The execution result is:

```
Invoice info
Grand Total: $4,087.03

Get order info
Product name: Java
Total quantity: 35
Total Amount: $3,139.15
```

13.3 Map and Its Collections

From Figure 13.1 we may see that **Map** and **Collection** are two branches in the Java Collection Framework. **Map** includes **HashMap** and **TreeMap** in which each class requires that a data pair consisting of a key and value must be established to store an element in a map collection. They are objects and the key is used to search or retrieve the associated value. As an example, assume a map is used to store telephone numbers. A key:value pair might consist of the person's name (key) and telephone number (value).

In summary, in a map collection:

- The key and value must form a paired data entity. The data components are objects.
- No duplicate keys are allowed.

In this section, we use examples to discuss these two collections in **Map** and the differences between **Collection** and **Map**.

13.3.1 HashMap

HashMap implements the **Map** interface and uses a hash table to store the elements in the collection. It does not maintain any "sense" of the order in which elements are added to the collection. Table 13.9 lists commonly used constructors and methods in **HashMap**.

Table 13. 9 Commonly used constructors and methods in **HashMap**

Constructor/Method	Description Constructor/Method
HashMap()	Creates an empty HashMap with an initial capacity of 16 elements and a load factor of
HashMap(int capacity)	Creates an empty HashMap with an initial capacity of *capacity* elements.
void clear()	Removes all elements from collection.
boolean containsKey(Object key)	Returns true if collection contains specified key; otherwise returns false.
boolean containsValue(Object	Returns true if collection contains boolean containsValue(Object value)
V get(Object key)	Returns value to which specified key is mapped; returns null if this map contains no mapping for key.
boolean isEmpty()	Returns true if collection is empty; otherwise returns false.
Set<K> keySet()	Returns a Set view of all keys contained in map.
V put(K key, V value)	Associate specified *value* with specified *key* in this map. If map previously contained
V remove(Object key)	Removes specified *key* from map, if present. Returns previous value associated with *key*, or
int size()	Returns number of elements in collection.
Collection<V> values()	Returns a Collection view of all values Collection<V> values()
String toString()	Returns names of all key-value pairs in collection as String. If not over toString() in a progra key-value pairs reference.

The following are examples using constructors and methods in Table 13.9.

Example 1. Create collections of **HashMap**.

```
//Complete code called MapTest.java in Ch13 from the author's website
HashMap myMap = new HashMap(10); //Size 10 and type-safety is not checked

// Size 16 String type
HashMap<String, String> phonebook = new HashMap<String, String>();
```

The first statement creates a collection of **HashMap**. No type safety check is performed. The second statement creates a **String** type collection with a default size of 16 elements.

Example 2. Call **put()** method in **HashMap**.

```
//Complete code called MapTest.java in Ch13 from author's website
phonebook.put("Lee", "510-666-9900");            //Add key-value elements
phonebook.put("Smith", "408-322-2277");
String oldValue = phonebook.put("Lee", "925-333-5566");

System.out.println("old value = " + oldValue);
```

When "Lee" is entered as a key in the **put()** method, the associated value, i.e., Lee's telephone number, is returned as:

```
old value = 510-666-9900
```

Example 3. Continuing from the above example, call other methods in **HashMap**.

```
//Print valid key:  Smith
System.out.println(phonebook.containsKey("Smith");

//Phonebook does NOT contain data value:  510666-9900 [Note missing "-" between
//area code and telephone number prefis
System.out.println(phonebook.containsValue("510666-9900"));

String phone = phonebook.get("Lee");              //Return 925-333-5566
Set<String> phoneKeySet;                          //Declare as String type Set
phoneKeySet = phonebook.keySet();                 //Return all keys

//Iterate all elements
for (Iterator iterator = phoneKeySet.iterator(); iterator.hasNext();)
    System.out.println(iterator.next());
```

The result of execution is:

```
Smith
Lee
```

Because **HashMap** does not support Iterator, you may call the **keySet()** method and use the **Set** collection to refer to the keys in a **HashMap**, thereby allowing the creation of an **Iterator** to scan all key elements. For iterating value elements, you may call the **values()** method:

```
Collection<String> phoneValues = phonebook.values();
for (Object value : phoneValues)
    System.out.println(value);
```

Executing the above code snippet displays the values, i.e., telephone numbers, contained in the **phonebook**:

```
408-322-2277
925-333-5566
```

13.3.2 TreeMap

TreeMap is similar to **HashMap** in that both implement the **Map** interface and use a key-value pair to operate on an element. Their differences are:

- **TreeMap** uses a tree structure to store a key-value pair; **HashMap** uses **Hash Table** to store a key-value pair.
- **TreeMap** uses the sequence of key to order the element; **HashMap** has no sequence of ordering the elements.
- In **TreeMap** the memory space is used more efficiently than **HashMap**, but in **HashMap**, the specified memory location generated by the **Hash Table** must be used to store the elements.

Table 13.10 lists commonly used constructors and methods in TreeMap.

Table 13.10 Commonly used constructors and methods in TreeMap

Constructor/Method	Description
TreeMap()	Creates an empty TreeMap using the natural ordering of its keys. All keys inserted into map must use Comparable interface. No type-safety checking is performed.
TreeMap(Comparator<? super K> comparator)	Creates an empty TreeMap, ordered according to the given comparator. All keys inserted into map must be mutually comparable as defined by specified comparator in form of: comparator.compare(key1, key2).
TreeMap(Map<? extends K, ? extends V> M)	Creates new TreeMap containing same mappings as given map. Mappings are ordered according to natural ordering of its keys. All keys inserted into map must implement Comparable interface.
K ceilingKey(K key)	Returns least (smallest) key in collection greater than or equal to specified key. Returns null if key does not exist.
void clear()	Removes all elements from collection.
Comparator<? super K> comparator()	Returns comparator used to order keys or null if map uses natural ordering of its keys.
boolean containsKey(Object key)	Returns true if collection contains specified key; otherwise returns false.
boolean containsValue(Object value)	Returns true if collection contains specified value; otherwise returns false.
K firstKey()	Returns first(lowest) key in collection.
K floorKey(K key)	Returns greatest key in collection less than or equal to specified key; returns null if *key* does not exist.
V get(Object key)	Returns value to which specified key is mapped; returns null if this map contains no mapping for key.
K higherKey(K key)	Returns least(smallest) key in collection greater than but not equal to specified key. Returns null if key does not exist.
Set<K> keySet()	Returns a Set view of all keys contained in map.
K lastKey()	Returns last key in collection.
K lowerKey(K key)	Returns greatest key in collection less than or equal to specified key; returns null if specified key does not exist.
V put(K key, V value)	Associate specified *value* with specified *key* in this map. If map previously contained mapping for key, old value is replaced. Returns previous value associated with *key*, or null if no mapping for *key* is present.
V remove(Object key)	Removes specified *key* from map, if present. Returns previous value associated with *key*, or null if no mapping for *key* is present.
int size()	Returns number of elements in collection.
Collection<V> values()	Returns a Collection view of all values contained in map.
String toString()	Returns names of all key-value pairs in collection as String. If not over toString() in a programmer-defined collection, it also returns address of key-value pairs reference.

More Info: *Natural ordering or sequence referring to alphabetical ordering or numerical ordering; special characters are using Unicode in ordering.*

Example 1. Create collections of **TreeMap**.

```
//Complete code called MapTest.java in Ch13 from author's website
TreeMap treeMap = new TreeMap();     //Create a collection with type check

//Create a collection with String as key type and value type
TreeMap<String, String> tMap = new TreeMap<String, String>();
```

Example 2. Use email address as key to reflect people's name using **TreeMap**.

```
TreeMap treeMap = new TreeMap();//Create a collection without type safety check
TreeMap<String, String> emailMap = new TreeMap<String, String>();
emailMap.put("zhao123@yahoo.com", "Zhao Xiao");
emailMap.put("qian_li@hotmail,com", "Li Qian");

String firstKey = emailMap.firstKey();
System.out.println("first key = " + firstKey);

String lowerKey = emailMap.lowerKey("zhao123@yahoo.com");
System.out.println("lower key = " + lowerKey);

String value = emailMap.get("Zhao Xiao");
System.out.println("value = " + value);

System.out.println(emailMap);
```

The execution result is:

```
first key = qian_li@hotmail.com
lower key = qian_li@hotmail.com
value = null
{qian_li@hotmail,com=Li Qian, zhao123@yahoo.com=Zhao Xiao}
```

13.3.3 Use of Comparator

Implementation of the **Comparator** interface, provided in **java.util**, allows changes to the natural ordering of the elements in **TreeMap**. Table 13.11 lists the methods that need to be implemented in **Comparator**.

Table 13.11 Methods in Comparator interface

Method	Description
int compare(T obj1, T obj2)	Compares its two arguments for natural order: returns a negative integer if obj1 is less than obj2; returns 0 if obj1 and obj2 are equal; returns positive integer if obj1 greater than obj2. Implementor must ensure that: a.) sgn(compare(x, y)) == -sgn(compare(y, x)) for all x and y; b.) relation is transitive:

	((compare(x, y)>0) && (compare(y, z)>0)) implies compare(x, z)>0.; and c.) compare(x, y)==0 implies sgn(compare(x, z)) == sgn(compare(y, z)) for all z.
boolean equals(Object obj)	Returns true if object is equal to comparator; otherwise returns false.

As an example, let us assume there are two types of product keys: a four-digit key representing each hardware product and a four-character key representing each software product. We need to order the products such that software products are ordered before hardware products. The required order is an "unnatural" ordering, and we must implement the Comparator interface to achieve the desired ordering:

```
//Complete code called MapTest.java in Ch13 from the author's website
class CodeComparator implements Comparator {            //Implement Comparator
   public int compare(Object key1, Object key2) {
      int flag = key1.toString().compareTo(key2.toString());
      return -flag;                               //Return unnatural ordering flag
   }
}
```

The comparison returns a negative integer if **key1** is greater than **key2**. As such, this represents an unnatural ordering of the sequence. Because **Object** already implements the **equal()** method, there is no requirement for coder implementation.

The following code specifies the ordering of the key:

```
//Create CodeComparator to specify the ordering of the key
TreeMap<String, String> productMap =
   new TreeMap<String, String>(new CodeComparator());
productMap.put("Java", "JDK1.70 with a new IDE"); //Add element
productMap.put("1111", "Solaris Server");

System.out.println(productMap);                          //Display all elements
```

and displays a typical result of execution:

```
{Java=JDK1.70 with a new IDE, 1111=Solaris Server}
```

Modifying the statement:

```
return flag;
```

eliminating the negation of flag results in the traditional natural ordering of the sequence, wherein alphabetic characters precede numbers.

13.3.4 Application example

The following application uses **HashMap** to create a collection in which the product ID is used as a key to reflect the product description. The application also records the number of products purchased and the total amount of the purchase. The application contains three classes: **Product**, **Invoice**, and **HashMapInvoiceApp**.

The **Product** class includes name, order number, and price of the product. Its code is similar to the example we discussed in Section 13.2.5. The **Invoice** class uses **HashMap** to create the collection and perform necessary operations:

```
//Complete code called Invoice.java in Ch13 from the author's website
class Invoice {
   private HashMap<String, Product> orderMap;        //Declare HashMap
   private Collection<Product> orderList;            //Declare Collection

   NumberFormat currency = NumberFormat.getCurrencyInstance(); //Currency format

   public Invoice(){                                      //Constructor
      orderMap = new HashMap<String, Product>();
   }
   public void addOrder(String code, Product product){   //Add element
      orderMap.put(code, product);
   }
   public String search(String code){                     //Use key to search product
      String message = null;
      Product product = orderMap.get(code);
      double total = product.getQuantity()* product.getPrice();

      message = "Product: " + product.getName()
                            + "\nQuantity: " + product.getQuantity()
                            + "\nPrice: " + currency.format(product.getPrice())
                            + "\nTotal: " + currency.format(total) + "\n";
      return message;                          //Return the message
   }
   public String getOrderInfo(String name) {        //Search order info
      orderList = orderMap.values();           //Return the order collection
      int totalQuantity = 0;
      double totalAmount = 0.0;
      String message;
      for (Product order : orderList) {             //Iterator
         if (name.equals(order.getName()))
            totalQuantity += order.getQuantity();
            totalAmount += order.getPrice();
         }

         totalAmount *= totalQuantity;
         message = "Product name: " + name + "\nTotal quantity: "
                                    + totalQuantity + "\nTotal amount: "
                                    + currency.format(totalAmount) + "\n";

         return message;             //Return the message
   }
```

```
    public String getInvoiceTotal() {                    //Compute total
        orderList = orderMap.values();
        double total = 0.0;
        for (Product order : orderList)
            total += order.getPrice() * order.getQuantity();
        return "Grand Total: " + currency.format(total) + "\n";  //Return total
    }
}
```

Methods **getOrderInfo()** and **values()** of **HashMap** return a **HashSet** collection to hold the ordered products. The following is the driver code of this application:

```
//Complete code called HashMapInvoiceApp.java in Ch13 from the author's website
public class HashMapInvoiceApp {
   public static void main(String[] args) {

     Invoice invoice = new Invoice(); //Create object
     invoice.addOrder("1122", new Product("Java", 15, 89.69));          //Add
elements
     invoice.addOrder("1133", new Product("JSPS", 12, 78.99));
     invoice.addOrder("1124", new Product("Java", 20, 89.69));

     System.out.println("Product info\n" + invoice.search("1133")); //Search
     System.out.println("Get order info\n" + invoice.getOrderInfo("Java"));
     System.out.println("Invoice info\n" + invoice.getInvoiceTotal());
   }
}
```

The execution result is:

```
Product info
Product: JSPS
Quantity: 12
Price: $78.99
Total: $947.88

Get order info
Product name: Java
Total quantity: 35
TotalAmount: $9,042.95

Invoice info
Grand Total: $4,087.03
```

13.4 Data Structures and Algorithms

Linked lists, trees, and hash tables are basic data structures used in collections. They can be used to generate more application-oriented data structures, such as stacks and queues. The Java API provides for classes of stacks and queues with a variety of static methods for sorting, searching, shuffling, and related operations in highly efficient and reliable ways.

In this section we discuss how to use these static methods as they relate to **Collections** with examples.

13.4.1 Stacks

Statics are commonly used data structures with particular rules restricting the access of the elements in the collection. Elements in a stack are stored in a LIFO (Last In, First Out) manner, i.e., the last element added "pushed" onto the stack will always be accessed "popped" from the stack first. Class **Stack** is provided in **java.util**. It is inherited from **Vector** and utilizes **LinkedList** to form the structure of a stack. Table 13.2 lists commonly used constructors and methods in the **Stack** class.

Table 13.12 Commonly use constructors and methods in Stack

Constructor/Method	Description
Stack<E>()	Creates an empty Stack of specified object.
boolean empty()	Returns true if stack is empty; otherwise returns false.
E peek()	"Looks", i.e., returns at object at top of stack without removing it from stack.
E pop()	Removes and returns object at top of stack.
E push(E item)	Pushes element onto top of the stack. Returns pushed element.
int search(Object obj)	Returns position of specified element in stack; first position is designated as 1.

The following is example code using the constructor and methods in **Stack**.

```
//Complete code called StackTest.java in Ch13 from the author's website
Stack<String> stack = new Stack<String>();          //Create a stack of String
stack.push("abc");                                  //Push
stack.push("xyz");
int pos = stack.search("abc");                      //Return 2
System.out.println("The position of abc: " + pos);

boolean empty = stack.empty();             //Return false
String obj = stack.peek();                 //Return xyz; but do not pop
String top = stack.pop();                  //Pop and return xyz

System.out.println("The top of the stack: " + top);
```

The execution result is:

```
The position of abc: 2
The top of the stack: xyz
```

13.4.2 Queues

Queues are another commonly used data structure in applications. A queue accesses its elements in a FIFO (First In, First Out) ordering. Interface **Queue** is a sub-interface of **Collection** and uses **LinkedList** to form the queues themselves. In the Java API, classes implementing **Queue** include **AbstractQueue**, **LinkedBlockingQueue**, and **PriorityQueue**. In this section API classes relating to **Queue** are not discussed; rather, a programmer-defined structure using **LinkedList** is created to perform the basic operations involving FIFO operations.

The following code is an example of a programmer-defined queue called **GenericQueue**:

```
//Complete code called GenericQueue.java in Ch13 from the author's website
import java.util.*;

public class GenericQueue {
   private LinkedList<E> que = new LinkedList<E>();      //Create a collection
   public void inQue(E item) {
          que.addLast(item);                              //Enqueue
   }
   public E deQue() {                                     //Dequeue
          return que.removeFirst();
   }
   public int size() {                                    //Call method
          return que.size();
   }
   public boolean empty() {                               //Call isEmpty()
          return que.isEmpty();
   }
   public String toString() {                             //Call toString()
          return que.toString();
   }
}
```

The following is the driver code of **GenericQueue**:

```
//Complete code called GenericQueueTest.java in Ch13 from the author's website
public class GenericQueueTest {
   public static void main(String[] args) {

   GenericQueue<String> myQue = new GenericQueue<String>(); //Create collection

   myQue.inQue("One");                                 //pushes
   myQue.inQue("Two");
   myQue.inQue("Three");

   int myQueSize = myQue.size();               //myQueSize = 3
   System.out.println(myQue);
```

```
  while(myQue.size() > 0)
         System.out.println(myQue.deQue());              //Deque all elements
  }
}
```

The result of execution is:

```
[One, Two, Three]
One
Two
Three
```

13.4.3 Sorting

There are many static methods provided in **Collections** to perform sorting. Table 13.13 lists the commonly used ones.

Table 13.13 Commonly used methods in sorting in Collections

Method	Description
static void reverse(List<?> list)	Reverses order of elements in specified list.
static <T> Comparator<T> reverseOrder()	Returns comparator imposing reverse of natural ordering, i.e., ordering
static <T extends Comparable<? super T>> void	Sorts list into ascending order, according to its natural ordering.
static <T> void sort(List<T> list, Comparator<? super	Sorts list into order specified by Comparator.

Methods with **Comparator** as an argument are used to sort programmer-defined objects in collections. A class must be coded that implements the **Comparator** interface. Objects of the class are then created.

Let's first discuss an example code that uses methods listed in Table 13.13. We will then discuss how to sort programmer-defined elements in a collection in **Example 2**.

Example 1. Call sorting methods in **Collections**.

```
//Complete code called SortTest.java in Ch13 from the author's website
ArrayList<Double> doubleList = new ArrayList<Double>(); //Create a collection

doubleList.add(120.99);                          //Add elements
doubleList.add(87.03);
doubleList.add(89.67);

System.out.println("Before reverse: " + doubleList);           //Display
Collections.reverse(doubleList);                       //Call reverse()
System.out.println("After reverse: \t" + doubleList);    //Display result
```

```
Collections.sort(doubleList);                          //Call sort()
System.out.println("After sort: \t" + doubleList);      //Display result

Collections.sort(doubleList, Collections.reverseOrder()); //Call reverseOrder()
System.out.println("After reverse again: \t" + doubleList);
```

Executing the above code produces the following result:

```
Before  reverse:  [120.99,  87.03,  89.67]
After  reverse:    [89.67,  87.03,  120.99]
After sort:      [87.03, 89.67, 120.99]
After reverse again:    [120.99, 89.67, 87.03]
```

Example 2. Sort a collection of programmer-defined elements. Assume the following programmer-defined class **Items**:

```
//Complete code called Items.java in Ch13 from the author's website
class Items      { private
   int number; private
   String name;
   Items(int number, String name) {                //Constructor
      this.number = number;
      this.name = name;
   }
   public void setNumber(int number) {
      this.number = number;
   }
   public int getNumber() {
      return number;
   }
  public void setName(String name) {
      this.name = name;
     }
     public String getName() {
      return name;
   }
  public String toString()  {              //Override toString()
     return "Number: " + number + " Name: " + name;
  }
}
```

The following code implements Comparator in class **NumberComparator** to perform sorting:

```
//Complete code called Items.java in Ch13 from the author's website

//class for Items to implement Comparator
class NumberComparator implements Comparator<Items> {
   public int compare(Items Item1, Items Item2) {
      if (Item1.getNumber() < Item2.getNumber()) //Sorting number in natural order
         return -1;
```

```
        if (Item1.getNumber() > Item2.getNumber())
            return 1;

        return 0;
    }
}
```

The driver code is:

```
//Complete code called ItemsSortTest.java in Ch13 from the author's website
List<Items> list = new LinkedList<Items>();       //Create the Items collection

Items myItem = new Items(100, "software");        //Create the objects
Items hisItem = new Items(10, "hardware");
Items herItem = new Items(15, "middleware");

list.add(myItem);                                 //Add elements
list.add(hisItem);
list.add(herItem);

Collections.sort(list, new NumberComparator());          //Call sort()
System.out.println(list);
```

In calling method **sort**(), an anonymous object, **NumberComparator**, is used for the sorting specification. The execution result is:

```
 list = [Number: 10 Name: hardware, Number: 15 Name: middleware, Number: 100 Name:
software]
```

More Info: *Calling either method **reverseOrder()** or exchanging the return value in **compare()** in **NumberComparator** will perform "unnatural" or a reverse ordering of the values.*

13.4.4 Searching

There are two methods provided in **Collections** to perform searching. Table 13.14 lists these two methods.

Table 13.14 Searching methods in Collections

Method	Description
static <T> int binarySearch(List<? extends Comparable<? super T>> list, T key)	Searches for element with specified key in specified list. List must be subclass of T including T and implements Comparator. Returns index of element if found; otherwise returns a negative integer if element is not found. Index of elements is not certain if multiple elements are found. List must be sorted first.

int binarySearch(List<? extends T>list, T key, Comparator<? super T> c)	Same as above, but combine the implementation of Comparator into the searching method.

Example 1. Call the first method in Table 13.14 to perform binary searching.

```
//Complete code called BinarySearchTest.java in Ch13 from the author's website
List<Integer> iList = new LinkedList<Integer>();
iList.add(88);
iList.add(888);
iList.add(8);

Collections.sort(iList);                         //Sort first in natural order
int index = Collections.binarySearch(iList, 88);  //Call searching

System.out.println("iList = " + iList);
System.out.println("index of 88 = " + index);
```

Execution result is:

```
iList = [8, 88, 888]
index of 88 = 1
```

Example 2. Use the second binary searching method to perform searching in a collection with programmer- defined elements.

```
//Complete code called BinarySearchTest.java in Ch13 from the author's website
List<Items> list = new LinkedList<Items>();        //Create a collection of Item
Items myItem = new Items(100, "software");
Items hisItem = new Items(10, "hardware");
Items herItem = new Items(15, "middleware");

list.add(myItem);
list.add(hisItem);
list.add(herItem);

index = Collections.binarySearch(list, hisItem, new NumberComparator());

System.out.println("list = " + list);
System.out.println("index of number in hisItem = " + index);
```

Execution result is:

```
list = [Number: 100 Name: software, Number: 10 Name: hardware, Number: 15 Name:
middleware]
index of number in hisItem = 1
```

13.4.5 Shuffling

The **shuffle()** methods provided in Collections perform shuffling, i.e., element rearrangement is a prescribed random order. Table 13.15 lists two methods dealing with shuffling.

Table 13.15 shuflling methods in Collections

Method	Description
static void shuffle(List<?> list)	Randomly permutes, "shuffles", specified list using default source of
static void shuffle(List<?> list, Random random)	Similar to above,but list "shuffled" according to specified random mode.

The following is an example using these methods to shuffle elements in a collection.

```
//Complete code called CardShuffleTest.java in Ch13 from the author's website

import java.util.*;
public class CardShuffleTest {
   public static void main(String[] args) {

      String[] cardArray = new String[]{"2", "3", "4", "5", "6", "7", "8",
                                       "9", "10", "J", "Q", "K", "A"};
      List<String> cardList = Arrays.asList(cardArray); //Copy array to list

      Collections.shuffle(cardList);               //Call shuffling

      System.out.println("cardlist = " + cardList);      //Display

      Collections.shuffle(cardList, new Random(10));     //Call with random
      System.out.println("cardlist = " + cardList);      //Display
   }
}
```

The following are two example results of random shuffling:

```
cardlist = [10, 6, 5, A, K, 3, 9, Q, J, 2, 4, 7, 8]
cardlist = [2, 8, A, Q, 6, J, 9, 3, K, 7, 4, 10, 5]
```

You may create an application that shuffles an entire deck of cards.

13.4.6 Summary of collections

In the above sections, we have discussed the major methods dealing with algorithms in **Collections**. The **Collections** class also provides many lesser-known methods to perform operations associated with collections. Table 13.16 lists a summary of these methods.

Table 13.16 Other methods in Collections

Method	Description	Example
static <T> boolean addAll(Collection<? super T> c, T ...a)	Adds specified elements to c; elements must be superclass of T including T; returns true if adding is successful; otherwise returns false.	Collections.addAll(list, "ab", "xy"); Collections.addAll(list, myArray);
static <E> Collection<E>	Returns dynamically type-safe view	Collections.checkedCollection(list,

checkedCollection(Collection<E> c, Class<E> obj)	of specified collection. Throws ClassCastException if obj is not a specified type in c.	product);
static <T> void copy(List<? super T>dest, List<? extends T> src)	Copies all elements of one list to another. Detailed discussion found in Section 13.1.3.	Same as examples in Section 13.1.3
static boolean disjoint(Collection<?> c1, Collection<?> c2)	Returns true if specified collections share no elements in common.	Collections.disjoint(lis1, list2);
static final List<T> emptyList()	Returns empty and serialized list of T.	List<String> sList = Collections. emptyList();
static <T> void fill(List<? super T> list, T obj)	Replaces all elements of list with specified element. List must be supeclass of T including T.	Collections.fill(list, "Java");
static int frequency(Collection<?> c, Object obj)	Returns number of elements in specified collection equal to specified object.	int n = Collections.frequency(list, "Java");
static <T extends Object & Comparable<? super T>> T max(Collection<? extends T> c)	Returns maximum element in c according to its natural ordering; it must be subclass of T including T.	String s = Collections.max(list);
static <T extends Object & Comparable<? super T>> T min(Collection<? extends T> c)	Returns minimum element in c according to its natural ordering; it must be subclass of T including T.	String s = Collections.min(list);
Static <T> boolean replaceAll(List<T> list, T oldObj, T newObj)	Replaces specified element in collection with *newObj*; returns true if successful; otherwise returns false.	Collections.replaceAll(list, "x", "y");
static void rotate(List<?> list, int dist)	Rotates elements in list by specified distance.	Collections.rotate(list, 3);
static void swap(List<?> list, int i, int j)	Swaps elements with specified indices in list.	Collections.swap(list, 0, 12);
static <T> Collection<T> sychronizedCollection(Collection <T> c)	Returns synchronized, i.e., thread-safe, collection.	Collection<Double> list = Collections.sychronizedCollection (dList);
static <K,V> Map<K, V> synchronized Map (Map<K, V> map)	Returns synchronized, i.e., thread-safe, map.	Map<String, Integer> sMap = Collections.synchronizedMap(map);

13.4.7 Application in collection

We will use **TreeMap** to create an application simulating a telephone directory, **Phonebook**. It can store, add, search, and delete phone numbers. In adding a phone number, it may display information indicating if there is a duplicate name in the phone book and ask for another entry of the name, or prompting to use an email address as a name. Users can search for a telephone number by entering either a name or email address. The code also displays information indicating if there is no such person in the phone book if the name or email does not match the search. It also will ask the user if the telephone number is to be added into the phone book. Although file I/O is discussed in Chapter 21, simple file I/O operations to store and update the phone book are also used.

```
//Complete code called Phonebook.java in Ch13 from the author's website
import java.util.*;
import java.io.*;
import javax.swing.JOptionPane;

class Phonebook {
   private String name, phone;                        //Instance data
   Map<String, String> phones;                        //Declare a map

   public Phonebook() throws IOException {            //For file I/O
      name = phone = null;
      phones = new TreeMap<String, String>();         //Create TreeMap collection
      readPhonebooks();                               //Read in the file
   }
   private void readPhonebooks() throws IOException{
      File phoneData = new File("phones.txt");        //Create a file object
      BufferedReader in = new BufferedReader(new FileReader(phoneData));
      String line = in.readLine();                    //Read a record
      while (line != null){                           //Continue to read
           StringTokenizer token = new StringTokenizer(line, "\t");
           name = token.nextToken();        //Name
           phone = token.nextToken();                 //Phone number
           phones.put(name, phone);                   //Add to collection
           line = in.readLine();                      //Read next record
      }
      in.close();                                     //Close the file
   }
   ...
```

Phonebook uses **TreeMap** in which the name or email address key reflects the telephone number. The constructor calls **readPhonebooks()** to read the records from an existing file, **phones.txt**. Because file I/O requires checked exception handling, **IOException** is thrown to its caller, and the exception is propagated to the JVM for handling. This processing is presented in the driver code. Each file record is of the form:

```
   Li zhongyi   (408) 655-1255
...
```

wherein each record field is separated by a tab. When the record is read in, method **nextToken()** in the **Tokenizer** class separates the fields, which are then added to **phones**. This processing is continued until the end-of-file is encountered in the while loop. A detailed discussion of file I/O is presented in Chapter 21.

Adding a record to the collection is performed by the **addRecord()** method:

```
public void addRecord() throws IOException {
   String message = null;
   String choice = null;
   name = JOptionPane.showInputDialog(null, "Please enter the name: ");
   phone = JOptionPane.showInputDialog(null, "Please enter the phone number:  ");

   processDuplicate();                      //Process duplicated name

   phones.put(name, phone);                 //Add new element
```

```
    updatePhonebooks(name, phone);              //Update phonebooks

    message = "The following record has been added to the phonebook: \n"
                 + "Name/Email: " + name + "\n" + "Phone number:  " + phone + "\n";
    JOptionPane.showMessageDialog(null, message);
}
```

After the user enters a name a phone number in method **updatePhonebooks()**, **processDuplicate()** is invoked to check for duplicate names in the collection. The user is prompted to reenter a name or use an email address in the event of duplicate names in the directory. The name is added before the phone number for a better directory display:

```
phone = name + " " + phone;
name = email;
```

Because name and phone are defined as instance data, each method in **Phonebook** can directly access them. After a new element is added into the collection, **updatePhonebooks()** is called to record the new key-value pair in the file for updating purposes. The updated record is reported back to the user.

The following is the code of method **processDuplicate()**:

```
public void processDuplicate() {
   String email = null,
          message = null,
          choice = null;

   while (phones.containsKey(name)) {              //Loop to check for duplicates
       message = "There is a duplicated name in the phone book...\n"
                 + "Enter 1 to use other name\n" //Use other name
                 + "Enter 2 to use email: ";          //Or use email
       choice = JOptionPane.showInputDialog(null, message);
       if (choice.equals("1")) {                   //Get new name
         name = JOptionPane.showInputDialog(null, "Enter the new name:");
       }
       else if (choice.equals("2")) {                    //If use email
              email = JoptionPane.showInputDialog(null,
                                                 "Enter the email addresss: ");
              phone = name + " " + phone; //Add name before phone
              name = email;                                //email as name
       }
   }
}
```

he following is the code of **updatePhonebooks():**

```
public void updatePhonebooks(String name, String phone) throws IOException {
   //Create object for file output - append new records to end of file
   PrintWriter out = new PrintWriter(new FileWriter("phones.txt", true));
   out.println(name + "\t" + phone);

   out.close();
}
```

The denotation of the second argument in the API class **FileWriter** constructor as **true** indicates that records are to be appended at the end of the file.

Method **search()** searches for the phone number after the user enters the name or email address. Method **display()** is called if the name or email address matches the key in the collection. If the key is not present, the user is prompted to add the entry as a new record in the **phonebooks**. Method **addRecord()** is called if the user wants to add such a new record.

The following is the code of **search()**:

```
 public void search() throws IOException {
   String choice = null,
          message = "Enter the name or email address you want to search the
phone #: ",
          name = JOptionPane.showInputDialog(null, message);

   if (phones.containsKey(name)) {
      phone = phones.get(name);
      display(name, phone);
   }
   else {
      message = "This name or email is not in the phonebook...\n"
                        + "Do you want to add into the record? (y/n): ";
      choice = JOptionPane.showInputDialog(null, message);
      if (choice.matches("[y|Y]"))
        addRecord();
   }
 }
```

Method **deleteRecord()** checks if the name key is in the collection, and then calls **remove()** in **TreeMap** to delete the element from the collection. In real world applications, records are stored in a database, rather than a file, so this demonstration application does not perform file updating.

The following is the code of **deleteRecord()**:

```
public void deleteRecord() {
   String message = null;
   name = JoptionPane.showInputDialog(null,
                    "Please entry the name/email you want to delete: ");
    if (phones.containsKey(name)) {          //Check if name is in the collection
       phone = phones.remove(name);
    }
    else {                                   //If is it not in, prompt the info
         message = "Name you entered: " + name + " is not in the phone book."
                   + "Please check your entry and try again...";
         JOptionPane.showMessageDialog(null, message);
    }
}
```

Other two methods in **Phonebook** print the name, phone number, and good bye info, respectively:

```
public void display(String name, String phone) {
   String message = "Name/Email: " + name + "\n" + "Phone number: " + phone;
   JOptionPane.showMessageDialog(null, message);
}
public void goodBye() {
   JOptionPane.showMessageDialog(null, "Thank you for using the phonebook.  Good
bye!");
   System.exit(0);
}
```

The application driver code, **PhonebookApp**, is:

```
//Complete code called PhonebookApp.java in Ch13 from author's website
import javax.swing.JOptionPane;

public class PhonebookApp {
   public static void main(String[] args) throws IOException { //Throw to JVM
   String again = "y";

   Phonebook phonebook = new Phonebook();                 //Create Phonebook object
   while (again.matches("[y|Y]")){                        //Use regular expressions
        String choice = phonebook.makeChoice();//Call menu display
        switch (Integer.parseInt(choice)) {
                case 1: phonebook.addRecord();            //Add record
                        break;
                case 2: phonebook.search();               //Search
                        break;
                case 3: phonebook.deleteRecord(); //Delete
                        break;
                case 4: phonebook.goodBye();              //Call goodBye()
        }
        again = JOptionPane.showInputDialog(null, "Continue? (y/n): ");
   }
   phonebook.goodBye();
}
```

The **main()** method propagates any thrown exception from **updateRecord()** to the JVM for handling. Method **makeChoice()** displays a menu selection for the user and processes the user's selection. This could be modified as a real menu (see Chapter 17).

Method **makeChoice()** in **Phonebook** as follows:

```
public String makeChoice() {
  String choice = null,
         message = "Welcome to phonebook...\n"
                        + "Enter 1 to add phone record\n"
                        + "Enter 2 to search phone number\n"
                        + "Enter 3 to delete a record\n"
                        + "Enter 4 to exit\n";
   boolean done = false;

   while (!done) {                 //Continue until it is done
        choice = JOptionPane.showInputDialog(null, message);
        if (choice.matches("[1|2|3|4]"))         //Must be 1-4
          done = true;
        else                                     //Continue to select if wrong
          JoptionPane.showMessageDialog(null,
                                    "Wrong choice.  Please try again...");
   }
   return choice;                                //Return the choice
}
```

Exercises

1. Use examples to explain what principles must be applied in deciding whether to use an array or a collection for a given application.
2. Use examples to explain the differences between the **List** interface and the **Map** interface.
3. What are the characteristics of generic types?
4. Use examples to explain the meaning of the following terms and statements:
    a. Wildcard
    b. Upper bounded wildcard
    c. Lower bounded wildcard
    d. Collection<Double> list = new LinkedList<Double>();

e. boolean myMethod(List<?> list) { .... }

f. Collection<? Super T> list

5. Write code to create the following collections:

   a. Create a collection of **ArrayList** with a size of 100 **String** elements.

   b. Use of a for-each loop to initialize each element in the above collection to "Java".

   c. Create a collection of **LinkedList** and referred by **List** with size of 10 integer elements.

   d. Use of a **for-each** loop to initialize all elements with values from 10, 20, 30, ..., to 100.

   e. Use at least five methods provided in Table 13.7 in writing a driver code to manipulate in some manner the collection created in the above example. Print each element in the collection. Run and save all files.

6. Programming Project: Create an application to record student courses and grades. The application should also print a student's transcript. There are for programmer-defined classes in the application:

   Course – record the course title, credit and final grade.

   Transcript – create a collection of **Course** to perform record adding, deleting, sorting, searching, and printing operations.

   Validator – verify all data entries until all input data are valid.

   TranscriptApp – the driver code.

   You should also document the **Transcript** class and save the HTML files to a subdirectory, **docs**. Run and save all files.

7. Programming Project: Create an application that can use a cell phone to search for a friend's name, mailing address, and email address. The following programmer-defined classes should be included in the application:

   MySohu – create a collection; carry out adding, deleting, searching, sorting, and printing operations.

   Validator – Verify all data entries from the user. You may use regular expression processing in your code.

   MySohuApp – the driver code.

   Document **MySohu** class and save all generated HTML files in a sub folder called docs. Run and save all files.

8. Programming Project: Use sorting, searching, and shuffling methods provided in **Collections** to create an application with the following functions:

    a. Shuffling a deck of cards

    b. Sorting the cards and deck by the four suits.

    c. Shuffling a deck to 2 players or 4 players based on the choice from user.

    d. Search to determine if an adjacent pair of cards, e.g., two 4s, exists in

       the shuffled deck and report its position within the deck.

"When I walk along with two others, from at least one I will be able to learn."

– Confucius

Chapter 14 Multithreading

Multithreading refers to two or more tasks executing concurrently within a single program. A thread is an independent path of execution within a program. Many threads can run concurrently within a program. Java does not rely on the multithreading functions of the underlying operation system, but, instead, has its own robust multithreading API classes to handle such coding requests. As an example, there is at least one thread in each Java application, **main**, which serves as the starting point for the JVM to begin execution. The JVM may create many other threads, e.g., garbage collection, finalization of the object, and functions for clearing and resetting, during the course of program execution. Other examples, such as client-server applications, toolkits in the user-interface of Swing or AWT, are executed by their own threads. These internal threads are hidden from programmers by running inside the JVM.

Mulithreading can increase code efficiency. However, synchronization problems may occur if multiple threads share a common resource. This chapter provides examples to explain the concept of and coding skills related to multithreading and its synchronization.

14.1 Analysis of Multithreading

In this section, we discuss the basic concepts of threads and the five statuses of a programming thread.

14.1.1 How threads work

Figure 14.1 shows the comparison between a single thread and multiple threads executing the same operations. Assume there are two tasks, **task1** and **task2**, in a code: **task1** performs file reading and writing; **task2** maintains a networking connection with another application. If only one thread is allowed, as shown at the top of Figure 14.1, **task2** must wait until all codes in **task1** has completed execution. However, if two threads are utilized, as shown at the bottom of the figure, the efficiency of execution for both tasks is improved. This efficiency is achieved because when **task1** is waiting for I/O from the operating system, the idled CPU loads **task2** for execution until the waiting time of **task1** expires or the time for executing **task2** expires. Because CPU speed is measured in nanoseconds, we, as humans, cannot perceive the many swapping operations occurring and the fact that different tasks are executing concurrently. The synchronization and coordination among the threads are major activities performed by the JVM and thread scheduler in the operating system.

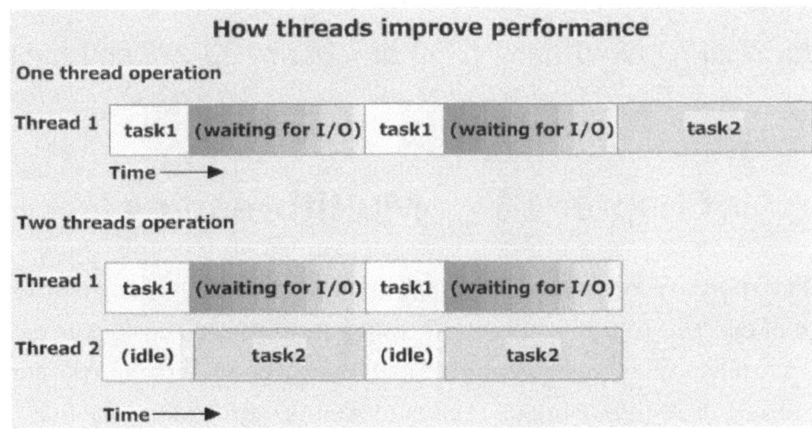

Figure 14.1 Single thread vs. multiple threads

14.1.2 Multitasking and multiprocessing

The operation performed at the bottom of Figure 14.1 is also called a multitasking process. The terms multitasking process and multithreading are interchangeable and refer to such operations performed on a computer with a single main CPU. Multithreads can also be executed in multi-CPU systems, known as multiprocessing. In multiprocessing, multithreads are executed in parallel, and the threads are not frequently swapped for execution by the CPU. Although many modern computers have multi-core CPUs, it still considered as a single main CPU system. This chapter focuses on multithreading in a single main CPU system.

Figure 14.2 shows how a three CPU system executes the two tasks discussed in Figure 14.1. It is obvious the speed of execution is many times faster than with a single CPU, as waiting times are either reduced to a minimum or eliminated.

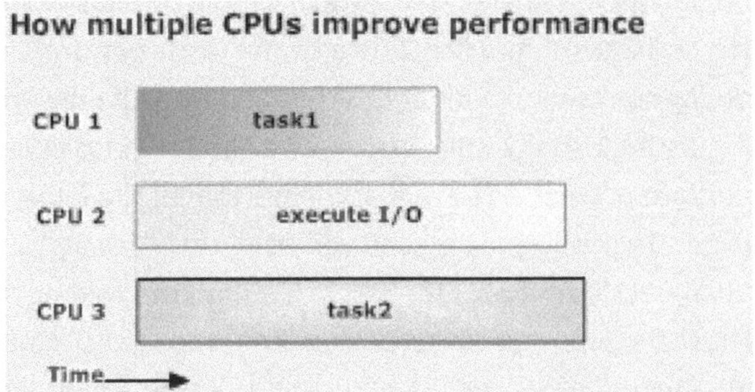

Figure 14.2 Multiprocessing

14.1.3 Multithreading in applications

All Java applications use multithreading even though some operations may not be directly coded in threads by the programmer. Multithreading is commonly used in the following operations:

- Improvement of applications dealing with multiple file I/O, e.g., downloading and uploading files, development of software dealing with file I/O via the Internet.
- Improvement of GUI programming through the performance of event handling operations, e.g., event handling of buttons or menu selections, audio play, image and animation operations that may frequently request CPU time.
- Development of client-server applications that allow multiple clients to access shared resources concurrently by sending requests and asking for responses.
- Development of simulative applications, such as banking or management simulations, event handling, system programming, optimization, scientific research, and military applications. Multithreading often reduces development costs, simplifies design, and improves efficiency.
- Utilization of multi-CPU resources. Most modern operating systems, such as Linux, Unix, and Windows, support multithreading. Multithreading may improve efficiency and reduce program execution risks.

14.1.4 Five statuses of a thread

Before we start developing code using multithreading, we will discuss the five statuses of a thread to gain a better understanding of its behavior. Figure 14.3 shows the life cycle of a thread:

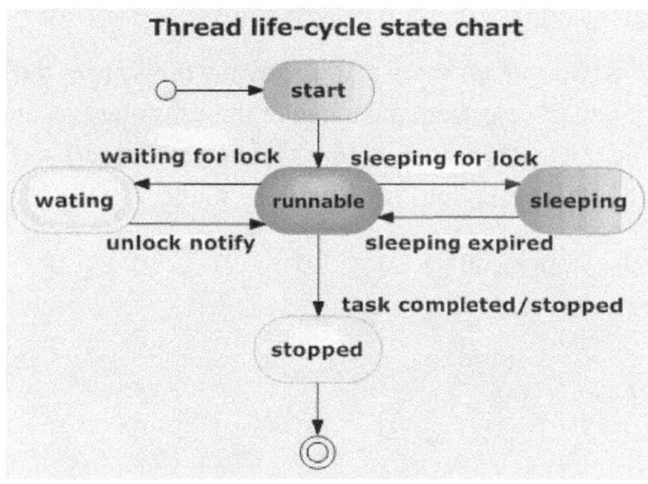

Figure 14.3 The five statuses of a thread

You may see from the figure that when a thread object is created, its **start()** method is called. At this point, the thread will be in the start or ready status waiting for a CPU so it can begin executing. A thread will be in a runnable status when the CPU is scheduled by the operating system to run the thread. There will be three statuses when a thread is runnable: the thread is stopped after completion of its tasks; the thread may be sleeping and will wake up after the sleeping time is expired and returns to runnable status; and the thread may be waiting, upon which, after becoming unlocked, it will be runnable. **Thread** class methods **stop()**, **sleep()**, **wait()** and **notify()** can be called to perform such status changes in a thread object.

14.1.5 A simple example

Study the following code to see how two threads are executed alternately to print a "Hello World" message:

```
//Complete code called SimpleThreadTest.java in Ch14 from the author's website
public class SimpleThreadTest {
   public static void main(String[] args) {
      System.out.println(Thread.currentThread().getName()); //Print thread name
      Thread thread1 = new HelloThread();                     //Create a thread
      Thread thread2 = new HelloThread();                //Create another thread

      thread1.start();                                       //Get each thread ready
      thread2.start();
   }
}
class HelloThread extends Thread {                        //Inherit Thread
   public void run() {                                    //Override run()
      for (int i = 0; i < 10; i++)                        //Print message 10 times
         System.out.println("Hello world! " + this.getName() + " is running...");
   }
}
```

This example shows how the two threads share and display the message in the overridden **run()** method. In addition to printing the message, the name of the currently executing thread printing the message is also displayed by calling **Thread** class methods **currentThread()** and **getName()**. The constructors and commonly used methods in **Thread** can be found in Table 14.1.

The following is a typical execution result:

```
main
Hello world! Thread-0 is running...
Hello world! Thread-0 is running...
Hello world! Thread-0 is running...
Hello world! Thread-0 is running...
Hello world! Thread-0 is running...
Hello world! Thread-0 is running...
Hello world! Thread-0 is running...
Hello world! Thread-0 is running...
Hello world! Thread-1 is running...
Hello world! Thread-1 is running...
Hello world! Thread-1 is running...
Hello world! Thread-1 is running...
Hello world! Thread-1 is running...
Hello world! Thread-1 is running...
Hello world! Thread-1 is running...
Hello world! Thread-1 is running...
Hello world! Thread-1 is running...
Hello world! Thread-1 is running...
Hello world! Thread-0 is running...
```

```
Hello world! Thread-0 is running...
```

You may see the execution result differ if the code is executed several times—the number of executions of a thread may vary. This is caused by the thread scheduling mechanisms in the JVM and the operating system. We discuss this in more detail in later sections.

The following points may be drawn:

1. **main()** method has its own independent thread called **main**.
2. After instantiating a thread, its **start()** method is called to put the thread into the ready or runnable status, waiting for execution.
3. Each thread executes the **run()** method independently and concurrently.
4. If two threads having the same priority are to be executed (as in the above example), the currently executing thread will be swapped out after a certain time period and the other thread will be swapped in and executed in turn.

14.2 Creating Threads

All API classes dealing with threads are provided in the default package **java.lang**. In addition to creating a thread using the **Thread** class, you can also implement the **Runnable** interface, in particular its **run()** method, to instantiate a thread. Table 14.1 shows commonly used constructors and methods in the **Thread** class and **Runnable** interface.

Table 14.1 Commonly used constructors and methods in Thread and Runnable interface

Constructor/Method	Description
Thread()	Creates object of Thread with default priority.
Thread(Runnable obj)	Creates object of Thread containing an object whose run() method is called.
Thread(String name)	Creates object of Thread with specified name.
Thread(Runnable obj, String name)	Creates object of Thread containing an object whose run() method is called. The new object will be of the specified name.
interface Runnable () { void run(); }	Runnable interface. When object implementing Runnable interface is used to create a thread, starting thread calls object's run() method in that separately executing thread. Method must be implemented.
static Thread currentThread()	Returns reference to the currently executing thread object.
String getName()	Returns name of currently executing thread object.
void run()	When object implementing Runnable interface is used to create a thread, starting thread calls object's run() method in that separately executing thread; otherwise, method does nothing and returns.
void start()	Causes thread to begin execution. The JVM calls run() method of this thread.

The following sections discuss the use of the constructors, methods, and interface listed in Table 14.1 through examples.

14.2.1 Inheriting a Thread

Let's first discuss how to inherit a thread created from the **Thread** class by coding an application that prints two different messages using two threads. The first message designed to print "Java SE" and the second print "Programming Art", but they are coded in separate statements for testing.

The steps to code this simple application are as follows:

1. Code two classes, **MessageOne** and **MessageTwo**, that are inherited from **Thread**.
2. In each class, override the **run()** method to carry out the specified task of printing the message.
3. Code the driver code to test the application.

The following is the code of **MessageOne** and **MessageTwo**:

```
//Complete code called MessageOne.java in Ch14 from the author's website
class MessageOne extends Thread {              //thread MessageOne
   public void run() {                         //Override run()
      System.out.print("Java ");
      System.out.print("SE ");
   }
}
class MessageTwo extends Thread {              //thread MessageTwo
   public void run() {                         //Override run()
      System.out.print("Programming ");
      System.out.print("Art ");
   }
}
```

These two threads print different messages.

The following is the driver code:

```
//Complete code called ThreadBasicApp.java in Ch14 from the author's website
public class ThreadBasicApp {
   public static void main(String[] args) {
      // Create two objects of Thread and get ready
      new MessageOne().start();
      new MessageTwo().start();
   }
}
```

There are various output message sequences that may be displayed after executing the code several times:

```
Java Programming SE Art
Java Programming Art SE
```

```
Java SE Programming Art
```

The last display one is the result we are expecting, but it will not be guaranteed without thread synchronization. Synchronization in multithreading is discussed in Section 14.4.

14.2.2 Implementing interface Runnable

The **Runnable** interface is also used to create threads by implementing its **run()** method. Let's modify the example in the above section to implement the **Runnable** interface to perform the same threaded message displays:

```
//Complete code called Message.java in Ch14 from the author's website
class Message {
   public void display(String letters) {                    //Display message
      System.out.print(letters);
   }
}
class MessageJava extends Message implements Runnable {
   public void run() {                                      //Implement run()
      display("Java ");                                     //Call method
      display("SE ");
   }
}
class MessageProgramming extends Message implements Runnable {
   public void run() {                                      //Implement run()
      display("Programming ");
      display("Art \n");
   }
}
```

Message serves as a superclass providing the **display()** method for its subclasses to use. The **Runnable** interface, in particular the **run()** method, is implemented in **MessageJava** and **MessageProgramming** to perform the display of each respective message.

The driver code is modified to create two threads and call their respective **start()** methods to get ready for execution:

```
//Complete code called RunnableBasicApp.java in Ch14 from the author's website
public class RunnableBasicApp {
   public static void main(String[] args) {
      Thread messageJava = new Thread(new MessageJava());       //Create threads
      Thread messageProgramming = new Thread(new MessageProgramming());

      messageJava.start();
      messageProgramming.start();
```

```
    }
}
```

The execution result is the same as in the previous example.

14.2.3 The first look at a producer-consumer application

Producer-consumer interaction is a classical example using multithreading. This model shows the importance of synchronizing the relationship between each party – "producers" producing the products and "consumers" who consume the products. In a more complex situation, there are often many producers and consumers in existence with extensive interactions, thereby requiring synchronization among the multiple threads serving as the key to maintain program integrity.

The following example is a simple simulation of a producer-consumer relationship using two threads only: one for the producer and one for the consumer. The basic concepts and problems associated with using threads are revealed by the example to provide a better basis for the discussion of multithreading synchronization in later sections of this chapter.

Assume the existence of a class called **Shop** containing two threads:

Shop – class to conduct the business between a producer and a consumer. **Producer** provides the product for the shop; **Consumer** buys the product at the shop.

Producer – thread that produces the product.

Consumer – thread that buys/consumes the product.

In order to better understand the concept of this simple use of threads, we display the information provided by both the **Producer** and **Consumer** to indicate the existence of the relationship interaction without performing any "commercial" operations by either party. More complicated applications of multithreading are discussed in later sections.

The following are the steps in establishing the producer-consumer threaded interaction model:

1. Code the class **Shop** containing two static methods, **producing()** and **consuming()**.
2. Code threads **Producer** and **Consumer**, inherited from the **Thread** class, respectively.
3. In the **Producer** and **Consumer** classes, override the **run()** method to perform the specified tasks via methods **producing()** and **consuming()**, respectively.
4. Code the driver code to test the simulation.

The following is the code of **Shop**:

```
//Complete code called Shop.java in Ch14 from author's website
```

```
class Shop {
   private static int numOfProduct = 0;     //Static data showing the business
   public static void producing() {         //Display the producing
      numOfProduct++;
      System.out.println("Number of products available: " + numOfProduct);
   }
   public static void consuming() {         //Display the consuming
      numOfProduct--;
      System.out.println("Number of products available: " + numOfProduct);
   }
}
```

In **Shop**, method **producing()** is accessed by the **Producer** thread to increment the current number of available products, and display the thread name and product information. Thread **Consumer** calls **consuming()** to decrement the number of available products and display the thread name and product information.

The following is the code for **Producer** and **Consumer**:

```
//Complete code called Producer.java in Ch14 from author's website
class Producer extends Thread {                      //Thread Producer
   public void run() {                               //Override run()
      System.out.print(this.getName());              //Print name of thread
      System.out.println( "is producing...");        //Print the product info
      Shop.producing();                              //Call business
   }
}

class Consumer extends Thread {                      //Thread Consumer
   public void run() {                               //Override run()
     System.out.println((this.getName() + " is consuming...");
     Shop.consuming();
   }
}
```

In the overridden method **run()** of **Producer**, **getName()** is called to display the thread name for tracking purposes. It also calls static method **producing()** in the **Shop** class to show associated production information. Similar functionality is found in the overridden **run()** method of **Consumer**.

The following is the driver code:

```
//Complete code called ProducerConsumerBasicApp.java in Ch14 from author's website
public class ProducerConsumerBasicApp {
   public static void main(String[] args) {
      Thread[] producer = new Producer[4];          //Define Producer array
      Thread[] consumer = new Consumer[4];          //Define Consumer array
      for (int i = 0; i < 4; i++) {                 //Create producers and consumers
```

```
            producer[i] = new Producer();
            producer[i].start();                    //Ready for run
            consumer[i] = new Consumer();           //Create Consumer array
            consumer[i].start();                    //Ready
            System.out.println("consumer thread name: " +
                                consumer[i].getName() + " is created...");
        }
        System.out.println("Thread name: " + Thread.currentThread().
        getName());                                 //Print the current thread name
    }
}
```

In the driver code, two arrays of **Producer** and **Consumer**, each containing four elements, are created to perform the producer-consumer simulation. Because no form of synchronization is used, it is possible a consumer may consume a product that does not exist, i.e., **productNumber** is less than or equal to 0. The following is a typical execution result:

```
consumer thread name: Thread-1 is created...
Thread-0 is producing...
Number of products available: 1
Thread-1 is consuming...
Number of products available: 0
Thread-2 is producing...
Number of products available: 1
consumer thread name: Thread-3 is created...
consumer thread name: Thread-5 is created...
consumer thread name: Thread-7 is created...
Thread name: main
Thread-3 is consuming...
Number of products available: 0
Thread-4 is producing...
Number of products available: 1
Thread-5 is consuming...
Number of products available: 0
Thread-7 is consuming...
Number of products available: -1
Thread-6 is producing...
Number of products available: 0
```

You may see that when the number of products available is less than or equal to 0, Thread-7 is still buying/consuming the product.

14.3 Control of Threads

Table 14.2 lists commonly used methods in the **Thread** and Object classes used to control and synchronize threads.

Table 14.2 Commonly used methods of **Thread** and **Object** classes to control and synchronize threads

Method	Description
void interrupt()	Interrupts this currently running thread.
boolean isInterrupted()	Tests to determine if thread is interrupted. If thread is not alive at time of interruption, false is returned.
void join()	"Join" in execution and block currently running thread until completion of execution. Wait for thread to die.
void notify()	Wake a single thread waiting on this object's monitor. The selection of the thread is implementation dependent. Thread waits on object's monitor by calling one of its wait() methods.
void notifyAll()	Wake all threads waiting on this object's monitor. Thread waits on object's monitor by calling one of its wait() methods.
void setPriority(int n)	Sets priority of thread for execution to smaller of specified priority "n" and maximum allowed priority of thread's thread group.
static void sleep(long milliseconds)	Causes currently executing thread to "sleep," i.e., temporarily halt execution, for specified number of milliseconds.
static void yield()	Causes currently executing thread to temporarily pause and allow other threads to execute.
void wait()	Causes currently executing thread to wait until another thread invokes notify() or notifyAll() method for this object.
void wait(long timeout)	Causes currently executing thread to wait until another thread invokes notify() or notifyAll() method for this object or until the specified timeout elapses.

The following sections discuss these methods by examples.

14.3.1 setPriority()

Different operating systems handle priorities in thread executions in varying manners. Under Unix/Linux, the processing of thread execution is based solely upon thread priorities. When the JVM thread scheduler sends threads and their assigned priorities to the operating system, the thread scheduler puts the threads in the waiting queue for the CPU to execute based on their priorities. In this system, a thread with a higher priority may always execute while threads with lower priorities are always in a waiting mode. In the Windows operating system, however, the order of thread executions is based both on priority and assigned time allotment. As such, a thread with a higher priority may cease execution when its time allotment has expired, thereby allowing a thread with a lower priority to be executed.

The range of a thread's priority is determined by the thread's group; typically, this is from 1 (lowest) to 10 (highest), with a default priority of 5. The coder may call **setPriority**() to set the priority of a thread to a desired value. The following code modifies **ThreadBasicApp**, discussed in the previous section, so thread **MessageOne** is assigned the highest priority and is always executed before thread **MessageTwo**:

```
//Complete code called ThreadPriorityApp.java in Ch14 from the author's website
...
Thread messageOne = new MessageOne();
Thread messageTwo = new MessageTwo();
```

```
messageOne.setPriority(10);
messageTwo.setPriority(1);
messageOne.start();
messageTwo.start();
...
```

The expected result of execution is:

```
Java SE Programming Art
```

It is important to note there is no guarantee **messageOne** will complete execution before **messageTwo** even though its priority is higher. This is especially true in the Windows operating system. You must apply other thread synchronization techniques to ensure the desired goal is achieved.

14.3.2 yield()

Method **yield()** causes the currently running thread to temporarily pause, thereby allowing other threads in the ready queue the opportunity to execute. Techniques using **yield()** are the most common form of alternately or interweaving execution between threads.

Example 1. Modify **SimpleThreadTest.java** so it calls **yield()** to alternate the execution between two threads.

```
//Complete code called SimpleThreadYieldTest.java in Ch14 from the author's website
public class SimpleThreadYieldTest {
   public static void main(String[] args) {
      System.out.println(Thread.currentThread().getName());
      Thread thread1 = new HelloThread2();
      Thread thread2 = new HelloThread2();

      thread1.start();
      thread2.start();
   }
}

class HelloThread2 extends Thread {
   public void run() {                        //Override run()
      for (int i = 0; i < 10; i++) {
         System.out.println("Hello world! " + this.getName() + " is running...");
         Thread.yield();                      //Yield to another thread
      }
   }
}
```

A result of executing the code is:

```
main
Hello world! Thread-0 is running...
Hello world! Thread-1 is running...
Hello world! Thread-0 is running...
Hello world! Thread-1 is running...
Hello world! Thread-0 is running...
Hello world! Thread-1 is running...
Hello world! Thread-0 is running...
Hello world! Thread-1 is running...
...
```

You may observe that while the two threads are executed alternately, their distribution may not be even. If you run the code many times, the results may vary. Synchronization techniques are required to guarantee the threads will be executed in an evenly distributed alternating pattern.

14.3.3 sleep()

Static method **sleep()** causes the currently executing thread to "sleep," i.e., temporarily halt execution, for a specified number of milliseconds. It is commonly used for delaying thread execution. After the sleep time has expired, the JVM automatically sets the thread to the ready status, where it waits for execution. This method throws a checked **InterruptedException**, for which the programmer must provide an exception mechanism to handle.

We now modify **SimpleThreadTest** so it uses sleep() to delay thread execution:

```
//Complete code called MessageLanguage.java in Ch14 from the author's website
class MessageLanguage extends Thread {
   public void run() {                          //Override run()
      System.out.print("Java ");
      System.out.print("SE ");
   }
}
class MessageProgramming2 extends Thread {
   public void run() {                          //Override run()
      try {
            //Cause thread to sleep 500 milliseconds to (help) allow
synchronization
            Thread.sleep(500);
            System.out.print("Programming ");
            System.out.println("Art ");
      }
      catch (InterruptedException e) {
            System.out.println(e);
      }
   }
}
```

In this example, **MessageProgramming2** calls **sleep()** to delay the thread's execution for 500 milliseconds (0.5 seconds), thereby allowing the **MessageLanguage** thread to be executed first. The checked exception is handled by a **try-catch** block. In the driver code below, you may see that although the two threads have the same priority and **messageProgramming2** has been waiting for execution before **messageLanguage**, **sleep()** guarantees **messageLanguage** will be executed first.

```
//Complete code called ThreadSleepApp.java in Ch14 from the author's website
//demo: basic threads application using sleep()

public class ThreadSleepApp {
   public static void main(String[] args) {
      Thread messageLanguage = new MessageLanguage();
      Thread messageProgramming = new MessageProgramming2();
      messageProgramming.start();
      messageLanguage.start();
   }
}
```

Using **sleep()** for simple synchronization guarantees the execution result will always be:

```
Java SE Programming Art
```

14.3.4 join()

If a thread requires execution until another thread dies, you can "join" the first thread onto the end of the second thread using method **join()**. For example, if thread **B** is to execute only until thread **A** completes its operations, then thread **B** must join thread **A**. If the joined thread is interrupted, an **InterruptedException** is thrown, and the joined execution is stopped. Method **interrupt()** is discussed in Section 14.3.5. It is important to note that if the caller is executing an infinite loop, the other thread may not have a chance to execute. To prevent such a situation wherein a thread may dominate the execution, Java provides two overloaded **join()** methods setting time limits for the join operation.

In mathematics, the Gregory-Leibniz series: 4 – 4/3 + 4/5 – 4/7 + 4/9 ... is often used to estimate the value of pi. The following example calls **join()** to print the estimated value of pi using the formula "carried" by the thread **Estimate**:

```
//Complete code called ThreadJoinApp.java in Ch14 from the author's website
public class ThreadJoinApp {
   public static void main(String[] args) {
      Thread demo = new Estimate();
      demo.start();
      try {
```

```
            demo.join();              //Block out the main until demo finishes
        }
        catch (InterruptedException e) {
        }
        System.out.println("PI = " + Estimate.PI);  //Display the value
    }
}
//Complete code called Estimate.java in Ch14 from author's website
class Estimate extends Thread {
    public static double PI = 0.0;
        private int sign = 1;

        public void run() {                              //Override run()
        for (long i = 1; i <= 9999999; i += 2)   {   //Estimate PI
            PI += 4.0 * ((double)sign/i);
            sign = -sign;
        }
    }
}
```

The execution result is:

```
PI = 3.1415924535897797
```

Omitting (or commenting out) the statement: **demo.join()** produces an execution result of:

```
PI = 0.0
```

because the **main** thread completes its task first, thereby expiring the life time of the code.

14.3.5 interrupt()

Method **interrupt()** is used to interrupt, i.e., temporarily halt execution, of the currently running thread. When a thread is interrupted it will throw **InterruptedException** and change the thread's status such that calling **isInterrupted()** will return true. Note that **interrupt()** will not affect the execution of the **main** thread.

The following example uses **interrupt()** to monitor a user's keyboard entries:

```
//Complete code called ThreadInterruptApp.java in Ch14 from the author's website
import java.util.Scanner;
public class ThreadInterruptApp {
    public static void main(String[] args) {
        System.out.println("current thread = " + Thread.currentThread().getName());
       System.out.println("Is thread interrupted? " +
Thread.currentThread().isInterrupted());
        Thread service = new Service();              //Create thread
        service.start();                             //Ready for execution
        Scanner sc = new Scanner(System.in);         //Scan the keyboard entry
        String choice = "";
```

```
        while (!choice.equals("stop"))          //If not stop, continue
              choice = sc.next();                       //Waiting for user entry

        service.interrupt();  //If it's stop, call interrupt()
    }
}
class Service extends Thread {                          //Thread Service
    private int count = 1;                              //Counter set to 1
    public void run() {
        while (!isInterrupted()) {
              //Print service information
              System.out.println(this.getName() + " providing service " + count++);
              System.out.println("Type stop to interrupt...");
              try {
                    Thread.sleep(2500);                 //Sleep 2.5 seconds
              }
              catch (InterruptedException e){           //Handle the exception
                    break;                              //Stop the execution
              }
        }
        System.out.println("Thread service is interrupted by user...");
    }
}
```

In this example, if the user enters **stop** on the keyboard, **service.interrupt()** is called to interrupt—in this case halt—execution. However, the code continues to run if any other character is entered. The following is a typical result of execution:

```
Thread-0 providing service 1
Type stop to interrupt...
Thread-0 providing service 2
Type stop to interrupt...
Thread-0 providing service 3
Type stop to interrupt...
Thread-0 providing service 4
stop
Thread service is interrupted by user...
```

14.3.6 Application examples

Example 1. Code an application that uses multithreading to search for the maximum number in a two-dimensional array. You may visualize this as an array of threads having the same number of rows as a two-dimensional array containing random numbers. Each thread is coded to find the maximum number in a given row. As such, it will concurrently and efficiently perform the search for the maximum number in each row, thereby allowing us to finally find the largest number among the threads. Assume we have a 100 x 200 double precision array filled with random numbers and 200 threads created as follow:

```
//Complete code called ThreadFindMaxApp.java in Ch14 from the author's website
public class ThreadFindMaxApp {
   public static void main(String[] args) {
      final int ROW = 100,                                 //2-D array bounds
                COL = 200;
      long startTime = 0,
           endTime = 0;

      MaxThread[] eachMaxThread = new MaxThread[ROW];    //Thread array - 200
      double[][] matrix = Matrix.generator(ROW, COL);    //Random generator
      double max = Double.MIN_VALUE;                   //Max initialization

      for (int i = 0; i < eachMaxThread.length; i++) {   //Create thread array
          eachMaxThread[i] = new MaxThread(matrix[i]);
          eachMaxThread[i].start();                      //Ready for run
      }
      try {
           startTime = System.currentTimeMillis();       //Get the starting time
           System.out.println("start time: " + startTime);
           for (int i = 0; i < eachMaxThread.length; i++) {
              eachMaxThread[i].join();                   //Let each thread finish
              max = Math.max(max, eachMaxThread[i].getMax()); //Get maximum
           }
           endTime = System.currentTimeMillis();
           System.out.println("end time: " + endTime);
      }
      catch (InterruptedException e) {
           System.out.println(e);
      }
      System.out.println("Max of the matrix is: "+ max); //Display maximum found
      //Print execution time
      System.out.println("Completion time: " + (endTime - startTime) + "ms.");
   }
}
//Complete code called MaxThread.java in Ch14 from the author's website
class MaxThread extends Thread {                         //MaxThread class
   private double max = Double.MIN_VALUE;                //Max initialization
   private double[] eachArray;                           //For each row

   public MaxThread(double[] eachArray) {                //Constructor
      this.eachArray = eachArray;
   }
   public void run() {                                   //Override run()
      for (int i = 0; i < eachArray.length; i++) {       //Find maximum
```

```
        max = Math.max(max, eachArray[i]);
      }
    }
    public double getMax() {
      return max;
    }
}
class Matrix {                          //Create 2-D array with random numbers
    public static double[][] generator(int row, int col) { //Static method
      double[][] matrix = new double[row][col];
      for (int i = 0; i < row; i++)
         for (int j = 0; j < col; j++)
            matrix[i][j] = Math.random() * 101;
      return matrix;
    }
}
```

A sample execution result is:

```
start time: 1383069293407
end time: 1383069293408
Max of the matrix is: 100.99867204926774
Completion time: 1 ms.
```

You will see it takes 1 millisecond to let 200 threads find the maximum number in a 100 x 200 array. The execution time will vary in different computer systems.

For comparison purposes, the following code snippet performs the same task without using multithreading:

```
//Complete code called MaxWithoutThreadApp.java in Ch14 from the author's website
...
    long startTime = 0,                //Define the starting time
         endTime = 0;                  //Initialize the ending time
    double[][] matrix = Matrix.generator(ROW, COL); //Or: new double[ROW][COL];
    double max = Double.MIN_VALUE;
    startTime = System.currentTimeMillis(); //Begin time to search
    System.out.println("start time: " + startTime);
    for (int i = 0; i < ROW; i++)
       for (int j = 0; j < COL; j++)
          max = Math.max(max, matrix[i][j]);
    endTime = System.currentTimeMillis();          //End time for search
    System.out.println("end time: " + endTime); System.out.println("Max of
    the matrix is: " + max); System.out.println("Completion time: " +
    (endTime - startTime) + "ms.");
```

```
...
```

The result of execution is:

```
start time: 1383069678895
end time: 1383069678898
Max of the matrix is: 100.99550336335037
Completion time: 3 ms.
```

It is clear that multithreading improves the execution efficiency of the programming task.

14.4 Thread Synchronization

Threads must be synchronized to perform producer-consumer operations. This is critical in situations where threads are using shared resources. For example in Section 14.2.3, **numberOfProduct** is shared by all threads of **Producer** and **Consumer**. A producer cannot produce more products if the number of products exceeds a maximum; a consumer cannot consume a product if none are in the inventory, i.e., **numberOfProduct** = 0. Real world applications usually involve multiple producers and consumers with access to shared resources. The following synchronization problems must be solved in this model:

- When any producer produces a product and increases the inventory, other threads must wait until it completes the production.
- When a consumer buys a product or reduces the inventory, other threads must wait until it completes the consumption.
- The program must control the inventory. In other words, when the inventory reaches an upper limit, producers must stop production and wait until the inventory is reduced to a certain level.
- When the inventory reaches either 0 or certain minimum limit, consumers must stop and wait until the inventory is increased to a level allowing purchases to be made.

14.4.1 Concept of synchronization

Java provides a series of coding techniques to solve synchronization problems in multithreading:

- Use keyword **volatile** to ensure persistence in accessing a shared resource.
- Use keyword **synchronized** to ensure coordination and the proper order of accessing a shared resource.
- Call **wait()** to place the currently executing thread in a waiting status until the other thread calls either **notify()** or **notifyAll()** to wake it up and return it to a ready status.
- Call other methods in **Thread** to control thread execution, e.g., **sleep()**, **join()**, **yield()**, **interrupt()**, **setPriority()**.

Following sections discuss examples using synchronization techniques in multithreading.

14.4.2 Volatile data

Memory cache technology allows for the highly efficient storage of data in memory. However, at any given moment data in main memory may differ from its supporting cache due to the memory updating process. This is especially true in a multithreading environment. A thread accesses the shared data in the temporary cache but not in the destination main memory location. Use of the keyword **volatile** ensures the data a thread accesses is from main memory, not from the cache. This will maintain data integrity and allow persistence.

Example 1. Use of **volatile** in a producer-consumer application.

```
private volatile int consumerNumber = 0;
private volatile String consumerInfo = null;
```

Example 2. Assume many threads share data in an array. Multiple threads sort the array while other threads print the maximum and minimum values of the array. The following code defines the shared data as **volatile**:

```
//Complete code called ThreadSynchronizationApp.java in Ch14 from author's website
...
static final int SIZE = 100;
static volatile int nums[] = new int[SIZE];
static volatile int first = 0;
static volatile int last = 0;
static volatile boolean ready = false;
...
```

Important Note: *Keyword* ***volatile*** *can only be used for primative data types. It only ensures that the data a thread accesses is from main memory rather than cache. It does not coordinate or control the order of execution among the threads.*

14.4.3 Synchronized data access

Java provides the keyword **synchronized** to solve synchronization problems through code monitor and lock techniques. Keyword **synchronized** can be used to define a block of code or an entire method. Monitor and lock techniques ensure that only one thread can access the specified portion of code, and other threads must wait until the currently executing thread completes its task, allowing the lock to be opened and waiting threads to resume execution. Keywords **synchronized** and **volatile** are often used together to ensure data persistence and coordination among the threads.

Example 1. Use **synchronized** to define a block of code so two threads can be synchronized to perform sorting and printing tasks.

```
//Complete code called SynchronizationTest.java in Ch14 from the author's website
public class SynchronizationTest {
   static Shared sharedObject = new Shared();            //Create shared data
   private static class DemoThread1 extends Thread {     //Inner static thread
      public void run() {                                //Override run()
         synchronized (sharedObject) {                   //Define synchronized
block
            sharedObject.sorting();                      //Call sorting()
         }
      }
   }
   static class DemoThread2 extends Thread {      //Another inner static thread
      public void run() {                         //Override run()
         synchronized (sharedObject) {            //Define synchronized block
            sharedObject.printing();       //Call printing()
         }
      }
   }
   public static void main(String[] args) {       //Driver code
         new DemoThread1().run();                 //Create and ready
         new DemoThread2().run();
   }
}
```

For demonstration purposes, the code uses static inner classes to define two threads. The **synchronized** blocks are defined in the overridden **run()** methods of each thread, allowing each to carry out its respective task. When a thread is executing the synchronized block, the other thread must wait until the lock is released. In the driver code, the statement:

```
new DemoThread1().run();
```

is the same as:

```
new DemoThread1().start();
```

This creates an anonymous object of **DemoThread** and calls its **start()** method. This action, however, does not ensure the correct execution result if the keyword **synchronized** is omitted. The code of a programmer-defined class, **Shared**, is:

```
//Complete code called Shared.java in Ch14 from the author's website
import java.util.Arrays;
public class Shared {
   static final int SIZE = 100;                  //Define the array
   static volatile int nums[] = new int[SIZE];   //Use volatile for shared data
   static volatile int first = 0;
   static volatile int last = 0;
```

```
   static volatile boolean ready = false;           //Initialize
   public void sorting() {                          //sorting() method
      ready = false;                                //Not ready
      for (int i = 0; i < nums.length; i++) {       //Array initialization
          nums[i] = (int)(Math.random() * 10000);
      }
      Arrays.sort(nums);                            //Perform array sorting
      for (int num : nums)
         System.out.print(num + " ");               //Print the result
      System.out.println();
      first = nums[0];                              //Minimum data value
      last = nums[SIZE-1];                          //Maximum data value
      ready = true;                                 //Complete
   }
   public void printing() {                         //printing()
      if (ready) {
        System.out.println("the first number: " + first);
        System.out.println("the last number: " + last);
      }
   }
}
```

Example 2. Modify the above example so methods **sorting()** and **printing()** are **synchronized** in their entirety:

```
//Complete code called SynchronizationTest2.java in Ch14 from author's website
private static class DemoThread1 extends Thread {
   public void run() {
      sharedObject.sorting();        //sorting() is a synchronized method
   }
}
static class DemoThread2 extends Thread {
    public void run() {
      sharedObject.printing();       //printing() is a synchronized method
    }
}
```

In a newer version of **Shared** class, **Shared2**, methods **sorting()** and **printing()** are modified to be **synchronized**:

```
//Complete code called Shared2.java in Ch14 from auhtor's website
public synchronized void sorting() {
   ...
}
```

14.4.4 wait()

The **wait()** method is used in conjunction with **notify()** and **notifyAll()** to perform synchronization in multithreading where shared resources are accessed by threads. Method **wait()** throws a checked **InterruptedException**. For example, in the code snippet:

```
try {
     if (!ready)
       wait();
     ...
}
...
```

the use of **wait()** ensures all other threads must wait in a locked mode until ready for execution or until any thread calls **notify()** or **notifyAll()**, for example:

```
if (ready)
   notifyAll();
...
```

This will wake any thread waiting for execution.

Overloaded method **wait(long timeout)** specifies a thread's waiting time (milliseconds), so any thread will not be placed in the extreme case of infinitely waiting for execution. An example of this is discussed in Section 14.4.6.

Note: *Any thread that is in a waiting or sleeping status will change its status due to calling* ***interrupt()****.*

More Information: ***wait(), notify(),*** *and* ***notifyAll()*** *are methods in the* ***Object*** *class. Method* ***wait(long timeout)*** *is an overloaded method of* ***wait()****.*

14.4.5 notify() and notifyAll()

Methods **notify()** and **notifyAll()** are used with **wait()** to wake a waiting thread or all waiting threads, respectively. The following example uses **wait()** in conjunction with **notifyAll()**.

Example 1. We will modify the example previously discussed using searching to find the minimum and maximum values in an array, so the respective results will be guaranteed by using **wait()** and **notifyAll()**:

```
//Complete code called WaitNotifyAllTest.java in Ch14 from the author's website

import java.util.*;
public class WaitNotifyAllTest {
   static Shared3 sharedObject = new Shared3();
   static class DemoThread1 extends Thread {
      public void run() {
         sharedObject.sorting();
```

```
      }
   }
   static class DemoThread2 extends Thread {
      public void run() {
         sharedObject.printing();
      }
   }
   public static void main(String[] args) {
      final int NUM = 1000;
      DemoThread1[] demoSorting = new DemoThread1[NUM];
      DemoThread2[] demoPrinting = new DemoThread2[NUM];
      for (int i = 0; i < demoSorting.length; i++) {
         demoSorting[i] = new DemoThread1();
         demoPrinting[i] = new DemoThread2();
         demoSorting[i].start();
         demoPrinting[i].start();
      }
   }
}

//Complete code called Shared3.java in Ch14 from the author's website

class Shared3 {
   static final int SIZE = 20;
   static volatile int nums[] = new int[SIZE];
   static volatile int first = 0;
   static volatile int last = 0;
   static volatile boolean ready = false;
   public synchronized void sorting() {
      try {
            if (!ready) {
              for (int i = 0; i < nums.length; i++) {
                 nums[i] = (int)(Math.random() * 10000);
              }

              Arrays.sort(nums);
              for (int num : nums)
                 System.out.print(num + " ");
              System.out.println();

              first = nums[0];
              last = nums[SIZE - 1];
              ready = true;

               wait();                //Current thread must wait
             } //if
            else
              ready = false;
```

```
        } // try
        catch (InterruptedException e) {
              System.out.println(e);
        }
    }
    public synchronized void printing() {
        if (ready) {
          notifyAll();          //Notify all other threads to be ready
          System.out.println("the first number: " + first);
          System.out.println("the last number: " + last);
        }
    }
}
```

The execution result is the same as in the previous code.

14.4.6 Application of multithreading with synchronization

We will now use the classical example in multithreading – the simulation of producers and consumers – extending the above discussion to reflect problems in multithreading synchronization:

- **Product** class encapsulates product data and is used by the Producer class.
- Multiple objects of **Producer** and **Consumer** make business transactions in the market place Shop class.
- When a producer is producing or updating product inventory, other threads must wait until it completes.
- When a consumer is consuming or updating product inventory, other threads must wait until it completes.
- A consumer cannot consume a product if the inventory is (less than) 0 and can only consume the same product once.
- Producers and consumers need a certain amount of time to make and buy a product, respectively. Each product has unique product ID.
- Objects of **Producer** and **Consumer** have the same priority in threading.

Based on these assumptions, the **Product** class can be coded as follows:

```
//Complete code called Product.java in Ch14 from the author's website import
java.text.*;                                         //Currency format class
Product {
   private int productID;                            //Product ID
   private double price;                             //Product price
   public Product(int productNumber) {               //Constructor
      productID = productNumber;
```

```
        price = Math.random() * 100 + 5;            //Generate random product prices
    }
    public String toString() {                      //Override toString()
      String amount = NumberFormat.getCurrencyInstance().format(price);
      return "Product ID: " + productID + "\tPrice: " + amount;
    }
}
```

The following is the code of **Shop2**, modified from the original version of **Shop**:

```
//Complete code called Shop2.java in Ch14 from the auhtor's website
import java.util.*;                           //Support for LinkedList<E>
class Shop2 {
   //Product list
   private volatile LinkedList<Product> productQue = new LinkedList<Product>();
   public synchronized void producing(Product product) {//Synchronized method
      while (productQue.size() > 5 ){                  //Product out of bounds
           try {
                wait(100);                             //Wait 0.1 second
                System.out.println("Products are overstocked.
                     Waiting for consumer to buy...");
                System.out.println("Producer " + Thread.
                currentThread().getName() + " is waiting...");
           }
           catch (InterruptedException e) {
                System.out.println(e);
           }
      }
      notifyAll();                                 //Notify all waiting threads
      productQue.addLast(product);                 //Produce the product
                                                   //Display product count
      System.out.println("Number of products available: " + productQue.size());
   }
   public synchronized Product consuming() {       //Synchronized method
      while (productQue.size() == 0) {             //No inventory
           try {
                wait();                            //Wait for inventory
                System.out.println("Number of products available: " +
                productQue.size());
                System.out.println("Consumer " +
                       Thread.currentThread().getName() + " is waiting...");
           }
           catch (InterruptedException e) {
                System.out.println(e);
           }
      }
      return productQue.removeFirst();             //Otherwise consume the product
```

```
    }
    public synchronized int getSize() {                    //Synchronized method
        return productQue.size();                          //Return the inventory number
    }
}
```

In the code, all entities dealing with shared resources, e.g., **productQue**, **producing()**, **consuming()**, and **getSize()**, use keywords **volatile** and **synchronized** to achieve thread synchronization. At any given moment, only one thread is allowed to enter these methods or access shared data and perform an update or transaction operation.

In **producing()**, if the number of products exceeds the upper bound of 5, all producers must wait 0.1 second until they are notified to resume product production.

In **consuming()**, a consumer consumes a product if the inventory is greater than 0, otherwise, all consumers must wait until the number of products meets this requirement. A consumer updates the inventory with each transaction.

A thread may be updating the inventory while another thread access the quantity of inventory. As such, **getSize()** must also be synchronized.

The following is the producer's code, **Producer2**:

```
//Complete code called Producer2.java in Ch14 from the author's website
class Producer2 extends Thread {                                   //Producer thread
    private static volatile int productNumber;                     //Shared data
    private Shop2 shop;
    public Producer2(Shop2 shop) {                                 //Constructor
        this.shop = shop;                                          //The market
    }
    public void run() {                                            //Override run()
        try {
            productNumber++;                                       //Update Product ID
            Product product = new Product(productNumber);//Create product
            Thread.sleep((int)(Math.random() * 1000 + 200));       //Time to make
            shop.producing(product);                               //Product to shop
            System.out.println(product + " produced by " + this.getName());
        }
        catch (InterruptedException e) {
            Thread.currentThread().interrupt();     //Interrupt
        }
    }
}
```

In the code, **productNumber** is defined as **static** and **volatile** because it is shared among all threads. The constructor brings all threads into the market, **shop**. In overriding **run()**, the method first creates a new **productID** and uses it to instantiate a product. Synchronized method **producing()** "brings" the product to the market for consumers to trade. We use a random generator to create a sleep time of 200 to 1199 milliseconds to represent the time needed to make a product. Method **interrupt()** is called if an exception occurs during the production phase.

The following is the code for consumer threads, **Consumer2**:

```
//Complete code called Consumer2.java in Ch14 from the author's website
class Consumer2 extends Thread {                       //Consumer thread
   private Shop2 shop;
   public Consumer2(Shop2 shop) {                      //Constructor
      this.shop = shop;                                //enter the market
   }
   public void run() {                                 //Override run()
      Product product;
      try {
           Thread.sleep((int)(Math.random() * 1000 + 300)); //Create time to trade
           product = shop.consuming();                 //Buy product
           //Print buying information
           System.out.println(product + " is consumed by " + this.getName());
      }
      catch (InterruptedException e) {
           Thread.currentThread().interrupt(); //Interrupt
      }
   }
}
```

The processes associated with a consumer thread are similar to those of a producer thread. Note that different sleeping times are used with each thread category, thereby increasing the difficulty of synchronization among the threads.

The producer-consumer driver code is:

```
//Complete code called ProducerConsumerApp.java in Ch14 from the author's website
public class ProducerConsumerApp {                               //Driver code
   public static void main(String[] args) {
      final int SIZE_OF_PRODUCER = 150;                          //Can be any number
      final int SIZE_OF_CONSUMER = 150;
      Thread producer[] = new Producer2[SIZE_OF_PRODUCER];       //Thread array
      Thread consumer[] = new Consumer2[SIZE_OF_CONSUMER];

      Shop2 shop = new Shop2();                                  //Create the market

      for (int i = 0; i < producer.length; i++) {        //For all threads
```

```
            producer[i] = new Producer2(shop);                    //Share the market
            producer[i].start();                                  //Ready
        }
        for (int i = 0; i < consumer.length; i++) {           //All consumers
            consumer[i] = new Consumer2(shop);                    //Shared
            consumer[i].start();                                  //Ready
        }
    }
}
```

Figure 14.4 shows a typical execution result of this application.

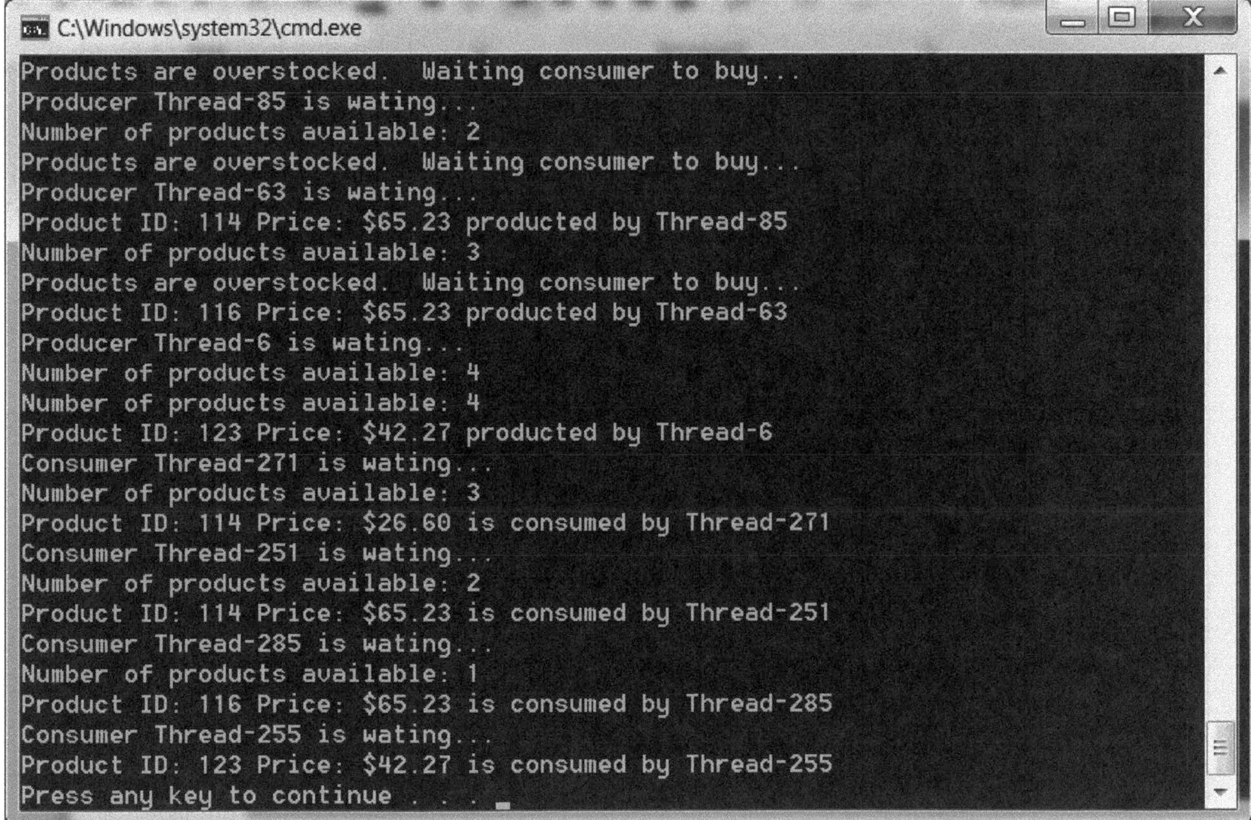

Figure 14.4 A typical execution result of producer-consumer application

14.5 More Multithreading

Multithreading in Java uses monitor and lock techniques to perform synchronized coding applications. We may also have to pay attention to safety and security issues as well as ensuring that resource deadlocks do not occur. Java also provides a variety of collection classes in **java.util.concurrent** to simplify concurrent processing in multithreading and ensure the safety, security, and deadlock issues regarding shared resources. The following sections discuss these topics.

14.5.1 A walk into monitor and lockroom

A monitor technique is used in synchronizing threads with access to shared resources. This is achieved in either a block of code or an entered method by using the Java keyword **synchronized**. When the JVM executes such code, it uses mutual exclusion and a lock technique to ensure only one thread owns the monitor and accesses the shared data or code at a given moment. We call the thread owning the monitor a locked thread.

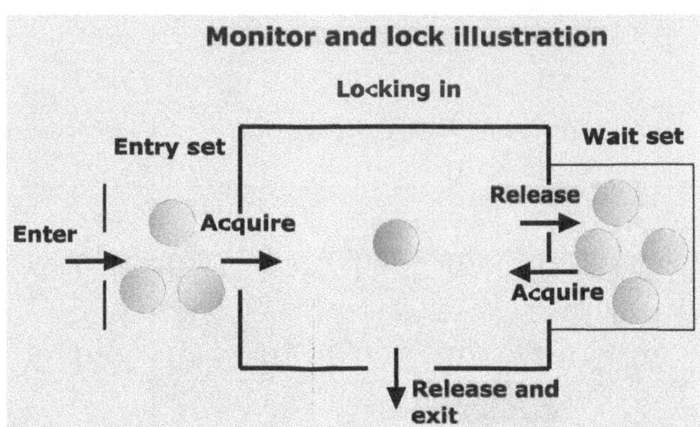

Figure 14.5 Monitor and lock techniques in Java

A thread may experience the following five statuses in a monitor and lock scenario:

1. Entry: a thread may enter the "entry" set and wait for a lock. Many threads may be in the entry set simultaneously.

2. Lock: The JVM randomly selects a waiting thread from either the entry set or waiting room and permits it to own the lock.

3. Wait: a locked thread may give up its locked status and go into the waiting room.

4. Notify: a thread in the waiting room may be selectively notified via random selection performed by the JVM to become locked.

5. Stop: a locked thread that completes its task will give up its lock and exit the monitor.

The JVM randomly selects a thread by a technique called the signal-continue mechanism. This technique may not be the best or most equitable way to allow a thread to own the lock, because a thread with a higher priority and/or a thread that has been waiting for a longer time may not be selected.

14.5.2 Terms in multithreading and techniques

We will now discuss frequently used terms in multithreading and then their use in coding.

Mutability and immutability. If all data in a thread is defined as **final**, this thread class is called a mutable thread or thread with mutability. This technique provides an easy manner to handle synchronization, safety, and security problems in coding. A thread with variable data is called an immutable thread or thread with immutability.

Semaphore. Java semaphores are provided as a class in the **java.util.concurrent** package. Semaphores are used to handle a lock request, lock release, lock tracking, lock limit, and other issues in dealing with synchronization. Detailed discussion of **Semaphore** is beyond this text.

Barrier. A thread on the way to a lock phase will pass through a barrier in order to own the lock. This provides a synchronization aid that allows a set of threads to all wait for each other in reaching a common barrier point. Class **CyclicBarrier** is provided in **java.util.concurrent** to allow programmers define the barrier, but in most cases it is unnecessary to change the system barrier defined by the JVM.

Blocking. Blocking describes the producer-consumer relationship. A producer will be in a blocking mode if it produces an excess amount of product that cannot be consumed; a consumer will be in a blocking if it consumes non-existing product.

Condition variable. Condition variable refers to the current status of the lock and shows the current thread associated with the lock.

Deadlock. Deadlock is a classical problem in multithreading, wherein two threads are locked forever, each awaiting the resources of the other, which can not or will not be released.

Mutex. Mutex is the same as mutual exclusion.

The following techniques are recommended in coding multithreading applications:

- Avoid or reduce the use of immutable data or code.
- Keep synchronized code short and straightforward.
- Avoid or reduce the use of the **interrupt()** method, as it will generate more complexity in synchronization.
- (Try to) avoid creating a new object and calling its method while a thread is in the monitor and lock room in order to reduce deadlock.

14.5.3 Concurrent classes

Many API classes in **Collections** dealing with multithreading have been provided in **java.util.concurrent** since JDK 1.5. For example, **SynchronousQueue** class method **put()**, which automatically blocks the addition of an element in the queue if the number of elements exceeds a defined limit, and **take()**, which automatically blocks the operation of attempting to remove a non-existing element from the queue, make these methods ideal for working with a producer-consumer relationship. Table 14.3 lists commonly used classes and interfaces provided in the **java.util.concurrent** package.

Table 14.3 Commonly used interfaces and classes in Collections dealing with multithreading

Interface/Class	Description
BlockingQueue<E>	Interface for collection with waiting when attempting to consume element in empty queue or production of new element in filled queue.
Callable<V>	Similar to Runnable interface, but will return result and throw checked exception.
Delayed	Interface with method that performs specified delay.
ArrayBlockingQueue<E>	Class using array to set upper limit of elements in queue to perform FIFO operations. It supports synchronization in waiting for consuming an element when queue is empty and for production of new element when queue is full.
ConcurrentLinkedQueue<E>	Unbounded queue based on linked list. Returns null when attempting to consume from empty queue and does not allow production of null element. Used in synchronization of multithreads with share resources.
DelayQueue<Extends Delayed>	Unbounded blocking queue of delayed elements from which element can only be taken when its delay has expired. Returns null if no delay and no head element. Does not allow production of null element.
LinkedBlockingQueue<E>	Queue with optional upper limit based on linked list. Better in efficiency than ArrayBlockingQueue, but execution result may not be predictable in multithreading.
PriorityBlockingQueue<E>	Unbounded blocking queue using same ordering rules as PriorityQueue. Provides blocking element retrieval operations.
SynchronousQueue<E>	Blocking queue in which each element insertion operation must wait for a corresponding element removal operation by another thread, and vice versa.

Example 1. Use of **SychronousQueue** in multithreading.

```
//Complete code called Producer3.java in Ch14 from the author's website
import java.util.concurrent.*;
import java.text.*;
class Producer3 extends Thread {                      //Producer threads
   private final BlockingQueue<Product> bQue;       //Use interface as parameter
   private static int productNumber;
   Producer3(BlockingQueue<Product> que) { bQue = que; }      //Constructor

   public void run() {                                //Override run()
      try {
            Thread.sleep(1000);
            bQue.put(producing());             //Call synchronized put()
      }
      catch (InterruptedException e) { System.out.println(e); }
   }
   Product producing() {                              //Produce product
      productNumber++;
```

```
      Product product = new Product(productNumber);
      return product;                              //Return product
   }
}

class Consumer3 extends Thread {                   //Consumer threads
   private final BlockingQueue<Product> bQue;
   Consumer3(BlockingQueue<Product> que) { bQue = que; }
   public void run() {                             //Override run()
      try {
           consuming(bQue.take());                 //Call synchronized take()
      } catch (InterruptedException e) { System.out.println(e); }
   }
   void consuming(Object product) {
      System.out.println(product + " consumed by " +
                        Thread.currentThread().getName());
   }
}

//Complete code called Product.java in Ch14 from the author's website
class Product {
   private int productID;
   private double price;
   public Product(int productNumber) {
      productID = productNumber;
      price = Math.random() * 100 + 5;             //Randomly generate price
   }
   public String toString() {
      String amount = NumberFormat.getCurrencyInstance().format(price);
      return "Product ID: " + productID + "\tPrice: " + amount;
   }
}

//Complete code called BlockingQueueTest.java in Ch14 from the author's website
public class BlockingQueueTest {                            //Driver
   public static void main(String[] args)  {
      SynchronousQueue<Product> bQue = new SynchronousQueue<Product>();
      Producer3 producer1 = new Producer3(bQue);            //Create two producters
      Producer3 producer2 = new Producer3(bQue);
      Consumer3 consumer1 = new Consumer3(bQue);            //Create two consumers
      Consumer3 consumer2 = new Consumer3(bQue);
      new Thread(producer1).start();               //Ready
      new Thread(consumer1).start();
      new Thread(consumer2).start();
      new Thread(producer2).start();
   }
}
```

A typical execution result is:

```
Product ID: 1   Price: $77.50 produced by Thread-4
Product ID: 1   Price: $77.50 consumed by Thread-6
Product ID: 2   Price: $78.23 produced by Thread-7
Product ID: 2   Price: $78.23 consumed by Thread-5
```

Because **SynchronousQueue** implements **BlockingQueue**, **put()** and **take()** have synchronized wait operations to avoid placing products in a full queue and consuming products from an empty queue, respectively.

Example 2. **DelayQueue** specifies a delay time to put elements in and take elements from a queue. We will use it to code an application delaying the operations on the elements. In using **DelayQueue**, all elements must implement the **Delayed** interface, i.e., method **getDelay(TimeUnit unit)**. **TimeUnit** is an enumeration type data and specifies the units of delay time, e.g., **TimeUnit.SECOND**, **TimeUnit.MILLISECOND**, or **TimeUnit.NANOSECOND**. Method **getDelay()** returns the remaining delay time and will automatically be called in delay operations, allowing the JVM to decide if it is time to perform a put or take operation. **DelayQueue** orders elements in the queue based upon their time delay specifications. Therefore, it requires implementation of the **compareTo()** method of the **Comparable** interface if the element type is programmer-defined. The following code, **NanoDelay**, implements **Delayed**, and is used in the driver code as the elements in **DelayQueue**.

```
//Complete code called NanoDelay.java in Ch14 from the author's website
import java.util.concurrent.*;
class NanoDelay implements Delayed {                //Implement Delayed
   long trigger;
   NanoDelay(long i) {                              //Constructor
      trigger = System.nanoTime() + i; //Call system provided nanosecond plus i
   }
   public int compareTo(Delayed d) {        //Override compareTo()
      long i = trigger;
      long j = ((NanoDelay)d).trigger;
      int returnValue;
      if (i < j) {                                  //See which one is greater
        returnValue = -1;
      } else if (i > j) {
        returnValue = 1;
      } else {
        returnValue = 0;
      }
      return returnValue;
   }
   public long getDelay(TimeUnit unit) {            //Implement getDelay()
      long n = trigger - System.nanoTime();         //Compute delay time
      return unit.convert(n, TimeUnit.NANOSECONDS);       //Convert to nanoseconds
```

```
    }
    public long getTriggerTime() {                    //Return the trigger time
        return trigger;
    }
}
```

The trigger time for adding an element to **DelayQueue** is determined by calling **System.nanoTime()**, which returns the system time plus a random number. The purpose is to generate a different delay time each time an element is created. The difference between the first time and the second time in calling **System.nanoTime()** is the delay time, **n**. The time unit is converted by calling **convert()**, an enumeration type class in **TimeUnit**.

The following is the driver code to test **NanoDelay**:

```
//Complete code called DelayQueueTest.java in Ch14 from the author's
website import java.util.*;
import java.util.concurrent.*;
public class DelayQueueTest {
    public static void main(String args[]) throws InterruptedException {
        Random random = new Random();
        DelayQueue<NanoDelay> queue = new DelayQueue<NanoDelay>();
        for (int i=0; i < 5; i++) {
            queue.add(new NanoDelay(random.nextInt(1000))); //Add element
        }
        long last = 0;
        for (int i=0; i < 5; i++) {
            NanoDelay delay = (NanoDelay)(queue.take());           //Consume
            long triggerTime = delay.getTriggerTime();
            System.out.println("Trigger time: " + triggerTime);
            if (i != 0)
              System.out.println("Delta: " + (triggerTime - last));

            last = triggerTime;
        }//for
    }
}
```

The following is a typical execution result:

```
Trigger time: 21267396780276
Trigger time: 21267396853112
Trigger time: 173921955437154
Trigger time: 173921955457900

Delta: 20746
Trigger time: 173921955465284
Delta: 7384
```

```
Trigger time: 173921955467706
Delta: 2422
Trigger time: 173921955470131
Delta: 2425
```

Exercises

1. What are the features of multithreading? How is code execution speed improved using multithreading? List at least three application examples using multithreading.

2. Use examples to explain the differences and similarities between multitasking and multiprocessing.

3. What are the five statuses of a thread? Which method triggers a thread's runnable status? Explain the difference between the **start()** and **run()** methods.

4. If we can use the **Thread** class to inherit a customized thread in an application, why do we need and use the **Runnable** interface?

5. Use the **Thread** class to code an application in which two threads print the odd and even numbers between 1 and 50, inclusive. One thread will print the odd numbers and its thread name; the other thread prints the even numbers and its thread name. Use the **yield**() method to alternate between the two threads. Assume each thread has the same priority. Write a driver to test your code. Save all files.

6. Based on Exercise 5 above, modify your code as follows:

    a. Assign each thread a different priority. Run the code and observe the execution result. Save all files.

    b. Assign different sleeping times to each thread using the **sleep()** method to alternate execution between the two threads. Remove the existing **yield()** method. Run the code and observe the execution result. Save all files.

7. Use the **Runnable** interface to code an application in which two threads print the odd and even numbers between 1 and 50, inclusive. One thread will print the odd numbers and its thread name; the other thread prints the even numbers and its thread name. Use the **yield**() method to alternate between the two threads. Assume each thread has the same priority. Write a driver to test your code. Save all files.

8. Based on Exercise 7 above, modify your code as follows:

    a. Assign each thread a different priority. Run the code and observe the execution result. Save all files.

b. Assign different sleeping times to each thread using the **sleep()** method to alternate execution between the two threads. Remove the existing **yield()** method. Run the code and observe the execution result. Save all files.

9. Why must threads be synchronized in application codes? List the ways to synchronize threads in coding.
10. What are the differences between **join()** and **interrupt()**? Use example to explain their uses.
11. What is the function of synchronization in multithreading? Use examples to explain multithreading synchronization problems and solutions in coding.
12. What is **volatile** data? Use examples to explain the nature and use of **volatile** data.
13. **Programming Project**: Use multithreading and thread synchronization to code an application simulating a bank deposit and withdrawal process. Set up an account containing an initial balance of $1000.00 with two shared threads, **Husband** and **Wife**. When a thread makes a deposit in an account, the other thread must wait. If the account balance is $0.00, no withdrawals are permitted. Assume a deposit transaction requires 0.2 seconds to complete and a withdrawal transaction requires 0.5 seconds to complete. Establish a list of randomly assigned deposit and withdrawal operations, using integers 1 and 2, respectively. Write a driver to test your application. Save all files.
14. **Programming Project**: Use multithreading and synchronization to code an application simulating bank-rule services and shop-rule services and compare the efficiency of each service model. In the bank-rule model, customers wait in one line to be called to receive service; the shop-rule service model allows multiple lines for customers corresponding to the number of point-of-sale stations. Code two classes, **BankService** and **ShopService**, to simulate these different operations. In each model, assume 100 customers are waiting for service from 5 clerks. You may use one **ArrayList** to store the customers and another to store the clerks. Assume each customer requires 0.2 seconds to be served. Write a driver to test your application and display the service efficiency of each model. Save all files.

"To know what you know and what you do not know, that is true knowledge."

– Confucius

Chapter 15 GUI Components and Programming

The GUI (Graphical User Interface) is an important part of the Java API. GUI components, or GUI API classes, are used to develop user interfaces in a variety of applications. GUI programming involves many Java techniques, such as concepts dealing with components, containers, event handling, and layout managers. In web development, graphical user interfaces are employed via applets, HTML, browsers, and the JVM. "A picture is worth a thousand words;" GUI components bring the effect of "look and feel" by creating a user-friendly environment.

15.1 General Discussion

GUI API classes, considered as components, include windows, buttons, menus, icons, and other GUI widgets in general. Figure 15.1 illustrates an example of some commonly used components.

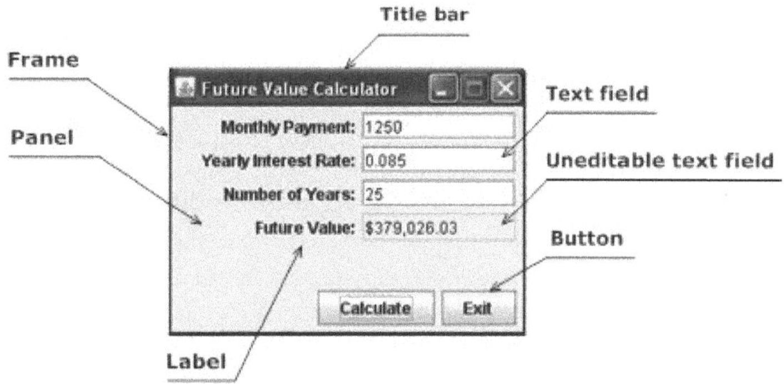

Figure 15.1 Commonly used GUI components

In Java, the component that makes up a window is called a "frame." Normally a component uses a control panel, or simply "panel," to display and perform the desired operations. The window "Future Value Calculator" contains ten GUI components: four(4) labels, four(4) text fields, and two(2) buttons. The last text field is non-editable and is provided for output. In addition to displaying the title of the window, a drop-down menu containing a Java coffee icon, maximum and minimum fields, and an option to close the window are also present. These features are created automatically as the default representation when the frame is initialized. You may recall using **showInputDialog()** and **showMessageDialog()** in the **JOptionPane** class to create input and output windows. They are good examples of rapid coding using GUI components.

15.1.1 AWT and Swing

The Java API provides two types of GUI components: AWT (Abstract Window Toolkit) components and Swing components, each representing a different Java technology.

All Java GUI components developed before JDK 1.2 are AWT components. In AWT, all GUI components dealing with the operating system are coded in low-level machine language and, as such, are not 100% platform independent. AWT components are known as "heavyweight" components because of their dependence upon the underlying native graphics library of a given platform. One problem with an AWT component is that its appearance may differ between various operating systems. In the Java doc specification, all GUI components that do not begin with the letter "J", for example, **Button**, **Frame**, **Menu**, etc., are AWT components.

On the other hand, all GUI components beginning with the letter "J" form the basis of Swing components. Swing components were first introduced in JDK 1.2, thereby allowing Java to become a 100% platform independent language. All GUI components in the Swing package use underlying Java code for their implementation and are known as "lightweight" components.

When Swing components first became available for general use, many internet browsers incorporating both Java applets written in AWT as well as newly released Swing components required the use of the HTML Converter provided in the JDK to convert the code or the downloading of a Java plug-in under which the browsers could run.

All current browsers support Swing components and most applets are coded using Swing components.

In this chapter, we discuss Swing GUI components. Java applets are discussed in Chapter 19.

15.1.2 The inheritance hierarchy

Figure 15.2 shows the inheritance hierarchy of major GUI components.

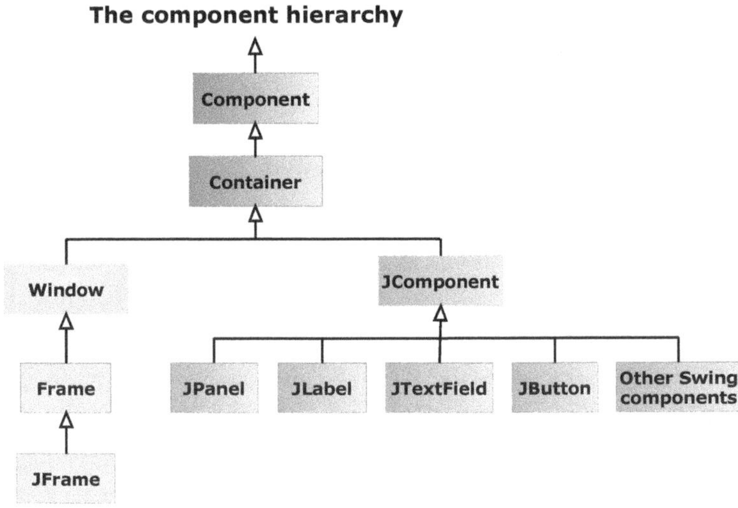

Figure 15.2 The inheritance hierarchy of major GUI components

In Figure 15.2, the **Component** and **Container** classes, serving as superclasses of all other GUI components, are inherited from **Object**. The left side of the figure shows a simplified inheritance of AWT components with one exception: **JFrame**; all other Swing components are inherited from **JComponent**. Other Swing components not shown in Figure 15.2, e.g., **JBox**, **JComboBox**, **JTextArea**, **JList**, and **JMenu**, are discussed in Chapter 17.

All AWT components are provided in the **java.awt** package; Swing components are contained in the **javax.swing** package.

15.1.3 Commonly used methods in Component

The **Component** class provides the basic operations for all GUI components. These operations include setting or returning information regarding the status, size, and location of the displayed component. Table 15.1 lists some commonly used methods in **Component**.

Table 15.1 Commonly used methods in Component class

Method	Description
String getName()	Returns the name of the displayed component.
Component getComponentAt(int x, int y)	Determines if component or one of its immediate subcomponents contains location (x,y). If so, returns the containing component; if false, returns null.
Locale getLocale()	Returns the locale name of the object.
void setSize(int width, int height)	Sets the size of displayed component in *width* and *height* in pixels.
void setLocation(int x, int y)	Sets the location of displayed component. Places the top-left corner of the component at location (x,y) in coordinates of the parent's component.
void setBounds(int x, int y, int width, int height)	Moves and resizes component. The new location of the top-left corner of component is at location (x,y) and the new size is specified by *width* and *height*.
void setEnabled(boolean flag)	Enables or disables component, depending on the value of parameter *flag*. An enabled component can respond to user input and generate events. Components are enabled initially by default.
void setVisible(boolean flag)	Displays component if *flag* is true; otherwise hides object.
void setFocusable(boolean flag)	Sets the focusable state of the component.
boolean isEnabled()	Returns true if component is enabled; otherwise returns false. An enabled component can respond to user input and generate events.
boolean isShowing()	Returns true if component is displayed; otherwise returns false.
boolean isValid()	Returns true if component is valid; otherwise returns false. A component is valid means it's correctly sized and positioned within its parent container and all its children are also valid.

Because all GUI components are inherited from the **Component** class, methods provided by **Component** can be called by all GUI objects. Many setter (setXxx()) methods of this class have corresponding getters (**getXxx()**) methods, and vice versa. The reader is advised to see the Java documentation for complete information.

It is important to note the measurement of all locations and size dimensions (width (x-dimension) and height (y-dimension)) are specified in pixels. Section 15.2.3 discusses how to use the API toolkit to obtain the monitor information of the local computer, including the size and resolution of the display monitor. The upper left corner of the monitor screen is defined as coordinate location (0,0).

The methods listed in Table 15.1 are discussed in the following sections.

15.2 Frame is a Window

As previously discussed, a frame is an object consisting of other GUI components. The following sections discuss the coding of frames.

15.2.1 Display frame

The **JFrame** class provides a variety of methods for coding frames. These methods include creating, initializing, displaying, positioning, (re-)sizing, and returning frame information, as well as event handling and threading. Most of these methods may be categorized as getters, setters, isXxx(), et cetera. You may review the full range of the class methods by referring to the API documentation.

Example: Use **setTile(), setResizable()**, and **setBounds()** in **JFame** to code a window.

```
import javax.swing.*;                                //Load JFrame
class ExampleFrame extends JFrame {
   public ExampleFrame() {                           //Constructor
      setTitle("Example Frame");                     //Set the title
      setBounds(300, 250, 320, 200);         //Set location and size
      setResizable(false);                           //Set resize status
   }
}
```

The example code represents a commonly used form of frame creation. **setResizable()** sets the "resizability" status for the window. In this example, the status is set as false, thereby prohibiting the window from being resized. The default status is true. The following is the driver code for the example:

```
//Complete code called ExampleFrameTest.java in the author's website
public class ExampleFrameTest {
   public static void main(String[] args) {
      JFrame frame = new ExampleFrame();             //Create a window
      frame.pack();                                  //Auto adjust display size
      frame.setVisible(true);                        //Display
   }
}
```

The frame shown in Figure 15.3 is generated as a result of executing the above code.

Figure 15.3 A simple window

15.2.2 Close window

The above example does not include a means of handling the event associated with closing the window. Therefore, when the close button on the top right corner of the window is clicked, the operating system will not display any information associated with the window closing. Method **setDefaultCloseOperation()** in **JFrame** handles such an event. Table 15.2 lists commonly used static fields in the method associated with handling a window closing event.

Table 15.2 Commonly used static fields in method **setDefaultCloseOperation()**

Method/Static field	Description
void setDefaultCloseOperation()	Uses default mode to close the window.
void setDefaultCloseOperation(int action)	Uses specified mode to close the window.
JFrame.EXIT_ON_CLOSE	Exits the application using the current System exit mode and return to the operating system.
WindowConstants.DO_NOTHING_ON_CLOSE	Closes window without any specified mode; the closing code must be provided in the event handling.
WindowConstants.HIDE_ON_CLOSE	The default mode for closing the window.
WindowConstants.DISPOSE_ON_CLOSE	Closes the window and exits the JVM (equivalent to System.exit()).

Example: Set **System.exit()** to be invoked when the window is closed.

```
import javax.swing.*;
class ExampleFrame extends JFrame {
   public ExampleFrame() {
      setTitle("Example Frame");
      setBounds(300, 250, 320, 200);
```

```
        //Exit from JVM upon closing the window
        setDefaultCloseOperation(WindowConstants.DISPOSE_ON_CLOSE);
        setResizable(false);
    }
}
```

15.2.3 Position and size controls

Because the specifications of computer monitors can vary, it is important to know this data to allow positioning and sizing of the displayed window. The **Toolkit** and **Dimension** classes provide many methods to retrieve such information from the local computer. **Toolkit** and **Dimension** belong to the **java.awt** package. Abstract class **Toolkit** can be used to get many important data, e.g., current content of the clipboard, location of the mouse pointer, desktop properties, fonts and font families, color specifications, screen data, and system events, et cetera, associated with the local computer. **Dimension** is used in obtaining and setting the width and height of a GUI component. It is most often used in conjunction with **Toolkit**. Other important classes, such as **GraphicsEnvironment**, **Rectangle**, and **Point**, are also included in the **java.awt** package. **GraphicsEnvironment** is used to obtain the list of available fonts, the specification of display devices, and data of input/output devices of the local computer. The **Rectangle** and **Point** classes are used to encapsulate the data involved in the drawing of rectangle objects and the establishing of coordinate systems. Because the return type of **GraphicsEnvironment** is either a **Rectangle** or **Point** object, we discuss these two classes as well.

Table 15.3 lists commonly used methods in **Toolkit** and **Dimension** dealing with data of the screen in the local computer. Other methods in these two classes are discussed in Chapter 20.

Table 15.3 Commonly used methods in Toolkit and Dimension

Method	Description
static Toolkit getDefaultToolkit()	Toolkit method. Returns object with property data of local computer.
Dimension getScreenSize()	Toolkit method. Returns a Dimension object with screen width and height of local computer.
double getHeight()	Dimension method. Returns height of screen in Dimension object.
double getWidth()	Dimension method. Returns width of screen in Dimension object.
static GraphicsEnvironment getLocalGraphicsEnvironment()	GraphicsEnvironment method. Returns object of GraphicsEnvironment with data of the graphic environment of local computer.
Point getCenterPoint()	GraphicsEnvironment method. Returns coordinates of central position of the object of GraphicsEnvironment.
Rectangle getMaximumWindowBounds()	GraphicsEnvironment method. Returns window size encapsulated in object of

	Rectangle.
double getX()	Rectangle method. Returns x-coordinate of component's origin in the object of Rectangle.
double getY()	Rectangle method. Returns y-coordinate of component's origin in the object of Rectangle.
Point getLocation()	Rectangle method. Returns Point object with coordinate data of the upper left corner of the displayed object.

More Info: ***Dimension also provides static fields of the width and height of the current object by which the data may be accessed using dot notation. Methods involving coordinate operations in the Point class are similar to those in the Rectangle class.***

Example: Using methods in Table 15.3 to obtain screen data from the local computer.

```
//Complete code called ToolkitTest.java in Ch15 from the author's website
import java.awt.*;
Toolkit tk = Toolkit.getDefaultToolkit(); //Call method to return Toolkit object
Dimension d = tk.getScreenSize();          //Call method to get screen size

System.out.println("My screen width: " + d.getWidth());         //Display width
System.out.println("My screen height: " + d.getHeight());       //Display height

//Get the graphic environment of local computer
GraphicsEnvironment environment = GraphicsEnvironment.
getLocalGraphicsEnvironment();
Rectangle rec = environment.getMaximumWindowBounds();    //get maximum window size

System.out.println("Centered width: " + rec.getCenterX());    //Display x
System.out.println("Centered Height: " + rec.getCenterY());   //Display y
System.out.println("My Screen dimensions: " + rec);           //Display screen size

Point point = environment.getCenterPoint();                   //Get center coordinates
System.out.println("Center of screen: " + point); //Display coordinates

point = rec.getLocation();                                    //Get screen coordinates
System.out.println("Location of my screen: " + point);  //Display it
```

The following is the result of execution displaying data associated with the current graphics environment and hardware of a particular computer:

```
My screen width: 1024.0
My screen height: 768.0
Centered width: 512.0
Centered Height: 369.0
My Screen dimensions: java.awt.Rectangle[x=0,y=0,width=1024,height=768]
Center of screen: java.awt.Point[x=512,y=369]
Location of my screen: java.awt.Point[x=0,y=0]
```

15.2.4 More examples

Write a program to open a window centered on the screen that is one-half the size of the monitor.

```
//Complete code called ExampleFrameTest.java in Ch15 from the author's website
import javax.swing.*;
import java.awt.*;
class ExampleFrame extends JFrame {
   Toolkit tk = Toolkit.getDefaultToolkit();      //Return object of Toolkit
   Dimension d = tk.getScreenSize();         //Return object of Dimension
   public ExampleFrame() {
      setTitle("Example Frame");
      setSize(d.width/2, d.height/2);
      //Call method JFrame's setSize() to access the data
      setDefaultCloseOperation(WindowConstants.DISPOSE_ON_CLOSE);
      centerWindow(this);     //Call user-defined method for centering display
      setResizable(false);
   }

   //User-defined method to display a window at the center of the screen
   private void centerWindow(JFrame frame){
      //Compute center coordinates of window
      int centeredWidth = ((int)d.getWidth() - frame.getWidth())/2;
      int centeredHeight = ((int)d.getHeight() - frame.getHeight())/2;

      setLocation(centeredWidth, centeredHeight); //Set the center position
   }
}
...
```

In this example, we use **d.width** and **d.height** to directly access the static fields encapsulated in object **d**. Methods **d.getWidth()** and **d.getHeight()** will also perform the same operations. It is important to note the return type of **getWidth()** and **getHeight()** are both **double**; however, the argument type of **setLocation()** is **integer**. You must therefore convert the double data to integer type. The data obtained using **d.width** and **d.height** can be directly used with **setLocation()**, as they have been converted to integer types by the JVM.

15.3 Control panel - JPanel

JPanel is one of the more important subclasses in **JComponent**. For good practice in sophisticated applications requiring a more polished interface, displaying, positioning, event handling, controlling, and other operations are all performed through **JPanel**. Although applications programmers do not normally concern themselves with the internal details of how **JPanel** functions, further information about **JPanel** will help in coding and can be found on some popular Java websites.

15.3.1 Example

In the example of Section 15.1, we created a window—an empty window with no defined component. Although GUI components may be directly displayed in a window without the use of **JPanel**, it is highly recommended the programmer to use **JPanel** to organize and manage all components.

```
//Complete code of ButtonPanel.java, ButtonFrame.java, and
//ButtonFrameTest.java are in Ch15 of the author's website

import javax.swing.*;
import java.awt.*;

class ButtonPanel extends JPanel {          //Button panel
   private JButton myButton;                //Declare button
   public ButtonPanel() {                   //Constructor
      myButton = new JButton("My button"); //Create two buttons, or code as:
      this.add(myButton);                   //add(myButton); add button
   }
}
class ButtonFrame extends JFrame {
   Toolkit tk = Toolkit.getDefaultToolkit();
   Dimension d = tk.getScreenSize();
   public ButtonFrame() {
      setTitle("Example Button Frame");
      setSize(d.width/2, d.height/2);
      setDefaultCloseOperation(WindowConstants.DISPOSE_ON_CLOSE);
      centerWindow(this);                   //Call central display method
      JPanel panel = new ButtonPanel();//Create object of the panel
      this.add(panel);                      //Add the panel to window
      setResizable(false);
   }
   ...
}
```

ButtonPanel inherits from the **JPanel** class. The constructor creates an object of **JButton**, **myButton**, that is then added to the panel. The **ButtonFrame** class creates an object of **ButtonPanel**, then adds this object to the window along with functionality to set the window's title, size, and closing mode. A user-defined method is called to display the window at the center of the screen. A window one-half the size of the screen with a button, **myButton**, at the top center is displayed upon executing the code.

Because we did not provide any code for event handling, nothing happens when the button is clicked. Furthermore, **myButton** is placed at the top center of the window because the default layout manager is automatically applied to the frame. Event handling and layout managers are discussed in later sections of the chapter.

15.3.2 Steps in GUI coding

The basic steps in GUI component coding can be summarized based upon the examples we have discussed:

1. Code a class inheriting **JPanel** to allow better control and management of the GUI components. Using this class, GUI components can be created and added to the panel. You may use either **add(nameOfComponent)** or **this.add(nameOfComponent)** for improved readability. The above codes are usually written in the constructor of the panel class.

2. Code event handling capabilities in the panel class. Event handling of GUI components is discussed in Section 15.14.3.

3. Code the layout manager in the panel class for positioning each of the GUI components. Layout managers are discussed in Chapter 16.

4. Code a class inheriting from **JFrame** to allow more flexible control and management of the panels and windows. In this class, the panel object is created and added to the frame by calling either **add(nameOfPanel)** or **this.add(nameOfPanel).** The title, position, size, and closing mode of the window are also coded in this class.
5. Code the driver to test the components displayed in the window.

The following sections discuss each of these five steps in detail.

15.4 Buttons

Buttons are the most frequently used GUI components. Table 15.4 lists commonly used constructors and methods in **JButton.**

Table 15.4 Commonly used methods in JButton

Constructor/Method	Description
JButton()	Creates a button without button name(text) or icon.
JButton(String name)	Creates a button with specified name or text.
JButton(Icon icon)	Creates a button with specified icon image.
JButton(String name, Icon icon)	Creates a button with specified name and icon image.
void addActionListener(ActionListener listener)	Adds ActionListener capabilities to button for event handling.
String getText()	Returns button text.

void setBackground(Color bg)	Sets background color of button.
void setEnabled(boolean b)	Sets button as enabled if true; otherwise disable button.
void setForeground(Color fg)	Sets foregrond color of button.
void setFont(Font font)	Sets font of displayed characters.
void setName(String name)	Sets name (text) of button.
void setSize(int width, int height)	Sets width and height of button.
void setVisible(boolean b)	Sets visibility of button: visible, if true; invisible if false.

Note: *All setXxx() methods have corresponding getXxx() methods.*

The following section discusses examples of these commonly used methods in coding buttons. Please note additional GUI-related methods may also be employed in the examples. An example relating to the coding of button color, font, and icon attributes is discussed in Chapter 20.

15.4.1 Examples in buttons

Example 1. Create a button.

```
JButton ok = new JButton();                //Create button without display name
JButton exit = new JButton("Exit"); //Create a button named Exit
```

Example 2. Get the name of the button.

```
String buttonName = exit.getName();        //Return the button's name: "Exit"
```

Example 3. Use the **setXxx()** methods in **JButton** class.

```
ok.setEnabled(false);         //Disable the button so its event cannot be handled.
ok.setName("Ok");             //Set the button's name as Ok
ok.setSize(50, 20);           //Change button's width and height in pixels.
ok.setVisible(false);         //Hide the button.
```

Example 4. Display **Ok** and **Exit** buttons in a window. Follow the steps listed in Section 15.3.2 and write the code:

```
//Complete code called TwoButtonPanel.java in Ch15 from the author's website
import javax.swing.*;
class TwoButtonPanel extends JPanel {        //Code the panel to arrange the buttons
   private JButton okButton, exitButton;     //Declare two buttons
   public TwoButtonPanel() {                 //Constructor
      okButton = new JButton("Ok");          //Create two buttons
      exitButton = new JButton("Exit");
      this.add(okButton);                    //Add buttons to panel
      this.add(exitButton);                  //Or code as:  add(okButton);
                                             //             add(exitButton);
```

```
    }
}
//End of the panel class

//Code the frame class
//Complete code called TwoButtonFrame.java in Ch15 from the author's website
import javax.swing.*;
import java.awt.*;
class TwoButtonFrame extends JFrame {
   Toolkit tk = Toolkit.getDefaultToolkit();
   Dimension d = tk.getScreenSize();
   public TwoButtonFrame() {
      setTitle("Two Button Frame");
      setSize(300, 200);                   //Width 300, Height 200 in pixels
      setDefaultCloseOperation(WindowConstants.DISPOSE_ON_CLOSE);
      centerWindow(this);                  //Call the method
      JPanel panel = new TwoButtonPanel(); //Create object of the panel
      this.add(panel);                     //Add the panel to the frame
   }
   //Method to display window at center of screen
   private void centerWindow(JFrame frame) {
      int centeredWidth = ((int)d.getWidth() - frame.getWidth())/2;
      int centeredHeight = ((int)d.getHeight() - frame.getHeight())/2;
      setLocation(centeredWidth, centeredHeight); //Set display location
   }
}

//Complete driver code TwoButtonFrameTest.java in Ch15 from the author's website
public class TwoButtonFrameTest {
   public static void main(String[] args) {
      JFrame frame = new TwoButtonFrame();
      frame.setVisible(true);
   }
}
```

The execution result is shown in Figure 15.5.

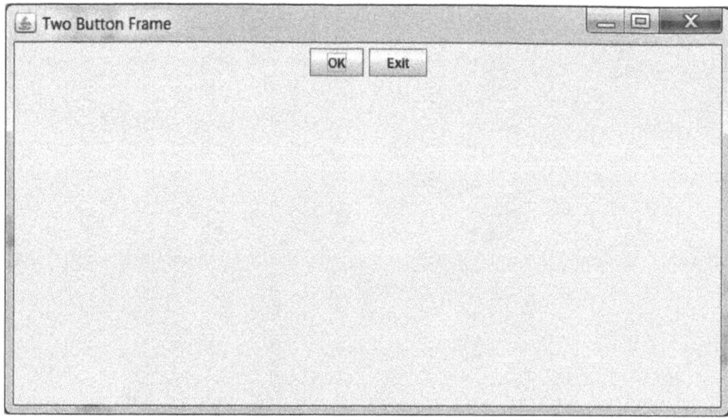

Figure 15.5 Two buttons in a window

Example 5. Use the **pack()** method in **JFrame** to automatically adjust displayed components. Method **pack()** automatically makes adjustments allowing the preferred size and layout of the components. Assume the following statement that purposely sets the window size smaller than the space required to completely display the image is used in **TwoButtonFrame**:

```
setSize(30, 20);//purposely set size smaller than required display space
```

We then add the **pack()** method to the driver code:

```
JFrame frame = new TwoButtonFrame();
frame.pack();                    //Automatically adjust button display
frame.setVisible(true);
```

Figure 15.6 shows the comparison of the display before and after using the **pack()** method in the code.

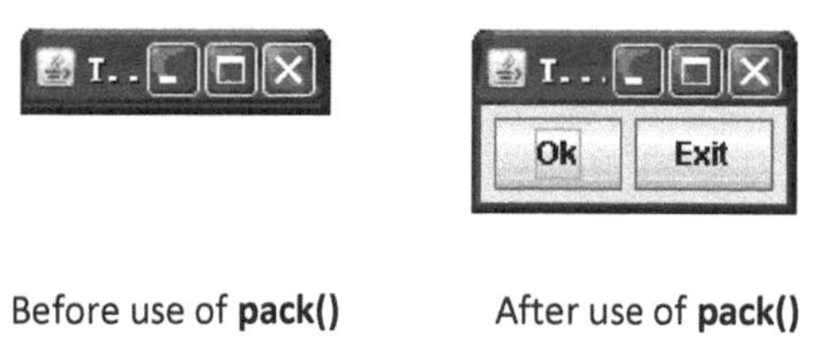

Before use of **pack()**   After use of **pack()**

Figure 15.6 Comparison using **pack()** method

15.4.2 Default layout manager

You may notice we did not explicitly specify the location for the buttons to be displayed in the window, yet the buttons are displayed in the top center of the window. In Java, if the code does not supply the specified display location using the layout manager, the default location—top center of the frame—will be used. The following code snippet shows how the **TwoButtonPanel** class may be written using the default layout manager scenario:

```
class TwoButtonPanel extends JPanel {      //Code the panel to arrange the buttons
   private JButton okButton, exitButton;   //Declare two buttons
```

```
    public TwoButtonPanel() {                        //Constructor
        //Code (italicized) representing default layout manager
        this.setLayout(new FlowLayout(FlowLayout.CENTER));
        okButton = new JButton("Ok");                //Create two buttons
        exitButton = new JButton("Exit");
        this.add(okButton);                          //Add buttons to panel
        this.add(exitButton);                        //Or code as:  add(okButton);
                                                     //             add(exitButton);

    }
}
```

The **FlowLayout** class is one of six layout managers provided by the Java API. It is considered the most basic layout and is used as the default layout manager of **JPanel** objects. The location of a GUI component can be specified in the display frame using the three **FlowLayout** fields: **LEFT**, **CENTER**, and **RIGHT**. The default specifier is **CENTER**. The **FlowLayout** manager's default positioning of the components is from left-to-right starting with the specified location. It will position a component on the next line with the specified location if no space is available for display on the previous line. As such, under **FlowLayout** the actual location of a component may vary depending on the size of the window in which it is displayed.

Layout managers are discussed in Chapter 16.

More information: *Although **setX()** and **setY()** methods are provided in GUI programming to position a component, the use of a layout manager to design, arrange, and control the location of a component is highly recommended.*

15.4.3 Button event handling

When a user "mouse clicks" a component such as a button, the clicking operation actually triggers an event; in this case, a button event. No action will be performed if event handling functionality associated with the button is absent from the code. Java provides many interfaces that may be implemented to handle a variety of events. The most common event handling mechanism is the **ActionListener** interface. The interface has only one method to be implemented: **actionPerformed()**. When an event occurs in the code, **actionPerformed()**, if present, is automatically executed to handle the event. Event handling, including keyboard events and mouse events, is discussed in detail in Chapter 20.

A variety of ways exist to code event handling procedures within Java. The following steps are recommended to perform basic event handling of commonly used GUI components:

1. Import the **java.awt.event** package and implement the **actionListener** interface:

```
import java.awt.event.*;
```

```
class TwoButtonPanel extends JPanel implements ActionListener { ... }
```

2. Call method **addActionListener()** to register or add the event associated with the component to be handled in the code.

```
componentName.addActionListener(this);
```

3. Code the **actionPerformed()** method to handle the processing of the event:

```
public actionPerformed(ActionEvent e) {
   Object source = e.getSource();
   if (source == componentName) {
            //The operations performed by the event
      ...
   }
   else ...
}
```

The following snippet uses the steps above to handle the events associated with the two buttons coded in the example discussed in Section 15.4.1:

```
//Provide event handling in the control panel
//Complete code called TwoButtonPanel2.java in Ch15 from the author's website
import javax.swing.*;
import java.awt.*;
import java.awt.event.*;      //Import the package for event handling

//Inherits JPanel and implements the ActionListener interface
class TwoButtonPanel2 extends JPanel implements ActionListener{
   private JButton okButton, exitButton;    //Declare two buttons
   public TwoButtonPanel2() {               //Constructor
      okButton = new JButton("Ok");         //Create two buttons
      exitButton = new JButton("Exit");
      this.add(okButton);
      this.add(exitButton);
      //Add ActionListener event handling capabilities to each button
      okButton.addActionListener(this);
      exitButton.addActionListener(this);
   }
   public void actionPerformed(ActionEvent e){ //Implement method to handle event
      //Obtain source of triggered event
      Object source = e.getSource();
         if (source == okButton) {          // Event source:  okButton
            JOptionPane.showMessageDialog(null, "Ok button is pressed...");
```

```
        }
        else if (source == exitButton) {    //Event source:  exitButton
            JOptionPane.showMessageDialog(null, "Goodbye!\nPress Exit to
close window...");
            System.exit(0);                    //exitButton event is handled
        }
    }
}
```

During execution of the above code, an event will be triggered when a button receives a mouse click. The event will automatically call method **actionPerformed()** and obtain the name of the event source object (either **okButton** or **exitButton**) to serve as the method's parameter. Calling method **getSource()** of the **EventObject** class allows us to determine which of the two buttons actually triggered the event, thereby allowing the event to be properly handled by executing the appropriate code associated with each respective button. In the example, when **okButton** is pressed, the message “Ok button is pressed...” is displayed; when **exitButton** is pressed, the message “Goodbye! Press Exit to close window...” is displayed and program execution is terminated.

15.5 Lables and Text Fields

Labels, in the form of text or images, are used to explain the meaning of other components. **JLabel** is commonly used to provide accompanying text fields. **JTextField** provides a mechanism for accepting keyboard input or displaying output information. Java also provides a security-enhanced text field for entering passwords with **JPasswordField**. The following section discusses these GUI components.

15.5.1 JLabel

Table 15.5 lists commonly used constructors and methods in **JLabel**.

Table 15.5 Commonly used constructors and methods in JLabel

Constructor/Method	Description
JLabel()	Creates a label with an empty string for the title.
JLabel(String text)	Creates a label displaying the specified text.
JLabel(Icon icon)	Creates a label displaying specified icon image.
Icon getIcon()	Returns the graphic image displayed in the label.
String getText()	Returns the text displayed in the label.
setIconTextGap(int space)	Sets specified space (pixels) between displayed text and icon image.

The following examples use these constructors and methods to create and display fields.

Example 1. Create a panel to display 3 labels.

```
//Complete code called DisplayPanel.java in Ch15 from the author’s website
class DisplayPanel extends JPanel {        //Code the panel to display labels
private JLabel productLabel, quantityLabel, totalLabel;
```

```
    public DisplayPanel() {                                    //Constructor
        productLabel = new JLabel("Enter product name:");      //Create 3 labels
        quantityLabel = new JLabel("Enter quantity:");
        totalLabel = new JLabel("Total amount:");
        this.add(productLabel);                                //Add labels
        this.add(quantityLabel);
        this.add(totalLabel);
    }
}
```

Example 2. Since labels are normally used without event handling, the object name of the label is not important. The following code creates three unnamed labels and displays them in the top right corner of the window.

```
//Complete code called DisplayPanel.java, DisplayFrame.Java, and
//DisplayFrameTest.java are available from the author's website
import javax.swing.*;
import java.awt.*;
class DisplayPanel extends JPanel {                        //Code panel to display
    public DisplayPanel() {                                //Constructor
        setLayout(new FlowLayout(FlowLayout.RIGHT));       //Display on right side
        add(new JLabel("Enter product name:"));            //Create 3 unnamed labels
        add(new JLabel("Enter the quantity:"));
        add(new JLabel("The total amount:"));
    }
}
```

Figure 15.7 shows the execution result.

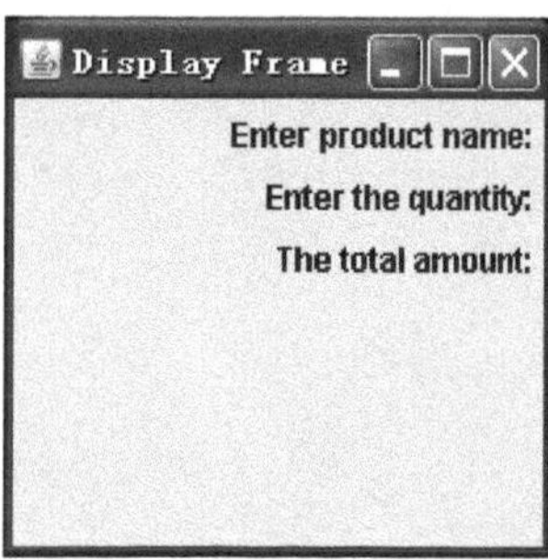

Figure 15.7 Display 3 labels in a window

15.5.2 JTextField

Table 15.6 lists commonly used constructors and methods of **JTextField**.

Table 15.6 Commonly used methods in JTextField

Constructor/Method	Description

JTextField()	Creates a text field with an initial string of null and the number of displayed columns set to 0.
JTextField(String text)	Creates a text field with the specified text displayed.
JTextField(int columns)	Creates a text field with the specified number of columns.
JTextField(String text, int columns)	Creates a text field with specified text displayed and length in columns.
void addActionListener(ActionListener listener)	Adds the specified ActionListener to receive action events associated with the text field.
int getColumns()	Returns the displayed length (columns) of the text field.
String getText()	Returns the displayed text in the text field component.
void setColumns(int columns)	Sets the specified length (columns) of the text field.
void setText(String text)	Sets the specified text for display in the text field.
void setEditable(boolean b)	Sets the specified boolean indicating if the text field is editable (true) or non-editable (false). The default is true.

The following examples use these **JTextField** constructors and methods in establishing text fields.

Example 1. Create three text fields.

```
//Complete code called DisplayFrame2Test.java in Ch15 from the author's website
import javax.swing.*;
import java.awt.*;
class DisplayPanel2 extends JPanel {  //Code the panel to display the text fields
  private JTextField productField, quantityField, totalField;
  public DisplayPanel2() {                          //Constructor
     setLayout(new FlowLayout(FlowLayout.RIGHT));        //Right alignment

     //Create a text field with 18 columns and add it to the panel
     productField = new JTextField(18);
     add(productField);

     //Create a text field with 15 columns and add it to the panel
     quantityField = new JTextField(15);
     add(quantityField);

     //Create a non-editable (display-only) text field with 10 columns containing
     //the associated displayed text and add it to the panel
     totalField = new JTextField("$0.00", 10);
     totalField.setEditable(false);
     add(totalField);
  }
}
```

Figure 15.8 shows the result of executing the above code. Note the bottom text field is non-editable and contains the specified text.

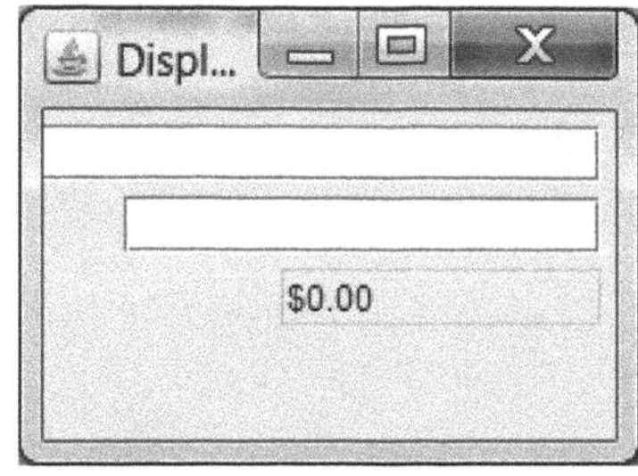

Figure 15.8 Three text fields are displayed in a window

Example 2. Example coding snippets illustrating other methods in **JTextField**.

```
//Display the text ($0.00) contained in the text field totalField
System.out.println(totalField.getText());

//Set the displayed text of text field productField to:  Laptop
productField.setText("Laptop");

//Set and display the length, as measured in text columns, (15) of quantityField
quantityField.setColumns(15);
System.out.println(quantityField.getColumns());
```

15.5.3 Event handling in text fields

Text field events are normally triggered by other components, such as buttons. For example, we may call the **getText()** method to retrieve the contents in a text field after a "submit" button is mouse-clicked. Of course, we may also use the button's own interface, e.g., **TextListener**, to handle a text field event. This is discussed in later chapters. This section focuses on the handling of events triggered by buttons.

The following code segment shows modifications made to the above example to handle events associated with the computation and display of product information or stopping code execution when the appropriate button is clicked.

```
//Complete code is called ProductCalculatorPanel.java, ProductCalculatorFrame.java
//and ProductCalculatorApp.java from the author's website

//Declare components and content data
private final double CD_PRICE = 2.99, DVD_PRICE = 19.89;
private JLabel productLabel, quantityLabel, totalLabel;
private JTextField productField, quantityField, totalField;
private JButton okButton, exitButton;

//Create and add components to panel and handle event
public ProductCalculatorPanel() {
   //Add components to panel
   ...
   //Add event handling
   okButton.addActionListener(this); //Add Ok button for event handling
```

```
   exitButton.addActionListener(this);      //Add Exit button for event handling
}
public void actionPerformed(ActionEvent e){  //Implement event handling interface
   Object source = e.getSource();                    //Get the source of the event
   if (source == okButton) {                         //If event source is Ok button
      if (productField.getText().equals("CD")) {  //Get the product name
         int quantity = Integer.parseInt(quantityField.getText());     // Get
number
         double total = CD_PRICE * quantity;      //Compute and display total
         totalField.setText(NumberFormat.getCurrencyInstance().format(total));
      }
      else if (productField.getText().equals("DVD")) {   //Get product name
            int quantity = Integer.parseInt(quantityField.getText());
            double total = DVD_PRICE * quantity;
            totalField.setText(NumberFormat.getCurrencyInstance().format(total));
      }
      else {                                  //Wrong product name
           JOptionPane.showMessageDialog(null, "Entry error!\n
               + Please check product name and try again...");
           System.exit(0);                    //Stop execution
      }
   }
   else if (source == exitButton) { //If event source is exitButton
           JOptionPane.showMessageDialog(null, "Goodbye!\nPress OK to close
              window...");
           System.exit(1);                    //Stop execution
   }
}
...
```

We may also use method **getActionCommand()** to identify the component triggering the event:

```
public void actionPerformed(ActionEvent e) {              //Implement the method
   if (e.getActionCommand().equals("Ok"))  {              //If the event from Ok
      if (productField.getText().equals("CD")) {          //Get the product name
         //All other codes are the same
             ...
      }
   }
}
```

The complimentary method **setActionCommand()** can be used to set the event triggered by the specified component for example,

```
okButton.setActionCommand("OK");    //Set the event triggered by OK
```

The simulated event may then be handled as:

```
if (e.getActionCommand().equals("OK")  {   //If OK triggered the event
   ...
```

```
}
```

We discuss more about event handling in Section 15.7.

15.5.4 JPasswordField

JPasswordField is similar to **JTextField** and is used to handle text field input requiring a measure of safety. It displays the entered string as a user-defined character, e.g., "*", in the input field. Table 15.7 lists commonly used constructors and methods in **JPasswordField**.

Table 15.7 Commonly used constructors and methods in JPasswordField

Constructor/Method	Description
JPasswordField()	Creates a password text field with a null starting string and a column length of 0.
JPasswordField(String text)	Creates a password text field initialized with the specified character display.
JPasswordField(int columns)	Creates a password text field with specified column length.
void addActionListener(ActionListener listener)	Adds the specified action listener to receive action events from the text field component.
int getColumns()	Returns the length in columns of the password text field.
char getEchoChar()	Returns the character to be displayed in the password text field. Default: "*".
void setEchoChar(char c)	Sets the "echoed", i.e., displayed, character in the password text file. Note that this is largely a suggestion, since the installed view can use any desired graphic techniques to represent the field. Setting a value of 0 allows the entered text to be seen as it is typed, similar to the behavior of a standard **JTextField**.
char[] getPassword()	Returns the password entered in the password text field.

Example 1. Create an object of **JPasswordField** and add event handling capabilities.

```
public PasswordPanel() {

  //Display password field of column length 15 containing echo character "*"
  private JPasswordField passwordField = new JPasswordField(15);

  add(passwordField);                                  //Add to the panel
  passwordField.addActionListener(this);               //Add to event handling
}
```

Example 2. Use of other methods in **JPasswordField**.

```
passwordField.setEchoChar('a');       //Set the displayed character as 'a'
System.out.println(passwordField.getPassword()); //Display the entered password
String password = new String(passwordField.getPassword()); //Retrieve the password
```

15.5.5 Application example

The following modifies the example in Section 15.5.3 by requiring the user to enter a password before running the application. Figure 15.9 shows the data input window:

Figure 15.9 The input window showing the password entry

A panel enabling the application password is coded as follows:

```
//Complete code called PasswordPanel.java in Ch15 from the author's website
import javax.swing.*;
import java.awt.*;
import java.awt.event.*;
class PasswordPanel extends JPanel implements ActionListener{
  private JPasswordField passwordField;           //Declare a password text field
  private JButton okButton, exitButton;
  public PasswordPanel() {                        //Constructor
     setLayout(new FlowLayout(FlowLayout.RIGHT));
     add(new JLabel("Enter your password:"));     //Create and add label
     //Create password field of length(columns) 10
     passwordField = new JPasswordField(10);
     add(passwordField);                    //Add the password field to the panel
     okButton = new JButton("Ok");          //Create two buttons
     exitButton = new JButton("Exit");
     add(okButton);                         //Add Ok button to the panel
     okButton.addActionListener(this);      //Add Ok button for event handling
     add(exitButton);                       //Add exit button to the panel
     exitButton.addActionListener(this);    //Add exit button for event handling
  }
  public void actionPerformed(ActionEvent e) {   //Implement event handling
     Object source = e.getSource();         //Get the source of the event
     if (source == okButton) {      //If okButton triggered the event
         String password = new String(passwordField.getPassword());
         if (password.equals("abc123")) {//If password is correct
```

```
            this.setVisible(false);//Remove password display
            JFrame frame = new ProductCalculatorFrame();
            frame.setVisible(true);//Display window
        }
        else {                          //Password input error
              JOptionPane.showMessageDialog(null, "Entry error!\n
                 + Please check password and try again...");
              System.exit(0);           //Stop execution
              }
      }
      else if (source == exitButton) {//If exitButton triggered event
              JOptionPane.showMessageDialog(null, "Goodbye!\nPress OK
                 to close window...");
              System.exit(1);           //Handle event
      }
   }
}
```

Within the event handling code segment, the entry of the correct password, **abc123**, causes the program to close the password text field and establish and display the product calculation window. Because **getPassword()** returns the entered password as a string, we create a string object and use its constructor to encapsulate the password.

The window for processing the password is similar to the one for performing the product calculation; you may refer to the code **PasswordFrame.java** in Ch15 from the author's website. The following is the driver code to run this application:

```
//Complete code called PasswordApp.java in Ch15 from the author's website
import javax.swing.*;
public class PasswordApp {
   public static void main(String[] args) {
      JFrame frame = new PasswordFrame();          //Create the window
      frame.pack();                                //Auto adjust
      frame.setVisible(true);                      //Display the window
   }
}
```

15.6 JTextArea

A text area is used to enter, edit, and display a block of text that is typically in a format containing multiple lines. Table 15.8 lists commonly used constructors and methods of **JTextArea**. Many methods in **JTextArea** are the same as those in **JTextField**; they are not listed in the table.

Table 15.8 Commonly used constructors and methods in **JTextArea**

Constructor/Method	Description

JTextArea()	Creates a text area with an initial string of null and the number of columns and rows set to 0.
JTextArea(String text)	Creates a text area with specified displayed text content. The number of columns and rows is set to 0.
JTextArea(int row, int columns)	Creates an empty text area with the specified number of columns and rows.
JTextArea(String text, int row, int columns)	Creates a text area containing the specified text with specified number of columns and rows.
void append(String text)	Appends the specified text to the end of text area.
void insert(String text, int position)	Inserts the specified text at the specified position.
String setText(String text)	Sets the specified text in the text area.
void setLineWrap(boolean wrap)	Sets the line wrapping policy of the component. If *wrap* is true, characters exceeding the width of the text area are wrapped back to the next line; if *wrap* is false, the lines will be unwrapped. Default is false
void setWrapStyleWord(boolean word)	Sets the style of wrapping if line wrapping is enabled. If set to true, lines too long to fit in the allocated space will be wrapped at word (whitespace) boundaries ; if false, lines will be wrapped at character boundaries. Default is false.

The following section discusses the use of the **JTextArea** constructors and methods.

NOTE: *Columns and rows are measured by the number of characters currently in use.*

15.6.1 Create text areas

Example 1. Create a text area with 8 rows and 30 columns to display the specified content.

```
private JTextArea exampleArea;         //Declare an object of JTextArea
exampleArea = new JTextArea(8, 30);    //Create an object with 8 rows and 30
columns
exampleArea.setWrapStyleWord(true);    //Wrap words in display
exampleArea.setText("Example text displayed in the text area. ");  //Display it

add(exampleArea);                      //Add to the panel
```

The above code will display a text area measuring 8 rows by 30 columns with the content:

```
Example text displayed in the
text area.
```

You may note the words are automatically wrapped onto the next line when the text line length exceeds the number of specified columns. However, the wrapped text portion will not be displayed if **setWrapStyleWord()** is omitted or set to false. As such, the wrapped text, “text area”, would not be displayed.

Example 2. Use of other methods in **JTextArea**.

```
//Create the specified text area
JTextArea textArea = new JTextArea("another example of text area. ", 2, 20);
add(textArea);                                   //Add to the panel
//Insert content at beginning of text area
textArea.insert("This is an ", 0);
//Append content to end of text area
textArea.append(" This is another example of text area.");
System.out.println(textArea.getText());    //Output the content on the console
```

15.6.2 JScrollPane

JScrollPane is used to provide horizontal and vertical scroll bars in the text area, thereby allowing any content exceeding the size of the allotted text area to be viewed. **JScrollPane** is provided in the **javax.swing** package. Table 15.9 lists commonly used constructors and static fields in **JScrollPane**.

Table 15.9 Commonly used constructors and methods in JScrollPane

Constructor/Static fields	Description
JScrollPane (Component name)	Creates an object of JScrollPane for the specified GUI component. Scroll bar(s) will be displayed when the contents are larger than the view.
JScrollPane(Component name, int vertical, int horizontal)	Creates an object of JScrollPane for the specified GUI component with the specified scroll bar modes.
static final int VERTICAL_SCROLLBAR_ALWAYS	Always display vertical scroll bar.
static final int VERTICAL_SCROLLBAR_AS_NEEDED	Display vertical scroll bar if needed.
static final int VERTICAL_SCROLLBAR_NEVER	Do not display vertical scroll bar
static final int HORIZONTAL_SCROLLBAR_ALWAYS	Always display horizontal scroll bar.
static final int HORIZONTAL_SCROLLBAR_AS_NEEDED	Display horizontal scroll bar if needed.
static final int HORIZONTAL_SCROLLBAR_NEVER	Do not display the horizontal scroll bar.

Note: ***JScrollPane*** *provides many methods and fields not listed in Table 15.9. Please refer to the* ***JScrollPane*** *documentation for further information.*

The steps to effectively code a **JScrollPane** component are:

1. Create a GUI component that may require the use of scroll bars.
2. Create an object of **JScrollPane** by encapsulating the object requiring scroll bars to the constructor of **JScrollPane**.
3. Add the object of **JScrollPane** to the panel.
4. Add the GUI component to the panel along with any required event handling capabilities. Implement the interface for event handling, as required.
5. Add the panel to the frame.

6. Create an object of **JFrame** and call the method to display the window.

15.6.3 Application example

The following application modifies the example discussed in Section 15.6.1 to use a scroll pane and event handling to copy the content in the text area to an output window of **JOptionPane**.

```
//Complete code called TextAreaPanel.java is available in Ch15 of author's website
import javax.swing.*;
import java.awt.event.*;
class TextAreaPanel extends JPanel implements ActionListener{
   final int vScroll = JScrollPane.VERTICAL_SCROLLBAR_AS_NEEDED,
             hScroll = JScrollPane.HORIZONTAL_SCROLLBAR_ALWAYS;
   private JTextArea textArea;
   private JScrollPane scroll;
   private JButton copyButton;
   public TextAreaPanel() {                                  //Constructor
      textArea = new JTextArea("another example of text area. ", 2, 20);
      //Create a text area
      textArea.setWrapStyleWord(true);
      textArea.setLineWrap(true);
      add(textArea);                          //Add the text area to panel
      //Create scroll pane for the text area
      scroll = new JScrollPane(textArea, vScroll, hScroll);
      add(scroll);                            //Add scroll pane to the panel
      copyButton = new JButton("Copy >>"); //Create a button
      add(copyButton);                        //Add the button to panel
      copyButton.addActionListener(this); //Add the button for event handling
   }
   public void actionPerformed(ActionEvent e) {    //Implement the interface
      Object source = e.getSource();          //Get event source
      if (source == copyButton) {                    //If event source is the button
         //Add content to beginning of text area
         textArea.insert("Welcome to Text Area and Scroll Application.  This is ",
0);
         //Append additional text to above content textArea.append("This is
         another example of text area. "); JOptionPane.showMessageDialog(null,
         textArea.getText());                                      //Copy content
      }
      else                                           //Otherwise
         System.exit(0);                             //Stop the execution
   }
}
```

The code creates a scroll pane for a text area, a text field, and a button using the first four steps of the **JScrollPane** component coding guidelines described above. It uses methods **insert()**, **append()**, and

getText() to insert content at the beginning of the text area and append content to the end of the text area before copying the entire body of text to the **JOptionPane** window.

The code of **TextAreaPanel**, **TextAreaFrame**, and the driver code are similar to other examples discussed in the chapter. You may refer to examples in **TextAreaFrame.java** and **TextAreaApp.java** in Ch15 from the author's website. Figure 15.10 shows a typical execution result.

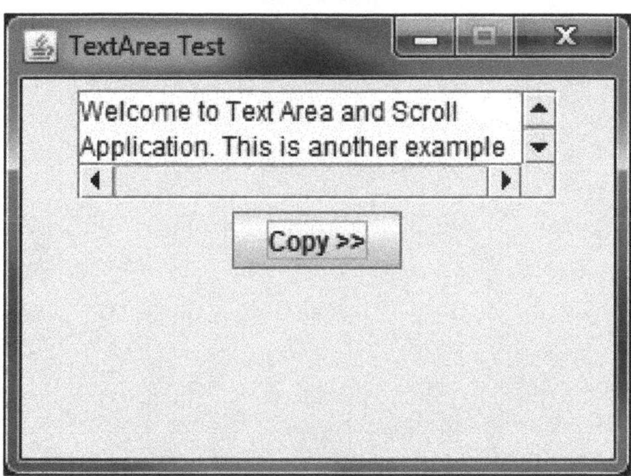

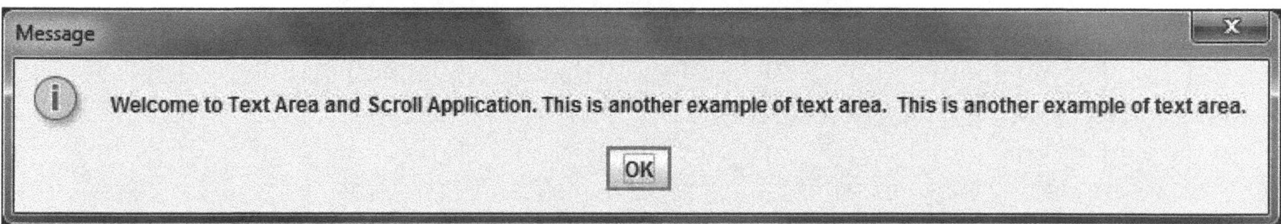

Figure 15.10 Execution result of the application with scrolling pane

15.7 JCheckBox

Check boxes provide a mechanism for making selections in a GUI window. Multiple check boxes can be organized for managing the choices. A check box may have its own label or image representing the description of the choice. A check box can be set as the default when the box is created. Table 15.10 lists commonly used constructors and methods in **JCheckBox**.

Table 15.10 Commonly used constructors and methods in **JCheckBox**

Constructor/Method	Description
JCheckBox(String text)	Creates object with displayed text and an initially unselected check box.
JCheckBox(String text, boolean selected)	Creates object with displayed text and specifies if check box is initially selected (true) or unselected (false).
JCheckBox(Icon icon)	Creates object with displayed icon and an initially unselected check box.
JCheckBox(String text, Icon icon)	Creates object with displayed text and icon and initially unselected check box.
void addActionListener(ActionListener listener)	Adds action listener event handling capabilities to the object.

boolean isSelected()	Returns true if check box is selected; otherwise returns false.
void setSelected(boolean selected)	Sets state of check box: selected if true; unselected if false.
String getActionCommand()	Returns name of the check box in the triggered event.
void setActionCommand(String command)	Sets name of the check box for the selection action command.

Note: *You may refer Chapter 20 for information about check boxes with icon displays.*

Example 1. Create three check boxes.

```
private JCheckBox pingPongBox, swimmingBox, tennisBox;  //Declare 3 check boxes.
pingPongBox = new JCheckBox("Pingpong", true);    //Create and set default
selection
swimmingBox = new JCheckBox("Swimming");          //Create other 2 check boxes.
tennisBox = new JCheckBox("Tennis");
add(new JLabel("Select your habit:"));      //Create a label and add to the panel
add(pingPongBox);                           /Add the check box to the panel
pingPongBox.addActionListener(this);//Add the event handling
...
```

Example 2. Call various methods in **JCheckBox**.

```
if (swimmingBox.isSelected())                    //If swimmingBox is selected
    JOptionPane.showMessageDialog(null, "Your selection is swimming." );
//Display
pingPongBox.setActionCommand("Pingpong");        //Set the event as Pingpong
if (inputField.getText().equals("Tennis"))       //If the selection is Tennis
    tennisBox.setSelected(true);                 //Set the selection is true
```

15.7.1 Event handling in JCheckBox

When a check box changes its selection status, an event is triggered and the information is sent to the implemented **actionPerformed()** in **Actionlistener**. This sequence of operations is similar to handling events in text fields. As such, we need to code event handling in the **actionPerformed()** method. For example:

```
JCheckBoxTestPanel extends Panel implements ActionListener {
  //Create objects
  ...
  public void actionPerformed(ActionEvent e) {
     Object source = e.getSource();
     if (source == pingPongBox && pingPongBox.isSelected())
        JOptionPane.showMessageDialog(null, "Your hobby is playing ping pong" );
        //Other code in the event handling
```

```
        ...
    }
}
```

You may also use **getActionCommand()** to perform the same activity:

```
public void actionPerformed(ActionEvent e) {
   if (e.getActionCommand().equals("Pingpong"))
       JOptionPane.showMessageDialog(null, "Your hobby is playing ping pong." );
       //Other code in event handling
       ...
}
```

15.7.2 Application example

The following example uses check boxes, labels, text fields, and buttons in an application designed to search for book publication information. The user is first prompted to enter a book code in the text field. After the user clicks the button, the complete book title and two check boxes containing author and publisher information are displayed. Additional data is displayed after a verification check box selection is clicked.

```
//Complete code called BookInfoPanel.java, BookInfoFrame.java and BookInfoApp.java
//in Ch15 from the author's website

class BookInfoPanel extends JPanel implements ActionListener{
  private JLabel entryLabel;
  private JTextField entryField, titleField;
  private JCheckBox authorBox, publisherBox;                 //Declare check boxes
  private JButton okButton;
  public BookInfoPanel() {                                   //Constructor
   entryLabel = new JLabel("Enter the book code:");
   add(entryLabel);
   entryField = new JTextField("Java or C/C++", 12);         //Default display text
   add(entryField);
   entryField.addActionListener(this);
   titleField = new JTextField(43);
   titleField.setEditable(false);                    //Output only
   titleField.setVisible(false);                     //Hide display first
   add(titleField);
   authorBox = new JCheckBox("Author", true);        //Create the box and selected
   authorBox.setVisible(false);                      //Hide first
   add(authorBox);                                   //Add to the panel
   authorBox.addActionListener(this);                //Add to the event handling
   publisherBox = new JCheckBox("Publisher");        //No default selection
   publisherBox.setVisible(false);                   //Hide display first
   add(publisherBox);                                //Add to the panel
   publisherBox.addActionListener(this);             //Add to the event handling
```

```
    okButton = new JButton("Ok");
    add(okButton);
    okButton.addActionListener(this);
  }
...
}
```

You may note the **setVisible(false)** method is called in association with the objects in **BookInfo** to hide the display of **titleField**, **authorBox**, and **pressBox**. The following code segment provides event handling to update the display statuses for these three components after the user enters the correct book title:

```
public void actionPerformed(ActionEvent e) {      //Implement the interface
   Object source = e.getSource();                 //Get the source of the event
   String info = null;
   if (source == okButton) {
       if (entryField.getText().equals("Java")) {
           titleField.setText("Programming Art in Java");
           info = titleField.getText();
           setVisibles();  //Call method to update display status
       }
       else if (entryField.getText().equals("C/C++")) {
               titleField.setText("Complete Programming in C/C++");
               info = titleField.getText();
               setVisibles(); //Call method to update display status
       }
   }
   if (source == okButton && authorBox.isSelected()) {//If the button is selected
       info += getAuthorInfo();                 //Call method to get information
       titleField.setText(info);                //Display information
    }
   if(source == okButton && publisherBox.isSelected()) { //Similar to above
       info += getPressInfo();
       titleField.setText(info);
    }
}
```

The code calls three methods, **setVisibles()**, **getAuthorInfo()** and **getPressInfo()**, to update the display status of the components and retrieve the information about the author and publisher:

```
public void setVisibles() {                     //Method setVisibles()
   entryLabel.setVisible(false);                //Do not display the label
   entryField.setEditable(false);               //Do not display the text field
   titleField.setVisible(true);                 //Display the book title field
   authorBox.setVisible(true);                  //Display the author  box
   pressBox.setVisible(true);                   //Display the publisher box
```

```
}
public String getAuthorInfo() {              //Method getAuthorInfo()
   return ", Gao Yong Qiang, Ph.D."; //Return author's info
}
public String getPressInfo() {               //Method getPressInfo()
   return ", Tsinghua University Press.";  //Return publisher information
}
```

The code of **BookInfoFrame** and the associated driver code are similar to other examples previously discussed. Figure 15.11 shows the result of a typical code execution sequence. The top portion of the figure shows the window when the application is initially executed; it then displays the window in the lower portion of the figure after the user selects a book code, e.g., "Java", and presses the **Ok** button. The complete information of the selected book is displayed in an uneditable text field.

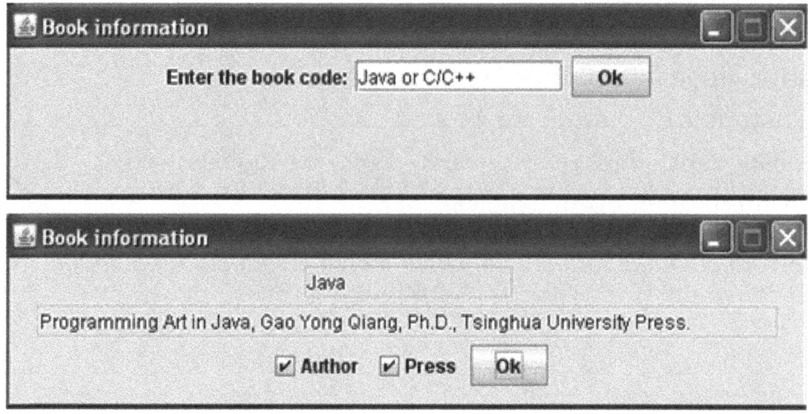

Figure 15.11 A typical execution result of check box application

15.8 JRadioButton

Radio buttons are commonly grouped together for selection. However, unlike check boxes, you may only select one radio button in the group. We use **ButtonGroup** to group radio buttons for synchronization.

Table 15.11 lists commonly used constructors and methods in **JRadioButton** and **ButtonGroup**.

Table 15.11 Commonly used constructors and methods in **JRadioButton** and **ButtonGroup**.

Constructor/Method	Description
JRadioButton(String text)	Creates an initially unselected radio button with the specified text.
JRadioButton(String text, boolean selected)	Creates a radio button of the specified selection state with the specified text.
JRadioButton(Icon icon)	Creates an initially unselected radio button with the specified icon.
JRadioButton(String text, Icon icon)	Creates an initially unselected radio button with the specified text and icon.
void addActionListener(ActionListener listener)	Adds action listener event handling capabilities to the object.
boolean isSelected()	Returns true if the radio button is selected; otherwise

	return false.
String getActionCommand()	Returns name of the radio button in the triggered event.
setActionCommand(String command)	Sets name of the radio button for the selection action command.
void add(AbstractButton name)	Adds the specified object to the button group.
void clearSelection()	Clears the selection such that no button in the button group is selected.
int getButtonCount()	Returns the number of buttons in the button group.

The following steps describe the procedures for creating, adding, and establishing event handling capabilities for radio buttons:

1. Create an object of **JRadioButton**.
2. Add the object to the control panel.
3. Create the button group using **ButtonGroup**.
4. Add the radio button to the button group.
5. Add event handling capabilities to be associated with the radio button.
6. Implement the interface for event handling.
7. Repeat Steps 1, 2, 4, 5, and 6 for each remaining button in the specified button group.

Example: Use of constructor and methods to create radio buttons.

```
//Create three buttons; set "check" button as "selected"
check =  new JRadioButton("Check", true);
creditCard = new JRadioButton("Credit Card");
debitCard = new JRadioButton("Debit Card");

//Add radio buttons to the panel
add(check);
add(creditCard);
add(debitCard);

//Create button group and add each radio button to the group
ButtonGroup paymentGroup = new ButtonGroup();
paymentGroup.add(check);
paymentGroup.add(creditCard);
paymentGroup.add(debitCard);

//Add event handling capabilities for each radio button
check.addActionListener(this);
creditCard.addActionListener(this);
debitCard.addActionListener(this);
```

15.8.1 Event handling with radio buttons

As with check boxes, radio buttons may trigger an event. Although you may use the **ItemListener** interface to handle events occurring with radio buttons, in certain cases radio button events are handled in association with other GUI components, such as button. The **ItemListener** interface is discussed in Chapter 17.

Assume we have created and added the three radio buttons as discussed in above section. The following code snippet creates other components, e. g., labels and buttons, to handle the radio button event:

```
//Complete code called JRadioButtonPanel.java, JRadioButtonFrame.Java, and
//JRadioButtonTest.java from the author's website
public void actionPerformed(ActionEvent e) {  //Implement the event handling
   Object source = e.getSource();            //Get the source of the event
   if (source == okButton) {
      //If OK triggered event and if radio button is selected, display information
       if (check.isSelected())
           JOptionPane.showMessageDialog(null, "Check is selected...");
       else if (creditCard.isSelected())
                 JOptionPane.showMessageDialog(null, "Credit card is selected...");
       else if (debitCard.isSelected())
                 JOptionPane.showMessageDialog(null, "Debit card is selected...");
   }
   if (source == check)                 //If the event source is the radio button
       JOptionPane.showMessageDialog(null, "check triggered the event...");
   if (source == creditCard)            //And if the event is triggered by creditCard
       JOptionPane.showMessageDialog(null, "creditCard triggered the event...");
   if (source == debitCard)                      //If the event is triggered by
debitCard
       JOptionPane.showMessageDialog(null, "debitCard triggered the event...");
}
```

Figure 15.12 shows the result of the execution:

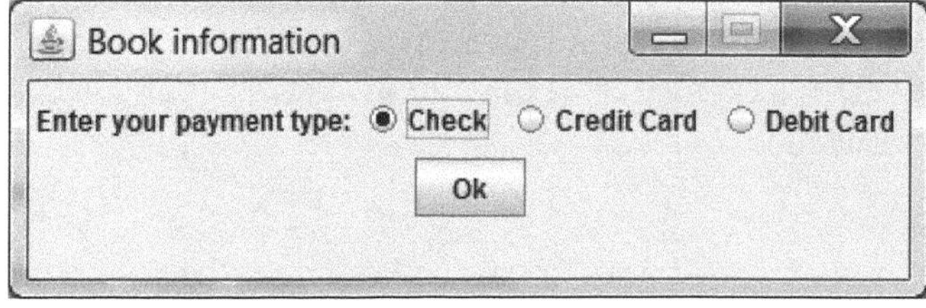

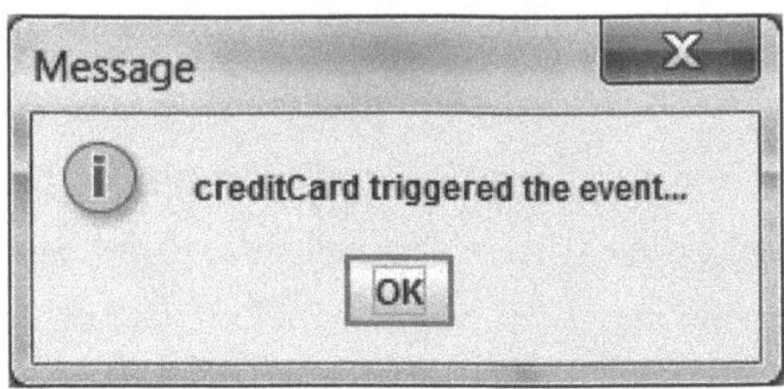

Figure 15.12 The typical execution result for radio button event handling

15.8.2 Application example

This application uses the **JLabel**, **JCheckBox**, **JRadioButton**, **JButton** , and **JTextArea** classes along with event handling to make a user survey of the fast food franchises: Pizza, Hamburgers, and KFC. The application first displays a window containing three check boxes associated with each franchise, and two radio buttons from which the user can register satisfaction (or lack thereof) of the food served by the respective franchise. When the user clicks the **OK** button to submit the survey selections, a text area is displayed at the bottom showing the survey results. The following snippet shows the code of the control panel:

```
//Complete code called FoodSurveyPanel.javaFoodSurveyFrame.java and
//FoodSurveyFrameApp.java in Ch15 from the author's website
import java.awt.*;
import java.awt.event.*;
import javax.swing.*;
public class FoodSurveyPanel extends JPanel implements ActionListener {
   //Define member data
   private int pizzaLikeCount, hamburgerLikeCount, kfcLikeCount;
   private int pizzaDislikeCount, hamburgerDislikeCount, kfcDislikeCount;

   //Define GUI components
   private JLabel selectLabel;
   private JTextArea displayTextArea;
   private JCheckBox pizzaBox, hamburgerBox, kfcBox;
   private Jbutton addButton;

   //Declare radio buttons and button group
   private JRadioButton likeRadioButton, dislikeRadioButton;
   private ButtonGroup buttonGroup;

   public FoodSurveyPanel() {        //Constructor
      //initialize survey
      pizzaLikeCount = hamburgerLikeCount = kfcLikeCount = 0;
      pizzaDislikeCount = hamburgerDislikeCount = kfcDislikeCount = 0;
      createGUIComponents();
   }
...
```

The constructor in the above code, in addition to initializing the data for the survey statistics, calls a method, **createGUIComponents()**, to carry out the creation and adding of the GUI components to the panel and event handling.

```
//Method createGUIComponents()
private void createGUIComponents() {
   //Create and add label and check boxes
   selectLabel = new JLabel("Please select one you like or dislike: ");
   add(selectLabel);
   pizzaBox = new JCheckBox("Pizza");
   add(pizzaBox);
   hamburgerBox = new JCheckBox("Hamburger");
   add(humbuggerBox);
   kfcBox = new JCheckBox("KFC");
   add(kfcBox);
   likeRadioButton = new JRadioButton("Like",true); //Create and add radio buttons
   dislikeRadioButton = new JRadioButton("Dislike");
   add(likeRadioButton);
   add(dislikeRadioButton);
   buttonGroup = new ButtonGroup();  //Create button group and add radio buttons
   buttonGroup.add(likeRadioButton);
   buttonGroup.add(dislikeRadioButton);
   addButton = new JButton("Add");           //Create button add(addButton);
                                             //Add the button to panel
   addButton.addActionListener(this);        //Add the button for event handling
   setupTextArea();                          //Call method to establish text area
   displayTextArea.setVisible(false);        //Don't display it first
}
```

Another method, **setupTextArea()**, is written for creating an area to contain the survey statistics. Initially hidden from view, this text area will be shown when the user clicks the **Add** button. The following is the code of method **setupTextArea()**:

```
//Method setupTextArea()to create and add the text area
private void setupTextArea() {
  displayTextArea = new JTextArea();                   //Create
  displayTextArea.setBounds(16, 55, 315, 93);                  //Specify the size
  displayTextArea.setEditable( false );                        //Not editable
  add(displayTextArea);                                        //Add to the panel
}
```

In regard to event handling, if the user presses the **Add** button to submit the survey data, the code checks the status of each check box and radio button before accumulating the survey data:

```
//Implement actionPerformed()for event handling
```

```
public void actionPerformed(ActionEvent e) {
   Object source = e.getSource();                    //Get the source of the event
   if (source == addButton) {                        //If Add button is pressed
       //If Pizza is selected, increment survey selection choice
       if (pizzaBox.isSelected()) {
           if (likeRadioButton.isSelected())
               pizzaLikeCount++;
           else
               pizzaDislikeCount++;
       }
       //Perform same handling methodology of remaining survey selection choices
       if (hamburgerBox.isSelected()) {
           if (likeRadioButton.isSelected())
               hamburgerLikeCount++;
           else
               hamburgerDislikeCount++;
       }
       if (kfcBox.isSelected()) {
           if (likeRadioButton.isSelected())
               kfcLikeCount++;
           else
               kfcDislikeCount++;
           }
           updateTextArea();                      //Call method to update survey results
   }
}
```

After obtaining the survey data, method **updateTextArea()** updates the text area by displaying the survey statistics report:

```
//Method updateTextArea() to update the survey statistics report
private void updateTextArea() {
   String info = "\tLike\tDislike\n"
      + "Pizz\t" + pizzaLikeCount + "\t" + pizzaDislikeCount + "\n"
      + "Hamburger\t" + hamburgerLikeCount + "\t" + hamburgerDislikeCount + "\n"
      + "KFC\t" + kfcLikeCount + "\t" + kfcDislikeCount;
   displayTextArea.setText(info);
   displayTextArea.setVisible(true);
}
```

The code for managing the frame and the driver code are similar to other examples we have discussed. The complete code for this application can be found in **Ch15** from the author's website. Figure 15.13 shows an example result of execution of this application:

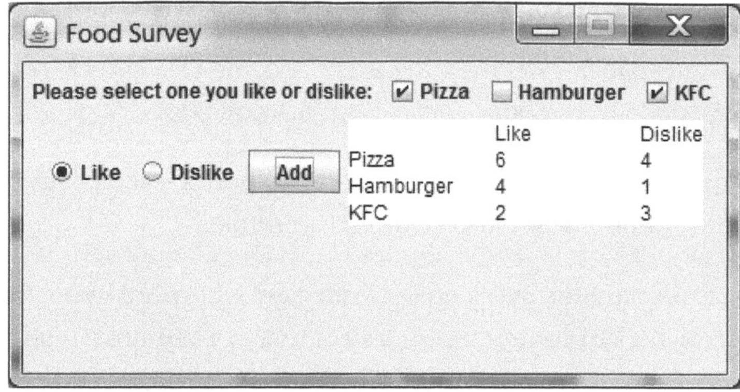

Figure 15.13 A typical execution result of the Fast Food Survey

Exercises

1. Use examples to explain and define GUI frames, windows, containers, and components.
2. What are the differences between AWT and Swing?
3. Write code displaying a frame that will always be located in the upper left corner of the screen. The frame is to be one-half the width and height of the monitor.
4. What is a panel? Use examples to explain the relationship between a panel and a frame.
5. Using the steps for coding GUI components in a frame, write an application that will convert kilometers to miles. The application must display a label and text field prompting the user to enter a quantity of kilometers then display the equivalent number of miles in another text field. The window is to be displayed in the center of the screen; its dimensions are to be one-half the screen width and height. You may decide where to position the GUI components. Write a driver code to test your application and save all files.
6. Add two buttons, **Submit** and **Exit**, to the application you wrote for Exercise 5 above. Each button is to be displayed at the bottom of the window. When the user clicks the **Submit** button, the value representing the mileage equivalent of the specified quantity of kilometers is to be displayed in the text field. When the **Exit** button is pressed, the program stops executing. Add exception handling capabilities to the code associated with the **Submit** button such that when the button is pressed without any data in the input text field the user is prompted to enter correct input data. Write a driver code to test the application and save all files.
7. Use examples to explain the differences in functionality, display, layout managers, and event handling between text fields and text areas.
8. Describe how to use horizontal and vertical scroll bars in a text area.
9. Write an application using text areas, buttons, labels, and other GUI components of your choice to display statistics showing the quantity of words entered in the text area. When the user

presses the **Submit** button, the statistical result is to be displayed as a label. The text area is to have word wrapping capabilities. When the user clicks the **Exit** button, program execution is to stop. Write a driver code to test your application. Save all files.

10. Use examples to explain the differences between radio buttons and check boxes. Why do we need to use button groups in association with radio buttons?

11. Write an application using three check boxes associated with word wrapping, line wrapping, and the presence of scroll bars to control the display of text in a text area. You may initially display some default text in the text area with a default check box selected. Write a driver code to test your application. Save all files.

12. Write an application using radio buttons and any other required GUI components that will convert kilometers-to-miles, kilograms-to-pounds, and Celsius-to-Fahrenheit. A group of radio buttons will provide these selections. When the user presses a radio button, a label prompting the user to enter the data in a text field will be displayed. When the user presses the **Submit** button, the convert result will be displayed in another text field in the window. When the user clicks the **Exit** button, the program will terminate. You may use a layout manager of your choice to position the GUI components. Write a driver code to test your application. Save all files.

"Learning without thought is labor lost; thought without learning is perilous."

– Confucius

Chapter 16 Layout Managers of GUI Components

In the previous chapter all examples use the default layout manager, **FlowLayout** class, with the **FlowLayout.CENTER** field to position the GUI components in a window. This chapter discusses six layout managers provided in Java using examples. More sophisticated positioning techniques of GUI components using nested layout managers are also introduced.

16.1 General Discussion

A layout manager refers to the design and placement a GUI component in a specified position in a window. In addition to **FlowLayout**, Java also provides **BorderLayout**, **BoxLayout**, **GridLayout**, **GridBagLayout**, and **JTabbedPane** for managing and positioning GUI components. These layout managers are in the **java.awt** and **java.swing packages**. Table 16.1 lists the characteristics of these six layout managers.

Table 16.1 Six Layout Managers in Java

Name	Description
FlowLayout (java.awt)	A component can be placed in 3 positions: LEFT, CENTER, and RIGHT. The default is FlowLayout.CENTER. The position of a component is not fixed, dependent upon the size of the window, or number and type of components.
BorderLayout (java.awt)	A component can be placed in 5 positions: NORTH, WEST, CENTER, EAST, and SOUTH. The position of a component is not fixed, dependent upon the size of the window, or number and type of components.
JTabbedPane (javax.swing)	Components are positioned in different layers and activated for display by a tab key.
BoxLayout (javax.swing)	Components are placed in horizontal rows or vertical columns. Each cell displays one component.
GridLayout (java.awt)	Components are placed in evenly divided columns and rows. Each cell contains one component.
GridBagLayout (java.awt)	Similar to GridLayout, but a component may occupy more than one cell, and each cell may have a different size. This is a more sophisticated layout manager and careful design is required. It is usually nested with other layout managers to achieve a sophisticated design and display of components. The positions of components will not change.

The following sections discuss the use of these six layout managers to position GUI components through examples.

16.2 FlowLayout

As discussed in Chapter 15, **FlowLayout**, in particular with the **FlowLayout.CENTER** field, is the default Java GUI layout manager for placing components. Table 16.2 lists commonly used constructors, methods, and static final fields in **FlowLayout**.

Table 16.2 Commonly used constructors, methods, and static final fields in **FlowLayout**

Constructors, methods, and fields	Description
FlowLayout()	Creates an object of **FlowLayout** with default alignment CENTER.
FlowLayout(int alignment)	Creates an object of **FlowLayout** with the specified alignment.
JFrame void setLayout(LayoutManager layoutName)	Adds the object to the container for management.
static int LEFT	Value indicates each row of components should be left-justified.
static int CENTER	Value indicates each row of components should be centered. Default.
static int RIGHT	Value indicates each row of components should be right-justified.

16.2.1 Positions of display

Because the position of a GUI component is changeable depending on the size of the displayed window and underlying hardware, when using **FlowLayout** you may consider using the following techniques to avoid repositioning:

1. Properly design and code the window with the components to be displayed and disable the window resizing capability: **this.setResizeable(false)**; or

2. Use other layout managers nested and in conjunction with **FlowLayout**, thereby allowing your design to be sophisticated enough to maintain the components in fixed positions. We discuss how to do this in Section 16.3.2.

The following code uses **FlowLayout** to place two right-justified buttons using **FlowLayout.RIGHT**:

```
//Complete code called TwoButtonsFrameTest.java in Ch16 from the author's website
public ButtonsPanel extends JPanel {
   //Create the object with RIGHT alignment
   FlowLayout flowLayout = new FlowLayout(FlowLayout.RIGHT);
   setLayout(flowLayout);                   //Add the object for the management
   add(new JButton("Button One");           //Create two buttons
   add(new JButton("Button Two");
}
```

Figure 16.2 shows the result of execution:

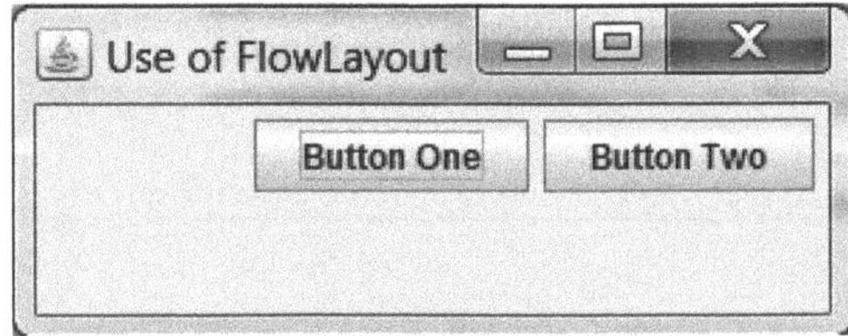

Figure 16.1 Buttons right-justified using **FlowLayout.RIGHT**

16.2.2 More examples

The following code demonstrates the placement of a button in three different positions within a window using **FlowLayout**. When the user presses the button, the button's position will change as it cycles through the left-, center-, and right-justified positions. The example uses an anonymous inner class to handle the event processing. More coding techniques to handle events are discussed in Chapter 17.

```
//Complete code called ButtonClickFrame.java in Ch16 from the author's website
import java.awt.*;
import java.awt.event.*;
import javax.swing.*;
class ButtonClickFrame extends JFrame {
   private FlowLayout flowLayout;
   private JButton button;
   private int postCount = 0;     //Compute the display position
   private Container container; //Declare an object of Container to manage layout
   public ButtonClickFrame() {
      setTitle("Use of FlowLayout");
      flowLayout = new FlowLayout(FlowLayout.LEFT);       //Display on left
      container = getContentPane();                        //Get the layout info
      setLayout(flowLayout);                               //Add the layout
      button = new JButton("Click me");                    //Create a button
      add(button);                                         //Add the button
      button.addActionListener(new ActionListener() {     //Anonymous inner class
         public void actionPerformed(ActionEvent e) {
            //0 = left-justified; 1 = centered-justified; 2 = right-justified
            flowLayout.setAlignment(postCount++ % 3);
            flowLayout.layoutContainer(container);         //Update the display
         }
      });
   }
}
```

The following event handling code does not use an anonymous inner class; it is equivalent to the event handling code above:

```
class ButtonClickFrame2 extends JFrame implements ActionListener{
   ...
   public void actionPerformed(ActionEvent e) {
      Object source = e.getSource();
      if (source == button) {
          flowLayout.setAlignment(postCount++ % 3);
          flowLayout.layoutContainer(container);
      }
   }
}
```

In addition to using an anonymous inner class to handle the event, the code segment also uses the **Container** class methods **getContentPane()** and **layoutContainer()** to update the current button position. When the user clicks the button, the code **postCount++ % 3** computes an integer in the range: 0 – 2 (inclusive), representing left-, center-, and right-alignment, respectively, corresponding to **FlowLayout.LEFT**, **FlowLayout.CENTER**, and **FlowLayout.RIGHT** in the **FlowLayout** manager. The demonstration uses the default panel provided by the JVM, eliminating the need to create a control panel and manage the components in simple code scenarios. The window closing and display size of the window are coded in the driver code.

```
//Complete code called ButtonClickFrameTest.java in Ch16 from the author's website
public class ButtonClickFrameTest {
   public static void main(String[] args) { JFrame frame = new
      ButtonClickFrame();
      frame.setDefaultCloseOperation(JFrame.EXIT_ON_CLOSE); //Window closing
      frame.setSize(450, 80);                             //Size of the window
      frame.setVisible(true);
   }
}
```

Figure 16.2 shows the execution result in which the button are placed in three different positions:

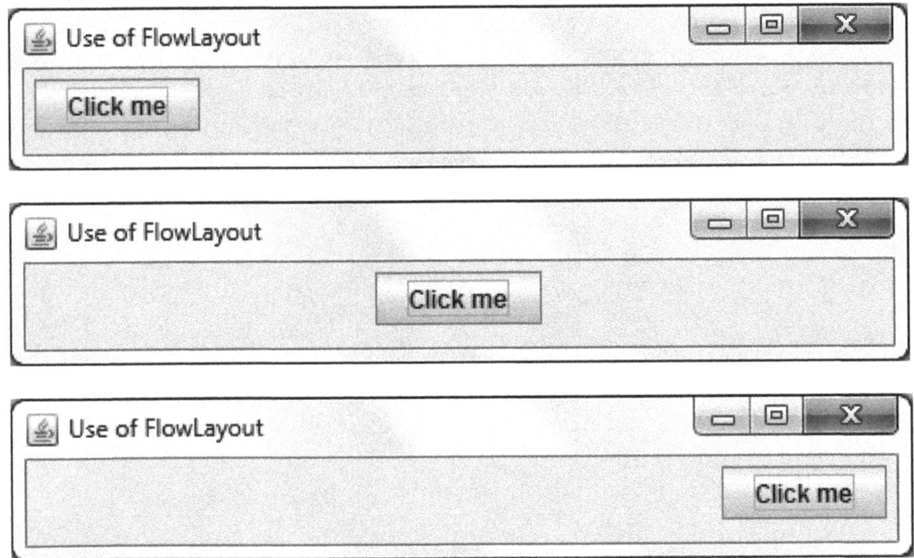

Figure 16.2 Three button positions using **FlowLayout** alignments

16.3 BorderLayout

The **BorderLayout** manager contains five regions: **EAST**, **WEST**, **NORTH**, **SOUTH**, and **CENTER** (default). **BorderLayout** is often coded in conjunction with other layout managers to allow greater flexibility in positioning GUI components. Table 16.3 lists commonly used constructors, methods, and static fields of **BorderLayout**.

Table 16.3 Commonly used constructors, methods, and five regions of **BorderLayout**

Constructors, methods, and static fields	Description
BorderLayout()	Creates an object of BorderLayout with no gaps between regions.
BorderLayout(int hGap, int vGap)	Creates an object of BorderLayout with the specified gaps between regions.
JFrame void setLayout(LayoutManager layoutName)	Adds the object to the container for management.
void add(Component comp, int regionField)	Method of Container. Adds specified layout object and the region to the panel.
Static final String NORTH	North (top of container) positioning constraint.
Static final String SOUTH	South (bottom of container) positioning constraint.
Static final String EAST	East (right side of container) positioning constraint.
Static final String WEST	West (left side of container) positioning constraint.
Static final String CENTER	Center of container positioning constraint. Default.

16.3.1 Five regions

The following code snippet displays a button in each of the five regions of the **BorderLayout** manager in a window:

```
//Complete code called BorderLayoutPanel.java and BorderLayoutFrameTest.java in
//Ch16 from the author's website
...
private JButton[] buttons;          //Declare array of buttons
private BorderLayout layout;        //Declare object of BorderLayout
private int post;                   //Used for naming the button
public BorderLayoutPanel() {
   buttons = new JButton[5];        //Create 5 elements of buttons
   post = 0;                        //Initialize
   layout = new BorderLayout(5, 5); //Create the object with 5 pixel space
   setLayout(layout);               //Add layout manager
   for (int i = 0; i < 5; i++)      //Create buttons
     buttons[i] = new JButton("button" + post++); //button0 to button4
   add(buttons[0], BorderLayout.NORTH);    //Add each button to the specified
region
   add(buttons[1], BorderLayout.SOUTH);
   add(buttons[2], BorderLayout.WEST);
   add(buttons[3], BorderLayout.EAST);
   add(buttons[4]);                          //Default is CENTER
```

It should be noted there is no static final data to replace the names of the five regions in **BorderLayout.** The default region is **BorderLayout.CENTER**. Figure 16.3 shows the result of execution:

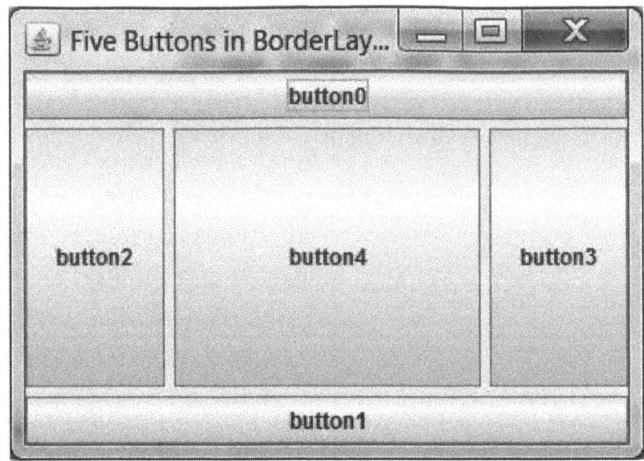

Figure 16.3 Five buttons displayed in five regions using BorderLayout

16.3.2 Nested Layouts

Layout managers are often nested to create a desired positioning of GUI components within a window display. The follow example uses **BorderLayout** and **FlowLayout** to display two buttons in the bottom right corner of a window. We first create a panel using **FlowLayout** to position the two right-aligned buttons, and then we create the panel of this frame using **BorderLayout** to display the button panel in the South region.

```
//Complete code called BorderLayoutFrameTest2.java in Ch16 from the author's website
class BorderLayoutPanel2 extends JPanel {
   private JButton okButton, exitButton;
   public BorderLayoutPanel2() {
      JPanel buttonPanel = new JPanel();    //Create right-aligned button panel
      buttonPanel.setLayout(new FlowLayout(FlowLayout.RIGHT));
      okButton = new JButton("Ok");
      exitButton = new JButton("Exit");
      buttonPanel.add(okButton);                      //Add the buttons to the panel
      buttonPanel.add(exitButton);
      setLayout(new BorderLayout());        //Create object of BorderLayout
      add(buttonPanel, BorderLayout.SOUTH);           //Add button panel to the border
   }
}

class BorderLayoutFrame2 extends JFrame {
   . . . .
   JPanel panel = new BorderLayoutPanel2();           //Create the border panel
   this.add(panel);                                   //Add the panel to frame
   . . .
}
```

Figure 16.4 shows the result of execution. Note the use of nested layout managers places the two buttons in the desired fixed position.

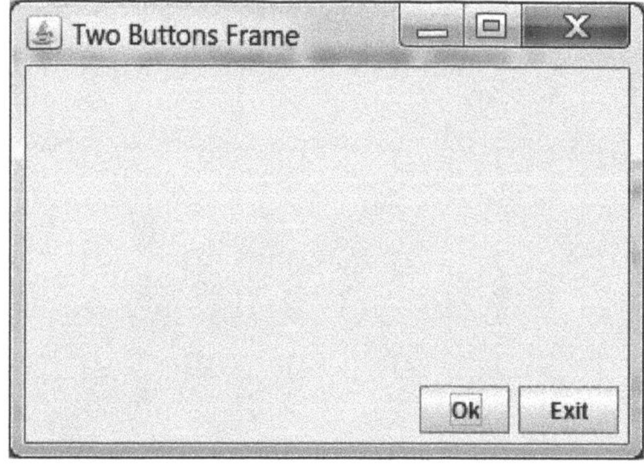

Figure 16.4 Use of nested layouts to place two right-aligned buttons in the bottom panel

The following steps should be followed in designing a GUI window display using nested layout managers:

1. Group GUI components according to their display positions, then determine the number of panels to hold the groups of components.
2. In the panel performing the nested layout, code each panel, e.g., **componentPanel()**, in which the group of components is created and added to the panel.
3. Call **setLayout(LayoutManager layoutName)** to position the components within the panel.
4. Add event handling capabilities, as required, for desired GUI components.
5. In a frame, create an object of the nested layout panel and add it to the frame.

We discuss more examples of nested layouts in later chapters.

16.3.3 More examples

The five regions of **BorderLayout** are relative to each other, and the positions of components using this manager may be uncertain depending on which regions are selected for use. For example, if no component is positioned at **NORTH**, the components placed in **WEST**, **CENTER**, and **EAST** will occupy the space in the top region. In the following example, we expand the code discussed in Section 16.3.1 to handle events demonstrating the changing of button positions within the regions of **BorderLayout**. The example also adds a counter to reset all buttons to their original positions once the entire cycle of positioning has been completed.

```
//Complete code called BorderLayoutFrameTest3.java in Ch16 from author's website
public void actionPerformed(ActionEvent e) {
   Object source = e.getSource();
   if (count < 4) {                     //Still have buttons in display
      for (int i = 0; i < 5; i++)      //See which button triggered event
         if (source == buttons[i]) {
            buttons[i].setVisible(false); //Do not display
            count++;                      //Counter update
```

```
            }
    }
    else {                              //Reset when no button in display
        for (JButton button : buttons)
            button.setVisible(true); //Set each button to be displayed
        count = 0;                              //Reset the counter
    }
}
```

16.4 Border

Although the use of a border is superficially an embellishment to better display grouped components, its implicit function is to reflect graphically the internal design of the panel to users. Applying the concept "A picture is worth a thousand words" allows the display of a more user-friendly display with the use of borders. Figure 16.5 displays commonly used borders. The supporting codes are discussed in Section 16.4.2.

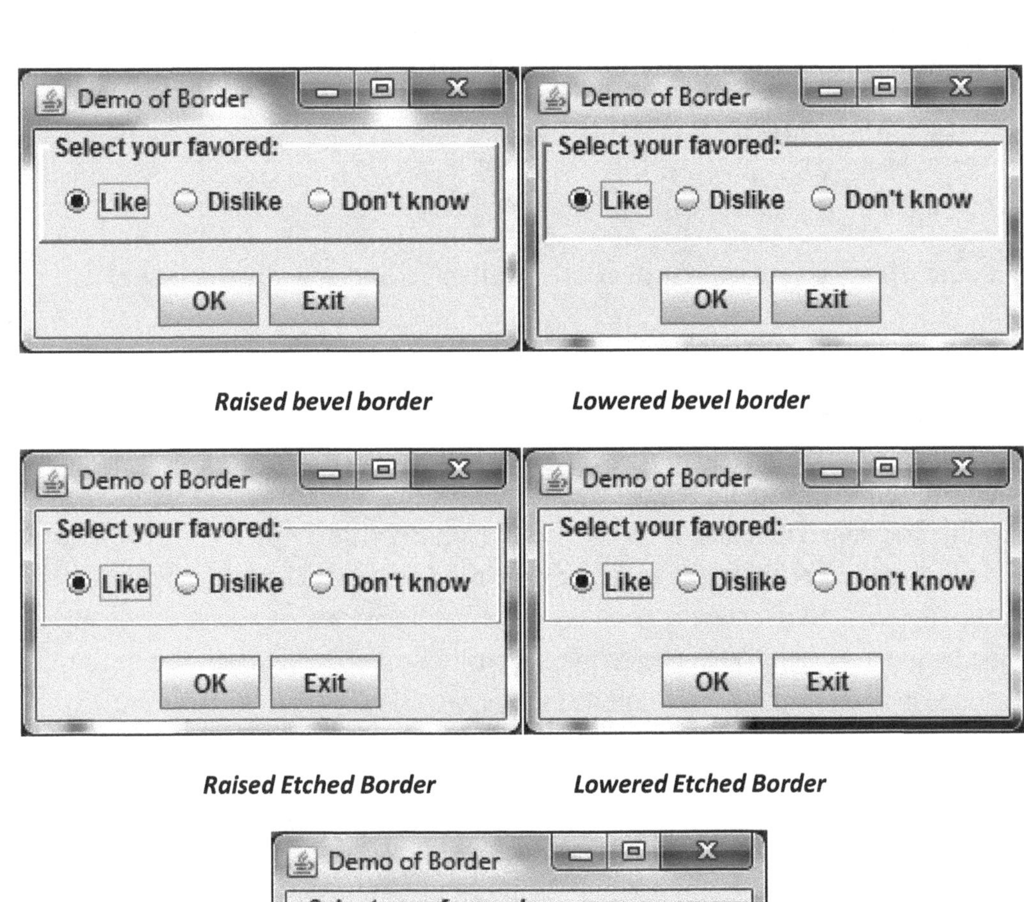

Raised bevel border ***Lowered bevel border***

Raised Etched Border ***Lowered Etched Border***

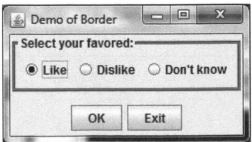

Colored Line Border

Figure 16.5 Five commonly used borders

It should be noted a border with a title can be used to further explain the enclosed components.

We use the **javax.swing.border** package **BorderFactory** class to create a border. Table 16.4 lists commonly used static methods in **BorderFactory**.

Table 16.4 Commonly used static methods in **BorderFactory** and method in **JComponent**

Static Methods and Methods	Description
static Border createBevelBorder(int type)	Creates object with specified beveled border type: BevelBorder.LOWERED or BevelBorder. RAISED.
static Border createEtchedBorder(int type)	Creates object with specified etched border type: EtchedBorder.LOWERED or EtchedBorder.RAISED.
static Border createLineBorder(Color color, int thickness)	Creates object with specified line color and thickness.
static TitledBorder createTitledBorder(Border border, String title)	Adds a title to an existing border, with default positioning (sitting on top line), default justification (leading), and default fond and text color (determined by current look-and-feel).
JComponent void setBorder(Border border)	Sets border object to its panel or components.

16.4.1 The steps in coding a border

The basic steps in coding a border are:

1. Code the GUI components to be placed within a surrounding border.
2. Select a desired valid border style and call the **BorderFactory** method to return the object. For example, the following Java statement creates an etched lower border style:

```
Border selectBorder = BorderFactory.createEtchedBorder(EtchedBorder.LOWERED);
```

3. Call method **createTitledBorder()** to include a title in the border, if desired:

```
selectBorder = BorderFactory.createTitledBorder(selectBorder, "Make selection:  ");
```

4. Call method **setBorder()** to add the border to the panel or component:

```
selectPanel.setBorder(selectBorder);
```

or you may combine Steps 3 and 4 together:

```
selectPanel.setBorder(BorderFactory.createTitledBorder(selectBorder,
"Make selection: "));
```

The following code snippet uses the above steps to create a beveled lower border for the text area:

```
//Complete code called BorderFrameTest.java in Ch16 from author's website
textArea = new JTextArea("This is a demo...", 5, 20);
Border selectBorder = BorderFactory.createBevelBorder(BevelBorder.LOWERED);
selectBorder = BorderFactory.createTitledBorder(selectBorder, "enter your story");
textArea.setBorder(selectBorder);
add(textArea);
...
```

Figure 16.6 shows the execution result:

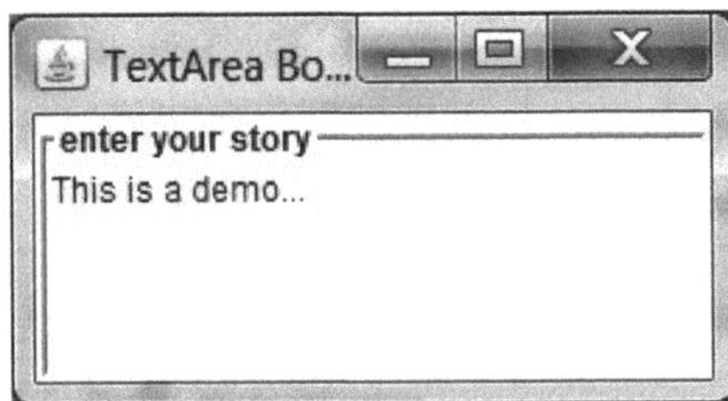

Figure 16.6 The execution result of the text area with a border

16.4.2 Application example

The following code creates a raised beveled border, as shown in the first picture of Figure 16.4.

```
//Complete code called BorderDemoFrameTest.java in Ch16 from the author's website
class BorderDemoFrame extends JFrame {
   private JPanel borderDemoPanel, buttonPanel;
   private JRadioButton likeRadioButton, dislikeRadioButton, dontKnowRadioButton;
   private ButtonGroup buttonGroup; private
   JButton addButton, exitButton; Toolkit tk
   = Toolkit.getDefaultToolkit(); Dimension
   d = tk.getScreenSize();

   public BorderDemoFrame() {
      setLayout(new BorderLayout());         //Create border layout

      borderDemoPanel = new JPanel();
      borderDemoPanel.setLayout(new FlowLayout(FlowLayout.LEFT));
      likeRadioButton = new JRadioButton("Like", true);
      dislikeRadioButton = new JRadioButton("Dislike");
      dontKnowRadioButton = new JRadioButton("Don't know");
      borderDemoPanel.add(likeRadioButton);
      borderDemoPanel.add(dislikeRadioButton);
      borderDemoPanel.add(dontKnowRadioButton);
```

```
        buttonGroup = new ButtonGroup();
        buttonGroup.add(likeRadioButton);
        buttonGroup.add(dislikeRadioButton);
        buttonGroup.add(dontKnowRadioButton);

        BorderFactory.createBevelBorder(BevelBorder.LOWERED);

        //You may replace the above statement with:

        //BorderFactory.createEtchedBorder(EtchedBorder.RAISED);,
        //BorderFactory.createEtchedBorder(EtchedBorder.LOWERED); and
        //BorderFactory.createLineBorder(Color.red, 3);

        //to show different border styles

        Border selectBorder = BorderFactory.createBevelBorder(BevelBorder.RAISED);
        selectBorder = BorderFactory.createTitledBorder(selectBorder, "Select your
favored:");
        borderDemoPanel.setBorder(selectBorder);

        add(borderDemoPanel, BorderLayout.NORTH);   //Display at the top

        buttonPanel = new JPanel();
        borderDemoPanel.setLayout(new FlowLayout(FlowLayout.LEFT));
        addButton = new JButton("OK");
        buttonPanel.add(addButton);
        exitButton = new JButton("Exit");
        buttonPanel.add(exitButton);
        add(buttonPanel, BorderLayout.SOUTH);

        setTitle("Demo of Border");
        setSize(250, 140);                          //Display size
        setDefaultCloseOperation(WindowConstants.DISPOSE_ON_CLOSE);
    }
}
```

If we modify the above code:

```
Border selectBorder = BorderFactory.createBevelBorder(BevelBorder.RAISED);
//Create the border
```

using the different methods of **BorderFactory** representing the five border styles discussed above, you will see the other four border displays.

16.5 JTabbedPane

JTabbedPane is provided by the **javax.swing** package. It is used to create graphical file folder labels ("tabs"), in which components can be placed in each file folder and accessed by clicking on the folder labels (see Figure 16.6: a window with two tabbed panels). **JTabbedPane** is often nested with other layout managers so it can be placed in specified locations of a window. Table 16.5 lists commonly used constructors and methods in **JTabbedPane**.

Table 16.5 Commonly used constructors and methods in JTabbedPane

Constructor/Method	Description

JTabbedPane()	Creates the object with the default tab location JTabbedPane.TOP.
JTabbedPane(int tabPlacement)	Creates the object with the specified tab location: JTabbedPane.TOP, JTabbedPane.BOTTOM, JTabbedPane.LEFT, or JTabbedPane.RIGHT.
JFrame void setLayout(LayoutManager layoutName)	Adds the object to the container for management.
Component add(Component component)	Adds the tabbed pane to the frame.
Component add(String name, Component component)	Adds the tabbed pane to the frame with the specified name.
void addTab(String title, Component component)	Adds the component to the tabbed pane with the specified title.
void addTab(String title, Icon icon, Component component)	Adds the component to the tabbed pane with the specified title and icon.
Component getSelectedComponent()	Returns currently selected component.
int getTabCount()	Returns the number of tabs in this tabbed pane.
void setTabPlacement(int tabPlacement)	Set the tabbed pane to the specified position: JTabbedPane.TOP, JTabbedPane.BOTTOM, JTabbedPane.LEFT, or JTabbedPane.RIGHT.

JTabbedPane provides five static final fields for aligning the position of a tabbed pane:

```
BOTTOM_ALIGNMENT        CENTER_ALIGNMENT          LEFT_ALIGNMENT
RIGHT_ALIGNMENT         TOP_ALIGNMENT
```

In real world applications, a tabbed pane is usually used to open another panel containing components positioned by a different layout manager. We may consider tabbed pane as a general control panel in which other (sub)panels are placed. The object of **JTabbedPane** is always directly added to the frame. The steps to create a tabbed pane in an application are:

1. Code all panels with their respective layout manager(s) to place all components. Code all event handling capabilities, as required.
2. Code the frame and create the tabbed pane object and each panel object.
3. Add each panel object created in Step 2 to the tabbed pane object.
4. Add the tabbed pane object to the frame.
5. Create the frame object and display it in the driver code.

16.5.1 Use of JTabbedPane

Example 1. Assume classes **ButtonsPanel** and **BorderLayoutPanel** are provided. Code a frame using a tabbed pane incorporating these two panels. Display the result in a window.

```
//Complete code called JTabbedPaneFrameTest.java in Ch16 from author's website
```

```
import java.awt.*;
import javax.swing.*;
class JTabbedPaneFrame extends JFrame {
   private JTabbedPane tabbedPane;           //Declare the object of JTabbedPane
   private ButtonsPanel buttonsPanel;
   private BorderLayoutPanel borderLayoutPanel;

   public JTabbedPaneFrame() {               //Constructor
      super("Demo: use of JTabbedPane");//Or: setTitle("Demo: use of
JTabbedPane");
      tabbedPane = new JTabbedPane();        //Create JTabbedPane object
      buttonsPanel = new ButtonsPanel();     //Create two panels
      borderLayoutPanel = new BorderLayoutPanel();
      tabbedPane.addTab("Buttons", buttonsPanel);    //Add the panels to tabbed pane
      tabbedPane.addTab("BorderLayout", borderLayoutPanel);
      add(tabbedPane);                       //Add the tabbed pane to frame
   }
}
```

Figure 16.7 shows the execution result.

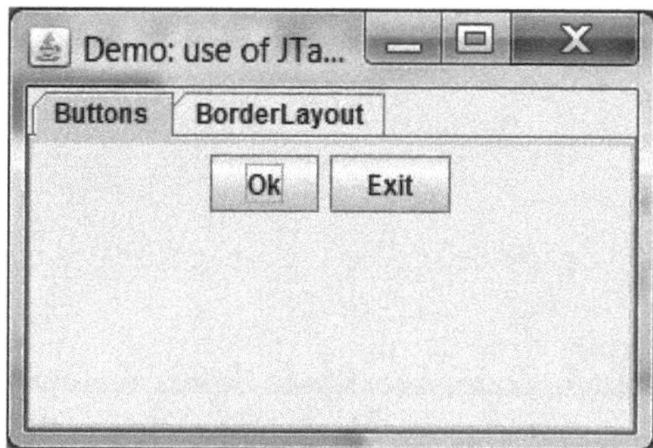

Figure 16.7 Result of executing the above code to construct a window containing two tabbed pane panels.

Example 2. Use of other methods in **JTabbedPane** in the above code.

```
System.out.println("Number of tabs: ", tabbedPane.getTabCount());//Return number 2
tabbedPane.setTabPlacement(RIGHT_ALIGNMENT); //Display tabbed panes aligned right
...
if (tabbedPane.getSelectedComponent() == button0) //If button0 is pressed
   JOptionPane.showMessageDialog(null, "button0 in BorderLayout is selected...");
```

16.5.2 Application example

We will use a tabbed pane in modifying the examples to calculate and display product purchasing information in **ProductCalculatorPane** discussed in Section 15.5.3 and the book information provider in **BookInfoPanel** discussed in Section 15.7.2. These two panels are displayed in a window using **JTabbedPane**. The user must first enter the password (Section 15.5.5) to verify accessibility to the window. The following code snippet is the event handling procedure performed by method **actionPerformed()** of **PasswordPanel**:

```
//Complete code called PasswordPanel.java, PasswordFrame.java,
//JTabbedPaneFrame2.java, ProductCalculatorPanel.java, BookInfoPanel2.java,
//and JTabbedPaneFrameApp.java from the author's website

public void actionPerformed(ActionEvent e){         //Implement the interface
   Object source = e.getSource();                    //Get the source of event
   if (source == okButton) {                         //If okButton triggered event
      String password = new String(passwordField.getPassword());
      if (password.equals("abc123")) {               //If password is correct
          setVisible(false);                         //Hide the password
          JFrame frame = new JTabbedPaneFrame2();//Create a frame
          frame.setVisible(true);                    //Set as display
      }
      else {                                         //If password incorrect
            JOptionPane.showMessageDialog(null, "Entry error!\n"
                 + "Please check password and try again...");
            System.exit(0);                          //Stop run
      }
   }
   else if (source == exitButton) {          //If exitButton triggered event
            JOptionPane.showMessageDialog(null, "Good bye!\nPress OK to close
   window...");
            System.exit(1);                          //Handle the event
   }
}
```

When the frame is created in the driver code, a text field is displayed prompting the user to enter the password. The code hides the password, then creates an object of **JTabbedPane**.

The following code creates the tabbed panes and displays the result of selecting either product purchasing information or book search information in the **JTabbedPaneFrame2** window.

```
//Complete code called JTabbedPaneFrame2.java in Ch16 from the author's website
import java.awt.*;
import javax.swing.*;
class JTabbedPaneFrame2 extends JFrame {
   private JTabbedPane tabbedPane;                          //Declare tabbed pane
   private PasswordPanel passwordPanel;
   private ProductCalculatorPanel productCalculatorPanel;
   private BookInfoPanel2 bookInfoPanel;
   Toolkit tk = Toolkit.getDefaultToolkit();
   Dimension d = tk.getScreenSize();
   public JTabbedPaneFrame2() {
      super("JTabbedPane Applications");
      tabbedPane = new JTabbedPane();                       //Create tabbed pane
      passwordPanel = new PasswordPanel();
      productCalculatorPanel = new ProductCalculatorPanel();
      bookInfoPanel = new BookInfoPanel2();
      tabbedPane.addTab("Products", productCalculatorPanel);
      //Add the panels to tabbed pane
```

```
        tabbedPane.addTab("Books", bookInfoPanel);
        add(tabbedPane);                    //Add the tabbed pane to frame
        setSize(550, 200);
        centerWindow(this);
    }
    private void centerWindow(JFrame frame) {//Display at the center of the screen
        int centeredWidth = ((int)d.getWidth() - frame.getWidth())/2;     //Width
        int centeredHeight = ((int)d.getHeight() - frame.getHeight())/2; //Height
        setLocation(centeredWidth, centeredHeight);      //Display location
    }
}
```

The driver code first displays **PasswordFrame**, prompting the user to enter the password. This window is closed upon entering the correct password. A new window displaying the tabbed pane consisting of two panels is then made visible.

To better organize the GUI components, we modified the original code by using the **FlowLayout** and **BorderLayout** managers to display the input components (labels, text field, and check boxes) at the top of the window and to display the right-aligned **Ok** and **Exit** buttons at the bottom of the window. This code is discussed in Section 16.3.2 and may be referenced for additional details. The top portion of Figure 16.8 shows the window prompting the user to enter the password; the lower part of the figure shows the panel of book information chosen in executing the code.

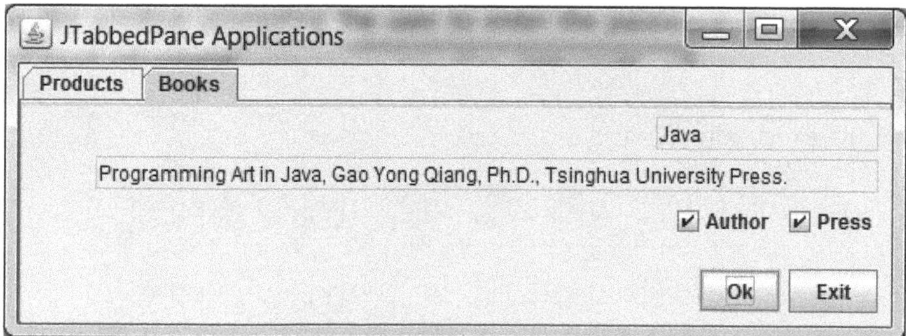

Figure 16.8 A typical result of executing the above tabbed pane application

16.6 BoxLayout and GradLayout

BoxLayout and **GridLayout** are two other commonly used layout managers. **BoxLayout** is provided by **javax.swing**. **GridLayout** is included in the **java.awt** package. Components in a **BoxLayout** layout can be arranged along horizontally (x-axis) or vertically (y-axis), but only one component can be placed within each cell, or box (see Figure 16.8 and Figure 16.9). In **GridLayout** the display window is divided into evenly-sized cells, with each cell containing a single component. Positions of the components placed in these two layout managers will not change when the window size is changed.

Table 16.6 lists commonly used constructors, methods, and static fields in **BoxLayout**.

Table 16.6 Commonly used constructors, methods, and static fields in **BoxLayout**

Constructor/Method/Static Field	Description
BoxLayout(Container target, int axis)	Creates the object with components laid out along the specified axis.
int getAxis()	Returns the axis used to layout the components.
Container getTarget()	Returns the container that holds the layout manager.
static int X_AXIS	Specifies components should be laid out horizontally from left to right.
static int Y_AXIS	Specifies components should be laid out vertically from top to bottom.

Example 1. Use **X_AXIS** to place the components horizontally.

```
//Complete code called BoxLayoutFrameTest.java in Ch16 from the author's website
import javax.swing.*;
import java.awt.*;
class BoxLayoutPanel extends JPanel {
   BoxLayout boxLayout;
   public BoxLayoutPanel() {
      //Create a box layout with horizontal component placement
      boxLayout = new BoxLayout(this, BoxLayout.X_AXIS);
      setLayout(boxLayout);                    //Add the box layout
      add(new JLabel("Label"));                //Create and add the components
      add(new JTextField("Text Field"));
      add(new JButton("Button"));
      add(new JCheckBox("Check Box"));
   }
}
```

Figure 16.9 shows the execution result:

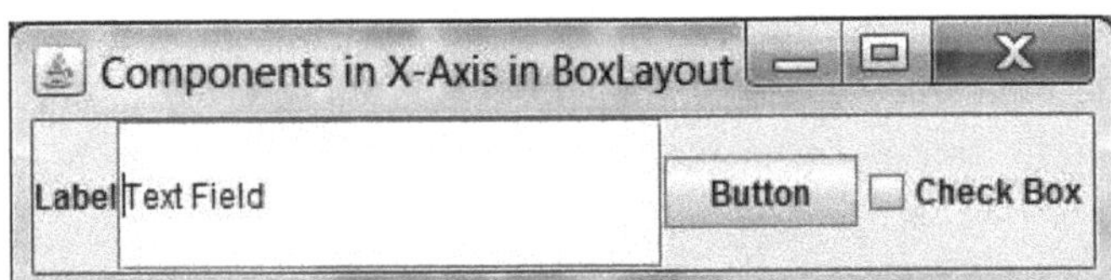

Figure 16.9 The execution result of a horizontal box layout

Example 2. Modify the code in **Example 1** to display the components in the box layout vertically. We need only replace the axis specifier to Y_AXIS:

```
//Create box layout with vertical component placement
setLayout(new BoxLayout(this, BoxLayout.Y_AXIS));//Create box layout with vertical
```

Figure 16.10 shows the execution result:

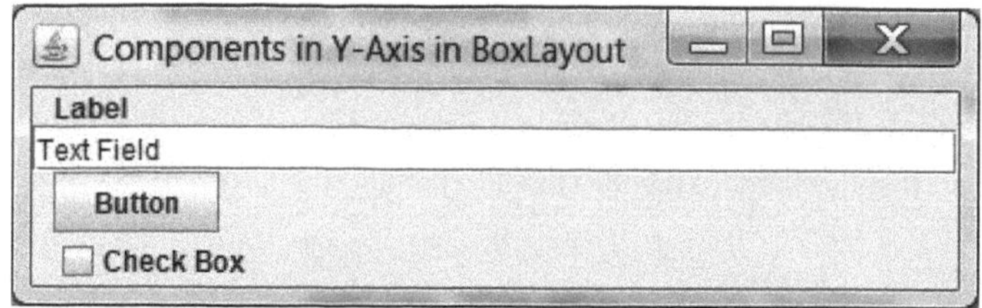

Figure 16.10 Components displayed in box layout vertically

Table 16.7 lists commonly used constructors and methods in **GridLayout**.

Table 16.7 Commonly used constructors and methods in **GridLayout**

Constructor/Method	Description
GridLayout()	Creates the object with one column per component, in a single row (default).
GridLayout(int rows, int cols)	Creates the object with the specified number of rows and columns.
void addLayoutComponent(String name, Component comp)	Adds the specified component with the specified name to the layout.
int getColumns()	Returns the number of columns in the layout.
int getRows()	Returns the number of rows in the layout.

Example 3. Use **GridLayout** to display components in a window containing 3 rows and 2 columns.

```
//Complete code called GridLayoutFrameTest.java in Ch16 from the author's website
import javax.swing.*;
import java.awt.*;
class GridLayoutPanel extends JPanel {
   public GridLayoutPanel() {
      //Create a grid layout containing 3 rows and 2 columns
      setLayout(new GridLayout(3, 2));
      add(new JLabel("Label"));                      //Create and add components
      add(new JTextField("Text Field"));
      add(new JButton("Button"));
      add(new JCheckBox("Check Box"));
      add(new JTextArea("Text Area"));
   }
}
```

We used the grid layout to create a window with five components placed within three rows and two columns. You can see each cell, including the last one containing no component, has the same space allotment:

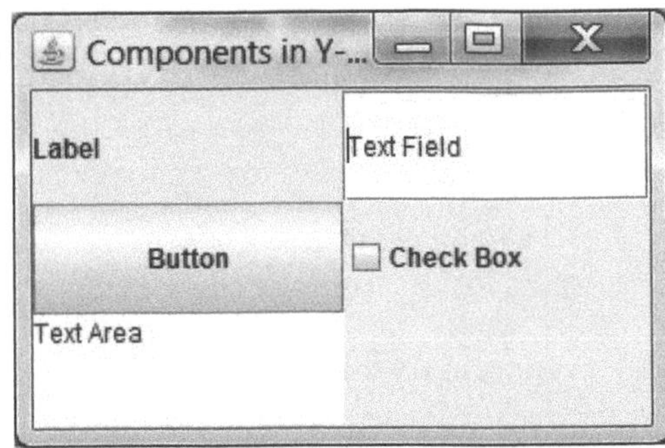

Figure 16.11 Five components displayed in a ~~box~~ grid layout

Example 4. Other commonly used methods in **BoxLayout and GridLayout**.

```
//Display component information
System.out.println(boxLayout.getTarget());

//Display axis orientation of object
System.out.println(boxLayout.getAxis());

//Display number of columns in grid layout object
System.out.println(gridLayout.getColumns());

//Display number of rows in grid layout object
System.out.println(gridLayout.getRows());
```

16.6.1 Nested layouts

As with other layout managers, **BoxLayout** and **GridLayout** are often nested to create more flexible layouts for components in the final display. The following examples show how to nest these layout managers.

Example 1. Use of **BoxLayout** and **BorderLayout** to place a label, text field, check box, and button in a window (see Figure 16.11). The label and text field are displayed at the top of the window. The check box and button are displayed at the bottom of the window. We use two panels to contain the two position's groups for the components. **ComponentPanel1** uses **BoxLayout** to manage the label and text field displayed with a vertical orientation. **ComponentPanel2** uses **BoxLayout** to position the check box and button horizontally. Two static fields, **BorderLayout.NORTH** and **BorderLayout.SOUTH**, are used to place the two panels in the window.

```
//Complete code called BoxLayoutFrameTest3.java in Ch16 from the author's website
import javax.swing.*;
import java.awt.*;
class BoxLayoutFrame3 extends JFrame {
   Toolkit tk = Toolkit.getDefaultToolkit();
   Dimension d = tk.getScreenSize();
```

```
    public BoxLayoutFrame3() {
      //Create panel with vertical component placement
      JPanel componentPanel1 = new JPanel();
      componentPanel1.setLayout(new BoxLayout(componentPanel1, BoxLayout.Y_AXIS));
      componentPanel1.add(new JLabel("Label"));//Add components
      componentPanel1.add(new JTextField("Text Field"));

      //Create another panel with horizontal component placement
      JPanel componentPanel2 = new JPanel();
      componentPanel2.setLayout(new BoxLayout(componentPanel2, BoxLayout.X_AXIS));
      componentPanel2.add(new JCheckBox("Check Box"));    //Add components
      componentPanel2.add(new JButton("Button"));

      //Use border layout to place panel at top
      add(componentPanel1, BorderLayout.NORTH);
      //Use border layout to place panel at bottom
      add(componentPanel2, BorderLayout.SOUTH);

      setTitle("Components in nested Layouts");
      setSize(220, 200);              //Width 220, height 200 pixels
      setDefaultCloseOperation(WindowConstants.DISPOSE_ON_CLOSE);
      centerWindow(this);      //Call programmer-defined method to center display
    }
    ...
}
```

Figure 16.12 shows the execution result.

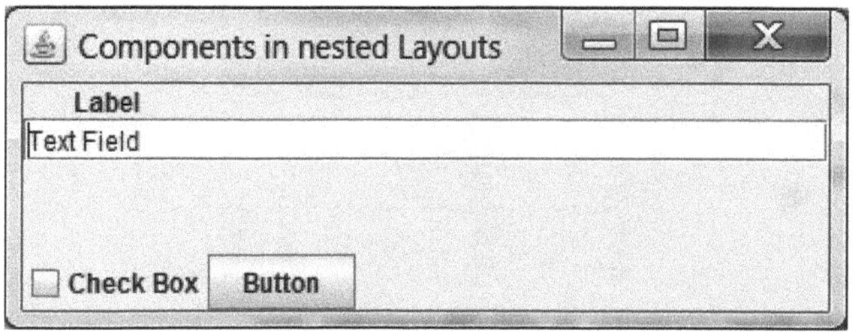

Components in nested Layouts
Label
Text Field
Check Box Button

Figure 16.12 The execution result of the above example using **BoxLayout** and **BorderLayout**

Example 2. Modify the above example using **GridLayout** and **BorderLayout** to perform the same operations. We need only modify the following three lines in the code:

```
//Complete code called GridLayoutFrameTest2.java in Ch16 from the author's website
GridLayout gridLayout = new GridLayout(1, 2);     //Create grid layout with 1X2
componentPanel1.setLayout(gridLayout);            //Add to the first panel
...
```

```
componentPanel2.setLayout(gridLayout);              //Add to the second panel
...
```

The execution result ~~shows~~ is shown in Figure 16.13.

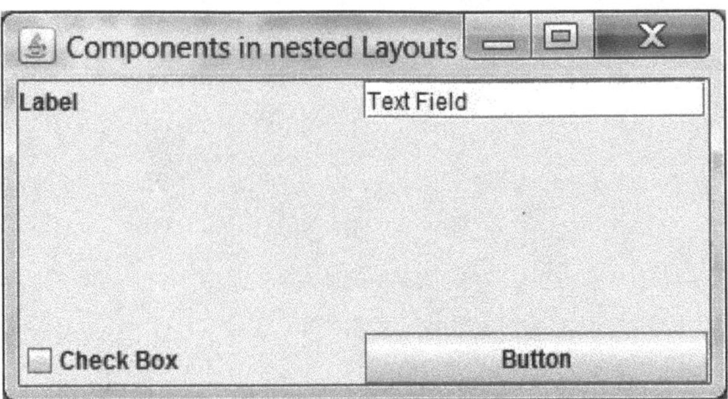

Figure 16.13 The execution result of example using **GridLayout** and **BorderLayout**

16.6.2 Simulation of a calculator (Part 1)

We will use GUI components and layout managers to design the layout of a calculator. The following example is the first part of a simulation—the graphical design and layout of calculator components. Event handling, color assignment, fonts, images, drawing, and audio capabilities are discussed in later chapters. The complete simulation of the calculator is also discussed in later chapters. Figure 16.14 shows the display of the calculator:

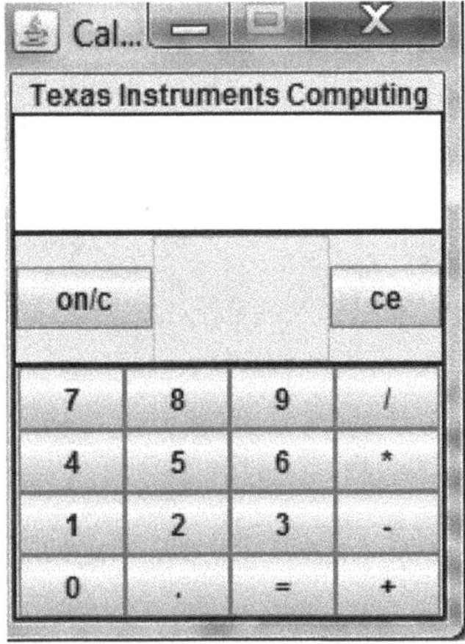

Figure 16.14 A simulated calculator (Part 1)

```
//Complete code called CalculatorFrameAppl.java in Ch16 from the author's website
CalculatorFrame() {                                       //Constructor
   displayPanel = new DisplayPanel();                     //Create display panel
   displayPanel.setLayout(new BoxLayout(displayPanel, BoxLayout.Y_AXIS));//Box layout

   controlPanel = new ControlPanel();                     //Create control panel
   controlPanel.setLayout(new BoxLayout(controlPanel, BoxLayout.X_AXIS));//Box layout
```

```
    controlPanel.setBorder(new LineBorder(Color.BLACK)); //Border

    entryPanel = new EntryPanel();                        //Create input panel
    entryPanel.setLayout(new GridLayout(4, 4));           //Grid layout 4X4
    entryPanel.setBorder(new LineBorder(Color.BLACK));    //Border

    add(displayPanel, BorderLayout.NORTH);                //Display at the top
    add(controlPanel, BorderLayout.CENTER);               //Display at the center
    add(entryPanel, BorderLayout.SOUTH);                  //Display at the bottom

    setTitle("Calculator");                               //Name of the window
    setSize(190, 260);                                    //Size of the window
    setResizable(false);                                  //image is not resizable
    setVisible(true);                                     //Set to display
    }
}
```

The calculator consists of three panels: input/output display, panel of control keys Esc and C, and the keyboard. **LineBorder()** and **setBorder()** construct the black borders bounding each panel. Event handling and other functions in the simulation are discussed in Section 18.3.3. The following code, **DisplayPanel**, constructs the calculator's input/output display panel. Code for **ControlPanel** and **EntryPanel** are similar in nature; the complete code can be found on the author's website.

```
class DisplayPanel extends JPanel {
    private JLabel name;
    private JTextArea display;
    DisplayPanel() {
        name = new JLabel("  ");                          //Display the empty space
        add(name);                                        //Add to the panel
        display = new JTextArea(3, 20);                   //Create text field
        display.setEditable(false);                       //Non-editable
        display.setBorder(new LineBorder(Color.BLACK));   //Set border
        add(display);                                     //Add to the panel
    }
}
```

16.7 GridBagLayout

The **GridBayLayout** class is included in **java.awt**. It provides a vast number of resources allowing the user much flexibility and complexity in designing a GUI component layout. It is similar to **GridLayout**, in which the components are placed in same-sized cells; however, in **GridBagLayout**, the sizes of the rows and columns can vary allowing a component to occupy more than one cell. Furthermore, **GridBagLayout** provides static fields and variables, e.g., **GridBagLayoutConstraints** and the **Insets** class, to adjust the space between components and the space inside a component. **GridBagLayout** is often nested with other layout managers to achieve finer positioning and management of the components. In addition, the locations of components placed in **GridBagLayout** are fixed and will not change as the size of a window changes. Table 16.8 lists the **GridBagLayout** constructor and commonly used methods of the class.

Table 16.8 Constructor and commonly used methods in **GridBagLayout**

Constructor/Method	Description
GridBagLayout()	Creates a GridBagLayout object.
GrigBagConstraints getConstraints(Component component)	Gets constraints for the specified component. A copy of the object of GridBagLayoutConstraints is returned.
float getLayoutAlignmentX(Container parent)	Returns the x-Axis alignment between the components. The value range is from 0 – 1.
float getLayoutAlignmentY(Container parent)	Returns the y-Axis alignment between the components. The value range is from 0 – 1.
void removeLayoutComponent(Component comp)	Removes specified component from the layout. Most applications do not call this method directly.
void setConstraints(Component component, GridBagConstraints constraints)	Sets constraints of the specified component.

In using the **GridBagLayout** manager to position GUI components, you will create an object of **GridBagLayoutConstraints**, then specify the adjustment space between components and the alignments inside a component. We discuss coding examples using this practice in the next section. Table 16.9 lists commonly used constructors and variables associated with **GridBagLayoutConstraints** and **Insets**.

Table 16.9 **GridBagConstraints** and **Insets** constructors; commonly used variables

Constructor/Variable	Description
GridBagConstraints()	Creates a GridBagConstraints object with default values.
int gridx	Specifies the cell containing the leading edge of the component's display area, where the first cell in a row is `gridx=0`.
int gridy	Specifies the cell at the top of the component's display area, where the topmost cell is `gridy=0`.
int gridwidth	Specifies number of cells in a row of the display area.
int gridheight	Specifies number of cells in a column of the display area.

double weightx	The percent of the weight of the component in the X-Axis (0 – 100).
double weighty	The percent of the weight of the component in the Y-Axis (0 - 100).
int ipadx	Specifies the horizontal pixel adjustment padding if there is a space inside the component.
int ipady	Specifies the vertical pixel adjustment padding if there is a space inside the component.
int anchor	Determines where, within the display area, to place the component. Adjusts the position of the component with the specified field as NORTH, SOUTH, WEST, EAST, CENTER, NORTHEAST, or SOUTHEAST if there is a space in the cell.
int fill	Determines how, within the display area, to re-size a component. Adjusts the position of the component in the cell with the specified filed as NONE, HORIZONTAL, VERTICAL, or BOTH, if there is a space. May not be used together with an anchor field.
Insets(int top, int left, int bottom, int right)	Creates an object with the specified insets. You may not use this constructor if weightx and weighty are used.

16.7.1 Steps in design and coding GridBagLayout

Let's use the following GUI window design (Figure 16.15) to discuss the steps in coding with a **GridBagLayout** manager.

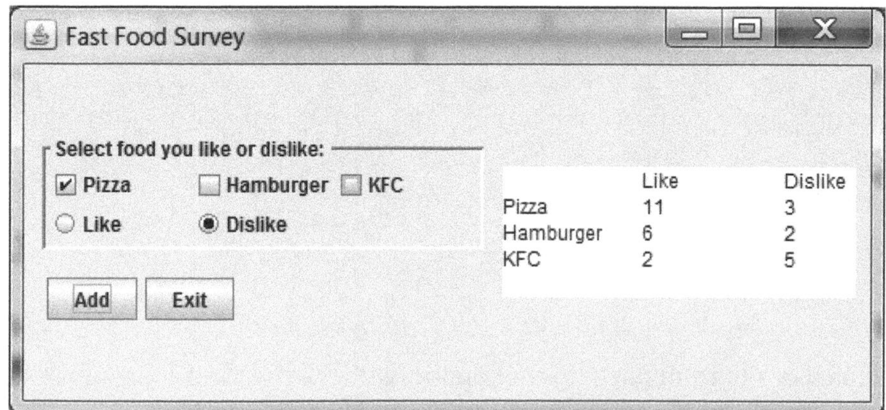

Figure 16.15 A typical GUI design using GridBagLayout

The common steps in coding **GridBagLayout** are:

1. Use a grid to design the component layout. You may divide the components into groups based upon function, so each group becomes a panel (see Figure 16.16). You may also consider using nested layouts in the design.

2. Create an object of **GridBagLayout**, e.g., **setLayout(new GridBagLayout());**

3. Create an object of **GridBagConstraints** to position and adjust the components:

```
GridBagConstraints c = new GridBagConstraints();
```

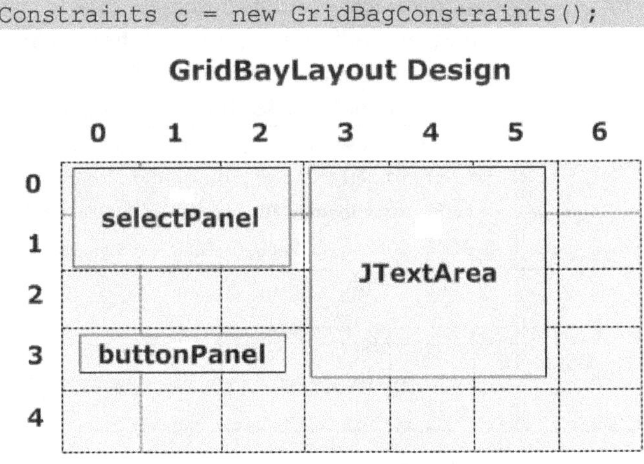

Figure 16.16 Design of the GridBagLayout

4. For each panel, code each component using the specified layout manager. Go to Step 5 if there is no panel present in the design.
5. Use the **GridBagConstraints** fields to position each component, e.g., **selectPanel**, **buttonPanel**, et cetera (see Figure 16.15).

```
c.gridx = c.gridy = 0; //c is an object of GridBagConstraints
c.gridwidth = 3;
c.gridheight = 2;
c.insets = new Insets(5, 5, 5, 5);
c.ipadx = c.ipady = 4;
c.fill = GridBagConstraints.WEST;
```

6. Add the panel or the component to the window with the specified constrains:

```
add(selectPanel, c);
```

7. Repeat Steps 4 to 6 until the coding of all components is completed.

Normally, we write a method incorporating the code shown in Step 5 for re-use and simplification of the coding procedure. In addition, you must also code event handling mechanisms for all components triggering events. We discuss event handling for this example in the next section.

16.7.2 Application example using GridBagLayout

The following example uses the steps listed above to code a **GridBagLayout** design in the application shown in Figure 16.14.

```
//Complete code called FoodSurveyPanel2.java, FoodSurveryFrame2.java and
//FoodSurveyFrame2App.java in Ch16 from the author's website
import java.awt.event.*; import javax.swing.*;
import javax.swing.border.*;

public class FoodSurveyPanel2 extends JPanel implements ActionListener {
   private Border loweredBorder;     //Declare border
   private GridBagConstraints c;     //Declare Gridbag constraints
   //Declare components
   private int pizzaLikeCount, hamburgerLikeCount, kfcLikeCount;
   private int pizzaDislikeCount, hamburgerDislikeCount, kfcDislikeCount;
   private JCheckBox pizzaBox, hamburgerBox, kfcBox;
   private JRadioButton likeRadioButton, dislikeRadioButton;
   private ButtonGroup buttonGroup;
   private JButton addButton, exitButton;
   private JTextArea displayTextArea;
   //Constructor
   public FoodSurveyPanel2() {
      pizzaLikeCount = hamburgerLikeCount = kfcLikeCount = 0;
      pizzaDislikeCount = hamburgerDislikeCount = kfcDislikeCount = 0;
      loweredBorder = BorderFactory.createBevelBorder(BevelBorder.LOWERED);
      createGUIComponents();                    //Call user-defined method
   }
   private void createGUIComponents() {
      setLayout(new GridBagLayout());       //Create object of GridBagLayout
      c = new GridBagConstraints();         //Create object of GridBagConstraints

      JPanel selectPanel = new JPanel();          //Create the panel
      selectPanel.setBorder(BorderFactory.createTitledBorder(loweredBorder, "Select
food you like or dislike:"));
      selectPanel.setLayout(new GridLayout(2, 3));       //Use GridLayout
      pizzaBox = new JCheckBox("Pizza");                 //Add the component
      selectPanel.add(pizzaBox);
      humburgerBox = new JCheckBox("Hamburger");
      selectPanel.add(hamburgerBox);
      kfcBox = new JCheckBox("KFC");
      selectPanel.add(kfcBox);

      likeRadioButton = new JRadioButton("Like", true);
      dislikeRadioButton = new JRadioButton("Dislike");
      selectPanel.add(likeRadioButton);
      selectPanel.add(dislikeRadioButton);
      buttonGroup = new ButtonGroup();
      buttonGroup.add(likeRadioButton);
      buttonGroup.add(dislikeRadioButton);
```

```
    //Call user-defined method
     setupConstraints(0, 1, 3, 2, GridBagConstraints.WEST);
     add(selectPanel, c);          //Add the constrains to frame
     ...
```

The above code describes the layout for GUI components in **selectPanel**. Other panels or components, such as **buttonPanel** and **displayTextArea**, are similar to this code. You may note the user-provided method **setupConstraints()** is created to simplify the code by assigning constraints to each component:

```
private GridBagConstraints setupConstraints(int gridx, int gridy, int gridwidth,
         int gridheight, int anchor) {
   GridBagConstraints c = new GridBagConstraints(); //For returning constraints
   c.gridx = gridx;
   c.gridy = gridy;
   c.insets = new Insets(5, 5, 5, 5);       //Set the pixels for adjustment
   c.ipadx = c.ipady = 0;                   //No adjustment inside a component
   c.gridwidth = gridwidth;
   c.gridheight = gridheight;
   c.anchor = anchor;                       //Adjust anchor in the cell
   return c;                  //Return the object encapsulating the constraints
}
```

16.8 UIManager

The API class **UIManager** is used to manage the style of a GUI display. It is part of **javax.swing**. These styles are often called the "look-and-feel" (L&F) of a display and describe the visual effect of the GUI components. The default style is the cross-platform Java "look-and-feel" known as "metal." All of our examples discussed so far use the "metal" look-and-feel. Java provides the following three look-and-feel styles:

javax.swing.plaf.metal.MetalLookAndFeel – default Java look-and-feel; also known as "metal"

com.sun.java.swing.plat.MotifLookAndFeel – style SUN Solaris Motif look-and-feel

com.sun.java.swing.plaf.windows.WindowsLookandFeel – style for Microsoft Windows versions

Figure 16.17 shows these 3 styles.

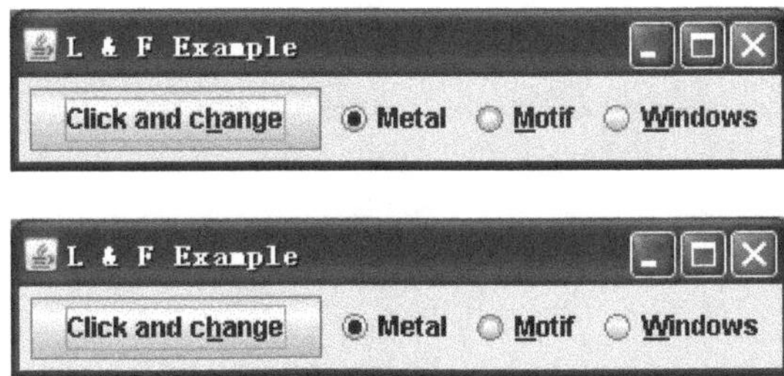

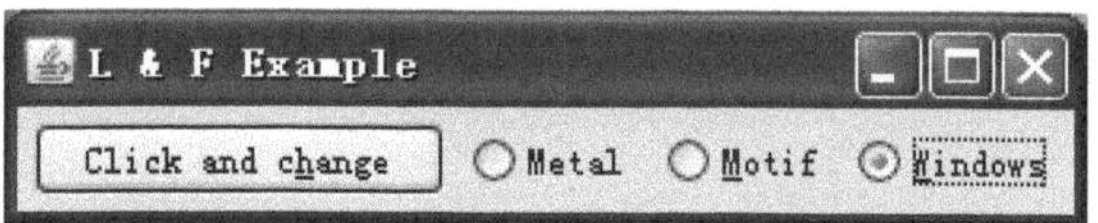

Figure 16.17 Three display styles in UIManager

UIManager is not used only to control display styles. It can also be used to retrieve the platform default properties of GUI components, such as colors, fonts and font sizes, borders, L&F, and related exception handling. Other functionality, such as nested L&F loading and managing, local L&F loading, distinguishing, and defining L&F in XML, are beyond our discussion. Our focus is using **UIManager** to set different styles of components.

16.8.1 Commonly used UIManager capabilities

UIManager is provided by the **javax.swing.UIManager** package. It includes many static methods to be called by the **LookAndFeel** class to set the style of a display. In addition, after setting the style, another static method, **updateComponentTreeUI()**, in the **SwingUtilities** class is called to update the display. Table 16.10 lists some of these commonly used static methods.

Table 16.10 Commonly used static methods in **UIManager**, **LookAndFeel**, and **SwingUtilities** to set the styles of display

Static method	Description
LookAndFeel getLookAndFeel()	Returns an object of LookAndFeel.
static void setLookAndFeel(LookAndFeel laf)	Sets current style to the specified look-and-feel style.
static void setLookAndFeel(String className)	Loads the LookAndFeel specified by the class name.
static void updateComponentTreeUI(Component c)	Method of SwingUtilities to update the current style of display.

Example 1. Get the current L&F style in the system.

```
System.out.println("The current look and feel is: " + UIManager.getLookAndFeel());
```

The following result will be displayed if the system is currently using the default L&F:

```
The current look and feel is: [The Java(tm) Look and Feel - javax.swing.plaf.
metal.MetalLookAndFeel]
```

Example 2. Set the current L&F to the Microsoft Windows style and update the setup:

```
try {
   setLookAndFeel("com.sun.java.swing.plaf.windows.WindowsLookAndFeel");
   SwingUtilities.updateComponentTreeUI(this);
}
```

```
catch (IllegalAccessException e) {
   Systen.err.println(e);
}
```

The last display shown in Figure 16.16 is the result of executing the above code. Note that method **setLookAndFeel()** requires handling of the **UnsupportedLookAndFeelException** and other exceptions:

```
ClassNotFoundException
InstallationException
IllegalAccessException
UnsupportedLookAndFeelException
```

16.8.2 Application example

We will modify the example discussed in Section 16.7.1 to display three look-and-feel styles in the window. Three buttons are added, located at the top of the text area, to select the three different display styles. The modified application also provides the required event handling code for updating the look-and-feel.

```
//Complete code called FoodSurveyPanel3.java, FoodSurveryFrame3.java, and
//FoodSurveyFrame3App.java in Ch16 from the author's website

//set three different look-and-feel styles
private final String metalClassName = "javax.swing.plaf.metal.MetalLookAndFeel",
              motifClassName = "com.sun.java.swing.plaf.motif.MotifLookandFeel",
              windowsClassName = "com.sun.java.swing.plaf.windows.WindowsLookAndFeel";
//Declare three radio buttons
private JRadioButton metalRadioButton, motifRadioButton, windowRadioButton;
private ButtonGroup buttonGroup, buttonGroup2;    //Arrange them in the button
group
public FoodSurveyPanel3() {
   ...
   JPanel lafPanel = new JPanel();                  //Create the panel
   lafPanel.setBorder(BorderFactory.createTitledBorder(raisedBorder, "Select your
favored style: "));
   lafPanel.setLayout(new GridLayout(1, 3));        //1 X 3
   metalRadioButton = new JRadioButton("Metal", true);//Create 3 radio buttons
   motifRadioButton = new JRadioButton("Linux");
   windowRadioButton = new JRadioButton("Windows");
   lafPanel.add(metalRadioButton);                  //Add to the panel
   lafPanel.add(motifRadioButton);
   lafPanel.add(windowRadioButton);
   metalRadioButton.addActionListener(this);        //Add for event handling
   motifRadioButton.addActionListener(this);
   windowRadioButton.addActionListener(this);
   buttonGroup2 = new ButtonGroup();          //Button group
   buttonGroup2.add(metalRadioButton);
   buttonGroup2.add(motifRadioButton);
```

```
    buttonGroup2.add(windowRadioButton);
    c = setupConstraints(3, 0, 3, 1, GridBagConstraints.WEST); //Set constraints

    add(lafPanel, c);                                         //Add to the frame
    ...
}
```

Note that the code also uses the border to display the three radio buttons. The following code snippet shows the event handling required by the radio button:

```
try {
    if (source == metalRadioButton)
        UIManager.setLookAndFeel(metalClassName);
    if (source == motifRadioButton)
        UIManager.setLookAndFeel(motifClassName);
    if (source == windowRadioButton)
        UIManager.setLookAndFeel(windowsClassName);
    SwingUtilities.updateComponentTreeUI(this);
}
catch (Exception ex) {
    System.err.println(ex);
}
```

Figure 16.18 shows the execution result where the Linux L&F style is selected:

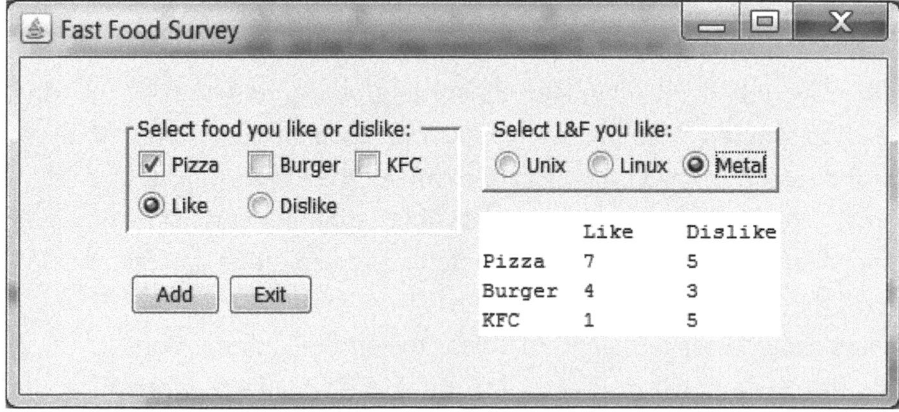

Figure 16.18 Linux L&F style is displayed in the execution result

Exercises

1. What are the commonly used layout managers provided by Java? Use examples in describing their features.

2. What is a nested layout? List the steps to design a nested layout.

3. What is a border? Why should a border be used? List the steps to properly code a border.

4. Modify **Exercise 9** in Chapter 15 to display the text field and button in a border titled: "Input the Info:." Delete the label. Display the second text field in another border titled: "The result of statistics:." Write the driver code to test your modified code. Save all files.

5. Modify **Exercise 6** in Chapter 15 to display the label and text field in a border titled: "Kilometer/Mile Converter." Display the two buttons in another border titled: "Operation." Write the driver code to test your modified code. Save all files.

6. What is a tabbed pane? List the steps to properly code a tabbed pane.

7. Modify **Exercise 6** in Chapter 15 to use a tabbed pane, instead of radio buttons, to select the different conversion methods. Write the driver code to test your modified code. Save all files.

8. Use the proper GUI layout manager(s) and nested layout manager(s), as required, to code a window displaying a simple calculator, as shown in Figure 16.19.

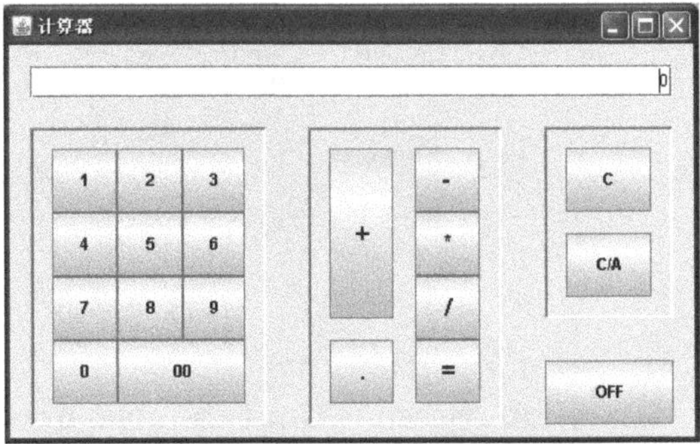

Figure 16.19 The GUI layout for Exercise 8

9. Use **GridBagLayout** and any other layout managers, as required, to code the window shown in Figure 16.20 to simulate customer payments. Your code must contain all required event handling. If a customer selects credit card payment, the display will show a list of acceptable credit cards. A text field for entering a valid credit card number must be provided. Pull down lists, as shown in the figure, for setting the credit card expiration date are required. After the user presses the **Accept** button, the program will use method **JOptionPane.showMessageDialog()** to display the entered information. If the user opts to pay using cash, the program will display the associated cash payment information after the **Accept** button is clicked. Write the driver code to test your modified code. Save all files.

Figure 16.20 GUI layout for Exercise 9

10. What is the purpose of **UIManager**? What are the three "look-and-feel" styles? What style is the system default?

11. Modify Exercise 12 in Chapter 15 using **UIManager** to include selections for displaying the three look-and-feel styles. You may decide the placement and the default selections using radio buttons. Write the driver code to test your modified code. Save all files.

"One picture is worth a thousand words."

– Fred R. Barnard

Chapter 17 More GUI Components and Event Handling

In this chapter, we continue to discuss more GUI components: combo box, list, menu, slider, progress bar, color chooser, table, tree, and desktop pane. We also discuss event handling of these components and other event handling techniques for mouse and keyboard. A summary of five different coding methods for event handling is also discussed.

17.1 Drop Down Menu - JComboBox

A combo box provides a drop down menu for selecting an item. It allows you to select only one item at a time. Figure 17.1 shows a typical combo box. When the user clicks on the triangle tab, a drop down list appears displaying all items in the collection.

Figure 17.1 A typical example of the combo box

Table 17.1 lists commonly used constructors and methods in **JComboBox**. In the following sections, we discuss how to use them.

Table 17.1 Commonly used constructors and methods in JComboBox

Constructor/Method	Description
JComboBox()	Creates an empty combo box with the default model.
JComboBox(Object[] items)	Creates a combo box with the specified items in the array.
void addActionListener(ActionListener e)	Adds event handling to the combo box using ActionListener.
void addItem(Object item)	Adds the specified item to the combo box item list.
void addItemListener(ItemListener e)	Adds event handling to the combo box using ItemListener.
Object getItemAt(int index)	Returns the item at the specified index.
int getItemCount()	Returns the quantity of items in the list.
Object getSelectedItem()	Returns the selected item.
int getSelectedIndex()	Returns the first item in the list matching the given item.
void insertItemAt(Object item, int index)	Inserts specified item into list at the specified index.
boolean isEditable()	Returns true if the combo box is editable; otherwise

	returns false.
void removeItem(Object item)	Removes specified item from the item list.
void removeItemAt(int index)	Removes item at the index. This method works only if JComboBox uses a mutable data model.
void setEditable(Boolean flag)	Sets editable status of the combo box.
void setMaximumRowCount(int rows)	Sets the maximum number of rows of displayed items in the combo box.
void setSelectedItem(int index)	Selects the selected item by specified index.

17.1.1 Examples

Example 1. Declare and create a combo box.

```
String[] books = {"Programming Arts in Java", "All C/C++ Programming", "JSP and
Servlets"};
JComboBox bookComboBox = new JComboBox(books);    //Create a combo box with 3 rows
...
JComboBox myComboBox;                             //Declare a combo box
myComoBox = new JComboBox();                      //Create an empty combo box
myComboBox.addItem("Pizza");                      //Add the items into the combo
box
myComboBox.addItem("Hamburger");
myComoBox.addItem("KFC");
```

Example 2. Call commonly used methods in combo box.

```
//Continued from Example 1
System.out.println(bookComboBox.getItemAt(0)); //Display Programming Arts in Java
System.out.println(bookComboBox.getItemCount()); //Print 3
myComboBox.insertItemAt("French Fries", 2);      //Insert the item before KFC
System.out.println(bookComboBox.isEditable());   /Display true
bookComboBox.removeItem("JSP and Servlets");     //Delete the item
myComboBox.setSelectedItem(1);               //Set the selected item as Hamburger
bookComboBox.setEditable(false);             //Set the combo box as uneditable
myComboBox.setMaximumRowCount(2);            //Set the maximum row of display as 2
```

Example 3. Add the combo box for display.

```
//More and complete coding examples can be found in ComboBoxFrameTest.java and
//ComboBoxFrame2Test.java in Ch17 from the author's website

add(bookComboBox);                                //Add to the frame
JPanel selectPanel = new JPanel();                //Create a panel
selectPanel.add(myComboBox);                      //Add to the panel
```

17.1.2 Event handling

The following code snippet is an example of event handling in a combo box.

```
//Complete code called ComboBoxFrame2Test.java in Ch17 from the author's website
myComboBox.addActionListener(this);                    //Add event handling
...
public actionPerformed(ActionEvent e) {
   Object source = e.getSource();
   if (source == myComboBox) {                         //If the combo box triggered
event
      if (myComboBox.getSelectedItem() == "Pizza")
         JOptionPane.showMessageDialog(null, "You have selected Pizza.");
      else if (myComboBox.getSelectedItem() == "Hamburger")
         JOptionPane.showMessageDialog(null, "You have selected Hamburger.");
      else if (myComboBox.getSelectedItem() == "French Fries")
         JOptionPane.showMessageDialog(null, "You have selected French Fries.");
      else
         JOptionPane.showMessageDialog(null, "You have selected KFC.");
   }
}
```

17.1.3 Use of ItemListener

You may have noticed in Table 17.1 the **ItemListener** interface can be used to handle an event in a combo box. **ItemListener** can be used to handle events of components with multiple items, e.g., list, menu, tabbed pane, in addition to combo box. The selection of an item generates three(3) events: two items events and one action event. When a user clicks the combo box and selects an item, the previous item is "unselected", the chosen item is "selected", and a selection event is triggered. We use these features to write the event handling code. Of course, the event of the combo box can be handled by any other button click to submit the selection in many applications. We discuss this in our examples, as well.

Interface **ItemListener** is provided by the **java.awt.event** package. It is similar to **ActionListener**, in that only one method, **itemStateChanged()**, needs to be implemented by the code writer. In addition, class **ItemEvent** is used to handle events involving multiple items. There are many useful methods in **ItemEvent** that may be conveniently called to handle such events. Table 17.2 lists commonly used methods in **ItemListener**, **ItemEvent**, and **EventObject**.

Table 17.2 Commonly used methods of ItemListener, ItemEvent, and EventObject

Method	Description
void ItemStateChanged(ItemEvent)	Method in interface ItemListener. Invoked when an item is selected or deselected by the user.

void addItemListener(ItemListener)	Adds event handling using ItemListener.
Object getSource()	Returns the object on which the event initially occurred.
Object getItem()	Method of ItemEvent. Returns the item affected by the event.
int getStateChange()	Method of ItemEvent. Returns the state change, SELECTED or DESELECTED, indicating whether the item was selected or deselected, respectively.

Example. Modify the example discussed in Section 17.1.2 so it uses **ItemListener** to handle the combo box event.

```
//Implement ItemListener interface
class SelectPanel2 extends JPanel implements ItemListener {

   JComboBox myComboBox;                          //Declare a combo box

   public SelectPanel2() {                        //Constructor
      ...                                         //Create and add the combo box
      myComboBox.addItemListener(this);           //Add it to item event handling
   }
   //Implement itemStateChanged()
   public void itemStateChanged(ItemEvent e) {
      Object source = e.getSource();
      if (source == myComboBox) {             //If the combo box triggered the event
         if (e.getItem() == "Pizza" && e.getStateChange() == ItemEvent.SELECTED)
            JOptionPane.showMessageDialog(null, "You have selected Pizza.");
         else if (e.getItem() == "Hamburger" && e.getStateChange() ==
                  ItemEvent.SELECTED)
            JOptionPane.showMessageDialog(null, "You have selected Hamburger.");
         else if (e.getItem() == "French Fries" && e.getStateChange() ==
                  ItemEvent.SELECTED)
            JOptionPane.showMessageDialog(null, "You have selected French
Fries.");
         else if (e.getItem() == "KFC" && e.getStateChange() ==
ItemEvent.SELECTED)
            JOptionPane.showMessageDialog(null, "You have selected KFC.");
      }
   }
}
```

As discussed previously, any item status change triggers two status changes in the selection. In the above code, in confirming if a new item triggers an event, we must first verify the particular item and then its state is changed to **SELECTED**.

We may also use method **getSelectedItem()** of **JComboBox** to simplify verification of the selected item:

```
if (source == myComboBox) {           //If the combo box triggered an event
   if (myComboBox.getSelectedItem() == "Pizza")   //If selected item is Pizza
      JOptionPane.showMessageDialog(null, "You have selected Pizza.");
   else if (myComboBox.getSelectedItem() == "Hamburger") //If selected is hamburger
     JOptionPane.showMessageDialog(null, "You have selected Hamburger.");
```

```
    else if (myComboBox.getSelectedItem() == "French Fries") //If it's French Fries
            JOptionPane.showMessageDialog(null, "You have selected French Fries.");
    else
        JOptionPane.showMessageDialog(null, "You have selected KFC.");
}
```

17.1.4 An application example

Let's discuss an application that uses combo box to list commonly used terms in OOP and displays the selected term with an explanation in a text area. In the GUI design, we use **GridBagLayout** to position the combo box at the top left and a text area at the top right of the window. Under the combo box, we place a button, **New Term**, that can insert a new OOP term into the combo box and another button, **Exit**, to conclude the application. When the user clicks **New Term**, a new window with a text field allowing the user to enter a new term, a text area to enter the description of the new term, and a **Submit** button are displayed. After the user presses **Submit**, the new term and its description are stored in the combo box and an associated linked-list, the window is hidden, and the display is restored to its original status. Figure 17.2 shows a typical result of execution.

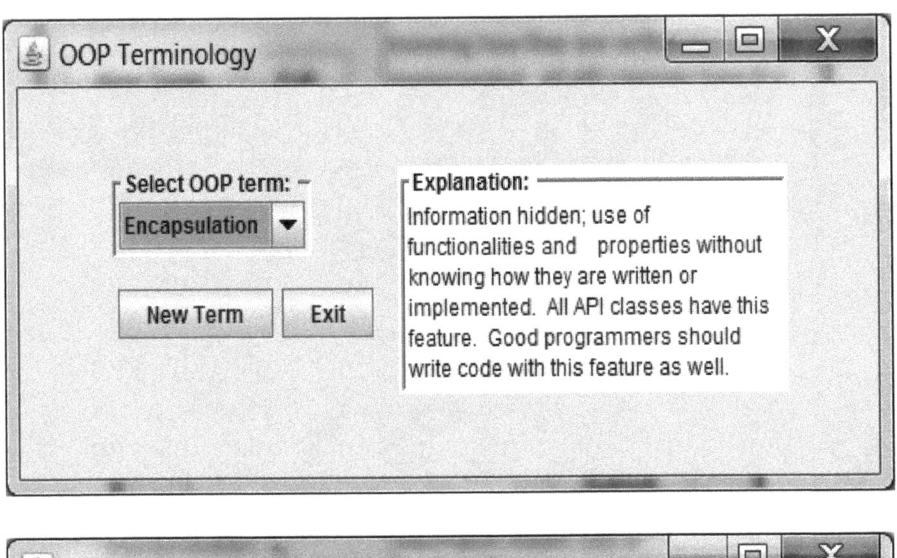

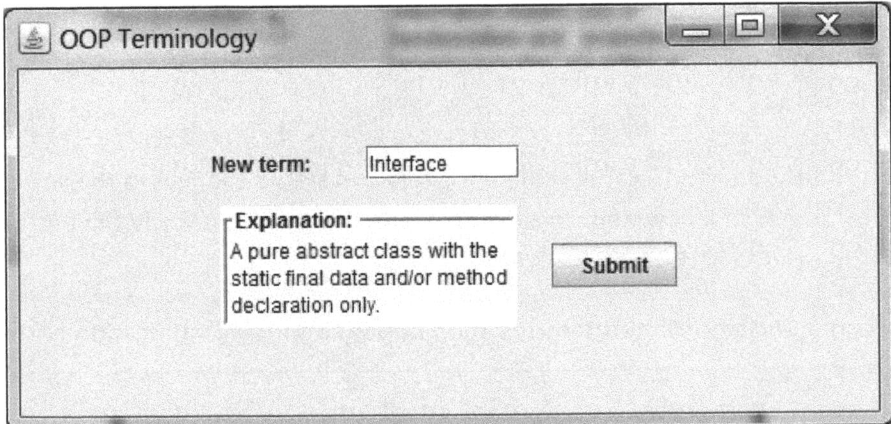

Figure 17.2 Combo box application

In this application code, we use two arrays of String to store three OOP terms and their descriptions. A linked list is used to conveniently insert new terms and descriptions into the application.

```
//Complete code called OOPPanel.java in Ch17 from the author's website
private String[] OOPs = {"Encapsulation", "Inheritance","Polymorphism"};
//Term array
private String[] explains = {"Information hidden; use of functionalities and
properties "    //Description array
         + "without knowing how they are written or implemented.  "
         + "All API classes have this feature.  Good programmers "
         + "should write code with this feature as well.",
           "Inherit properties, including variables and methods, "
         + "by a subclass from superclass(es), saving time "
         + "in case the code is re-written.",
         "A method can carry out a variety of functionalities depending on "
         + "the object that overrides and dynamically calls it."
         };
private LinkedList<String> explainList = new LinkedList<String>(Arrays.
asList(explains));//Insert to the linked list
```

After discussing file I/O in Chapter 21, we may store all terms and descriptions in files or a database to expand our application.

To better utilize **GridBagLayout**, all components except the text area are organized in their corresponding panels: **ComboBoxPanel** to manage the combo box; **ButtonPanel** to manage the **New Item** and **Exit** buttons; **TextPanel** for label and text field management; **TextAreaPanel** for entering a new term and its description; and **Button2Panel** to manage activities associated with **Submit**. All panels are managed by a general panel, **OOPPanel**. The following is the code for all panels:

```
//Complete code called OOPPanel.java, OOPFrame.java and OOPFrameApp.java from
//the author's website


  public OOPPanel() {
      loweredBorder =
BorderFactory.createBevelBorder(BevelBorder.LOWERED);//Border
createGUIComponents();      //Call programmer-defined method to handle layout
 }
 private void createGUIComponents() {
   setLayout(new GridBagLayout());        //Create GridBagLayout
   c = new GridBagConstraints();
```

```
comboBoxPanel = new JPanel();            //Create the combo box panel
comboBoxPanel.setBorder(BorderFactory.createTitledBorder(loweredBorder,
                        "Select an OOP term: "));
comboBoxPanel.setLayout(new GridLayout(1, 2)); //Nested with 1X2 grid layout
comboBox = new JComboBox(OOPs);                       //Create the combo box
comboBox.addActionListener(this);              //Add event handling
comboBoxPanel.add(comboBox);                          //Add to the panel
c = setupConstraints(0, 0, 2, 1, GridBagConstraints.WEST); //Call user-defined
add(comboBoxPanel, c);                                //Add to OOPPanel

buttonPanel = new JPanel();                           //Create button panel
//Nested with flow layout
buttonPanel.setLayout(new FlowLayout(FlowLayout.LEFT));
newItemButton = new JButton("New Term");
buttonPanel.add(newItemButton);
newItemButton.addActionListener(this);
exitButton = new JButton("Exit");
buttonPanel.add(exitButton);
exitButton.addActionListener(this);
c = setupConstraints(0, 3, 2, 1, GridBagConstraints.WEST);
add(buttonPanel, c);

textPanel = new JPanel();                      //Create text panel
textPanel.setLayout(new GridLayout(1, 2));
termLabel = new JLabel("New term: ");
termField = new JTextField(8);
textPanel.add(termLabel);
textPanel.add(termField);
c = setupConstraints(0, 0, 2, 1, GridBagConstraints.WEST);
add(textPanel, c);
textPanel.setVisible(false);                   //Default as hidden

textAreaPanel = new JPanel();                  //Create text area panel
textAreaPanel.setLayout(new FlowLayout(FlowLayout.LEFT)); explainTextArea
= setupTextArea(explainTextArea, 3, 15, true);
textAreaPanel.add(explainTextArea);
c = setupConstraints(0, 1, 2, 3, GridBagConstraints.WEST);
```

```
    add(textAreaPanel, c);
    textAreaPanel.setVisible(false);                //Default as hidden

    button2Panel = new JPanel();                    //Create button2 panel
    button2Panel.setLayout(new FlowLayout(FlowLayout.LEFT));
    submitButton = new JButton("Submit");
    button2Panel.add(submitButton);
    submitButton.addActionListener(this);
    c = setupConstraints(2, 3, 1, 1, GridBagConstraints.WEST);
    add(button2Panel, c);
    button2Panel.setVisible(false);                 //Default as hidden

    displayTextArea = setupTextArea(displayTextArea, 5, 20, true);

//Create text area at the right side of the window for new term description
    comboBox.setSelectedIndex(0);
    updateTextArea(0);                              //Call programmer-defined method
    c = setupConstraints(3, 0, 3, 5, GridBagConstraints.WEST);
    add(displayTextArea, c);
}
```

The code first sets all panels of components dealing with the entry of new terms as "investable," i.e., not displayed, until the user presses **New Term**; they are then set to display the status. This methodology is discussed in the event handling code. There are four programmer-defined methods written to provide convenience and efficiency in implementing the layout and display functions: **createGUIComponents()**, **setupConstraints()**, **setupTextArea()**, and **updateTextArea()**. The following is the code of **setupTextArea()**:

```
private JTextArea setupTextArea(JTextArea textArea, int rows, int cols, boolean
editable) {
   textArea = new JtextArea(rows, cols);
   textArea.setLineWrap(true);                           //Display style
   textArea.setWrapStyleWord(true);                      //Word wrap return
   textArea.setEditable(editable);
   textArea.setBorder(BorderFactory.createTitledBorder(loweredBorder,
                    "Explanation: "));                   //Create the border
   return textArea;
}
```

This method manages the content display and initialization of the text area. It is a modification and extension of the code discussed in Section 16.7.2. Another programmer-defined method, **updateTextArea()**, updates the displayed content in the text area:

```
private void updateTextArea(int index) {
   displayTextArea.setText(explainList.get(index)); //Set the displayed content
```

```
   displayTextArea.setVisible(true);                    //Set the display
}
```

Methods **createGUIComponents()** and **setupConstraints()** have been discussed previously.

The following is the code to handle the events:

```
public void actionPerformed(ActionEvent e) {
  int index = 0;
  Object source = e.getSource();                        //Get the source of the event
   if (source == exitButton) {
         System.exit(0);
   }
   else if (source == comboBox) {                       //If it is triggered by combo box
         index=comboBox.getSelectedIndex();             //Get the index of selected item
         updateTextArea(index);                         //Call the method
   }
   else if(source == newItemButton) {                   //If it's triggered by new term
         comboBoxPanel.setVisible(false);               //Hit the combo box
         buttonPanel.setVisible(false);                 //Hit two buttons
         displayTextArea.setVisible(false);             //Hit the text area
         textPanel.setVisible(true);                    //Display the text field
         textAreaPanel.setVisible(true);                //Display the text area
         button2Panel.setVisible(true);                 //Display Submit button
   }
   else if (source == submitButton) {                   //If it's triggered by submit
         comboBox.addItem(termField.getText());         //Update the combo box
         explainList.addLast(explainTextArea.getText());//Add the item to the list
         comboBoxPanel.setVisible(true);                //Display the combo box
         buttonPanel.setVisible(true);                  //Display New Term and Exit
                                                                                       }
           displayTextArea.setVisible(true);            //Display the text area
         textPanel.setVisible(false);                          //Hide the text field
         textAreaPanel.setVisible(false);                      //Hide the text area
         button2Panel.setVisible(false);                       //Hide the submit

}
```

17.2 List - JList

A list is similar to a combo box in its ability to select items; a list, however, allows the selection of multiple items. **JList** is in the **javax.swing** package. A scroll bar can be used to display items not visible in the list window. **ListSelectionListener** is commonly used to handle list events.

Figure 17.3 shows a typical list with a vertical scroll bar. The code for creating this list is discussed in Example 2 of Section 17.2.1. The size of a list can be fixed or variable by calling the proper methods. Table 17.3 describes commonly used constructors and methods of lists.

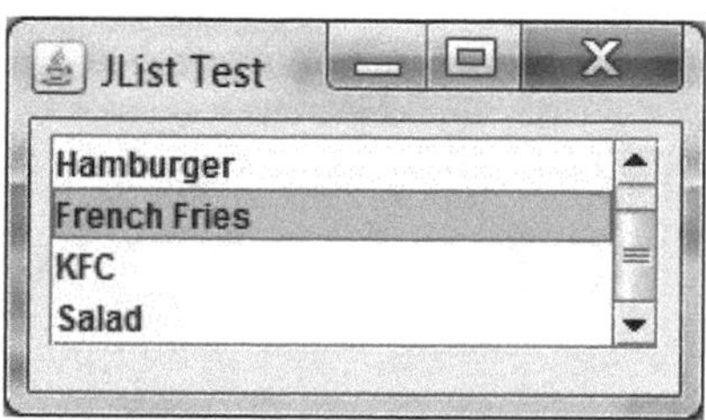

Figure 17.3 A typical list with vertical scroll bar

Table 17.3 Commonly used constructors and methods in **JList**

Constructor/Method	Description
JList()	Creates an empty list with a null, read-only model.
JList(ListModel listModel)	Creates a list with the specified list model (see Section 17.2.3).
JList(Object[] items)	Creates a list displaying the items specified in the array.
void clearSelection()	Clears all selections. After calling this method, isSelectionEmpty() is set to be true.
int getSelectedIndex()	Returns the index of selected item.
int[] getSelectedIndices()	Returns an array of all selected indices, in increasing order.
Object getSelectedValue()	Returns the name of the selected item.
Object[] getSelectedValues()	Returns an array containing the names of all selected items.
boolean isSelectedIndex(int index)	Returns true if the specified item is currently selected.
void setFixedCellWidth(int width)	Set the width (pixels) of the each cell in the list.
void setListData(Object[] items)	Creates a read-only list model from an array of objects. Attempts to modify the array after calling this procedure result in undefined behavior.
void setSelectedIndex(int index)	Use specified index to set an item as selected item.
void setSelectedIndices(int[] indices)	Use array of indices to set multiple selected items.
void setSelectionMode(int mode)	Set the selection mode for the list: ListSelectionModel.SINGLE_SELECTION – only one list index can be selected at a time. ListSelectionModel.SINGLE_INTERVAL_SELECTION – only one contiguous interval can be selected at a time. ListSelectionModel.MULTIPLE_INTERVAL_SELECTION – no restriction on what can be selected (default).

17.2.1 Examples

Example 1. Create a list with the specified items and options.

```
String[] items = {"Yellow", "Blue", "Green", "White", "Black"};
JList list = new JList();                          //Create an empty list
list.setListData(items);                           //Insert the items
```

```
list.setSelectionMode(SINGLE_SELECTION);          //Set as single selection
list.setVisibleCellWidth(200);                    //The width 200 pixels
list.setVisibleRowCounts(4);                      //Set the number of visible cells
                                                  //in the list:  4
add(new JScrollPane(list));                       //Add the vertical scroll bar
```

You may also directly set the items into the list when you create it:

```
JList list = new JList(items);
```

Example 2. A list is often managed by its panel:

```
//Complete code called ListFrameTest.java in Ch17 from the author's website
class JListFrame extends JFrame {
   String[] foods = {"Pizza", "Hamburger", "French Fries", "KFC", "Salad"};
   JList foodList;                                //Declare a list
   JPanel foodPanel;                              //Declare a panel
   public JListFrame() {
      foodPanel = new JPanel();                   //Create the panel
      foodList = new JList(foods);         //Create list with the specified items
      foodList.setFixedCellWidth(200);            //Set width
      foodList.setVisibleRowCount(4);             //Set the visible cells as 4
      foodList.setSelectedIndex(0);        //Set first item as default selection
      foodList.setSelectionMode(ListSelectionModel.SINGLE_INTERVAL_SELECTION);
                      //Set selection mode
      foodPanel.add(new JScrollPane(foodList));//Create scroll bar, add to panel

      add(foodPanel);                             //Add panel to frame
      ...
   }
}
```

Figure 17.3 (above) shows the execution result of this code example.

Example 3. Call other commonly used methods in **JList**:

```
System.out.println(foodList.getSelectedValue()); //Display the selection items
String[] choices = new String[5];
choices = foodList.getSelectedValues();     //Return the selected items to choices
```

If the selected items are **Pizza**, **KFC**, and **Salad**, the elements in **choices** are:

```
choices[0] = "Pizza"          choices[1] = "KFC"          choices[2] = "Salad"
```

17.2.2 ListSelectionListener interface

JList uses the **ListSelectionListener** interface to handle events associated with lists. It does not support the **ActionListener** and **ItemListener** interfaces. Sometimes a list event may be handled by another component, such as a button, for which **ActionListener** may still be used to handle the event.

ListSelectionListener is provided by the **javax.swing.event** package. It contains a single method **valueChanged(ListSelectionEvent)**, to be implemented as shown in Table 17.4.

Table 17.4 **ListSelectionListener** and methods used to handle list events

Method	Description
void valueChanged(ListSelectionEvent e)	Method to be implemented in ListSelectionListener interface. Called when the value of the selection changes.
void addListSelectionListener(ListSelectionListener e)	Adds a listener to the list, to be notified each time a selection change occurs. The preferred way of listening for selection state changes.
Object getSource()	Returns the event source.

Example. Use of **ListSelectionListener** to handle a list event.

```
 //Complete code called ListFrame1Test.java in Ch17 from the author's website
import javax.swing.event.*;   //Import package for ListSelectionListener
class JListPanel extends JPanel implements ListSelectionListener{     //Implement
   String[] foods = {"Pizza", "Hamburger", "French Fries", "KFC", "Salad"};
   JList foodList;
   public JListPanel() {
      //All other code list
      ...
      foodList.addListSelectionListener(this);    //Add the event
   }
   public void valueChanged(ListSelectionEvent e) {      //Implement the method
      Object source = e.getSource();
      if (source == foodList) {
         String selected = (String) foodList.getSelectedValue();
         if ( selected == "Pizza")
            JOptionPane.showMessageDialog(null, "You have selected Pizza.");
         else if (selected == "Hamburger")
            JOptionPane.showMessageDialog(null, "You have selected Hamburger.");
         else if (selected == "French Fries")
            JOptionPane.showMessageDialog(null, "You have selected French 
Fries.");
         else if (selected == "KFC")
            JOptionPane.showMessageDialog(null, "You have selected KFC.");
         else if (selected == "Salad")
```

```
            JOptionPane.showMessageDialog(null, "You have selected Salad.");
        }
        else
           System.exit(0);
    }
}
```

17.2.3 More operations in JList

Package **javax.swing** provides another API class, **DefaultListModel**, used exclusively to carry out the operations in **JList**. **DefaultListModel** implements the **ListModel** interface, so we may use the constructor **Jlist(ListModel)** to create an object of **JList**, encapsulating the information of **DefaultListModel**. Table 17.5 lists the constructor and commonly used methods in **DefaultListModel**.

Table 17.5 Commonly used constructor and methods in **DefaultListModel**

Constructor/Method	Description
DefaultListModel()	Creates a list model.
void add(int index, Object item)	Adds the specified item at the specified index in list model.
void addElement(Object item)	Adds the specified item at the end of the list model.
void clear()	Removes all items from the list model.
boolean contains(Object item)	Returns true if the specified item is contained in the list; otherwise returns false.
Enumeration<?> elements()	Returns an enumeration of the items in the list.
Object get(int index)	Returns the item at the specified index in the list.
Boolean removeElementAt(int index)	Removes the first (lowest-indexed) occurrence of the specified item from the list. Returns true if the item is present in the list; otherwise returns false.
int size()	Returns the number of items in the list model.

Example 1. Use **DefaultListModel** to create a list:

```
String[] items = {"Yellow", "Blue", "Green", "White", "Black"};
DefaultListModel listModel = new DefaultListModel();    //Create a list model
for(String item : items)
   listModel.addElement(item);                      //Add each item to the list model
JList list = new JList(listModel);                  //Create the list
```

Example 2. Use of other commonly referenced methods in **DefaultListModel**.

```
//Continued from above example
listModel.add(0, "Red");                            //Add item Red as the first item
System.out.println(listModel.contains("Black");    //print true
System.out.println(listModel.get(4));               //print Black
System.out.println(lisModel.removeElementAt(0);    //Delete the first item Red
```

```
System.out.println(listModel.size());              //print 5
listModel.clear();                                 //Delete all items
System.out.println(listModel.size());              //Display 0
...
```

17.2.4 Application example

We will modify the example discussed in Section 17.1.4 to use a list, instead of a combo box, to display terms associated with OOP. Figure 17.4 shows the result of executing the modified application:

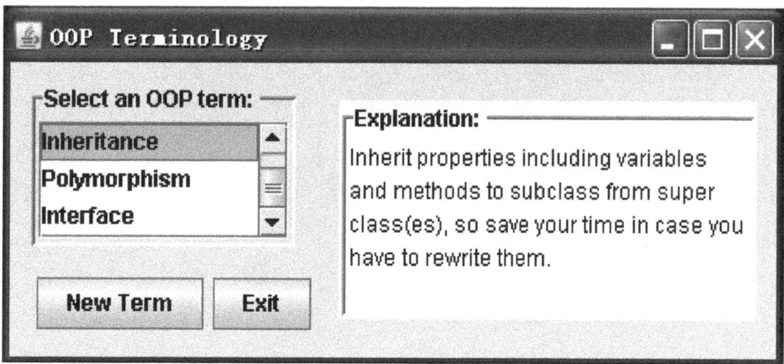

Figure 17.4 Use of list to display the terms in OOP

The following code snippet is the major part of the modified code:

```
//Complete code called OOPListPanel.java, OOPListFrame.java, and
//OOPListFrameApp.java in Ch17 from the author's website

import java.awt.event.*;
import javax.swing.*;
import javax.swing.event.*;  //For ListSelectionListener to handle events in JList
import javax.swing.border.*;
import java.util.*;

//Implement the interface to handle list event
public class OOPListPanel extends JPanel implements ListSelectionListener,
ActionListener {
   private Border loweredBorder;
   private GridBagConstraints c;
   private JPanel listPanel, buttonPanel, button2Panel, textPanel, textareaPanel;
   private JList OOPList;                          //Declare a list
   private DefaultListModel OOPListModel;          //Declare the default model
   ...
   private void createGUIComponents() {
      setLayout(new GridBagLayout());
      c = new GridBagConstraints();
```

```
        listPanel = new JPanel();
        listPanel.setBorder(BorderFactory.createTitledBorder(loweredBorder,
                            "Select an OOP term: "));
        listPanel.setLayout(new GridLayout(1, 1));
        OOPListModel = new DefaultListModel();         //Create the default model
        for(String item : OOPs)                        //Add the item to the list
            OOPListModel.addElement(item);
        OOPList = new JList(OOPListModel);             //Create the model
        OOPList.setVisibleRowCount(2);         //Set number of visible cells
        OOPList.setFixedCellWidth(120);                //Set width 120 pixels
        OOPList.addListSelectionListener(this);        //Add to event handling
        listPanel.add(new JScrollPane(OOPList));       //Create the scroll bar and add
                                                       //to the panel

        c = setupConstraints(0, 0, 3, 1, GridBagConstraints.WEST);
        add(listPanel, c);
        ...
    }
}
```

17.3 More GUI components

In addition to the GUI components previously discussed, Java provides many other components used for special purposes: slider, progress bar, file chooser, color chooser, table, tree, desktop pane, et cetera. These components are included in the **javax.swing** package. We discuss these components in the following sections.

17.3.1 JSlider

Sliders are used to graphically display the value currently chosen in a given range. Figure 17.5 shows a typical slider ranging from 0 – 100 with the slider indicator currently set at 50.

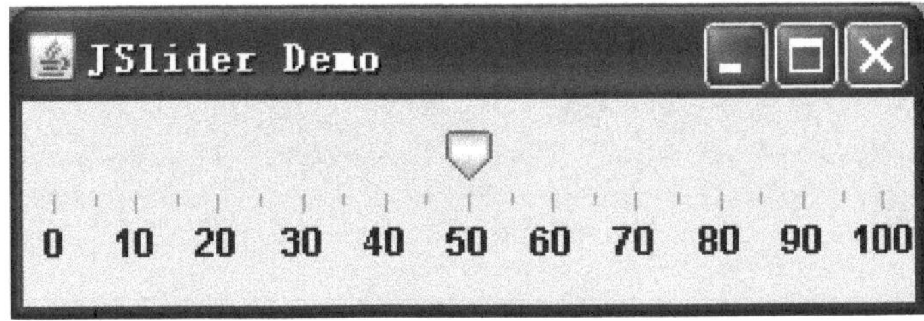

Figure 17.5 A typical slider ranged from 0-100

A slider can be displayed horizontally or vertically. The range and subintervals are specified using methods provided by **JSlider**.

Although many interfaces can be used to handle slider events, **ChangeListener** and **ChangeEvent**, provided by **javax.swing.event**, are most commonly used to handle such events. To handle a slider event, you need only implement method **stateChanged()**. The following example uses two sliders to convert between Celsius and Fahrenheit temperatures. Figure 17.6 displays a typical result of execution.

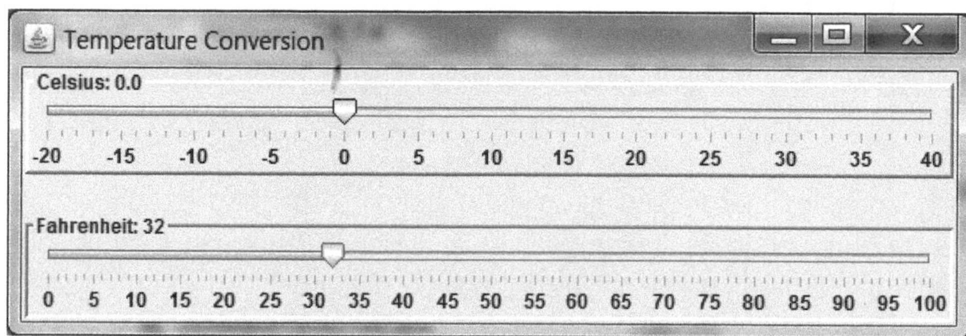

Figure 17.6 A typical execution result in temperature conversion using sliders

The following code snippet shows the steps in creating and adding sliders for display and event handling in a frame:

```
//Complete code called TempConvertFrameApp.java in Ch17 from the author's website
class TempConvertFrame extends JFrame {
   JSlider fSlider, cSlider;                        //Declare two sliders
   Border loweredBorder, raisedBorder;
   JPanel cSliderPanel, fSliderPanel;
   double cTemp, fTemp;
   TempConvertFrame() {
      super("Temperature Conversion");
      loweredBorder = BorderFactory.createBevelBorder(BevelBorder.LOWERED);
      raisedBorder = BorderFactory.createBevelBorder(BevelBorder.RAISED);
      cSliderPanel = new JPanel();
      cSliderPanel.setLayout(new BoxLayout(cSliderPanel, BoxLayout.Y_AXIS));
      cSlider= new JSlider (-20, 40);       //Create a slider with range -20 to 40
      cSlider.setMinorTickSpacing(1);              //Interval is 1
      cSlider.setMajorTickSpacing(5);              //Length is 5
      cSlider.setPaintTicks(true);          //Set the tick display
      cSlider.setPaintLabels(true);         //Set the paint label display
      cSlider.setBorder(BorderFactory.createTitledBorder(raisedBorder,
                     " Celsius: " + 10));               //Create the border
      ChangeListener changeListener = new SliderChangeListener();
      //Create event handling object
      cSlider.addChangeListener(changeListener); //Add the event handling
```

```
        cSliderPanel.add (cSlider);                    //Add to the panel
        add(cSliderPanel, BorderLayout.NORTH);              //Display at the top

        fSliderPanel = new JPanel();
        fSliderPanel.setLayout(new BoxLayout(fSliderPanel, BoxLayout.Y_AXIS));
        fSlider = new JSlider (0, 100);  //Create another slider with range 0-100
        fSlider.setMinorTickSpacing(1);
        fSlider.setMajorTickSpacing(5);
        fSlider.setPaintTicks(true);
        fSlider.setPaintLabels(true);
        fSlider.setBorder(BorderFactory.createTitledBorder(loweredBorder,
                          "Fahrenheit: " + 50));
        changeListener = new SliderChangeListener();
        fSlider.addChangeListener(changeListener);
        fSliderPanel.add(fSlider);
        add(fSliderPanel, BorderLayout.SOUTH);
    }
    ...
}
```

The following code snippet implements the **stateChanged**() method in the **ChangeListener** interface for slider event handling:

```
class SliderChangeListener implements ChangeListener {  //Implement the interface
    public void stateChanged(ChangeEvent e) {           //Code the method
        Object source = e.getSource();
        if (source == fSlider) {
            if (!cSlider.getValueIsAdjusting()) {//If another slider doesn't move
                cTemp = fToCConvert(fSlider.getValue()); //Call the conversion method
                cSlider.setValue((int)cTemp);  /Move the slider to the converted value
                cSlider.setBorder(BorderFactory.createTitledBorder(raisedBorder,
                                  "Celsius: " + cTemp)); //Update the display
                fSlider.setBorder(BorderFactory.createTitledBorder(loweredBorder,
                                  "Fahrenheit: " + fSlider.getValue()));
            }
        }
        else
        if (source == cSlider) {
            if (!fSlider.getValueIsAdjusting()) {
                fTemp = cToFConvert(cSlider.getValue());
                fSlider.setValue((int)fTemp);
                fSlider.setBorder(BorderFactory.createTitledBorder(loweredBorder,
                                  "Fahrenheit: " + fTemp));
                cSlider.setBorder(BorderFactory.createTitledBorder(raisedBorder,
```

```
                                     "Celsius: " + cSlider.getValue()));
            }
        }
    }
}
```

Two programmer-defined methods, **cToFConvert()** and **fToCConvert()**, perform the desired temperature conversions:

```
double cToFConvert(int cTemp) {
   return 9.0/5.0 * cTemp + 32;
}
double fToCConvert(int fTemp) {
   return 5.0/9.0 * (fTemp - 32);
}
```

More Information: *A more detailed discussion and examples of* ***JSlider*** *can be found in the* ***JSlider*** *class of the Java API documentation.*

17.3.2 JProgressBar

A progress bar displays the amount of progress, i.e., the percent of completion, of a specified process in a graphical format. We often see a progress bar displayed showing the amount of a file that has successfully been transferred when being downloaded from the internet. Since a progress bar reflects real-time progress, a thread is normally used to monitor the process implementing the **ActionListener** interface.

Figure 17.7 shows a typical progress bar. The following code snippet is used to generate the progress bar.

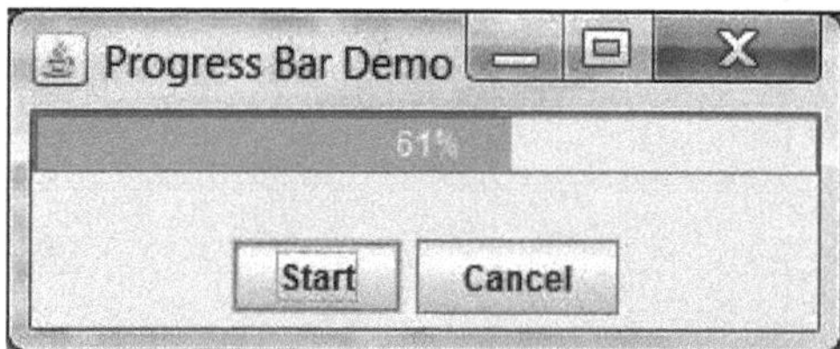

Figure 17.7 A typical progress bar

```
//Complete code called ProgressBarFrameApp.java in Ch17 from the author's website
ProgressBarFrame() {
   super("Progress Bar Demo");
   progressBar = new JProgressBar(0, 100); //Create progress bar with range 0-100
   progressBar.setStringPainted(true);             //Set the display
   add(progressBar, BorderLayout.NORTH);

   minimum = progressBar.getMinimum();             //Get the minimum
   maximum = progressBar.getMaximum();             //Get the maximum
```

```
    panel = new JPanel();
    panel.setLayout(new FlowLayout());
    startButton = new JButton("Start");
    panel.add(startButton);
    cancelButton = new JButton("Cancel");
    panel.add(cancelButton);

    add(panel, BorderLayout.SOUTH);
    startButton.addActionListener(this);
    cancelButton.addActionListener(this);

    setDefaultCloseOperation(JFrame.EXIT_ON_CLOSE);
}
```

The following code implements the **actionPerformed()** method in **ActionListener**:

```
public void actionPerformed(ActionEvent e) {//Implement ActionListener
   Object source = e.getSource();
   if (source == cancelButton)
      System.exit(0);
   else if (source == startButton)
         new Thread(new BarThread()).start();//Create thread and call start()
}
```

BarThread is a programmer-defined inner class that implements the **Runnable** interface. It is used to monitor the real-time progress of the specified process:

```
public void run(){
   for (int i=minimum; i<=maximum; i++){  //The range of the progress
         progressBar.setValue(i);          //Set the value of the change
         progressBar.repaint();            //Update the display
         try{Thread.sleep(DELAY);}
         catch (InterruptedException err){}
   }
}
```

In real-world applications, e.g., downloading a file, some user-defined coding is typically required to determine the (estimated) length of time remaining for completion of the given process. This value can then be provided to the **setValue()** method for updating the progress bar.

More Information: *A more detailed discussion and examples of **JProgressbar** can be found in the **JProgressbar** class of the Java API documentation.*

17.3.3 JFileChooser

File chooser provides functions for graphically creating and selecting files. Figure 17.8 shows an example using a file chooser to select files and calculate the total number of words in the selected text files. File I/O is discussed in Chapter 21.

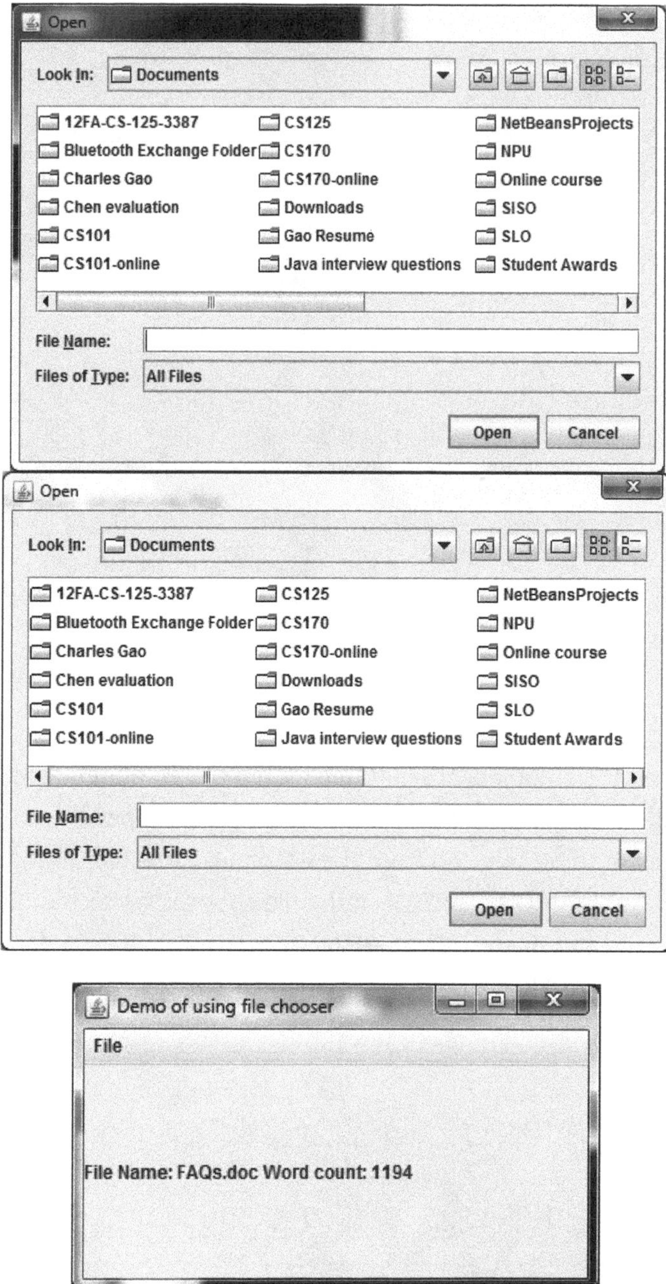

Figure 17.8 The execution result of the demo using file chooser

The following code creates a menu and labels to display the selected file name and word count in the file:

```
//Complete code called FileChooserFrameApp.java in Ch17 from author's website
class FileChooserFrame extends JFrame {
   JMenuBar menuBar;
   JMenu fileMenu;
   JMenuItem openItem, saveItem, exitItem;
   JLabel statusLabel;

   FileChooserFrame() {
      menuBar = new JMenuBar();
      fileMenu = new JMenu("File");
      menuBar.add(fileMenu);
      openItem = new JMenuItem("Open");
      fileMenu.add(openItem);
      fileMenu.insertSeparator(1);
      exitItem = new JMenuItem("Exit");
      fileMenu.add(exitItem);
      setJMenuBar(menuBar);
      statusLabel = new JLabel("It will display the file name and the statistics
of the word count...");
      add(statusLabel);
      ...
   }
}
```

In this example, an anonymous inner class handles the event of menu selection. The implementation of **actionPerformed()** first creates an object of **JFileChooser** then calls **JFileChooser** method **showOpenDialog()** to add the display. The method's **null** argument specifies the opening of a new dialog window, allowing a file to be selected from the list of available files in the current directory. The method returns **JFileChooser.APPROVE_OPTION** if the file chooser is successfully accessed. When the user successfully selects a file and presses **Open**, **JFileChooser** method **getSelectedFile()** is called to return the object of the requested file. The program then calls programmer-defined method **countWordsInFile()** to return the total word count in the file. Method **setText()** displays the file name and word count.

```
//Use an anonymous inner class to handle menu item event
openItem.addActionListener(new ActionListener() {
   public void actionPerformed(ActionEvent e) {
      JFileChooser chooser = new JFileChooser();
      int wordsCount = 0;
      //chooser.setMultiSelectionEnabled(true);
      int option = chooser.showOpenDialog(null);
      if (option == JFileChooser.APPROVE_OPTION) {
          File file = chooser.getSelectedFile();
          wordsCount = countWordsInFile(file);
```

```
          statusLabel.setText("File Name: " + file.getName() + " Word count: " +
wordsCount);
      }
      else {
            statusLabel.setText("You have canceled the file selection.");
      }
   }
});
```

Code for the programmer-defined method **countWordInFile()** is as follows:

```
int countWordsInFile(File file) {
   int numberOfWords = 0;
   String word = null;
   try {
        Scanner sc = new Scanner(file);
        while (sc.hasNext()) {
               word = sc.next();
               numberOfWords++;
        }
        sc.close();
   } catch (FileNotFoundException e) {
            JOptionPane.showMessageDialog(null, e);
   }
   return numberOfWords;
}
```

Because file I/O requires checked exception handling, we must provide for this in the code. File I/O is discussed in Chapter 21.

In a manner similar to handling the menu item event, an anonymous inner class is coded to handle the **exitItem** event:

```
exitItem.addActionListener(new ActionListener() {
   public void actionPerformed(ActionEvent e) {
   System.exit(0);
   }
});
```

More Information: *A more detailed discussion and examples of **JFileChooser** can be found in the **JFileChooser** class of the Java API documentation.*

17.3.4 JColorChooser

API class **Color** is discussed in Chapter 20. In this section, the basics of using **JColorChooser** to select a particular color are introduced. Color palettes HSV, HSL, RGB, and CMYK are presented as sliders provided by **JColorChooser**. A color sample is provided before issuing the selection. **JColorChooser** is in the **javax.swing.colorchooser** package and includes Class **ColorSelectionModel** for proper conversion between color models and event handling. Event handling, however, is often performed through **ChangeListener** in **javax.swing.event** through implementation of method **stateChanged()**. Figure 17.9 shows a typical color chooser.

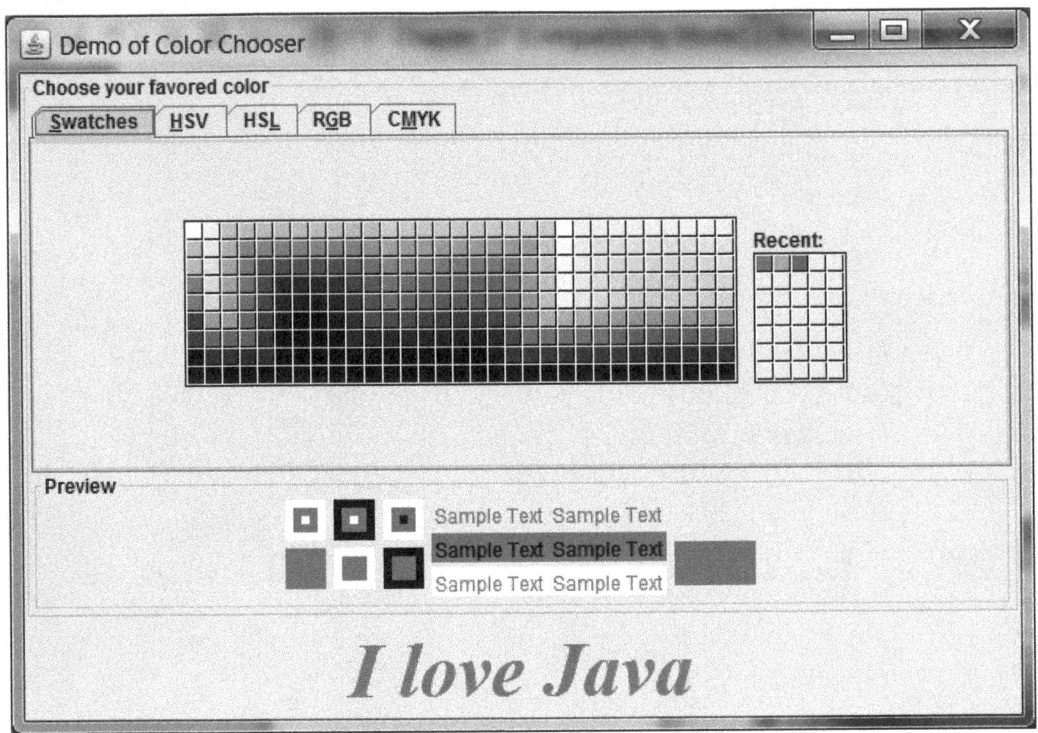

Figure 17.9 A typical color chooser

The following is the code of a color chooser application:

```
//Complete code called ColorChooserFrameApp.java in Ch17 from the author's website
class ColorChooserFrame extends JFrame{
   JColorChooser colorChooser;
   ColorSelectionModel model;
   JLabel label;
   ChangeListener changeListener;
   ColorChooserFrame() {
      super("Color Chooser Application");
      label = new JLabel("I love Java", JLabel.CENTER);
      label.setFont(new Font("Serif", Font.BOLD + Font.ITALIC, 48));
      add(label, BorderLayout.SOUTH);

      colorChooser = new JColorChooser(label.getBackground());
```

```
        colorChooser.setBorder(BorderFactory.createTitledBorder("Choose your
    favored color"));
        add(colorChooser, BorderLayout.CENTER);

        changeListener = new ChangeListener() {
           public void stateChanged(ChangeEvent changeEvent) {
              Color newForegroundColor =
              colorChooser.getColor();
              label.setForeground(newForegroundColor);
           }
        };
        model = colorChooser.getSelectionModel();
        model.addChangeListener(changeListener);
        setDefaultCloseOperation(JFrame.EXIT_ON_CLOSE)
        ;
      }
    }
```

More Information: *A more detailed discussion and examples of **JColorChooser** can be found in the **JColorChooser** class of the Java API documentation.*

Exercises

1. What is a combo box? What is the difference between a combo box and a list?

2. Summarize the differences and similarities between the **ActionListener** and **ItemListener** interfaces.

3. Referring to the examples discussed in Section 17.1.4, develop an application using **JComboBox** to explain a minimum of three(3) terminologies associated with event handling. The explanation is to be displayed in a text area. When the user presses an **Add** button, your application should allow the entering of a new term, addition of the term to the combo box, and addition of the term definition in the text area of the display. Test and run the code. Save all files.

4. Referring to the examples discussed in Section 17.2.4, develop an application using **JList** to explain a minimum of three(3) terminologies associated with event handling. The explanation is to be displayed in a text area. When the user presses an **Add** button, your application should allow the entering of a new term, addition of the term to the list, and addition of the term definition in the text area of the display. Test and run the code. Save all files.

5. Use **JSlider** to code an application that can convert between miles and kilometers. Test your code and save all files.

6. Use **JSlider** to code an application that can convert between pounds and kilograms. Test your code and save all files.

7. Use **JSlider** to code an application that can convert between feet and meters. Test your code and save all files.

8. Use **JFileChooser** to code an application that can open any text file in the folders and count the number of words, lines, and pages in the selected file. Use **showMessageDialog()** in **JOptionPane** to display the statistics. Test and run your code. Save all files.

9. Use **JColorChooser** to code an application to display the text typed in a text field by the user and display it in the color chooser. The text will change color accordingly when the user selects different colors in the color chooser. Test and run your code. Save all files.

10. Use **JTable** to code an application displaying a table containing the square root, square, and cube of the integers from 1 to 10, inclusive. Test and run your code. Save all files.

11. Use **JDesktopPane** to write an application containing three(3) windows for each of the three conversion applications in Exercises 11, 12, and 13 (above), respectively. Upon selecting a window, the user will be asked to enter the data to be converted. When the users presses the **Submit** button, the conversion result will be displayed in the proper location of the window. You may consider using **JSlider** to assist in the development of this application. Test and run your code. Save all files.

"When you see a good person, think of becoming like her/him. When you see someone not so good, reflect on your own weak points."

- Confucius

Chapter 18 More Event Handling

In this chapter we continue to discuss more event handling capabilities of GUI components as well as handling mouse and keyboard events. We also summarize different ways to code event handling.

18.1 More Event Handling In GUI Components

We have experienced many instances of using event handling in association with GUI components. Let's explore more details by discussing how events are handled by the JVM, characteristics of coding event handling procedures, and the use of adapters in handling events.

18.1.1 Explore events in GUI components

We have discussed that Java is a 100% OOP programming language. In addition, Java is also an event-driven language. How is an event handled internally after it has occurred?

We already know the handling of a GUI component event requires the addition or registering of an event handling interface together with the implementation of the interface method to handle the event:

```
button.addActionListener(this);                              //Add event handling
...

public void actionPerformed(ActionEvent e) {                 //Implement the interface
  ...
}
```

or:

```
button.addActionListener(actionEventHandler);     //Add    the    event    handling
interface
...

public void actionPerformed(ActionEvent e) {                 //Implement the interface
   ...
}
```

You may also code an anonymous inner class to add and implement the event handling interface:

```
button.addActionListener(new ActionListener() {//Anonymous inner class to handle
   public void actionPerformed(ActionEvent e) {
```

```
        ...
);
```

Adding or registering an event of a GUI component performs two tasks:

1. Initialization of the event handling argument **listenerList**. Every GUI component registered for event handling has an event monitoring parameter, **listenerList**. It is used as an index in an array of **EventListenerList** objects, provided by **javax.swing.event**, created after the event has been added and the interface has been implemented. Each element in this array encapsulates the data and methods necessary to handle an event triggered by the GUI component. Note that a GUI component may add more than one event handler.

2. Creation of an object in **EventHandler**. An object of **EventHandler**, provided by **javax.swing.event**, is created. The keyword **this** in a typical event handling code also represents the object created to handle the added event of the component if the event interface is implemented by the panel or frame. This object, e.g., **eventHandler**, is created and works together with the **EventListenerList** array in handling the event. The registration of more than one event handler with a GUI component is called multi-event handling.

A component may also cancel event handling by calling:

```
button.removeActionListener(this); //Cancel the event handling
```

Array **eventListenerList** coordinates with **EventHandler** to complete the event handling process as follows: when a GUI component triggers an event, e.g., pressing a button, the JVM sends **EventID**, i.e., **java.awt.Event: public final static int ACTION_EVENT**, to **eventListenerList** and creates an object of **ActionEvent**. This object, including the signature of the calling method, is sent to the event handler, so the method can be called. For example, in a button event, **actionPerformed(ActionEvent)** is called after the event is triggered. If a component triggers multiple events, each event will be handled in a similar manner using multi-threading.

The processing of an event is also called event dispatching. The information or data provided by the object of **ActionEvent** includes:

- The object name of the event source. NOTE: Mouse and keyboard events do not have this data.
- The time (system milliseconds) of the triggered event.
- The ID of the event.
- The x-y coordinates of the event location. NOTE: Mouse event only.
- Code of the keystroke(s). NOTE: Keyboard event only.
- The number of times the mouse key was pressed. NOTE: Mouse event only.
- The name of the object triggering the event, e.g., the name displayed on a button.

If the code has provisions for mouse event handling, the JVM will also send **MOUSE_MOVED** and a **MouseEvent** object to **MouseMotionListener** and call method **MouseMoved(MouseEvent)**. Similarly, when the mouse key is pressed, the JVM calls **MousePressed(MouseEvent)**; releasing the mouse key causes the JVM to call **MouseReleased(MouseEvent)**. If the event is canceled, the JVM will not send **EventID** and the object of the event, thereby not handling the event.

Using a button event as an example, Figure 18.1 shows the processing of the button event.

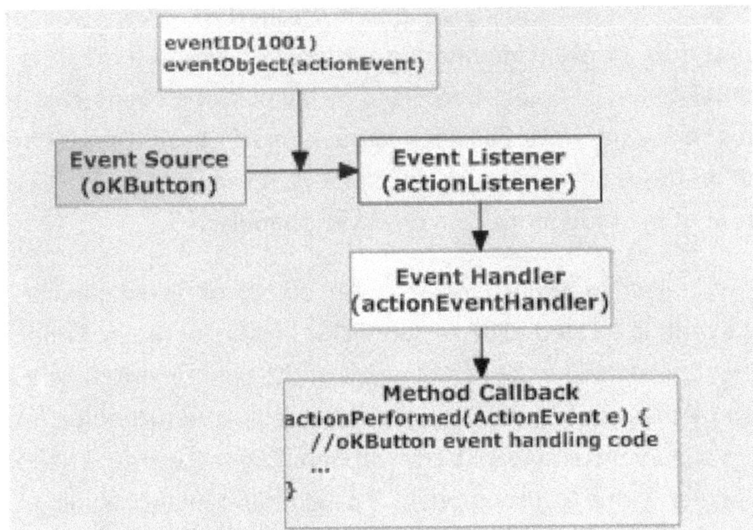

Figure 18.1 Event handling in GUI components

Given the high sophistication of JVM event handling capabilities, programmers only need to concentrate on the following three requirements in coding event handling functionality:

1. Select the correct event handling interface;
2. Select the correct event handling interface;
3. Implement the event handling interface by properly writing the event handling code.

18.1.2 Commonly used interfaces in event handling

Most event handling interfaces are provided by **java.awt.event** and **javax.swing.event**. These interfaces are inherited from **EventListener**. Table 18.1 lists commonly used interfaces in **java.awt.event**.

Table 18.1 Commonly used interfaces for event handling in java.awt.event

Interface/Method	Description
ActionListener	The most commonly used event handling interface in GUI components.
actionPerformed(ActionEvent)	The method needs to be implemented.
AdjustmentListener	The interface used for events in sliders and progress bars.
adjustmentValueChanged(AdjustmentEvent)	The method needs to be implemented.
ComponentListener	The interface used for changes in size, display status, and move events.
componentHidden(), componentMoved(),	The methods need to be implemented. The parameter is

componentResized() and componentShown()	ComponentEvent.
FocusListener	The interface used for focus in keyboard events.
focusGained()、focusLost()	The methods need to be implemented.
ItemListener	The interface used for event handlings in menu and components with multiple items.
itemStateChanged(ItemEvent)	The method needs to be implemented.
KeyListener	The interface use for keyboard events.
keyPressed()、keyReleased()、keyTyped()	The methods need to be implemented. The parameter is KeyEvent.
MouseListener	The interface used for mouse events.
mouseClicked()、mouseEntered()、mouseExited()、mousePressed()、mouseReleased()	The methods need to be implemented. The parameter is MouseEvent.
MouseMotionListener	The interface for mouse motion events.
mouseDragged()、mouseMoved()	The methods need to be implemented. The parameter is MouseEvent.
TextListener	The interface used for document or text events.
textValueChanged(TextEvent)	The method needs to be implemented.
WindowListener	The interface used for windows events.
WindowActivated()、windowClosed()、windowClosing()、windowDeactivated()、windowDeiconified()、windowIconified() windowOpened()	The methods need to be implemented. The parameter is WindowEvent.

Methods of the form **addXxxListener(XxxListener)** are called to add or register event handling of the interfaces listed in Table 18.1. For example:

```
MousePanel.addMouseListener(this);  //Add event handling to the panel
addMouseListener(mouseHandler);     //Add event handling to frame or current
object
```

Table 18.2 lists commonly used event handling interfaces and methods requiring implementation in **javax.swing.event**.

Table 18.2 Commonly used interfaces for event handling in javax.swing.event

Interface/Method	Description
ChangeListener	Used for components in status changes.
stateChanged(ChangeEvent)	Method needs to be implemented.
DocumentListener	Used for documenting events.
changedUpdate(), insertUpdate(), removeUpdate()	Methods need to be implemented. Parameter is DocumentEvent.
ListSelectionListener	Used for components with multiple items.
valueChanged(ListSelectionEvent)	Method needs to be implemented.
MenuListener	Used for menu events.
menuCanceled(), menuDeselected(), menuSelected()	Methods need to be implemented. Parameter is MenuEvent.

PopupMenuListener	Used for popup menu events.
popupMenuCanceled(), popupMenuWillBecomeInvisible(), popupMenuWillBecomeVisible()	Methods need to be implemented. Parameter is PopupMenuEvent.
TreeSelectionListener	Used for tree events.
valueChanged(TreeSelectionEvent)	Method needs to be implemented.

Methods of the form **addXxxListener(XxxListener)** are called to add or register event handling of the interfaces listed in Table 18.2. For example:

```
textArea.addDocumentListener(this); //Add textArea event handling to the frame
textArea.addDocumentListener(textAreaEventHandler);      //Add textAreaEventHandler
```

18.1.3 Adapters

Adapters are used in Java to speed up the process of coding event handlers if there are multiple methods requiring implementation in the corresponding interface. For example, in a window event handler using **WindowAdapter**, one only need to override the method of interest, e.g., **windowActivated(WindowEvent)**, in **WindowAdapter** without concern for developing code for the remaining methods of the adapter class. Compare this technique to the use of **WindowListener** in preparing event handlers, wherein one must implement all seven methods of the interface.

An adapter provides the skeleton containing an empty body of code for each method of its corresponding interface, thereby relieving the programmer of preparing the code structure manually. Adding event handling capabilities is exactly the same for inheriting an adapter or implementing an interface to handle an event.

Table 18.3 Commonly used adapters and their corresponding interfaces

Adapter	Corresponding Interface
ComponentAdapter	ComponentListener
FocusAdapter	FocusListener
KeyAdapter	KeyListener
MouseAdapter	MouseListener
MouseMotionAdapter	MouseMotionListener
WindowAdapter	WindowListener

18.1.4 Examples

The following are examples using adapters.

Example 1. Use **FocusAdapter** to automatically handle the selection of content in a text area. Method **selectAll()** is provided by superclass **JTextComponent** of **JTextArea**. Assume the **textArea** object has been created and added for event handling:

```
public class autoSelectTextArea extends FocusAdapter {
   public void focusGained(FocusEvent e) {
      Object source = e.getSource();
      if (source == textArea)
          textArea.selectAll();
   }
}
```

Example 2. Use **WindowAdapter** to handle a window closing event:

```
public static void main(String[] args) {
   JFrame frame = new JFrame("Window Adapter Demo");
   WindowListener listener = new WindowAdapter() {        //Use the adapter
      public void windowClosing(WindowEvent e) {
         System.exit(0);
      }
   };
   frame.addWindowListener(listener);
   frame.setSize(280, 200);
   frame.setVisible(true);
}
```

18.2 Mouse Event Handling

Most events associated with GUI components are triggered by mouse clicks. **MouseAdapter** and **MouseMotionAdapter** and their corresponding interfaces **MouseListener** and **MouseMotionListener**, provided by **javax.awt.event**, are commonly used to handle these events. Please refer to Table 18.1 for details of methods requiring implementation in these two interfaces.

18.2.1 Types of events

In addition to the more traditional mouse operations such as pointing and clicking over a GUI components, e.g., a button, to trigger an event, there are three other types of mouse events used in applications:

1. To handle events of GUI components, e.g., using right mouse button clicks to handle a popup menu event.
2. To handle events of the right mouse button click, e.g., positioning the mouse cursor over a picture to trigger the event and perform the specified task.

3. To handle events of the mouse itself, e.g., using mouse clicks to draw pictures, write text, or play games.

Section 18.2.3 illustrates an application that uses mouse to draw pictures.

18.2.2 Adapters and interfaces

Table 18.4 lists adapters and interfaces used in mouse event handling.

Table 18.4 Commonly used adapters and interfaces used in mouse event handling

Adapter/Interface	Method	Description
MouseListener	ouseClicked(MouseEvent e)	Methods are called when the mouse is pressed and then released.
	ouseEntered(MouseEvent e)	Method is called when the mouse entering to the border of the component.
	ouseExited(MouseEvent)	Method is called when the mouse is leaving from the component.
	ousePressed(MouseEvent)	Method is called when the mouse is pressed.
	ouseReleased(MouseEvent e)	Method is called when the mouse is released.
MouseMotionListener	mouseDragged(MouseEvent e)	Method is called when the mouse is dragged.
	mouseMoved(MouseEvent e)	Method is called when the mouse is moved.
MouseAdapter		Mouse adapter corresponding to MouseListener.
MouseMotionAdapter		Mouse adapter corresponding to MuseMotionListener.

18.3 Keyboard Event Handling

KeyListener and **KeyAdapter**, provided by **java.awt.event**, are used to handle keyboard or key events. In addition to monitoring keystrokes, key events also include the following occurrences:

- Events triggered by Keyboard mnemonics and short-cut keys;
- Events triggered by custom-defined keys to display special characters, numbers, symbols, and drawings; and
- Events triggered by keys for filtering specified numbers, characters, or function keys.

The steps in handling a keyboard event are:

1. Use of **KeyListener** or **KeyAdapter** to implement or override the methods. Use the methods in **KeyEvent** to gain or modify the keyboard data, or carry out the keyboard operations.
2. Use **addKeyListener** to add or register ~~the~~ keyboard event handling.

18.3.1 Interface and adapter

Table 18.5 lists adapters and interfaces used in keyboard and key stroke event handling.

Table 18.5 Adapters and interfaces used in keyboard and key stroke events

Interface/Adapter	Method	Description

KeyListener	keyPressed(KeyEvent e)	Trigger the method when a key is pressed.
	keyReleased(KeyEvent e)	Trigger the method when a key is released.
	keyTyped(KeyEvent e)	Trigger the method when a key is pressed and released.
KeyAdapter		Keyboard adapter.

18.3.2 Commonly used methods in KeyEvent

KeyEvent is contained in **java.awt.event** and is used to retrieve or modify data in keyboard event handling. Table 18.6 lists commonly used methods and static fields in **KeyEvent**.

Table 18.6 Commonly used methods and static fields in KeyEvent

consume()	Consume the current keystrokes event so it will not be handled.
char getKeyChar()	Return the Unicode character of the current keystroke (function and special keys are not included).
int getKeyCode()	Return the key code represented by the keystroke. It returns VK_UNDEFINED in calling keyTyped().
String getKeyText(int keyCode)	Return the name of the key code.
boolean isActionKey()	Return true if the event is triggered by a function key; otherwise returns false.
boolean isAltDown()	Returns true if the event is triggered by Alt key; otherwise return false.
boolean isControlDown()	Return true if the event is triggered by a Ctrl key; otherwise returns false.
boolean isShiftDown()	Return true if the event is triggered by a Shift key; otherwise returns false.
setKeyChar(char ch)	Define the key with the specified character.
setKeyCode(int keyCode)	Define the key using the specified key code.

More Information: *Superclasses **InputEvent** and **ComponentEvent** of class **KeyEvent** also provide many useful methods associated with keyboard event handling. Complete information can be found in the Java API documentation.*

KeyEvent also provides a number of static fields as virtual key code in the standard keyboard. This code is using **VK_** plus the capital letter of the key:

```
VK_0 - VK_9(Number keys)     VK_A - VK_Z (Letter keys)     VK_ASTERISK (* key)
VK_AT (@ key)                VK_ALT (Alt)                  VK_CTRL (Ctrl)
VK_SHIFT (Shift)             VK_CAPS_LOCK  (lette keys)
VK_COLON (;)                 VK_COMMA (,)                  VK_DELETE(Delete key)
VK_DIVIDE (/)                VK_DOLLAR ($)                 VK_ENTER (Return)
VK_EQUALS (=)                VK_ESCAPE (Esc)               VK_F1 - F23 (Function)
VK_HOME (Home key)           VK_INSERT (Insert)            VK_LESS (<)
VK_MINUS (-)                 VK_SPACE (Space bar)          VK_TAB (Tab)   ...
```

It is important to note that the returned virtual key code value of **getKeyCode()** in any particular computer system may not exactly match the specifications above. Please check the documentation of **KeyEvent** for the complete list of virtual key codes.

Example 1. Filter all letter entries.

```
public void keyPressed(KeyEvent e) {
   if (e.getKeyCode() >= KeyEvent.VK_A && e.getKeyCode() <= KeyEvent.VK_Z)
      consume();                //Withdraw the event
   ...
}
```

Example 2. Define "$" as "¥". Assume **display** is an object of an output component.

```
display.addKeyListener(new KeyAdapter() {
   public void keyTyped(KeyEvent e) {
      if (e.getKeyChar() == '$')
         display.setText("¥");             //Or:display.append("¥");
   }
);
```

Example 3. Use **setKeyChar()** to convert all lowercase letters to uppercase letters.

```
display.addKeyListener(new KeyAdapter() {
   public void keyTyped(KeyEvent e) {
      e.setKeyChar(Characher.toUpperCase(e.getKeyChar()));
   }
);
```

18.3.3 Simulation of a calculator (Part 2)

In Chapter 16 we discussed Part 1 of a calculator simulation using GUI components. Now we include event handling to complete the simulation. For our demonstration, in addition to using the more traditional **ActionListener** to handle events, we will also use **KeyAdapter** to simulate the calculator keypad. Users may also use the standard keyboard of their computer system to perform all functions and operations. Figure 18.2 shows the result of a typical operation performed on the simulated calculator.

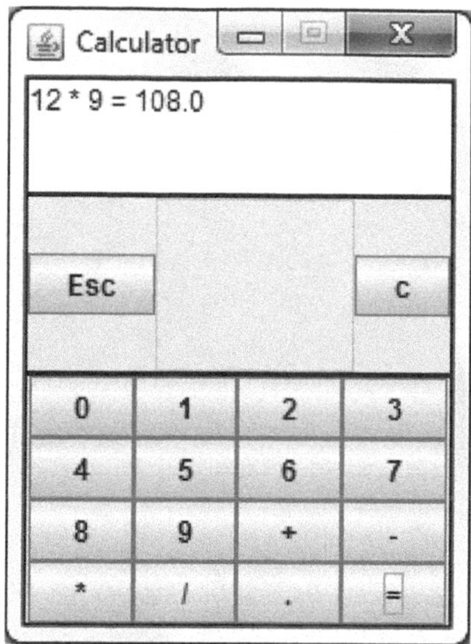

Figure 18.2 A typical execution result of simulated calculator

Note that **getKeyCode()** is used to obtain the virtual key code of a pressed key due to the inability of **getKeyChar()** to return special key codes, e.g., **ESC**, '=', **Return**, et cetera. When the '=' button on the calculator, the '=' key on the keyboard, or **Return** key on the keyboard is pressed, a programmer-defined method, **showResult()**, displays, calculates, and shows the final result of the entered expression in the calculator window.

```
//Complete code called CalculatorFrameApp2.java in Ch18 from the author's website
//Programmer-defined method showResult()
private void showResult() {
   try {                                              //Exception handling
        expression = display.getText();               //Get the expression
        parseExpression();                            //Call the method
        display.append(" = " + currentTotal);         //Show the result
        done = true;                                  //Set the status
   }
   catch (Exception ex) {     //If there is any exception
         JOptionPane.showMessageDialog(null, "Incorrect entry.  Click on the
         display and try again...");
         display.setText("");                         //Clear the display
         done = true;                                 //Change the status
         display.requestFocus();                      //Focus gain in the display
   }
}
```

Another programmer-defined method, **parseExpression()**, is called to evaluate the entered expression and assign the result to **currentTotal**. If an exception occurs, e.g., entering an illegal expression, invalid operands or operators, an exception is thrown and an error message is displayed. Method **parseExpression()** uses **StringTokenizer()** to parse the expression, thereby allowing the tokens to be used by **compute()** in completing the calculation. You may find a detailed discussion of the above in Section 10.5.4 of Chapter 10.

```
//Programmer-defined method parseExpression()
private void parseExpression() {
   String operatorStr;
   char[] operatorArray = new char[1];
   StringTokenizer tokens = new StringTokenizer(expression);
   currentTotal = Double.parseDouble(tokens.nextToken());

   while (tokens.hasMoreTokens()) { operatorStr =
         tokens.nextToken(); operatorArray =
         operatorStr.toCharArray(); operator =
         operatorArray[0];
         operandValue = Double.parseDouble(tokens.nextToken());
         compute();
   }
}
private void compute() {
   switch (operator) {
      case '+':  currentTotal += operandValue;
                 break;
      case '-':  currentTotal -= operandValue;
                 break;
      case '*':  currentTotal *= operandValue;
                 break;
      case '/':  currentTotal /= operandValue;
                 break;
      default:   System.out.println("Illegal operator...");
                 break;
   }
}
```

18.4 Coding Techniques In GUI Component Programming

Many Java coding techniques using the API classes we have discussed in previous chapters and sections can be applied to GUI component programming. We summarize the techniques of GUI component coding, so you may choose the techniques that best fit your applications.

18.4.1 Six coding methods to implement GUI components

Depending on the complexity of the GUI application, there are typically six different coding techniques:

1. Code the components and event handling directly in a frame inherited from **JFrame**. This technique is suitable for simple and short coding. For example:

```
//Complete code called ColorChooserFrameApp.java in Ch18 from the author's website
class SimpleFrame extends JFrame implements ActionListener {
   SimpleFrame() {
      JButton button1 = new JButton("button1");   //Create GUI components
      add(button1);                    //Or: add(button1, BorderLayout.NORTH);
      button1.addActionLister(this);        //Add event handling
      ...
      //Create other components

      //Implement event handling
      public void actionPerformed(ActionEvent e) {
         //Event handling code
         ...
      }
}
```

2. Code a separate panel inherited from **JPanel** and create GUI components in the panel. Then create an object of the panel and add event handling in a frame inherited from **JFrame**. This technique is suitable for relatively complex coding involving detailed component positioning requirements in GUI applications. For example:

```
//Complete code called BoxLayoutFrameTest.java in Ch16 from the author's website

class SimplePanel extends JPanel implements ActionListener {
   SimplePanel() {
      setLayout(new FlowLayout(FlowLayout.RIGHT));
      JButton button1 = new JButton("button1");   //Create components
      add(button1);                             //Or:add(button1,
BorderLayout.NORTH);
      button1.addActionListner(this);             //Add event handling
      ...                                         //Create and add other components

      //Implement event handling
      public void actionPerformed(ActionEvent e) {
         //Event handling code
         ...
      }
   }
}
class PanelFrame extends JFrame {    //Code the frame
   PanelFrame() {
      super("Title of the frame");
      JPanel panel = new SimplePanel();    //Create object of the panel
      add(panel);                          //Add the panel, or: this.add(panel);
      //Other code
      ...
   }
```

```
}
```

3. Code multiple panels inherited from **JPanel** according to the grouping and functionality(ies) of the GUI components. Then code a frame inherited from **JFrame**, creating and adding each panel in the frame. Event handling procedures are coded in each respective panel. This technique is suitable for complex GUI applications involving many components, event handling, and component positioning requirements. It is an extension of the above coding technique. For example:

```
//Complete code called OOPListPanel.java in Ch18 from the author's website

class PanelOne extends JPanel implements ActionListener {
   PanelOne() {
      setLayout(new BorderLayout(BorderLayout.NORTH));  //Layout
      JButton button1 = new JButton("button1");          //Create components
      add(button1);                          //Or: add(button1, FlowLayout.LEFT);
      button1.addActionListner(this);        //Add for event handling
      ...
      //Create other components
   }

   //Implement event handling
   public void actionPerformed(ActionEvent e) {
      //Event handling code
      ...
   }
}
//End of PanelOne

class PanelTwo extends JPanel implements ActionListener {
   PanelTwo() {
      setLayout(new BorderLayout(BorderLayout.SOUTH));  //Layout
      //Other components
      ...
   }
   //Event handling code
   ...
}
//End of PanelTwo

//More panels
...

class PanelsFrame extends JFrame {          //Code a frame
   PanelsFrame() {
      super("Title of the frame");
      //Create and add each panel object
      JPanel panelOne = new JPanel();
```

```
        add(panelOne);                          //Add the panel; or: this.
    add(panelOne);
        JPanel panelTwo = new JPanel();
        add(panelTwo);
        ...
        //Other code
        ...
    }
}
```

4. Group the GUI components according to their functionality and location in the application. Code inner panel classes for each component grouping inside a frame, then create and add each panel in the frame. This technique is suitable for complex GUI applications with different component location requirements and their respective event handling. This is a modification of the above technique. For example:

```
//Complete code called CalculatorFrame2.java in Ch18 from the author's website

class PanelsFrame extends JFrame {                  //Code the frame
    PanelsFrame() {
        super("Title of the frame");
        JPanel panelOne = new InnerPanelOne();      //Create the panel
        add(panelOne);                          //Add the panel; or: this.
    add(panelOne);
        JPanel panelTwo = new InnerPanelTwo();      //Create and other panels
        add(panelTwo);                          //Add the panel
        ...                                     //Create and add more panels
        //Other code
        ...
    }
    class InnerPanelOne extends JPanel implements ActionListener {
        InnerPanelOne() {
            setLayout(new BorderLayout(BorderLayout.NORTH));  //Layout
            JButton button1 = new JButton("button1");         //Create component
            add(button1);                       //Or: add(button1, FlowLayout.LEFT)
            button1.addActionLister(this);      //Add the event handling
            ...                                 //Create and add other components
        }
        //Implement event handling
        public void actionPerformed(ActionEvent e) {
            //Event handling code
            ...
        }
    } //End of InnerPanelOne
    ...          //Other inner panels
```

```
} //End of PanelsFrame
```

5. Group the GUI components according to their positioning requirements and functionality. Code each inner panel class in a general panel and add each to the general panel. Then create and add the general panel to a frame. This technique is suitable for GUI applications with multiple components in multiple locations and event handling in multiple groups. It is a variation of the above coding techniques. For example:

```
class PanelsFrame extends JFrame {                    //Code the frame
   PanelsFrame() {
      super("Title of the frame");
      JPanel panelOne = new InnerPanelOne();          //Create panel
      add(panelOne);
      JPanel panelTwo = new InnerJPanelTwo();         //Create other panel
      add(panelTwo);                                  //Add the panel
      ...                                             //Create and add more panels
      //Other code
      ...
   }
   class InnerPanelOne extends JPanel implements ActionListener {
      InnerPanelOne() {
         setLayout(new BorderLayout(BorderLayout.NORTH));//Layput
         JButton button1 = new JButton("button1");          //Create component
         add(button1);  //Add the component; //or: add(button1,FlowLayout.LEFT);
         button1.addActionLister(this);      //Add event handling
         ...                                 //Create and add other components
      }
      //Implement event handling
         public void actionPerformed(ActionEvent e) {
               //Event handling code
               ...
         }
   } //End of InnerPanelOne
   ...         //Other inner classes
} //End of PanelsFrame
```

6. Create a panel (or multiple panels) with a layout manager(s) in a frame implementing event handling. This technique is suitable for GUI applications with simple event handling requirements but having a complex code structure in the layout manager requirements. For example:

```
//Complete code called FoodSurveyFrame5.java in Ch17, and GridLayoutFrameTest2.java
//in Ch16 from the author's website

class FoodSurveyFrame5 extends JFrame implements ActionListener {
   JPanel menuPanel, selectPanel, buttonPanel, lafPanel; //Declare panels
```

```
    private JMenuBar menuBar;                                    //Declare components
    private JMenu selectMenu, likeMenu, dislikeMenu, displayMenu, aboutMenu;
    ...

    FoodSurveyFrame() {
       CreateGUIComponents();           //Call programmer-defined method
       //Other code
       ...
    }
    void CreateGUIComponents() {              //Programmer-defined method
       menuPanel = new JPanel();              //Create panel
       menuPanel.setLayout(new FlowLayout(FlowLayout.LEFT));      //Layout
       menuPanel = new JPanel();                                 //Create panel
       menuBar = new JMenuBar();                                 //Create component
       menuPanel.add(menuBar);                            //Add the component
       add(menuPanel);                                    //Add the panel to frame
       //Create and add more components
       ...
    }
}
```

Of course, you can apply any one or more of the coding techniques to achieve greater control and flexibility according to the particular situations of your GUI applications.

18.4.2 Six techniques of coding event handling

You may have already noted there are many ways of coding event handling procedures discussed in both this and previous chapters. We may summarize them as follows:

1. Code the event handling in a frame or panel. We have discussed this technique in previous sections. It is most suitable for relatively simple event handling requirements.

2. Code the event handling using a separate class. This technique is suitable for complex event handling requirements. For example:

```
public class GUIEventHandler extends MouseAdapter implements ActionListener {
   public void actionPerformed(ActionEvent e) {
      //Component event handling code
      ...
   }
   public void mouseClicked(MouseEvent e) {
      //Mouse event handling code
      ...
   }
}
```

3. Code a separate event handling class for each component that triggers an event. This technique is suitable for complex event handling in each component may use different interfaces or adapters. For example:

```
//Button event handling
public class ButtonEventHandler implements ActionListener {
    public actionPerformed(ActionEvent e) {
        //Button event handling code
        ...
    }
}
//Item event handling
public class ItemEventHandler implements ItemListener {
    public void itemStateChanged(ItemEvent e) {
        //Item event handling code
        ...
    }
}
//Keyboard event handling
public class KeyEventHandler extends KeyAdapter {
    public void keyTyped(KeyEvent e) {
        //Keyboard event handling code
        ...
    }
}
```

4. Code event handling procedures using an inner class. This technique is best suited for custom-designed, relatively short and independent, and less-complex event handling requirements for each component triggering an event. For example:

```
class GUIPanel extends JPanel {
    //Code for creating and adding components
    private class InnerButtonEventHandler implements ActrionListener {
        public void actionPerformed(ActionEvent e) {
            //Button event handling code
            ...
        }
    } //End of InnerButtonEventHandler
    private class InnerKeyEventHandler extends KeyAdapter {
        public void keyPressed(KeyEvent e) {
            //Keyboard event handling code
            ...
        }
    } //End of InnerKeyEventHandler
}
```

5. Code event handling procedures using anonymous inner class. This technique is similar to the coding technique discussed above and is suitable for custom-designed, relatively short and independent, less-complex event handling requirements. For example:

```
class GUIPanel extends JPanel {
   //Creating and adding components
   ...
   button1.addActionListener(new ActionListener() {
      public void actionPerformed(ActionEvent e) {
         //Button1 event handling code
         ...
      }
   });
   button2.addActionListener(new ActionListener() {
      public void actionPerformed(ActionEvent e) {
         //Button2 event handling code
         ...
      }
   });
}
```

6. Code event handling procedures directly using an inner class. This technique is a combination of using an inner class and an anonymous inner class, as discussed above. It is suitable for simple event handling code. For example:

```
class GUIPanel extends JPanel {
   ChangeListener changeEventHanlder;       //Declare event handling class
   //Creating and adding components
   ...
   changeEventHandler = new ChangeListener(){//Directly create event
handling class
      public void stateChanged(ChangeEvent changeEvent) {
         //Event handling code
         ...
      }
   };
   colorChooserModel.addChangeListener(changeEventHandler);
   radioButton.addChangeListener(changeEventHandler);
   ...    //Other event handling code
}
```

You can apply any one or more of the coding techniques, or one of your own design, to achieve greater control and flexibility according to the particular situations of your GUI applications.

Exercises

1. What is “event-driven” programming? Why is Java called an “event-driven” programming language? Why is event handling incorporated in code?

2. What is an adapter? What is the difference between an adapter and an interface? Use examples to explain why the use of an adapter may be preferred to that of an interface.

3. Referring to the **Calculator (Part 2)** example discussed in this chapter, add another key, **CE**, between the **Esc** and **C** keys. The purpose of the **CE** key is to provide the function of clearing the current entry. Test your code and save all files.

4. Summarize the six common coding techniques of GUI programming and explain their respective purposes in programming.

5. Summarize the six common coding techniques associated with event handling procedures and explain their respective purposes in event handling coding.

6. Code an application to simulate the operation and display of a computer keyboard. The simulated keyboard should be displayed in the lower part of the screen. When the user presses any key in the computer, the corresponding key of the simulated keyboard is to be displayed with a specified color of your choice (see Chapter 20) to indicate the key has been pressed. In the upper part of the screen, display the content of the keystrokes. Test the code and save all files.

"Trying may not lead to success, but giving up definitely leads to failure."

– Yao Ming

Chapter 19 Applet Programming

Applets are client-side web programs and form an important part of web services. In this chapter we first introduce the features of applet programming, then discuss the calling, testing, and debugging of applets. You will also learn the similarities and differences between desktop application programming and applet programming, how to convert an application to an applet, and vice versa.

19.1 General Discussion

An applet is a program that can be executed in a web browser. Current popular browsers, e.g., Internet Explorer, Firefox, Google Chrome, Mozilla, Safari, all come with the Java Runtime Environment (JRE). Beginning with JDK 1.6, installation of the JDK automatically installs the JRE and Java Plug-in to the browsers, allowing Java applets to be executed.

The coding, testing, and debugging of an applet are usually completed on a local computer before uploading it to the web server with the HTML file. The applet can then be displayed in a webpage and work together with server-side programs, such as Servlets and JSP, to become client-server application.

19.1.1 History

Applet components developed before JDK 1.2 were built upon AWT. After the introduction of the JDK 1.2 Swing package, the **Applet** class now had its counterpart, **JApplet**, and related API classes starting with the letter **J**. Although most browsers of that time kept upgrading from the updated JRE to keep current, Microsoft stopped updating the JRE in their browser shortly thereafter.

To solve the problem of allowing updated applets to be executed under Internet Explorer, Sun Microsystems provided a website (in 1997), **www.java.com**, for downloading the current JRE and Java Plug-in. The 1998 introduction of Swing with JDK 1.2 added a new program, **HTML Converter**, to the JDK, allowing the conversion of any code that could not be executed in the older browsers; Swing features using **JApplet** could now be supported.

In 2007, due to Microsoft's announcement canceling support of the JRE, Sun Microsystems decided to automatically install JRE and Java Plug-in with the JDK starting with JDK 1.6.

19.1.2 Safety issues

In real world applications, applets are downloaded from web servers to the user's computer system, and the results can be viewed by browsers on the local machines. This procedure may cause safety and security issues if there are not protections. Applets are <u>prohibited</u> from performing the following tasks on the local computer:

- Read, update, and delete files.
- Run another applet within an applet.
- Make a network connection.

Applets can retrieve the Java version, name of the operating system, directory listing, and path name. Java provides signed applet and digital signature techniques, indicating the source is coming from a secure web server, so access can be granted. Signed applets and digital signatures are related to **keytool**, **jarsigner**, safety policy applications, and similar techniques are beyond the scope of this text.

19.1.3 Commonly used methods

JApplet is provided by javax.swing and its inheritance hierarchy is as follows:

```
java.lang.Object
   java.awt.Component
      java.awt.Container
         java.awt.Panel
            java.applet.Applet
               javax.swing.JApplet
```

Table 19.1 lists commonly used methods in **JApplet**. These methods are inherited from **Applet**, **Container**, and **Component**.

Table 19.1 Commonly used methods in **JApplet**

Method	Description
void destroy()	Release the resources used by the applet; automatically called after stop() when the browser is closed. This method is not typically called directly by the applet programmer.
URL getCodeBase()	Return the URL object encapsulating the directory of the applet.
URL getDocumentBase()	Return the URL object of the document in which this applet is embedded.
void init()	Called by browser or applet viewer to inform the applet that it has been loaded into the system. It is always called the first time before start() is called.
void resize(int width, int height)	Resizes the display dimension of the applet.
void start()	Called by browser or applet viewer to inform the applet that it should start its execution. It is called after init() and each time the applet revisits a web page.
void stop()	Called by browser or applet viewer to inform the applet that it should stop its execution. It is called when the web page containing this applet is replaced by another web page and just before the applet is to be destroyed.
void paint(Graphics g)	Paints the component or the object of the Graphics. Inherited from JComponent.
void repaint()	Repaints the component or the object of the Graphics. Automatically called by paint() for updating.

The five methods in **JApplet** listed in Table 19.1 have the special feature of constructing the life cycle of applet execution: **init()** is automatically called when the browser loads the applet by executing the embedding HTML file. Method **start()** is then automatically called. The JVM provides **init()** and **start()** if such method(s) is not in the applet code. Method **paint()** is normally called to draw graphics, and

repaint() is called during event handling to update graphics. In actuality, **repaint()** calls **paint()** to update the drawing. When the browser is closed, **stop()** is called first to halt execution of any currently running operations, e.g., threads, audio, et cetera, before invoking **destroy()** to release the resource(s), e.g., memory, thread schedules, system queue, and CPU request, through JVM garbage collection method **gc()**.

We use the features in the above five commonly used **JApplet** methods to code our applets: Initialization is performed in **init()**, and the statements must first be executed via **start()**. Java does not recommend overriding the **paint()**, **stop()**, and **destroy()** methods. It is also recommended not to directly call **destroy()**; is should be called by the JVM or JRE. We may, of course, use all other methods from **JApplet** and its superclasses in applet coding.

19.1.4 Example

Let's modify the example of using the color chooser to paint text, as discussed in Section 17.5.4, to be an applet.

```
//Complete code called ColorChooserApplet.java in Ch19 from the author's website

import java.awt.*;
import javax.swing.*;
import javax.swing.colorchooser.ColorSelectionModel;
import javax.swing.event.*;

public class ColorChooserApplet extends JApplet{          //Inherit JApplet
   JColorChooser colorChooser;
   ColorSelectionModel model;
   JLabel label;
   ChangeListener changeListener;
   public void init() {                         //Create components in init()
      label = new JLabel("I love Java", JLabel.CENTER);
      label.setFont(new Font("Serif", Font.BOLD + Font.ITALIC, 48));
      add(label, BorderLayout.SOUTH);
      colorChooser = new JColorChooser(label.getBackground());
      colorChooser.setBorder(BorderFactory.createTitledBorder("Select your favored
color: "));
      add(colorChooser, BorderLayout.CENTER);

      changeListener = new ChangeListener() {                    //Event handling
         public void stateChanged(ChangeEvent changeEvent) {
            Color newForegroundColor = colorChooser.getColor();
            label.setForeground(newForegroundColor);
         }
      };
```

```
        model = colorChooser.getSelectionModel();
        model.addChangeListener(changeListener);
    }
}
```

Note that the applet is easier and simpler to code than the desktop version of this application. Figure 19.1 shows the result of executing the applet in the applet viewer.

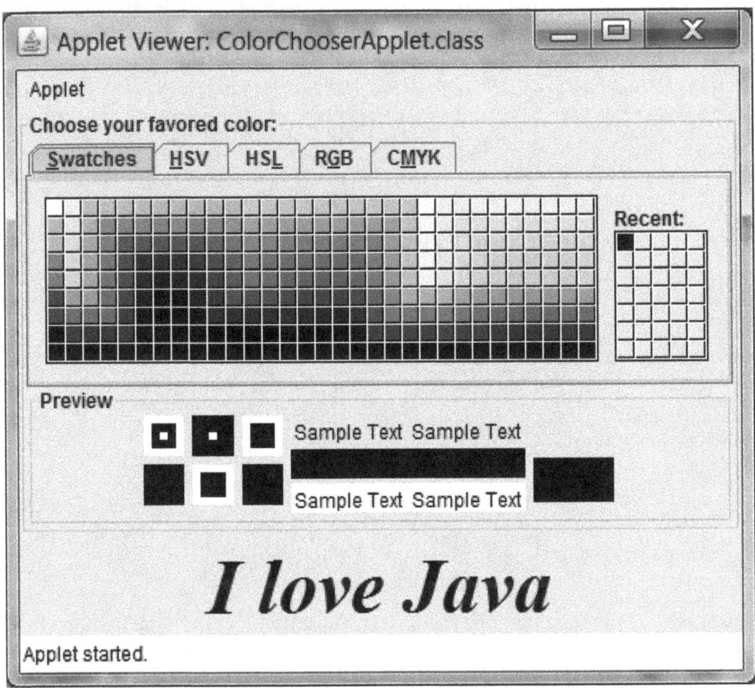

Figure 19.1 The execution result of ColorChooserApplet

19.2 Applet Coding

Although the coding of desktop applications and applets is not significantly different, albeit some differences in their purposes and areas of usage, applet coding has its own special features and coding steps.

19.2.1 Feature analysis

Using our **ColorChooserApplet** example, we may note the following coding features relating to applets:

- There is no need to perform event handling in the window itself. For example, you do not need to provide code to close and exit the opened window. The browser automatically handles these events.

- There is no need to code requirements for the display, location, and size of the frame. These functions are performed by the HTML file or the IDE that calls the applet class (see example below).
- There is no **main()** method in an applet. The applet is loaded and executed by the browser.
- There is no title of the **window** in the code. It may be specified in the HTML file.
- The **init()** and **start()** methods function in a manner akin to a constructor, and we may place all the code that is necessary to be executed at the start of the program, e.g., object declaration and creation, adding objects for event handling and display, component layout, in **init()** and **start()**.
- Barring an special requirements, there is no need to call **stop()** and **destroy().** These are called automatically by the JVM or JRE.
- Methods **paint()**, **paintComponent()**, and **repaint()** are normally used together for dynamically updating the displayed images or pictures. An applet with animation is a good example. You should override **paint()** or **paintComponent()** by providing your own code for the applet; **repaint()** should be called only in event handling code for updating, because **repaint()** will automatically call **paint()** or **paintComponent()**.

19.2.2 Coding steps

The coding steps of applet can be as follows:

1. Begin the applet code by inheriting the **JApplet** class and implementing the specified interface(s):

```
PainterApplet extends JApplet implements ActionListener {
    //init()and other methods
    ...
}
```

or:

```
AnimatorApplet extends JApplet implements Runnable, MouseMotionListener {
    //init()method
    ...
    //start()method
    ...
    //run()method
    ...
    //paint()or paintComponent() method
    ...
}
```

2. Override **init()** and code other necessary methods, such as **start()**, **run()**, or **paint()**.
3. You may also code inner classes in the applet to carry out specified tasks, e.g., **Validator**, **GUIPanel**, **EventHandler**, et cetera. These can, of course, be separate classes.
4. Compile the applet source code and generate the bytecode file.
5. Code the HTML file to call the generated applet class file. You do not need to supply the HTML file when using an IDE to execute an applet; the IDE will automatically produce an HTML file for you in which to run the applet.
6. Use the JDK **appletviewer** to test the applet by calling the HTML file.
7. Modify or debug the applet, as necessary.
8. To test the applet under a variety of web browsers to ensure it works well in different environments.
9. Upload to the web server and test if it works.

If you develop a client-server application, it will be necessary to coordinate with the servlet and test the result.

19.2.3 Using HTML to call applet

The **<Applet>** tag in HTML loads the applet bytecode file (.class) and executes the applet. The following is an example of HTML code that calls the **ColorChooserApplet** applet:

```
<!—HTML Comment Line - optional  -->
<HTML>
   <Head>
          <Title>applet Title - optional</Title>
   </Head>
   <Body>
          <Applet code = "ColorChooserApplet.class" width = 400 height = 500>
             <!— If it is not executed, the following line will be displayed -->
                 <P>applet error: Check the version of Java</P>
          </Applet>
   </Body>
</HTML>
```

We code **<P>applet error: Check the version of Java</P>** before the **</Applet>** tag, which ends the **<Applet>** block. This code message will only be executed and displayed if there is an error in running the applet.

A much simpler HTML file that calls the applet without the several options is as follows:

```
<html>
   <applet code = "ColorChooserApplet.class" width = 400 height = 500>
   </applet>
</html>
```

Actually, this is the code an IDE automatically generates when executing the applet using an IDE.

Note: *HTML is not case sensitive. Use a meaningful name to save the HTML file.*

19.2.4 More examples

Example 1. Modify FoodSurveyFrame5 discussed in Chapter 17 to an applet.

```
//Complete code called FoodSurveyApplet.java in Ch19 from the author's website

//Applet:  Use of JApplet, JPopupMenu, JMenu, L&F, GridBagLayout, JLabel,
//JCheckBox, JRadioButton, JTextArea, and event handling to take an opinion survey
//of various foods.
import java.awt.*;
import java.awt.event.*;
import javax.swing.*;
import javax.swing.border.*;

public class FoodSurveyApplet extends JApplet implements ActionListener {
   private Border loweredBorder, raisedBorder;
   private final String
      metalClassName = "javax.swing.plaf.metal.MetalLookAndFeel",
      motifClassName = "com.sun.java.swing.plaf.motif.MotifLookAndFeel",
      windowsClassName = "com.sun.java.swing.plaf.windows.WindowsLookAndFeel";
   private GridBagConstraints c;
   private JPanel menuPanel, selectPanel, buttonPanel, lafPanel;
   private int pizzaLikeCount, hamburgerLikeCount, kfcLikeCount;
   private int pizzaDislikeCount, hamburgerDislikeCount, kfcDislikeCount;

   private JMenuBar menuBar;
   private JMenu selectMenu, likeMenu, dislikeMenu, displayMenu, aboutMenu;
   private JMenuItem pizzaItem, hamburgerItem, kfcItem, metalItem, motifItem,
      winItem, contactItem, copyrightItem;
   private JMenuItem dPizzaItem, dHamburgerItem, dKfcItem, exitItem;

   private JCheckBox pizzaBox, hamburgerBox, kfcBox;
   private JRadioButton likeRadioButton, dislikeRadioButton;
   private JRadioButton metalRadioButton, motifRadioButton, windowRadioButton;
   private ButtonGroup buttonGroup, buttonGroup2;
   private JButton addButton;

   private JTextArea displayTextArea;
   private JPopupMenu popupMenu;
   private JMenuItem loweredPopupItem, raisedPopupItem;

   public void init() {
      pizzaLikeCount = hamburgerLikeCount = kfcLikeCount = 0;
      pizzaDislikeCount = hamburgerDislikeCount = kfcDislikeCount = 0;
      loweredBorder = BorderFactory.createBevelBorder(BevelBorder.LOWERED);
      raisedBorder = BorderFactory.createBevelBorder(BevelBorder.RAISED);
```

```
        createGUIComponents();
}

   private void createGUIComponents() {
      //The code is the same as previous version
      ...
   }
   public void actionPerformed(ActionEvent e) {
      //The code is the same as previous version
      ...
   }
   //Other methods are the same as previous version
   ...
}
```

The HTML file for this applet is:

```
<HTML>
   <Applet code = "FoodSurveyApplet.class" width = 620 height = 220>
   </Applet>
</HTML>
```

Figure 19.2 shows the execution result of this example.

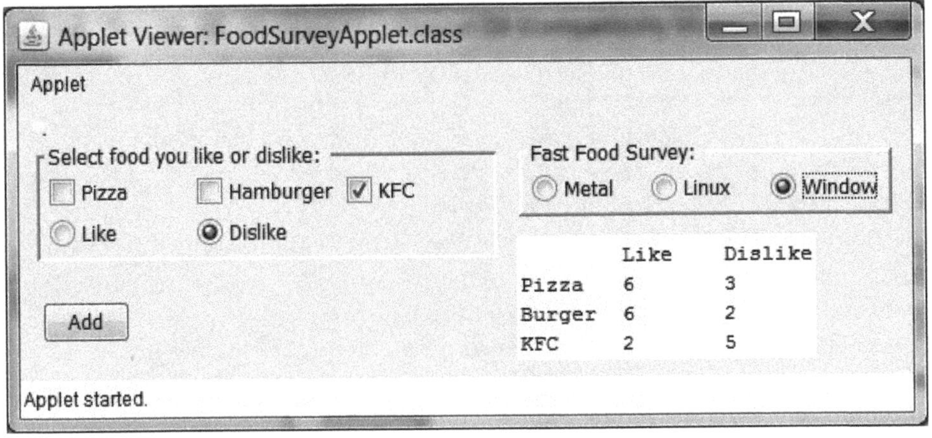

Figure 19.2 A typical execution result of the applet

Example 2. An applet with animation.

```
//The complete code called MovingBannerApplet.java in Ch19 from the author's website
public class MovingBannerApplet extends Applet implements Runnable {
  //Declare thread to control the speed of moving banner
   private Thread bannerThread;    private int x;
   public void init(){
      x = 10;
   }
   public void start() {
```

```
      if (bannerThread == null) {
         bannerThread = new Thread(this);
         bannerThread.start();
      }
   }
   public void run() {                                   //Override run()
      Thread myThread = Thread.currentThread();
      while (bannerThread == myThread) {
         try{
            Thread.sleep(100);                           //Control animation speed
         }
         catch (InterruptedException e){}

         repaint();
      }
   }
   public void paint(Graphics g) {                       //Override paint()
      x += 5;
      Dimension d = getSize();                           /Get the screen dimension
      if (x > (d.width - 10))                            //d.width - Screen width
         x = 10;                                         //Reset x
      g.setFont(new Font("SansSerif", Font.BOLD, 24)); //Set the fonts and size

      g.setColor(Color.red);                             //Set the color
      g.drawString("Java SE 7 is out now!", x, 50); //Drawing the banner
   }
   public void stop() {               //Override stop()
      bannerThread = null;            //Release the thread
   }
}
```

The applet calls **getSize()** of the **Dimension** class in **java.awt** to get the object d containing the screen dimension of the current computer system. It also uses **setFont()**, **setColor()**, and **drawString()** to define and display the moving banner. For this demonstration, the applet overrides the **JApplet** class **stop()** method to halt execution and release the resource held by the thread. Figure 19.3 shows the screen shot of the movin banner.

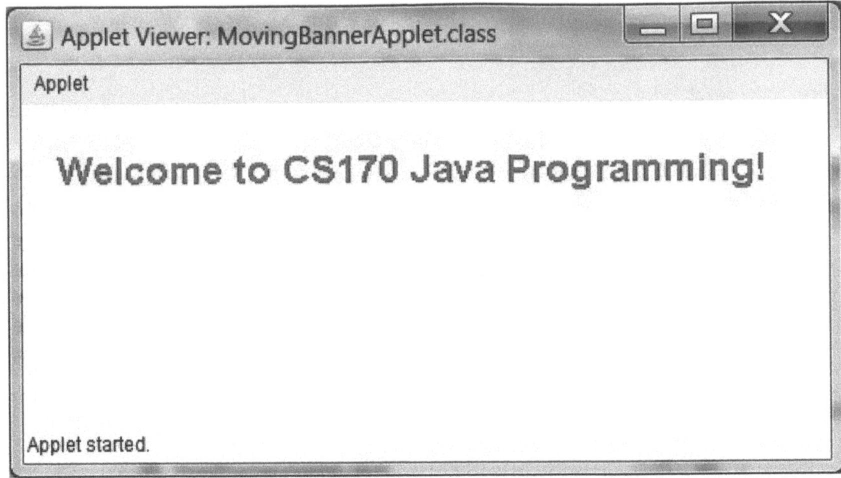

Figure 19.3 The screenshot of moving banner applet

19.3 Inside of Applets

Applet coding reflects the idea of using Java API classes in a way to achieve program modularization. It can be described with the following points:

- **Separation of common features from application-specific specialization.** Applet design can be divided into two categories: Standard components that use or inherit API classes, such as GUI components, and the specialized code (or behavior-oriented code), such as layout, event handling, control, and operations. These must be coded by the developer using implementation and overriding of existing classes and interfaces.
- **Modular design approach.** Use API classes as building blocks that can be reused as modules by other applets.
- **Utilizing the Java application framework.** Java provides the basic structure allowing separation of the common code features from the application-specific portion as well as modular design. These principles are automatically applied in the coding of an applet because you have no choice in following applet design requirements. The use of applets can simplify code design, thereby improving coding efficiency. In fact, applets serve as good proof for the ideal of "write once, run anywhere," because they are called by platform-independent HTML files for execution.

19.3.1 How to execute an applet

The following are the typical steps in executing an applet:

1. When the user clicks on the browser and opens a web page, the HTML file will be loaded into the user's computer.

2. When the <applet> tag in the HTML file is executed, the specified **.class** applet file will be loaded from the web server to the user's computer. If the browser cannot find the class file, it will search the user's computer using CLASSPATH. If the file cannot be found, an error message will be displayed.

3. The browser calls the JRE and Java Plug-in to run the loaded applet code.

4. When the user opens the web page, the applet will call **stop()** and then **destroy()** to halt applet execution and release the resources held by the applet, respectively.

Note that an applet cannot be executed correctly if the JRE or browser's Java Plug-in do not support the features in the applet code. In this case you must download and install the current versions of the JRE or Java Plug-in.

19.3.2 Applet testing and debugging

Let's first list three different ways in testing your applet:

1. Use an IDE, such as Eclipse or TextPad, to execute your applet after compilation. These IDEs automatically generate the HTML file that calls your applet if you do not provide such a file. In practice, the IDEs call **appletviewer**, installed in the JDK, to run the applet.

2. Run your applet under the operating system. You must code a HTML file that calls the applet. After compiling the applet and generating the class file, you may need to navigate to the directory containing the HTML and the applet's bytecode files before issuing the JDK's **appletviewer** command. In the Windows operating system, an example of these operations is:

```
C:\java\Ch19\appletviewer LittlePainterApplet.html
```

3. Run your applet in a browser. In a browser, you may open the HTML file that calls the applet to run the applet. It should be noted an applet may run correctly in **appletviewer** but may not necessarily run the same way in a commercial browser. It is strongly recommended you test your applet with different browsers to insure it runs correctly in multiple environments.

Current browsers can also be used to debug an applet and trace its execution using the Java console. In the Windows operating system, the console is displayed as a Java icon in the taskbar, as shown in Figure 19.4, when the HTML file is opened in a browser. Since the default option of the Java console is hidden, you may need to enable the **Java Console** option in the **Control Panel** by selecting **Java Panel** to select **Java Console** via the **Advanced** tab.

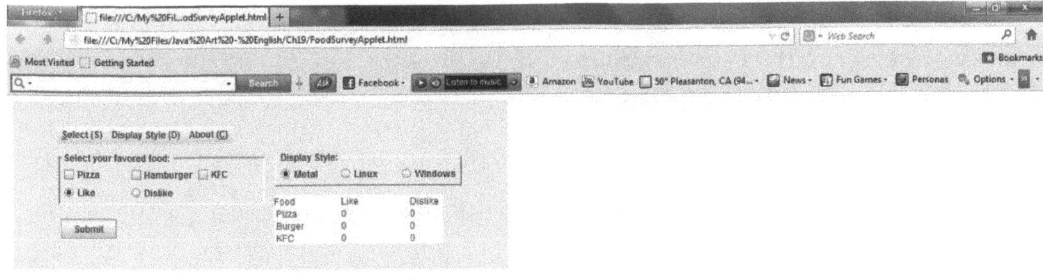

Figure 19.4 Java Console displayed at the taskbar in Firefox

Java console will display the information for testing and debugging as shown in Figure 19.5.

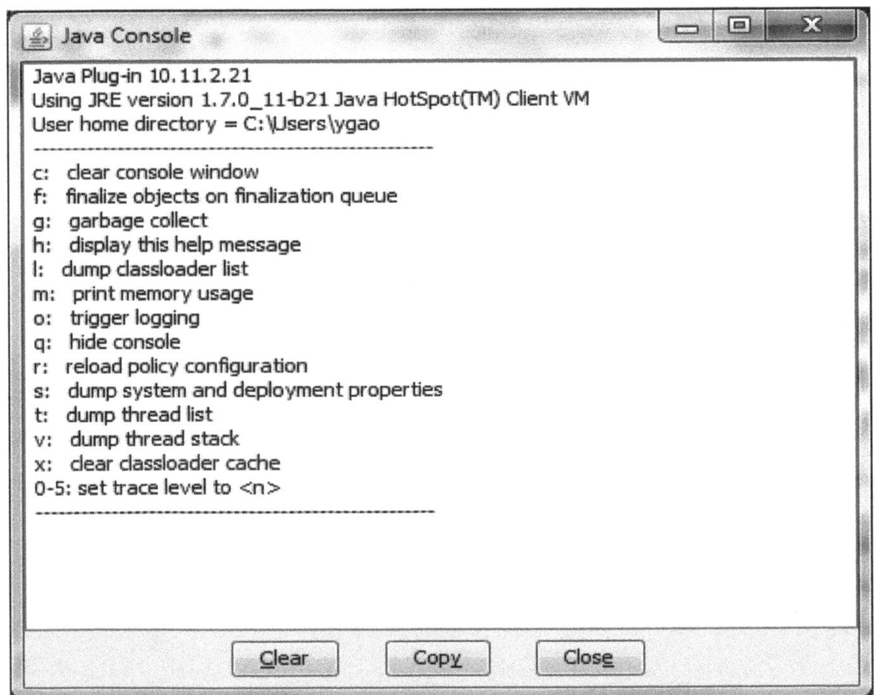

Figure 19.5 Java console displays the options for applet testing and debugging

Clicking on **Java Console** produces the display shown in Figure 19.4. In this state, you may enter any option indicated in the window to display the selected data. For example, entering **t** displays thread dump information, e.g.,

```
Memory: 16,000K  Free: 10,338K  (64%) ... completed.
```

19.3.3 JAR files

In applet coding, it is a common occurrence that you will have to zip the supporting classes used by the applet into a JAR (Java Archive) file, so it can be specified in the HTML file. The JDK provides the **jar** command to create the required **jar** file. Table 19.2 lists commonly used options of the **jar** command. When you type the command **jar** without an option, it will display a list of all available options.

Table 19.2 Commonly used options of the **jar** command

Option	Description
c	Creates a jar file, e.g., *jar cf jar_file input_files*
f	Specifies the jar file name after f.
t	Lists the contents in the jar file without unzip
u	Updates the jar file, adding or replacing files, as required.
v	Lists the information associated with the zipping process.
X	Unzips the jar file .

A jar file is typically created after the bytecode files are generated. Using **OOPListApplet** (see Section 19.3.5) with all bytecode files stored in directory **C:\Temp\Java Art\Ch19\OOPListApplet** as an example under the Windows operating system, the steps to create a **jar** file are as follows:

1. In the operating system window, change to the specified directory:

```
cd C:\Temp\Java Art\Ch19\OOPListApplet
```

2. In this directory, issue the following **jar** command:

```
jar cvf OOPListApplet.jar *.class
```

The following information about the zip process will be displayed in the window:

```
jar cfv OOPListApplet.jar *.class
added manifest
adding: OOPListApplet.class(in=356)(out=256)(deflated 28%)
adding:OOPListPanel2.class(in=5859)(out=3063)(deflated 47%)
C:\Temp\Java Art\Ch19>
```

3. After the **jar** file is created, you may call it in the HTML file as:

```
<HTML>
   <Head>
          <Title>OOP List Applet</Title>
   </Head>
          <Applet archive = "OOPListApplet.jar" code = "OOPListApplet.class"
```

```
        width = 530 height = 250>
                <P>This applet requires JDK 1.6 or above to run</P>
        </Applet>
</HTML>
```

When the browser loads the HTML file, the specified jar file will also be loaded, unzipped, and executed by the JVM and JRE.

The **jar** command can also be used to unzip a **jar** file. The following command unzips the **OOPListApplet.jar** file and displays the extracted information:

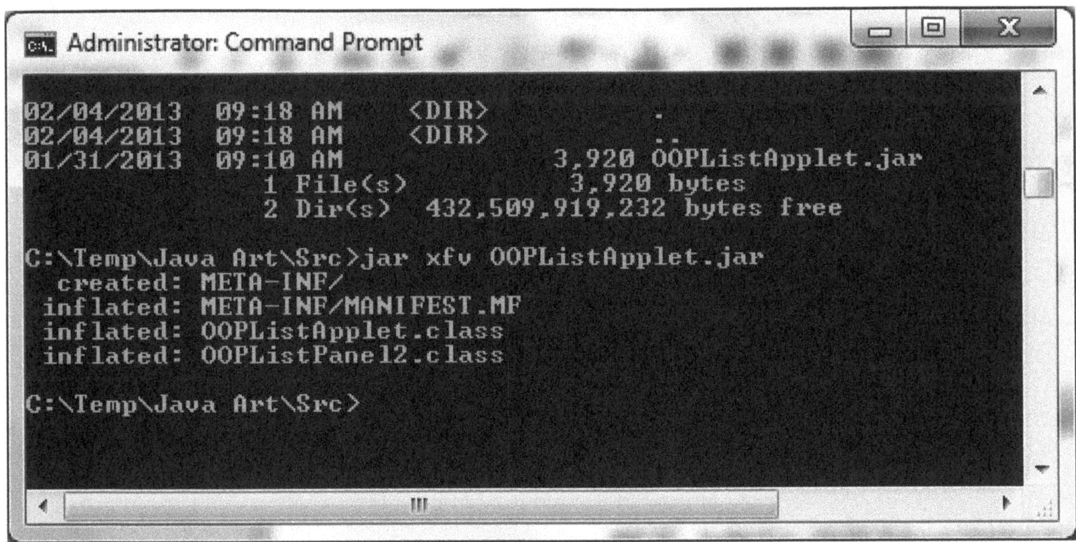

Figure 19.6 Use of the jar command to unzip a jar file

More Information: ***jar*** *files are commonly used for an applet containing one or more supporting classes. Under an IDE, e.g., Eclipse, the* ***jar*** *file is created automatically.*

19.3.4 Application example

The following example modifies **OOPListApp.java** (see Section 17.2.4) to become an applet:

```
//Complete code called OOPListApplet.java and OOPListPanel2.java in Ch19 from
//the author's website
import javax.swing.*;
import java.awt.*;

public class OOPListApplet extends JApplet {
   public void init() {
      JPanel panel = new OOPListPanel2();   //Create a panel
      this.add(panel);                      //Add the panel to applet
   }
}
```

The code of **OOPListPanel2** is the same as the code used in **OOPListApp.java** except for the omission of the **Exit** button, which is not required, in the applet.

To demonstrate how we can use the archive parameter in the HTML file to call the applet with the jar file, the steps discussed in the previous section are followed to create the jar file and the following <Applet> tag used in calling the applet:

```
<Applet archive = "OOPListApplet.jar" code = "OOPListApplet.class"
      width = 480 height = 250>
      <P>This applet requires JDK 1.6 or above to run</P>
</Applet>
```

Figure 19.7 shows the execution result of the applet:

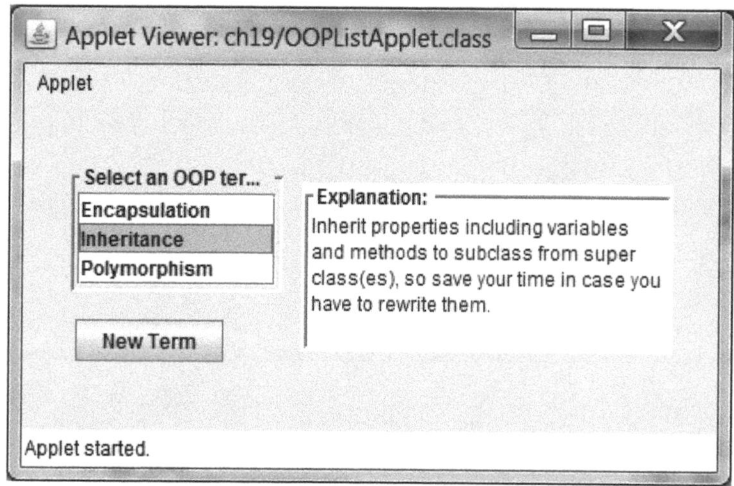

Figure 19.7 The execution result of the applet example

Exercises

1. What is an applet? What are the differences between an applet and an application?
2. Use examples to explain the differences between **AWT** and **Swing** components.
3. What features may be achieved or realized by coding an applet? What are the functions performed by **paint()** and **repaint()** in an applet?
4. What are the nine steps in coding an applet? Use an example to support your answer.
5. Why is it unnecessary to create your own HTML file to run an applet if you use a Java IDE? In what directory is the HTML file stored?

6. Modify the following exercises in Chapter 17 to transform each traditional application into an applet: Exercises 3, 4, 6, 9, 10, 11, 12, 13, 14, 15, 16, and 17. Test and run each applet. Save all files.

7. Modify the Calculator simulation discussed in Chapter 18 to become an applet. Code your own HTML file. Test and run the applet. Save all files.

"Red, orange, yellow, green, indigo, blue and purple:
Who is dancing in the sky with a rainbow?
After rain the sinking sun is again seen;
Passes and hills reveal a deep green. "

– Chairman Mao

Chapter 20 Fonts, Colors, Images, and Sounds

Fonts, colors, images, and sounds are important parts of multimedia programming. We have discussed some simple examples of how to use the **Font** and **Color** classes for GUI programming in previous chapters. In this chapter we discuss how Java supports fonts and the structure of fonts, how to define and create colors, terms related to defining images, coding techniques associated with photographs and drawings, and sound and audio processing in Java.

20.1 Fonts

Java uses mapping techniques in the **Font** class, so a **Font** object provides the information needed to map sequences of characters to sequences of glyphs and to render sequences of glyphs in **Graphics** and **Component** objects. Let's first discuss some important concepts and terms used in fonts.

20.1.1 Commonly used terms in fonts

- Characters and glyphs. Characters are symbols, including letters, numbers, punctuation, and strings in general. Glyphs refer to the visualized physical form of a character using a sequence of pixels in its display. Because there can many different designs of a particular character, there is no one-to-one relationship between a character and a glyph. An object of **Font** provides the set of glyphs for a particular character with a list reflecting the sequences.

- Physical fonts. Font libraries contain glyph data and tables to map from character sequences to glyph sequences using a font technology such as **TrueType** or **PostScript Type 1**. Java supports only **TrueType** fonts. **Helvetica**, **Palatino**, and **HonMincho** are a few examples of physical font names.

- Logical fonts. There are five font families defined by the Java platform that must be supported by any Java runtime environment: **Serif**, **SansSerif**, **Monospaced**, **Dialog**, and **DialogInput**. These logical fonts are not actual font libraries. Instead, the logical font names are mapped to physical fonts by the Java runtime environment. The mapping is implementation and (usually) locale dependent.

- Font families. A font can have many faces, such as heavy, medium, oblique, Gothic, and regular. Each face has a similar typographic design, referred to as a font family. There are three different names associated with a **Font** object. The *logical font name* is simply the name used to construct the font. The *font face name* or *font name* is the name of a particular font face, e.g., **Helvetica Bold**. The family name is the name of the font family the determines the typographic design across several faces, e.g., **Helvetica**. You may call **getLocalGraphicsEnvironment()** in **GraphicsEnvironment** to retrieve the font families of your local computer system. Examples are discussed in later sections of this chapter.

- Font styles. Java supports three display styles of a font: plain, **bold**, and *italic*. You may call **deriveFont(int style)** of **Font** to copy the current font object and specify the display style.

20.1.2 Commonly used methods

The **Font** class, provided by the **java.awt** package, contains the constructors and methods used to create, display, and set fonts. In addition, the **GraphicsEnvironment** class, also provided in this package, is used to retrieve data related to fonts in the local computer system. Table 20.1 lists commonly used constructors and methods in **Font** and **GraphicsEnvironment**.

Table 20.1 Commonly used constructors and methods in **Font** and **GraphicsEnvironment**

Constructor/Method	Description
protected Font(Font font)	Creates a Font object of the specified font.
Font(String name, int style, int size)	Creates a Font object from the specified name, style, and point size.
String getFamily()	Returns the name of this font family.
String getFontName()	Returns the font face name of this font.
String getName()	Returns the logical name of this font.
int getSize()	Returns the point size of this font, rounded to the nearest integer.
boolean isBold()	Returns true if this font's object style is BOLD.
boolean isItalic()	Returns true if this font's object style is ITALIC.
boolean isPlain()	Returns true if this font's object style is PLAIN.
abstract String[] getAvailableFontFamilyNames()	Method of GraphicsEnvironment. Returns an array containing the font family names in the locale computer system.
static GraphicsEnvironment getLocalGraphicsEnvironment()	Method of GraphicsEnvironment. Returns an object of GraphicsEnvironment in the local computer system.

Example 1. Create fonts.

```
Font myFont = new Font("SimSun", Font.PLAIN, 18); //Create a specified font
Font yourFont = new Font(myFont);                 //Copy a font
```

Example 2. Call other methods in **Font**.

```
System.out.println(myFont.getFamily());           //Print the font family
System.out.println(myFont.getFontName());         //Print the font name
```

```
System.out.println(myFont.setSize());              //Print the size 18
System.out.println(yourFont.isBold());             //Print false
System.out.println(yourFont.isPlain());            //Print true
```

Example 3. GraphicsEnvironment to retrieve the local graphics environment from the current computer system.

```
//Return the environment from the local computer
GraphicsEnvironment ge = GraphicsEnvironment.getLocalGraphicsEnvironment();

//Get the font family names from the local computer

String[] fontFamilies = ge.getAvailableFontFamilyNames();
   for (String font : fontFamilies)                      //Print the family
names
       System.out.println(font);
```

Component and **Graphics** In **java.awt** also provide two methods dealing with fonts, as listed in Table 20.2.

Table 20.2 Methods in Component and Graphics dealing with fonts

Method	Description
Font getFont()	returns the font object.
setFont(Font font)	sets the specified font object.

Example 4. Set the font of the button names.

```
JButton myButton = new JButton("Press Me");
myButton.setFont(new Font("Arial", Font.BOLD,16));   //Set the font Font
myButtonFont = myButton.getFont();                  //Return the font
System.out.println(myButtonFont.getName());         //Print the font name
```

Example 5. Display the string in the specified font.

```
public void paint(Graphics g) {              //Or: paintComponent(Graphics g);
   g.setFont(new Font("Arial", Font.BOLD, 30));   //Set font
   String text = "I love life, I love Java.";
   g.drawString(text, 30, 40);                    //Draw string at x=30,y=40
}
```

20.1.3 An application using fonts

We will write an application to display the font families installed in the local computer, including the name and size of three font styles. A specified string will be displayed in the selected font, size, and style. Figure 20.1 shows the result of this application.

Figure 20.1 Display the font families installed in the local computer system

In this application, we use **FontsPanel** to layout and manage the GUI components of the display and implement **ItemListener** to handle events. Method **paintComponent()** is called to draw the text. The following is the application code:

```
//Complete code called FontsPanel.java and FontsFrameApp.java in Ch20 from
//the author's website
class FontsPanel extends JPanel implements ItemListener{//control panel
   JComboBox fontComboBox, sizeComboBox;    //Declare components
   JCheckBox boldCheckBox, italicCheckBox;
   Font font;                               //Declare font
   public FontsPanel(){                     //Constructor
      GraphicsEnvironment ge;
      ge = GraphicsEnvironment.getLocalGraphicsEnvironment(); //Get local
      fontComboBox = new JComboBox(ge.getAvailableFontFamilyNames());

      fontComboBox.setSelectedItem("SimSun");

      fontComboBox.addItemListener(this);              //Add event handling

      String[] sizes = {"8", "10", "12", "14", "16", "18", "20", "22", "24",
      "26", "28", "30"};                         //Size
      sizeComboBox = new JComboBox(sizes);       //To combo box
      sizeComboBox.setSelectedItem("18");        //Set the size
      sizeComboBox.addItemListener(this);        //Add event handling

      boldCheckBox = new JCheckBox("Bold");             //Display style
     boldCheckBox.setFont(new Font("Times New Roman", Font.BOLD, 14));
```

```
        boldCheckBox.addItemListener(this);        //Add event handling
        italicCheckBox = new JCheckBox("Italic");
        italicCheckBox.setFont(new Font("Times New Roman", Font.ITALIC, 14));
        italicCheckBox.addItemListener(this);

        JPanel northPanel = new JPanel();          //Nested panels
        northPanel.add(fontComboBox);
        northPanel.add(sizeComboBox);
        northPanel.add(italicCheckBox);
        northPanel.add(boldCheckBox);

        setLayout(new BorderLayout());             //Layout manager
        add(northPanel, BorderLayout.NORTH);       //Add to the layout
        font = new Font("Calibri", Font.PLAIN, 18); //Set font
    }
public void itemStateChanged(ItemEvent e){         //Implement even handling
     String fontFamily = (String) fontComboBox.getSelectedItem();
                  int style = Font.PLAIN;          //Set the style
        String sizeInt = (String) sizeComboBox.getSelectedItem();
        int size = Integer.parseInt(sizeInt);  //Covert
        if ((boldCheckBox.isSelected()) && (italicCheckBox.isSelected()))
           style = Font.BOLD + Font.ITALIC;
        else if (boldCheckBox.isSelected())
           style = Font.BOLD;
        else if (italicCheckBox.isSelected())
           style = Font.ITALIC;
        font = new Font(fontFamily, style, size);         //Set the font
        repaint();              //It will automatically call paintComponent()
    }
    public void paintComponent(Graphics g){
        super.paintComponent(g);               //call method in superclass
        g.setFont(font);                       //Set the font
        String text = "I love life, I love Java";  //Display

        g.drawString(text, 100, 80);           //display string at x=100, y=80
    }
}
```

The code overrides **paintComponent()** of **JComponent** to carry out the drawing function. Although **repaint()** automatically calls **paintComponent()**, **super.paintComponent(g)** is called first to ensure the existing drawing is cleared and not overwritten before the remaining code is executed.

We may also code **FontsPanel** as an applet to perform the same drawing operation.

```
//Complete  code  called  FontsPanel.java  and  FontsApplet.java  in  Ch20  from
//the author's //website
public class FontsApplet extends JApplet{                              //applet
   public void init(){
      FontsPanel panel = new FontsPanel();                             //Create panel
      add(panel);                //add to applet
   }
}
```

20.2 Colors

Multimedia would be lacking a basic "life component" without color. Java defines three color components (red, green, and blue) each ranging from 0 to 255, or 0.0 to 1.0, allowing the generation of 1,677,216 different colors. Class **Color** from the **java.awt** package not only provides many constructors and methods for creating and manipulating colors but also supplies eighteen commonly used static color fields. In addition, **JColorChooser** in **javax.swing**, as previously discussed, makes the use of colors in visualized and convenient ways.

20.2.1 Commonly used terms in colors

HSB – Hue, Saturation, and Brightness. Hue refers to a particular color, e.g., yellow, red, or orange. Saturation is the degree of color "dilution" with white. Brightness is the color intensity level.

RGB – Red, Green, and Blue. RGB is the basic color component scheme. Different colors are made with varying ratios of RGB components.

HSL – Hue, Saturation, and Lightness.

20.2.2 Commonly used methods

Table 20.3 lists commonly used constructors and methods in **Color** and **JColorChooser**.

Table 20.3 Commonly used constructors and methods in **Color** and **JColorChooser**

Constructor/Method/Static	Description
Color(float r, float g, float b)	Creates an opaque color in the standard RGB color space in the range: 0.0 –
Color(int r, int g, int b)	Creates an opaque color in the standard RGB color space in the range: 0 –
Color brighter()	Returns a new **Color** that is a brighter version of **Color**.
Color darker()	Returns a new **Color** that is a darker version of **Color**.
JColorChooser()	Creates a color chooser pane with an initial color of white.
JColorChooser(Color color)	Creates a color chooser pane with an initial specified *color*.
static Color getColor(String nm)	Finds a color in the system properties. Parameter *nm* is the system
void setColor(Color color)	Method in class **JColorChooser**. Sets the current color of the color chooser
void setColor(int r, int g, int b)	Method in class **JColorChooser**. Sets the current color of the color chooser

The following static fields are provided in **Color** class:

BLACK BLUE CYAN DARK_GRAY GRAY GREEN LIGHT_GRAY
MAGENTA ORANGE PINK RED WHITE YELLOW

More Info: *The static color fields can be lower-case letters.*

Example 1. Create colors and color choosers.

```
Color redColor = new Color(255, 0, 0);      //Create color red
Color yellowColor = new Color(255, 255, 0);       //Create color yellow
Color darkGray = new Color(0.5f, 0.5f, 0.5f);     //Create color dark gray.
JColorChooser myColorChooser = new JColorChooser();      //Create a color
chooser

//Create a color chooser with specified color red.
JColorChooser herColorChooser = new JColorChooser(redColor);
```

Example 2. Call commonly used methods in **Color**.

```
Color brighterYellow = yellowColor.brighter();    //Call brighter()
Color darkerYellow = yellowColor.darker();        //Call darker()
```

Example 3. Call commonly used methods in **JColorChooser**.

```
Color hisColor = myColorChooser.getColor(); //Get the current selected color
herColorChooser.setColor(Color.BLUE);       //Set the color as blue
myColorChooser.setColor(255, 255, 255);    //Set the color as white
```

In **Component** and **Graphics** of **java.awt**, some useful methods that manipulate colors are also provided:

Table 20.4 Commonly used methods manipulating colors in **Component** and **Graphics**

Methods	Description
abstract Color getColor()	Method of Graphics. Returns the graphics context's current
abstract void setColor(Color color)	Method of Graphics. Sets this graphics context's current color
Color getBackground()	Method of Component. Returns the background color of this component.
Color getForeground()	Method of Component. Returns the foreground color of this component.
void setBackground(Color color)	Method of Component. Sets the background color of this component.
void setForeground(Color color)	Method of Component. Sets the foreground color of this component.

Example 4. Call commonly used methods in Component.

```
myButton.setBackground(Color.PINK);                  //Set the background as pink
myButton.setForeground(Color.BLUE);                  //Set the foreground as blue
Color myBackground = myButton.getBackground();     //Return the background
Color myForeground = myButton.getForeground();     //Return the foreground
```

Example 5. Set the colors in the frame or applet.

```
public void paintComponent(Graphics g){
      super.paintComponent(g);         //call method in superclas
      g.setFont(font);                 //Set the font
      g.setColor(Color.red);           //Set the color as red
      String text = "I love life, I love Java";          //Define text
      g.drawString(text, 100, 80);            //Draw at x=100, y=80
  }
```

20.2.3 Application example

Figure 20.2 shows the result of executing an applet that uses fonts and a color chooser to display the specified text with different size, styles, and colors.

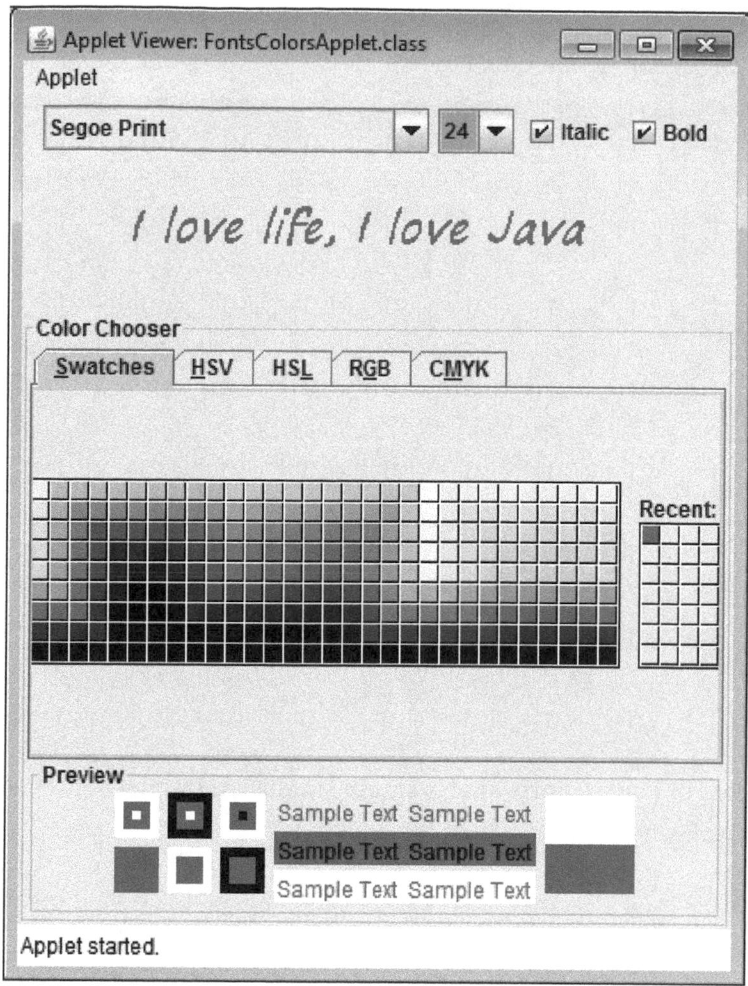

Figure 20.2 Execution result of FontsColorsApplet

```
//Complete code called FontsColorsPanel.java in Ch20 from the author's website
class FontsColorsPanel extends JPanel implements ItemListener{
   JComboBox fontComboBox, sizeComboBox;
   JCheckBox boldCheckBox, italicCheckBox;
   Font font;

   JColorChooser colorChooser;
   ColorSelectionModel model;
   Color newColor;
   ChangeListener changeListener;
   public FontsColorsPanel(){
     //Code for creating and set layout manager
      ...
      colorChooser = new JColorChooser();         //Create color chooser
              colorChooser.setBorder(BorderFactory.createTitledBorder("Color
Chooser"));
```

```
                add(colorChooser, BorderLayout.SOUTH);

            changeListener = new ChangeListener() { //Event handling
                public void stateChanged(ChangeEvent changeEvent) {
                  newColor = colorChooser.getColor();
                  repaint();
                }
        };
        model = colorChooser.getSelectionModel();
                model.addChangeListener(changeListener);
            }
  //Code for event handling
  ...
  public void paintComponent(Graphics g){
     super.paintComponent(g);
     g.setFont(font);
     g.setColor(newColor);
     String text = "I love life, I love Java";
     g.drawString(text, 60, 80);
  }
}
```

The object of **FontsColorsPanel** is created and added to the applet within the **init()** method for use in displaying the graphics of the applet:

```
//Complete code called FontsColorsApplet.java in Ch20 from the author's website
public class FontsColorsApplet extends JApplet{
   public void init() {
      FontsColorsPanel panel = new FontsColorsPanel();
      add(panel);
   }
}
```

20.3 Shape Drawing

It is easy to use traditional drawing methods contained in the **Graphics** class to draw a variety of shapes:

```
//Complete code called GraphicsShapesApplet.java in Ch20 from author's website
public void paint(Graphics g) {
   g.drawLine(100, 30, 50, 100); //Beginning at (100, 30), ending at (50, 100)
   //Upper left corner(120, 30), width 70 and height 65
   g.drawRect(120, 30, 70, 65);
  //Upper left corner (210, 30), width 70, height 40, 30 degree bend to x and
  //30 degree bend to y
   g.drawRoundRect(210, 30, 70, 40, 30, 30); //Round rectangle
   //Upper left corner (250, 30), width 80, height 60
   g.drawOval(250, 30, 80, 60);
   //Upper left corner (30, 90), width 70, height 40, beginning angle 30, and
```

```
    //ending angle 120
    g.drawArc(30, 90, 70, 40, 30, 120);

    int[] xPoints = {120, 155, 190};                //Coordinates of x's
    int[] yPoints = { 130, 90, 130};                //Coordinates of y's

    //Create polygon object - triangle
    Polygon triangle = new Polygaon(xPoints, yPoints);
    g.drawPolygon(triangle);                        //Draw triangle
}
```

The above code draws a line, rectangle, rectangle with rounded corners, oval, arc, and a triangle, as shown in Figure 20.3. We may also draw the shapes will filled colors using methods of the form **g.fillXXX()**, e.g., such as **g.fillRect()**, **g.fillRoundRect()**, **g.fillOval**, **g.fillArc()**. This is discussed later in the chapter.

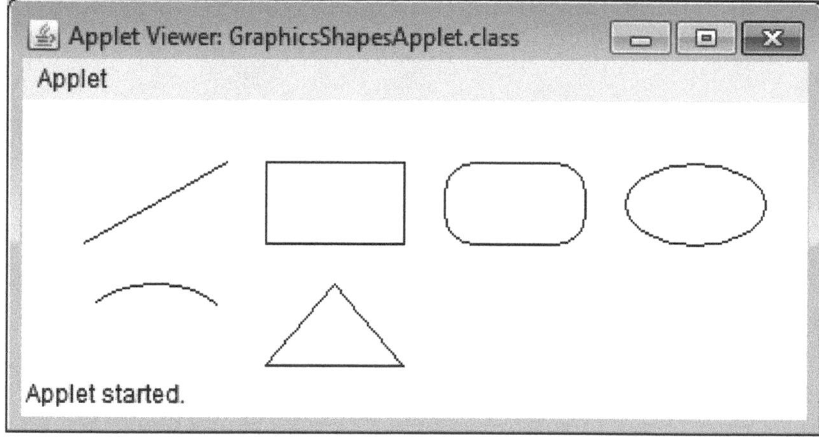

Figure 20.3 Commonly drawing shapes in Graphics class

Graphics2D, an abstract subclass of **Graphics**, provides three additional features associated with shape drawing:

- More powerful drawing functions.;
- Improved quality in drawing, e.g., higher line resolution.; and
- Capabilities for treating drawings as objects.

Java also provides capabilities for working with three-dimensional drawings and more sophisticated geometry functionality in its API classes. These capabilities are not part of the JDK foundational libraries and require separate downloading. A discussion of these capabilities and techniques is beyond the scope of this text. The user is referred to articles and texts written with an emphasis on these topics.

More Info: *The coordinate system of Java sets (x=0, y = 0) at the upper left corner of the container, e.g., frame, panel, et cetera. Both the x-axis (horizontal) and y-axis (vertical) are measured in pixels. This mode is called the logical coordinate system. You may use the **GraphicsEnvironment** and **GraphicsConfiguration** classes to convert a logical coordinate system to the "world coordinate system" of the objects being rendered on the drawing device for ease in computation and rendering. Further discussion of this topic is beyond the scope of this text.*

20.3.1 Steps in drawing with Graphics2D

The use of **Graphics2D** to draw shapes may follow these sequence of steps:

1. In **paint()** or **paintComponent()** method, cast the **Graphics** object to **Graphics2D**:

```
public void paint(Graphics g) { //Or: public void paintComponent  (Graphics g)
 {
   Graphics2D gg = (Graphics2D) g;         //Cast to Graphics2D
   ..
 }
```

2. Create an object of the drawing class provided by **java.awt.geom**:

```
Ellipse2D e = new Ellipse2D.Double(250, 30, 80, 60); //Create an oval object
```

3. Draw the shape:

```
gg.draw(e);      //Draw an oval at (250, 30) with width 80 and height 60 pixels
```

```
public void paint(Graphics g) {
   Graphics2D gg = (Graphics2D) g;
   Ellipse2D e = new Ellipse2D.Double(250, 30, 80, 60);
   gg.draw(e);
}
```

***Note**: You should call **super.paintComponent()** in **paintComponent()** before casting the object to **Graphics2D** as shown in some previous examples.*

20.3.2 Java2D API

The **Java2D** API contains the classes necessary to perform the drawing of geometric shapes, select colors and fonts, display and dynamically update two-dimensional graphics drawings in a convenient manner. It belongs to the foundational Java API libraries included in the JDK. The **Java2D** API contains the following packages:

```
java.awt     java.awt.font      java.awt.color      java.awt.geom      java.awt.image
java.awt.print          java.awt.image.renderable
```

Examples of using these classes are discussed in this chapter.

20.3.3 Commonly used methods in Graphics2D

Graphics2D, an abstract subclass of **Graphics**, is included in the **java.awt** package. In addition to being able to call all the methods in **Graphics**, commonly used methods for shape drawings of **Graphics2D** are listed in Table 20.5.

Table 20.5 Commonly used methods in **Graphics2D**

Method	Description
abstract void draw(Shape	Strokes the outline of the specified **Shape** using the settings of the current
abstract void fill(Shape s)	Fills the interior of the specified **Shape** using the settings of the current **Graphics2D**
abstract void setPaint(Paint paint)	Sets the **Paint** attribute for the **Graphics2D** context. May use **GradientPaint** class that implemented the **Paint** interface to set this type of painting. See Table 20.6.
abstract void setStroke(Stroke s)	Sets the **Stroke** attribute for the **Graphics2D** context of the stroke. May use **BasicStroke** that implemented **Stroke** interface to set the width.

In Table 20.5, **Shape** is the interface of all classes that carry out the drawing of a shape. In the next section, commonly used classes that implement this interface are discussed with examples. **Paint** and **Stroke** are interfaces in the **java.awt** package. **Color** and **GradientPaint** are classes that implement **Stroke**. **BasicStroke** implements **Stroke** and is used for setting the width of a drawing stroke. Table 20.6 lists commonly used constructors and methods in the **GradientPaint** and **BasicStroke** classes.

Table 20.6 Commonly used constructors and methods in GradientPaint and BasicStroke

Constructor/Method	Description
GradientPaint(float x1, float y1, Color c1, float x2, float y2, Color c2)	Creates an acyclic GradientPaint object starting with color *c1* at (x1, y1) and ending with color *c2* at (x2, y2).
GradientPaint(float x1, float y1, Color c1, float x2, float y2, Color c2, boolean cyclic)	Constructs a cyclic or acyclic GradientPaint object depending on the boolean parameter.
getColor1()、getColor2()、getPoint1()、getPoint2()、isCyclic()	Methods in GradientPaint: Returns the colors of the starting and ending points, the coordinates of the starting and ending points, and *true* if the gradient cycles
BasicStroke()	Constructs a BasicStroke object using defaults: solid line
BasicStroke(float width)	Create a BasicStroke object with specified width and the
float getLineWidth()	Method of BasicStroke: Returns the line width in user

Example. Use **Graphics2D**, **GradientPaint** and **BasicStroke** to draw shapes.

```
//Complete code called ShapeTestApplet.java in Ch20 from the author's website
Public class ShapeTestApplet extends JApplet {
   public void paint(Graphics g) {
         Graphics2D gg = (Graphics2D) g;                  //Cast
         Shape e = new Ellipse2D.Double(30, 30, 150, 85);//Create an oval
         gg.setPaint(new GradientPaint(30, 30, Color.red, 120, 70, Color.
         yellow, true));                                  //Set gradient
         gg.fill(e);                                      //Draw with filling
         gg.setPaint(Color.BLUE);                         //Set color
         gg.setStroke(new BasicStroke(6.0f));           //Set the  stroke width
```

```
        gg.draw(new Rectangle2D.Double(20, 20, 170, 105));//Draw rectangle

    }
}
```

Figure 20.4 shows the execution result of this applet.

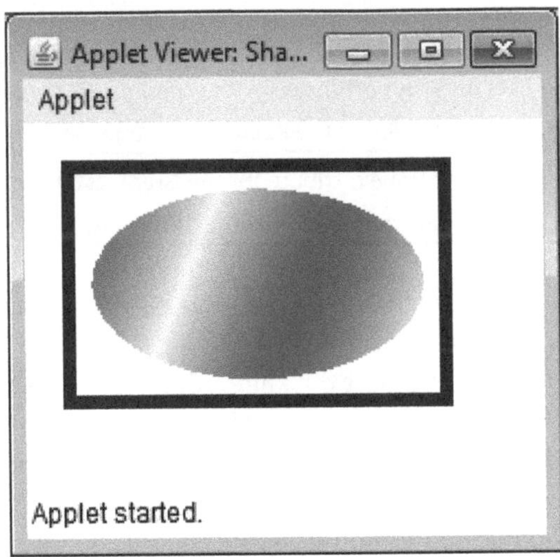

Figure 20.4 The execution result of ShapeTestApplet

20.3.4 Shape classes in java.awt.geom

There are many classes provided in **java.awt.geom** that are exclusively designed for 2D shape drawings. Table 20.7 lists commonly used ones.

Table 20.7 Commonly used classes in java.awt.geom in shape drawings

Class	Description
Point class: Point2D.Double(double x, double y)	Creates and initializes a point at the specified location.
Line class: Line2D.Double(double x1, double y1, double x2, double y2)	Creates and initializes a line starting (x1， y1) and ending (x2， y2).
Rectangle class: Rectangle2D.Double(double x, double y, double width, double height)	Creates and initializes a rectangle with the specified upper corner (x, y), width and height.
Rounded rectangle class: RoundRectangle2D.Double(double x, double y, double width, double height, double arcWidth, double arcHeight)	Creates and initializes a rounded rectangle with the upper corner (x, y), width, height, and the arc width and height.
Oval class: Ellipse2D.Double(double x, double y, double width, double height)	Creates and initializes an oval with the upper corner (x, y), width and height.
Arc class: Arc2D.Double(double, x, double y, double width, double height, double startAngle, double arcAngle, int arcType)	Creates and initializes an arc with the upper corner (x, y), width, height, starting angle, arc angle, and type of the arc - OPEN, CHORD, or PIE.

Quad curve classes: QuadCurve2D.Double(), QuadCurve2D.Double (double x1, double y1, double ctrlx, double ctrly, double x2, double y2)	Creates and initializes a QuadCurve2D object. The first form of the constructor creates and initializes this object with starting point coordinates (0.0,0.0), control point coordinates (0.0,0.0), and ending point coordinates (0.0,0.0). The second form of the constructor creates and initializes this object with specified starting point coordinates, control point coordinates, and ending point coordinates.

More Info: *Each class listed in Table 20.7 has a corresponding class using **Float** type arguments, e.g., **Line2DFloat(float x1, float y1, float x2, float y2)**. In addition, each class provides many methods to set, change, get, and test the shape. Please refer to the documentation of the classes for details.*

20.3.5 Application example

We will use the classes discussed in the above sections to draw different shapes with selected colors and fill styles chosen via drop down menus and radio buttons. The following is the code of the applet panel:

```
//Complete code called ShapesApplet.java in Ch20 from the author's website
class ShapesPanel extends JPanel {
   Shape shape;                                  //Use Shape as reference
   JComboBox  shapeComboBox, colorComboBox;      //Declare the combo boxes
   JRadioButton drawButton, fillButton;          //Declare the radio buttons
   boolean fill;                                 //Filling status
   Color color;                                  //Declare color
   public ShapesPanel() {                        //Constructor
      //Shape array
      String[] shapes = {"Line", "Rectangle", "Round Rectangle","Ellipse",
"Arc"};
      shapeComboBox = new JComboBox(shapes);     //Create the combo box
      shapeComboBox.setSelectedItem("Rectangle");//Default as rectangle
      shape = new Rectangle2D.Double(100, 60, 200, 60);
      shapeComboBox.addItemListener(new ShapeEventHandler());  //Event handling
      String[] colors = {"Black", "Red", "Blue", "Green", "yellow"};//Color array
      colorComboBox = new JComboBox(colors); //Create the combo box
      colorComboBox.setSelectedItem("Black");    //Default color as black
      colorComboBox.addItemListener(new ColorEventHandler());  //Event handling
      drawButton = new JRadioButton("not fill"); //Create radio button
      fillButton = new JRadioButton("fill");
      ButtonGroup drawGroup = new ButtonGroup(); //Create button group
      drawGroup.add(drawButton);                 //Add to the button group
      drawGroup.add(fillButton);
      drawButton.addItemListener(new DrawEventHandler()); //Event handling
      fillButton.addItemListener(new DrawEventHandler());
      JPanel northPanel = new JPanel();          //Panel for layout
      northPanel.add(shapeComboBox);        //Set FlowLayout.CENTER
```

```
    northPanel.add(colorComboBox);
    northPanel.add(drawButton);
    northPanel.add(fillButton);
    setLayout(new BorderLayout());         //Position to the top
    add(northPanel, BorderLayout.NORTH);
  }
  public void paintComponent(Graphics g) {         //Painting
    super.paintComponent(g);
    Graphics2D gg = (Graphics2D)g;         //Cast
    gg.setColor(color);                            //Set color
    if (fill)                                      //if it is filling ...
      gg.fill(shape);                              //   Call the filling method
    else
      gg.draw(shape);                              //   Else not filling
  }
  //The following code is for event handling
  ...
}
```

You may see that internal layout panel **northPanel** is created to position the two combo boxes and two radio buttons in the center of the panel at the top of the applet. Three inner classes, **ShapeEventHandler**, **ColorEventHandler, and DrawEventHandler**, are coded to carry out event handling and drawing. The following is the code of **ShapeEventHandler**:

```
//ShapeEventHandler is an inner class of ShapesPanel
class ShapeEventHandler implements ItemListener {//Event handling code
  public void itemStateChanged(ItemEvent e) {     //Implement
    String shapeString = (String)shapeComboBox.getSelectedItem(); //Get shape
    int x = 100, y = 60, w = 200, h = 60;               //Set the drawing
    if (shapeString.equals("Line"))                     //Draw a line
      shape = new Line2D.Double(x, y, w + 100, h + 100);
    else if (shapeString.equals("Rectangle"))           //Draw a rectangle
      shape = new Rectangle2D.Double(x, y, w, h);
    else if (shapeString.equals("Round Rectangle")) //Draw a rounded rectangle
      shape = new RoundRectangle2D.Double(x, y, w, h, 40, 40);
    else if (shapeString.equals("Ellipse"))             //Draw an ellipse
      shape = new Ellipse2D.Double(x, y, w, h);
    else if (shapeString.equals("Arc"))                 //Draw an arc

      shape = new Arc2D.Double(x, y, w, h, 30, 210, Arc2D.CHORD);
    repaint();                               //repaint() calls paintComponent()
  }
}
```

In the **init()** method of this applet, a **ShapesPanel** object is created to display the drop down menus and radio buttons and perform the drawing:

```
public class ShapesApplet extends JApplet{
   public void init(){
      JPanel panel = new ShapesPanel();
      add(panel);
   }
}
```

Figure 20.5 shows a typical execution result of this applet.

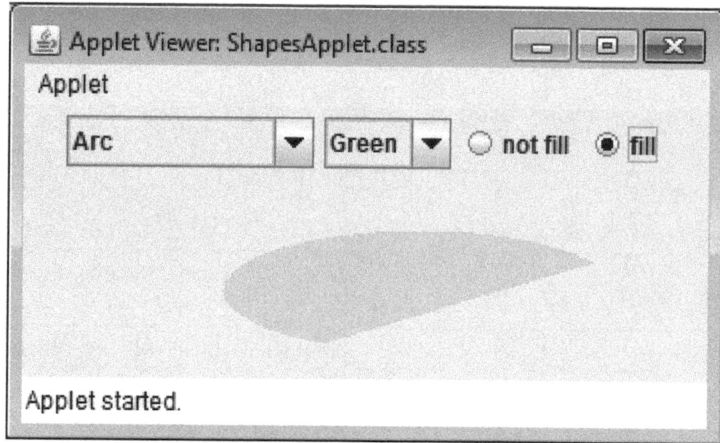

Figure 20.5 A typical execution result of the applet

20.3.6 Catching balls game

The "Catching Balls" game requires the user to use the mouse in attempting to catch six balls of differing color and size moving in random directions. The score is recorded, showing the highest score attained and the time (seconds) used in finishing the game. Pressing the "Play Again" button allows the player to advance to the next level, featuring smaller balls moving at higher velocities. The player's name, score, and game timer are displayed on the game board during play. Game coding techniques include painting, shape drawing, GUI design, multi-threading, event handling, exception handling, timer programming, and random number generation methods. Audio programming, (discussed later in this chapter) featuring different sound clips at different playing levels, makes the game more fun to play.

20.4 Images

Java API **Image** and **ImageIcon** classes are provided in the **java.awt** and **javax.swing** packages, respectively. In addition, Java provides an advanced image processing library, **Java Advanced Imaging** API. This API is not included in the standard JDK; it requires a separate downloading. Images are usually processed using methods in the **Applet** class. If images are displayed in a frame, you may need to use methods in **Toolkit**. Both image displaying venues require calling methods in **Graphics**.

In this section, we discuss image processing in Java using examples.

20.4.1 Image formats

Java supports many image formats, including GIF (Graphics Interchange Format), JPEG (Joint Photographic Experts Group), and PNG (Portable Network Graphics). The default file extensions of these formats is **.gif**, **.jpg**, and **.png**, respectively.

The **javax.imageio** package (beginning in JDK1.4) provides many API interfaces to handle image I/O, format conversion, save, and other operations. In this chapter we discuss the three standard default image default formats in Java.

20.4.2 Commonly used methods

Table 20.8 lists commonly used methods in the **Applet**, **Toolkit,** and **Graphics** classes of the **java.awt** package.

Table 20.8 Commonly used methods in Applet. Toolkit and Graphics in java.awt

Method	Description
Image getImage(URL url)	Method of Applet. Returns an Image object that can be
Image getImage(URL url, String name)	Method of Applet. Returns an Image object that can be
URL getDocumentBase()	Method of Applet. Returns the absolute URL of the image file.
URL getCodeBase()	Method of Applet. Returns the URL containing the applet
static Toolkit getDefaultToolkit()	Static method of Toolkit. Returns a default Toolkit object of the current computer.
abstract Image createImage(String fileName)	Method of Toolkit. Creates and returns an Image object that gets image bit data from the specified file.
abstract Image getImage(URL url)	Method of Toolkit. Returns an Image object that gets data from the specified URL.
abstract Image getImage(String filename)	Method of Toolkit. Returns an Image object that gets data from the specified file, whose format can be GIF, JPEG, or
abstract boolean drawImage(Image image, int x, int y, Color bgColor, ImageObserver observer)	Method of Graphics. Draws as much of an image as is possible beginning at coordinates (*x*,*y*) in the graphics context's coordinate space. Transparent pixels are drawn
abstract boolean drawImage(Image image, int x, int y, ImageObserver observer)	Method of Graphics. Draws as much of an image as is possible beginning at coordinates (*x*,*y*) in the graphics context's coordinate space. Transparent pixels do not
abstract boolean drawImage(Image image, int x, int y, int width, int height, ImageObserver observer)	Method of Graphics. Draws as much of an image as is possible scaled to fit in the specified rectangle. Transparent pixels do not affect whatever pixels are

20.4.3 Examples

Example 1. Read and display the specified file in an applet.

```
//Complete code is called ImagesTestApplet.java in Ch20 from the author's website
import java.awt.*;
import javax.swing.*;
public class ImagesTestApplet extends JApplet {
   private Image flowers, myPhoto;          //Declare two images
   public void init() {
```

```
      //Read the file from the directory of the HTML file
      flowers = getImage(getDocumentBase(), "flowers.gif");
      //Read the file in the subdirectory starting from the applet directory
      myPhoto = getImage(getCodeBase(), "images/ygao.jpg");
   }
   public void paint(Graphics g) {
      g.drawImage(flowers, 0, 0, this);     //Display the image in applet
      g.drawImage(myPhoto, 265, 0, this);
   }
}
```

In the above example, both the HTML file and applet code file are stored in the same directory. As such, **getDocumentBase()** and **getCodeBase()** return the same directory name. If the image files are stored in a subdirectory of the folder containing the HTML and applet files, e.g., "**\image**", this may be specified (in the above case) as "**\image\\gao.jpg**".

Because the applet is the component that implements **ImageObserver**, you may use the keyword **this** when the **drawImage()** method is called. Figure 20.7 shows the result of executing the applet.

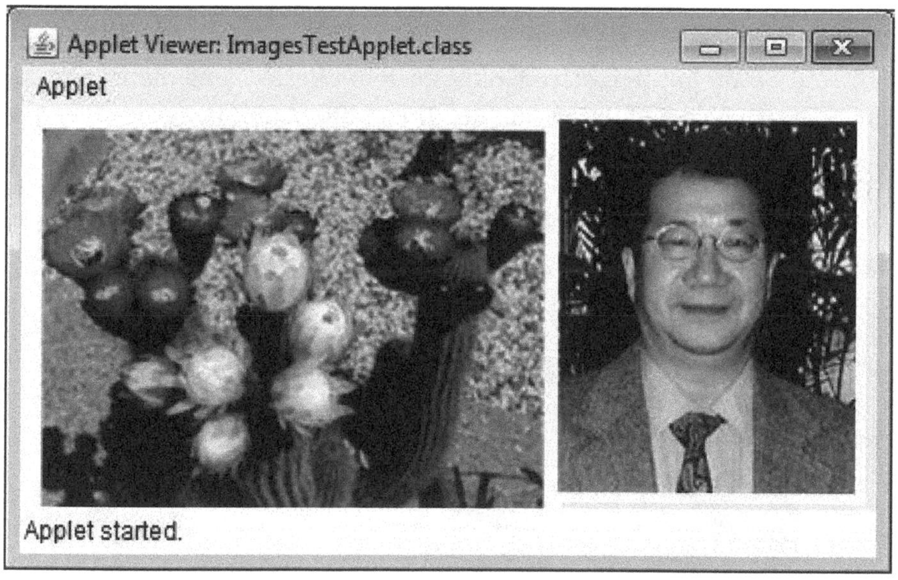

Figure 20.6 The execution result of the image applet

Example 2. Use methods in **ToolKit** to get and display the images in the panel or frame.

```
//Complete code called ImagePanel.java in Chh20 from the author's website
import javax.swing.*;
import java.awt.*;
import java.net.*;

class ImagePanel extends JPanel {
   Toolkit tk;                                             //Declare variables
   Image flowers, myPhoto , javaLogo;
   URL imageUrl;

   public ImagePanel(){                                    //Constructor
```

```
        tk = Toolkit.getDefaultToolkit();
        flowers = tk.createImage("flowers.gif");           //From the current folder
        myPhoto = tk.getImage("images\\ygao.jpg");         //From the subfolder
        try {
            //Image from a website
            imageUrl = new URL("http://img9.3lian.com/c1/vector2/03/07/03.jpg");
            javaLogo = tk.getImage(imageUrl);
        }
        catch (MalformedURLException e) {}
    }

    public void paintComponent(Graphics g){
        super.paintComponent(g);
        Graphics2D gg = (Graphics2D)g;
        gg.drawImage(flowers, 0, 0, this);                 //Display
        gg.drawImage(myPhoto, 265, 5, this);
        gg.drawImage(javaLogo, 480, 0, this);
    }
}
```

In this example, three images from different source locations are read and created using different techniques: The flower image is stored in the current directory and method **createImage()** of **Toolkit** is called to create an object of the image file. The photographic image is stored in subdirectory "images," and method **getImage()** of **Toolkit** is called to get the image file. The Java logo is from a website specified in the URL and the URL constructor instantiates the object of the URL encapsulating the image file. These three images are displayed in the frame by calling the **Graphics** class method **drawImage()**. Figure 20.8 shows the result of executing the example.

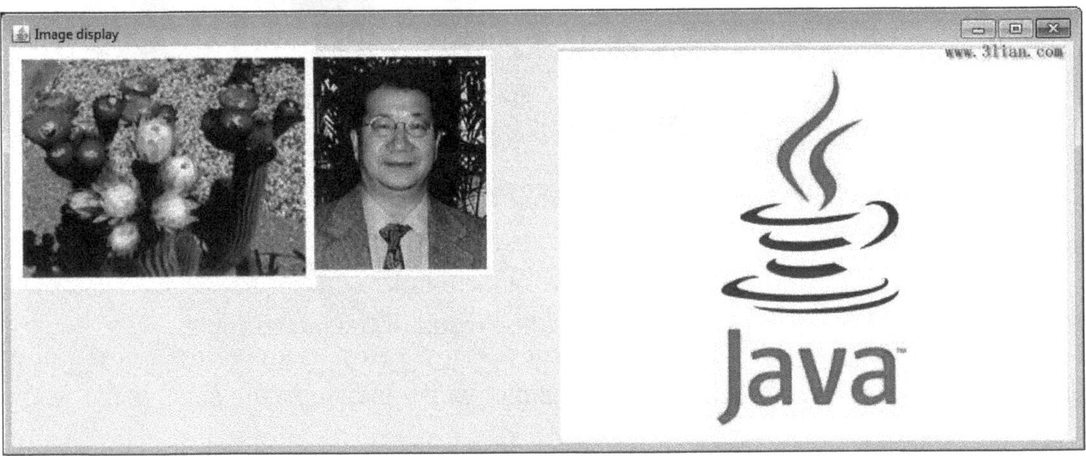

Figure 20.7 The execution result of Example 2

Example 3. A URL can also be used to create directories in a local computer system. The following code snippet show how to create objects of directories in which the image files are saved. The image files in these directories can later be retrieved. For safety purposes, the URLs are not used in applets.

```
//Complete code called LocalImagePanel.java and LocalImageFrameTest.java
try {
   //Create local directory object using URL
   flowersUrl = new URL("file:" + new File(".").getCanonicalPath() +
   "\\flowers.jpg");  //From the current folder
   myPhotoUrl = new URL("file:" + new File(".").getCanonicalPath() +
   "\\images\\gao.jpg");  //From a subfolder
   tk.getImage(flowersUrl);          //Get the image

    //Print the path
   System.out.println("file:" + new File(".").getCanonicalPath() +
   "\\flowers.jpg");
}
catch (IOException e) {                        //Exception handling
   System.out.println(e);
]
catch (MalformedURLException e) {
   System.out.println(e);
}
```

If a path or URL is specified relative to the local computer system, Java requires that it must start with the keyword **file** when creating a **URL** object. Constructor **File**, provided in **java.io**, is used to create an anonymous **File** object in which a dot "." is used to represent the root directory, e.g., under Windows: **c:**. Method **getCanonicalPath()** in **File** returns the path from the root to the directory in which the file is stored. The image file name or subdirectory storing the file is specified as the last part of the path. An example of these technique under the Windows operating system is:

```
file:C:\Java Art - English\Ch20\ch20\gao.gif
```

Method **getCanonicalPath()** throws a checked exception. Code must be provided to handle the exception.

Note: *The pathes of images showing in these examples are in TextPad. they may be different if you use different IDEs. You need to verify the path in the particular IDE and modify it accordingly.*

20.4.4 A movable image

Through the use of image processing techniques and Java threading, we may code a movable image applet:

```
//Complete code called AnimatedImageApplet.java in Ch20 from the author's website
import java.awt.*;
import javax.swing.*;
public class AnimatedImageApplet extends JApplet implements Runnable {
   private Image photo;
   private int imageWidth, imageHeight;
   public void init() {
      //Get the image
      photo = getImage(getCodeBase(), "images\\javaLogo.gif");
      imageWidth = getWidth() - 300; //Get the size and make it smaller
      imageHeight = getHeight() - 150;
   }
   public void start() {
      Thread thread = new Thread(this);     //Create a thread
      thread.start();                       //Call start()
   }
   public void paint(Graphics g) {
      //Display it according to the specified changing size
      g.drawImage(photo,10,10,imageWidth,imageHeight,this);
   }
   public void run() {
      int dx=10, dy=5;          //Beginning coordinates
      while (true) {
         for (int i=0; i<20; i++) {          //Change image position 20 times
              imageWidth += dx;              //Increase width
              imageHeight += dy;             //Increase height
              repaint();                     //Repaint
              try {
                   Thread.sleep(280);        //Waiting
              }
              catch(InterruptedException e) {
                   e.printStackTrace();
              }
         }
         dx = -dx; dy = -dy;                 //Reset the coordinate
      }
   }
}
```

20.5 Icons

There is no significant difference between an image and an icon, except for the size of the picture: smaller images can be treated as icons. Icons are routinely used in GUI programming on task bars to represent a variety of computer operations, company logos, et cetera. Many GUI components, such as labels, buttons, and menus, incorporate icons to make them more intuitive and provide a better "look and feel." Java icon files follow the format conventions of image processing files and be in the format of **GIF**, **JPEG**, or **PNG**.

Figure 20.8 shows a group of icons displayed in a frame. The "smiley face" is an animated icon.

Figure 20.8 A group of icons are displayed in a window

20.5.1 Commonly used methods

Table 20.9 lists commonly used constructors and methods provided in the **ImageIcon** class of the **java.swing** package.

Table 20.9 Commonly used constructors and methods in ImageIcon class

Constructor/Method	Descripti
ImageIcon ()	Creates an uninitialized icon.
ImageIcon(Image image)	Creates an ImageIcon from an Image object.
ImageIcon(Image image, String description)	Creates an ImageIcon from an Image object and a
String getDescription()	Returns the brief textual description of the image.
int getIconHeight()	Returns the height of the icon.
int getIconWidth()	Returns the width of the icon.
Image getImage()	Returns the icon as an Image object.
void setDescription(String description)	Sets the brief textual description of the icon.
void setImage(Image image)	Sets the image displayed by this icon.

The **JFrame** class of **java.swing** also provides the method **setIconImage(Image image)** to process icons. The method displays an icon at the beginning of the title bar in a frame, as shown in Figure 20.9.

Example 1. Create an icon and call some commonly used methods.

```
ImageIcon javaIcon = new ImageIcon();              //Create an unspecified icon
javaIcon.setImage("java.jpg");                     //Set and display the icon
ImageIcon jugglerIcon = new ImageIcon("juggler.gif");   //Create a specified
icon
setIconImage(jugglerIcon);                    //Display the icon in the title bar
```

```
ImageIcon nextIcon = new ImageIcon("next.gif", "Next Icon");    //Create
specified
System.out.println("Icon height: " + javaIcon.getIconHeight()); //Print height
System.out.println("Icon width: " + javaIcon.getIconWidth());  //Print width
System.out.println("The description: " + nextIcon.getDescription());
   //Description
Image javaImage = javaIcon.getImage();      //Return the icon as an image
```

Example 2. Create labels and buttons with icons.

```
JLabel myLabel = new JLabel(new ImageIcon("smiley.gif")); //Create an icon
label
//Create an icon button
JButton myButton = new JButton(new ImageIcon("javaIcon.png"));
```

Or:

```
//Read and create the specified icon
ImageIcon icon = new ImageIcon("images\\javaIcon.gif");
JButton myButton = new JButton();                //Create a button
myButton.setIcon(icon);                          //Display the icon on the
button
```

20.5.2 More examples

Display the icons shown in Figure 20.8 (see above).

```
//Complete code called IconFrameTest.java in Ch20 from the author's website
public class IconFrameTest extends JFrame {
   private ImageIcon numberIcon;
   public IconFrameTest(){
      setTitle("Icon frame test");
      numberIcon = new ImageIcon("images\\number.gif"); //Create icon
      Image numberImage = numberIcon.getImage();       //Get the icon
      setIconImage(numberImage);                      //Display icon in title bar
      IconPanel panel = new IconPanel();               //Create the panel
      this.add(panel);                                 //Add panel to frame
      ...
   }
}
```

IconPanel creates and positions the icons in the example. For demonstration purposes these buttons with displayed icons are created using different constructors:

```
class IconPanel extends JPanel{
      private ImageIcon javaIcon,jugglerIcon, numberIcon,nextIcon,
```

```
        javaLogoIcon;
        private JButton startButton, jugglerButton, introButton, nextButton;
        public IconPanel(){
        javaIcon = new ImageIcon("images\\javaIcon.png");     //Create icon
        startButton = new JButton("Start Java", javaIcon );   //Create button
        jugglerIcon = new ImageIcon("images\\jugglerIcon.png"); //Create icon

        jugglerButton = new JButton("Juggler");               //Create button
        jugglerButton.setIcon(jugglerIcon);                   //Set an icon
          //Create button with icon
        introButton  =  new  JButton(new  ImageIcon("images\\numberIcon.gif"));


        nextIcon = new ImageIcon("images\\next.gif");  //Create icon
        nextButton = new JButton(nextIcon); //Create button with icon

        JPanel buttonPanel = new JPanel();
        buttonPanel.add(startButton);
        buttonPanel.add(jugglerButton);
        buttonPanel.add(introButton);
        buttonPanel.add(nextButton);
        buttonPanel.setBackground(Color.red);
        setLayout(new BorderLayout());
        add(buttonPanel, BorderLayout.SOUTH);
        }
        public void paintComponent(Graphics g){
    super.paintComponent(g);
    javaLogoIcon = new ImageIcon("images\\smiley.gif");      //Create icon
    Image javaImage = javaLogoIcon.getImage();               //Get the icon
    g.drawImage(javaImage, 260, 50, this);                   //Display
        }
}
```

20.5.3 An alphabet learning game

An alphabet learning game for preschool children can be developed using icons, buttons, and other Java coding techniques. The game displays one letter at a time, and upon recognizing the letter the child presses the corresponding button showing the letter at the bottom of the screen. The score is displayed showing the number of correct and incorrect recognitions. Three audio clips are played during the game to stimulate the child's playing interest. Audio programming is discussed in a later section of this chapter. Figure 20.9 shows a typical screenshot of this game.

There are six programmer-defined classes in the alphabet learning game:

GameFrame – Creates the frame, sets the size and position of the letter, handles window closing, and creates and adds the game panel.

GamePanel – Creates the GUI components, performs event handling, processes the player's answer, updates the score, and controls the audio clip and playing.

GameLetterPanel – Creates a randomly colored letter. A thread is used to control the "dropping" of the letter within the display, and returns the letter selected by the player.

RanNum – Random letter and color generator. Supports **GamePanel** and **GameLetterPanel**.

PlaySound – Creates and plays game audio clips.

GameApp – Driver code to create and display the game window.

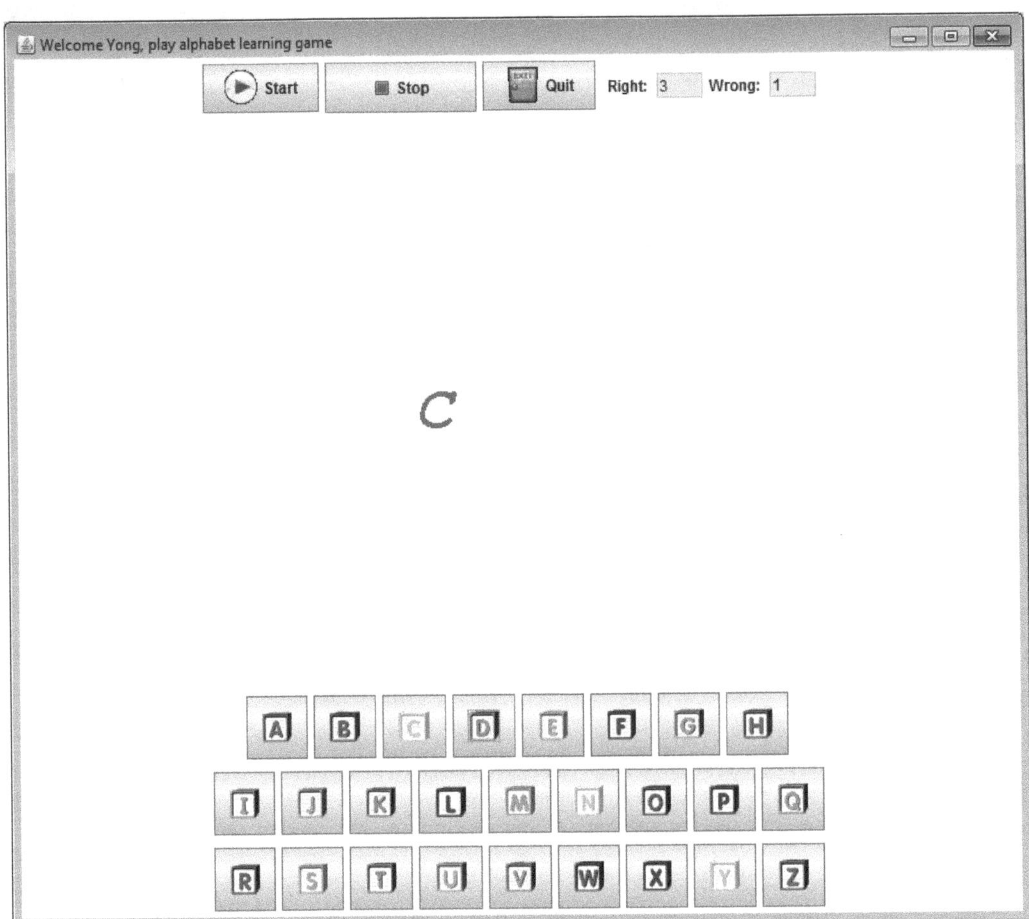

Figure 20.9 A typical screenshot of the game

The complete code of the game is available in Ch20 from the author's website.

20.6 Audio And Audio Coding

Java has three packages providing API classes in JDK for audio processing and coding:

java.applet – Contains APIs for reading audio files and performing operations (play, loop, and stop) on audio clips. It supports audio file types **au**, **wav**, and **aif**.

javax.sound.sampled – Contains APIs for sampling or digitalizing audio, as well as playing audio.

javax.sound.midi – Contains APIs for transporting and sequencing MIDI events and for synthesizing sound from those events.

Java also supplies the following sound and audio processing APIs. These APIs are not included in JDK

SE and require separate downloading:

JMF (Java Media Framework) – JMF API contains classes that are exclusively designed for video and audio processes and operations. The ranges of applications using these classes include web-based video conferencing, video telephoning, and internet gaming.

javax.media.j3d and **com.sun.j3d.audioengines** – Contains APIs for 3D sound application development.

Topics relating to the above two non-JDK SE packages are beyond the scope of this text.

20.6.1 Commonly used methods

Table 20.10 lists commonly used methods provided in the **Applet** class of the **java.applet** package. The **AudioClip** interface also provides three audio operations: **play()**, **loop()**, and **stop()**. Methods **getAudioClip()** and **newAudioClip()** implement the interface and return an object of **AudioClip**, allowing the three methods of audio operations to be called.

Table 20.10 Commonly used methods in audio

Method	Description
AudioClip getAudioClip (URL url)	Returns the AudioClip object specified by the URL.
AudioClip getAudioClip(URL url, String name)	Returns the named AudioClip object located at the
static final AudioClip newAudioClip(URL url)	Static method. Returns the AudioClip object specified by
void play(URL url)	Plays the AudioClip object specified by the URL.
void play(URL url, String name)	Plays the named AudioClip object located at the specified
void play()	Method of getAudioClip() and newAudioClip(). Plays the audio clip. Each time this method is called, the clip is
void loop()	Method of getAudioClip() and newAudioClip(). Plays the audio clip in a loop.
void stop()	Method of getAudioClip() and newAudioClip(). Stops the audio clip.

***Note**: The **java.applet** package does not provide a class to directly create an object of **AudioClip**. The object is created by calling **getAudioClip** and **newAudioClip**. These procedures implement **AudioClip** and return an object of **AudioClip**.*

Note: *Path of an audio file may be different if you use different IDEs. Please check the IDE you are using and modify the path accordingly.*

Example 1. Call methods that return an object of **AudioClip** in an applet.

```
import java.applet.*;
class SoundPlayApplet extends JApplet {
   AudioClip sound1, sound2;                        //Define audioClip references
   public void init() {
      sound1 = getAudioClip(getDocumentBase(), "sounds//event.au");
      sound2 = getAudioClip(getCodeBase(), "file:joy.wav");
   }
   ...
}
```

Method **init()** calls **getAudioClip()** in two different manners: **AudioClip sound1** is retrieved from a subdirectory of the directory storing the HTML file; **AudioClip sound2** is retrieved from the current directory containing the applet source code.

Example 2. Call methods that return an object of **AudioClip** in a frame.

```
import java.applet.*;
import javax.swing.*;
import java.net.*;

class SoundPlayFrame extends JFrame {
   URL soundUrl;
   AudioClip yourSound, herSound;
   String soundFile;
   Applet soundApplet;
   SoundPlayFrame() {
      //Create the audio file using URL
      soundUrl = new URL("http://www.prankcallsunlimited.com/freesound2/
                       siren03.wav");
      yourSound = Applet.newAudioClip(soundUrl); //Return the sound
      soundApplet new Applet();                  //Create an object of Applet
      soundFile = "sound\\joy.wav";              //Specify the sound file

      //Return the sound object
      herSound = soundApplet.getAudioClip(getCodeBase(), soundFile);
          }
   ...
}
```

Applet class static method **newAudioClip()** is called to return an object of **AudioClip** In the frame. Because no problem of web safety exists within a frame, we may access a sound file from a website by specifying its URL address. Of course, you may also create an object of **Applet** and then call **getAudioClip()** to return the object.

Example 3. Continue from the above example; call the methods in **AudioClip** to operate the sound.

```
sound1.play();                                  //Play
sound2.loop();                                  //Loop
...
yourSound.stop();                               //Stop
soundApplet.play(soundUrl);             //Directly play the web sound file
...
play(getDocumentBase(),"sound\\event.au");  //Play specified sound in applet
```

20.6.2 Free download the audio clips

Many websites provide sound files that may be freely downloaded or from which the sound files may be directly played. The following list contains several such websites:

```
www.freeaudioclips.com
www.partnersinrhyme.com/pir/PIRsfx.shtml
www.prankcallsunlimited.com
www.make4fun.com/audio-clips.htm
```

Of course, all sound files with a format of **au**, **wav, mid**, or **aif** can be played using **AudioClip**.

20.6.3 Example of playing music

Example 1. Play music in an applet.

```
//Complete code called SoundPlayApplet.java in Ch20 from the author's website
import java.awt.*;
import java.applet.*;
import javax.swing.*;
public class SoundPlayApplet extends JApplet {
   AudioClip sound;
   public void init() {
      sound = getAudioClip(getCodeBase(), "file:sounds\\event.au");
      sound.play();
   }
   public void start() {
      sound.loop();              //Loop
   }
   public void stop() {
      sound.stop();              //Stop the play when applet is closed
   }
   public void paint(Graphics g) {
      Graphics2D g2D = (Graphics2D)g;
      g2D.drawString("Playing Event Sound, Click Close Window to Stop....", 10,
20);
   }
}
```

Example 2. Play music in a frame.

```
//Complete code called SoundFrameApp.java in Ch20 from the author's website
class SoundFrame extends JFrame {
   SoundFrame() {
      JPanel soundPanel = new SoundPanel();         //Create panel
      add(soundPanel);                              //Register
```

```
        setTitle("Sound Play Frame");
        setSize(250, 80);
        setDefaultCloseOperation(WindowConstants.DISPOSE_ON_CLOSE);
        centerWindow(this);
    }
    //Code for centerWindow
    ...
}
public class SoundFrameApp {
    public static void main(String[] args) {
        JFrame frame = new SoundFrame();
        frame.setVisible(true);
    }
}
class SoundPanel extends JPanel implements ActionListener {         //Music panel
    JButton playButton, stopButton;
    String musicName;                                    //Declare the file
    AudioClip music;
    URL localUrl;                                        //Declare file address
    SoundPanel() {
        playButton = new JButton("Play");                //Create play button
        add(playButton);
        playButton.addActionListener(this);
        stopButton = new JButton("Stop");                //Create stop button
        add(stopButton);
        stopButton.addActionListener(this);
        musicName = "sounds//event.au";                  //Define file name
        try {
            //Define the path of the file
            localUrl = new URL("file:" + new File(".").getCanonicalPath()
                                  + "//" + musicName);
            music = Applet.newAudioClip(localUrl);  //Return AudioClip object
        }
        catch (IOException e) {
            System.out.println(e);
        }
    }
    public void actionPerformed(ActionEvent e) {   //Event handling
        Object source = e.getSource();
        if (source == playButton)
            music.loop();                                //Loop
        else if(source == stopButton)
                music.stop();                            //Stop
    }
}
```

The example uses the "try-catch" mechanism to provide exception handling for the **IOException** required in working with the **URL**. In the **try** block, **new File(".")** returns an object of **URL**, and we use **getCanonicalPath()** to retrieve the complete file path including the root to the current directory.

You may also the web address as the URL to play the music remotely:

```
URL soundUrl = new URL("http://www.prankcallsunlimited.com/freesounde-
ffects/chicken.wav");
AudioClip music = Applet.newAudioClip(soundUrl);
music.play();
```

Exercises

1. Use examples to explain the differences between characters and glyphs and the differences between logical fonts and physical fonts. What is a font family? What is a font style?

2. Use examples to explain the differences between **AWT** and **Swing** components.

3. What are the commonly used terms in defining and describing color? Use examples to explain their meanings and usages.

4. Summarize the commonly used steps and techniques used in Java coding of colors.

5. Use examples to explain the differences between images and icons. Use examples to summarize the steps in the coding of images and icons.

6. Referring to examples discussed in this chapter about fonts and colors, use the font family provided on your local computer to write Java code allowing the user to select a font size (8 to 30 points), font style, and font color (minimum of five colors), and draw a text string in the lower part of the window. Run, test, and save your file(s).

7. Write a Java application code to draw a multi-colored robot in a style of your choice. Run, test, and save your file(s).

8. Write a Java applet to draw a multi-colored robot in a style of your choice. Run, test, and save your file(s).

9. Write a Java application code to design and draw a "No Smoking" sign or logo. Run, test, and save your file(s).

10. Write a Java applet to design and draw a "No Smoking" sign or logo. Run, test, and save your file(s).

11. Write a Java application code to design and draw a "No Food or Drink" sign or logo. Run, test, and save your file(s).

12. Write a Java applet to design and draw a "No Smoking" sign or logo. Run, test, and save your file(s).

13. Develop a Java application using drawn shapes, colors, GUI components, and sound effects in a mathematics learning game for preschool children. The game must randomly generate a minimum of ten mathematics questions and display the score of each round. Run, test, and save the file(s).

14. Develop a Java applet using drawn shapes, colors, GUI components, and sound effects in a mathematics learning game for preschool children. The game must randomly generate a minimum of ten mathematics questions and display the score of each round. Run, test, and save the file(s).

15. Develop a Java application using drawn shapes, colors, GUI components, and sound effects in an alphabet learning game for preschool children. The game must randomly generate a minimum of twenty-six letter-related questions and display the score of each round. Run, test, and save the file(s).

16. Develop a Java applet using drawn shapes, colors, GUI components, and sound effects in an alphabet learning game for preschool children. The game must randomly generate a minimum of twenty-six letter-related questions and display the player's name and score of each round. Run, test, and save the file(s).

17. Develop a Java application using drawn shapes, colors, GUI components, and sound effects in a color learning game for preschool children. The game must randomly generate a minimum of ten colors and display the player's name and score of each round. Run, test, and save the file(s).

18. Develop a Java applet using drawn shapes, colors, GUI components, and sound effects in a color learning game for preschool children. The game must randomly generate a minimum of ten colors and display the player's name and score of each round. Run, test, and save the file(s).

19. Develop a Java application using drawn shapes, colors, GUI components, and sound effects in a English word learning game for preschool children. The game must randomly generate a minimum of ten simple words and display the player's name and score of each round. Run, test, and save the file(s).

20. Develop a Java applet using drawn shapes, colors, GUI components, and sound effects in a color learning game for preschool children. The game must randomly generate a minimum of ten colors and display the player's name and score of each round. Run, test, and save the file(s).

"Running water is never stagnant and door hinges never get worm-eaten—practice keeps one always fit."

– Lüshi chunqiu

Chapter 21 File I/O

File input and output, or file I/O, is an important function in Java. Java has a broad definition of data file resources and supports many file formats. In previous chapters dealing with image and audio operations, we discussed how to use the **Image**, **ImageIcon**, and **AudioClip** classes to read image or sound files. We also discussed using **JFileChooser** (Chapter 17) to code basic file I/O. Regardless of file format, Java uses the concept and technology of a "stream" to perform files I/O. The **java.io** package provides powerful API classes used exclusively for file I/O operations in a variety of ways.

In this chapter we introduce the concept of "streams" in Java, emphasizing their role with file data. We will present examples to discuss using the API class in **java.io** to code applications using file I/O, in particular text I/O, binary I/O, random access I/O, and compressed file I/O.

21.1 Data Streams and Files

Data saved in a file has a permanency in use. Java file I/O is not limited to reading or writing files in a local computer system; files may be saved on or retrieved from a website. Java socket files provide the functionality to perform file operations from any I/O device. Java supports operations on text, binary, object, and compressed files.

The concept of data streams simplifies the understanding of Java file I/O operations. A data stream is a collection of data with a defined byte length and direction of movement. An input data stream refers to data movement, or "reading in," from a storage device to the program. An output data stream represents data "moving out," or being written, from the program to a destination device, such as a hard drive. This concept is illustrated in Figure 21.1.

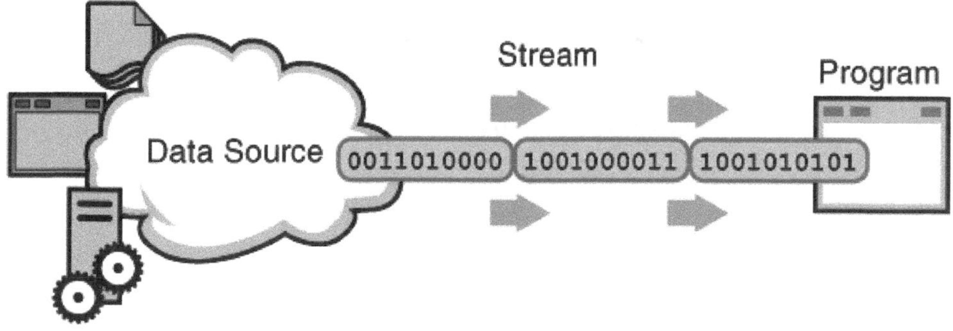

Data input Stream

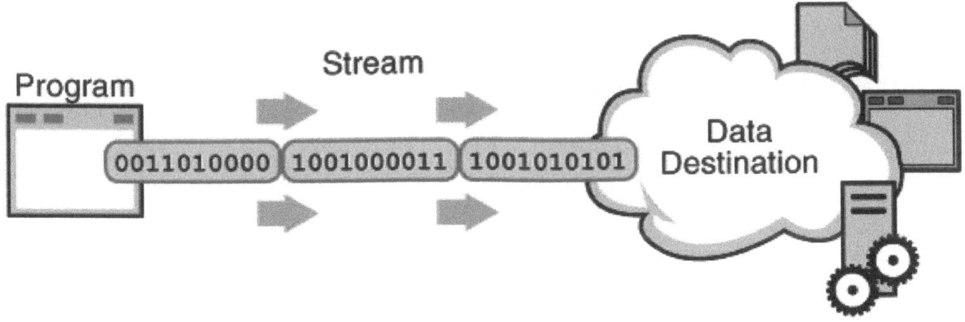

Data output stream

Figure 21.1 Conception of data input and output streams

Although I/O streams contain data in bytes, the content of the bytes can represent different data formats:

Text file – formatted as ASCII or Unicode.

Binary file – formatted as binary code.

Object file – formatted as a computer code's object, i.e., machine-readable, file with its data

Compressed file – formatted as a JAR, ZIP, GZIP, or other similar file incorporating data compression.

Java provides API classes to support the operations necessary for ~~all~~ each of above format of data streams.

21.1.1 "Must know" information for file I/O

Based on our discussion above, we must know the following information before coding file I/O operations:

- The format of the file.
- The content organization of the file—especially important in working with binary files.
- The direction of the data stream: input or output.
- The file path – the directory of the file.
- Buffer – if an I/O buffer is necessary.

The following sections discuss file paths, the **File** class and its commonly used methods, the concept of buffered I/O, and exception handling in file I/O.

21.1.2 File path

A file path or directory may or may not include a file name. Because the path definition is operating system-specific or IDE-specific, you must follow the requirements specified in the operating system or IDE. This text uses Windows OS as examples without consideration of any IDEs.

Table 21.1 lists commonly used directory path notations and their meanings in UNIX/Linux and Windows OS.

Table 21.1 Commonly used paths and their meanings in Unix/Linux and Windows

Path	Unix/Linux	Windows
/a/b/c/	From root directory including a and b to subdirectory c	From the current directory including a and b to the subdirectory c; or \a\b\c\
c:\a\b\	Illegal path	From the root directory c: including a to the subdirectory b; or c:\a\b\,:/a/b/
data.txt	The file name in the current directory	The file name in the current directory
/a/b/c/data.txt	From the root directory including a and b to the subdirectory with the file name	From the current directory including a and b to the subdirectory with the file name
.	Current directory	Current directory
..	Return to the above level from the current directory	Return to the above level from the current directory
..\b\c\	From the current directory return to the above level, and then go to subdirectory b\c\	From the current directory return to the above level, and then go to subdirectory b\c\
..\b\c\data.txt	Same as above; but including the file name	Same as above; but including the file name

21.1.3 Commonly used methods of file directory notation

An absolute file path refers to the defined path from the root directory to specified subdirectory. It may include the current directory or directory at the level above the current directory. An absolute path in UNIX/Linux might be specified as:

```
/a/b/c/..
./../c/d/data.txt    //Assume current directory is "b"and path is in
alphabetical order
```

or under Windows OS as:

```
C:\d\e\..
./../f/h/data.txt    //Assume current directory is e: and path is in
alphabetical order
```

A canonical path carries out the execution of the code in the current directory or the above level directory. For example:

```
Absolute path: C:\abc\..\abc\file.txt
Canonical path: C:\abc\file.txt
```

21.1.4 URI, URL, and URN

A uniform resource identifier (URI) includes a uniform resource locator (URL) and uniform resource name (URN). They are used to define files stored on remote computer systems in a network or on the internet. In the **java.net** package, the **URI** and **URL** classes are used to create objects of their classes. A URN is used to create an object in which the directory path starts with double forward slashes:

```
String mySharedFile = "//serverName/sharedFiles/java/Ch21/myFiles/myData.txt";
```

The above string defines a text file stored in the specified server *serverName*.

URLs and URNs are commonly used in defining paths of data files for text and binary file I/O. A URL is more likely used to define a path for multimedia files.

21.1.5 File class

The **File** class is provided in the **java.io** package. It is used to create the object of a **File**, so information about the file can be obtained. Table 21.2 lists commonly used constructors and methods of the **File** class.

Table 21.2 Commonly used constructors and methods in File class

Constructor/Method	Description
File(String pathname)	Creates new File instance by converting specified file pathname into an abstract pathname.
File(String, pathname, String fileName)	Creates new File instance from parent pathname and child pathname string.
File(URI uri)	Creates new File instance by converting file URI into an abstract pathname.
boolean canRead()	Returns true if file can be read; otherwise return false.
boolean canWrite()	Returns true if file can be modified; otherwise return false.
boolean createNewFile()	Creates a null File object if and only if a file with this name does not yet exist.; throws IOException if file cannot be created.
boolean delete()	Deletes File object or directory denoted by abstract pathname.
boolean exists()	Returns true if file or directory denoted by abstract pathname exists; otherwise returns false.
String getAbsolutePath()	Returns absolute pathname of this abstract pathname.
String getCanonicalPath()	Returns canonical pathname of this abstract pathname. Throws IOException if path cannot be returned.
String getName()	Returns name of file or directory denoted by this abstract pathname.
String getParent()	Returns pathname string of this abstract pathname's parent, or `null` if this pathname does not name a parent directory.
String getPath()	Converts this abstract pathname into a pathname string.
boolean isDirectory()	Returns true if object is file path, i.e., directory; otherwise returns false.
boolean isFile()	Returns true if object is a path including file name; otherwise returns false.
long length()	Returns length(bytes) of file denoted by the abstract pathname.
String[] list()	Returns array of strings naming files and directories in directory denoted by this abstract pathname.

File[] listFiles()	Returns array of abstract pathnames denoting files in directory denoted by this abstract pathname.
boolean mkdirs()	Creates directory named by this abstract pathname, including any necessary but nonexistent parent directories. Returns true if director(ies) are created.
boolean setReadOnly()	Marks file or directory named by this abstract pathname so that only read operations are allowed. Returns true if operation is successful; otherwise returns false.
boolean setWritable(boolean writable)	Convenience method to set owner's write permission for this abstract pathname. Returns true if operation is successful; otherwise returns false.

More Information: *According to the Java naming convention, a text file uses "txt" as its file extension; a binary file uses "dat" as its file extension.*

Example 1. Create a local file object.

```
String myFilePath = "C:/java/Ch21/myFiles/"; //Create specified object path
File myFile = new File(myFilePath + fileName);/Or: new
File(myFilePath,filename);
System.out.println("my file exists: " + myFile.exists());
```

Note this does not actually create the directory specified in the above example; it only registers or adds the path and encapsulates it in the object. The following statement:

```
System.out.println("my file exists: " + myFile.exists());
```

will display:

```
my file exists: false
```

Method **createNewFile()** can be called to establish the specified path:

```
if (!myFile.exists())
   myFile.createNewFile();
```

Example 2. Creates object with the specified remote file pathname.

```
//Use URI to create object with a remote file path
URI uri = new URI ("http://www.freeskytech/shared/myFiles/webFile.htm");
//Use URNs to create object with a remote file path

String serverFile = "//hostIPAddress/shared/myFiles/webFile.htm";

File webFile = new File(uri);  //Create the specified file object
```

```
File webFile2 = new File(serverFile);//Create the specified file object
```

Example 3. Call method **mkdirs()** to create the specified directories.

```
String yourFilePath = "C:/java/Ch21/yourfiles/";
if (!yourFile.exists())
    yourFile.mkdirs();
System.out.println("yourFile path: " + yourFile.getPath());
```

The above code creates the following file path:

```
yourFile path: C:\java\Ch21\yourfiles
```

Example 4. Call the methods to display the file name and the status of file operations.

```
if (!myFile.exists())
    myFile.createNewFile();
System.out.println("File name: " + myFile.getName());
System.out.println("Can read myFile: " + myFile.canRead());
System.out.println("Can write myFile: " + myFile.canWrite());
System.out.println("File name: " + yourFile.getName());
System.out.println("Can read yourFile: " + yourFile.canRead());
System.out.println("Can write yourFile: " + yourFile.canWrite());
```

The above code generates the following execution result:

```
File name: myData.txt
Can read myFile: true
Can write myFile: true
File name: yourfiles
Can read yourFile: false
Can write yourFile: false
```

Because object **yourFile** encapsulates the file path, **yourFile.getName()** only returns the subdirectory **yourFiles** and indicates the file cannot be read or modified.

Example 5. Call the methods that display the absolute file path and canonical file path.

```
System.out.println("Absolute path: " + myFile.getAbsolutePath());
System.out.println("Canonical path: " + myFile.getCanonicalPath());

String absolutePath = new File(".\\..").getAbsolutePath();
System.out.println("Absolute path: " + absolutePath);

String canonicalPath =  new File(".\\..").getCanonicalPath();
System.out.println("Canonical path: " + canonicalPath);

System.out.println("Parent path: " + myFile.getParent());
System.out.println("File path: " + myFile.getPath());
```

```
System.out.println("Path and myFile exist: " + myFile.isFile());
System.out.println("Length of myFile: " + myFile.length());
```

In the above example, we create anonymous file objects in two instances to show the differences between an absolute path and a canonical path. The following is the result of execution:

```
Absolute path: C:\java\Ch21\myFiles\myData.txt
Canonical path: C:\Java\Ch21\myFiles\myData.txt
Absolute path: C:\Documents and Settings\YGao\My Documents\Temp\JavaBook\.\..
Canonical path: C:\Documents and Settings\YGao\My Documents\Temp
Parent path: C:\java\Ch21\myFiles
File path: C:\java\Ch21\myFiles\myData.txt
Path and myFile exist: true
Length of myFile: 0
```

21.1.6 Buffers

A buffer is a portion of memory used to temporarily hold data during file I/O. The purpose of using a buffer is to increase the efficiency of frequent file I/O operations. Figure 21.2 shows the processing associated with using a buffer during file I/O. Comparing this figure to Figure 21.1, you may see that during buffered file I/O, data read by an input data stream or written by an output data stream are temporarily stored in the memory buffer. When any one of the following conditions is true the data stream in the buffer will be read into the program or written to the specified device, as appropriate:

- The buffer is full.
- The file is closed.
- The buffer is flushed.

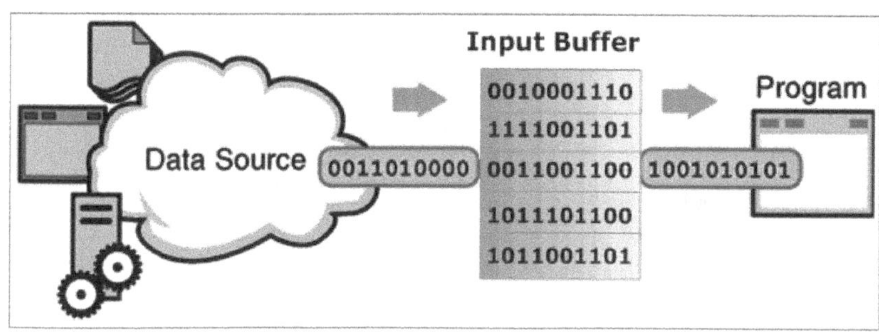

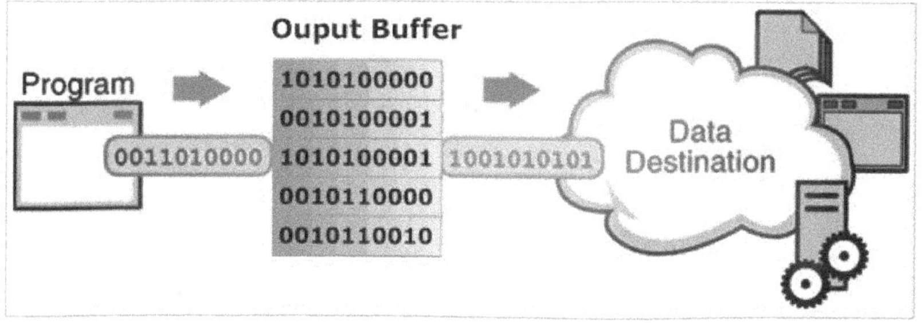

Figure 21.2 Concept of buffered file I/O

21.1.7 Exceptions in file I/O

The exceptions in file I/O are all checked exceptions. The programmer must provide exception handling code using the **try-catch** mechanism or throw the exception(s) to the next higher level for handling.

Commonly occurring checked exceptions in file I/O are:

IOException – occurs when an error is encountered during the processing of file I/O.

EOFException – occurs when the code attempts to read data past the end of the file.

FileNotFoundException – occurs when the code attempts to open a nonexistent file.

IOException is the superclass of **EOFException** and **FileNotFoundException**. It is a subclass of **Exception**.

21.2 Text File I/O

Although a text file may occupy more storage space than a binary file, text files are often used where direct human recognition of the readable characters or strings is required. The content of a text file can also be directly read by a text editor. **Writer** and **Reader** in **java.io** are the superclasses for all other classes of file I/O in Java. We will first discuss text file output, the text file input.

21.2.1 File output

Table 21.3 lists commonly used constructors in file output classes **PrintWriter**, **BufferedWriter**, and **FileWriter**.

Table 21.3 Commonly used constructors in file output

Constructor	Description
PrintWriter(File file)	Creates new PrintWriter object, without automatic line flushing, of the specified file.
PrintWriter(Writer writer)	Creates new PrintWriter object without automatic line flushing.
PrintWriter(Writer writer, boolean flush)	Creates new PrintWriter object with automatic line flushing if *flush* is true and methods println, printf, or format are used.
BufferedWriter(Writer writer)	Creates buffered character-output stream that uses default-sized output buffer.
FileWriter(File file)	Constructs new FileWriter object given a File object. Throws IOException if specified file is a directory, does not exist and cannot be created, or cannot be opened for any reason.
FileWriter(File file, boolean append)	Constructs new FileWriter object given a File object. If *append* is true, bytes will be added to the end of the file rather than the beginning. Throws IOException if specified file is a directory, does not exist and cannot be created, or cannot be opened for any reason.

FileWriter(String fileName)	Constructs new FileWriter object of *filename*. Throws IOException if specified file is a directory, does not exist and cannot be created, or cannot be opened for any reason.
FileWriter(String fileName, Boolean append)	Constructs new FileWriter object of *filename*. If *append* is true, bytes will be added to the end of the file rather than the beginning. Throws IOException if specified file is a directory, does not exist and cannot be created, or cannot be opened for any reason.

Writer is an absolute class. **PrintWriter** implements the methods particular file output operations allowing output data streams to be written with the assigned data format. **BufferedWriter** is used for buffered output. **FileWriter** is the lowest class level for file output. It makes connections with the **File** class or specified file name for file output operations. You should follow the order of class designations from specific to general, e.g., **File** → **BufferedWriter** (optional) → **FileWriter**, in creating specified objects for file output. If a buffer is not required for file output, use of **PrintWriter(File file)** could directly create a specified object. Coding examples of these classes will be shown in the next section.

Table 21.4 lists commonly used methods in **PrintWriter**.

Table 21.4 Commonly used methods in **PrintWriter**

Method	Description
void print(argumentExpression)	Writes specified argument expression to text file. File pointer will be placed at the end of the expression.
void println(argumentExpression)	Writes specified argument expression to text file. File pointer will be placed at the next new line of the expression.
void flush()	Flushes buffer. Throws IOException if error occurs.
void close()	Closes buffer. Throws IOException if error occurs.

21.2.2 Examples of file output

Example 1. Unbuffered file output.

```
//Complete code called TextFileWriteTest.java in Ch21 from author's website
String fileName = "myData.txt";
String myFilePath = "C:/java/Ch21/myFiles/";
try {
   //Create specified file object using the file name
   File myFile = new File(myFilePath + fileName);
   //or: new File(myFilePath, fileName)
   PrintWriter out = new PrintWriter(myFile);     //Create file output
   out.println("This line will be written to the file. ");//Call output
   out.print("Version" + 1.01);
   out.print("\tAuthor: Yong Gao");
   out.println();
   out.println("File name: " + filename);
```

```
        out.close();                        //Close file; or: out.flush()
}
catch (IOException e) {
    System.out.println(e);
}
```

The code writes the following data to file **myData.txt** in the specified directory using unbuffered file I/O:

```
This line will be written to the file.
Version: 1.01   Author: Yong Gao
File name: myData.txt
```

Example 2. Modify the above example to perform buffered file output:

```
//Complete code called TextFileBufferedWriteTest.java in Ch21 from author's
//website
try {
     //Create the specified file object using the file name
     File myFile = new File(myFilePath + fileName);
     //Or: new File(myFilePath, fileName)
     //Create buffered output
     PrintWriter out = new PrintWriter(new BufferedWriter(new
FileWriter(myFile)));
     out.println("This line will be written to the file. ");  //Call output
     out.print("Version" + 1.01);
     out.print("\tAuthor: Yong Gao");
     out.println();
     out.println("File name: " + filename);
     out.close();        //Close file output; or: out.flush()
}
catch (IOException e) {
     System.out.println(e);
}
```

In both Example 1 and Example 2, the contents of the file will be cleared each time the code is run. Occasionally you may want to append new data to the end of the currently existing file content. This action may be achieved by using the **FileWriter** constructor with the *append* parameter set to **true** (see Example 3). This will not clear the existing data in the file.

Example 3. Enable file data appending using the **FileWriter** constructor.

```
...
//enable data file appending
```

```
PrintWriter out = new PrintWriter(New FileWriter(myFile, true));
...
```

or:

```
//enable data file appending with buffering
PrintWriter out = new PrintWriter(new BufferedWriter(new FileWriter(myFile,
true));
```

You may also code this as:

```
//enable data file appending with buffering
PrintWriter out = new PrintWriter(
                           new BufferedWriter(
                                       new FileWriter("myData.txt", true)));
```

Execution of this code will store file **myData.txt** with appending enable in the current directory.

Example 4. Write various numerical type data to the text file.

```
//Complete code called TextFileBufferedWriteTest2.java in Ch21 from author's
//website
import java.io.*;
public class TextFileBufferedWriteTest2 {
   public static void main(String[] args) {
      short age = 89;
      int count = 100;
      float price = 89.56f;
      long population = 1300000000;
      double invest = 678900000;
      //Create buffered output with data appending implemented
      try {
           PrintWriter out = new PrintWriter(
                                 new BufferedWriter(
                                     new FileWriter(
                                         new File("numberData.txt"), true)));
           out.println(age);          //Call output
           out.println(count);
           out.println(price);
           out.println(population);
           out.println(invest);
           out.println(invest/population);
           out.close();
      }
      catch (IOException e) {
           System.out.println(e);
      }
   }
}
```

Upon executing this code the first time, the following data will be written into **numberData.txt**:

```
89
100
89.56
1300000000
6.789E8
0.05222307692307693
```

Because argument *append* in the constructor sets as **true**, the data will be appended to end of the file following subsequent executions of the code.

21.2.3 File Input

Table 21.5 lists commonly used constructors in text file input provided in the **java.io** package.

Table 21.5 Commonly used file input constructors in **BufferedReader** and **FileReader**

Constructor	Description
BufferedReader(Reader in)	Creates buffering character-input stream using default-sized input buffer.
FileReader(File file)	Creates new `FileReader object`, given the `File` to read from. Throws FileNotFoundException if specified file is a directory, does not exist and cannot be created, or cannot be opened for any reason.
FileReader(String fileName)	Creates new `FileReader object`, given the name of the file to read from. Throws FileNotFoundException if specified file is a directory, does not exist and cannot be created, or cannot be opened for any reason.

Reader is the abstract class of **BufferedReader** and **FileReader**. **BufferedReader** implements **Reader**. Table 31.6 lists commonly used methods in **BufferedReader**.

Table 21.6 Commonly used methods in **BufferedReader**

Method	Description
Int read()	Reads a single character in Unicode format; returns -1 if end of input stream has been reached. Throws IOException if an error occurs.
String readLine()	Reads a line of text. A line is considered to be terminated by any one of a line feed ('\n'), a carriage return ('\r'), or a carriage return followed immediately by a linefeed.; returns -1 if end of input stream has been reached. Throws IOException if an error occurs.
long skip(long chars)	Skips specified quantity of characters. Returns actual number of characters it skipped. Throws IOException if an error occurs.
void close()	Closes stream and releases any associated system resources. Once stream has been closed, further read(), ready(), mark(), reset(), or skip() invocations will throw IOException. Closing a previously closed stream has no effect.

Note: *Trying to read in a file that doesn't exist will throw* ***IOException***.

The default file input schema is buffered read: **BufferedReader → FileReader**.

21.2.4 Examples of file input

Example 1. Create a text file input object and use **readLine()** to read in the content of a file.

```
//Complete code called TextFileReadLineTest.java in Ch21 from author's
website
import java.io.*;
public class TextFileReadLineTest {
   public static void main(String[] args) {
      String fileName = "myData.txt";
      String myFilePath = "C:/java/Ch21/myFiles/";
      try {
           File myFile = new File(myFilePath + fileName);
           BufferedReader in = new BufferedReader( //Create input file

           new FileReader(myFile));
           String line = in.readLine();     //Read in a line from file

           while (line != null) {                          //Not in EOF
              System.out.println(line);                    //Display the line
              line = in.readLine();                        //Continue to read in
           }
           in.close();                              //Close input file
       }
      catch (IOException e) {
             System.out.println(e);
      }
   }
}
```

A **null** is returned when the end of the file is reached. This feature is used to control the **while** loop. The above example displays the file content:

```
This line will be written to the file.
Version: 1.01    Author: Yong Qiang Gao
File name: myData.txt
```

read from the input file.

Example 2. Use **read()** and **skip()** in file input. Method **read()** returns -1 when an end-of-file condition is reached. This feature can be used to control a loop governing the reading process. Assume we need to skip the line "Author: Yougqiang Gao" contained in the input file.

```
//Complete code called TextFileReadTest.java in Ch21 from author's website
import java.io.*;
public class TextFileReadTest {
   public static void main(String[] args) {
      String fileName = "myData.txt";
      String myFilePath = "C:/java/Ch21/myFiles/";
      try {
           File myFile = new File(myFilePath + fileName);
           BufferedReader in = new BufferedReader(new FileReader(myFile));
           String line = "";  //Initialization
           int ch = in.read();                      //Read in a character
```

```
            while (ch != -1) {                      //Not at the EOF
              line += (char)ch;                     //Form a string
              if (ch == '\n') {                     //If it is next line
                  System.out.print(line);           //Display the line
                  line = "";                        //Reset
              }
              else if (ch == '\t')                  //If read in a tab
                  in.skip(16);                      //Skip 16 characters
              ch = in.read();                       //Continue to read
        }
        in.close();
    }
    catch (IOException e) {
           System.out.println(e);
    }
  }
}
```

The execution result is:

```
This line will be written to the file.
Version: 1.01
File name: myData.txt
```

The line “Author: Yong Qiang Gao” is skipped, as expected.

Example 3. Read in the character representation of numbers and convert to the proper numerical data types.

```
//Complete code called TextFileReadLineTest2.java in Ch21 from author's
website
import java.io.*;
public class TextFileReadLineTest2 {
   public static void main(String[] args) {
      short age = 0;
      int count = 0;
      float price = 0.0F;
      long population = 0L;
      double invest = 0.0,
             total = 0.0,
             average = 0.0;
      try {
          //Create input file object
          BufferedReader in = new BufferedReader(new
          FileReader("numberData.txt"));
          String line = in.readLine();  //Read age as characters
```

```
            age = Short.parseShort(line);                     //Convert
            line = in.readLine();
            count = Integer.parseInt(line);  //Read count as characters
            price = Float.parseFloat(in.readLine());          //Convert
            population = Long.parseLong(in.readLine());
            invest = Double.parseDouble(in.readLine());
            total = count * price;                            //Compute total
            System.out.println("Total: " + total);
            //Read in, convert, and display
            System.out.println("Average: " + Double.parseDouble(in.readLine()));
            in.close();
        }
        catch (IOException e) {
            System.out.println(e);
        }
        catch (NumberFormatException e) {
            System.out.println(e);
        }
    }
}
```

The content format of the file must be known exactly before performing conversion of the data from the input character format to the desired numerical format, otherwise **NumberFormatException** is thrown when **parseXxx()** is called.

You may also use **valueOf()** in the wrapper class to convert the data:

```
Age = Short.valueOf(line);
```

The execution result of above example is:

```
Age: 89
Population: 1300000000
Invest: 6.789E8
Total: 8956.0
Average: 0.5222307692307693
```

21.2.5 File I/O application

Example 1. Write an application to generate a text file for a company's product data. The following classes should be coded in the application:

TextFileWriter – Provides constructor to create the object of the output file, write the data, and close the file.

ProductTextWriterFrame – Provides a GUI window to allow input of data. Creates and displays panel. Closes the window.

ProductTextFileWriterApp – The driver code application.

Figure 21.3 is a typical execution result of the application.

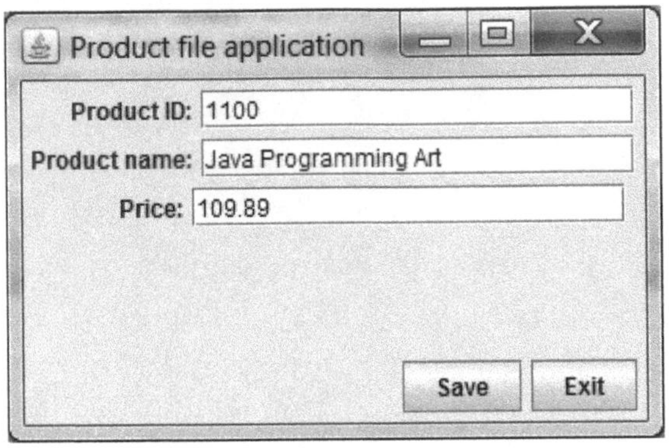

Figure 21.3 A typical execution result of the product file application

The following is the code of **TextWriter**:

```
//Complete code called TextFileWriter.java in Ch21 from author's website
import java.io.*;
class TextFileWriter {
   PrintWriter out;
   public TextFileWriter(String fileName, boolean append) throws IOException {
      out = new PrintWriter(new BufferedWriter(new FileWriter(filename,
append)));
   }
   public final void output(String...text) {      //Use variable arguments
      for (String s: text)
           out.print(s + "|");                    //Data delimiter
           out.println();
      }
   public final void closeFile() {                //Close file
      out.close();
   }
}
```

You may note a variable argument type is used in **output()** to allow any length of **String** type can be written to the file.

The following is the major code segment of **ProductTextFileWriterFrame**:

```
//Complete code called ProductTextFileWriterFrame.java and the driver code
called //ProductTextFileWriterApp.java in Ch21 from author's website
   ...
```

```
    try {
        fileWriter = new TextFileWriter(fileName, true);  //Create output file
    }
    catch (IOException e) {
        System.out.println(e);
    }
    count = 0;                                       //Product counter
}
public void actionPerformed(ActionEvent e) {
    Object source = e.getSource();
    if (source == exitButton) {                      //If Exit button is pressed
        fileWriter.closeFile();                      //Close the file
        System.exit(0);                              //Exit
    }
    else if (source == saveButton) {                 //If Save button is pressed
        String ID = IDTextField.getText();           //Get ID
        String title = titleTextField.getText();     //Get name
        String price = priceTextField.getText();     //Get price
        fileWriter.output(ID, title, price);         //Call output
        IDTextField.setText("");                     //Reset
        titleTextField.setText("");
        priceTextField.setText("");
        infoLabel.setVisible(true);                  //Display the path and name
        infoTextField.setVisible(true);
        infoTextField.setText(fileName);
        countLabel.setText("Record count:      " + ++count); //Display
    }
}
...
```

Example 2. Code an application that can read in, display, and compute the product price from the product file generated from **Example 1**. This application includes the following classes:

TextFileReader – Provides the constructor to create the input file object. Reads the input data, and closes the file.

ProductTextFileReaderFrame – Provides a GUI window to allow input of data. Displays the control panel and closes the window.

Formatter – Performs data formatting of double precision data and currency values.

ProductTextFileReadApp – The driver code of the application.

Figure 21.4 shows a typical execution result of this application.

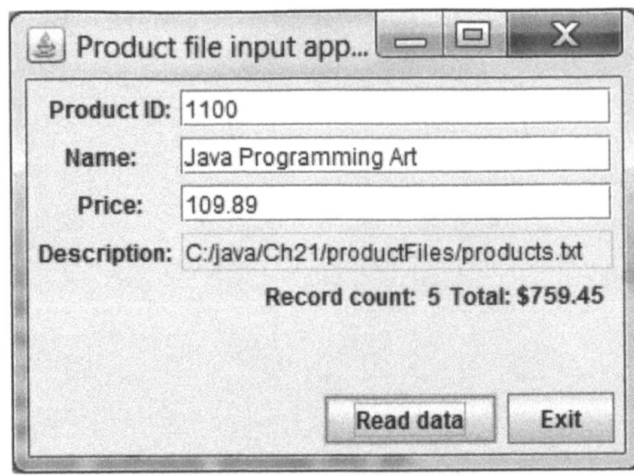

Figure 21.4 A typical execution result of product file input

The following is the code of **TextFileReader**:

```
//Complete code called TextFileReader.java in Ch21 from author's website
import java.io.*;
class TextFileReader {
   BufferedReader in;
   public TextFileReader(String fileName) throws IOException {  //Constructor
      in = new BufferedReader(new FileReader(fileName));
   }
   public final String getData() throws IOException {
      return in.readLine();  //Read in a line of input data
   }
   public final void closeFile() throws IOException {          //Close file
      in.close();
   }
}
```

The following is a code snippet from **ProductTextFileReaderFrame** that creates the text file input file object and performs event handling related to the display of product data, data accumulation, and displaying the product total:

```
//Complete code called ProductTextFileReader.java in Ch21 from author's
website
   ...
   try {
        fileReader = new TextFileReader(fileName);       //Create input file
   }
   catch (IOException e) {
        System.out.println(e);
   }
   count = 0;                                       //Product counter
   total = 0.0;                                     //Initialization
}
public void actionPerformed(ActionEvent e) {
   Object source = e.getSource();
```

```
    if (source == exitButton) {                  //If the exit button is pressed
        try {
            fileReader.closeFile(); //Close file
        }
        catch (IOException io) {
            System.out.println(io);
        }
        System.exit(0);                           //Exit
    }
    else if (source == readButton) {           //If Read in button is pressed
        try {
            String data = fileReader.getData();             //Read in data
            if (data != null) {                             //If it's not EOF
                token = new StringTokenizer(data, "|"); //Separate the string
                String ID = token.nextToken();             //Get ID
                IDTextField.setText(ID);                   //Display the ID
                String title = token.nextToken(); //Get the title
                titleTextField.setText(title);             //Display it
                String price = token.nextToken(); //Get the price
                priceTextField.setText(price);             //Display it
                infoLabel.setVisible(true);       //Display path and file name
                infoTextField.setVisible(true);
                infoTextField.setText(fileName);
                countLabel.setText("Record count:  " + ++count); //Display

                total += Double.parseDouble(price);      //Compute the total
                String totalString = Formatter.currency(total);

                totalLabel.setText("Total:  " + totalString); //Display total
                data = fileReader.getData();               //Read in next data
            }
            else
                endFileLabel.setText("End of the file."); //Complete read
        }
        catch (IOException ioe) {
            System.out.println(ioe);
        }
    }
}
```

Formatter is a programmer-defined class to format the currency display. The following is the code of **Formatter**:

```
//Complete code called Formatter.java in Ch21 from author's website
import java.text.*;
public class Formatter {
```

```
    public static final String currency(double currency) {
    //Static method to format the currency
    String currencyStr;
    NumberFormat currency = NumberFormat.getCurrencyInstance();
    currencyStr = currency.format(currency);
    return currencyStr;
  }
}
```

21.3 Binary File I/O

Java uses data streams, e.g., **DataInputStream** and **DataOutputStream** in the **java.io** package, to perform binary file I/O. In this section, we discuss binary file input, binary file output, and applications in binary file I/O.

21.3.1 Binary file output

Table 21.7 lists commonly used binary file output classes and constructors in **java.io**.

Table 21.7 Commonly used binary output file classes and constructors

Constructor	Description
DataOutputStream(DataOutput outStream)	Creates new data output stream to write data to the specified underlying output stream.
BufferedOutputStream(OutputStream outStream)	Creates new buffered output stream to write data to the specified underlying output stream.
FileOutputStream(File fileObj)	Creates file output stream to write to the file represented by specified `File` object. A new `FileDescriptor` object is created to represent this file connection. Throws FileNotFoundException if file exists but is a directory rather than a regular file, does not exist but cannot be created, or cannot be opened for any other reason.
FileOutputStream(File fileObj, boolean append)	Creates file output stream to write to the file represented by specified `File` object. If *append* is `true`, then bytes will be written to the end of the file rather than the beginning. A new `FileDescriptor` object is created to represent this file connection. Throws FileNotFoundException if file exists but is a directory rather than a regular file, does not exist but cannot be created, or cannot be opened for any other reason.
FileOutputStream(String fileObj)	Creates file output stream to write to the file with specified name. A new `FileDescriptor` object is created to represent this file connection. Throws FileNotFoundException if file exists but is a directory rather than a regular file, does not exist but cannot

	be created, or cannot be opened for any other reason.
FileOuputStream(String fileName, boolean append)	Creates file output stream to write to the file with specified name. If *append* is `true`, then bytes will be written to the end of the file rather than the beginning. A new `FileDescriptor` object is created to represent this file connection. Throws FileNotFoundException if file exists but is a directory rather than a regular file, does not exist but cannot be created, or cannot be opened for any other reason.

In the above table, **DataOutput** is the interface and **DataOuputStream** implements the methods in **DataOutput**. **OutputStream** is the abstract class of **BufferedOutputStream**. It will throw **FileNotFoundException** if one of the following conditions is encountered when **FileOutputStream** is used to create the object:

- The file specified is only the path of the file.
- File cannot be created in the specified path.
- File object can be created, but the file cannot be opened.
- Any other cases preventing the opening of the existing file.

The format of a binary output file process is: **DataOutputStream → BufferedOutputStream** (optional) → **FileOutputStream**. Although using a buffered output is optional, it is recommended this output mode be used to increase the efficiency of binary file I/O.

Table 21.8 lists commonly used methods in **DataOuputStream**.

Table 21.8 lists commonly used methods in **DataOuputStream**.

Method	Description
void close()	Closes this output stream and releases any system resources associated with the stream. Throws IOException if an I/O error occurs.
void flush()	Flushes this data output stream, forcing any buffered output bytes to be written out to the stream. Throws IOException if an I/O error occurs.
final int size()	Returns length (bytes) of the file data read in.
final void writeBoolean(boolean v)	Writes out a boolean type data. Throws IOException if an I/O error occurs.
final void writeByte(byte v)	Writes out a byte type data. Throws IOException if an I/O error occurs.
final void writeChar(char v)	Writes out a char type data. Throws IOException if an I/O error occurs.
final void writeChars(String v)	Writes out a String type data. Throws IOException if an I/O error occurs.
final void writeDouble(double v)	Writes out a double type data. Throws IOException if an I/O error occurs.
final void writeFloat(float v)	Writes out a float type data. Throws IOException if an I/O error occurs.
final void writeInt(int v)	Writes out a int type data. Throws IOException if an I/O error occurs.
final void writeLong(long v)	Writes out a long type data. Throws IOException if an I/O error occurs.

final void writeShort(short v)	Writes out a short type data. Throws IOException if an I/O error occurs.
final void writeUF(String v)	Writes out a string type data in modified UTF-8 format. Throws IOException if an I/O error occurs.

You may note each data type has its own method to write the data. Method **writeUTF()** writes a string using the modified UTF-8 machine-dependent format. In this data format, the first two bytes indicate the length of the data, and each character uses one byte. For example, writing the output string "Java" requires 6 bytes (2 bytes + 4 bytes) when invoked by **writeUTF("Java")**. However, calling **writeChars("Java")** requires 8 bytes (4 bytes * 2 bytes) of output data storage.

21.3.2 Examples

Example 1. Create a binary output file object and write the file in the current directory.

```
//Complete code called BinaryFileBufferedWriteTest.java in Ch21 from author's
//website
...
   try {
        DataOutputStream out = new DataOutputStream(
                                     new BufferedOutputStream(
                                          new FileOutputStream("myData.dat")));
   ...
}
catch (FileNotFoundException e) {
   System.out.println(e);
}
```

Example 2. Create a binary output file object with specified path and append option.

```
String filePath = "C:\java\Ch21\yourFiles\";        //Windows OS format
String filename = "yourData.dat";
File yourFile = new File(filePath, filename);
try {
     DataOutputStream out = new DataOutputStream(
                                 new BufferedOutputStream(
                                      new FileOutputStream(yourFile, true)));
   ...
}
catch (FileNotFoundException e) {
    System.out.println(e);
}
```

The above may also be performed without using a buffer, though this practice is not recommended:

```
...
try {
```

```
    DataOutputStream out = new DataOutputStream(
  new FileOutputStream(filePath + filename, true)));
  ...
}
catch (FileNotFoundException e) {
    System.out.println(e);
}
```

Example 3. Continue from the above example, call other methods in **DataOutputStream:**

```
//Complete code called BinaryFileBufferedWriteTest.java in Ch21 from author's
//website
try {
    ...
    out.writeBoolean("false");      //Write out a Boolean data
    out.writeChar('A');             //Write out a char; or out.writeChar(65);
    out.writeChars("Java");         //Write out a string (Unicode format)
    out.writeUTF("Java");           //Write out a string (UTF format)
    out.writeByte(99);              //Write out a byte
    out.writeShort(age);            //Write out a short
    out.writeInt(count);            //Write out an int
    out.writeLong(population);      //Write out a long
    out.writeFloat(price);          //Write out a float
    out.writeDouble(invest);        //Write out a double
    out.close();                    //Close the file
}
catch (IOException e) {
    System.out.println(e);
}
```

Because all of the binary output operations throw **IOException**, you must provide the exception handling mechanism to handle such exception.

Example 4. Continue from the example above, call the **size()** method to display the length of the file in bytes written to the file:

```
System.out.println("File size: " + out.size() + " bytes");
```

The execution result is:

```
File size: 44 bytes
```

21.3.3 Binary file Input

Table 21.9 lists commonly used constructors for binary file input in **java.io**.

Table 21.9 Commonly used constructors for binary file input

Constructor	Description
DataInputStream(DataInput input)	Creates DataInputStream using specified underlying InputStream.
BufferedInputStream(InputStream inputStream)	Creates `BufferedInputStream` and saves input stream *`inputStream`*, for later use. An internal buffer array is created and stored in *`buf`*.
FileInputStream(File file)	Creates `FileInputStream object` by opening connection to an actual file, *`file`*, in the file system. A new `FileDescriptor` object is created to represent this file connection. Throws FileNotFoundException if file does not exist, is a directory rather than a regular file, or for some other reason cannot be opened for reading.
FileInputStream(String filename)	Creates `FileInputStream object` by opening connection to an actual file named by the path name *`filename`*, in the file system. A new `FileDescriptor` object is created to represent this file connection. Throws FileNotFoundException if file does not exist, is a directory rather than a regular file, or for some other reason cannot be opened for reading.

DataInput is the file interface providing all operations for binary file input. **DataInputStream** implements this interface. **InputStream** is an abstract class of **BufferedInputStream**. During binary file data input operations, **FileInputStream** will throw **FileNotFoundException** if any of the following conditions occurs:

- File does not exist.
- File cannot be opened.
- The file path does not include the file name.
- File cannot be read.

The format for binary file input is: **DataInputStream → BufferedInputStream** (recommended option) → **FileInputStream**.

Table 21.10 lists commonly used methods in binary file input.

Table 21.10 Commonly used methods in binary file input

Method	Description
Int available()	Returns (estimated) quantity of bytes in file that have not been read (or skipped).
void close()	Closes this output stream and releases any system resources associated with the stream. Throws IOException if an I/O error occurs.
Int skipBytes(int bytes)	Makes an attempt to skip over *bytes* quantity of byte data from the input stream, discarding the skipped bytes. Returns quantity of bytes actually skipped. Throws IOException if an I/O error occurs.
boolean readBoolean()	Reads in a Boolean type data. Throws IOException if an I/O error occurs.
byte readByte()	Reads in a byte type data. Throws IOException if an I/O error occurs.
char readChar()	Reads in a char type data. Throws IOException if an I/O error occurs.
double readDouble()	Reads in a double type data. Throws IOException if an I/O error occurs.
float readFloat()	Reads in a float type data. Throws IOException if an I/O error occurs.

void readFully(byte[] b)	Reads some bytes from an input stream and stores them into buffer array *b*. Quantity of bytes read is equal to the length of *b*.
int readInt()	Reads in a int type data. Throws IOException if an I/O error occurs.
long readLong()	Reads in a long type data. Throws IOException if an I/O error occurs.
short readShort()	Reads in a short type data. Throws IOException if an I/O error occurs.
String readUTF()	Reads in a string type data in modified UTF-8 format. Throws IOException if an I/O error occurs.

21.3.4 Examples

Example 1. Create a binary file input object; assume the file is stored in the current directory.

```
//Complete code called BinaryFileBufferedReadTest.java in Ch21 from author's
//website
try {
     DataInputStream in = new DataInputStream(
                                new BufferedInputStream(
                                    new FileInputStream("myData.dat")));
   ...
}
catch (FileNotFoundException e) {
     System.out.println(e);
}
```

Example 2. Create a binary file input object with the specified path.

```
String filePath = "C:\java\Ch21\yourFiles\";      //Windows OS format
String filename = "yourData.dat";
File yourFile = new File(filePath, filename);
try {
     DataInputStream in = new DataInputStream(
                                new BufferedInputStream(
                                    new FileInputStream(yourFile)));
    ...
}
catch (FileNotFoundException e) {
     System.out.println(e);
}
```

The following code snippet demonstrates the above example without using an input buffer. This method is <u>not</u> recommended.

```
...
try {
     DataInputStream in = new DataInputStream(new FileInputStream(yourFile));
     ...
}
```

```
catch (FileNotFoundException e) {
     System.out.println(e);
}
```

Example 3. Continuing from **Example 1**, call commonly used methods associated with binary file input.

```
//Complete code called BinaryFileBufferedReadTest.java in Ch21 from author's
//website
...
boolean flag = in.readBoolean();
char grade = in.readChar();
String code ="";
for (int i = 0; i < 4; i++)                         //Read in 4 bytes of data
     code += in.readChar();                         //Convert to a string

System.out.println("String code = " + code);        //Print the string String
code = in.readUTF();                                //Read in as UTF string
byte n = in.readByte();                             //Read in a byte type data
short age = in.readShort();                         //Read in a short type data
int count = in.readInt();                           //Read in an int type data
long population = in.readLong();                    //Read in a long type data
float price = in.readFloat();                //Read in a float type data

System.out.println("flag = " + flag);               //Display
System.out.println("grade = " + grade);
System.out.println("UTF code = " + code);
System.out.println("byte n = " + n);
System.out.println("short age = " + age);
System.out.println("int count = " + count);
System.out.println("long population = " + population);
System.out.println("float price = " + price);
System.out.println("invest = " + in.readDouble());//Read and display a double

double total = price * count;                //Demo verification of numerical
                                                    //format

System.out.println("total = " + total);             //Display result
in.close();
...
```

It is important to note when reading binary data that the input data format match the "format" of the data reading method. If the two forms do not agree, an **IOException** will be thrown. It should also be noted **DataInputStream** does not provide methods to read **String** or multiple **char** data.

Method **readChar()** can convert multiple **char** data to a string, as shown in the example above. The result of executing the above example code is:

```
String code = Java
flag = false
grade = A
UTF code = Java
byte n = 99
short age = 89
int count = 100
long population = 1300000000
float price = 89.56
invest = 6.789E8
total = 8956.0
```

21.3.5 Application in binary file I/O

Example 1. Modify the product text file example discussed in Section 21.2.5 to use binary file output. The GUI window and other functions should remain the same.

The following code processes the binary file output:

```
//Complete code called BinaryFileOutput.java in Ch21 from author's website
import java.io.*;
class BinaryFileOutput {
   DataOutputStream out;
   public BinaryFileOutput(String fileName, boolean append) throws IOException
{
      //Constructor to create binary output file
      out = new DataOutputStream(
                  new BufferedOutputStream(
                      new FileOutputStream(fileName, append)));
   }
   public final void outUTF(String text) throws IOException {

      out.writeUTF(text);     //Output as UTF
   }
   public final void outString(String text) throws IOException {
      out.writeChars(text);   //Output as string
   }
   public final void outDouble(double value) throws IOException {
      out.writeDouble(value); //Output as double
   }
   public final void outInt(int value) throws IOException {
      out.writeInt(value);    //Output as int
   }
```

```
        public final void outChar(char ch) throws IOException {
        out.writeChar(ch);      //Output as char
    }
    public final void closeFile() throws IOException {
        out.close();
    }
}
```

Because all methods dealing with binary file output throw **IOException**, this code example throws the exception to its caller. You may also note the control panel deals with event handling through **try-catch** mechanism to handle the variety of exceptions that may be encountered. The following code snippet illustrates working with binary file output with the product data example:

```
//Complete code called ProductBinaryFileOutputFrame.java and the driver code
//called ProductBinaryFileOutputApp.java in Ch21 from author's website
...

class ProductFileOutputPanel extends JPanel implements ActionListener {
    ...
    private BinaryFileOutput fileOutput;    //Declare the binary file output
    private String fileName = "C:/java/Ch21/productFiles/products.dat";
    public ProducttFileOutputPanel() {
        ...
        try {
            fileOutput = new BinaryFileOutput(fileName, true); //Create binary

        }
        catch (IOException e) {
            System.out.println(e);
        }
        ...
        public void actionPerformed(ActionEvent e) {       //Event handling
            Object source = e.getSource();
            if (source == exitButton) {             //If it is exit
                try {
                    fileOutput.closeFile();                 //Close file
                }
                catch (IOException io) {
                    System.out.println(io);
                }
                System.exit(0);                             //Stop run
            }
            else if (source == saveButton) {                //If it is save
                String ID = IDTextField.getText();          //Get ID
                String title = titleTextField.getText();    //Get name
                String price = priceTextField.getText();    //Get price
                try {
                    fileOutput.outUTF(ID);                  //Call UTF output
                    fileOutput.outUTF(title);
                    //Call double output
```

```
                fileOutput.outDouble(Double.parseDouble(price));
            }
            catch (IOException ioe) {
                System.out.println(ioe);
            }
            IDTextField.setText("");                        //Clear
            titleTextField.setText("");
            priceTextField.setText("");
            countLabel.setText("Record count:       " + ++count);
        }
    }
}
```

Example 2. Continuing from **Example 1**, modify the application discussed in Section 21.2.5 to read the binary file produced in **Example 1**. The GUI window and rest of the code remain the same. The result of code execution is shown in Figure 21.4.

The following is the code import dealing with binary file input:

```
//Complete code called BinaryFileInput.java in Ch21 from author's website
import java.io.*;
class BinaryFileInput  {
   DataInputStream in;
   public BinaryFileInput(String fileName) throws IOException {
      in = new DataInputStream(              //Create binary file input
               new BufferedInputStream(
                  new FileInputStream(fileName)));
   }
   public final boolean hasMore() throws IOException {//If there is more
      if (in.available() != 0)
         return true;
      else
         return false;
   }
   public final String getUTF() throws IOException {            //Read in UTF
      return in.readUTF();
   }
   public final double getDouble() throws IOException { //Read in double
      return in.readDouble();
   }
   public final int getInt() throws IOException {        //Read in int
      return in.readInt();
   }
   public final char getChar() throws IOException {             //Read in char
```

```
        return in.readChar();
    }
    public final void closeFile() throws IOException {          //Close file
        in.close();
    }
}
```

The following code snippet deals with binary file input in the product data application example:

```
//Complete code called ProductBinaryFileInputFrame.java in Ch21 from author's
//website
...
class ProductBinaryFileInputPanel extends JPanel implements ActionListener {
    //Control panel
     ...
    private BinaryFileInput fileReader;     //Declare binary file input
    private String fileName = "C:/java/Ch21/productFiles/products.txt";
     ...
    public ProductBinaryFileInputPanel() {
        ...
        public void actionPerformed(ActionEvent e) {        //Event handling
            Object source = e.getSource();
            if (source == exitButton) {                 //If it is exit button
                try {
                    fileReader.closeFile();                 //Close file
                }
                catch (IOException io) {
                    System.out.println(io);
                }
                System.exit(0);                             //Stop run
            }
            else if (source == readButton) {                //If it is read in
                try {
                    if (fileReader.hasMore()) {             //There is data
                        String ID = fileReader.getUTF();            //Read ID
                        String title = fileReader.getUTF();         //Read name
                        double price = fileReader.getDouble();      //Read price
                        IDTextField.setText(ID);                    //Display
                        titleTextField.setText(title);
                        priceTextField.setText("" + price);    //Display
                        countLabel.setText("Record count:  " + ++count);
                        total += price;                     //Compute the total

                        String totalString = Formatter.currency(total);
                        totalLabel.setText("Total:  " + totalString);
```

```
                    }
                    else
                                                                    //File end
                        endFileLabel.setText("End of the file. ");
                }
                catch (IOException ioe) {
                    System.out.println(ioe);
            }
        }
    }
}
```

21.4 Serializable Objects in File I/O

Just as data streams support I/O of primitive data types, object streams support I/O of objects. When writing or reading data as an object, or an object that refers to another object, you must make each object serializable during file I/O. Most classes support serialization of their objects if they implement the **Serializable** interface.

21.4.1 Object serialization

The purpose of object serialization is to retain the object's persistence during file I/O. Object serialization encapsulates the object and records metadata regarding the object's data. It may also provide information to which the object refers. During file input, this serialized information is used to "reconstruct" the stored object.

21.4.2 How to serialize an object

A serialized object must be an object implemented by the **Serializable** interface. This interface is included in the **java.io** package. Although the interface does not have any methods that must be implemented:

```
public class Product implements Serializable {
    //statements
}
```

writing the serialized object during file output operations requires use of the **writeObject()** method:

```
private void writeObject(ObjectOutputStream out)
```

when writing a serialized object. This method throws **IOException**, and the coder must provide the exception mechanism to handle the exception.

Deserializing the object during file input requires use of the **readObject()** method:

```
Private void readObject(ObjectInputStream in)
```

This methods throws **IOException** and **ClassNotFoundException**, and the coder must provide the exception mechanisms to handle each respective exception.

ObjectOutputStream and **Object InputStream** are API classes in the **java.io** package used for object serialization.

21.4.3 Commonly used methods in object serialization

Table 21.11 lists commonly used methods for object serialization of file output. These methods are contained in the **ObjectOutputStream** class of the **java.io** package.

Table 21.11 Commonly used methods in object serialization for file output

Constructor/Method	Description
ObjectOutputStream (OutputStream out)	Creates an ObjectOutputStream that writes to specified OutputStream. Throws IOException if an error is encountered while writing the stream header.
void close()	Closes stream. Throws IOException if an I/O error occurs.
void flush()	Flushes stream buffer. Throws IOException if an I/O error occurs.

OutputStream is an abstract class of **ObjectOutputStream**.

Table 21.11 lists commonly used methods for object serialization of file input. These methods are contained in the **ObjectInputStream** class of the **java.io** package.

Table 21.12 Commonly used methods in object serialization for file input

Constructor/Method	Description
ObjectInputStream(InputStream in)	Creates an ObjectOutputStream that reads from specified InputStream. Throws IOException if an error is encountered while reading the stream header.
int available()	Returns number of bytes than can be read without blocking. Throws IOException if I/O errors occur while reading from the underlying input stream.
void close()	Closes stream. Throws IOException if an I/O error occurs.
final Object readObject()	Reads serialized object from underlying ObjectInputStream. Throws IOException and ClassNotFoundException; throws IOException and ClassNotFoundException if an I/O error occurs or the class of a serialized object cannot be found, respectively.

21.4.4 Steps in object serialization

The steps required for object serialization for file I/O are:

1. Create a class that implements the **Serializable** interface and encapsulate all data types.

2. Code a class that will operate on serialized objects for file I/O. This class creates the serialized objects and an object to perform the file I/O, and calls **writeObject()** and **readObject()**. The format of serialized object output is:

```
ObjectOutputStream out = new ObjectOutputStream(new
    FileOutputStream(fileName));
```

The format of serialized object input is:

```
ObjectInputStream in = new ObjectInputStream(new
    FileInputStream(fileName));
```

The use of an I/O buffer is mandatory when performing serialized object file I/O.

3. Code the application and driver code.

The following section discusses how to use these three steps to perform serialized object file I/O.

21.4.5 Application in serialized object file I/O

We will now code an application that performs serialized object file I/O. The **Product** object includes the code, price, and description of the product. For purposes of our example, another class, **Item**, is created to provide the title and price of the product. The following classes are included in the application:

Product – Implements the **Serializable** interface. It also includes another class, Item, representing the serialized object.

ObjectOutput – Performs serialized object output.

ObjectInput – Performs serialized object input.

ProductFileOutput – Performs serialized object file output.

ProductFileInput – Performs serialized object file input.

ProductFileInputApp – Driver code of the serialized object file input application.

The following is the code of **Product**:

```
//Complete code called Product.java in Ch21 from author's website
import java.io.*;
class Product implements Serializable {
   private String ID;
   private Item item = new Item();  //another referred object

   Product(String ID, String title, double price) {  //Constructor
      this.ID = ID;
      item.setTitle(title);
      item.setPrice(price);
   }
```

```
    String getID() {
      return ID;
   }
   String getTitle() {
      return item.getTitle();
   }
   double getPrice() {
      return item.getPrice();
   }
}

//Demonstration class for serialization
class Item implements Serializable {    //Must be serializable
   private String title;
   private double price;

   public void setTitle(String title) {
      this.title = title;
   }
   public void setPrice(double price) {
      this.price = price;
   }
   public String getTitle() {
      return title;
   }
   public double getPrice() {
      return price;
   }
}
```

The following is the code of **ObjectOutput**:

```
//Complete code called ObjectOutput.java in Ch21 from author's website
import java.io.*;
class ObjectOutput {
   ObjectOutputStream out;                                        //Declare
   public ObjectOutput(String fileName) {                         //Constructor
      try {
          out = new ObjectOutputStream(new FileOutputStream(fileName));
          }
      catch (IOException ioe) {
          System.out.println(ioe);
      }
   }
   public final void outObject(Object obj) {                      //Output
      try {
          out = writeObject(obj);
```

```
        }
    catch (IOException ioe) {
         System.out.println(ioe);
    }
  }
  public final void closeFile() {                              //Close file
    try {
         out.close();
        }
    catch (IOException ioe) {
         System.out.println(ioe);
    }
  }
}
```

The following is the code of **ObjectInput**:

```
//Complete code called ObjectInput.java in Ch21 from author's website
import java.io.*;
class ObjectInput {
  ObjectInputStream in;                                  //Declare
  boolean status = true;                                 //File can be read
status
  public ObjectInput(String fileName) {                  //Constructor
    try {
         in = new ObjectInputStream(                     //Create
         new FileInputStream(fileName));
    }
    catch (IOException ioe) {
         System.out.println(ioe);
    }
  }
  public final Object getObject() {             //Read in serialized object
    Object obj = new Object();
    try {
         obj = in.readObject();
    }
    catch (EOFException eof) {                           //Exception occurred
         System.out.println("End of the file."); //Display exception info

         status = false;                                 //Update status
         return null;
    }
    catch (IOException ioe) {
         System.out.println(ioe);
```

```
        }
        catch (ClassNotFoundException cnf) {
            System.out.println(cnf);
        }
        return obj;                                    //Return object
    }
    public final boolean hasMore() {                   //"Can be read" status
        return status;
    }
    public final void closeFile() {                    //Close
        try {
            in.close();
        }
        catch (IOException ioe) {
            System.out.println(ioe);
        }
    }
}
```

You may use many different techniques to write the serialized object to the file. In this example, the **Scanner** class is used to accept the user's product input data. A serialized object of the product is created to encapsulate the data and prepare the serialized object for file output. The application uses a loop to continually accept input until the application is terminated. In the exercises at the end of this chapter, you will be asked to use a GUI to obtain the user's product data.

The following is the code of **ProductFileOutput**:

```
//Complete code called ProductFileOutput.java in Ch21 from author's website
import java.util.*;
import java.io.*;
public class ProductFileOutput {                       //Constructor
    ObjectOutput out;                                  //Declare
    public void createOutputfile(String fileName) {   //Create
        out = new ObjectOutput(fileName);
    }
    public void createData() {                         //Product data
        Product product;
        String productID;
        String title;
        double price;
        Scanner sc = new Scanner(System.in);       //Create Scanner object
        String choice = "y";
        while (choice.equalsIgnoreCase("y")) {         //Get the data
            try {
```

```
                System.out.print("Enter the product ID: ");
                productID = sc.next();
                sc.nextLine();
                System.out.print("Enter the product title: ");
                title = sc.nextLine();
                System.out.print("Enter the price: ");
                price = sc.nextDouble();

                //Create the serialized product object
                product = new Product(productID, title, price);
                System.out.println("Product ID: " + product.getID());
                System.out.println("Product tile: " + product.getTitle());
                System.out.println("Product price: " + product.getPrice());
                out.outObject(product);                    //Output
            }
            catch (Exception e) {                          //Exception
                sc.nextLine();//Clear the buffer of scanner
                System.out.println("Error! Invalid price. Try again.\n");
                continue;                                  //Next loop
            }
            System.out.print("Continue? (y/n): "); //Continue or not?
            choice = sc.next();                            //Get the answer
            System.out.println();
        } //while
    }
    public void closeOutputFile() {                        //Close the file
        out.closeFile();
    }
}
```

The code uses **ObjectOutput** to perform serialized object file output. This technique provides better coding structure and allows the driver code to be simplified:

```
//Complete code called ProductObjectFileOutputApp.java in Ch21 from author's
//website
public class ProductObjectFileOutputApp {
    public static void main(String[] args) {
        String fileName = "C:/java/Ch21/productFiles/objects.dat";

        ObjectFileOutput out = new ObjectFileOutput();          //Create
        out.createOutputfile(fileName);    //Call the method
        out.createData();
        out.closeOutputFile();
    }
```

```
}
```

The following is a typical execution result of the application:

```
Enter the product ID: 1100
Enter the product title: Art of Java programming
Enter the price: 89.88
Product ID: 1100
Product tile: Art in Java programming
Product price: 89.88
Continue? (y/n): y
...
Enter the product ID: 2201
Enter the product title: 27" Flat panel monitor
Enter the price: 6500.67
Product ID: 2201
Product tile: 27" Flat panel monitor
Product price: 6500.67
Continue? (y/n): n
```

The following is the code of **ProductFileInput**. It uses **ObjectInput** to carry out the file input of the serialized product object, perform deserialization of the product object, read in the record counter, calculate the total, and display the result. You may also use a GUI to perform the above operations. We used **System.out** to display the result. In the exercises at the end of this chapter, you will be asked to modify this code using a GUI and other components to improve the application's display.

```
//Complete code called ProductFileInput.java in Ch21 from author's website
public class ProductFileInput {
   ObjectInput in;                                          //Declare
   Object object;
   Product product;
   int count = 0;                                   //Product record counter
   double price = 0.0,
          total = 0.0;                                      //Total

   public void createInputfile(String fileName) { //Create input
      in = new ObjectInput(fileName);
   }
   public void showData() {;                                //Read in and display
      while (in.hasMore()) {                                //Loop
         object = in.getObject();                           //Read in
         if (object instanceof Product) {                   //If it is product
            product = (Product)object;                      //Convert
            System.out.println("Data " + ++count);          //Display counter
            System.out.println("Product ID: " + product.getID());
            System.out.println("Product tile: " + product.getTitle());
            price = product.getPrice();    /Get price
            System.out.println("Product price: " +
            Formatter.currency(price));
```

```
            total += price;                             //Accumulate total
        }
        else break;                                     //End reading of data
    } //while
    System.out.println("Price total: " + Formatter.currency(total));
  }
  public void closeInputFile() {                        //Close file
    in.closeFile();
  }
}
```

The diver code is:

```
//Complete code called ProductFileInputApp.java in Ch21 from author's website
public class ProductFileInputApp {
   public static void main(String[] args) {
      String fileName = "C:/java/Ch21/productFiles/objects.dat";
      ProductFileInput in = new ProductFileInput();      //Create input object
      in.createInputfile(fileName);                      //Call the methods
      in.showData();
      in.closeInputFile();
   }
}
```

The following is a typical execution result of this application:

```
Data 1
Product ID: 1100
Product tile: Art of Java Programming
Product price: $89.88
Data 2
Product ID: 1101
Product tile: JSP programming
Product price: $67.09
Data 3
Product ID: 1102
Product tile: Java EE and EJB programming
Product price: $76.08
Data 4
Product ID: 2200
Product tile: 27" Flat panel monitor
Product price: $6,500.87
Data 5
Product ID: 2201
Product tile: Photo Quality Color Printer
```

```
Product price: $855.00
End of the file.
Price total: $7,588.92
```

21.5 Random Access File I/O

The file I/O we have discussed to this point is considered as sequential file I/O—the data records are read in and written out in a sequential order. However, we often need to access data randomly, i.e., directly, in a file. Java provides API classes designed exclusively for random access file I/O. Compared with other computer languages, such as C or C++, Java actually simplifies the random access file I/O process, as well as making it convenient and reliable. Random access file I/O in Java can be used for text as well as binary data files.

21.5.1 Commonly used classes and methods

Table 21.13 lists commonly used methods in the **RandomAccessFile** class provided in **java.io**.

Table 21.13 Commonly used methods in **RandomAccessFile**

Constructor/Method	Description
RandomAccessFle (File file, String mode)	Creates random access file stream to read from, and optionally to write to, file specified by File argument. A new FileDescriptor object is created to represent this file connection. Throws IllegalArgumentException and FileNotFoundException.
RandomAccessFile(String fileName, String mode)	Creates random access file stream to read from, and optionally to write to, file specified by *filename* argument. A new FileDescriptor object is created to represent this file connection. Throws IllegalArgumentException and FileNotFoundException.
void close()	Closes this random access file stream and releases any system resources associated with the stream. Throws IllegalArgumentException.
long getFilePointer()	Returns current offset from beginning of file, i.e., current file pointer, in this file. Throws IOException.
long length()	Return length of the file (bytes). Throws IOException.
void seek(long position)	Sets file-pointer offset, measured from beginning of this file, at which the next read or write occurs. Throws IOException.
void setLength(long length)	Sets file length with specified bytes. Throws IOException.

int skipBytes(int n)	Attempts to skip over *n* bytes of input from current file pointer position discarding skipped bytes. Actual number of bytes skipped is returned. If *n* is negative, no bytes are skipped. It will not throw and EOFException when end-of-file is encountered. Throws IOException.

The **RandomAccessFile** constructor's `mode` specifies the access mode in which the file is to be opened. The permitted access modes and their definitions are:

Mode	**Definition**
`"r"`	Open for reading only. Invoking any `write` method will throw an IOException.
`"rw"`	Open for reading and writing. If file does not already exist, an attempt will be made to create it.
`"rws"`	Open for reading and writing, as with `"rw"`, and also require every update to the file's content or metadata be written synchronously to the underlying storage device.
`"rwd"`	Open for reading and writing, as with `"rw"`, and also require every update to the file's content be written synchronously to the underlying storage device. The metadata may not be updated.

The `"rwd"` mode can be used to reduce the number of I/O operations. Using `"rwd"` only requires updates to the file's content to be written to storage. However, the `"rws" modes` requires updates to both the file's content and its metadata to be written.

RandomAccessFile provides many methods, e.g., **readInt()**, **writeInt()**, et cetera, for file I/O that are similar to methods provided in **DataOutputStream** (see Table 21.10), so they are not repeated in Table 21.13. It should also be noted that **RandomAccessFile** provides **read()** and **readline()** methods for use in randomly access data in a text file.

21.5.2 Records and positions

A record refers to a complete "unit" of related data stored in a file. It is vital in random access file I/O to determine the position of the record so that file pointer can be correctly placed, via the **seek()** method, at the beginning of the record. Records stored in a random access file must be the same size and must have a fixed length. This means the size of a record cannot change. A formula is employed to calculate the offset position to the beginning of each record.

recordPosition = record_size * (n – 1)

wherein,

recordPosition – the beginning location of a record in the file.

record_size – the length (bytes) of a record.

n – record number in the file requiring access (the first record number is 1).

For example, the beginning position, *recordPosition*, of the first record in a file is 0.

21.5.3 Examples

Example1. Create random access file objects.

```
try {
    String filename = "c:/java/Ch21/productFiles/products.dat";
    File productFile = new File(fileName);

    //Create random access file object
    RandomAccessFile randomFile = new RandomAccessFile(productFile,"rw");
}
catch (FileNotFoundException e) {
    System.out.println(e);
}
```

You may also directly use the file name as the first argument:

```
RandomAccessFile randomFile = new RandomAccessFile("products.dat", "rw");
```

Example 2. Call various methods in random access file operations.

```
try {
    //Print the file pointer position
    System.out.println("File pointer position: " +
randomFile.getFilePointer());
    //Print file length
    System.out.println("File length: " + randomFile.getLength());
    randomFile.skipBytes(4);        //Forward file pointer 4 bytes
    randomFile.setLength(0); //Set the length of file: 0

}
catch (IOException io) {
    System.out.println(io);
}
```

Example 3. Calculate the file pointer position and use **seek()** to move the pointer to the specified location. Assume a product record (50 bytes in length) includes the following data:

```
String ID;      //4 characters written in UTF-8 format:  6 bytes.
String title;   //34 characters (maximum) written in UTF-8 format: 36 bytes.
double price;   //double precision type data:  8 bytes
```

We will also assume the complete product data file, **productData.dat**, will contain a maximum of 100 records stored in a binary format, as shown in the following code snippet:

```
final int RECORD_SIZE = 50;          //Define the length of each record
try {
     //Set pointer to beginning of file, i.e., record #1
     randomFile.seek(0);
     //Get file length:  fileSize = 5000 bytes
     int fileSize = randomFile.length();
     //Set pointer to end of file:  Position 4950
     randomFile.seek(fileSize - RECORD_SIZE);

     int recordPos = (RECORD_SIZE * n) - RECORD_SIZE;
     //Set pointer to beginning of record "n"
     randomFile.seek(reconrdPos);
}
catch (IOException ioe) {
     System.out.println(ioe);
}
```

Example 4. Modify an added record that exceeds the file length, so it will avoid an exception.

```
...
         //Continue from Example 3
if (recordPos < 0 && recordPos > fileSize){       //Exceeds the length
   randomFile.seek(fileSize);  //Pointer to the end of the file
   randomFile.writeUTF(ID);                         //Write out
   randomFile.WriteUTF(title);
   randomFile.writeDouble(price);
}
...
```

Example 5. Modify an added record that exceeds the file length such that it will replace the last record currently in the file.

```
...
//Continuing from Example 4
if (recordPos < 0 && recordPos >= fileSize) {  //Exceeds the length
   //Set position indicator to beginning of last record in file
   randomFile.seek(fileSize - RECORD_SIZE);
   System.out.println("Attempt to read record beyond file size...");
   System.out.println("Read the last record instead...");
   ID = randomFile.readUTF();                  //Write out
   title = randomFile.readUTF();
   price = randomFile.readDouble();
}
...
```

Exercises

1. Use examples to explain the relationship and difference(s) between a data stream and a file.
2. What information must be known to correctly perform file I/O?
3. Use examples to explain and distinguish a path, an absolute path, and a canonical path.
4. Use examples to explain and distinguish a URL, URI, and URN.
5. Use examples to explain what a data I/O buffer is and how it is used.
6. List three possible exceptions that may be thrown in the course of performing file I/O. Use examples to explain how to handle each exception.
7. List the basic coding steps in performing text file input and text file output.
8. Use text file I/O to code an application that counts the number of lines of source code in an application file. The program will use **JFileChooser** to prompt the user to select a source code file. After reading in the code and counting the number of lines containing source code (note: blank lines containing only whitespace are not counted), the input file will be saved in a file with the extension "**txt**" in the current directory. Run, test, and save all files. Use file I/O in coding an application to calculate the number of classes contained in a Java program. Use **JFileChooser** to prompt the user in selecting a file for analysis. Use **showMessageDialog()** in **JOptionPane** to display the result. Assume proper Java naming conventions are used in the source code files. Run, test, and save all files.
9. Use file I/O to code an application that can search for a user-specified keyword in a Java source code file. The program will display a GUI window a prompt the user to enter a keyword as a search "key." Searching will begin after the **OK** button is pressed in the prompt window. The search result will be displayed in another GUI window, showing the keyword, the number of occurrences in the source code, and the line numbers containing the keyword. The program will continue to search for additional keywords until the **Exit** button is pressed. Run, test, and save all files.
10. Use examples to explain the differences between a text file and a binary file. What are the features (techniques) used in coding binary file I/O.
11. Use a GUI window and binary file I/O to code an application that stores student grade data. A grade report consists of grades relating to homework assignments (0 – 400 grades), midterm examinations (0 – 200 grades), and file examinations (0 – 400 grades). A GUI window prompts the user to enter a student name and three(3) scores. After the **OK** button is pressed, the code computes the grade in percentage and writes the data (student name, 3 grades, and percent) to a binary file, **grades.dat**. Properly display the current grade information and total records written to the file in the GUI window. The program will continue to execute until properly halted by the user. Run, test, and save all files.
12. Use the binary file generated in the above exercise to compute the average, and the highest and lowest values in the grade. Display these results in a GUI window. Run, test, and save all files.

13. What is object serialization? Why is it needed and how is it used? Explain you answer with examples.

14. List the steps to perform object serialization.

15. Use a GUI window and object serialization in modifying **ProductFileOutput.java**, discussed in the chapter, so it will create GUI components to perform user data entry. After the user presses the **OK** button, the application will write the serialized object to the file. The program will halt execution when the **Exit** button is pressed. Run, test, and save all files.

16. Use examples to explain the features of random access file I/O. How do you calculate the beginning position of a record?

17. Assume that a student record includes the following data:

```
Student ID:                     4 characters Student
Name:                           20 characters
Assignment Score:               integer, 2 bytes
Midterm Examination Score:      double precision Final
Examination Score:              double precision
```

Code an application that can write student records containing the data listed above in a random access file according to the user's specifications for record placement. Assume there are 50 records in the file. Your application should first display a window for recording student grades on a random basis. Text fields can be used to enter the student record data. Several buttons can be created to specify record placement within the

file, e.g., first record, last record, previous record, next record, et cetera. An **OK** button is used to submit the record into the file. An **Exit** button is used to stop execution. When the user completes the entry of the data and specification of the record position, the record will be written to the correct record position in the file **studentScores.txt**. The program will display an error message and permit the user to reenter any data requiring correction or completion. Use a layout manager(s) to position GUI components. Run, test, and save all files.

18. Modify the application created in **Exercise 18** so the student file will be a binary file called **studentScores.dat**. Run, test, and save all files.

19. Modify the example **MyFile.java** discussed in the chapter to perform compressed file I/O operations via a GUI window. Refer to **ProductObjectFileOutputApp.java** for additional information and details. Run, test, and save all files.

20. Modify the example **MyFile.java** discussed in the chapter to perform decompressed file I/O operations via a GUI window. Refer to **ProductObjectFileOutputApp.java** for additional information and details. Run, test, and save all files.

21. Modify **Exercise 11** to use the **Scanner** class in performing file input. Run, test, and save all files.

Index

V

Y

W